CIVIL LITIGATION

Seventh Edition

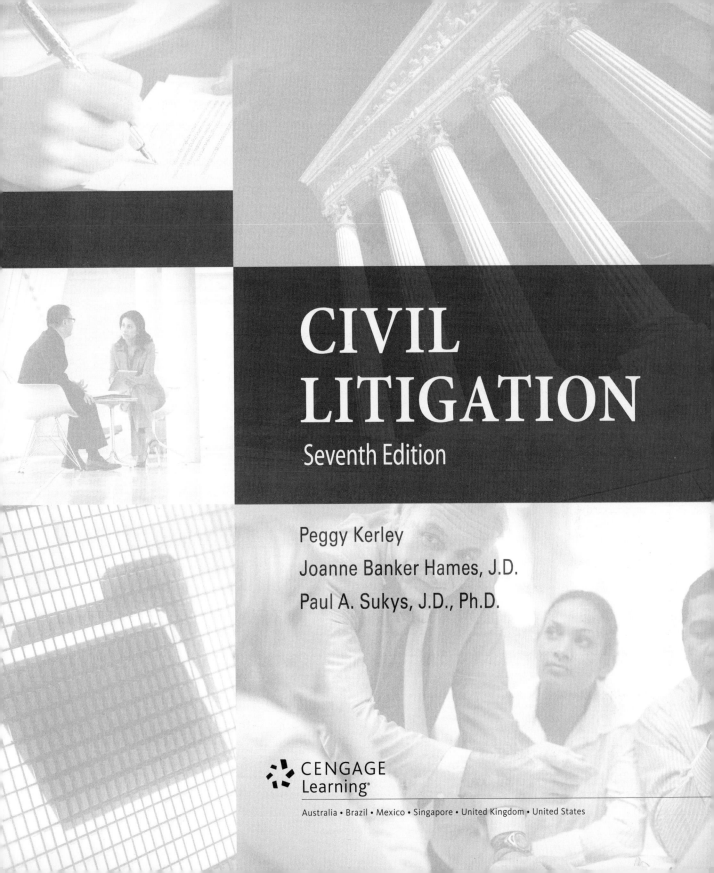

CIVIL LITIGATION

Seventh Edition

Peggy Kerley

Joanne Banker Hames, J.D.

Paul A. Sukys, J.D., Ph.D.

CENGAGE
Learning

Australia • Brazil • Mexico • Singapore • United Kingdom • United States

CENGAGE
Learning®

Civil Litigation, Seventh Edition
Peggy Kerley, Joanne Banker Hames, J.D., and
Paul A. Sukys, J.D., Ph.D.

Vice President and General Manager-Skills and
    Product Planning: Dawn Gerrain

Senior Director, Development-Global Product
    Management, Skills: Marah Bellegarde

Senior Product Development Manager:
    Larry Main

Senior Content Developer: Melissa Riveglia

Product Assistant: Diane E. Chrysler

Market Development Manager: Jonathan
    Sheehan

Marketing Manager: Scott Chrysler

Senior Production Director: Wendy Troeger

Production Manager: Mark Bernard

Content Project Management and Art Direction:
    PreMediaGlobal

Senior Technology Project Manager: Joe Pliss

Media Developer: Deborah Bordeaux

Cover images: digital file: © Pavel Ignatov/
    Shutterstock.com; US Supreme Court building: ©
    fstockfoto/Shutterstock.com; hand signing
    documents: © Sergei Butorin/Shutterstock.com;
    business meeting: © Yuri Arcurs/Shutterstock.
    com; man and woman business meeting: ©
    Monkey Business Images/Shutterstock.com

For product information and technology assistance, contact us at
Cengage Learning Customer & Sales Support, 1-800-354-9706

For permission to use material from this text or product,
submit all requests online at **www.cengage.com/permissions**
Further permissions questions can be e-mailed to
permissionrequest@cengage.com

Library of Congress Control Number: 2013951171

ISBN-13: 978-1-285-44918-0

Loose-leaf Edition:

ISBN-13: 978-1-337-41390-9

Cengage Learning
200 First Stamford Place, 4th Floor
Stamford, CT 06902
USA

Cengage Learning is a leading provider of customized learning solutions with
office locations around the globe, including Singapore, the United Kingdom,
Australia, Mexico, Brazil, and Japan. Locate your local office at
www.cengage.com/global

Cengage Learning products are represented in Canada by Nelson Education, Ltd.

To learn more about Cengage Learning, visit **www.cengage.com**

Purchase any of our products at your local college store or at our preferred online
store **www.cengagebrain.com**

Printed in the United States of America
3 4 5 6 7 20 19 18 17 16

Brief Contents

PART I

INTRODUCTION TO CIVIL LITIGATION

PART II

INITIATING LITIGATION

PART III

DISCOVERY

PART IV

PRETRIAL, TRIAL, AND POSTTRIAL

Contents

PART I

INTRODUCTION TO CIVIL LITIGATION

PART II

INITIATING LITIGATION

CHAPTER 4   **Investigation and Evidence**   92

CHAPTER 5   **The Complaint**   123

CHAPTER 6   **Responses to the Complaint**   169

PART III

DISCOVERY

PART IV

PRETRIAL, TRIAL, AND POSTTRIAL

Preface

The paralegal profession remains one of the fastest growing professions in the United States. One reason for the phenomenal growth of this relatively young profession is the unique role that the paralegal plays within the legal system. The paralegal bridges the gap between the attorney and the legal secretary by bringing to the law office a body of knowledge and a set of skills developed specifically for the day-to-day practical realities of the practice of law.

THE REASON FOR THE DEVELOPMENT OF CIVIL LITIGATION

Paralegal education requires a skillful blend of the principles of the law with its practical application. Nowhere in the law is that skillful blend of theory and practice more imperative than in the study of litigation. The litigation paralegal meets new and different challenges each day on the job. These daily challenges mean that, from the very first hour on the job, the paralegal must be prepared to understand not only what is required in a specific situation but also why it is required. The paralegal is expected to know the most efficient, the most effective, and the most economical way to accomplish the task at hand. In recent years this often involves the use of technology. Familiarity with the many uses of technology, including the Internet, is essential to a litigation paralegal. *Civil Litigation* was planned and written with these specific goals in mind.

While paralegal educators have recognized the requirements of proper paralegal training, many of the available textbooks have not satisfied those requirements, either concentrating too heavily on legal theory or containing one form after another with little or no discussion of the relevant law. Too many times paralegal instructors have had to supplement texts by creating their own practical assignments or by filling in all the legal blanks. This textbook combines theory and practice and includes numerous practical assignments for students. Also, although this is not a computer text, each chapter addresses the use of technology, including the Internet, in litigation.

Additional factors also prompted our development of this text. Civil litigation instructors know that one of the most difficult tasks is covering both federal and state law and doing it in a way that does not confuse students. Although the text emphasizes federal litigation practice and forms, it also incorporates common state practice and forms. Furthermore, several individual state supplements for this text have been prepared and are available for students.

To successfully acquaint the fledgling paralegal student with this intricate mix of legal theory and practical legal skills, we have remained attuned to the fact that, for many students, civil litigation will be their first legal studies course. Consequently, we have been careful to present the study of litigation in a straightforward, yet lively, fashion that should not only inform but also challenge both student and instructor. All legal terms are in bold type and defined in the text, a necessity for beginning paralegal students. We also begin each chapter with a hypothetical case that is fully developed as the chapter unfolds. Our objective in doing this is to show students that the law deals not only with books and documents but also with people—usually people in trouble, often people who have been hurt or unfairly treated and who have turned to the law and to legal professionals for help. The hypothetical cases, found in the chapter opening case commentaries, deal with a variety of factual and legal problems illustrating the breadth of civil litigation in the legal system. In addition, so that students can follow the progression of two cases, we have included assignments in each chapter that refer back to the cases introduced in the Chapter 1 Commentary. It is our belief that this approach will give a realistic and energetic flavor to the study of litigation.

THE ORGANIZATION OF CIVIL LITIGATION

For clarity and ease of understanding, we have chosen to use chronological order throughout the text. The book has been divided into four parts representing the four major stages in the litigation process. In Part I we introduce the student to the role of the paralegal in the litigation process. The two chapters in this section also provide an overview of the court system and the litigation process, along with a discussion of the concepts of jurisdiction and venue.

In Part II we begin the study of litigation in earnest by walking the student through the opening stages of a lawsuit. Naturally, this means concentrating on the preliminary legal and practical concerns that must be taken into consideration at the onset of a lawsuit. Consequently, these early chapters focus on such things as interviewing and investigation skills, the role of evidence in litigation, the writing and filing of initial and responsive pleadings, and an understanding of motion practice. To accomplish our objective of making the text a practical guide for students, we have explained the requirements for pleadings and motions found in the Federal Rules of Civil Procedure and have included many examples and sample documents. We have also provided detailed explanations and guidelines for drafting various legal documents.

Following our chronological plan, Part III explores the discovery process. Because the paralegal has an extensive role in discovery, we have devoted one of the six chapters in this section to an overview of the process, including a lengthy discussion of the most recent changes to the Federal Rules of Civil Procedure relating to discovery. The remaining five chapters discuss specific discovery techniques. Separate chapters cover depositions, interrogatories, requests for physical and mental examinations, requests for the production of documents, and requests for admission. Part III also includes the new amendments to the Federal Rules of Civil Procedure, which were added recently to deal with the growing use of electronically stored information (ESI) in the litigation process. Again, in keeping with our objective of providing students with a practical guide, we have explained in great detail the day-to-day role of the paralegal during each stage of the discovery process. These chapters combine theory with practice, covering the discovery rules in the Federal Rules of Civil Procedure. We have also included an extensive array of sample documents, including requests for physical and mental examinations, requests for the production of documents, and requests for admissions. As a supplement to Part III, Appendix A provides a sample deposition based on the case scenario that serves as the basis for the examples and samples in Chapter 9.

Part IV provides the student with an in-depth view of the final stages in the litigation process. We have devoted one chapter to pretrial settlements, dismissals, and alternative dispute resolution; one to the trial itself; and one to posttrial procedures. Again, in keeping with our goal of making *Civil Litigation* a practical guide, we have provided students with a wide variety of suggestions for making the trial process run as smoothly as possible. Some of these tips include how to prepare a trial notebook, how to arrange for accommodations during the trial, how to contact court personnel, how to prepare a jury profile, and how to use shadow juries among many others. We have included a wide variety of practical illustrations and sample documents, including releases and dismissals, a settlement summary, a settlement letter, a detailed settlement agreement, a notice of appeal, and a motion for enlargement of time, among others. Sample letters, charts, and diagrams also are included, as are appropriate references to the Federal Rules of Civil Procedure and the Federal Rules of Appellate Procedure.

Chapter Organization

Each chapter follows the same organizational pattern. Chapters begin with a case commentary, establishing a realistic setting for the material to be covered in the chapter. This is followed by a statement of the chapter objectives. The student immediately identifies the learning goals of the specific chapter. Text material is presented along with multiple charts, diagrams, and sample forms. Where applicable, reference is made to the facts described in the commentary. All legal terms are bold and defined. Special features in each chapter address the application of technology and the Internet to litigation practice. Each chapter ends with a chapter summary, questions for review, chapter exercises, and a major chapter project. At the end of each chapter are assignments relating to the fictional *Bennett* and *Douglass* cases, which are introduced in Chapter 1.

Teaching and Learning Features

The practical nature of *Civil Litigation* makes it an ideal text for use in and beyond the classroom. Because of its many forms, letters, memos, charts, and diagrams, it can easily serve as a reference manual for the paralegal in the litigation section of a law firm. Nevertheless, the primary objective of the book is to serve as a textbook for a basic civil litigation course for paralegal students. Consequently, we have included several important features to enhance this objective and to make the book the best in its market. Those features include:

- an outline at the beginning of each chapter pointing out the major topics to be covered in the chapter
- case commentaries at the beginning of each chapter that illustrate the varied nature of civil litigation, demonstrate the practical application of the matters contained within the chapter, and give a realistic color to the study of litigation

- a list of learning objectives at the beginning of each chapter to provide the student with a sense of direction
- a set of review questions at the end of each chapter to provide students with a sense of continuity with the learning objectives and to guarantee that students understand the chapter material
- definitions of all legal terms in the chapter material (all terms are bold), in a running glossary and in a full glossary at the end of the text
- chapter exercises at the end of each chapter that include questions for analysis and practical assignments, including those that require students to investigate specific state statutes and apply them to the topics covered in the chapter
- a chapter project that offers a chance for the student to undertake a major paralegal task related to the matter in the chapter, including such activities as writing letters and memos; drafting pleadings, motions, and affidavits; and preparing discovery devices
- case assignments in each chapter based on the same cases to give students the opportunity to work one case from start to finish
- an Automated Litigation Support feature in each chapter that relates the effective use of technology to the material in the chapter
- a Finding It on the Internet feature in each chapter that describes Internet applications to the material in the chapter and includes several Web sites as well as Internet assignments
- an appendix containing the transcript of a deposition
- an appendix containing research material and forms to enable students to complete the case assignments based on the Chapter 1 hypothetical cases
- state-specific supplements for Florida, New York, Texas, California, Ohio, and Pennsylvania are provided on the Instructor Companion Site and MindTap.

THE SEVENTH EDITION OF CIVIL LITIGATION

When we first wrote this text, our basic plan was to present the litigation process in chronological order, emphasizing the practical aspects of litigation and the role of the paralegal in the process. Comments from instructors and students who have used the book convince us that this is the correct approach. However, nothing in the law, including litigation, remains static. Of course, there have been changes in the law. But more important, the development and use of technology, including the Internet, have resulted in tremendous changes in the way litigation is practiced. The increased utilization of paralegals in law firms, especially in the area of litigation, has also affected litigation practice. Attorneys have come to recognize the full potential of paralegals and are now giving them more and more responsibility. We have revised this text with these thoughts in mind. Accordingly, the following matters have been revised.

- Where applicable, legal concepts have been updated to reflect revisions of the U.S. Code and Federal Rules.
- Where applicable, the feature illustrating the ways that technology plays a role in the litigation process was updated.

- Where applicable, Internet references were updated so as to allow students to avail themselves of the wealth of information currently related to litigation. Of primary importance are sites containing the U.S. Code, the Federal Rules of Civil Procedure, and the Federal Rules of Evidence. Accessing these rules through the Internet assures that students will be reading the latest version of the law, something that would not happen if the rules were included as an appendix to the text.

- Material on ethical concerns raised by the use of technology in the law firm was added, including telephone appearances for motion hearings.

- The extensive changes made to the time limits related to amendments, responsive pleadings, and motions are discussed.

- The discovery chapters were revised to include new amendments to the Federal Rules of Civil Procedure, especially those related to handling electronically stored information (ESI), new material on the Sedona Conference including the Fourteen Principles of ESI that formed the groundwork for the amendments to the Federal Rules of Civil Procedure. The discovery chapters also include new material on the EU Data Protection Directive and the Safe Harbor Principles enforced by the U.S. Department of Commerce.

- New material was added on the Genetic Information Nondiscrimination Act of 2008 and how it may relate to the rules governing physical and mental examinations.

- Additional material relating to the Uniform Arbitration Act of 2000 is included.

- Major revisions on the presentation of evidence at trial and jury deliberation and verdicts are discussed.

- Appendix B contains additional documents related to the Bennett case, a hypothetical employment law case that allows students to work on all stages of one case. In addition, documents from a new case were added to give students the opportunity to work on a case in state court.

HOW TO USE THIS TEXT

This text was designed to follow the litigation process from beginning to end. Following this pattern, we believe, gives the student a realistic and complete picture of the litigation process and the role of the paralegal at the various stages of litigation. We do offer some suggestions about the various chapter features.

- Students can be required to answer the Questions for Review in writing. Alternatively, they can be used for discussion in class either with the entire class or in small groups.

- The Chapter Exercises provide opportunities for students to explore state law and to engage in factual analysis. Students can, of course, be assigned all of the exercises. Alternatively, with exercises requiring outside research, small groups in the class can each be assigned a different exercise and asked to report their findings to the class. The exercises requiring analysis can be assigned for writing or for discussion.

- The Chapter Project provides an important opportunity for students to engage in realistic litigation tasks. For the most part, the projects at the end of each chapter relate to the case commentary. Students are given the experience of working on different cases, just as litigation paralegals commonly do. Additionally students can work on one case from start to finish by completing the assignments found at the end of each chapter relating to the *Bennett* and *Douglass* cases. Selected hypothetical documents from these cases are found in Appendix B.

- Internet access gives students the opportunity to read actual code sections (both federal and state) and case law. Relevant Web sites are included in the chapters.

- The chapters in the state-specific supplements relate state law to the material in the corresponding chapter in the text. In those states for which there is a state-specific supplement, reading assignments should include both the text and the corresponding chapter in the supplement.

SUPPLEMENTAL TEACHING AND LEARNING MATERIALS

Instructor Companion Site

Instructor's Manual

The Instructor's Manual has been revised to incorporate changes in the text and to provide comprehensive teaching support. The Instructor's Manual contains the following: Syllabus and lesson plans for each chapter

- Chapter outlines
- Answers to exercises in the text
- Test Bank and answer key

PowerPoint Presentations

Customizable PowerPoint® Presentations focus on key points for each chapter. (PowerPoint® is a registered trademark of the Microsoft Corporation.)

Cengage Learning Testing Powered by Cognero is a flexible, online system that allows you to:

- author, edit, and manage test bank content from multiple Cengage Learning solutions
- create multiple test versions in an instant
- deliver tests from your LMS, your classroom, or wherever you want

Start Right Away!

Cengage Learning Testing Powered by Cognero works on any operating system or browser.

- No special installs or downloads needed
- Create tests from school, home, the coffee shop—anywhere with Internet access

What Will You Find?

- **Simplicity at every step.** A desktop-inspired interface features drop-down menus and familiar, intuitive tools that take you through content creation and management with ease.
- **Full-featured test generator.** Create ideal assessments with your choice of 15 question types (including true/false, multiple choice, opinion scale/likert, and essay).

Multi-language support, an equation editor, and unlimited metadata help ensure your tests are complete and compliant.

- **Cross-compatible capability.** Import and export content into other systems.

To access additional course materials, please go to login.cengage.com, then use your SSO (single sign on) login to access the materials.

MindTap 🟠 MindTap™

MindTap for Civil Litigation is a highly personalized fully online learning platform of authoritative content, assignments, and services offering you a tailored presentation of course curriculum created by your instructor. MindTap for Civil Litigation guides you through the course curriculum via an innovative learning path where you will complete reading assignments, annotate your readings, complete homework, and engage with quizzes and assessments. MindTap includes a variety of web-apps known as "MindApps" — allowing functionality like having the text read aloud to you as well as MindApps that allow you to synchronize your notes with your personal Evernote account. MindApps are tightly woven into the MindTap platform and enhance your learning experience.

How MindTap Helps Students Succeed?

- Use the Progress App to see where you stand at all times—individually and compared to highest performers in your class
- ReadSpeaker reads the course material to you
- MyNotes provides the ability to highlight text and take notes—that link back to the MindTap material for easy reference when you are studying for an exam or working on a project
- *Merriam Webster Dictionary* and a glossary are only a click away
- Flashcards are pre-created to help you memorize the key terms

Not using MindTap in your course?

- It's an online destination housing ALL your course material and assignments . . . neatly organized to match your syllabus
- It's loaded with study tools that help you learn the material more easily
- To learn more go to www.cengage.com/mindtap or ask your instructor to try it out

---

Please note that the Internet resources are of a time-sensitive nature and URL addresses may often change or be deleted.

Acknowledgments

Civil Litigation is the result of the planning and input of many individuals and entities. With grateful appreciation, we would like to acknowledge and give our thanks to our editors; to Bob Nirkind, who supported the authors in the original ideas for the book; to the former Southeastern Paralegal Institute, which initially introduced Peggy Kerley to the exciting field of paralegal textbook publishing; to our former and present students for the positive comments about the text; to Mark Hames, for his support, encouragement, and especially his assistance with technology questions and issues; to Kerry Hames, attorney, for her assistance; to Terry Ellis, director of the Administration of Justice program at DeAnza College, for his support and flexibility and to all of the paralegal students at DeAnza College who have helped in the development of this edition; to Addie Tackett, former director of the Radiologic Technology Department of North Central State College, and Dale Maurer, a registered radiologic technologist, who provided the medical details for the sample deposition; to L. Dan Richards, John Falls, Diane Hipsher, and Judith Sturgill of North Central State College for their support of the paralegal program at the college; to the spring quarter 1991 advanced business law students at North Central State College for their enthusiastic willingness to test several of the cases in the text; to John and Louise Sukys, Jennifer Ann Chiocco, Ashley Gentille, Megan Gentille, and Susan Sukys for their patient understanding and loyal encouragement; and to the many paralegal students whose enthusiasm and intelligence continually motivate us. The authors gratefully acknowledge the encouragement and support and extend their sincere appreciation to these individuals and entities.

In addition, we acknowledge the contributions of the following reviewers, whose suggestions and insights have helped us enormously:

Sally Bisson
College of St. Mary
Omaha, NE

Howard Sokol
Athens Area Technical Institute
Athens, GA

Tamara McIntosh
Cincinnati State Technical and
Community College
Cincinnati, OH

About the Authors

Peggy N. Kerley is a litigation paralegal, working with the law firm of Weil, Gotshal & Manges, and a former paralegal instructor at Southeastern Paralegal Institute, in Dallas, Texas. She has more than 45 years of legal experience. Ms. Kerley received her undergraduate degree in political economy from the University of Texas at Dallas and her paralegal certificate from the University of Oklahoma. She is also the author of another paralegal text, *Employment Law for the Paralegal*.

Joanne Banker Hames is a California attorney and instructor in the paralegal program at DeAnza Community College, located in Cupertino, California. She earned her J.D. degree from Santa Clara University. For several years Ms. Hames was employed as an attorney in a busy litigation law firm. During that time she was involved in all aspects of civil litigation, including pretrial preparation, jury trials, and appeals. For the past several years, she has been involved primarily in paralegal education, teaching at DeAnza Community College and previously at Santa Clara University Paralegal Institute. Civil litigation is among the classes she teaches. She is also a co-author of three other paralegal texts, *Constitutional Law: Principles and Practice, Introduction to Law,* and *Legal Research, Analysis, and Writing*.

Paul A. Sukys is a professor of philosophy, law, and legal studies in the Humanities Department of North Central State College in Mansfield, Ohio. He is co-author of *Business and Personal Law* and *Business Law with UCC Applications*, and author of *Lifting the Scientific Veil: Science Appreciation for the Nonscientist*, a text that explores the complex relationships that exist among science, law, philosophy, and politics. Dr. Sukys is also a former member of the advisory committee for the paralegal program at North Central State College and was instrumental in designing the curriculum for that program. He received his bachelor's and master's degrees from John Carroll University in Cleveland. Dr. Sukys received his law degree from Cleveland State University and his Ph.D. from The Union Institute and University in Cincinnati. He also serves as an adjunct professor at Mount Vernon Nazarene University and at Ashland University. He is a member of the Ohio Bar.

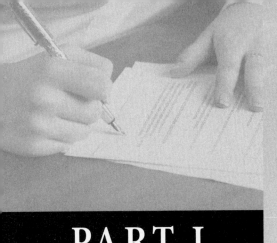

PART I

Introduction to Civil Litigation

CHAPTER 1 # Litigation and the Paralegal

CHAPTER OUTLINE

INITIAL CASE ASSIGNMENTS

You have just started your first day working as a litigation paralegal. You were hired as a paralegal by a litigation law firm consisting of numerous attorneys, paralegals, legal secretaries, and word processors. The law firm has several groups specializing in different areas of litigation. Areas of specialty include employment law, intellectual property, real property, civil rights, personal injury, insurance, and securities. Your supervisor tells you that currently the firm has several pending cases in different phases of litigation. Some of these cases are in federal court and others are in state court. Eventually you may be asked to assist in these cases. Initially you are assigned to the following two cases:

Bennett v. Rikards-Hayley

In this case, Alice Bennett, the firm's client, maintains that she was denied a promotion and eventually fired from her job at Rikards-Hayley because of sex discrimination. She claims that she suffered extreme emotional distress and was out of work for a considerable time. She believes she is entitled to money damages from her former employer.

Hewitt v. Portman and Douglass Financial Services, Inc.

In this case, the firm's client, Douglass Financial Services, Inc., is threatened with a lawsuit by Jessica Hewitt. Ms. Hewitt is claiming damages as a result of an automobile accident. The driver of the vehicle that collided with Ms. Hewitt is Evan Portman, an employee of the firm's client. Prior to the collision, Evan Portman attended a Douglass Financial office party where he consumed alcohol. Ms. Hewitt claims that Douglass Financial, the firm's client, is liable for the accident because it provided alcohol to Evan Portman.

Your first assignment is to familiarize yourself with the office files for these cases.

This chapter introduces you to the area of legal practice known as civil litigation and presents an overview of such topics as the nature of civil litigation, the distinction between criminal and civil litigation, and the role of the paralegal in civil litigation. After reading this chapter, you should be able to:

- differentiate between civil and criminal procedure.
- identify the role of substantive law and procedural rules to civil litigation.
- outline the basic litigation process.
- identify different types of civil litigation cases.
- list alternatives to litigation.
- differentiate between primary and secondary sources of law.
- explain the role of technology to litigation.
- list tasks performed by litigation paralegals.
- identify skills required of litigation paralegals.
- describe activities that lead to a paralegal's success in a litigation law firm.

INTRODUCTION TO CIVIL LITIGATION

civil litigation
The process of resolving private disputes through the court system.

trial
A court proceeding in which parties to a lawsuit present their evidence to a judge or jury and the judge or jury make a decision in favor of one party.

substantive law
Laws that determine parties' rights and obligations as opposed to the procedures used to enforce those rights.

procedural law
Laws that set forth legal procedures or methods used by parties to enforce their rights or to oppose claims made against them.

criminal law
Laws that prohibit conduct that society deems harmful and provide for punishment in the form of jail, fines, or probation.

In a perfect society, discrimination would be nonexistent, businesses would not infringe on the legally protected rights of others, parties would not act negligently, and all business transactions would be conducted with fairness and honesty. The cases introduced in the Commentaries of each chapter illustrate that we do not live in a perfect society. As a result, disputes arise. When the parties are unable to resolve their disputes, they rely on the legal system. Although the legal system provides various methods to help parties resolve disputes, one of the most important is the process of civil litigation.

Civil litigation is the process of resolving private disputes through the court system. Unless the parties are able to resolve their dispute, the litigation process usually results in a **trial**, or hearing, where the parties present their evidence to a judge or jury, who then decide the dispute. Before this happens, however, a great deal of investigation, research, and preparation takes place. Although most of this occurs outside of the courtroom, it is an important part of the litigation process. Litigation attorneys and their paralegals often spend considerable time gathering and analyzing the facts as well as researching the law. Formal legal documents must be prepared and filed with the court, witnesses must be interviewed, and other evidence must be identified and located.

Differences between Criminal and Civil Cases

The U.S. court system handles both criminal and civil disputes. However, criminal and civil cases are very different. They are based on different substantive laws and the cases are subject to different procedural rules. **Substantive laws** create, define, or explain our rights or obligations. **Procedural laws** set forth the methods used to enforce those rights or obligations. Criminal cases are based on substantive **criminal laws** such as murder, theft, and possession of drugs. Substantive civil laws include such areas as contracts, real estate and construction, commercial and business transactions, intellectual property, and consumer rights. One of the most common areas of substantive law resulting in litigation is the area of tort law, especially the tort of negligence. This area, often referred to as personal injury litigation, includes lawsuits stemming from automobile accidents, professional malpractice, and product liability. The cases presented in the Commentary at the beginning of this and subsequent chapters are all based on different substantive *civil* laws.

In some instances, the same case may result in both a civil action and a criminal case. In such an instance, the underlying substantive law, as well as the procedural rules, differs. For example, consider the *Hewitt* case described in the commentary. Evan Portman, one of the defendants in the case, may be civilly liable to Hewitt because of the substantive law of negligence. On the other hand, he may be subject to criminal prosecution if he was driving under the influence of alcohol. Procedurally, the two cases would be very different, as described below. Knowing the differences between a criminal case and civil case is important for any litigation paralegal.

Criminal Cases   Whereas the goal of a civil case is to compensate an individual who has been damaged, criminal cases are concerned with punishing individuals who commit a crime. This punishment is jail, a fine, or probation. A criminal case is generally initiated and prosecuted by a government prosecutor and the case is filed on behalf of the state or federal government. The victim is usually a witness in the case. The procedures and rules that apply when an individual is accused of committing a crime are known as the rules of **criminal procedure**. To a large extent, the Bill of Rights found in the U.S. Constitution governs the rules of criminal procedure. In a criminal case the defendant enjoys various rights, such as the right not to testify against himself. The defendant also has the right to a court-appointed counsel if he is indigent and is entitled to a speedy trial—all rights found in the Constitution. None of these rights exist in civil cases.

For example, consider the *Hewitt* case mentioned in the Commentary. Driving under the influence of alcohol is a crime. A local prosecutor could file criminal charges against Portman and if he is found guilty, the punishment could be jail. Ms. Hewitt would need to file a separate civil case to obtain money damages for her injuries and her pain and suffering. The government prosecutor would not be involved in the civil case. When the same act results in both a civil action and a criminal case, the two legal cases are always kept separate. They are never tried together. In part, this is because a different standard, or burden of proof, is required in the criminal case. The standard of evidence used to judge the criminal case is higher than the standard applied in civil cases.

Considerable differences between civil and criminal cases also exist in the documents that are filed in court, the proceedings that occur before trial, the hearings that take place in court, and the kinds of relief or remedies the court can order. The documents, proceedings, and kinds of remedies discussed in this and subsequent chapters apply only in civil cases.

Civil Cases   The rules of civil litigation, sometimes referred to as **civil procedure**, apply only if a substantive **civil law** is involved. The procedures and rules that would govern these lawsuits are known as the rules of civil procedure. The law of civil litigation consists of both procedural and substantive laws. Procedural law sets forth the methods we use to enforce our rights. In civil cases, procedural law answers questions such as these:

- In what court should an action be filed?
- What types of documents should be filed?
- What are the technical requirements for documents filed in court?
- How must the defendant be notified of the lawsuit?
- What are the time requirements for the various procedures?

This book concentrates on familiarizing you with the basic procedures for civil cases. Substantive law determines what rights a party has. As your paralegal education continues, you will take specific courses in the various areas of substantive law. Today, the basic procedures in a civil case require the use of technology. As you proceed through this text, you will also be introduced to the role that technology plays. Along with taking courses in substantive laws, to be an effective litigation paralegal you should continue to develop your technology skills.

See Exhibit 1-1 for a comparison of civil and criminal cases in the Hewitt matter.

criminal procedure
The rules that apply in a criminal case and determine how a criminal case proceeds through the legal system; these are based on federal and state constitutions, codes, rules of court, and cases.

civil procedure
The rules that apply in a civil case and determine how a civil case proceeds through the legal system; in federal courts many of the rules are found in the Federal Rules of Civil Procedure and the Federal Rules of Appellate Procedure.

civil laws
Laws dealing with private disputes between parties.

EXHIBIT 1-1 Comparison of a Civil and a Criminal Case

	CRIMINAL CASE	CIVIL CASE
Parties	*State v. Portman*	*Hewitt v. Portman*
Documents	Usually only one pleading: a complaint filed by a government prosecutor or an indictment filed by the Grand Jury.	Both sides must file pleadings and often more than one pleading is filed.
Pretrial Proceedings	Defendants usually appear in court for arraignments and other hearings. Some proceedings are handled by attorneys, but in some states defendants must also appear.	Most pretrial proceedings are handled by attorneys, and the parties make no appearance until trial.
Trial	Jury or nonjury; defendant is found guilty or not guilty; to prevail the prosecutor must prove the case beyond a reasonable doubt.	Jury or nonjury; defendant is found liable or not liable; to prevail the plaintiff must prove the case by a preponderance of the evidence.
Remedy	Jail, fine, or probation.	Money damages or other specific relief; never jail.
Appeal	Only the defendant can appeal a trial verdict.	Either side can file an appeal.

Copyright © 2015 Cengage Learning®

plaintiff
The party who initiates a civil or criminal lawsuit in court.

defendant
The party who is sued in either a civil or criminal case.

complaint
Usually the first document filed in court in connection with a lawsuit; this sets forth the allegations or contentions of the plaintiff and states the basis for the action and the type of relief requested from the court.

petition
An initial document filed with the court asking the court for some order. Sometimes petitions are filed in conjunction with a complaint (e.g., asking the court to appoint a guardian for a party who cannot file a lawsuit); sometimes petitions are filed in lieu of a complaint (e.g., in certain jurisdictions petitions and not complaints are used in divorce cases).

An Overview of Civil Litigation

The rules and procedures followed in the litigation process vary from court to court. Rules or procedures applicable in one state may not apply in another state, and rules applicable in a state court may not apply if the action is in a federal court. However, the general litigation process is similar from one court to another.

The Parties   The parties in the litigation process are known as the **plaintiff**, the party bringing the lawsuit, and the **defendant**, the person or entity who is sued. Most often the parties hire lawyers to represent them. Attorneys are not parties to the actions.

Pleadings   Pleadings are documents that describe the nature of the dispute and, most often, contain the factual contentions of the parties. In a contested case, both the plaintiff and the defendant file pleadings. The process of civil litigation formally begins when the plaintiff files a written document in court. This document is generally called a **complaint**, although in some instances it is referred to as a **petition**. In the complaint, or petition, the plaintiff alleges or claims that the defendant has done something, or has failed to do something, that entitles the plaintiff to relief. As noted earlier, the relief is frequently money but may involve nonmonetary matters, such as determining the validity of a will, issuing an injunction (an order requiring the defendant to do something or to stop doing something), or ordering specific performance of a contract (an order requiring the defendant to comply with the terms of an agreement).

After the complaint or petition is filed, the defendant is served with a copy of the complaint and is given the opportunity to contest the lawsuit. If the defendant challenges the factual basis of the lawsuit, he or she files a document called an **answer**. In an answer, the defendant states why the plaintiff is not entitled to any relief. If a defendant challenges the lawsuit on the basis of a legal issue, a defendant may file other documents. (This method of responding to a complaint is discussed in detail in Chapters 6 and 7.) A defendant who was served with a complaint also has the option of doing nothing and ignoring the complaint. If this is done, the defendant is said to **default**. In most cases the plaintiff then obtains a **judgment**, an award of money damages or other relief.

Discovery   If both the plaintiff and defendant filed appropriate pleadings with the court, litigation proceeds with **discovery**. Discovery is an extremely important part of the litigation process. During this process, parties uncover facts, documents, and other evidence in possession of the opposing party, or in some cases in possession of a third party. Discovery allows the parties to determine the strengths and weaknesses of their case and be better prepared for trial. Paralegals play an important role in the discovery process.

Motions   Prior to trial, parties may request orders from the court related to the case. These requests range from very simple procedural issues, such as requests for more time in which to file a pleading, to more complicated legal issues, such as a request to dismiss the case. These requests are known as **motions**. Some motions, if granted, dispose of the case before any trial takes place. For example, if one party makes a motion to dismiss the case and that motion is granted, there is no trial. The matter was decided without any need for a trial (however, an appeal may result from this kind of order). Motions can also occur during or after a trial.

Trial and Judgments   If the parties do not settle their dispute, and the case is not disposed of by a motion, the parties eventually go to court and present evidence to support their claims. This occurs at a trial, and a judge or jury decide the case. The litigation process does not necessarily end at trial because in a civil case both sides have the right to appeal to a higher court. The higher court (the appellate court) considers whether a substantial legal error was committed (see Exhibit 1-2). Even if no appeal is filed, if the plaintiff wins the case, collecting or enforcing the judgment may require further court action. The plaintiff may need to obtain a **writ of execution**, a document that allows the plaintiff to seize and sell the defendant's property and use the proceeds to satisfy the judgment.

TYPES OF CIVIL LAWSUITS

Civil lawsuits range from very simple procedures to very complex court proceedings. Consider the following: Lombardi loans McNair $1,000. McNair signs a promissory note for that amount, promising to pay the money back in three months. At the end of four months McNair has still not paid back the money. Lombardi asks for the money, but McNair refuses to pay. The dispute between Lombardi and McNair is very simple, as are the legal issues involved in the case. Nonetheless, if McNair refuses to pay, Lombardi could

---

answer
The initial pleading filed by the defendant in a lawsuit, contesting the factual and/or legal basis for the lawsuit.

default
Failure to file an answer or other responsive pleading within the proper time; can eventually lead to a default judgment.

judgment
In a civil court action, the final decision from the trial court.

discovery
In a civil case, the procedures by which all parties have the right to obtain information from other parties, and in some cases from witnesses; includes such procedures as depositions, interrogatories, and production of documents.

motion
A request that a judge make a ruling or take some other action, most often in connection with a pending lawsuit.

writ of execution
A court order authorizing the seizure and sale of a person's property to satisfy a judgment against that party.

EXHIBIT 1-2 The Litigation Process

```
                    ┌─────────────────────────────────────┐
                    │  Plaintiff Files and Serves a Complaint  │
                    └─────────────────────────────────────┘
                              │
               ┌──────────────┴──────────────┐
    ┌──────────────────┐   or    ┌──────────────────┐
    │ Defendant Responds │        │ Defendant Defaults │
    └──────────────────┘          └──────────────────┘
               │                             │
    ┌──────────────────┐          ┌──────────────────┐
    │ Discovery Commences │        │  Judgment Entered  │
    └──────────────────┘          └──────────────────┘
               │
    ┌──────────────────┐
    │  Pretrial Motions  │
    │    (If Needed)     │
    └──────────────────┘
               │
    ┌──────────────────┐
    │       Trial        │
    │ (By Judge or by Jury) │
    └──────────────────┘
               │
    ┌──────────────────┐
    │  Judgment Entered  │
    └──────────────────┘
               │
    ┌──────────────────┐
    │    Either Side     │
    │    Can Appeal      │
    └──────────────────┘
```

file a lawsuit against McNair. Such a case has one plaintiff, Lombardi, and one defendant, McNair. The complaint itself will be short and straightforward.

Many cases are more complex. Consider the following: Best Roofing Material manufactures a synthetic shingle used primarily for reroofing of houses. The material is very popular and installed on thousands of homes by various roofing contractors. After a few years numerous roofs leak, resulting in personal property loss because of water. Many of the homeowners want the roofs replaced, and some want additional damages for individual property losses. The manufacturer claims that damages are the responsibility of various installers. Installers claim the roofing material is defective. Before any lawsuits are filed, the manufacturer filed bankruptcy. The issues in this case are extremely complex. Complex cases like this present many practical problems. Several legal and procedural questions also arise, as does the need for extensive pretrial preparation. Often voluminous documents must be organized, analyzed, and indexed. Technology plays a critical role in these cases.

Many courts have developed special procedures and rules for complex litigation. The Federal Judicial Center, an education and research agency for the federal courts, publishes a *Manual for Complex Litigation,* describing approaches that trial judges have found useful for complex cases in federal court. (The *Manual,* along with many other publications, can be found on the Web site for the Federal Judicial Center <http://www.fjc.gov/>.) However, whether Lombardi sues McNair for $1,000 or multiple homeowners sue several defendants, the basic litigation procedures outlined in this section apply.

Civil lawsuits are not only categorized as simple or complex but often also are described by the type of substantive law involved. The following are some common types of civil lawsuits:

Personal injury litigation	Litigation resulting from physical or emotional injuries. Types of personal injury litigation are automobile accidents, accidents occurring on another's property, product liability, and medical and other professional malpractice.
Employment litigation	Litigation related to employment disputes, such as claims of unlawful discharge or discrimination.
Intellectual property litigation	Litigation related to rights in intellectual property, such as patents, trademarks, trade names, and copyrights.
Construction litigation	Litigation related to claims of faulty construction; damages may include claims for property damage or, in some cases, injuries resulting from the faulty construction.
Securities litigation	Litigation related to stocks and other securities, which often involve class action claims by stockholders against a corporation or its directors and/or officers.
Business litigation	Litigation related to general business matters, such as contract disputes and partnership disputes.
Real estate litigation	Litigation related to real property, such as ownership rights, possession rights, and landlord–tenant issues.
Asbestos litigation	Litigation related to the various diseases and injuries caused by exposure to asbestos.
Civil rights litigation	Litigation related to damages claimed as a result of the violation of one's state or federal civil rights.

ALTERNATIVES AND LIMITATIONS TO LITIGATION

Not all civil disputes are resolved through litigation. In fact, most disputes are not litigated. Several other methods of resolving disputes exist.

alternative dispute resolution (ADR)
Ways to resolve a civil dispute without resort to a legal action.

negotiation (negotiate)
Discussion between opposing parties in an attempt to settle a case; usually involving compromise by both sides.

settlement
An agreement that resolves a dispute without the necessity of a court action.

mediation
A nonbinding process in which a neutral third party helps disputing parties reach a settlement.

mediator
The neutral third person who facilitates the mediation process.

arbitration
An out-of-court process in which disputing parties present their case to a neutral third person who listens to evidence from each disputing party and makes a decision; the decision is sometimes binding and sometimes not binding.

arbitrator
The neutral third party who presides over the arbitration process and makes a decision.

Alternative Dispute Resolution

Because of the time and expense involved in litigation, courts and attorneys have turned to alternative ways to settle disputes. The use of these alternative procedures is known as **alternative dispute resolution (ADR)**. The courts encourage the use of ADR, and many courts require parties to try these methods before trial. The term *alternative dispute resolution* applies to many of the procedures that parties use in an attempt to avoid litigation. Three common forms of ADR are negotiation, mediation, and arbitration. **Negotiation** involves the disputing parties' discussing their problems with one another and—it is hoped—reaching an agreement or **settlement** of those problems. **Mediation** is a form of settlement that uses a third person, known as a **mediator**, to help the parties come to an agreement to settle their differences. **Arbitration** is an out-of-court process in which a neutral party, known as an **arbitrator**, hears both sides of the dispute and then makes a decision. Alternative dispute resolution is discussed in more detail in Chapter 14.

Administrative Agency Hearings

Some civil disputes cannot be resolved through litigation because the law does not allow it. For example, if an individual has a dispute with the government over Social Security payments, that dispute is first presented to a special board or agency established to handle such disputes. Often, whether a case can be resolved through the courts is a question of state law. In many states, for example, absent special circumstances, employees who are injured on the job cannot sue their employers. However, employees are entitled to compensation for their injuries. When disputes arise regarding the extent of the compensation, they are resolved by a special board or agency that exists separate from the court system.

Legislative and Judicial Limitations

In recent years a great deal of criticism has been directed to the area of tort litigation relating to personal injury claims. Critics point out that these cases often result in fraudulent practices and abuses of the legal system, as well as contributing to the high cost of insurance premiums. Awards of punitive damages are also highly criticized. As a result, various state and federal legislatures have considered legislation to control this area. In the past, several states adopted laws, known as "no-fault" insurance laws, that prevent or severely limit a person in filing a lawsuit stemming from an automobile accident. Although a similar law has been considered by the U.S. Congress, it has never been passed.

More recently, legislatures have considered laws to regulate the areas of medical malpractice. The rising cost of medical care has led many states to limit the amount of damages for pain and suffering that can be awarded in medical malpractice cases.[1] At least one state court, though, has found this limit unconstitutional in that it denies the plaintiff the right to a jury trial.[2] The enactment of the Affordable Healthcare Act has led to discussion among federal legislators concerning limits for medical malpractice cases, but no action has yet been taken.[3]

Various laws also limit punitive damages. Some states impose restrictions, but more importantly, the U.S. Supreme Court has ruled that excessive punitive damages violate the Due Process Clause of the Constitution. Another area affected by recent legislation is the class action lawsuit. In 2005 Congress enacted, and the president signed, a new law known as the Class Action Fairness Act of 2005. Among the important provisions in this act are a limit on attorney fees and broader access to the federal courts. Critics claim that this will be prejudicial to plaintiffs.[4]

In recent years, the Supreme Court has also decided cases dealing with a variety of civil litigation topics, including jurisdiction, attorney fees, class actions, arbitration clauses, sovereign immunity, and discovery.

LOCATING THE LAW OF CIVIL LITIGATION

A litigation paralegal inevitably has questions about the rules or procedures that must be followed in particular cases. The ability to find the answers to these questions is an important skill often developed through legal research courses, usually a required part of your paralegal education. Familiarity with a law library is a must. Most law offices have a collection of legal books and often this collection is sufficient for regular research needs. You may need additional resources, however, and, therefore, you should also be familiar with a more comprehensive law library. Many counties maintain these for attorneys and the public. Familiarity with legal resources on the Internet is also a must. Many codes, rules, and cases are available online. Web sites maintained by the state, by local courts, by educational institutions, and even by commercial vendors often provide these resources without any cost. Two major fee-based legal databases, Westlaw and Lexis, provide as much, if not more, materials as any large library. There is a fee to access these sites, although many attorneys do subscribe.

One of the basic concepts when researching any question of law is the distinction between primary sources of law and secondary sources of law. **Primary sources** contain the actual law itself. The primary sources of the law are federal and state constitutions, codes (or statutes), rules of court, and opinions from the various courts. **Secondary sources** explain or describe the law. Form books and practice guides are important *secondary* sources of the law.

Primary Sources

The primary sources of the law of civil litigation are generally found in the same sources as are all our laws: constitutions, statutes, rules of court, and case law. If a case is litigated in federal court, then the U.S. Constitution, U.S. Code, the Federal Rules of Civil Procedure, and cases from the federal courts usually control. If a case is brought in state court, then the state constitution, state codes, state rules of court, and state case law are the usual sources of the law.

Constitutions provide some general guidelines that pertain to civil litigation. For example, the Seventh Amendment to the U.S. Constitution provides for the right to juries in common law cases exceeding $20. The Constitution also mandates that due process be followed in civil cases. Very briefly, this means that the procedures followed in a civil case must be fair to all parties, especially to the defendant. The authority and power of the various state courts in the litigation process are often found in state constitutions.

Codes and rules of court control more specific litigation matters. Rules of court are rules of procedure adopted by representatives of the federal and state courts under authority given by the respective legislatures. The Federal Rules of Civil Procedure are rules of practice that have been adopted for civil practice in the federal courts. They cover such matters as the content and filing of pleadings, descriptions of various motions, and types of discovery permitted. State codes and rules contain comparable provisions. Individual federal and state

primary sources
Print or electronic publications that contain the actual law (i.e., case reporters, codes, constitutions).

secondary sources
Print or electronic publications about the law, such as articles, treatises, and encyclopedias; these are not binding on a court.

local rules of court
Rules that are adopted by individual courts and apply only in those courts.

trial and appellate courts also adopt rules for practice within their local courts. These are known as **local rules of court**. In the federal system, these rules vary from district to district. In state systems, they vary from one local area to another. In other words, within one state some rules of procedure may be different from one court to another. Local rules of a court should always be checked before initiating any litigation within that court.

Case law, law that results from court decisions, is also a major source of rules regarding civil litigation. The courts have the power and the duty to interpret the constitutions and statutes. The Supreme Court has frequently done this with the constitutional phrase *due process*. Moreover, even when a statute seems to be clear and explicit, case law cannot be ignored. For instance, California has the following statute relating to default judgments:

> The court may . . . relieve a party . . . from a judgment . . . taken against him . . . through his . . . mistake, inadvertence, surprise or excusable neglect. . . . Application for such relief . . . must be made within a reasonable time, in no case exceeding six months, after such judgment, order or proceeding was taken.

The phrase *in no case more than six months* seems to be clear and without need of further interpretation. Nonetheless, the courts of the state have repeatedly decided that if fraud exists, a party may apply for relief after six months. Case law tells us that "in no case" does not mean "never." When you rely on a statute, you must also review any case law relating to that statute. See Exhibit 1-3.

EXHIBIT 1-3 Primary Sources of Law

CIVIL LITIGATION: *PRIMARY* SOURCES OF LAW

Constitutions

- United States
- State

Statutes and Rules

- U.S. Codes
- Federal Rules

  - Federal Rules of Civil Procedure
  - Federal Rules of Appeal
  - Federal Rules of Evidence

- State Codes
- State Rules of Court
- Federal and State Local Rules of Court

Case Law

- U.S. Supreme Court Cases
- Federal Appellate Court Cases
- State Supreme Court Cases
- State Appellate Court Cases

EXHIBIT 1-4 Secondary Sources of Law

CIVIL LITIGATION: *SECONDARY* SOURCES OF LAW

- Legal Encyclopedias
- Practice Manuals
- Textbooks
- Form Books

Copyright © 2015 Cengage Learning®

Secondary Sources

When questions arise relating to litigation, the primary sources of the law are not the only reference materials used. A secondary source is often quicker and easier to use. A secondary source is one in which an author explains or describes the primary sources of the law. Many secondary sources exist for both state and federal procedure. Secondary sources include legal encyclopedias, practice manuals, textbooks, and various legal periodicals. See Exhibit 1-4.

A type of secondary source that is heavily relied upon in the area of litigation is the **form book**. As the name suggests, form books contain sample forms for all aspects of litigation, from complaints to judgments. Better form books also contain explanations of the laws relating to the various forms, and as such are valuable research tools. An example of a form from a secondary source is found in Appendix B. The secondary source, *American Jurisprudence Forms of Pleading and Practice Annotated*, contains numerous forms, including a form for wrongful discharge, as seen in Appendix B.

form books
Books containing sample forms for legal professionals to follow in preparing pleadings and other documents.

THE ROLE OF TECHNOLOGY IN LITIGATION

Technology and the Law Firm

Like any modern business office, the litigation law firm is dependent on technology. Documents, including client letters, settlement agreements, and pleadings, are prepared using word-processing software such as Microsoft Word or Corel's WordPerfect. At times documents are converted to a portable document format (PDF) format to prevent any changes. This is particularly important when documents are transmitted electronically to the court or to other offices. In addition, many firms use software specially created for the law office to handle such tasks as calendaring, billing, and case files. Spreadsheets and databases also find a place in the modern law office. Firms involved in complex litigation often use powerful case management software that allows the firm to organize and summarize extensive discovery. For trial, many attorneys use presentation software to emphasize their arguments to a jury or a judge.

In addition to computers, attorneys are often dependent on electronic devices such as smartphones and tablets, both with Internet access. Such handheld devices allow attorneys to keep accurate calendars and communicate by e-mail. Special applications ("Apps") for these devices allow the attorney to review documents or conduct online legal research at any location. Perhaps the most important technological instrument used by law firms

cloud computing
Electronic file storage where files are stored on the Internet rather than on the office computer.

is the Internet. Attorneys use this to do factual and legal research, file documents with the court, communicate with clients and other attorneys, and to advertise. Recently, many attorneys have found social media, such as Facebook and Twitter, useful for advertising. The Internet has also become a "storage shed" for lawyers who do not have sufficient physical office space. Documents, such as those found in case files, can be stored on-line rather than on the office computer; this is referred to as **cloud computing**. Without doubt, the law firm today is dependent on technology. However, the use of technology sometimes presents new problems for the law office. One of the most important is the ethical requirement of confidentiality. This topic is discussed in more detail in Chapter 3. An excellent source for information about technology in the law firm is found at http://technology.findlaw.com/. See Exhibit 1-5 for a screen from Findlaw showing some of the topics found on the Web site.

EXHIBIT 1-5 Findlaw Technology Links

FindLaw ▸ Legal Technology

Legal Technology

FindLaw's Legal Technology Center provides a wealth of free resources designed for solo and small law firms on law technology topics such as Electronic Discovery, Law Office Hardware, Legal Practice Software, Mobile, Networking, Data Storage, and Modern Law Practice. Making technology decisions for a solo or small law firm requires careful attention to technical and practical details. Whether you are a solo practitioner, or need to provide technical office support to many lawyers, FindLaw can help you make successful technology decisions.

Electronic Discovery
eDiscovery, Metadata, More...

Mobile
Mobile Devices, Legal Apps, More...

Legal Software
Case Management, Docket & Calendar, Time & Billing, More...

Law Office Hardware
Computers, Peripherals, Telephone & Conferencing, More...

Networking & Storage
Cloud Computing, Data Storage, Network Security, More...

Modern Law Practice
Legal Tech Events, Social Media, Tech Law News, More...

eDiscovery Guide
Records Management, Presentation, Collection, More...

eDiscovery Wizard
Duty of Disclosure, Privilege Claims, Safe Harbor, More...

Legal Technology and Practice News

Technology and the Courts

Like law firms, courts rely heavily on technology in both operation and design. All federal courts and many state courts maintain documents in electronic format and allow attorneys to file documents electronically. The federal court maintains a comprehensive system, known as CM/ECF (Case Management and Electronic Case Files). This system is utilized in all bankruptcy, district, and appellate courts.[5] One advantage of this is that the public, including attorneys, has easier access to court records. A recent report from the Administrative Office of the United States Courts indicates that over 6 million documents are filed each month.[6] Another use of technology includes videoconferencing and teleconferencing for various pretrial conferences and motions. This allows attorneys to handle brief court appearances from their offices rather than travel to the court. As with law firms, one of the most important technology tools is the Internet. All courts maintain Web sites, posting factual information about the court as well as providing access to local rules and forms. Many courts post court calendars and allow limited access to court records.

More than 20 years ago Congress enacted federal legislation, providing funds for the federal courts to plan and implement technology into the courts. As a result, courts today consider courtroom design to meet the needs of the digital age; attorneys can often expect to find courtrooms equipped with PC inputs at counsel tables, an evidence presentation system featuring a digital document camera, DVD player, CD player, and monitors for the judge and jury. While not all courtrooms are technologically state of the art, efforts are continually made to improve and update. Two judicial organizations, the Federal Judicial Center (www.fjc.gov) and the National Center for State Courts (www.ncsc.org), help to promote such efforts. Information about courtroom technology is found on both Web sites.

THE ROLE OF THE LITIGATION PARALEGAL

A paralegal plays an important role in a litigation law firm, although that role often varies, depending on the specialization and size of the law firm.

The Litigation Law Firm

Many differences exist among law firms that specialize in litigation. Some litigation firms primarily represent plaintiffs whereas others represent defendants. These latter firms often represent insurance companies whose insured has been sued. Litigation law firms are not necessarily large offices. Sometimes the firm consists of an attorney and the paralegal. On the other hand, some litigation firms are extremely large, consisting of several departments and hundreds of attorneys located in offices throughout the world. In such cases, the firm generally handles business matters in addition to litigation. In medium- and large-size firms, the paralegal is one member of a litigation team that may consist of an office manager, senior trial attorney, associate attorneys (usually a newer attorney), paralegals, legal secretaries, and word processors. See Exhibit 1-6 for a description of common law firm positions.

EXHIBIT 1-6 Common Positions in a Medium or Large Law Firm

THE LITIGATION LAW OFFICE—A TEAM EFFORT	
Managing Partner	A senior attorney who manages the other attorneys in the firm; as a partner, this attorney shares in the profits of the business in addition to receiving a salary
Partners	Experienced attorneys who receive a salary in addition to sharing in the profits of the business; some firms have both senior and junior partners
Associates	Newer attorneys who receive a salary, but do not share in profits
Office Manager	A professional who supervises nonlegal staff and is responsible for such activities as hiring, training, orientation, and day-to-day management of the firm
Paralegal	An individual who does substantial legal work under the supervision of an attorney; a paralegal cannot give legal advice or otherwise practice law; some firms have both senior and junior paralegals
Legal Secretary	An individual who assists the attorney in administrative matters; such as calendaring and document preparation
Word Processors	An individual who is responsible for generating documents

Although attorneys in private practice handle most civil litigation, attorneys working for various public agencies may also be involved in civil litigation. An example of a large public agency that is involved in many civil lawsuits is the U.S. Attorney General's Office, which litigates civil cases such as discrimination, civil rights, and securities violations. As with private law firms, the litigation paralegal working for a public agency is usually part of a litigation team.

As a litigation paralegal, your responsibilities also are influenced by the type of case. In a complex litigation case, as part of a litigation team your responsibilities may be limited to one aspect of the case. For example, you might be responsible for organizing and indexing documentary evidence in a case (e.g., contracts, purchase orders, letters between parties), whereas another paralegal in your firm is responsible for researching legal issues that arise. In smaller, less complex cases, you may be involved in all aspects of the case.

Litigation Paralegal Job Description

The following list contains some of the more common tasks that may be included in the job description of a litigation paralegal.

General Responsibilities

1. maintaining firm's calendaring system
2. organizing client files
3. assisting with technology

Prelitigation Facts Investigation

1. interviewing clients
2. interviewing witnesses
3. obtaining statements from witnesses
4. gathering evidence (police reports, photographs, etc.)
5. organizing and indexing documentary evidence
6. researching factual and legal issues using the Internet and other sources

Commencing Litigation

1. researching substantive law and procedural rules related to the case
2. drafting pleadings
3. coordinating service of process
4. reviewing pleadings from opposing party
5. drafting motions, including memoranda of points and authorities
6. preparing orders after motions
7. evaluating and using possible case-management software

Discovery

1. drafting written forms of discovery (interrogatories, requests to produce, requests for admissions)
2. assisting client in complying with discovery requests
3. reviewing discovery obtained from opposing parties
4. preparing client for deposition
5. setting up, reviewing, and summarizing depositions
6. organizing, analyzing, and coding documents for document production, and, where appropriate, creating a document database
7. assisting with the technology needs in the e-discovery process

Trial

1. organizing file and evidence for trial
2. serving witnesses with subpoenas
3. interviewing witnesses
4. preparing the client
5. drafting jury instructions
6. drafting proposed judgments
7. assisting with research and preparation of trial brief

8. preparing and organizing trial exhibits
9. coordinating technology needs with the court
10. assisting the attorney during trial

Posttrial

1. researching possible posttrial motions
2. drafting possible posttrial motions
3. drafting notice of appeal and requests for transcripts
4. assisting with research and writing of appellate briefs
5. preparing documents associated with enforcing judgments

What a Litigation Paralegal Cannot Do

Obviously, as a litigation paralegal, you perform many tasks in the course of a lawsuit and play an important role in the litigation law firm. However, the litigation paralegal is not an attorney and therefore cannot practice law. With very limited exceptions, the paralegal cannot appear in court, cannot ask questions at a deposition, and cannot give legal advice to a client. These and other ethical concerns are covered more fully in Chapter 3.

SKILLS REQUIRED OF THE LITIGATION PARALEGAL

As a litigation paralegal, you need some very definite skills. You must be able to communicate both orally and in writing. You cannot conduct intelligent interviews with clients or prospective witnesses without the ability to communicate orally. Nor can you help draft witness statements or pleadings without the ability to communicate in writing. As a litigation paralegal, you also must possess organizational and analytical skills. Reviewing and analyzing documentary evidence and pleadings is a task often given to paralegals. Likewise, you must sometimes organize documents, discovery information, and pleadings. The ability to do legal research, including familiarity with form books, is also important. Drafting court documents and preparing memoranda of points and authorities (discussion or analysis of legal questions) require this skill. In today's law office, a litigation paralegal must have strong technology skills and knowledge. This means you should be familiar with word-processing, database, and spreadsheet programs. You should also possess excellent research skills using the Internet. See Exhibit 1-7.

EXHIBIT 1-7 Paralegal Skills Checklist

DO YOU HAVE THE NECESSARY LITIGATION PARALEGAL SKILLS?

✓ Oral Communication Skills   ✓ Legal Research Skills
✓ Written Communication Skills   ✓ Factual Research Skills
✓ Organizational Skills   ✓ Computer/Technology Skills
✓ Analytical Skills

Continuing Legal Education

Litigation paralegals must keep current on changes that constantly occur in the area of litigation. Our laws are always subject to change. Codes and rules are often amended. New cases are frequently decided. In addition to changes in the law, technological advances, especially in computers and software packages, often affect the way litigation is practiced.

Local legal newspapers and professional journals generally report national and state judicial and legislative developments. They keep you updated on new practices adopted by the local courts, report on technological developments, and contain other valuable information about the practice of law and the paralegal profession. You should develop the habit of reading your local legal newspaper and professional journals regularly. Local and state bar associations and paralegal associations often sponsor seminars on selected areas of law. Paralegal schools may also offer courses or seminars that would benefit working paralegals. In addition, you can often find continuing legal education opportunities online. If you want to be a conscientious paralegal, you should take advantage of opportunities to attend these seminars and courses.

Professional Organizations

A good paralegal continuously strives for professional improvement as well as information about developments in the paralegal profession. One source for growth in the profession is affiliation with local, state, and national paralegal organizations. A partial list of national organizations includes the following:

National Association of Legal Assistants, Inc. (NALA)	**http://www.nala.org/**
National Federation of Paralegal Associations, Inc.	**http://www.paralegals.org/**
American Bar Association	**http://www.americanbar.org/aba.html** (search for "legal assistants" or "paralegal")
International Paralegal Management Association	**http://www.paralegalmanagement.org/**

PRACTICAL TIPS FOR SUCCESS IN THE LAW FIRM

Forms File—Invaluable Aid

As mentioned earlier, litigation paralegals often need to use form books. However, finding the proper form and adapting it to your particular needs is sometimes a time-consuming task. To find a proper form, a paralegal often spends considerable time researching and reviewing several possible forms. Revising or adapting sample forms to fit a particular need is then required. Not only is all of this a time-consuming task, but it is also a task that may be repeated because firms often deal with similar kinds of cases. Thus, a form needed for one case can easily be followed for another. One way to ease the task of finding proper

AUTOMATED LITIGATION SUPPORT

The 21st Century Law Office

SCENARIO

Congratulations! You were just hired as a paralegal by a prestigious litigation law firm, and it's your first day on the job. Your supervising attorney has asked you to read and summarize a case file. You are anxious to make a good impression. However, when you look for the case file, you find that it is nowhere to be found. A senior paralegal tells you not to worry. All case documents are scanned and stored electronically "in the cloud." When you ask about the use of technology in the firm, the senior paralegal also tells you that the firm uses the latest devices and software. Attorneys and paralegals use smartphones, tablets, and laptop computers. The firm is on a network and uses the latest technology in "automated litigation support," including several software applications that will make your job easier. These software programs handle document generation, calendaring, billing, and conflicts checks, as well as summarize, retrieve, and integrate discovery documents. You are also told that most legal research is performed using the online services of LEXIS and Westlaw, the Internet, and the firm's intranet. You are confident in your computer skills. In spite of this, you are overwhelmed!

PROBLEM

Your success as a litigation paralegal in any litigation law firm depends on your ability to adapt your knowledge of litigation rules and procedures to the use of technology. You are willing and even eager to do this. You have a basic understanding of computers. You do word processing and can access the Internet, but you are overwhelmed by the whole concept of automated litigation support. Where do you start?

SOLUTION

Adapting to the litigation law firm of the 21st century requires that you understand and can use the office technology. Two other aspects of technology are also important in a law office. Your use of technology must be consistent with legal ethical guidelines and you must also adhere to office policies related to technology use.

Today's law office is fully automated. In any office you can expect to see either laptop or desktop computers for all attorneys and support staff. Attorneys take laptop computers or tablets to court, to depositions away from the office, and for other times when the desktop computer is not available. You can also expect to see scanners, fax machines, and computerized copy machines. These copy machines allow the office to keep track of photocopies made on each client's case. Most attorneys also use smartphones with access to e-mail, phone, calendar, applications, and more.

Software found in a law office varies. In addition to common office software such as Microsoft Office, many firms use software specifically addressing different law office needs. In a litigation firm, this software is sometimes referred to generically as case-management software or litigation support software.

Many litigation law firms also have technology equipment designed for use during trial. In addition to their laptop computers, attorneys frequently have LCD projectors to project images from their computer screens and document cameras that can project three-dimensional objects onto large screens for easy viewing by the jury. Trial attorneys who do not own such equipment often rent it for trial. A successful paralegal takes the time to learn about the equipment and software in the law office as soon as possible.

The successful paralegal must also know the ethical guidelines that regulate the legal profession and guard against the abuse of these rules in the use of technology. For example, care must always be taken so as not to violate the confidentiality of client information that is created, stored, or communicated by means of any electronic equipment. The successful paralegal also takes time to become familiar with office policies regarding the use of office technology. For example, policies often regulate such issues as whether clients can be contacted by cell phones, whether e-mail are encrypted, whether a paralegal can work on office files at home, on a personal computer, and whether personal use of office computers is ever allowed.

EXHIBIT 1-8 Organizing a Forms File

ORGANIZING A FORMS FILE

Whether your forms file is in paper format or in electronic format, consider organizing it by the following categories. Using tabs in a binder or subfolders in a word-processing program will facilitate your use of the forms:

- Letters
- Pleadings: Plaintiff
- Pleadings: Defendant
- Motions
- Discovery
- Legal Memoranda and Briefs
- Settlement
- Appeal
- Miscellaneous

---

forms is for the law firm, or for you as a litigation paralegal, to maintain a forms file. When you start working as a paralegal, check to see whether the firm maintains its own forms file. Many do. If the firm has an intranet, be sure to check there for forms. Even if a forms file is maintained for the firm, as an individual litigation paralegal you would be wise to keep your own forms file, retaining copies of forms that you have prepared, as well as copies of forms prepared by others, that might be useful in the future. Forms that should be kept include pleadings, motions, memoranda of points and authorities, and briefs. (See Exhibit 1-8 for a list of possible ways to organize a forms file.)

How to Build a Litigation Procedures Manual

Another invaluable aid to litigation paralegals is a litigation procedures manual, in which the various tasks performed by the paralegals are described and step-by-step directions are given. In such a procedures manual, consideration should be given to two distinct procedures. In describing any paralegal task—for example, preparing and filing a complaint—all of the legal requirements must be set out. In addition, a procedures manual should detail office policy. A procedures manual might also include detailed instructions on preparing various legal forms. If a law firm has its own procedures manual, the new litigation paralegal should consult it. Experienced paralegals also will find it helpful when they are involved in new tasks or engaged in tasks that are infrequently performed. If a procedures manual does not exist, the litigation paralegals can work together to assemble one. An easy way to accomplish this is for you and the other paralegals in your firm to keep a checklist, or step-by-step directions, for each task that you and the others perform. These can be collated into a complete procedures manual. As a paralegal student, you can begin keeping your own reference manual by making checklists for each matter covered in class. See Exhibit 1-9 for a sample.

EXHIBIT 1-9 A Sample of a Litigation Training Manual

PREPARING AND FILING A COMPLAINT
(Personal Injury—Accident)

1. Review office file.
   a. Check client interview sheet.
   b. Review police reports.
   c. Review investigator's report.
   d. Verify statute of limitations.
2. Gather information for complaint.
   a. Plaintiffs.
      1) Names.
      2) Are all plaintiffs competent adults?
   b. Defendants.
      1) Names.
      2) Addresses for service.
   c. Location of accident.
   d. Description of injuries and expenses.
3. Were any preliminary notices or actions required?
   a. Is defendant a government entity?
   b. Is plaintiff a minor?
4. Determine which court complaint is to be filed in.
   a. Check local rules of court for any special requirements.
5. Prepare complaint.
   a. Check office forms file.
   b. Check form books if needed.
6. Prepare summons (see Training Manual—instructions for preparing summons).
7. Have attorney review complaint.
8. Check court for proper filing fee.
9. Obtain filing fee from bookkeeper.
10. Take check, complaint, and summons (original and three copies) to court for filing.
11. Return copies to office.
12. Give copies of complaint and summons to process server for serving.
    a. Calendar for 10 days to check on service.

FINDING IT on the Internet

An abundance of information about litigation, the courts, and the law in general can be found on the Internet. Many legal sites contain a variety of types of legal information. One way to find specific information on a Web site is to use the "search" feature, which is generally found on the home page of any Web site.

As explained in this chapter, litigation rules for the federal courts are found in the U.S. Code and Federal Rules of Civil Procedure. The following sites provide access to these:

<http://www.law.cornell.edu>

Select "U.S. Code" and "Federal Rules." Follow the links to the U.S. Codes and the Federal Rules of Civil Procedure. This site will also lead to state codes and rules. Click on "State Statutes by Topic" and then "civil procedure."

<http://www.uscourts.gov>

Follow the links: "Rules and Policies" > "Federal Rules of Practice and Procedure" > "Current Rules of Practice and Procedure" to access the Federal Rules of Civil Procedure. (You can also search for Federal Rules of Civil Procedure on the homepage.)

a. Search the Internet for your state's code and rules and identify the specific Web site addresses for these.

b. Law office technology is continually changing and keeping current is important. The Findlaw Web site mentioned in the chapter is a good resource. Two other good sources for information on this topic are Law Technology News, available on **<http://www.law.com>** (search the "publications" listed on the homepage) and **<http://www.americanbar.org/aba.html>** (search for "technology"). Access one of these sites and summarize an article dealing with litigation technology.

SUMMARY

- Civil litigation is the process through which parties resolve their civil disputes in court. Civil cases deal with private disputes between individuals or parties. Civil litigation does not include the pursuit of any criminal case. The substantive law of the case controls whether the parties have the right to sue. Procedural rules dictate how that case is handled in the court system. One cannot exist without the other. Civil litigation usually begins with the plaintiff filing a complaint in court and serving it on the defendant. The defendant then responds by filing an answer or other appropriate pleading. While the parties await trial, they try to find out as much about the other's case as possible by going through discovery. If problems with the case arise, the parties file court proceedings known as motions. After the trial has ended, either of the parties can appeal. Once the case is over, the prevailing party may use the court process to collect a judgment.

- Some civil lawsuits are very simple proceedings, whereas others are very complex. Regardless of the nature of the case, the basic litigation process remains the same. However, more complex cases can involve multiple parties, multiple pleadings, and voluminous documents. They might also require extensive legal research.

- Not all civil disputes are litigated. Other methods exist for resolving disputes. The term *alternative dispute resolution* applies to many of these methods, including such procedures as negotiation, mediation, and arbitration. Negotiation occurs when the parties discuss their problems in an effort to settle their dispute. Mediation resembles negotiation except that a neutral third party (the mediator) helps the parties settle their differences. Arbitration involves the parties submitting their dispute to a third, neutral party (the arbitrator) who decides the case. In addition to alternative dispute resolution methods, some disputes must be resolved by administrative agencies. In recent years various legislative and judicial action has begun to curb litigation, especially in the area of tort law.

- The laws of civil litigation are found primarily in constitutions, statutes and rules of court, and cases. Lawsuits brought in federal court are governed by the U.S. Constitution, federal statutes, federal rules of court, and federal cases. Cases brought in state courts are controlled by state constitutions, state statutes and rules of court, and cases. In both federal and state courts, attention must also be paid to local rules of the various courts. In researching a question of civil litigation, the paralegal may use primary sources or secondary sources. Primary sources are constitutions, code books, or case reporters. Secondary sources include textbooks, legal encyclopedias, legal periodicals, and form books. It is important for the litigation paralegal to be aware of changes that occur in the law. Reading local legal newspapers and professional journals, as well as joining professional associations helps.

- Technology is important to litigation. Law firms as well as the courts use technology to accomplish tasks. Law firms and courts use general business software in addition to software designed for the legal environment. The Internet is an important tool for both lawyers and the courts.

- Paralegals can perform a number of duties or jobs in the area of litigation. These include gathering evidence, interviewing clients and witnesses, preparing pleadings and motions, assisting with all aspects of discovery, and conducting factual and legal research.

- Litigation paralegals must be able to communicate orally and in writing. They must possess organizational and analytical skills. They must be able to do legal research. Strong technology skills are also required.

- Litigation paralegals will find their jobs somewhat easier if personal forms files and procedure manuals are available to them.

KEY TERMS

alternative dispute resolution (ADR)	arbitrator	cloud computing
	civil law	complaint
answer	civil litigation	criminal law
arbitration	civil procedure	criminal procedure

default	mediator	secondary sources
defendant	motion	settlement
discovery	negotiation	substantive law
form book	petition	trial
judgment	plaintiff	writ of execution
local rules of court	primary sources	
mediation	procedural law	

REVIEW QUESTIONS

1. What is the difference between civil procedure and criminal procedure?
2. Why are substantive laws and procedural rules important to civil litigation?
3. What are the steps in the litigation process?
4. Describe different types of civil litigation cases.
5. What are some of the alternatives to litigating a case?
6. What are the primary sources for finding the law of civil litigation? How do these sources differ from secondary sources?
7. How is technology used in litigation?
8. What are five tasks performed by litigation paralegals?
9. What skills must a litigation paralegal have? Why are these skills needed?
10. What activities lead to a paralegal's success in a litigation law firm?

CHAPTER EXERCISES

Where necessary, check with your instructor prior to starting any of these exercises.

1. Check job advertisements for paralegal positions. What are the job requirements? Are any particular skills described?
2. Locate the local rules of court for your local, state, and federal courts. Start by accessing the Web sites for these courts. If local rules are not posted, determine how you can obtain a copy of them.
3. Locate your local or state paralegal associations. How do you join? Do they ever sponsor seminars in the area of litigation?
4. Start your own procedures manual. As you go through each chapter in this book, prepare step-by-step directions or a checklist for each task described therein. As part of your procedure manual, include a glossary of terms and their definitions. This can be done by using a three-ring, loose-leaf binder or by creating a file in a word-processing program. If you create a document file, create subfolders for each chapter in the text.
5. Review the advertisements in a local bar journal or legal newspaper that deal with computer software advertised as "automated litigation support." Alternatively, "Google" the phrase. Make a list of some of the products and give a brief description of what the software does. Also make a list of products that provide an online tutorial.

6. Analyze the following factual disputes. Would these disputes result in a civil case, a criminal case, or both? Explain your answer. If a civil case would result, who would be the plaintiff and who would be the defendant?

   a. Baron and Finkle sign a written contract in which Baron agrees to build a room addition to Finkle's house. When the contract was signed, Finkle gave Baron a $1,000 deposit. Before construction was to begin, Baron called Finkle and told him he would not be able to do the work. Baron has not returned the $1,000 deposit.

   b. Martin sets fire to a building he owns in order to collect insurance.

   c. Reese works as a software engineer for DATA Corp. and has been involved in the design of a new computer chip. He has signed a confidentiality agreement with DATA Corp. and has agreed that all products developed by him while working for DATA belong to DATA. Reese has a dispute with DATA over salary and leaves. He sells the design for the computer chip to DISK Corp., his new employer. DISK knows that the chip design was developed while Reese was working for DATA.

   d. Bates, in a fit of anger, kills his wife. The couple has two minor children.

   e. Rosemond Corporation is engaged in a business that produces by-products that pollute water. It illegally dumps the by-products. Children in a nearby area develop a high incidence of cancer.

7. The following lawsuits eventually resulted in landmark Supreme Court cases. Read the factual basis for the cases and state whether the case was a civil case or criminal case. Explain your answer.

   a. In this lawsuit, a group of children sued to be allowed to attend nonsegregated schools. The Supreme Court found that separate schools were unequal and held in favor of the children. (*Brown v. Board of Education*, 347 U.S. 483 [1954])

   b. In this action, an indigent person was accused of committing a felony in the state of Florida. The state refused to provide him with a lawyer. He challenged his subsequent conviction claiming that his constitutional right to an attorney was denied. The Supreme Court agreed with the accused. (*Gideon v. Wainwright*, 372 U.S. 335 [1963])

   c. After a high school principal edited articles in the school paper, members of the high school newspaper filed a lawsuit seeking injunctive relief, money damages, and declaration that First Amendment rights were violated by censorship of certain articles. The Supreme Court ruled against the students. (*Hazelwood v. Kuhlmeier*, 484 U.S. 260 [1988])

   d. A teacher accused a minor student of smoking in the bathroom. When the student denied the allegation, the principal searched her purse and found cigarettes and marijuana paraphernalia. The state sought to have the young girl declared a delinquent. The minor claimed that the evidence found in her purse should be excluded at the delinquency hearing because it was obtained in violation of her Fourth Amendment rights. The Supreme Court ruled that her rights were not violated. (*New Jersey v. T.L.O*, 469 U.S. 325 [1985])

   e. Barbara Grutter sued the University of Michigan Law School for racial discrimination claiming that she was denied admission to the law school because the school unlawfully used race as an admission factor. The school admitted that race was one of many factors, but that it used race in order to achieve a diverse student population. The Supreme Court disagreed with Grutter and held that institutions of higher education have a legitimate interest in promoting diversity and in this case, the school used race in a narrowly tailored manner. (*Grutter v. Bollinger*, 539 U.S. 306 [2003])

f. A young man committed a murder when he was 17 and was convicted of the crime after he turned 18. He was sentenced to die, and he challenged the sentence as cruel and unusual punishment. A majority of the Supreme Court agreed with Roper, and it held that to execute him for his crime would violate the Eighth Amendment. (*Roper v. Simmons*, 543 U.S. 551 [2005])

g. Various local public officials sued the *New York Times* for libel as a result of a story printed by the paper. The newspaper claimed that the public officials should not be able to recover because of the First Amendment right of freedom of the press. The Court found that in order to recover, the public officials needed to prove that the articles were published maliciously. (*New York Times v. Sullivan*, 376 U.S. 254 [1964])

h. A company holding the copyright to selected television shows sued manufacturers of videotape recorders used by individuals to record shows to view at a later time. The plaintiff asked for an injunction and for damages. The Court held that making of individual copies of complete television shows for purposes of time-shifting does not constitute copyright infringement, but is fair use. (*Sony Corp. of America v. Universal City Studios, Inc.*, 464 U.S. 417 [1984])

i. An individual sued various secret service agents for money damages, claiming that they violated his rights when they questioned and arrested him because he made derogatory comments about the vice-president (whom the agents were guarding). The Court found that the officers had qualified immunity and could not be sued. (*Reichle v. Howards*, 132 S. Ct. 2088, 182 L. Ed. 2d 985 [2012])

CHAPTER PROJECT

Using a three-ring, loose-leaf binder, start your own forms file. From the table of contents of this book, set up a general index to the file. As you proceed through the course on Civil Litigation, add copies of all forms that you see or prepare.

THE *BENNETT* CASE

Read the case Commentary at the beginning of this chapter and the Bennett Case File in Appendix B containing information and documents related to the *Bennett* case.

Assignment for Chapter 1: Preliminary Research

Your supervising attorney wants to prepare for a meeting with Alice Bennett. To help the attorney, you have been asked to review the Web site for the Equal Employment Opportunity Commission (EEOC) (<http://www.eeoc.gov>). Write a memo summarizing information about sex discrimination found on the Web site. (Hint: Search information for employees relating to equal compensation and sex discrimination.)

In summarizing the material on the Web site, try to include the following information:

1. A list and brief description of laws that might apply to *Bennett*
2. A discussion of what constitutes sex discrimination and sexual harassment
3. The procedures for filing a claim with the EEOC
4. Requirements for filing a lawsuit
5. Responsibilities of an employer once the employer is notified by the EEOC that a claim of sex discrimination was made
6. Any other information you think is relevant to either the plaintiff or the defendant

THE *DOUGLASS FINANCIAL SERVICES, INC.* CASE

Read the case Commentary at the beginning of this chapter and the Douglass Financial Services, Inc. Case File in Appendix B containing information and documents related to the case.

Assignment for Chapter 1: Factual Summary

Your supervising attorney asks you to review the file in the Douglass Financial Services case. After reading the police report and witness statement, you are to prepare a brief memorandum summarizing the factual basis of the plaintiff's claim. Be sure to note any facts that might indicate liability on the part your client, defendant Douglass Financial Services, Inc. Your attorney also tells you that office memorandum in the firm always have a heading as follows:

TO:

FROM:

DATE:

RE:

ENDNOTES

1. Kelly, C, & Mello, M 2005, Are Medical Malpractice Damages Caps Constitutional? An Overview of State Litigation, *Journal of Law, Medicine & Ethics*, 33, 3, pp. 513–534, Academic Search Complete, EBSCO*host*, viewed 22 January 2013.
2. McCarter, W 2012, Statutory Cap on Damages in Medical Malpractice Cases Is Unconstitutional, *Journal of the Missouri Bar*, 68, 5, pp.248–254, Academic Search Complete, EBSCO*host*, viewed 22 January 2013.
3. Nelson, L, Morrisey, M, & Morrisey, D 2011, Medical Liability and Health Care Reform, *Health Matrix: Journal of Law-Medicine*, 21, 2, pp. 443–519, Academic Search Complete, EBSCO*host*, viewed 22 January 2013.
4. Nahrstadt, B, & Boyd, B 2005, The IDC Monograph: The Class Action Fairness Act of 2005—What Is It All About? *IDC Quarterly*, 15, 2, pp. 1–10, Academic Search Complete, EBSCO*host*, viewed 22 January 2013.
5. PACER, Public Access to Court Electronic Records, http://www.pacer.gov/cmecf/
6. Administrative Office of the United States Courts, 2010 Annual Report, http://www.uscourts.gov

The Courts and Jurisdiction

CHAPTER OUTLINE

COMMENTARY

THE *WEIGH TO GO* CASE

Your law firm was recently retained by Weigh To Go, a corporation that operates a chain of retail stores featuring high-tech exercise equipment and low-calorie foods. The corporation was formed 10 years ago under the laws of the state of Texas and met with such success that it now has stores in Texas, Nevada, and Oregon. Its corporate headquarters is in Oregon. Weigh To Go currently maintains a Web site advertising and selling its products online. Because Weigh To Go has substantial Internet sales from California residents, it plans to open stores in California. (In fact, its gross revenues from California is almost twice as that from Oregon.) Weigh To Go just learned that a few months ago another company started a similar business. This company calls itself Go A Weigh and has one store in San Francisco, California. Go A Weigh is incorporated under the laws of California. Go A Weigh also maintains a Web site on the Internet but does not allow online purchases. Your attorney tells you that the firm will be filing a lawsuit based on trade name infringement and asks you to research the following questions. Should the complaint be filed in federal or state court, or does it matter? If the complaint is to be filed in federal court, which district is the proper one? If the complaint is to be filed in state court, which state or states could hear the case?

OBJECTIVES

Chapter 1 introduced you to the general litigation process. Choosing the proper court in which to initiate a lawsuit is an important step in that process. After reading this chapter, you should be able to:

- describe the functions of trial and appellate courts in the civil litigation process.
- describe the structure of federal court system.
- define subject matter jurisdiction.
- list the types of cases that must be brought in federal court.
- distinguish exclusive jurisdiction from concurrent jurisdiction.
- determine if a court can obtain personal jurisdiction over a defendant.
- explain the relevance of long-arm statutes.
- contrast personal jurisdiction with in rem jurisdiction.
- identify how venue affects the location of the trial court.

THE COURTS AND LITIGATION

The attorneys in the *Weigh To Go* matter recognize that they must choose a proper court in which to file their lawsuit. Selecting a proper court first requires an understanding of the U.S. court systems. Different court systems exist for each of the states. A separate court system exists for the federal government. Within each system you also find many different courts. Although court systems differ from one another in many ways, they have some characteristics in common. All court systems have trial courts and courts of appeals or review. Many court systems have two levels of review courts: intermediate courts of appeals (in some jurisdictions called courts of appeal) and highest courts of appeal or courts of last resort (sometimes referred to as supreme courts). The function of all trial courts is

EXHIBIT 2-1 U.S. Court Systems

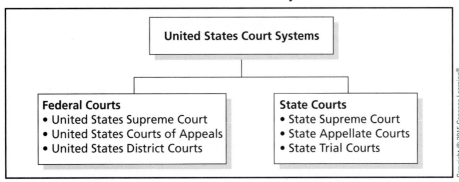

trial court
A court where the parties to a lawsuit file their pleadings and present evidence to a judge or jury.

lower courts
Another term for a trial court.

jurisdiction
The power that a court has to hear a particular case; requires that a court has the power to hear the type of case (subject matter) and that a court has power to render a decision against a particular defendant (personal) or over property (in rem).

original jurisdiction
The power of a court to conduct a trial in a case; confers a court the right to be the first court to hear the matter.

court of appeals
A court of review; this court reviews decisions from a trial court.

brief
A written analysis of the facts and law related to a case, written by the attorneys handling the case, and filed in a trial or appellate court. Briefs are also filed in the Supreme Court.

similar, as are the functions of courts of appeals and courts of last resort. The separate court systems are shown in Exhibit 2-1.

Trial Courts

The civil litigation process usually begins in a **trial court** where the parties to a lawsuit file pleadings and present evidence to a judge or jury. Trial courts are also called **lower courts**. The primary function of a trial court in civil cases is to resolve disputes between parties by first determining the true facts and then applying appropriate legal principles.

Example

Raeburn sues Cassidy for injuries he received in an automobile accident, claiming Cassidy failed to stop at a stop sign. Cassidy claims Raeburn ran the stop sign. In a jury trial, the jury determines the facts (i.e., who ran the stop sign). The jury then follows the judge's instructions in applying the law. In a trial before a judge only, the judge makes the factual and legal determinations.

Once a factual dispute is resolved, appropriate legal principles are applied to those facts—principles that for the most part have been established by the legislature and by higher courts. In the preceding factual situation, if a trial court judge or jury determines that Cassidy ran a stop sign, causing injuries to Raeburn, the legal principles of negligence are applied and the judge or jury could award Raeburn money damages. Because litigation usually begins in a trial court, this court is sometimes referred to as a court of original jurisdiction. **Jurisdiction** refers to the power or authority of a court to hear a particular case. A court of **original jurisdiction** is a court where the case begins and is tried.

Courts of Appeals

Courts of appeals (or appellate courts) are primarily courts of review. These courts examine the trial court proceedings to guarantee that parties receive a fair trial. A case is not retried in an appellate court. The appellate courts review the trial court's process by reviewing a written, verbatim transcript or record of the lower court documents and court proceedings. The parties also file legal **briefs** and may present oral arguments supporting their position.

legal error
A mistake in the way the court interprets or applies the law.

appellate jurisdiction
The power of a court to review the decision of a lower court or administrative agency.

higher court
Another term for a court with appellate jurisdiction.

affirm
An appellate court's upholding of the lower court's decision.

reverse
The act of an appellate court setting aside the decision of a lower court.

remand
The act of an appellate court sending a case back to the lower court after reversing a decision, often with specific instructions as to how the lower court must deal with the case.

supreme court
A name given to the highest court in the federal court system and to many, but not all, of the highest court in state court systems.

The appellate court's role is to determine if any legal errors occurred in the trial court and, if so, whether the error resulted in an unfair trial. A **legal error** is an error in the way the law is interpreted or applied to a situation. Examples of legal errors include a judge's misstating the law when instructing the jury or allowing attorneys to introduce evidence that is not relevant to the case or that has been improperly obtained. The appellate court is not allowed to substitute its judgment for that of the trial court on factual questions. If any reasonable basis for the factual findings exists, the appellate court must accept the trial court's findings.

Example

In the hypothetical case of *Raeburn v. Cassidy*, described earlier, the evidence in the case consisted of the following: Raeburn, a 19-year-old college student, testified that Cassidy ran the stop sign. Cassidy, a police officer who was off duty at the time of the accident, testified that Raeburn ran the stop sign. There are no other witnesses. If the trial court found in favor of Raeburn, an appellate court could not reverse just because an off-duty policeman seems more credible to it than a 19-year-old college student. The trial court already resolved this factual question, and the appellate court is bound by it.

Appellate review is usually conducted by a three-judge panel and cases are decided by a majority vote (two of the three). Because of their function, courts of appeals are called courts of **appellate jurisdiction**. The term **higher courts** is sometimes used to describe these courts. In exercising appellate jurisdiction, a reviewing court has the power to **affirm** the decision (uphold the lower court), **reverse** the decision (change the lower court's decision), or reverse and **remand** the case (change the lower court's decision and send it back to the trial court to be retried).

Courts of Last Resort

Many court systems have two levels of courts with appellate jurisdiction, intermediate courts of appeals and one court of last resort, often referred to as a **supreme court**. Like intermediate courts of appeals, courts of last resort are primarily courts of appellate jurisdiction. They review the proceedings at the trial level and at the intermediate appellate level. Unlike intermediate courts of appeals that *must* review cases in which the parties request a review, courts of last resort generally have *discretionary* right to review the cases. In other words, these courts hear only those appeals that they want to hear. See Exhibit 2-2 for a summary of the various court functions.

EXHIBIT 2-2 Court Functions

Trial Court	Evidence presented, facts determined, and appropriate law applied
Intermediate Court of Appeals	Trial court proceedings reviewed for legal errors that resulted in unfair trial; review is usually mandatory
Court of Last Resort (Supreme Court)	Discretionary review of trial court proceedings and appellate court decision

FEDERAL COURT SYSTEM

A federal court system was authorized by the U.S. Constitution, Article III, which created the Supreme Court and authorized Congress to create inferior courts. Today those inferior courts include trial courts and appellate courts. The trial courts are most commonly known as the U.S. district courts (or federal district courts), and include various specialized courts such as the U.S. Claims Court and the U.S. Court of International Trade. The appellate courts are known as U.S. courts of appeals (or federal courts of appeals). See Exhibit 2-3.

EXHIBIT 2-3 U.S. Federal Courts

The United States Federal Courts

SUPREME COURT	**UNITED STATES SUPREME COURT**
APPELLATE COURTS	**U.S. Courts of Appeals** 12 Regional Circuit Courts of Appeals 1 U.S. Court of Appeals for the Federal Circuit
TRIAL COURTS	**U.S. District Courts** 94 Judicial Districts U.S. Bankruptcy Courts **U.S. Court of International Trade** **U.S. Court of Federal Claims**
FEDERAL COURTS AND OTHER ENTITIES OUTSIDE THE JUDICIAL BRANCH	Military Courts (Trial and Appellate) Court of Veteran's Appeals U.S. Tax Court Federal administrative agencies and boards

Source: http://www.uscourts.gov/EducationalResources/FederalCourtBasics/CourtStructure/StructureOfFederalCourts.aspx

certiorari
A term used in connection with appellate proceedings indicating that the reviewing court wants the lower court to send the higher court its record, so that the proceedings can be reviewed. When parties ask the U.S. Supreme Court to hear a case, they often file a petition for writ of certiorari, which, if granted, means that the Supreme Court will review the record in the case.

U.S. District Courts

The United States and its territories are divided into 94 districts, each having a federal district court. Some larger districts are further subdivided into divisions. Each state has at least one federal district court in its boundaries and, depending on population, a state may have more. The number of judges assigned to each district varies according to need. District courts are trial courts. Thus, in the *Weigh To Go* case mentioned in this chapter's Commentary, if a lawsuit were pursued in the federal court system, it would start in a district court. The complaint and answer are filed in that court, and any trial takes place there.

Miscellaneous Federal Trial Courts

In addition to the U.S. district courts, the federal court system includes various specialized trial courts, including bankruptcy courts, the U.S. Court of International Trade, and the U.S. Claims Court. The bankruptcy courts are an "adjunct" to each district court. All bankruptcy proceedings originate there. The U.S. Court of International Trade deals with cases involving international trade and custom duties. The U.S. Claims Court handles suits against the federal government for money damages in numerous civil matters (except for tort claims that must be brought in district court).

U.S. Courts of Appeals

The United States is divided into 12 geographic appellate circuits, or regions. These courts hear appeals from district courts within their boundaries. The U.S. **courts of appeals** are primarily courts of review, having appellate jurisdiction. These courts review the proceedings that take place in a district court. In addition to the courts of appeals for each of the 12 geographic appellate districts, there is a 13th federal court of appeals with national jurisdiction. This court hears appeals in patent, copyright, and trademark cases from any district court and all appeals from the U.S. Claims Court and the U.S. Court of International Trade. Generally, when any of the courts of appeals reviews a lower court decision, that decision is reviewed by a three-judge panel, and the majority decision prevails. However, similar to the district courts, the total number of justices in each appellate court varies according to need. See Exhibit 2-4 for a map showing the federal circuits and districts.

U.S. Supreme Court

The U.S. court system has one Supreme Court, consisting of nine justices. The Court is located in Washington, D.C., and holds its sessions from October through June. Primarily, the Supreme Court exercises appellate jurisdiction. In most cases, the exercise of that appellate jurisdiction is discretionary. With limited exceptions, the Supreme Court is not required to hear cases in which a party requests review. In deciding whether to grant a hearing in a case, the Court considers the importance of the decision not only to the aggrieved parties but also to society as a whole. The Court also considers whether the courts of appeals have decided cases in contradictory ways. The Supreme Court often hears cases to resolve disagreements between various appellate courts.

To request a hearing in the Supreme Court, a party files with the Court a document called a *petition for a writ of* **certiorari**. In this petition the party explains why the Supreme Court should consider the case. The justices then consider each petition for writ of certiorari and vote on whether to grant it. For a petition to be granted, four of the nine justices

EXHIBIT 2-4 Shaded Areas Represent Various Circuits for the U.S. Courts of Appeal and Dotted Lines Reflect U.S. District Court Boundaries in States Having More Than One District

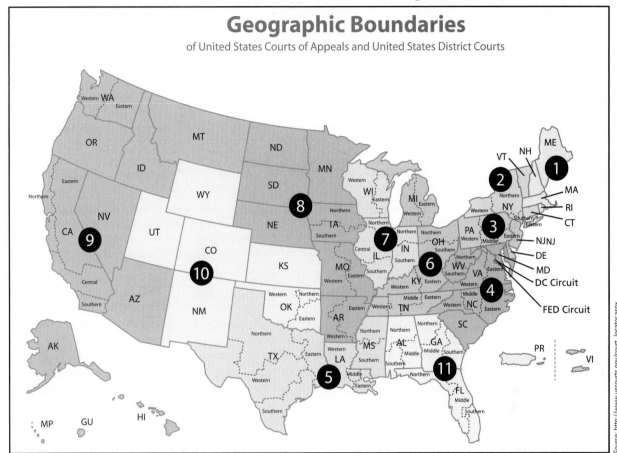

must agree. If the petition for the writ of certiorari is not granted, then the decision of the court of appeals stands. If a petition for writ of certiorari is granted, however, it does not mean that the party has won the case. The party has only managed to get a full hearing (review) by the Supreme Court. If the petition is granted and the writ is issued, the case proceeds much like an appeal in the appellate courts. The justices consider the lower court transcripts. The attorneys submit legal briefs and present oral arguments to the Court. To prevail before the Supreme Court, a party must have the vote of five out of the nine justices, or a simple majority. (In the event that fewer than nine justices are hearing the case, it takes a majority to win. Should there be a tie vote, the decision of the court of appeals stands.) See Exhibit 2-5 for an outline of the hearing process.

Although the Supreme Court is part of the federal court system, it can and does review cases originally tried in state courts, as long as some federal or constitutional issue exists. Again, there is usually no right to have such cases heard by the Supreme Court. As with appeals from federal court, Supreme Court review of state cases is discretionary.

EXHIBIT 2-5 Hearing Process for U.S. Supreme Court

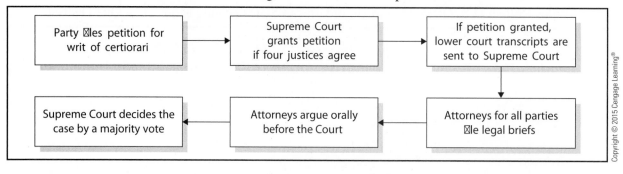

Although the Supreme Court is primarily a court of review, in certain cases it has original jurisdiction. Article III, Section 2 of the U.S. Constitution provides:

> In all cases affecting ambassadors, other public ministers and consuls, and those in which a state shall be a party, the Supreme Court shall have original jurisdiction. In all other cases before mentioned (Art. III, § 2.1) the Supreme Court shall have appellate jurisdiction, both as to law and fact, with such exception, and under such regulations as the Congress shall make.

STATE COURT SYSTEMS

Each state has a court system established pursuant to the laws of the state. For the most part, states pattern their court structures after the federal system. All states have trial courts and some sort of appellate, or review, courts. Most states also have a state supreme court or a court of last resort. The role of each of these courts is comparable to their equivalents in the federal system. The names, however, differ from state to state. For example, general trial courts in California are called superior courts. In New York, trial courts are called supreme courts. In other states, trial courts are known as circuit courts, city courts, county courts, surrogate courts, chancery courts, and courts of common pleas. Many states have additional specialty trial courts such as probate court, juvenile court, and family court. Some states have different levels of trial courts.

In addition, many state court systems have a *small claims court* (the people's court). In these courts, parties who are suing for small amounts of money go through a simplified litigation process. Attorneys are usually not involved, and all pleadings are extremely simple. These courts are intended to afford speedy legal relief in small cases where normal litigation costs would preclude other actions.

THE COURTS AND THE INTERNET

Today's courts, like most businesses, rely heavily on the Internet to function efficiently. A court's Web site provides essential factual and legal information for attorneys as well as litigants. You will generally find the following information:

- the court's physical address (or addresses), often with a link to an online map with directions

- the telephone numbers for the various departments within the court, often including telephone numbers for each judge's staff
- court hours (essential information for anyone filing documents)
- court calendars
- selected documents and other information about pending and past cases
- local rules of court
- local forms for use in the court
- instructions for electronic filing of documents

In addition to providing information, the Internet has changed the way courts conduct business. Many courts allow documents to be electronically filed. Many judges post "tentative rulings" in law and motion matters prior to the time for the hearing on the matter. In some proceedings, attorneys are allowed to appear by telephone, rather than personally. Litigation attorneys and paralegals must familiarize themselves with the various procedures and requirements connected with the court's use of the Internet. See Exhibit 2-6 for an example of one court's local policy on the use of equipment for telephone appearances.

EXHIBIT 2-6 Court Telephone Appearance Policy

subject matter jurisdiction

The authority that a court has to hear a particular type of case.

personal jurisdiction

The power or authority of the court to make a ruling affecting the parties before the court.

in rem jurisdiction

The authority of a court to hear a case based on the fact that property, which is the subject of a lawsuit, is located within the state in which the court is situated.

quasi in rem jurisdiction

Authority of a court to hear a case based on the fact that the defendant owns property that is located within the state, even though that property is not the subject of the lawsuit.

JURISDICTION

Jurisdiction is the power or authority that a court has to hear a particular case. Recall the hypothetical case of *Raeburn v. Cassidy* described earlier in the chapter. Assume that the automobile accident happened in San Francisco, California. An Internet search for courts in San Francisco results in your finding several different courts located in the city, including the San Francisco County Superior Court, the California Court of Appeal for the First District, the California Supreme Court, the U.S. District Court for Northern California, and the U.S. Court of Appeals for the Ninth Circuit. Before filing a lawsuit, the attorney for Raeburn must decide which of those many courts is appropriate for filing that lawsuit. This is a question of jurisdiction.

In many cases, the question of jurisdiction is relatively simple to answer. If a lawsuit arises under a state law and all of the parties are residents of that state, then jurisdiction is in the state courts. If a lawsuit arises under a federal law and all parties are residents of the same state, then jurisdiction is usually in the federal court located in the state of residence of the parties.

Example

In the hypothetical case of *Raeburn v. Cassidy* assume both parties reside in San Francisco, California, and the accident happened there. Because negligence is a matter of state law, and because both parties are residents of California, the state courts in California have jurisdiction. In this case, the attorney would file the action in the San Francisco County Superior Court.

However, not all cases are as obvious as *Raeburn v. Cassidy*. Where parties are not residents of the same state or where one party, especially a business, has a presence in several states, determining proper jurisdiction is more involved. The use of the Internet by businesses raises several jurisdiction questions.

Two factors are analyzed to determine which court has jurisdiction to hear a case: (1) the type of case (the subject matter of the lawsuit) and (2) the residence of the defendant (or in some cases where the defendant has property). To have jurisdiction to hear a case, a court must have both **subject matter jurisdiction**, the authority to hear the type of case before the court, and **personal jurisdiction**, authority or power over the parties, especially the defendant. Sometimes the defendant's property becomes a substitute for personal jurisdiction. This is referred to as **in rem jurisdiction** or **quasi in rem jurisdiction** (see Exhibit 2-7).

EXHIBIT 2-7 Jurisdiction

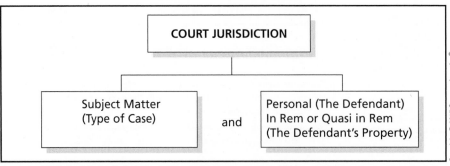

Subject Matter Jurisdiction

Subject matter jurisdiction determines whether a court has the power to hear a particular type of case. For example, review the *Weigh To Go* case in the Commentary at the beginning of this chapter. The plaintiff must file this lawsuit in a trial court that has the power to hear a case based on trade name infringement. The first issue in any case is to determine whether a case belongs in federal court or in state court. Various laws dictate the kinds of cases that can be brought in federal courts and the kinds that can be brought in state courts.

Subject Matter Jurisdiction of the Federal Courts The federal courts have limited subject matter jurisdiction. They hear cases only when the Constitution, treaties, or some federal law specifically confers jurisdiction on those courts. Generally, in criminal cases the federal courts have jurisdiction when the offense is a crime under federal law. In civil cases, the federal courts have subject matter jurisdiction in the following circumstances:

1. the case involves a constitutional issue;
2. the case involves a treaty;
3. the case involves a federal law, such as those that regulate bankruptcy, patent and copyright, discrimination, or maritime issues;
4. the U.S. government is a plaintiff or defendant in the lawsuit; or
5. the plaintiff and defendant are not citizens of the same state (**diversity of citizenship**).

Diversity of Citizenship Even though a particular type of case is usually in state court, such as automobile accidents, federal courts have subject matter jurisdiction if diversity of citizenship exists (28 U.S.C. § 1332). Jurisdiction based on diversity of citizenship has two requirements:

1. the plaintiff and defendant are not residents of the same state, and
2. if the case is a claim for money damages, the damages claimed must exceed $75,000.

Most cases require complete diversity before the federal court can hear a case. This means that no plaintiff and no defendant can be citizens of the same state. Diversity also exists when a dispute is between citizens of a state and citizens or subjects of a foreign state. For examples of how diversity is determined, see Exhibit 2-8. Complete diversity is not required for certain class action lawsuits. In these cases, if the amount in controversy exceeds $5,000,000, the federal courts have jurisdiction if diversity exists between any plaintiff and any defendant. Several special rules apply and the U.S. Code should always be checked (28 U.S.C. § 1332).

When plaintiffs and defendants in a case are individuals, state citizenship is normally determined by the individuals' primary residence. In contrast, corporate parties are considered citizens of both the state in which they are incorporated and the state in which they maintain their principal place of business. In a recent case, *Hertz Corp. v. Friend*, 559 U.S. 77 (2010), the U.S. Supreme Court ruled that the principal place of business for a

diversity of citizenship
A basis for federal court subject matter jurisdiction under 28 U.S.C. § 1332 existing when no plaintiff and no defendant are citizens of the same state and the amount in controversy exceeds $75,000, or when one party is a citizen of a state and the other is a citizen of a foreign state.

EXHIBIT 2-8 Determining Diversity of Citizenship

Recall the case of *Raeburn v. Cassidy* described earlier in the chapter. Rather than both parties being residents of San Francisco, California, assume the following situations at the time of the accident. Also assume that in all cases, the amount of damages exceeds $75,000:

1. Raeburn is a citizen of California and Cassidy is a citizen of Oregon, visiting a friend in California.

   Complete Diversity Exists

   Raeburn　　　　　　　v.　　　　　　*Cassidy*

   (citizen of California)　　　　　　**(citizen of Oregon)**

2. Raeburn is a citizen of California and has a passenger, Reese, also a citizen of California.

   Complete Diversity Exists

   Raeburn and Reese　　　　v.　　　　　*Cassidy*

   (both citizens of California)　　　**(citizen of Oregon)**

3. Raeburn is a citizen of California and Cassidy is a citizen of Oregon driving a vehicle owned by his friend, Pearlman, a citizen of California.

   Complete Diversity Does NOT Exist

   Raeburn　　　　v.　　　　*Cassidy*　　　　*and Pearlman*

   (citizen of California)　　**(citizen of Oregon)**　　**(citizen of California)**

corporation is based on its "nerve center," which the Court defined as "the place where a corporation's officers direct, control, and coordinate the corporation's activities." Corporations may thus be citizens of more than one state.

Example

Consider a hypothetical case of *Tech, Inc. v. Disk, Inc.* Tech, Inc. is a corporation incorporated in the state of Delaware but maintains its headquarters and principal business in Silicon Valley (California). Tech, Inc., the plaintiff, is a citizen of both Delaware and California. Disk, Inc., the defendant, is incorporated in the state of Delaware but maintains its headquarters and principal place of business in Texas. In this case, diversity of citizenship would not exist because both parties are considered residents of Delaware.

One question that sometimes arises in connection with the monetary limit required for diversity jurisdiction is whether several small claims can be aggregated to achieve the minimum requirement. Unfortunately, the answer to this question is not simple and depends on the nature of the claims to be aggregated. In general, however, claims cannot be added together to meet the $75,000 requirement if the claims are separate and distinct.

Example

Several people are injured in an automobile accident and individually each claim is under $75,000, but added together they exceed that amount. The federal court would not have diversity jurisdiction. Each person has a separate and distinct claim, even though they are related, and even though they could join in the same lawsuit.

Choice of Law   When a federal court exercises jurisdiction based on diversity of citizenship, the substantive law controlling the dispute is not found in federal law. If it were, subject matter jurisdiction would be based on that federal law rather than on the diversity of citizenship. When hearing a diversity case, therefore, the federal court must apply some state law to the substantive issues in the case. Usually, but not always, the federal court applies the substantive law of the state in which the federal court is situated.

Example

Again, consider the case of *Raeburn v. Cassidy*. Assume that the accident happens in California. If Raeburn is a citizen of California and Cassidy is a citizen of Oregon, the federal court has jurisdiction based on diversity (as long as Raeburn's claim exceeds $75,000). If the case is in a U.S. district court in California, California state substantive law applies to the case.

Exclusive versus Concurrent Jurisdiction   When federal courts have subject matter jurisdiction, sometimes state courts *also* have jurisdiction. Subject matter jurisdiction of the federal courts can be either exclusive or concurrent. **Exclusive jurisdiction** means that the action must be brought in federal court. **Concurrent jurisdiction** means that it can be brought either in federal court or in state court. Under federal law, certain types of cases must be in federal court. Examples of federal court exclusive jurisdiction include maritime cases, patent cases, and bankruptcy cases. However, other types of cases, such as employment discrimination or civil rights violations, can be litigated in either federal or state court. When federal jurisdiction is based on diversity of citizenship, jurisdiction is almost always concurrent with a state. For example, consider the *Weigh To Go* case described in the Commentary to this chapter. The facts indicate that this is a case of concurrent jurisdiction. (See Exhibit 2-9.)

Removal to Federal Court   In cases where concurrent jurisdiction exists, the plaintiff decides where to file the lawsuit. However, if the plaintiff chooses to file in a state court, the defendant usually has the right to have the case transferred or removed to the federal court. The defendant accomplishes this by following the requirements described in the U.S. Code (28 U.S.C. § 1446). After the plaintiff files a complaint in state court, removal occurs as follows:

1. Within 30 days of service or receipt of papers, the defendant files in federal court the following:
    a. a *notice of* **removal** (a document requesting that the case be transferred to the federal court) and
    b. copies of all process, pleadings, and orders that the defendant has received.

---

exclusive jurisdiction
Power or authority to hear a case that belongs to one court system only (i.e., federal or one state court system)

concurrent jurisdiction
Power or authority of more than one court system to hear a case.

removal
Generally, the transfer of a case from a state court to a federal court where concurrent jurisdiction exists and the case was initially filed in a state court.

EXHIBIT 2-9 Concurrent Jurisdiction for *Weigh To Go v. Go A Weigh*

CONCURRENT JURISDICTION

State Court Has Jurisdiction:

1. California statutory and case law provides protection to a trade name. This gives California subject matter jurisdiction.

2. Defendant Go A Weigh is a citizen of California. This gives California state court personal jurisdiction.

3. Because both subject matter and personal jurisdiction exist, state court in California has jurisdiction to hear case.

Federal Court Has Jurisdiction:

1. Plaintiff Weigh To Go is a citizen of Texas (state of incorporation) and Oregon (principal place of business). Defendant is a citizen of California. Diversity of citizenship exists, giving the federal court subject matter jurisdiction (assuming that damage minimums are requested). (Even though plaintiff does some business in California, California is not the place of incorporation or the principal place of business. Thus, plaintiff is not a citizen of California and diversity exists.)

2. Because the defendant is a citizen of California, the federal court in California has personal jurisdiction.

3. Because both subject matter and personal jurisdiction exist, the federal court located in California has jurisdiction to hear the case.

Conclusion

1. This is a case of concurrent jurisdiction. The plaintiff initially chooses the court. If the plaintiff chooses to file in state court, the defendant can remove the case to federal court. If the plaintiff files in federal court, the case remains there.

---

2. The defendant files these documents in the federal district and division located in the state where the plaintiff originally filed the complaint.

3. The defendant gives written notice to all adverse parties and the clerk of state court that notice of removal has been filed.

See Exhibit 2-10 for an example of a notice of removal.

Concurrent jurisdiction can also exist between two or more states. That is, where a case belongs in a state court system, more than one state may have subject matter jurisdiction. This would be determined by the facts of the case and the appropriate state laws.

supplemental jurisdiction
A federal court's right to decide a claim based on a nonfederal issue if this claim depends on the same set of facts as does a federal claim in the case before the court.

Supplemental Jurisdiction   Sometimes cases consist of more than one type of claim, one of which is a matter of federal law and the other of which is a matter of state law. Even if a matter is not normally within the subject matter jurisdiction of the federal courts, it is often heard in federal court if it is in conjunction with a case that is within the subject matter jurisdiction of the court. This is known as **supplemental jurisdiction**. This is also known as *pendent* or *ancillary jurisdiction*.

EXHIBIT 2-10 Notice of Removal

To the Honorable Judges of the United States District Court for the Northern District of California:

Defendants, Go A Weigh, a corporation, through its attorney, respectfully shows the court:

1. The above-entitled action was commenced in the Superior Court of the State of California, County of San Francisco, on January 10, _____, and is now pending in that court.

2. The above-mentioned action is a civil action for damages and injunctive relief based on alleged infringement of the trade name laws of the State of California.

3. All defendants that are required to join in this notice have joined.

4. The action is one of which the United States District Courts are given original jurisdiction under 28 U.S.C. § 1332 by reason of the diversity of citizenship of the parties.

5. The amount in controversy in the action, exclusive of interest and costs, exceeds $75,000.

6. A copy of the complaint was served on defendant at San Francisco, County of San Francisco, State of California, on January 3, _____.

7. Thirty days have not yet expired since the action thereby became removable to this court.

8. At the time of the commencement of this action, plaintiff was and now is a citizen of the State of Texas; at the time of the commencement of this action, defendants and each of them were and now are citizens and residents of the State of California.

9. Copies of all pleadings, process, and orders, served on petitioner in this action are attached and marked Exhibit A.

10. Defendants present and file with this notice a bond with a good and sufficient surety, as required by law, conditioned that defendants will pay all costs and disbursements incurred by reason of these removal proceedings, should it be determined that this action was not removable or was improperly removed.

Wherefore, defendants request that the above-entitled action be removed from the Superior Court of the State of California to the United States District Court for the Northern District of California.

Date: January 10, _____

Respectfully Submitted,

_____

Roberta Rios,

Attorney for Defendant

Example

Wilson works for Chipp Inc. as an electrical engineer. In the course of his employment, Wilson designs certain products, which are patented. Pursuant to a written agreement, the patent belongs to Chipp Inc. because it was developed as part of Wilson's job. Wilson leaves Chipp Inc. and starts his own company, manufacturing products that he designed at Chipp and for which Chipp holds the patent. This action on Wilson's part violates his written contract with Chipp as

general jurisdiction
The power or authority of a court to hear cases that are not within the exclusive jurisdiction of a different court.

well as Chipp's patents on the products. Chipp Inc. wishes to sue Wilson for breach of contract as well as patent infringement. Assuming that the parties are residents of the same state, a lawsuit for breach of an employment contract would not normally be within federal court subject matter. In the case of *Chipp v. Wilson*, because the federal court has jurisdiction over the patent case, it can also exercise jurisdiction over the related action based on breach of contract.

Multijurisdictional Litigation (28 U.S.C. § 1407)   Special jurisdictional rules can apply to complex cases where similar cases are filed in more than one U.S. district court. This may occur when a defective product, such as an automobile, results in injuries to numerous victims living in different states. Injured parties often file a lawsuit in the district in which they live, resulting in numerous cases arising out of the same conduct. The law allows these cases to be transferred to one district for the purpose of pretrial proceedings, hoping that the matters will settle. If a case does not settle, the matter is transferred back to the original court for trial.

Subject Matter Jurisdiction in the State Courts   Except for cases that must be brought in federal court, each state has the right to determine the subject matter jurisdiction of the courts within that state. Subject matter jurisdiction of state courts is determined by the laws of the state. If a dispute arises under those laws, the state courts generally have subject matter jurisdiction. Some federal laws, such as civil rights laws, also allow a state court to hear disputes arising under the federal law. See Exhibit 2-11 for examples of types of cases within the subject matter jurisdiction of the federal and state courts.

State court systems often have more than one level of trial court. Subject matter jurisdiction requires that a case be filed in the correct court. States usually have at least one trial court that has **general jurisdiction** in civil cases; that is, the power to hear any kind of case except those that must be brought in federal court. However, unlike the federal system,

EXHIBIT 2-11 Examples of Subject Matter Jurisdiction: Federal versus State

FEDERAL COURT	STATE COURT	FEDERAL OR STATE COURT
Cases involving federal laws • civil rights • discrimination • social security • broadcasting	Cases involving state constitutional or state law issues Most personal injury cases • automobile accidents • medical and other malpractice • product liability	State law disputes where diversity of citizenship exists Certain civil rights cases Federal constitutional issues Cases involving certain federal laws
Cases against the U.S. government	Real property disputes	
Intellectual property cases such as patent and copyright disputes	Landlord/tenant disputes	
Corporate securities cases	Contract disputes	
Admiralty cases (cases arising on the high seas)	Business disputes	
Cases involving rights under treaties	Family law cases	
Disputes between states	Probate matters	

where there is only one level of trial court, many states have created special trial courts that have limited subject matter jurisdiction. A court of **limited jurisdiction** has authority to hear only certain kinds of cases. For example, some courts have authority to hear limited types of cases, such as juvenile proceedings or family law matters; some courts with limited jurisdiction are only empowered to hear cases in which the amount of money in dispute is a limited amount. These courts are often known as municipal courts, district courts, or justice courts. See Exhibits 2-12 and 2-13.

limited jurisdiction
Authority to hear only certain kinds of cases.

EXHIBIT 2-12 Subject Matter Jurisdiction

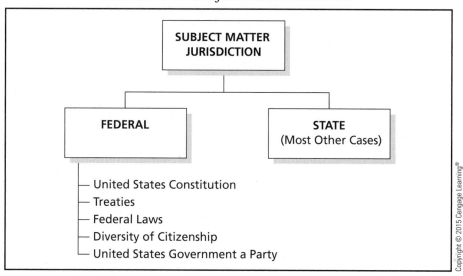

Copyright © 2015 Cengage Learning®

EXHIBIT 2-13 Analyzing Subject Matter Jurisdiction

ANALYZING A CASE FOR SUBJECT MATTER JURISDICTION

1. **Because federal courts have specific limited jurisdiction, analyze your case to see if it fits into any of the categories of federal court power:**
   a. Is this a dispute that arises under the Constitution?
   b. Is this a dispute involving a treaty?
   c. Is this a dispute where a specific federal law confers jurisdiction on federal courts?
   d. Does diversity of citizenship exist between the parties?
      1) Is there complete diversity so that no plaintiff and no defendant are citizens of the same state?
      2) Does the amount of the dispute exceed $75,000?
2. **If there is a basis for federal court jurisdiction, is that jurisdiction exclusive or concurrent?**
   a. If federal court jurisdiction is concurrent with state court jurisdiction, do you want to file in federal court or state court?
3. **If there is no basis for federal court jurisdiction, or if jurisdiction is concurrent, which state court has jurisdiction?**

Copyright © 2015 Cengage Learning®

Challenging Subject Matter Jurisdiction   A court that lacks subject matter juris-diction has no power to decide a case. If it attempts to do so, that judgment is void and can be challenged at any time. Subject matter jurisdiction can be challenged in different ways, depending on where the lawsuit is filed. One common way to attack subject matter jurisdiction is by filing a motion to dismiss the case.

Personal Jurisdiction

In addition to having jurisdiction over the subject matter of the case, a court must also have jurisdiction over the parties. This authority, known as *personal jurisdiction,* means that the court has the power to render a judgment that affects the rights of the parties before the court.

Jurisdiction over Plaintiff   Personal jurisdiction over the plaintiff seldom, if ever, presents any legal problems. The plaintiffs always file the lawsuit and select the trial court. Therefore, they cannot complain that the court has no power over them. Having asked the court to make a decision concerning their rights, plaintiffs have no basis to challenge the court's right to do so.

Jurisdiction over Defendant   Review the Commentary at the beginning of the chapter. Weigh To Go, a citizen of both Texas and Oregon, wants to file a lawsuit against Go A Weigh, a California citizen. Should Weigh To Go be allowed to file the lawsuit in ei-ther Texas or Oregon? If so, Go A Weigh, a company that does no business in either Texas or Oregon, would be required to appear in a Texas or Oregon court to defend itself. Is this fair? This is a question of personal jurisdiction.

No court has unlimited rights to exercise personal jurisdiction. Such a result is basi-cally unfair. All state courts have personal jurisdiction over those who reside within the state. Thus, if a person resides within a state, that person can be sued in any court within that state. Whether a court has jurisdiction over a nonresident defendant depends on two factors. First, the exercise of jurisdiction must be in accordance with the Due Process Clause of the Fourteenth Amendment to the U.S. Constitution. Second, the exercise of jurisdiction must be in accordance with state law. Federal courts generally have personal jurisdiction over defendants if the state courts in the state in which the federal court is located would have personal jurisdiction. In other words, if a state trial court in California has personal jurisdiction over a defendant, then the federal trial courts located in California also have personal jurisdiction.

Constitutional Limitations   The Fourteenth Amendment to the U.S. Constitution requires "due process of law" in civil as well as criminal cases. In the leading case of *Interna-tional Shoe Co. v. Washington,* the U.S. Supreme Court held that a state cannot exercise per-sonal jurisdiction over a nonresident defendant unless that defendant has sufficient contacts with the state to satisfy "traditional notions of fair play and substantial justice." Courts can usually exercise personal jurisdiction over a nonresident defendant if that person or entity is doing business within the state and therefore has the opportunity to avail itself of the state's laws and state's courts. The courts refer to this as "purposeful availment." However, it is not necessary that a defendant is actually conducting an ongoing business within the state. Constitutional requirements are often satisfied with less. In the *International Shoe* case, the

Supreme Court found that the state of Washington had personal jurisdiction over a business that hired shoe salesmen within the state and provided them with samples. Occasionally, the company rented rooms to display the shoes. The salesmen took orders that were transmitted to the company's office out of state. Products were shipped from out of state to Washington addresses. The company had no offices in the state of Washington. Read the reasoning of the Court in the excerpt from the case on page 49.

AUTOMATED LITIGATION SUPPORT

The 21st Century Law Office

THE ELECTRONIC COURTROOM

SCENARIO

Your supervising attorney, whose office is located in Texas, is anxious to file suit against Go A Weigh and has already determined that because of personal jurisdiction requirements the action must be maintained in California. She prefers to bring the case in federal court. She anticipates that this will eventually be a very complex trial. Handling numerous documents and presenting evidence will require the use of sophisticated technology. Your attorney asks you to check with the court and see what technology is available.

PROBLEM

Trial attorneys often depend on technology to manage and present evidence. If necessary equipment is not available, the trial attorneys may be responsible for providing their own, subject to rules and requirements of the court. Supplying extensive equipment may be more difficult when trial takes place in a distant and unfamiliar court. How do you help your attorney to be prepared for such a trial?

SOLUTION

When a case is tried in a far away location, logistic problems in arranging for equipment can arise. Today, many trial courts provide "electronic courtrooms" equipped with the latest technology. However, such courtrooms are not always available. To be prepared, the trial attorney must know what equipment is available at the court and what equipment must be supplied by the attorney. When a trial occurs in a local court, a paralegal can visit the court and see what is available. When a trial court is distant and unfamiliar, a good starting place is the court's Web site. For federal courts, you can locate the court's Web site from www.uscourts.gov. In searching the Web site for the federal court in San Francisco, you find the following information:

COURTROOM TECHNOLOGY

SOUND SYSTEMS

All courtrooms are equipped with state-of-the-art **sound systems** which include:

- Full room-wide public address (PA) system
- Wireless microphone for jury selection
- Hearing impaired/interpreter infrared headphones
- Jury masking system for sidebar conferences
- Teleconferencing
- Realtime translation court reporter transcript distributor

Evidence Presentation

Some of the courtrooms are **wired for evidence-presentation.** For **traditional** courtrooms, attorneys may either reserve one of the court's portable media carts equipped with evidence presentation equipment or provide their own equipment. See the charts on this page for details regarding a particular courtroom.

Evidence-Presentation-Ready ("Wired") Courtrooms

These courtrooms are equipped with:

- Dedicated evidence-presentation monitors at the bench, counsel tables and jury box
- An annotation monitor in the witness box
- Two large flat-screen monitors for viewing evidence from the gallery
- Additional laptop inputs at counsel tables
- Click here for info on how to use the evidence-presentation system.

INTRODUCTION TO CIVIL LITIGATION

Traditional courtrooms (those that are not yet wired for evidence presentation) do not have dedicated evidence-presentation monitors at the bench, counsel tables, jury box or witness stand. In San Francisco and Oakland, counsel may contact the courtroom deputy to reserve one of the court's portable media carts. These include:

- Document camera
- Microphone usable with the courtroom public address system
- Audio and video inputs for laptop-based presentations

- Annotation monitor (displays the image from the laptop or camera, and allows annotation of the image)
- DVD/CD player
- VHS player

Counsel must be prepared to provide their own evidence presentation equipment if they are not able to reserve a portable media cart and to provide back-up equipment in the event of equipment malfunction

Source: www.uscourts.gov

Although the court provides extensive equipment, it is clear that you still have work to do to make sure equipment is available for your trial.

---

long-arm statutes
A state law that defines the right of state courts to exercise jurisdiction over nonresident defendants.

On the other hand, personal jurisdiction was found to be lacking where defendants, an automobile wholesaler and a retailer, sold an automobile in New York. The buyers, claiming that the automobile was defective, sued the defendants in Oklahoma where they suffered an accident. Defendants had no other connection to Oklahoma.

In a series of recent cases, courts were asked to determine questions of personal jurisdiction of parties who maintain Web sites for their businesses. In general, courts find personal jurisdiction where there is some possibility of "interaction" with those visiting the Web site. That is, if a customer can order products through the site, personal jurisdiction probably exists. If the site is informational only, then personal jurisdiction probably will not exist.

State Long-Arm Statutes   Even though the exercise of jurisdiction may be constitutionally permissible, the state must also allow it. State laws describing the circumstances under which the state may exercise jurisdiction over nonresident defendants are known as **long-arm statutes**. The following is an example of a long-arm statute:

[A]ny person . . . whether or not a citizen or resident of this state, who in person or through an agent does any of the following enumerated acts, submits himself, and if an individual, his personal representative, to the jurisdiction of the courts of this state as to any claim arising out of or related to:

1. the transaction of any business within this state;

2. contracting to supply services or goods in this state;

3. the causing of any injury within this state whether tortious or by breach of warranty;

4. the ownership, use, or possession of any real estate situated in this state;

5. contracting to insure any person, property, or risk located within this state at the time of contracting. . . .

Utah Code Ann. § 78B-3-205

Waiver by Appearance   As mentioned, if a court lacks subject matter jurisdiction, any judgment rendered by the court is void. To an extent, the same is true of personal jurisdiction. However, although the parties to a lawsuit cannot waive, or give up, the requirement of subject matter jurisdiction, a defendant can waive, or give up, the requirement of personal

C A S E	*INTERNATIONAL SHOE CO. V. WASHINGTON,* 326 U.S. 310 (1945)

Mr. Chief Justice STONE delivered the opinion of the court.

The question for decision [is] whether, within the limitations of the due process clause of the Fourteenth Amendment, appellant, a Delaware corporation, has by its activities in the State of Washington rendered itself amenable to proceedings in the courts of that state. . . .

The Supreme Court of Washington was of the opinion that the regular and systematic solicitation of orders in the state by appellant's salesmen, resulting in a continuous flow of appellant's product into the state, was sufficient to constitute doing business in the state so as to make appellant amenable to suit in its courts.

• • •

Due process requires only that in order to subject a defendant to a judgment in personam, if he be not present within the territory of the forum, he have certain minimum contacts with it such that the maintenance of the suit does not offend "traditional notions of fair play and substantial justice."

• • •

It is evident that the criteria by which we mark the boundary line between those activities which justify the subjection of a corporation to suit, and those which do not, cannot be simply mechanical or quantitative. The test is not merely, as has sometimes been suggested, whether the activity, which the corporation has seen fit to procure through its agents in another state, is a little more or a little less. Whether due process is satisfied must depend rather upon the quality and nature of the activity in relation to the fair and orderly administration of the laws which it was the purpose of the due process clause to insure. That clause does not contemplate that a state may make binding a judgment in personam against an individual or corporate defendant with which the state has no contacts, ties, or relations. But to the extent that a corporation exercises the privilege of conducting activities within a state, it enjoys the benefits and protection of the laws of that state. The exercise of that privilege may give rise to obligations; and, so far as those obligations arise out of or are connected with the activities within the state, a procedure which requires the corporation to respond to a suit brought to enforce them can, in most instances, hardly be said to be undue. Applying these standards, the activities carried on in behalf of appellant in the State of Washington were neither irregular nor casual. They were systematic and continuous throughout the years in question. They resulted in a large volume of interstate business, in the course of which appellant received the benefits and protection of the laws of the state, including the right to resort to the courts for the enforcement of its rights. The obligation which is here sued upon arose out of these very activities. It is evident that these operations establish sufficient contacts or ties with the state of the forum to make it reasonable and just according to our traditional conception of fair play and substantial justice to permit the state to enforce the obligations which appellant has incurred there. Hence we cannot say that the maintenance of the present suit in the State of Washington involves an unreasonable or undue procedure.

• • •

AFFIRMED.

---

jurisdiction. A waiver of personal jurisdiction means that an individual voluntarily allows a court to hear a case against her even though the court would not otherwise have the power to do so. Furthermore, in some courts, if the defendant makes a general appearance in court and does not properly object to personal jurisdiction, she automatically waives any defect in personal jurisdiction. A defendant makes a **general appearance** whenever she files a pleading or takes part in the proceedings by doing anything other than objecting to jurisdiction.

Notice   Fairness demands that before a court can decide the rights of a defendant in a lawsuit, the defendant should be given proper notice of the action. This is known as *service*

general appearance
Either a physical appearance or filing of documents in a court, without specifically limiting the purpose of the appearance; a general appearance confers personal jurisdiction on the court on the party appearing.

special appearance
An appearance in court (either in person or by filing documents) for a limited purpose, often contesting jurisdiction.

motion to quash service of summons
A request that the court declare that service of the complaint and summons is invalid either because the court lacks jurisdiction over the defendant or because of some procedural problem with the service itself.

EXHIBIT 2-14 Personal Jurisdiction Checklist

PERSONAL JURISDICTION CHECKLIST

✓ Is defendant a resident of the state, *or* does defendant have sufficient contacts with the state?

And

✓ Has proper notice been given to defendant?

Copyright © 2015 Cengage Learning®

of process. How service can be accomplished is determined by the laws of the jurisdiction in which the lawsuit is pending. The different methods of service of process are described in Chapter 5. See Exhibit 2-14.

Challenging Personal Jurisdiction

A defendant must exercise care in challenging personal jurisdiction because doing so in an improper manner may inadvertently confer personal jurisdiction on the court. Although federal courts allow defendants to challenge personal jurisdiction in the answer to the complaint, in some courts personal jurisdiction must be attacked by a **special appearance** (an appearance for the sole purpose of questioning the court's jurisdiction). This is often done by filing a motion to quash service of summons. A **motion to quash service of summons** is a request that the court invalidate any service of the complaint and summons, thereby preventing the plaintiff from pursuing her lawsuit. In federal court, a motion to quash service of summons is an alternative way of challenging personal jurisdiction.

In Rem Jurisdiction

Sometimes, even though personal jurisdiction may be questionable or even nonexistent, the court can hear a case if it has jurisdiction over property that is the subject of a dispute. This is known as *in rem jurisdiction* and is a substitute in some cases for personal jurisdiction. See Exhibit 2-15.

Example

Ryan Flynn, a resident of Pennsylvania, dies and leaves an estate consisting of real and personal property, all of which is located in Pennsylvania. He is survived by two sons, Martin, a Pennsylvania resident, and Michael, a resident of Georgia. In his will, Flynn leaves all of his property to Michael. Martin wishes to challenge this. Even though Michael may have no connection to the state of Pennsylvania, because the property that is the subject of this dispute is located in Pennsylvania, the courts in Pennsylvania have jurisdiction to hear the matter. They have the right to determine ownership of property located within the state boundaries. This is in rem jurisdiction.

EXHIBIT 2-15 In Rem Jurisdiction Checklist

IN REM JURISDICTION CHECKLIST

✓ Does the lawsuit concern property located in the state?

And

✓ Has proper notice of the lawsuit been given to the defendant?

Copyright © 2015 Cengage Learning®

In exercising in rem jurisdiction, a court is limited to rendering judgments that affect only the property. The court cannot render personal judgments against the defendant that do not concern that property. For example, in the preceding case, suppose that Martin Flynn claimed that he was disinherited because of slanderous remarks made to his father by his brother. In addition to challenging the will, he might also wish to sue his brother for slander in the same action. For a court to hear this action, the Pennsylvania court would need to have personal jurisdiction over Michael.

attachment

Seizing property pursuant to a court order and giving the court the right to make orders regarding disposition of the property.

Quasi in Rem Jurisdiction

Another substitute for personal jurisdiction is quasi in rem jurisdiction. For quasi in rem jurisdiction to exist, various requirements must be met. First, a defendant must own some property within the state, although the property need not be the subject of the lawsuit. Second, any judgment is limited to the value of the property within the state. Third, that property is usually brought before the court at the beginning of the lawsuit through an attachment proceeding. In an **attachment** proceeding, the court usually orders that the property be seized and remain under the control of the court until the case is resolved.

If a court hears a case based on in rem or quasi in rem jurisdiction, due process still requires that the exercise of jurisdiction be fair and that the defendant be notified of the lawsuit. Notice is accomplished through service of process under the laws of the state in which the action is pending. See Exhibit 2-16 for an overview of jurisdiction.

EXHIBIT 2-16 Jurisdiction Overview

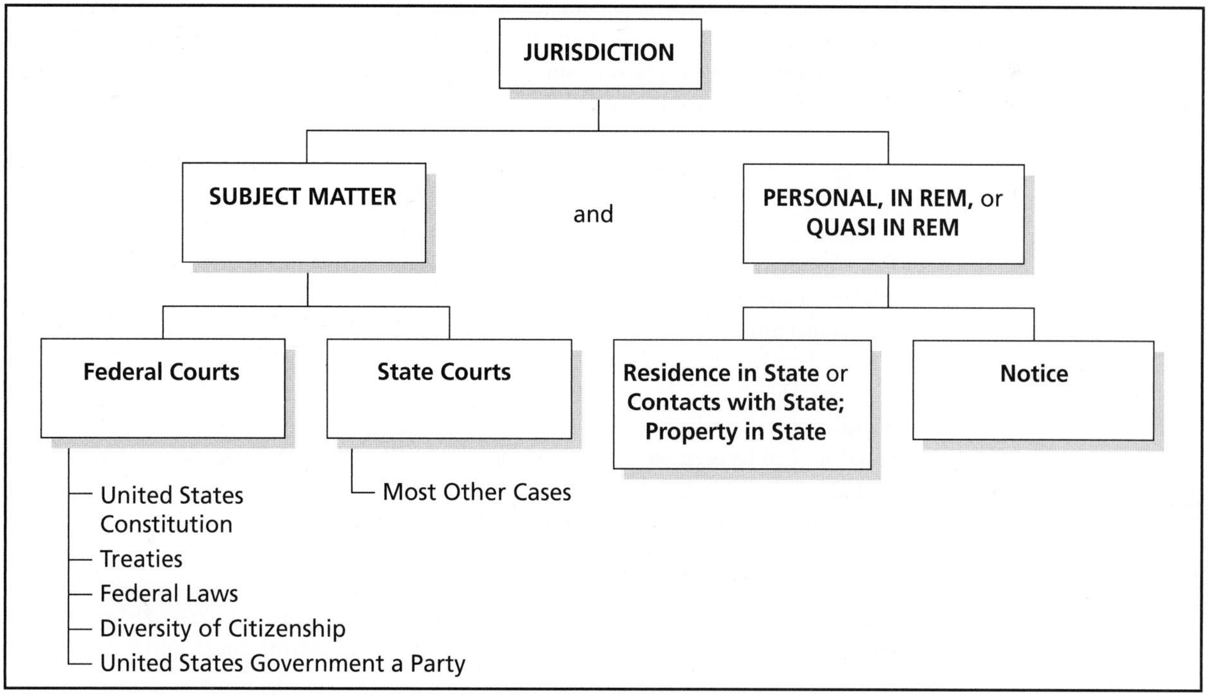

JURISDICTION

SUBJECT MATTER   and   PERSONAL, IN REM, or QUASI IN REM

Federal Courts   State Courts   Residence in State or Contacts with State; Property in State   Notice

— United States Constitution
— Treaties
— Federal Laws
— Diversity of Citizenship
— United States Government a Party

— Most Other Cases

venue

Among all the courts that have jurisdiction, venue defines the specific geographical location of the court or courts where an action should be brought. In the federal system, this determines which is the proper district. In state court systems, this often determines the proper county or counties.

VENUE

An analysis of subject matter jurisdiction tells a plaintiff whether to file an action in federal court or state court. An analysis of personal jurisdiction tells a plaintiff in which state or states to file. Personal jurisdiction is statewide. Choosing the court in the proper geographical area of the state is a question of **venue**.

Lawsuits should be filed and heard in a court that has proper venue. However, unlike jurisdiction, a court's lack of proper venue does not render a judgment void. If a defendant does not object to improper venue, she waives the right to object to the judgment rendered by the court.

Federal Court Venue

Some states have only one federal district court. Larger states, however, have more than one district located with their boundaries. Although all of the districts within the state have personal jurisdiction in a particular case, venue may be limited. The general venue statute for federal courts is 28 U.S.C. § 1391, but several different statutes control specific situations. The general statute provides two locations for proper venue and further provides that these locations are proper for cases based on diversity of citizenship or for cases not based on diversity:

1. the judicial district where any defendant resides, as long as all of the defendants reside in the same state, or

2. the judicial district where the acts that form the basis of the lawsuit occurred.

Where there are multiple defendants in a case, sometimes neither of these locations is possible.

If the action cannot be brought in any district meeting, these criteria (i.e., if all defendants do not reside in the same state or if the lawsuit arose from acts that took place in a location that no longer has personal jurisdiction 28 U.S.C. § 1391 provides an alternative venue: "[I]f there is no district in which an action may otherwise be brought as provided in this section, any judicial district in which any defendant is subject to the court's personal jurisdiction with respect to such action." See Exhibit 2-17.

Corporations present special issues with venue. In determining the residence of a defendant, a corporation is considered to reside in any judicial district in which it is subject to personal jurisdiction at the time the lawsuit is filed. If a state has more than one judicial district, however, the code provides that a corporation "shall be deemed to reside in any district in that State within which its contacts would be sufficient to subject it to personal jurisdiction if that district were a separate State, and, if there is no such district, the corporation shall be deemed to reside in the district within which it has the most significant contacts."

In addition to the general venue statute, other sections of the code provide special venue rules. For example, lawsuits relating to copyrights or trademarks may be brought in the district in which the defendant or his agent resides or may be found, and patent infringement actions may be brought in the judicial district where the defendant resides or where the defendant has committed acts of infringement and has a regular

EXHIBIT 2-17 Venue Analysis

BASIS FOR JURISDICTION	VENUE
Diversity of Citizenship	(1) a judicial district where any defendant resides, if all defendants reside in the same state, (2) a judicial district in which a substantial part of the events or omissions giving rise to the claim occurred, or a substantial part of property that is the subject of the action is situated, or (3) a judicial district in which any defendant is subject to personal jurisdiction at the time the action is commenced, if there is no district in which the action may otherwise be brought.
NOT Based on Diversity	(1) a judicial district where any defendant resides, if all defendants reside in the same state, (2) a judicial district in which a substantial part of the events or omissions giving rise to the claim occurred, or a substantial part of property that is the subject of the action is situated, or (3) a judicial district in which any defendant may be found, if there is no district in which the action may otherwise be brought.

and established place of business (28 U.S.C. § 1400). Any civil action by a stockholder on behalf of his corporation may be brought in any judicial district where the corporation might have sued the same defendants (28 U.S.C. § 1401). And generally, when the U.S. government is the defendant in a lawsuit, venue is proper in the judicial district where the plaintiff resides (28 U.S.C. § 1402). Special rules also apply to some complex litigation matters where similar cases have been brought in different courts. The code (28 U.S.C. § 1407) gives a special judicial panel on multidistrict litigation the power to make orders regarding venue for pretrial proceedings for the convenience of witnesses and interests of justice.

Sometimes, a statute that creates substantive rights also provides for venue. For example, the U.S. Code provides that employment discrimination lawsuits can be brought.

> in any judicial district in the state in which the unlawful employment practice is alleged to have been committed, in the judicial district in which the employment records relevant to such practice are maintained and administered, or in the judicial district in which the aggrieved person would have worked but for the alleged unlawful employment practice, but if the respondent is not found within any such district, such an action may be brought within the judicial district in which the respondent has his principal office. [42 U.S.C. § 2000e-5 (f) (3)]

Determining proper venue in federal cases can be a complicated process. Statutes must be carefully read and analyzed. See Exhibit 2-18.

State Court Venue

Venue in state court actions is, of course, determined by state law. As a general rule, however, actions usually can be maintained in the county in which the defendant resides

EXHIBIT 2-18 Venue Analysis

VENUE ANALYSIS

The large state of California has four court districts for federal trial courts:

Northern District	headquartered in San Francisco
Central District	headquartered in Los Angeles
Southern District	headquartered in San Diego
Eastern District	headquartered in Sacramento

Assume the following:

- P, a resident of Ohio, wants to sue D and E for injuries that P received in an auto accident that occurred in San Diego, California.
- Both D and E are California residents, but D lives in San Francisco and E lives in Los Angeles.

Jurisdiction exists in all four California districts because it involves California state law (negligence) and both defendants are residents of California.

Venue exists in:

1. *Northern District of California* because one defendant resides in this district and all defendants reside in the state of California.
2. *Central District of California* because one defendant resides in this district and all defendants reside in the state of California.
3. *Southern District of California* because the accident occurred here.

Conclusion: Plaintiff could file the lawsuit in any of these three districts; even though the Eastern District has jurisdiction, it does not have venue.

---

or where the cause of action arises. In different types of cases, other counties might also have proper venue. For example, in contract cases, actions can often be heard in the county in which the contract was made, was to be performed, or was breached. In lawsuits affecting title to real estate, the action is normally heard wherever the real estate is located.

Changing Venue

Because venue does not relate to the court's basic power to hear a case, under proper circumstances it can be changed. However, the place of trial can be changed only to another court that has jurisdiction. To change venue, a party makes a formal written request of the court where the lawsuit was filed. This is done by making a *motion for change of venue.* However, a court must have a good reason before it considers transferring the case to another location. Some of the more common reasons include the fact that in the original location the parties cannot get a fair trial, or the case was not filed in the proper court to begin with. A case might also be transferred for the convenience of the witnesses.

FINDING IT on the Internet

A paralegal working on the *Weigh To Go* case might be expected to locate addresses and other information concerning federal and state courts in different geographical regions. Information about federal courts can be found in the U.S. Federal Judiciary Web sites **<http://www.uscourts.gov>** and **<http://www.fjc.gov>**. Information about state courts can be accessed through the site for the National Center for State Courts at **< http://www.ncsc.org/>**.

a. Access the U.S. courts' site at **<http://www.uscourts.gov>** and, using the link feature, find the address for the district court in your region. This Web site contains several articles about the court that can be located by clicking on "Educational Resources." Find and summarize one article regarding the courts.

b. Access the Federal Judiciary site at **<http://www.fjc.gov>**. Locate the quizzes and take quiz 2 (How the Federal Courts Are Organized) and quiz 3 (Civil Cases). (From the Home page link to "Inside the Federal Courts Home" found under "Quizzes.")

c. Access the site containing information about state courts. Identify and list Web sites of the home pages for the state courts in your geographical area.

SUMMARY

- The litigation process revolves around the courts. Because many different courts exist in the United States, plaintiffs must choose the proper court in which to pursue their case. The court chosen must have jurisdiction, or authority, to hear the case. In general, court systems are made up of trial courts, courts of appeals, and a court of last resort. In the litigation process, the function of trial courts is to determine the facts of the dispute and apply appropriate legal principles. The primary purpose of the courts of appeals is to review the proceedings in the trial court. A court of last resort, often called a supreme court, generally has discretionary right to review lower court proceedings.

- The federal court system consists of three levels of courts, U.S. district courts, U.S. courts of appeals, and the U.S. Supreme Court. The U.S. district courts are primarily trial courts. This is where a case is originally heard. The U.S. courts of appeals and the U.S. Supreme Court are primarily courts of review. They examine the proceedings that occurred in the trial courts.

- The structure of any state court system is determined by the laws of that state. Although some differences do exist from state to state, most state court systems are similar to the federal court system. All state court systems have some sort of trial courts and courts of appeals. Most states also have a state supreme court. The functions of the various state courts are similar to their counterparts in the federal court system.

- Jurisdiction is the power or authority that a court has to hear a case. Proper jurisdiction requires that a court have the power to hear the kind of case before it (subject matter jurisdiction) and also power to make a decision binding the parties to the lawsuit (personal jurisdiction). The federal courts have subject matter jurisdiction in a case if the dispute arises under the Constitution, treaties, or federal laws. A federal court also has subject matter jurisdiction when there is diversity of citizenship and the amount in controversy exceeds $75,000. State law determines what kinds of cases can be brought in the state courts. If a court lacks subject matter jurisdiction, a judgment rendered is void. In addition to subject matter jurisdiction, a court must also have personal jurisdiction over the parties. A court (federal or state) has personal jurisdiction over those who voluntarily agree to submit to the court's jurisdiction or over those who reside within the state where the court is located. If a defendant resides outside of the state, then a court has personal jurisdiction only if the defendant has some substantial contacts with the state and state law authorizes the exercise of that jurisdiction. State laws that deal with the exercise of personal jurisdiction over nonresident defendants are known as long-arm statutes. Personal jurisdiction also requires that the defendant receive proper notice of the lawsuit. In rem jurisdiction and quasi in rem jurisdiction can sometimes substitute for personal jurisdiction. In rem jurisdiction exists when the subject matter of the lawsuit involves property that is located in a state. Quasi in rem jurisdiction can exist when the defendant owns any property within the state, but the plaintiff must satisfy any judgment from that property. In rem and quasi in rem jurisdiction also require that the exercise of jurisdiction be basically fair and that the defendant receive proper notice of the lawsuit.

- In choosing the proper court in which to initiate a lawsuit, an attorney must consider not only the question of jurisdiction but also the question of venue. Venue relates to selection of the court in the proper geographical area. In the federal courts, venue is usually proper where the cause of action arose or in the district in which the defendant resides. If the defendant is the U.S. government or if jurisdiction is based on diversity, it is also proper where the plaintiff resides. In the interest of justice, venue can be changed to another court of proper jurisdiction.

KEY TERMS

affirm	higher court	quasi in rem jurisdiction
appellate jurisdiction	in rem jurisdiction	remand
attachment	jurisdiction	removal
brief	legal error	reverse
certiorari	limited jurisdiction	special appearance
concurrent jurisdiction	long-arm statutes	subject matter jurisdiction
court of appeals	lower court	supplemental jurisdiction
diversity of citizenship	motion to quash service of	supreme court
exclusive jurisdiction	summons	trial court
general appearance	original jurisdiction	venue
general jurisdiction	personal jurisdiction	

REVIEW QUESTIONS

1. What are the functions of trial courts and courts of appeals in the litigation process?
2. How is the federal court system structured?
3. What are some of the different courts in state court systems?
4. What is subject matter jurisdiction?
5. What are three types of cases that can be brought in federal court?
6. What is the difference between exclusive jurisdiction and concurrent jurisdiction?
7. When does a court have personal jurisdiction over a party to a lawsuit?
8. Why do states have long-arm statutes?
9. What is the difference between personal jurisdiction and in rem jurisdiction?
10. What is venue?

CHAPTER EXERCISES

Where necessary, check with your instructor prior to starting any of these exercises.

1. Find out about the court structure in your state. List the various courts and the functions of each. Check the Web site for your state's courts.
2. Check the laws of your state to see if a long-arm statute exists. If it does, what does it provide?
3. Check the laws of your state to see how to do the following:
   a. Challenge subject matter jurisdiction.
   b. Challenge personal jurisdiction.
   c. Change venue from one court to another.

   Also check form books for your state to find proper forms to accomplish (a), (b), and (c).
4. Review the factual situation in the Commentary to this chapter. Assume that Go A Weigh is operating within your state instead of California. In which court or courts could an action by Weigh To Go against Go A Weigh be filed? Check the U.S. Codes and the laws of your state, and give some authority for your answer.
5. Analyze the following situations and determine whether the federal court has jurisdiction under diversity of citizenship.
   a. Brady and Jeffers, both citizens of North Dakota, wish to sue as a result of an automobile accident caused by the negligence of Crane, a citizen of Montana. The damages for each of them exceed $75,000.
   b. Same as in (a) except that Brady and Jeffers also want to name as a defendant, Dowd, the owner of the vehicle driven by Crane. Dowd is a citizen of North Dakota.
   c. Same as in (a) except that Brady is claiming damages of $50,000 and Jeffers is claiming damages of $40,000.

    d. Digicam, Inc., a manufacturer of digital cameras, is a corporation incorporated in the state of Delaware with its principal place of business in California. It distributes its product through several national retailers who do business in several states, including Washington State. Reider, a citizen of the state of Washington, buys a defective camera that "explodes" while Reider is holding it, injuring Reider. The retailer who sold Reider the camera has declared bankruptcy. Reider wishes to sue Digicam, Inc. for his injuries. Reider is claiming that his damages exceed $75,000.

6. Analyze the following situations and determine whether the forum state has personal jurisdiction.

    a. Review the Digicam, Inc. situation described in (d) of question 5. Based on the facts given, would the state of Washington have personal jurisdiction over Digicam?

    b. Go A Weigh, one of the corporations mentioned at the beginning of this chapter, maintains a Web site, <http://www.goaweigh.com>. The Web site contains a description and pictures of its equipment; a feature entitled "Frequently Asked Questions"; a list of names, addresses, and telephone numbers of vendors who sell the exercise equipment; and an e-mail address to contact the company for more information. You cannot order any equipment through the Web site. Marley is a resident of the state of Maine. Marley sees its Web site and wants to order equipment. Unfortunately, Go A Weigh does not distribute exercise equipment through any vendors in Maine. However, Marley calls a vendor (listed on the Web site) in New York. The vendor agrees to ship Marley equipment. Marley is seriously injured using the equipment and claims his injury is a result of a defectively designed product. Can Marley sue Go A Weigh in Maine? Business records show that the equipment manufactured by Go A Weigh is occasionally sold to Maine residents but that its total revenue for the state of Maine is less than 1%.

7. Answer the following questions regarding the case of *International Shoe Co. v. Washington* found in this chapter.

    a. Describe the contacts that International Shoe had with the state of Washington.

    b. Did the Court feel that these contacts were sufficient to give Washington personal jurisdiction over International Shoe?

    c. What was the reason for the Court's decision?

8. Recall the hypothetical case of *Raeburn v. Cassidy* described in the chapter. Assume that the case is tried in a state trial court. A jury returns a verdict in excess of a million dollars, even though Raeburn's medical bills are less than $5,000. Is there a basis for the defendant requesting a review in the U.S. Supreme Court? Explain your answer. (See *State Farm Mut. Auto. Ins. Co. v. Campbell*, 538 U.S. 408 [2003].)

9. Review the map in Exhibit 2-4. If a case was tried in Ohio in the U.S. District Court, in which circuit would an appeal be heard?

CHAPTER PROJECT

Review the case of *Raeburn v. Cassidy* presented earlier in this chapter. Assume that the facts described occurred in your city and that both Raeburn and Cassidy are residents of your state. Determine which court has original jurisdiction over the matter. Give the address of that court, as well as a reference to your state laws that determine jurisdiction and venue. If the case were to be appealed, which court in your state would hear the matter? Does this court have a Web site? If so, what is the Web address?

THE *BENNETT* CASE
Assignment for Chapter 2: Determining Jurisdiction

You have been given additional facts regarding the *Bennett* case (from Chapter 1 Commentary and Appendix B). Bennett's employer, Rikards-Hayley, an investment banking firm, is a corporation incorporated in Delaware with its principal place of business in San Francisco, California. It has offices in several states. Bennett is employed in the New York office, located in Manhattan. Your supervising attorney does not believe that this case will settle. It will probably go to trial. Preliminary research indicates that both state and federal laws exist regarding employment discrimination based on sex. Your supervisor asked you to review the Bennett research file (see Appendix B) and to write a memo addressing the following questions:

1. If the action is based on New York state law, does the New York trial court have both subject and personal jurisdiction over the defendant?
2. If the action is filed in a New York state court, locate the address for the court or courts that would have venue.
3. If the action is based on federal law (Title VII—42 U.S.C. § 2000e), which courts would have subject matter jurisdiction, personal jurisdiction, and proper venue?
4. If the action is filed in federal court under 42 U.S.C. § 2000e, can the federal court also hear a claim for infliction of emotional distress (based entirely on state law) suffered by Bennett as a result of the discrimination?

THE *DOUGLASS FINANCIAL SERVICES, INC.* CASE
Assignment for Chapter 2: Determining the Proper Court

Assume the automobile accident occurred in the city in which your school is located. What is the name and address of the court in which a lawsuit should be filed?

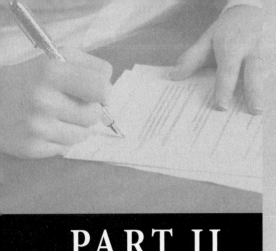

PART II

Initiating Litigation

CHAPTER 3 Preliminary Considerations and Procedures

CHAPTER OUTLINE

Determining the Existence of a Cause of Action

Feasibility of the Lawsuit

Turning Down a Case

Time Limitations

Ethical Considerations in Accepting a Case

Ethical Considerations after Accepting a Case

Ethical Considerations and Technology

Special Ethical Concerns for Paralegals

Law Office Procedures

THE *NGUYEN* CASE

Seven months ago Tara Nguyen was injured in an automobile–bus collision. The accident occurred when the brakes on the bus failed, resulting in the driver's inability to stop for a red light. The bus, in which Nguyen was a passenger, was hit broadside by a car entering the intersection at the green light. The bus, which was six months old, was owned and operated by the City of Cedar Pines. However, one month after the accident, the bus manufacturer, Euro Motors, Inc., issued a recall on the bus because of a possible defect in the braking system. After the accident, Nguyen did some Internet research on Euro Motors, Inc. and found that several customers had complained about the braking system on its busses for more than one year prior to her accident. Nguyen has requested that your firm represent her in a personal injury lawsuit for the injuries she sustained in the accident. Your attorney requested that you do some preliminary research to determine whether this lawsuit should be accepted and, if so, whether any immediate action is needed.

Chapter 2 covered the factors that determine the appropriate court for filing any lawsuit. However, before any action is filed in court, certain preliminary aspects of litigation must be considered and reviewed. After reading this chapter, you should be able to:

- analyze a factual situation to determine the existence of a cause of action.
- define the various types of time limitations on filing a lawsuit.
- explain the importance of tickler systems.
- list the practical considerations that affect the decision to accept a case.
- explain the procedure for turning down a case.
- identify ethical concerns and requirements that litigation attorneys and paralegals must consider.
- identify special ethical concerns related to the use of technology in litigation.
- analyze special ethical concerns for litigation paralegals.
- describe basic law office procedures.
- identify the types of technology that play a role in various law office procedures.

DETERMINING THE EXISTENCE OF A CAUSE OF ACTION

Although formal litigation begins when a lawsuit (a complaint) is filed in court, a litigator's responsibilities begin much earlier.

One of the first considerations facing an attorney is whether a potential client has a legitimate case. Before a party has a valid basis for a lawsuit, that party must have some

cause of action
A legal basis for a lawsuit based on the facts of the case and applicable law.

injury or damage caused in such a way that the law recognizes the right to sue. In other words, a legal right to recover damages must exist. This legally recognized right to relief is known as a **cause of action**. For example, suppose Bricker drives his motorcycle negligently and fails to stop at a stop sign. He is hit by Steinman, who is driving in a careful and prudent manner in accordance with all traffic laws. Bricker is the only one injured in the accident. Can Bricker recover his damages from Steinman? Obviously not. In this kind of case, where the defendant has done nothing wrong, no cause of action exists. The injured party has no valid basis for a lawsuit.

Whether a cause of action exists is a legal question and must be made by an attorney. However, as a litigation paralegal, you might assist in researching this issue. Your research requires that you examine both the law and the facts in the case. In examining the law you should determine what factors or elements must be present before a cause of action is created.

For example, the *Nguyen* case described in the Commentary to this chapter is controlled by the substantive law of torts. More specifically, it is covered in part by the tort of negligence. A review of the law of negligence reveals that for Nguyen to have a cause of action, the following elements must be shown:

1. the defendant must have a duty of due care toward the victim,
2. that duty must have been breached (a careless act),
3. the defendant's careless act must be the actual cause of the damages,
4. the defendant's careless act must be the proximate cause of the damages (i.e., the damages must be foreseeable), and
5. damages must have been sustained.

Once the elements of a cause of action are identified, the final step in determining whether a cause of action exists is to review the case itself to see if facts support each of the elements. Preparing a table or chart is helpful in this review. See Exhibits 3-1 and 3-2.

The conclusion you reach after reviewing Exhibit 3-2 is that Nguyen has a cause of action for negligence (assuming, of course, that all of the facts can be proven).

Identifying the elements of a cause of action is important in the litigation process for various reasons. Probably most important is that each of the elements must be proven at trial for the plaintiff to prevail. In other words, to win the case, the attorney

EXHIBIT 3-1 Steps in Determining the Existence of a Cause of Action

---

DETERMINING THE EXISTENCE OF A CAUSE OF ACTION

✓ Identify the general area of substantive law.
✓ Identify the more specific area of substantive law.
✓ Identify the legal elements required for a specific cause of action.
✓ Review the facts of your case.
✓ Determine if each legal element is satisfied by facts in your case.

EXHIBIT 3-2 Analyzing the Existence of a Cause of Action:
Nguyen v. Euro Motors, Inc.

ELEMENTS OF A CAUSE OF ACTION (NEGLIGENCE)	FACTUAL SUPPORT FOR EACH ELEMENT
1. Defendant must have a duty of due care toward the victim.	• A vehicle manufacturer owes a duty to all purchasers and users of vehicles that it sells. Because Nguyen was a passenger on the bus, Euro Motors, Inc. owed her a duty of due care.
2. That duty must have been breached (a careless act).	• The defendant had been put on notice about defective brakes and had failed to do anything about it. Thus, there is some evidence of a breach of the duty owed to users of that bus.
3. The defendant's careless act must be the actual cause of the damages.	• If the brakes had not failed, the accident would not have happened. Euro Motors, Inc.'s failure to notify purchasers that the brakes could be defective is, therefore, the actual cause of Nguyen's injuries.
4. The defendant's careless act must be the proximate cause of the damages (i.e., the damages must be foreseeable).	• Nguyen's injuries were a foreseeable consequence of Euro Motors, Inc.'s actions. This establishes proximate or legal causation.
5. Damages must have been sustained.	• Nguyen has sustained injuries and incurred expenses; this establishes damages.

must present evidence that supports each element of the cause of action. Also, in some state jurisdictions the initial pleading must allege facts that support each element of the cause of action.

Knowing the elements of the cause of action in a particular case is essential to any litigation paralegal assisting the attorney in pretrial preparation. Understanding what the attorney must prove at trial enables you to gather appropriate evidence and conduct relevant discovery. It also equips you to prepare pleadings that comply with legal requirements and to review opposing pleadings for legal deficiencies.

Identifying the elements of a cause of action in a particular case may take some research. The ultimate source for this information is generally statutory or case law (or both.) However, many secondary source books are of great help. Practice books and form books, which often contain explanations and legal analysis of the forms, are especially helpful. A popular resource is *Causes of Action 2d* published by Thomson Reuters. See Exhibit 3-3 for examples of the elements of some common causes of action. See Exhibit 3-4 for an example of the type of material found in *Causes of Action 2d*.

EXHIBIT 3-3 Elements of Different Causes of Action

FRAUD

1. The defendant misrepresented, concealed, or failed to disclose a fact.
2. The defendant knew of the falsity of the statement.
3. The defendant intended to defraud.
4. The plaintiff justifiably relied on the statement.
5. Damages resulted.

BREACH OF CONTRACT

1. A contract exists.
2. Plaintiff performed or was excused from performing his duties under the contract.
3. Defendant breached or failed to perform his duties.
4. Damages resulted.

STRICT LIABILITY—PRODUCTS LIABILITY

1. Defendant manufactured or distributed a product.
2. The product was defective.
3. The product was used in a foreseeable manner.
4. The defective product caused an injury.
5. Damages resulted.

FEASIBILITY OF THE LAWSUIT

Even though an attorney determines that a case has merit—that is, a cause of action exists—he may nevertheless decide that the lawsuit is not practical. Litigation takes a great deal of time and can cost a great deal of money, not only in attorney fees but also in costs. For example, it may be necessary to hire expert witnesses to establish certain facts. Experts charge substantial fees for their services. Numerous witnesses may need to be questioned and deposed. This also is costly. Before accepting a case, attorneys usually review it to see if it is practical. This involves reviewing the damages suffered by the plaintiff so that the value of the case can be determined. If the injured party's injuries are slight and result in little out-of-pocket expenses, the case might cost more than is reasonable. Preliminary investigation might also involve some research into the defendant's ability to pay a judgment. As a litigation paralegal, you might be asked to assist in doing this.

TURNING DOWN A CASE

If an attorney decides not to accept a case, she must clearly communicate this to the individual concerned. This should be done in writing so that there is a record of the fact. Many attorneys have been sued for malpractice by individuals who claim that the attorney led them to believe that their cases were being handled and learned only after the statute of limitations had expired that the attorney had not, in fact, accepted the case.

Source: From *Causes of Action 2d*. Reprinted with permission of Thomson Reuters.

EXHIBIT 3-4 Sample Page from *Causes of Action*

1 COA 1

Cause of Action for Motor Vehicle Brake Defects under Strict Products Liability

Approx. 62 pages

COA ACTION GUIDE

PRIMA FACIE CASE

- A prima facie case of strict liability in tort for injuries proximately caused by defective brakes in a motor vehicle requires proof:
  1. that the vehicle's brakes, or components thereof, are defective [§§ 4–7];
  2. in most jurisdictions, that the defect made the vehicle "unreasonably dangerous" or "dangerous beyond the contemplation of the ordinary consumer" [§ 3];
  3. that the defect existed at the time the vehicle left the hands of the manufacturer/seller [§ 8];
  4. that the claimant suffered an injury [§ 9]; and
  5. that the injury was proximately caused by the defect [§ 8].

PERSONS LIABLE

- Manufacturers, automobile dealers, lessors, component suppliers. § 16

PERSONS ENTITLED TO RECOVER

- Persons suffering personal physical or noncommercial economic damages as a proximate result of defective brakes. § 17

DEFENSES

- Contributory and comparative negligence or fault [§ 11], assumption of the risk [§ 12], misuse [§ 14], alteration or modification [§ 13], and state of the art [§ 15].

JURISDICTION

- Any state court of competent jurisdiction. § 18
- Federal courts when there is complete diversity of citizenship and the amount in controversy exceeds $10,000. § 18

VENUE

- In federal courts, venue in diversity actions is proper in the district where the plaintiff or the defendant resides, or where the claim arose. § 18

LIMITATIONS

- Controlled by state statute; tort, warranty, and/or product liability "repose" periods may apply. § 19

RECOVERY

- Actual damages. § 25
- Punitive damages; interest and attorneys' fees when permitted. § 26

EXHIBIT 3-5 Letter Turning Down a Case

OKIMURA & RESNICK
ATTORNEYS AT LAW

Robert Okimura	17 Plaza Square	Area Code 208
Leslie Resnick	Boise, Idaho 83707	Telephone 555-1212

Mr. Mark Jones
20 Birch Place
Boise, ID 83707

Dear Mr. Jones,

Thank you for contacting us regarding your dispute with ABC Corporation. As I explained to you on the telephone, our law firm is presently unable to represent you in this matter. Please note that our inability to accept your case is not a reflection or comment on the merits of your case. If you wish to pursue this matter you should obtain other legal advice. If you decide to do so, you should act as soon as possible. As we have previously explained to you, the statute of limitations in these kinds of cases is _____ years from the date of your injury. If you have not filed a lawsuit within that time you will be prevented from doing so.

Very truly yours,

Robert Okimura,
Attorney at Law

In turning down a case, an attorney must exercise care in stating an opinion regarding the merits of the case to the prospective client. Attorneys are sometimes sued for malpractice for advising a person that he has no case if later another attorney concludes otherwise. It is also advisable to warn the person about any possible statute of limitations. See Exhibit 3-5 for a sample letter.

TIME LIMITATIONS

If an attorney decides to accept a case, a number of considerations arise. One of the first relates to time limitations for filing a lawsuit in court. Consider the following. Martinez is injured in an automobile accident caused by a drunk driver. Martinez saw a doctor for more than one year and incurred thousands of dollars in expenses. Finally, three years after the accident happened, Martinez decides to consult with an attorney. The attorney tells Martinez that he no longer has a case because the state statute of limitations for this kind of action is two years. Even though the facts of the Martinez case satisfied all of the elements of a cause of action for negligence, Martinez is barred from pursuing the case because a lawsuit was not filed in court within proper time limits. Different time limits exist for different kinds of cases. As a paralegal you must be aware of these time limits. Any time a new case is accepted by a law office, it must be carefully calendared and reviewed so that a lawsuit is filed in court within the proper time limits.

Statute of Limitations

The basic time limit for filing a lawsuit in court is known as a **statute of limitations**. Unless a case is filed within the appropriate statute of limitations, it will be dismissed, regardless of the merits of the case. Statutes of limitations are found in state and federal codes and vary from one jurisdiction to another (see Exhibits 3-6 and 3-7). Statutes of limitations also differ depending on the type of case.

statute of limitations
The maximum time period in which any lawsuit must be filed in court.

EXHIBIT 3-6 Statutes of Limitations

(FEDERAL STATUTE—ACTIONS ARISING UNDER ACTS OF CONGRESS)

Time limitations on the commencement of civil actions arising under Acts of Congress:

(a) Except as otherwise provided by law, a civil action arising under an Act of Congress enacted after the date of the enactment of this section may not be commenced later than four years after the cause of action accrues.

(b) Notwithstanding subsection (a), a private right of action that involves a claim of fraud, deceit, manipulation, or contrivance in contravention of a regulatory requirement concerning the securities laws, as defined in section 3(a)(47) of the Securities Exchange Act of 1934 (a)(47), may be brought not later than the earlier of—

(1) Two years after the discovery of the facts constituting the violation; or

(2) Five years after such violation.

28 U.S.C. § 1658

(FEDERAL STATUTE—TIME FOR COMMENCING ACTION AGAINST UNITED STATES)

Time for commencing action against United States:

(a) Except as provided by the Contract Disputes Act of 1978, every civil action commenced against the United States shall be barred unless the complaint is filed within six years after the right of action first accrues. The action of any person under legal disability or beyond the seas at the time the claim accrues may be commenced within three years after the disability ceases.

28 U.S.C. § 2401(a)

(STATE OF CALIFORNIA STATUTE—ORAL CONTRACT ACTION)

The periods prescribed for the commencement of actions other than for the recovery of real property, are as follows:

Within two years: An action for assault, battery, or injury to, or for the death of an individual caused by the wrongful act or neglect of another.

Cal. Code Civ. Proc. §§ 335 and 335.1

Source: http://www.leginfo.ca.gov/.html/ccp_table_of_contents.html

EXHIBIT 3-7 Statutes of Limitations (Date of Discovery)

Source: http://www.leginfo.ca.gov/.html/ ccp_table_of_contents.html

> ### DATE OF DISCOVERY
>
> #### (State of California Statute—Legal Malpractice)
>
> . . . An action against an attorney for a wrongful act or omission, other than for actual fraud, arising in the performance of professional services, shall be commenced within one year after the plaintiff discovers, or through the use of reasonable diligence should have discovered, the facts constituting the wrongful act or omission, or four years from the date of the wrongful act or omission, whichever occurs first. . . .
>
> Cal. Code Civ. Proc. § 340.6

Commonly, statutes of limitations set time limits for filing a complaint and are easily determined and calculated. For example, a plaintiff might have two years from the date of an accident in which to file an action for personal injuries. Because the date of the accident is easily determined from police reports and witnesses, the statute of limitations is calculated with no difficulty.

In some cases, however, time limitations are not as easily determined. For example, in professional malpractice cases or in fraud cases, the statute of limitations might start to run not from the date of the malpractice or fraudulent act, but from the date that the plaintiff discovers or should have discovered the malpractice or fraud. This can be years after the defendant's wrongdoing. This kind of statute of limitations often presents numerous legal and factual questions, and proving the date on which the plaintiff discovered or should have discovered the wrongdoing becomes an important part of the trial process.

Calculating the Statute of Limitations   In calculating the statute of limitations, the code sections tell you not to count the first day, but do count the last day. The language is confusing but means only that if an accident happens on January 10 of one year, and the statute is a one-year statute of limitations, you must file the complaint on or before January 10 of the following year. However, if that day is a weekend or court holiday, you would have until the next court day to file your complaint. Consider the following examples:

1. Assume that Jeffers is in an automobile accident on July 1, 2013, and assume that this type of case has a two-year statute of limitations. The statute of limitations expires on July 1, 2015. This means that a lawsuit must be filed on or before July 1, 2015, unless July 1 falls on a Saturday or Sunday. In such a case the lawsuit would have to be filed on the following Monday.

2. Assume that Jeffers is in an automobile accident on July 4, 2013, and that this type of case has a two-year statute of limitations. The statute of limitations expires on July 4, 2015, but since this is a court holiday, Jeffers has until the next court day to file a lawsuit.

Tolling the Statute of Limitations   Certain events sometimes toll, or extend, the statute of limitations. When a statute of limitations is tolled, the time stops running. A common reason for tolling a statute of limitations is that the plaintiff is a minor. In such cases, the statute is tolled during the minority of the plaintiff and begins to run once the minor reaches the age of majority. Thus, if a 10-year-old child is injured in an automobile accident and the statute of limitations is normally two years, that two-year period does not begin to run until the child reaches the age of majority. The statute would expire on the child's 20th birthday (two years after reaching the age of majority). Do not assume, however, that the statute of limitations is always tolled during a child's minority. You must check the appropriate statutory law. For an example of a statute that incorporates a tolling period, refer to Exhibit 3-6 and read 28 U.S.C. § 2401(a). This statute is tolled during a person's legal disability or during any time the person is "beyond the seas."

Claim Statutes

Some types of cases are governed by special statutes known as **claim statutes**. This kind of statute requires that a written claim be presented to the defendant before a lawsuit is filed. The time for filing the lawsuit is usually determined by the date that the claim is denied. Claim statutes are common when a governmental entity is sued or when the defendant is deceased and a probate is pending. Naturally, there are time limits for presenting the claim, time limits that are often shorter than the statute of limitations for similar cases. For an example of a claim statute, see Exhibit 3-8.

Time limits for filing claims are often *not* tolled during minority or other legal disabilities. For example, the court has held that the tort claim statute found in Exhibit 3-8 is not tolled during a person's minority. You must be careful to check specific laws to determine this. Claim statutes usually contain a provision dictating when a lawsuit must be filed if the claim is denied. These time limits must be followed just as any statute of limitations. Read 28 U.S.C. § 2401(b), found in Exhibit 3-8. This claim statute requires that a lawsuit must be filed within six months after the claim is denied.

claim statute
A type of law that requires a written notice describing a claim to be presented to the defendant before a lawsuit can be filed.

EXHIBIT 3-8 Claim Statutes

> **FEDERAL STATUTES—CLAIMS AGAINST UNITED STATES**
>
> . . . An action shall not be instituted upon a claim against the United States for money damages for injury or loss of property or personal injury or death caused by the negligent or wrongful act or omission of any employee of the Government while acting within the scope of his office or employment, unless the claimant shall have first presented the claim to the appropriate Federal agency and his claim shall have been finally denied by the agency in writing and sent by certified or registered mail. The failure of an agency to make final disposition of a claim within six months after it is filed shall, at the option of the claimant any time thereafter, be deemed a final denial of the claim for purposes of this section. . . .
>
> 28 U.S.C. § 2675(a)
>
> A tort claim against the United States shall be forever barred unless it is presented in writing to the appropriate Federal agency within two years after such claim accrues or unless action is begun within six months after the date of mailing, by certified or registered mail, or notice of final denial of the claim by the agency to which it was presented.
>
> 28 U.S.C. § 2401(b)

Source: http://uscode.house.gov/lawrevisioncounsel.shtml

laches
An equitable doctrine preventing a party from pursuing certain types of lawsuits (equitable) because that party has delayed to the extent that it would be unfair to the opposing party.

Basically, a written claim requires the following:

- notification to a prospective defendant of intent to sue
- identifying information about the person making the claim
- description of the nature of the claim
- the amount of the claim

After the claim is properly submitted, the person against whom the claim is made has a certain time in which to accept or reject the claim. A lawsuit cannot be filed until this happens. See Exhibit 3-9 for an example of a claim form.

Laches

In addition to the statute of limitations, equitable cases (cases in which the plaintiff is asking for something other than money damages) are governed by another time limitation known as laches. **Laches** is an equitable principle that prevents lawsuits from being filed when, in fairness to the defendant, too much time has elapsed, even though the statute of limitations may not have expired.

Consider the following events that occur in a state with a four-year statute of limitations for actions based on a written contract:

February 10, 2011	In a written contract, Sargeant agrees to sell his house to Breyer for $100,000; escrow to close on April 8, 2011.
March 10, 2011	Sargeant backs out of the contract.
April 25, 2011	Breyer consults an attorney and decides that pursuing a lawsuit is not an economical choice; Breyer purchases another home.
January 25, 2014	Real estate values unexpectedly increased and the house is now worth substantially more than it was three years ago; Breyer now sues Sargeant for specific performance of the original contract. (This is an equitable action because Breyer is asking the court to order Sargeant to sell the house at the agreed price of $100,000.)

If Breyer files a lawsuit in January 2014, that suit is filed within the statute of limitations. However, fairness and equity tells us that at this point in time the court should not force Sargeant to sell his house to Breyer for substantially less than it is worth. Breyer waited too long to file his action. Thus, laches could prevent him from prevailing in his action.

Remember that laches applies only in equitable cases. If Breyer sued Sargeant for money damages for breach of the contract, and the appropriate statute of limitations was four years, time limitations would not be a bar. (However, under contract law, Breyer's damages would be the difference between the contract price and the fair market value of the house at the time the contract was to be performed [April 8, 2011], not the date that the action was filed.)

EXHIBIT 3-9 Claim Form

CLAIM FOR DAMAGE, INJURY, OR DEATH	INSTRUCTIONS: Please read carefully the instructions on the reverse side and supply information requested on both sides of this form. Use additional sheet(s) if necessary. See reverse side for additional instructions.	FORM APPROVED OMB NO. 1105-0008

1. Submit To Appropriate Federal Agency:	2. Name, Address of claimant and claimant's personal representative, if any. (See instructions on reverse.) (Number, Street, City, State and Zip Code)

3. TYPE OF EMPLOYMENT ☐ MILITARY ☐ CIVILIAN	4. DATE OF BIRTH	5. MARITAL STATUS	6. DATE AND DAY OF ACCIDENT	7. TIME (A.M. OR P.M.)

8. Basis of Claim (State in detail the known facts and circumstances attending the damage, injury, or death, identifying persons and property involved, the place of occurrence and the cause thereof. Use additional pages if necessary.)

9. **PROPERTY DAMAGE**

NAME AND ADDRESS OF OWNER, IF OTHER THAN CLAIMANT (Number, Street, City, State, and Zip Code).

BRIEFLY DESCRIBE THE PROPERTY, NATURE AND EXTENT OF DAMAGE AND THE LOCATION WHERE PROPERTY MAY BE INSPECTED. (See Instructions on reverse side.)

10. **PERSONAL INJURY/WRONGFUL DEATH**

STATE NATURE AND EXTENT OF EACH INJURY OR CAUSE OF DEATH, WHICH FORMS THE BASIS OF THE CLAIM. IF OTHER THAN CLAIMANT, STATE NAME OF INJURED PERSON OR DECEDENT.

11. **WITNESSES**

NAME	ADDRESS (Number, Street, City, State, and Zip Code)

12. (See instructions on reverse.) **AMOUNT OF CLAIM (in dollars)**

12a. PROPERTY DAMAGE	12b. PERSONAL INJURY	12c. WRONGFUL DEATH	12d. TOTAL (Failure to specify may cause forfeiture of your rights.)

I CERTIFY THAT THE AMOUNT OF CLAIM COVERS ONLY DAMAGES AND INJURIES CAUSED BY THE INCIDENT ABOVE AND AGREE TO ACCEPT SAID AMOUNT IN FULL SATISFACTION AND FINAL SETTLEMENT OF THIS CLAIM

13a. SIGNATURE OF CLAIMANT (See instructions on reverse side.)	13b. Phone number of person signing form	14. DATE OF SIGNATURE

CIVIL PENALTY FOR PRESENTING FRAUDULENT CLAIM	CRIMINAL PENALTY FOR PRESENTING FRAUDULENT CLAIM OR MAKING FALSE STATEMENTS
The claimant is liable to the United States Government for a civil penalty of not less than $5,000 and not more than $10,000, plus 3 times the amount of damages sustained by the Government. (See 31 U.S.C. 3729.)	Fine of not more than $10,000 or imprisonment for not more than 5 years or both. (See 18 U.S.C. 287, 1001.)

95-109	NSN 7540-00-634-4046	STANDARD FORM 95 PRESCRIBED BY DEPT. OF JUSTICE 28 CFR 14.2

Source: http://federal-tort-claims.com/images/form%2095.pdf.pdf

EXHIBIT 3-9 Claim Form (*continued*)

INSURANCE COVERAGE

In order that subrogation claims may be adjudicated, it is essential that the claimant provide the following information regarding the insurance coverage of his vehicle or property.

15. Do you carry accident insurance? ☐ Yes   If yes, give name and address of insurance company (Number, Street, City, State, and Zip Code) and policy number.   ☐ No

16. Have you filed a claim on your insurance carrier in this instance, and if so, is it full coverage or deductible?

17. If deductible, state amount.

18. If a claim has been filed with your carrier, what action has your insurer taken or proposed to take with reference to your claim? (It is necessary that you ascertain these facts.)

19. Do you carry public liability and property damage insurance? ☐ Yes   If yes, give name and address of insurance carrier (Number, Street, City, State, and Zip Code).   ☐ No

---

INSTRUCTIONS

Claims presented under the Federal Tort Claims Act should be submitted directly to the "appropriate Federal agency" whose employee(s) was involved in the incident. If the incident involves more than one claimant, each claimant should submit a separate claim form.

Complete all items - Insert the word NONE where applicable.

A CLAIM SHALL BE DEEMED TO HAVE BEEN PRESENTED WHEN A FEDERAL AGENCY RECEIVES FROM A CLAIMANT, HIS DULY AUTHORIZED AGENT, OR LEGAL REPRESENTATIVE, AN EXECUTED STANDARD FORM 95 OR OTHER WRITTEN NOTIFICATION OF AN INCIDENT, ACCOMPANIED BY A CLAIM FOR MONEY

Failure to completely execute this form or to supply the requested material within two years from the date the claim accrued may render your claim invalid. A claim is deemed presented when it is received by the appropriate agency, not when it is mailed.

If instruction is needed in completing this form, the agency listed in item #1 on the reverse side may be contacted. Complete regulations pertaining to claims asserted under the Federal Tort Claims Act can be found in Title 28, Code of Federal Regulations, Part 14. Many agencies have published supplementing regulations. If more than one agency is involved, please state each agency.

The claim may be filed by a duly authorized agent or other legal representative, provided evidence satisfactory to the Government is submitted with the claim establishing express authority to act for the claimant. A claim presented by an agent or legal representative must be presented in the name of the claimant. If the claim is signed by the agent or legal representative, it must show the title or legal capacity of the person signing and be accompanied by evidence of his/her authority to present a claim on behalf of the claimant as agent, executor, administrator, parent, guardian or other representative.

If claimant intends to file for both personal injury and property damage, the amount for each must be shown in item #12 of this form.

DAMAGES IN A <u>**SUM CERTAIN**</u> FOR INJURY TO OR LOSS OF PROPERTY, PERSONAL INJURY, OR DEATH ALLEGED TO HAVE OCCURRED BY REASON OF THE INCIDENT. THE CLAIM MUST BE PRESENTED TO THE APPROPRIATE FEDERAL AGENCY WITHIN <u>**TWO YEARS**</u> AFTER THE CLAIM ACCRUES.

The amount claimed should be substantiated by competent evidence as follows:

(a) In support of the claim for personal injury or death, the claimant should submit a written report by the attending physician, showing the nature and extent of injury, the nature and extent of treatment, the degree of permanent disability, if any, the prognosis, and the period of hospitalization, or incapacitation, attaching itemized bills for medical, hospital, or burial expenses actually incurred.

(b) In support of claims for damage to property, which has been or can be economically repaired, the claimant should submit at least two itemized signed statements or estimates by reliable, disinterested concerns, or, if payment has been made, the itemized signed receipts evidencing payment.

(c) In support of claims for damage to property which is not economically repairable, or if the property is lost or destroyed, the claimant should submit statements as to the original cost of the property, the date of purchase, and the value of the property, both before and after the accident. Such statements should be by disinterested competent persons, preferably reputable dealers or officials familiar with the type of property damaged, or by two or more competitive bidders, and should be certified as being just and correct.

(d) Failure to specify a sum certain will render your claim invalid and may result in forfeiture of your rights.

PRIVACY ACT NOTICE

This Notice is provided in accordance with the Privacy Act, 5 U.S.C. 552a(e)(3), and concerns the information requested in the letter to which this Notice is attached.
   A. *Authority:* The requested information is solicited pursuant to one or more of the following: 5 U.S.C. 301, 28 U.S.C. 501 et seq., 28 U.S.C. 2671 et seq., 28 C.F.R. Part 14.

B. *Principal Purpose:* The information requested is to be used in evaluating claims.
C. *Routine Use:* See the Notices of Systems of Records for the agency to whom you are submitting this form for this information.
D. *Effect of Failure to Respond:* Disclosure is voluntary. However, failure to supply the requested information or to execute the form may render your claim "invalid".

PAPERWORK REDUCTION ACT NOTICE

This notice is <u>solely</u> for the purpose of the Paperwork Reduction Act, 44 U.S.C. 3501. Public reporting burden for this collection of information is estimated to average 15 minutes per response, including the time for reviewing instructions, searching existing data sources, gathering and maintaining the data needed, and completing and reviewing the collection of information. Send comments regarding this burden estimate or any other aspect of this collection of information, including suggestions for reducing this burden, to the Director, Torts Branch, Attention: Paperwork Reduction Staff, Civil Division, U.S. Department of Justice, Washington, D.C. 20530.

SF 95   BACK

Tickler Systems

Missing a statute of limitations or a claim statute can result in a malpractice claim against the law firm. Therefore, all litigation firms have calendar or tracking systems to remind them of these and other important dates. These calendaring systems are known as **tickler systems**. Before the advent of computers in the law firm, reminders were kept by hand. A firm might have used a special calendar or a small file box organized by dates. Today, numerous software programs help firms keep track of important dates. Some of these programs are identified later in this chapter.

Even though a firm uses a computer, certain precautions should always be followed. First, when a case is tickled for the statute of limitations, it should be calendared early enough to allow for preparation of the complaint and for obtaining any necessary signatures. Second, the file should be re-calendared for a date near the statute of limitations, at which time it should be checked to verify that the complaint has in fact been filed. Third, if calendaring the case is not your responsibility as a litigation paralegal, you should still check cases assigned to you to make sure that proper calendaring has occurred. You might even wish to keep your own calendar, in addition to the firm's calendar, for cases assigned to you.

tickler system
A calendaring system.

AUTOMATED LITIGATION SUPPORT

Technology and Ethical Concerns

SCENARIO

Your attorney has accepted the *Nguyen* case and has made you part of the litigation team that will be handling the case. Your attorney tells you that this is a complex case and she expects that the attorneys working on the case will be extremely busy researching various legal issues as well as reviewing numerous documents, some of which may contain confidential information. She is concerned about ethical obligations and has asked you to review your state's rules of professional conduct and monitor the case for any problem areas.

PROBLEM

After reviewing your state's rules of professional conduct you identify several areas that could create potential ethical concerns, including concerns with client communication, competency, and confidentiality. In a busy law firm, attorneys often work on several cases simultaneously. In each case there will be numerous time limitations on work, as well as several court appearances and appointments for the attorney. From your experience working in a law firm you recognize that attorneys often have a difficulty finding time to return telephone calls from clients who want updates on their cases. In an overly busy office, it is also easy to miss important deadlines, actions that might call into question the competency of the firm. Also, the *Nguyen* case will involve e-mail communications between the firm, the client, and potential expert witnesses. You need to make sure that all e-mail communication maintains the strictest confidentiality.

SOLUTION

Various legal software products can help you monitor and prevent ethical violations. Numerous software products, referred to as "time and billing" or "case management" software, can provide the information and reminders needed to maintain good client communication and information about important dates. Programs such as Abacus Law, Amicus Attorney, and ProLaw allow you to maintain a contact list so that locating a telephone number or e-mail address is simple. Such programs also allow you to keep notes about the case so that you have quick access to current information. These programs also have features that provide you with reminders of court filing dates and other deadlines. If you are working on the *Nguyen* case, you will need to make certain that all information about the case is input into the appropriate office software.

Maintaining confidentiality in e-mail correspondence presents some different solutions. Although many offices include a statement on the e-mail itself that it is intended to be confidential, this really gives no protection. Confidentiality in e-mails can be strengthened by the use of encryption software, which is widely available. As a paralegal monitoring e-mail confidentiality, you need to make certain that employees of the law firm always use it in conjunction with confidential material. There is another consideration, however. The person receiving the e-mail must have software that allows a recipient of encrypted e-mail to "de-encrypt" the message. Thus, you may need to work with your client or expert witnesses to see that this is done.

Model Rules of Professional Conduct
American Bar Association rules setting standards for the ethical conduct of lawyers; while not binding in themselves, these rules form the basis for most state ethical rules.

conflict of interest
A situation in which, due to competing factors, one party (i.e., an attorney or paralegal) might be unable to act entirely for the benefit of party to whom a fiduciary duty is owed.

ETHICAL CONSIDERATIONS IN ACCEPTING A CASE

All attorneys are subject to a certain code of conduct. Ethical rules for attorneys are found in state law, although many states pattern their rules after the American Bar Association **Model Rules of Professional Conduct**. Ethical rules generally apply to attorneys rather than to paralegals, but you must still know and follow these rules. If a paralegal works under the direction or supervision of an attorney, and the paralegal violates any of the rules, the attorney is often held responsible and may face disciplinary action by the state bar. Ethical considerations control the entire litigation process, beginning with the decision to accept a case. Several ethical considerations influence the attorney's decision to accept or reject a case. Other ethical standards govern the attorney's and the paralegal's conduct during the course of litigation.

Competency to Handle the Case

Obviously, an attorney should not accept a case if he does not possess the ability, knowledge, or time to handle it. This decision is up to the attorney, and the paralegal has little, if any, input into it. However, competency means more than simply having the ability to handle a case. It also means that attorneys are prohibited from neglecting cases that they have accepted. This can concern a paralegal. When you are assigned to work on a case, you should make sure that the case is not ignored. A tickling or calendaring system should be established to remind the attorney or paralegal to regularly review all cases.

Frivolous Claims

Lawsuits that have no merit should not be pursued. Again, this is usually determined by the attorney, but the attorney may rely on your research in making this decision. If an attorney handles a frivolous case, he risks being sued himself by the defendant in the action, in addition to subjecting himself to disciplinary proceedings by the state bar association. Furthermore, pursuing any claim or defense that has no evidentiary support is also a violation of Rule 11 of the Federal Rules of Civil Procedure. Any attorney violating this rule is subject to sanctions or penalties imposed by the court. See Exhibit 3-10.

Conflict of Interest

A law firm generally cannot accept a case if a **conflict of interest** exists.
    Conflicts of interest can arise in a number of different situations:

1. A conflict might exist where the opposing party in the new case was a prior client of the firm or of any attorney in the law firm.
2. A conflict might exist if a paralegal worked on a prior case in which the prior client is now an opposing party.
3. A conflict might exist if any of the attorneys or paralegals have personal relationships with attorneys or paralegals representing the opposing party.

    A conflict of interest usually arises when a firm is asked to sue a party whom it currently represents or previously represented in another case. Although prior representation does not always result in a conflict, the potential for a conflict exists and must be closely examined before accepting the case. A conflict is determined by whom the firm represents, rather than by whom any

EXHIBIT 3-10 Rule 11 of the Federal Rules of Civil Procedure

Rule 11. Signing of Pleadings, Motions, and Other Papers; Representations to Court; Sanctions

(b) Representations to Court.

By presenting to the court (whether by signing, filing, submitting, or later advocating) a pleading, written motion, or other paper, an attorney or unrepresented party is certifying that to the best of the person's knowledge, information, and belief, formed after an inquiry reasonable under the circumstances—

1. it is not being presented for any improper purpose, such as to harass or to cause unnecessary delay or needless increase in the cost of litigation;

2. the claims, defenses, and other legal contentions therein are warranted by existing law or by a nonfrivolous argument for the extension, modification, or reversal of existing law or the establishment of new law;

3. the allegations and other factual contentions have evidentiary support or, if specifically so identified, are likely to have evidentiary support after a reasonable opportunity for further investigation or discovery; and

4. the denials of factual contentions are warranted on the evidence or, if specifically so identified, are reasonably based on a lack of information or belief.

(c) Sanctions.

If, after notice and a reasonable opportunity to respond, the court determines that subdivision (b) has been violated, the court may, subject to the conditions stated below, impose an appropriate sanction upon the attorneys, law firms, or parties that have violated subdivision (b) or are responsible for the violation.

Source: http://www.uscourts.gov/uscourts/RulesAndPolicies/rules/2010%20Rules/Civil%20Procedure.pdf

particular attorney in the firm represents. For example, in the case described in this chapter's Commentary, your firm would have to consider suing Euro Motors, Inc. Suppose, however, that one of the corporate attorneys in the firm had prepared and filed incorporation documents for that business on a previous occasion. Could a litigation attorney now sue the company? Probably not.

Before accepting a case, a firm must determine that no conflict exists. The larger the law firm, the more likely it is that some conflict may exist. As a litigation paralegal, you may be responsible for checking for conflicts. All law firms need to keep a centralized list of all clients. Without such a list, each attorney in the firm would have to be questioned about a possible conflict. This is not only time consuming but also unreliable. Most law firms, especially larger ones, now have centralized computerized lists of all clients. This makes the conflict check simple and more accurate.

Conflict problems also can arise when an attorney or a paralegal has changed jobs, and the prior law firm represented a party who is now a potential defendant. The prior relationship might result in a conflict of interest in the current litigation. Should you find yourself in such a situation, you should immediately inform the attorney handling the case. In these cases, a firm can sometimes continue to handle the case as long as they do not allow the attorney or paralegal with the conflict to have any involvement in the case. This is sometimes referred to as setting up an ethical wall.

Not all conflicts of interest revolve around the clients or parties in a potential case. Some conflicts are created by relationships between attorneys or paralegals in opposing law firms.

EXHIBIT 3-11 Ethical Considerations: Deciding to Accept a Case

---

ETHICAL CONSIDERATIONS: THE DECISION TO ACCEPT A CASE

✓ Does the law firm have the competency and time to handle the case?

✓ Does the case have legal merit?

✓ Is there any conflict of interest with the parties?

✓ Is there any conflict of interest between opposing lawyers or paralegals?

Even if a conflict does exist, the firm can still handle the case if the prior client agrees in writing to waive the problem and if the conflict does not interfere with the ability of the attorney to represent the client. In the event that a conflict is not waived, the firm cannot accept employment in the new case. See Exhibit 3-11.

ETHICAL CONSIDERATIONS AFTER ACCEPTING A CASE

Communication with the Client

Lawyers owe a duty to their clients to keep them advised about the status of their cases. Failure of lawyers to do this is the basis of one of the most common complaints against attorneys. Litigation can sometimes take years, and much of the litigation process does not personally involve the client. If a lawyer fails to communicate with his client on a regular basis, the client may think the attorney is doing nothing on the case. As a paralegal, you can be an asset to the attorney in maintaining communication with the client. In fact, parties often feel more comfortable dealing with the paralegal. In any event, if you have been assigned to a case, you should establish some procedure for regularly advising the client about the status of his action. This requires that you calendar cases for regular review. In addition, the most important rule to remember is to always return phone calls promptly. You should also keep a record of all telephone calls. Exhibit 3-12 is an example of a form that can be used.

Communication with the Opposing Party

Attorneys or paralegals violate ethical rules when they personally contact an opposing party who is represented by his own attorney. Contact must always be made with the attorney. If the opposing party is not represented by counsel, communication is allowed. If you are required to contact an opposing party, you should first verify that the opposing party is not represented. Naturally, an opposing party can be contacted to ascertain whether he is represented and who is representing him. However, once that information is disclosed, all further communication should cease.

One situation that sometimes occurs is that the opposing party, who is represented by an attorney, contacts you by telephone. (This is often a result of the failure of the opposing party's attorney to return telephone calls.) In such a situation you must tell the party that you cannot talk to him. You should also advise the party's attorney that her client attempted to talk to you about the case.

EXHIBIT 3-12 Telephone Call Memo Form

TELEPHONE CALL MEMO

Case Name: _____ Date ____/____/____/

Your Name: _____

     Telephone to _____   Telephone from _____

Telephone Number _____

_____ Left Message with _____ _____ Requested Callback

_____ Left Voicemail

Re:_____

_____

_____

_____

_____

_____

_____

_____

_____

_____

Time Billing (circle or fill in)   .1   .2   .3   .4   .5   _____

Confidentiality

Communication between a client and an attorney is confidential. The attorney is prohibited from disclosing any information revealed to him by his client. Even mentioning the client's name, without discussing the facts of the case, may be a violation of this ethical requirement. As part of the litigation team, the paralegal is bound by the same rules. Whether you are present during conferences between the client and the attorney, whether the client directly communicates with you, or whether information is relayed to you by the attorney, you must honor the confidentiality. You should not discuss the case with anyone not directly involved in the case.

Honesty

An attorney must never knowingly make a false representation about a case to a court or other tribunal. Although paralegals do not usually appear in court, you may frequently assist in the preparation of documents that are filed in court. You must be careful that factual and legal information is true and accurate.

    In addition to honesty with the court, attorneys and paralegals should always be honest in their dealings with other attorneys and other paralegals. Aside from basic ethical considerations, a firm's reputation will be destroyed if its attorneys and paralegals cannot be trusted by other firms.

flat fee
A legal fee based on a fixed sum rather than on an hourly rate or a percentage of a recovery.

hourly billing
A legal fee based on a fixed amount for each hour the law firm spends on the case.

contingent fee
A legal fee based on a percentage of the final settlement or recovery from a lawsuit.

costs
Out-of-pocket expenses incurred in pursuing a legal action (e.g., filing fees).

Attorney Fees and Ethics

Attorney fees present several ethical concerns. Only the attorney is allowed to set fees. Professional guidelines prohibit a paralegal from being involved in establishing fees in a case. However, you should be aware of the fee structure in case a question arises about a billing entry during the course of litigation. The fee should not be unreasonable or unconscionable. The fee arrangement, including any additional expenses, should be clearly explained to the client and it should be in writing. Some state laws require a written retainer agreement. Another important ethical rule prohibits sharing of fees with nonattorneys.

A fee in a litigation case can be set in a number of different ways. At the outset of the case, the attorney could simply set a **flat fee**, or fixed sum, to handle the case. For example, an attorney and client might agree that the attorney will handle the client's contract dispute for $10,000. Because the amount of time needed to properly litigate a case is hard to predict, it is rare to see a fee set in this manner. However, if the fee is set this way, the attorney must make a reasonable, good-faith effort to make the fee commensurate with the expected work in the case.

More commonly, the attorney and client will agree to an hourly billing. In an **hourly billing**, the client is charged a fixed amount for each hour the law firm spends on the case. The hourly rate cannot be excessive, but there are substantial differences in fees charged by lawyers, often depending on the attorney's experience. It is also common for firms to bill for paralegal time. For example, a firm handling some complicated business litigation might charge the client as follows: Senior Litigation Attorney—$350/hr; Junior Litigation Attorney—$225/hr; Paralegal—$125/hr. It is, of course, unethical to bill the client for time not spent on the case. See Exhibit 3-13 for an example of a form that can be used to keep accurate time records.

An alternative way of setting a fee in litigation is the **contingent fee**, a common arrangement in personal injury cases. In the contingent fee agreement, the attorney takes a percentage of whatever recovery is obtained. If no recovery is made, the attorney receives no fee. In this type of fee arrangement, there are times when an attorney receives a large fee for little time spent. Such a result, however, does not make the arrangement unreasonable. Contingent fees have been allowed on the theory that they permit people to pursue cases they could not afford otherwise.

A *fee* is the compensation that an attorney receives for his time and efforts in a case. However, it is not the only expense incurred during the litigation process. Courts require filing fees to process documents. Investigators and experts are often needed to help prove the case, and process servers have to be paid to serve papers. Out-of-pocket expenses such as these are known as **costs**. Most attorneys expect that the client will pay the costs of suit in addition to the fee that is charged. Even if the case is handled on a contingent fee basis, the attorney may request that the client put up funds to cover expected costs. Sometimes the attorney will advance or pay for these costs himself, expecting reimbursement (in addition to his fee) when the case is settled. It is important for the attorney to make this clear to the client.

In addition to ethical standards regarding the amount of fee a lawyer may charge, there are also standards regarding fee sharing. Generally, an attorney cannot share a fee in a case with a nonlawyer. This includes a paralegal.

The fee arrangement between the client and the attorney should always be in writing and signed by the client. In some jurisdictions, this is now required by law. However, even if not required, common sense dictates that the agreement should be clearly set forth

EXHIBIT 3-13 Time Sheet for Hourly Billing

Date _____ Daily Time Sheet of _____ Page _____ of ___

CASE NAME	CODE	DESCRIPTION OF WORK PERFORMED	TIME

BILLABLE CODES

ANA	Analyze	**DIS**	Discovery	**TLC**	Telephone Call
ANS	Answer Complaint	**MOT**	Motion	**TVL**	Travel
BRF	Brief	**RES**	Research	**TRP**	Trial Prep.
CON	Conference	**FIL**	Review File	**TRL**	Trial
CRT	Court Appear.	**SUM**	Summarize	**MSC**	Miscellaneous

in writing to avoid any dispute. The fee arrangement is usually included in a document referred to as a **retainer** agreement. See Exhibit 3-14 for a sample retainer agreement.

Property of Client—Trust Accounts

An attorney cannot commingle his own assets or property with property belonging to a client. To handle this kind of a situation, attorneys have special bank accounts, known as **trust accounts**, into which they deposit all money belonging to their clients. It is allowable to have one trust account for many clients, as long as accurate records are kept.

In litigation, trust accounts are used for two main purposes—advances by the client and settlement or satisfaction of judgments. First, if the client gives the attorney money that is specifically designated for costs, then the money should be deposited in a trust account until the cost is actually incurred. The attorney should not deposit the funds into his general account. Likewise, if the client gives the attorney a fee advance, that should also be deposited into the trust account until the fee is actually earned. Second, when a case is settled, the attorney must exercise care regarding any money he receives. A settlement check is primarily the property of the client. However, the attorney wants to be certain that he receives his fee and costs. In fact, the attorney may have a lien against the settlement if so provided in the

retainer
A legal fee imposed at the beginning of a legal action, usually intended to be applied to future attorney fees actually incurred.

trust account (trust deposit)
A special bank account used exclusively for handling money belonging to another, usually a client.

EXHIBIT 3-14 Retainer Agreement

THIS AGREEMENT IS BETWEEN TARA NGUYEN, hereafter referred to as "Client," and OKIMURA AND RESNICK, hereafter referred to as "Attorney." This agreement shall govern the respective rights and responsibilities of Client and Attorney, unless a subsequent agreement is made in writing.

1. **Claims Covered by Agreement.** Client retains Attorney to represent her in connection with a claim for damages for injuries suffered by Client while riding on a bus owned and operated by the City of Cedar Pines on or about April 4, ____. This Agreement does not cover any other possible related claims that may arise and may require legal services (for example, workers' compensation claims or disputes with Client's insurance company).

2. **Services to Be Performed by Attorney.** Attorney agrees to perform the following legal services, if necessary, with respect to the claim described above:

   - investigation of claim
   - preparing and filing lawsuit
   - negotiation
   - trial
   - if judgment is obtained, opposing motion for new trial. Attorney is authorized to associate or employ, at Attorney's expense, other counsel to assist in performing the services required by this Agreement.

3. **Services Not Covered by This Agreement.** The following services are not covered by this Agreement and if any are required to be done, additional fee arrangements shall be made between Attorney and Client:

   - defending any cross-complaint against Client in connection with above matter
   - any appeal in the above matter, regardless of who prevails at trial
   - any retrial ordered after posttrial motion or as a result of a mistrial, or after reversal on appeal
   - proceedings in connection with enforcing any judgment

4. **No Guarantee as to Result.** Client acknowledges that Attorney has made no guarantee as to the outcome or the amounts recoverable in the above matter.

5. **Contingency Fee to Attorney.** Client acknowledges that she has been advised by Attorney and is aware that any contingency fee arrangements are not set by law and that such a fee is negotiable between Attorney and Client. Client agrees that Attorney shall be paid thirty-three and one-third percent ($33\frac{1}{3}\%$) of any recovery, whether such recovery is by way of settlement, judgment, or compromise and Client agrees this is reasonable. Client further understands and agrees that costs and expenses incurred by Attorney shall be reimbursed before the contingency fee is computed.

6. **Litigation Costs and Expenses.** Attorney is authorized to incur reasonable costs and expenses in performing legal services under this Agreement. Client agrees to pay for such costs and expenses in addition to the contingency fee listed in paragraph 5.

   (a) **Particular costs and expenses:** The costs and expenses necessary in this case may include any or all of the following:

   - court filing fees
   - process serving fees
   - private investigator fees
   - photographic/graphic artist fees
   - fees to experts for consultation and/or appearance at deposition or trial jury fees
   - court reporter fees
   - mail, facsimile transmission, messenger and other delivery charges
   - transportation, meals, lodging, and all other costs of necessary out-of-town travel
   - long-distance telephone charges
   - photocopying (in office) at $.20/page

EXHIBIT 3-14 Retainer Agreement (*continued*)

> (b) **Client's responsibility to costs:** Attorney may advance such costs and expenses on Client's behalf but is not obligated to do so. Client agrees to reimburse Attorney upon demand for any such advances. Client is responsible for such reimbursement regardless of the status or outcome of the litigation.
>
> 7. **Effect of Discharge by Client.** Client shall have the right to discharge Attorney at any time upon written notice to Attorney. Such discharge shall not affect Client's obligation to reimburse Attorney for costs incurred prior to the discharge. Attorney shall be entitled to the reasonable value of legal services performed prior to such discharge to be paid by Client from any subsequent recovery on the claim covered by this Agreement.
>
> 8. **Attorney's Lien.** To secure payment to Attorney of all sums due under this Agreement for legal services, Client hereby grants Attorney a lien on Client's claim and on any recovery Client may obtain, whether by judgment or otherwise.
>
> 9. **Arbitration of Dispute.** Any dispute arising between Attorney and Client regarding fees charged or services rendered under this Agreement, including any claim for breach of contract, negligence or breach of fiduciary duty, shall be resolved by binding arbitration, conducted in accordance with the rules of the American Arbitration Association.
>
> Dated:
>
> Attorney: Client:
>
> _____   _____

retainer agreement. Because of the client's interest in the check, however, the attorney cannot deposit it into his personal account. The attorney must deposit the check into the trust account. After he makes certain that the settlement check has cleared, he can make proper disbursements from the trust account, paying the client his share and reimbursing himself for his costs and fee. If the trust account contains money for more than one client, the attorney should always make sure that the check has cleared before making any disbursements. Failure to do so could result in the property of one client being used for the benefit of another.

The importance of proper control and management of trust accounts cannot be overemphasized. Intentional misuse of clients' funds is theft and is punishable criminally. Negligent misuse of client funds results in disciplinary proceedings against the erring attorney. This is one area where bar associations are especially strict.

ETHICAL CONSIDERATIONS AND TECHNOLOGY

As with all businesses, the use of technology has affected the practice of law. Although it offers many advantages, technology creates many ethical concerns for legal professionals. A major area of concern is confidentiality.

Confidentiality and Client Communication

Technology offers convenient methods of communication with clients as well as with others. Cellular phones, e-mail, and facsimile transmissions have become standard modes of communication. Today, busy attorneys can send and receive e-mail through their "smartphones." However, using cellular phones and the Internet can present security risks. Communications over cellular phones and the Internet can be intercepted (either intentionally or accidentally). Greater risks result from simple misuse of the technology. For example, cell phones are easily used in public places where conversations can be overheard. In a careless moment, an individual can easily send fax transmissions to the wrong party. E-mails sent to a client might be retrieved by a client at work, exposing the communication to interception by the employer. A recent U.S. Supreme Court case allowed a government employer (a police department) to search the text messages of one of its officers. However, in its opinion, the Court recognized that many legal questions remain unanswered. The Court said, "Prudence counsels caution before the facts in the instant case are used to establish far-reaching premises that define the existence, and extent, of privacy expectations enjoyed by employees when using employer-provided communication devices. . . . At present, it is uncertain how workplace norms, and the law's treatment of them, will evolve." (*City of Ontario v. Quon*, 130 S.Ct. 2619, 2629–2630 [2010]). Whatever privacy rights do or do not exist, an ethical attorney or paralegal must use caution and common sense in using technology to communicate with clients.

Confidentiality and Client Information

In a modern law office, client information is stored in numerous, and sometimes unexpected, ways. Information is stored not only on the office computers. Copy machines, telephones, fax machines, and laptop computers may store copies of documents, e-mails, or text messages. Care must be taken to protect the confidentiality of this information, especially when equipment is "recycled."

Another current area of concern involves electronic transfer of documents. An electronic version of a document may contain "metadata." Metadata is information about the content and creation of the document and often includes confidential information, including the author of the document, date of creation of the document, and changes made in the document. Sending a document electronically makes that information available to anyone viewing the document unless methods are taken to protect the document. There are different ways of doing this. Various software programs will strip the metadata from the document. The document can be converted to a portable document format (PDF). Additionally, access to the document can be limited by adding a password.

Confidentiality issues are also a major concern today with the technology trend referred to as cloud computing. Traditionally, offices have used their desktop or laptop computers to create, manage, and store their documents. A recent technology trend changes this, by allowing these computer tasks to be accomplished without using software applications or storage capacity available on the office computer. Rather, an individual or business can access and use these with services provided by third parties over the Internet. (The term *cloud* is a metaphor used for the Internet.) The result is that documents are stored by a third party, and security and confidentiality are beyond the attorney's control. On the other hand, a law firm realizes many benefits. Not only is this trend financially beneficial, but it also offers the ability to share documents with clients or other attorneys. Additionally, the services offering cloud computing do provide security measures.

Document Retention Advice

The use of technology often results in the generation of a multitude of documents, either in paper or in electronic format. Most businesses have a policy regarding the destruction of these documents. Periodically paper documents are shredded and electronic documents deleted. However, once it becomes reasonably probable that a business might be sued, that business has an obligation to preserve all documents related to the litigation. Attorneys for such a business have a legal and ethical duty to become familiar with the business document

EXHIBIT 3-15 Ethical Considerations: The Litigation Process

ETHICAL STANDARDS: THE LITIGATION PROCESS

✓ Communicate regularly with your client.

✓ Do not communicate directly with an opposing party who is represented by an attorney.

✓ Keep all information about the case and the client confidential.

✓ Be honest in all representations to the court and to opposing counsel.

✓ Do not set unconscionable fees.

✓ Clearly explain fee arrangements to client and prepare written fee agreement if required by state law.

✓ Do not share fees with nonattorneys.

✓ Keep all client funds in a trust account.

✓ Never commingle personal or business funds with trust account funds.

✓ Use caution and common sense when using technology.

retention policy and to properly advise businesses about the obligation to retain documents related to probable litigation.

See Exhibit 3-15 for a checklist of ethical considerations throughout the litigation process.

SPECIAL ETHICAL CONCERNS FOR PARALEGALS

Although paralegals should be careful to follow all ethical standards imposed on attorneys, some concerns particularly affect legal assistants. Both the National Association of Legal Assistants (NALA) and the National Federation of Paralegal Associations (NFPA) have adopted ethical standards or guidelines for the paralegal profession. Included in those guidelines are the following:

1. Paralegals or legal assistants should disclose their status as a legal assistant at the beginning of any professional relationship.

2. Paralegals should protect or preserve all confidential information obtained by them.

3. Paralegals should not engage in any activity involving the unauthorized practice of law, including giving legal advice.

4. Paralegals should not establish the attorney–client relationship or set fees.

5. Paralegals should be honest and accurate in all timekeeping and billing records.

All of these ethical standards are important for the paralegal, but one that often poses many day-to-day questions involves the unauthorized practice of law. In part this is because the practice of law involves such a variety of activities. As a general rule, however, the unauthorized practice of law *prohibits* paralegals from:

1. making an appearance in a court proceeding on behalf of a client,

2. giving legal advice to a client (advice that calls for a legal opinion or legal judgment), and

3. signing pleadings or other documents filed in court on behalf of a client.

FINDING IT on the Internet

The Internet provides numerous sources for paralegals in the initial stages of litigation. There are several good Web sites dealing with legal ethics. The American Bar Association provides extensive information at **<http://www.abanet.org/cpr/home.html>**. One site that will give you current news, as well as links to the rules of professional conduct for the various states, is **<http://www.legalethics.com>**. This site has numerous news articles relating to the impact of technology on traditional ethical rules such as confidentiality and establishing the attorney–client privilege when using Web sites and chat rooms. The ethical rules for NALA and NFPA can be found on their Web sites, **<http://www.nala.org>** and **<http://www.paralegals.org>**.

a. The Internet also provides access to information from numerous companies that offer legal office software. Many provide online demonstrations or even trial versions of the software. Using any general search engine, locate the companies listed in this chapter that provide "time and billing" software and read or view information about the various products. Access the sites for NALA and NFPA and locate the ethical rules. (Search hint: On the NALA site follow the links to general information about the paralegal profession. On the NFPA site, follow the link to positions and issues.) Write a memo briefly summarizing each of the guidelines that would apply to the litigation paralegal working on the *Nguyen* case that has been discussed in this chapter.

b. Access the site for at least one software company described in this chapter. Write a memo briefly summarizing the key features of the software.

On the other hand, as a general rule, a paralegal can do the following without engaging in the unauthorized practice of law:

1. file documents in court or communicate with court staff regarding a case,
2. give factual information to a client, including general descriptions of legal proceedings, and
3. sign correspondence to clients, courts, or others, as long as the paralegal status is made clear and as long as the correspondence does not include any legal advice.

LAW OFFICE PROCEDURES

Litigation is a business, and as such a litigation law firm must follow accepted business practices. Those practices, however, must reflect the legal and ethical requirements and obligations discussed earlier in this chapter.

Basic Procedures

The following outlines typical litigation office procedures that occur when a law firm is faced with a new client:

1. As soon as a potential client contacts a firm, a conflicts check is done.
2. If no conflict exists, an attorney confers with the potential client and makes an initial assessment of the facts. (Client interviews are discussed in more detail in the next chapter.)

3. The attorney determines that a valid cause of action exists, that the statute of limitations has not run out, and that pursuing the case is reasonable. (Facts uncovered during the investigative stage of the case may alter this assessment.)

4. The attorney explains to the potential client the details of the law firm's representation, including the fee arrangements.

5. If the potential client agrees to pursue the case, a retainer agreement is prepared and signed by the client and the attorney.

6. An office file is created. The file must contain basic information about the case and contact information regarding the client. This information is usually kept in a physical file as well as in an electronic format.

7. A financial ledger sheet is created to keep track of all expenses and income related to the case.

8. If applicable, retainers and cost advances are deposited into an attorney trust account.

9. Dates for possible claim statutes and statutes of limitation are put in a tickler file. The file is also calendared for review.

10. The client is introduced to the paralegal, and the role of the paralegal is explained.

11. A letter is sent to potential defendants, or if applicable their attorney or insurance carriers, notifying them of representation.

With developments in technology, many of the typical office procedures have become automated. Numerous legal software programs now enable law offices to function in an electronic environment. Although some firms use generally designed calendar programs such as Microsoft Outlook, other firms choose calendaring software with features that are specifically designed for law offices. Such programs are often referred to as "time and billing" software. Examples of these are AbacusLaw, Amicus Attorney, ProLaw, Time Matters, Tabs3 Billing, Timeslips, and CaseMap. Some law firms use software programs specially designed for their firms.

Today most "time and billing" programs not only contain a calendar but also contain a to-do list, or memo pad, an address book, or contact list. These programs also allow the user to conduct conflict checks, share documents for editing, and maintain time and expense records for billing purposes. You can read more about these products on their Web pages.

In addition to using legal software to accomplish day-to-day office procedures, some of the more general case management software programs allow attorneys to manage all aspects of their cases. Some of these programs are featured in subsequent chapters of this text.

SUMMARY

- Before filing any lawsuit, an attorney must determine that a cause of action, or legally recognized right to sue, exists. Paralegals may assist the attorney in researching the law and analyzing the evidence in the case. The paralegal must understand the legal and factual basis for the cause of action to properly assist the attorney in preparing for trial.

- All lawsuits must be filed in a timely manner. Time limitations for filing lawsuits are known as statutes of limitations and claim statutes. The equitable concept of laches also limits the time in which to file suit. Time limits vary depending on the type of case and the jurisdiction. All firms maintain some type of tickler system to keep track of time requirements.

- In addition to reviewing the legal basis of the lawsuit and the ethical restraints in accepting a case, an attorney should consider the practicalities of the lawsuit. In particular, the damages and the ability of the defendant to pay a judgment must justify the cost of litigation.

- An attorney must clearly notify a prospective client if he decides not to take a case. He should also warn the individual of time limitations in pursuing the case. The attorney must also be careful in making any representations regarding the merits of the case.

- In deciding to accept a case, an attorney is bound by certain ethical standards. She cannot accept a case if she is not competent to handle it, if the case is without merit or frivolous, or if there is a conflict of interest.

- After accepting a case, the members of the law firm, especially the attorney and the paralegal, are bound by other ethical standards. They should keep the client advised about the status of the case. They must never communicate personally with an opposing party once they know that party is represented by his own attorney. They must honor the confidentiality of their client and not discuss the case with third parties. They must be honest in their dealings with the court and other law firms. Attorney fees should be reasonable and clearly explained to the client. In some cases written fee agreements are necessary. Any monies belonging to the client must be kept in a trust fund and not commingled with the attorney's personal property. When using technology, attorneys and paralegals should use caution to avoid disclosing confidential client information. Paralegals must be careful not to give legal advice and to properly identify themselves as nonlawyers to clients.

- Business practices in accepting a case, creating office files, and maintaining proper financial records must be in accordance with ethical rules governing the legal profession. The use of technology has impacted the legal office procedures.

KEY TERMS

cause of action	flat fee	retainer
claim statute	hourly billing	statute of limitations
conflict of interest	laches	tickler system
contingent fee	Model Rules of Professional	trust account
costs	Conduct	

REVIEW QUESTIONS

1. What is a cause of action?
2. What is the importance of a cause of action to the litigation process?
3. What are the various types of time limitations on filing a lawsuit?
4. What is a tickler system, and why is it important in a litigation law firm?
5. What practical considerations must be reviewed prior to accepting a case?

6. What is the proper procedure for turning down a case?

7. What are the various ethical standards that control an attorney's decision to accept a case?

8. What are the ethical responsibilities governing law firms that handle litigation?

9. What are the special ethical concerns of litigation paralegals?

10. Describe typical office procedures in a law firm?

CHAPTER EXERCISES

Where necessary, check with your instructor prior to starting any of these exercises.

1. Review the Commentary at the beginning of the chapter. Analyze the actions of Euro Motors, Inc., the city, the bus driver, and the driver of the other vehicle involved in the collision and determine whether a cause of action for negligence exists for each of the parties. Show your conclusions by completing charts for each of the parties as was done in Exhibit 3-2. In completing the charts, indicate if factual support for any element is lacking. Review Exhibit 3-4. Is there a cause of action against any of the parties for strict liability?

2. Research the laws of your state. Find the statutes of limitations for the following types of cases: an action for personal injuries based on negligence, an action for personal injuries based on strict liability, an action for personal injuries based on medical malpractice, an action for legal malpractice, an action for property damage based on negligence, an action based on a written contract, an action based on an oral contract, and an action for fraud.

3. Review your state rules of professional conduct. (You can probably find these rules on the Web site for your state bar association.) Summarize the rules that might affect a litigation paralegal.

4. During your client interview with Tara Nguyen, assume that she asks you the following questions. How should you respond?

   a. Do you think I have a good case?

   b. Should I take photos of the scene of the accident?

   c. How long will this case take if it has to go to trial?

   d. If the attorney files a lawsuit, what will court costs be?

   e. Based on your experience, what is my case worth?

5. Refer to Exhibit 3-3, Elements of Different Causes of Action. Analyze the following factual situations and determine which, if any, cause of action exists.

   a. Connors and Loewe enter into a written agreement whereby Connors agrees to purchase Loewe's house. Prior to signing the agreement, Connors asks Loewe about the condition of the roof. Loewe tells Connors that the roof is in good repair. In fact, Loewe recently had a roof inspection done and was told that the roof was in terrible condition and should be replaced immediately. Shortly after Connors moves into the premises, a storm occurs and the roof leaks in several places.

    b. Engels buys a preassembled student desk for her grammar-school son. When an overhead light goes out in her son's room, Engels stands on the desk to reach the light. The desk collapses and Engels is injured.

6. Refer to the various statutes of limitations set out in this chapter (see Exhibits 3-6 and 3-7). Consider the following cases. What would be the last date on which the complaint could be filed?

    a. On February 15, 2010, Jeffers and Holmes, both California residents, enter into an oral agreement whereby Holmes agrees to loan Jeffers money, which is due and payable on February 15, 2011. On February 15, 2011, Jeffers does not repay the money. Holmes wants to sue.

    b. Ruiz hires Baines and Baines, Attorneys at Law, to represent him in a lawsuit for personal injuries resulting from an automobile accident. Unfortunately, the attorneys miss the statute of limitations for the action and Ruiz's claim is barred. The complaint should have been filed March 1, 2010. On March 10, 2010, Ruiz calls the attorneys and asks about his case. They tell him that everything is going along and that he should be patient because lawsuits take a long time. After hearing nothing for four months, on July 12, 2010, Ruiz again calls the attorneys. This time he talks to a paralegal in the firm, who checks the file and tells him that she does not see any record of a complaint being filed. On July 20, 2010, Ruiz contacts another lawyer, who calls Baines and Baines. Finally, on July 30, 2010, Gerald Baines, one of the partners of Baines and Baines, admits that a complaint was never filed. Ruiz wants to sue Baines and Baines for malpractice. Apply California law (Exhibit 3-7).

    c. Rhonda Pedersen and her 12-year-old daughter are injured in a motor vehicle accident with a U.S. postal truck on March 15, 2010. They wish to sue the federal government for their injuries. By what date must a claim be filed? (See Exhibit 3-8.)

    d. Complete the claim form in Exhibit 3-9 on behalf of Rhonda Pederson. Assume the law firm of Okimura & Resnick is representing her (see Exhibit 3-5). Also assume that the accident occurred at the intersection of Fairfield Avenue and Albright Street in Boise. Ms. Pederson suffered a strained neck and back and the extent of her injuries is still unknown. Her vehicle sustained some damage and the repair estimate is $1,300. She has no insurance for her injuries or the damage to her car.

7. Assume that you are a litigation paralegal responsible for tickling or calendaring statutes of limitations for new cases. What date or dates would you calendar to make sure your office did not miss the statute of limitations for the cases mentioned in the previous question?

8. Assume that you are a litigation paralegal. Your law firm has decided to create a page for Facebook. What ethical considerations might affect this decision?

9. Find a recent article about ethics on <www.legalethics.com>. Prepare a brief oral presentation summarizing the article.

CHAPTER PROJECT

Review the Commentary at the beginning of the chapter. Research the following questions and present your findings in an interoffice memorandum:

1. What is the appropriate statute of limitations in your state for this case?
2. Do the laws of your state allow you to sue the city? If so, do any special claim statutes apply? If so, does Nguyen still have time to file a claim?
3. Are there other types of cases in your state that require a claim to be submitted prior to filing a lawsuit?

THE *BENNETT* CASE
Assignment for Chapter 3: Preliminary Claim

You have been given a copy of the Bennett research file along with a copy of the initial client interview form (see Appendix B). This file contains copies of relevant federal codes and regulations regarding discrimination claims under Title VII. The attorney handling the case is eager to pursue a claim under Title VII. Your supervisor tells you that before filing this type of lawsuit a claim with either the state or the EEOC must be submitted. Your supervisor tells you that the next step is to file a claim with the EEOC. The requirements for this claim are found in the Code of Federal Regulations. You are to read this rule (29 C.F.R. 1601), a copy of which is in the Bennett research file, and draft a claim. The needed factual information should be located in the client interview form. You should also review the Web site for the Equal Employment Opportunity Commission (<http://www.eeoc.gov>) for information on filing a charge of discrimination with the agency.

THE *DOUGLASS FINANCIAL SERVICES, INC.* CASE
Assignment for Chapter 3: Preparing a Time Sheet

Read the Interview of Braedon Douglass. Assume that following the interview, attorney Gretchen Reily asked paralegal Natalie Ortiz to write a summary of the interview, obtain a copy of the police report, and research the law about liability of employers for intoxicated employees. In one day, Natalie Ortiz spent 1.5 hours taking notes during the interview, 45 minutes summarizing her notes, 1 hour trying to obtain the police report, and 3.5 hours doing legal research. Using the form in Exhibit 3-13, complete the time sheet for Natalie for her day's work.

CHAPTER 4 Investigation and Evidence

CHAPTER OUTLINE

THE *SALDIVAR* CASE

Arturo Saldivar contacted your firm to represent him in a personal injury lawsuit against Greenwood Properties, Inc. Mr. Saldivar was recently diagnosed with mesothelioma, a form of cancer related to asbestos exposure. Several years ago, Mr. Saldivar worked as a warehouseman in a building owned by Greenwood Properties and leased to Saldivar's employer, Ryder Building Supplies. Recently, the building was torn down to make room for new construction. At this time, it was discovered that asbestos was widely used in the building. Mr. Saldivar's doctor advised him that his condition could have been caused by his continued exposure to asbestos.

Your attorney asked that you handle the preliminary arrangements for the interview, help determine whether the firm should accept the case, locate the necessary forms to gather information during and after the interview, and coordinate the interview. Your attorney explained that she would like for you to participate in the interview so that the client will be comfortable communicating with you throughout the expected lengthy litigation. You are to function as a member of the litigation team, which consists of a senior attorney, several junior associates, and several paralegals.

Chapter 3 discussed important preliminary considerations affecting the filing of a lawsuit. Interviewing and investigation are also important steps in beginning the litigation process. Knowledge of some basic rules of evidence helps in these two steps. After reading this chapter, you should be able to:

- outline the paralegal's responsibilities in preparing for the client interview.
- describe how to set up a client interview.
- prepare a client interview questionnaire.
- list forms or documents that might be needed during the client interview.
- explain the importance of maintaining a professional demeanor in dealing with clients, witnesses, and other legal professionals.
- identify potential sources for locating fact witnesses or elusive defendants.
- discuss the techniques for interviewing fact witnesses.
- identify rules that control the admissibility of different forms of evidence.
- describe methods for locating and preserving evidence.
- explain the functions of an expert witness.
- explain the paralegal's role in procuring an expert witness.

COMMENTARY

OBJECTIVES

THE CLIENT INTERVIEW

Successful litigation begins with proper preparation and investigation of both the facts and the law. This preparation and investigation often starts with the client interview. In most cases, the client is the most knowledgeable about the facts of the case. During a client interview, these facts are communicated to the attorney handling the case. The attorney is then able to determine what aspects of the case need further investigation or research.

Not only is the client interview an essential step in the fact-gathering process, but it also establishes the foundation for the long-term relationship between the client and the firm. The interview establishes the tone for the representation. If the interview goes smoothly, the client's impression of the firm will be favorable. However, if the paralegal and attorney are not prepared for the interview, have not researched the issues, and are not familiar with the basic facts of the potential representation, the client will have good cause to question his or her choice of counsel. The client will also question his or her choice of counsel if either the attorney or the paralegal does not present a professional demeanor.

The client interview affords the paralegal the opportunity to become an integral part of the litigation team. Although the attorney normally conducts an initial interview, a paralegal often plays an important role in the process. You may be asked to take various levels of responsibility for the interview, including:

1. researching potential causes of action or defenses,
2. scheduling the interview,
3. developing an interview questionnaire or form to fit the particular case,
4. gathering forms and documents the client will have to sign,
5. taking notes during the interview, and
6. producing a summary of the interview.

Preparing for the Initial Client Interview

Research Potential Causes of Action or Defenses
Preparation is essential to a successful interview. Once you are assigned a case such as the *Saldivar* case discussed in the Commentary of this chapter, you should review all information available on the subject matter of the potential litigation and the causes of action or defenses. In Chapter 3, sources for researching the elements of a cause of action were described. In addition, you should find out as much as you can about the factual subject matter of the lawsuit. Your firm's library, the local library, and the Internet offer an abundance of information on asbestos-related injuries and cases, including who has been sued, the outcome of jury trials, and reports on damage awards. You should also refer to medical journals covering the causes and effects of mesothelioma. Only by understanding the factual basis of the lawsuit are you able to ask relevant and pertinent questions during an interview.

Schedule the Interview
Once the attorney determines that a potential cause of action exists, the initial client interview can be scheduled. Before scheduling the interview, however, remember to check the firm's current and past client lists to rule out any conflict with any of the potential defendants. In scheduling the interview, the attorney's calendar should be checked for acceptable dates. You may contact the client by telephone to discuss available dates or suggest a tentative date by letter and request confirmation that the date is acceptable. If contact is made by telephone, a confirming letter should be sent. The date for the initial interview should be set as early as possible. When setting up the initial interview, the client should be instructed to bring along all necessary information for preparing the case. This information will vary depending on the nature of the case but may include such items as names and addresses of opposing parties and all witnesses, copies of

EXHIBIT 4-1 Letter Advising Client of Initial Interview Appointment

Schneider & Fenton
Attorneys at Law
45 North Main St.
San Antonio, Texas 78265
(512) 555-1312

Allyson Schneider   Anthony Fenton
Glen Bardwell   K.W. Post

Arturo Saldivar
189 Montalban Dr
San Antonio, Texas 78265

Dear Mr. Saldivar,
An appointment has been scheduled for you with attorney Allyson Schneider of our firm at 10 a.m. on Monday, June 15, at our offices to discuss your case. This interview should require approximately one hour. Please bring with you to the interview the following items checked on the list below:

(X) Social Security number
( ) Copy of insurance policy
(X) Information relating to the opposing party, such as insurance carrier, etc.
( ) Accident or incident reports
(X) Photographs and/or diagrams of injury site
(X) Newspaper clippings relating to injury
(X) Witness statements
( ) Description of automobiles involved in accident, including license tags, owner, and amount of damage
(X) Medical bills and information relating to treating physicians and hospitals
(X) Employment information concerning time lost because of injury
(X) Any other relative information or documents

Producing the information requested at the time of the interview will enable us to expedite the handling of your claim. Please call me if you have any questions about the items requested.

Sincerely,

Alan Berkshire
Paralegal

any correspondence between the client and the opposing party, and written verification of damages (medical bills, wage statements, etc.). Exhibit 4-1 is an example of an appointment-setting letter that asks the client to bring pertinent information to the interview.

representation letter
A letter from an attorney to a new client establishing the ground rules of the litigation, including fees, billing rates, retainer, and work to be performed by the law firm.

retainer agreement
An agreement between an attorney and a client setting forth the fee arrangement and details of the attorney's obligations.

release
Giving up a claim or right to sue.

authorization
A signed statement empowering someone (such as a doctor or employer) to give out information that might otherwise be treated as confidential.

The location of the interview is important. If the client is critically ill, has difficulty walking, or expresses reluctance to talk in the formal environment of the law firm, the interview may have to be held at the client's home, office, or hospital room. Most interviews in the law firm are conducted in either the attorney's office or a conference room. If a conference room is required, you may be asked to schedule the conference room and prepare it for the interview.

Enter the location and time of the interview on the attorney's calendar and on your calendar or reminder system. A follow-up telephone call or e-mail to the client the day before the interview ensures that the attorney's time is not wasted because of a last-minute cancellation.

Develop Interview Questionnaires or Forms
Preparing relevant questions for the interview is important and helps instill confidence. During any client interview, the attorney or paralegal first needs to elicit general background information, such as address, telephone number, employer, and so on. The heart of the interview, however, consists of questions specifically related to the case. Forms for client interviews containing sample questions are found in many form books and practice manuals in the law firm's library. However, interview forms are useful only if they are tailored to the specific case. An interview form that your attorney had used in a construction contract case would be worthless in a personal injury case. If you cannot find a form specifically tailored to your situation, you need to develop your own. Standard questions relating to identity, contact information, and general background information can be found on any client interview form; developing questions specifically addressing the facts and issues of your case requires some thought, effort, and research. One way to approach this kind of task is by identifying and listing the elements of all potential causes of action and using this list as an outline for organizing and writing your interview questions. Once you understand what the attorney has to prove at trial, you should be able to formulate questions geared toward gathering that information. Exhibit 4-2 is an example of an interview questionnaire containing general questions.

Gather Forms and Documents for Client Signature
Prior to the actual interview, you should locate copies of all forms that the client might need to sign. The first form to be filled out is the **representation letter** or **retainer agreement**, which establishes the ground rules of the litigation, including fees, billing rates, retainer, and work to be performed by the law firm. A sample retainer agreement was shown in Chapter 3 (Exhibit 3-14).

In Saldivar's case, the client's medical history and related expenses must be documented. Information concerning Saldivar's medical treatment by a hospital, doctor, physical therapist, or laboratory can be obtained only through a written release or authorization signed by Saldivar. A **release** or **authorization** is a signed statement by the client that authorizes someone (such as a doctor or employer) to give the attorney information regarding the client, information that otherwise might be treated as confidential. In drafting a medical release form you must be careful to use a form that complies with the privacy rights enumerated in the federal HIPAA law (Health Insurance Portability and

EXHIBIT 4-2 Client Interview Form

PERSONAL DATA:
Name: _____
Home Address: _____
Address for Billing: _____
Home Telephone: _____
Work Telephone: _____
Cellular Phone: _____
Fax Number: _____
E-mail: _____
Date of Birth: _____
Social Security No.: _____
Driver's License No.: _____
Spouse's Name: _____
Spouse's Work Phone: _____
Employer: _____
Address: _____

INFORMATION RELATING TO CLAIM:
Type of claim (EEOC, med. malpractice, etc.): _____
Date of incident leading to claim: _____
Brief statement of incident (or attach statement): _____
_____
_____
Itemize damages incurred to date: _____
_____
Do you anticipate additional damages? If so, describe: _____
_____
Name and address of any doctors you have seen: _____
_____
Identity, address, and telephone of any potential witnesses: _____
_____
Description and location of any documents or correspondence pertinent to litigation:
_____
_____
Have you made any statements to anyone (orally or in writing) regarding this case? If so,
describe. _____
_____
Do you have any insurance that covers this claim? If so, please describe. _____
_____
_____
Have you been served with any papers relating to this case? _____
Have you heard from any lawyers concerning this case? _____

PRIOR LITIGATION:
Type of litigation: _____
Date and place of litigation: _____
Outcome of litigation: _____
Attorney representing you: _____

EXHIBIT 4-3 Medical Authorization

AUTHORIZATION FOR RELEASE OF INFORMATION

I, Arturo Saldivar, hereby authorize _____ to release to the law firm of SCHNEIDER & FENTON, located at 45 North Main St., San Antonio, Texas 78265, telephone (512) 555-1312, or their authorized representative the information specified below pertaining to:

Arturo Saldivar, Birthdate: 10/25/1965. Social Security Number _____

Information/Type of Records Requested:
All records pertaining to medical treatment as a result of or related to exposure to asbestos and mesothelioma, including, but not limited to, all X-rays, medical records, nurses' notes, medical charts, diagnostic studies, and medical opinions.

For the Following Dates: 01/10/2000 and all dates forward

This disclosure is requested for the purposes of evaluation of a legal matter handled by SCHNEIDER & FENTON on behalf of Arturo Saldivar and this authorization expires at the time said legal matter is resolved.

I have read the above and also have been advised of my right to receive a true copy of this authorization. Further, I understand the contents of this written authorization in its entirety and have asked questions about anything that was not clear to me, and I am satisfied with the answers I have received.

I further acknowledge that I understand my right to revoke this authorization by presenting written notice to SCHNEIDER & FENTON. I further understand that if SCHNEIDER & FENTON has already served the authorization to the entity listed above, SCHNEIDER & FENTON has the right to dishonor my request to revoke the authorization.

It should be further noted that the information used or disclosed pursuant to this authorization may be subject to re-disclosure by the recipient.

A PHOTOSTATIC OR FACSIMILE COPY OF THIS AUTHORIZATION SHALL BE CONSIDERED AS EFFECTIVE AND VALID AS THE ORIGINAL.

Client/Patient Signature: _____ Date: _____

Accountability Act). Some states have additional privacy laws. Exhibit 4-3 shows a medical authorization form.

   To further establish damages as a result of the mesothelioma, Mr. Saldivar's employment records, tax returns, and/or earnings statements must be obtained. The Social Security earnings record, which offers a complete history of the client's employment and earnings, should be requested early in the investigative process of this case. Exhibit 4-4 shows a release for that employment information.

   Exhibit 4-5 presents a checklist of the steps in preparing for a client interview.

EXHIBIT 4-4 Authorization for Release of Information Relating to Employment and Earnings

I, ARTURO SALDIVAR, hereby authorize and permit the law firm of SCHNEIDER & FENTON, or its representative, to inspect, review, and make copies of any and all employment and/or earnings records regarding myself, including, but not limited to, employment application, vacation leave, sick or medical leave, W-2 forms, termination, and any other documents relating to my employment with _____. The release of this information is to be used for litigation purposes.

A copy of this authorization shall have the same effect and force as an original.

_____
ARTURO SALDIVAR

Copyright © 2015 Cengage Learning®

EXHIBIT 4-5 The Initial Client Interview Checklist

THE INITIAL CLIENT INTERVIEW: BE PREPARED

✓ Run a conflict check
✓ Research and identify elements of potential causes of action
✓ Research factual subject matter of potential lawsuit
✓ Schedule interview for time, date, and place convenient to both attorney and client
✓ Notify client of interview by telephone or in writing
✓ Advise client to bring relevant documents to interview
✓ Reserve conference room for interview if required
✓ Confirm interview with client the day before it is scheduled
✓ Develop an interview questionnaire
✓ Prepare forms and documents client might need to sign

Copyright © 2015 Cengage Learning®

The Paralegal's Role in the Interview

You have completed the research assignments and prepared all the necessary forms. The day of the interview has arrived. Your attorney should introduce you to the client and explain your role in the case. Giving clients a copy of your business card will assist them in contacting you should the need arise. This will facilitate information exchange between the firm and its clients.

Your attorney may ask that you take notes during the interview and have them transcribed for the file. You might also be asked to prepare a narrative interview summary. If you have prepared a questionnaire for the interview, give a copy to the attorney and keep a copy for yourself. You can then take notes on your copy of the questionnaire. This technique makes your note taking easier. If you do not understand an answer to a question, or are unsure of a name or word, ask questions. Sometimes it is necessary to ask the client to spell proper names that may appear later in pleadings filed with the court. Always make sure that you have the correct spelling of your client's name. Your notes should be complete and accurate.

medical diary
A document in which the client keeps track of medical treatment, daily health complaints, type and amount of medication, mileage to physicians' offices, and other related medical expenses.

During the interview, particular note should be made of the statute of limitations. As soon as the interview concludes, you should make sure that a reminder, or tickler, is entered in the firm's litigation tracking system.

Prior to concluding the interview, review the checklist of information that the client was asked to furnish. If any information is missing, make a written list of it and give it to the client. Be sure to calendar the file to check that you receive everything requested. In a personal injury case such as *Saldivar,* the client might also be asked to keep a **medical diary**, a document in which the client keeps track of medical treatment, daily health complaints, type and amount of medication, mileage to physicians' offices, and other related medical expenses. The client will be more receptive to keeping the journal up to date if he or she realizes that it will be used in calculating damages and evaluating the case for settlement. As the case progresses, the paralegal might periodically review the journal. Exhibit 4-6 shows a sample page from a medical diary.

EXHIBIT 4-6 Medical Diary

DATE: _____

MEDICAL TREATMENT:

VISIT TO DR. _____ (NAME)

REASON FOR VISIT: _____

DIAGNOSIS: _____

MEDICATION PRESCRIBED: _____

VISIT TO HOSPITAL OR OTHER MEDICAL SERVICE:

NAME: _____

REASON FOR VISIT: _____

DIAGNOSIS: _____

TYPE OF TREATMENT: _____

HEALTH COMPLAINTS:

TIME OF COMPLAINT: _____

DESCRIPTION OF HEALTH COMPLAINT: _____

MEDICATION:

NAME OF MEDICATION: _____

PRESCRIBED BY: _____

CONDITION FOR WHICH PRESCRIBED: _____

_____

AMOUNT OF MEDICATION TAKEN: _____

ADDITIONAL NOTES RELATIVE TO HEALTH:

_____

_____

_____

Interview Summary

Promptly upon completion of the interview, your interview notes should be summarized in a memorandum for the attorney's review and a copy placed in the client's file. The interview summary may reveal areas that need further development, either from a legal issue or factual standpoint. You may use the form to develop a to-do list for additional investigation.

Professional Demeanor

In performing your role as a paralegal you must always maintain a professional demeanor. Clients, supervising attorneys, coworkers, and even opposing counsel and paralegals expect that you will act in a professional manner at all times. The importance of this quality is recognized by almost every paralegal association and included either in the definition of a paralegal or in standards of conduct. There is no absolute definition of what this includes. One of the more important characteristics of this, however, is common courtesy. Remember that you have a professional relationship with your clients. In a world of informality, do not forget that you should not normally address clients by their first names. You must also take particular care in communicating with clients through e-mail. E-mail provides an efficient and speedy way of communicating, but your e-mails to clients and other paralegals or attorneys should always be written in a professional manner. Professional and courteous conduct should also be shown to opposing counsel and paralegals.

LOCATING FACT WITNESSES OR ELUSIVE DEFENDANTS

Prior to filing a lawsuit, all available facts should be gathered and organized. These facts are normally derived from the client, other witnesses, or documents. Mr. Saldivar's interview may yield many of the facts necessary to support filing a lawsuit on his behalf. However, more information may help his claims. For example, other employees who worked at the warehouse may have additional information. However, because this employment took place several years ago, finding these individuals will probably be difficult. Nevertheless, steps must be taken to locate and interview these potentially important fact witnesses.

In addition to locating fact witnesses, the defendant may need to be located prior to filing suit. Sometimes, pending litigation causes potential defendants to become elusive. You may be asked to research the opposing party's address for service of process. This effort should be made early in the investigation so that it does not hamper prompt service of the complaint or petition. Numerous sources are available to help you locate any person, including potential witnesses and defendants. The client can often provide you with names and contact information for witnesses as well as for potential defendants. Exhibit 4-7 provides a checklist of some traditional sources used to locate witnesses and potential defendants.

EXHIBIT 4-7 Checklist of Sources for Locating Fact
Witnesses or Elusive Defendants

✓ Client
✓ Internet
✓ Client's competitors
✓ Accident report
✓ Court records of prior litigation (often available on the court's Web site)
✓ Department of Motor Vehicles
✓ Friends and/or neighbors
✓ Employer and/or coworkers
✓ Professional organizations or unions
✓ County assessor or recorder
✓ Relatives
✓ Hospital and medical service providers
✓ Physicians
✓ Ambulance company

*agent for service of
process*

party designated by a
corporation who is authorized to
be served with a lawsuit against
the corporation.

Today, the Internet is the obvious starting point for information unknown to the client. Several free and fee-based sites provide substantial information about individuals and businesses. Many states and local governments make public documents available through their Web sites. As a result, you can often locate business and personal information through various business and court filings as well as through real property ownership records. Nationwide telephone directories and search engines such as Google will also help you uncover information about people and businesses. Popular social networks also help you locate people and businesses. See Exhibit 4-8 for a list of some popular Internet sites that can help you locate people and businesses.

Fee-based online legal research databases such as Westlaw also provide numerous sources that are helpful in locating individuals and businesses. See Exhibits 4-9 and 4-10 for sample Web pages showing sources that can be searched on Westlaw. You can also search for information related to judges, attorneys, and experts who might be involved in the case, as well as information about your client. (There is a good chance that the opposing side will seek information about your client.) See Exhibit 4-11.

Steps for Locating the Agent of Corporations or Partnerships

The opposing party in the *Saldivar* case is a corporation. Your client may know the physical address of the defendant. However, additional information is needed before the lawsuit can be filed. You will need the legal name of the company and the name and address of the party who should be served with the suit. This individual is known as the **agent for service of process**. If the defendant is a corporation, this information is available from the secretary of state's office and may be obtained by telephone or use of a research database,

EXHIBIT 4-8 Web Sites for Locating People and Businesses

WEB SITES FOR LOCATING PEOPLE AND BUSINESSES

Telephone and Address Directories

- http://www.infobel.com
- http://www.four11.com
- http://www.411.com/
- http://www.anywho.com
- http://www.switchboard.com
- http://www.whitepages.com/

National Listing of Real Estate Assessors

- http://indorgs.virginia.edu/portico/assessors.html

Company Information

- http://www.hoovers.com
- http://www.sec.gov/edgar.shtml

Social Networks

- http://www.facebook.com
- https://twitter.com/
- http://www.linkedin.com/

General Information

- http://www.google.com

such as Lexis or Westlaw. Other services on the Internet also provide this information. In many jurisdictions, the secretary of state has an online home page, making this information readily available. In some states, if a defendant is a partnership or limited partnership, this information may be available from the secretary of state's office; in other states this information may be filed in the county recorder's office in the county where the partnership has its principal place of business. This information should be obtained early in the investigative stage of the lawsuit.

TECHNIQUES FOR INTERVIEWING FACT WITNESSES

Once you locate a potential fact witness, make a telephone call to determine what information the witness has and whether the witness is willing to be interviewed. You should identify yourself as a paralegal working with the attorney representing Mr. Saldivar. The witness should clearly understand who the potential parties in litigation are and what claims are being made on behalf of Mr. Saldivar. If the witness has information that may be relevant to the case, a personal visit should be arranged to take his or her statement.

An interview form similar to the client interview form discussed earlier expedites the interview and helps elicit all pertinent facts from the witness. This form, a tape

EXHIBIT 4-9 Westlaw Databases—Locating People

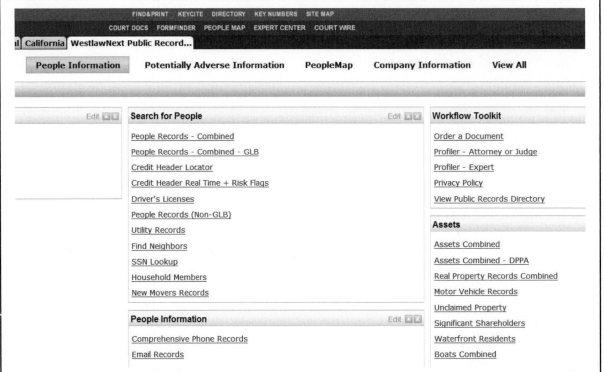

recorder, and a writing pad are necessary tools for the witness interview. A verbatim tape recording of the interview is preferable, but if the witness is reluctant to have his or her statement taped, you should be prepared. You should take written notes of the interview. In such a case, if possible, write out a statement and have the witness sign it before the interview concludes. Even if the statement is tape-recorded, you should take written notes in case the tape player malfunctions. Once the interview has been completed, a typed witness statement should be prepared, either from the recorded interview or from your written notes or statement. This typewritten statement can then be transmitted to the witness for review and signing. Never tape-record a witness's statement, in person or over the phone, without the witness's knowledge and permission. In some jurisdictions this is a crime.

Selecting the location for the interview is critical. Remember that this witness's statement is voluntary. You should exercise extreme courtesy and cooperation in scheduling the interview. The witness may prefer that the interview be in the evening so that it will not interfere with a job. Perhaps the witness does not want to travel downtown to the law firm and would rather have the interview at his or her home in a suburb. Flexibility is essential. You should make all arrangements for the interview to suit the witness's preferences.

EXHIBIT 4-10 Westlaw Databases—Locating Companies

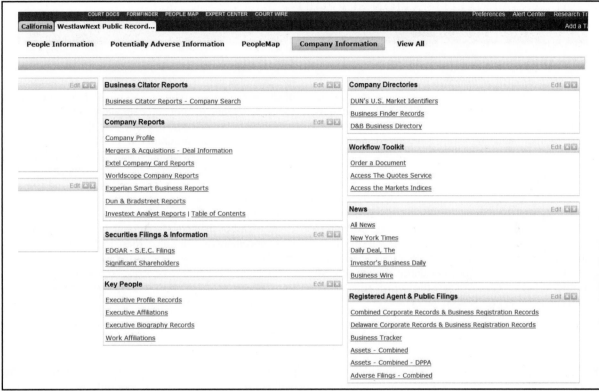

EXHIBIT 4-11 Westlaw Databases—Judge/Attorney/Expert Profiler

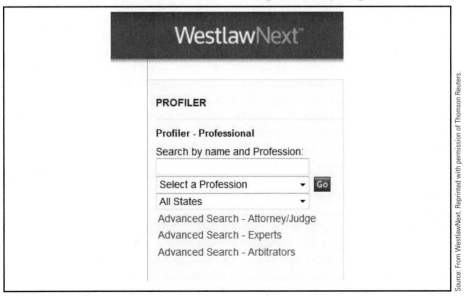

AUTOMATED LITIGATION SUPPORT

Case Management

SCENARIO

The *Saldivar* case will involve numerous documents, witnesses, and attorneys. It will also involve some complex facts and legal issues. Your attorney knows that she has a much better chance of a successful resolution of the case if all the information in the case is organized and carefully analyzed.

PROBLEM

Your attorney has asked your help to carefully organize and analyze all the potential evidence in the *Saldivar* case. Other paralegals and attorneys will also be working on this. You are concerned about how you will coordinate and analyze the significance of numerous documents, witness statements, and other evidence. You are also concerned about how to coordinate the work of other paralegals and attorneys working on the same case.

SOLUTION

In a complex case a thorough evaluation and analysis of all the evidence can be an arduous task. Fortunately, today, case management software allows attorneys and paralegals to better assess relevant facts, documents, and issues. One software program that provides such help is LexisNexisCaseMap. The program allows the users to create links between parties, witnesses, facts, documents, and legal issues. This allows the user to efficiently organize and assess the relevance of all evidence. Once the user has identified and listed the legal issues in the case, he or she can also create a "cast of characters," a chronology of events, and a list of documents and link all of these to the various issues in the case. The program can be used by several members of the legal team simultaneously. To read more about this software program go to http://www.lexisnexis.com/casemap/casemap.aspx

---

leading question
A question that generally calls for a yes or no answer and suggests the answer by the way it is phrased (e.g., beginning the question with "Isn't it true . . . ")

demeanor
The appearance of a person and the way in which a person acts as opposed to what he or she says.

The attorney may participate in the interview or request that you conduct the interview alone. Good planning will ensure that the interview goes quickly and smoothly. Preparation may include a review of the information on the interview form and facts about the witness from the earlier client interview.

Good interview techniques include listening attentively, taking detailed notes, and asking questions to clarify confusing or incomplete information. When asking questions, avoid **leading questions**. A leading question is a question that suggests the answer. For example, the question, "Isn't it true that Greenwood Properties had a reputation for not caring about the welfare of its tenants?" is a leading question. The witness feels that "yes" is the anticipated answer and will tend to respond accordingly. A better way to phrase the question is, "Could you tell me what Greenwood Properties' reputation was regarding the welfare of its tenants?" This type of question calls for the witness's own feelings and is not suggestive. A witness should be encouraged to tell a story in his or her own words. Avoid the appearance of rushing the narrative or reacting to the story as it unfolds.

At times, more information may be derived from the witness's body language than from his or her own words. You should learn to evaluate the body language as well as the testimony of a witness and make note of any discrepancies. You should also make notes regarding the **demeanor**, or appearance, of the witness. Would she make a good witness in court? Is he articulate or does he ramble on? Is she hostile? Your evaluation of a witness can be very helpful to an attorney.

Thoroughness is critical in a witness interview. Failure to be thorough can result in a witness's changing or adding to his or her testimony at the time of trial or deposition.

You should endeavor to obtain the most complete information about the client's claim as possible. Also, keep in mind that the rules of evidence generally do not allow an attorney to introduce a written witness statement at trial unless the witness is present in court and testifies in person. If a witness is unavailable at the time of trial, there is, however, a way of presenting that testimony to the court. A formal deposition (as described in Chapters 8 and 9) can be taken. At the time of the interview, therefore, you should determine whether the interviewee would be willing to testify at trial. You should also ask whether the witness plans to leave the area or might be unavailable at the time of trial for some other reason. The attorney can then take steps to legally preserve his or her testimony for trial.

When the interview concludes, prepare a narrative summary of the interview. This summary is then presented to the witness to read and sign, verifying its accuracy. Though a signed statement is not admissible as evidence at trial, even if it is signed under penalty of perjury, it can be used to attack a witness's credibility if the witness changes his or her testimony.

EVIDENCE

If a case goes to trial, parties must prove the allegations in their pleadings. They do this by presenting relevant and admissible information or evidence. Evidence takes many forms. At the trial of the *Saldivar* case, the finder of fact (judge or jury) will listen to the testimony of the witnesses, consider the documents, view photographs, and see charts or slide presentations. All of these are forms of evidence.

Proper investigation of any case requires a basic understanding of certain rules of evidence (either state or federal rules, depending on the court in which the matter is filed). These rules ultimately determine what information can be used at trial. Investigation of a case requires the paralegal to obtain information that will be admissible at trial. This does not mean, however, that an investigator should ignore inadmissible evidence; such evidence might lead to other important and admissible evidence.

Direct Evidence versus Circumstantial Evidence

Evidence may be either direct or circumstantial. **Direct evidence** is evidence that a witness personally observed, and which, if believed, directly establishes a fact. For example, consider the following situation. Pederson and Denton are involved in an intersection automobile accident. Waters, a fact witness, might testify that he personally observed Denton enter the intersection without stopping for a stop sign. This is direct evidence of the fact that Denton was at fault for the accident. **Circumstantial evidence** is evidence that does not directly establish a disputed fact. This type of evidence, however, often leads a judge or jury to infer a particular conclusion about the disputed facts. For example, in the case of Pederson and Denton, the witness might not have observed Pederson for sufficient time to have judged his speed. However evidence might be introduced that skid marks left by Pederson indicate he was traveling in excess of the posted speed limit. A jury could draw an inference that Pederson's speed may have contributed to the accident. Both direct and circumstantial evidence are important in proving your client's case.

direct evidence
Proof that establishes a fact without the necessity of other evidence or the drawing of inferences.

circumstantial evidence
Indirect evidence that helps to prove a fact, often requiring the trier of fact to draw reasonable and logical inferences.

presumption
A conclusion or assumption of fact that the law requires to be made from the proof of another fact. Presumptions can be rebuttable or conclusive.

judicial notice
A court's acceptance of the truth of a fact without the necessity of evidence, often because the facts are official acts or are so universally known that they cannot reasonably be disputed.

electronically stored information (ESI)
Computer-generated records such as those found in e-mail files, databases, calendaring programs, and all other relevant data files created by spreadsheets, word processing, or any analogous program.

Forms of Evidence

In any trial, attorneys use various forms of evidence to prove the elements of their case. For example, if the *Saldivar* case were to go to trial, the attorneys would have witnesses testify. They would present medical and employment records. They might also have old photographs of the warehouse and/or documents related to the construction, repair, and eventual destruction of the building. These documents might be in paper or electronic format. They might even have a piece of the building material that contained asbestos. The different forms of evidence would thus be testimony, photographs, and documents, both in paper and electronic format, and "real evidence"—an actual object that is offered as proof of an issue in the case. Testimony is the most common form of evidence and consists of statements made under penalty of perjury by witnesses in response to questions by the attorneys.

Other forms of evidence include demonstrative evidence, presumptions, and judicial notice. Demonstrative evidence consists of objects or items created for trial for illustrative purposes. For example, this might include diagrams, charts, summaries of evidence, or even a skeleton model. A recent trend in the use of demonstrative evidence is the production of animated, three-dimensional videos. Trial lawyers frequently use presentation software, such as PowerPoint, to help illustrate various points.

Presumptions and judicial notice are referred to as forms of evidence because they are ways that attorneys have of proving a point. However, they are very different from the forms of evidence that we see or hear. In a sense, these are legal ways of proving points without testimony or physical evidence. A **presumption** is a rule of law that allows the trier of fact to draw an inference—because one fact has been established by traditional evidence another fact also exists. For example, in many jurisdictions, if a party can prove that a letter was mailed, the jury can draw an inference (presume) that it was received. It is important to remember, however, that many presumptions can be rebutted or disproved by other evidence. **Judicial notice** allows a court to find that certain facts are true without the parties presenting evidence of the fact. Courts take judicial notice of facts that are commonly known or accepted. According to Federal Rules of Evidence, Rule 201, a court can take judicial notice of a fact not subject to reasonable dispute in that it is either (1) generally known within the territorial jurisdiction of the trial court or (2) capable of accurate and ready determination by resort to sources whose accuracy cannot reasonably be questioned.

Recently, the courts (and the Federal Rules of Civil Procedure) have specifically identified **electronically stored information (ESI)** as a form of evidence. Electronically stored information includes documents created on computers, e-mails, Web pages, and any other form of electronically created or stored information. See Exhibit 4-12 for a list of the forms of evidence.

Your role as a paralegal in the sample Commentary case would be to actively seek and maintain all of the evidence, whether in the form of fact, documents, or expert witness testimony. This might involve locating a copy of the client's employment records or finding an elusive witness who had knowledge of the existence of asbestos in Mr. Saldivar's workplace. It might also involve organizing, categorizing, and summarizing documents. The issue of whether evidence, once obtained, is admissible is an important one. To determine whether a particular piece of evidence, verbal or written, is admissible requires knowledge of the appropriate rules of evidence.

EXHIBIT 4-12 Forms of Evidence

FORMS OF EVIDENCE	
• Testimony	Statements from witnesses made under penalty of perjury
• Documentary	Documents such as medical or employment records; e-mails or other correspondence
• Real Evidence	A physical object used as proof of an issue
• Demonstrative	An item created for trial such as photographs, models, video, or PowerPoints
• Presumptions	Inferences allowed by law
• Judicial Notice	Allows the court to accept the truth of certain facts because the facts are common knowledge or are found in irrefutable sources
• Electronically Stored Information	Information created or stored in electronic format

Copyright © 2015 Cengage Learning®

Federal Rules of Evidence

The Federal Rules of Evidence govern the admissibility of evidence in civil and criminal cases in federal court. Although these rules do not apply in state courts, many states have patterned their state evidence rules after the Federal Rules of Evidence. The purposes of the Federal Rules of Evidence are set out in Rule 102: "These rules should be construed so as to administer every proceeding fairly, eliminate unjustifiable expense and delay, and promote the development of evidence law, to the end of ascertaining the truth and securing a just determination." A complete discussion of the rules of evidence and exceptions is impossible within this chapter or even this book. You will be introduced only to the general principles of the rules of evidence, including an overview of some specific rules of evidence that commonly affect litigation.

Relevancy

To be admissible, evidence must be **relevant**. Rule 401 states that "Evidence is relevant if (a) it has any tendency to make any fact more or less probable than it would be without the evidence and (b) the fact is of consequence in determining the action." No one piece of evidence need be sufficient in itself to persuade the judge or jury that a particular fact is true. It must only support the existence of the particular fact. In determining relevancy, a question often arises regarding background facts that may be necessary or helpful in understanding the ultimate disputed fact. For example, in the *Saldivar* case, the defense attorney might have evidence that Mr. Saldivar frequents gambling establishments on a regular basis. Obviously this has nothing to do with the facts of the case and, standing alone, would not be admissible. However, if the attorney can show that the gambling establishment has posted a warning about the presence of asbestos in the building's ceiling, then the fact that Mr. Saldivar gambles frequently can be introduced as evidence that he has been exposed to asbestos outside the workplace.

relevant evidence
Evidence that tends to prove or disprove any fact that is of consequence to the determination of the action.

The following facts generally are found to be irrelevant and inadmissible:

1. Subsequent remedial measures: Where an injury occurs because of some defective or dangerous property, the fact that the condition was repaired is not generally admissible.

2. Offer to compromise the claim: A party's offer to settle or compromise a claim is not admissible.

3. Promise to pay medical or other expenses: This is similar to a party's offer to settle and is not admissible as evidence of liability.

4. Existence of liability insurance: Whether or not one has insurance is not relevant to the issue of liability or damages.

However, not all relevant evidence is admissible evidence. Rule 402 specifically provides that relevant evidence can be made inadmissible by the United States Constitution, by any federal statute, by the Rules of Evidence, or by other rules prescribed by the Supreme Court pursuant to statutory authority. As a result, there are several instances in which relevant evidence is not admissible at trial. In a civil trial, two of the most important rules affecting the admissibility of relevant evidence are Rule 403 and the hearsay rule, Rules 801–807. Rule 403 permits exclusion of relevant evidence if "its probative value is substantially outweighed by a danger of one or more of the following: unfair prejudice, confusing the issues, misleading the jury, undue delay, wasting time, or needlessly presenting cumulative evidence."

The judge determines whether the negative aspects of the evidence outweigh its probative value. The hearsay rule is discussed in more detail in a later section of this chapter.

Evidence of Character and Habit

Rules 404 and 406 deal with the exclusion of another type of evidence that many consider relevant—**character evidence**. Character evidence includes testimony about a person's reputation in the community or whether the person is felt by friends and coworkers to be honest or dishonest. In a civil case, character evidence is not admissible if its purpose is to prove that an individual "acted in conformity" with his or her normal character traits on a particular occasion. Under Rule 406, evidence to establish **habit**—how a person responds to a particular situation—may be admissible if it develops sufficient evidence of a repeated pattern of behavior to the extent that it is an automatic response (e.g., unplugging the coffeemaker after pouring the last cup of coffee).

Documentary Evidence

Documentary evidence presents several evidentiary issues. Like all evidence, it must be relevant and not otherwise inadmissible (i.e., it must comply with all the rules of admissibility, including the hearsay rule). In addition, before documentary evidence will be admitted, the document must be authenticated and must meet the requirements of the best evidence rule.

Authentication
Rule 901(a) of the Federal Rules of Evidence describes the requirement of authentication (or identification) of a document. The person presenting the document as evidence must establish that the document is what it purports to be—a contract, warranty, deed, and so forth. This is called *authenticating* the document.

Many examples of methods of authentication are found in Rule 901(b), including testimony of witnesses with knowledge of the genuineness of the document, nonexpert opinion regarding handwriting, voice identification, telephone conversation, and public records or reports. For example, an individual who knew a decedent and often corresponded with him might be able to identify and authenticate a handwritten will. The witness would not have to be a handwriting expert; she would need only a basis for being able to identify the handwriting. Public records may be authenticated through testimony of an employee of the public office that the document in fact came from that office.

Because of its nature, electronic evidence presents potential problems with authenticity. However, it is subject to the same rules as any type of evidence.

Self-Authentication

Rule 902 of the Federal Rules of Evidence permits self-authentication of certain documents without the required testimony of a witness to establish that authenticity. The following types of documents can usually be introduced without any testimony or other evidence showing authenticity:

- public documents,
- certified copies of public records,
- official (government) publications,
- newspapers and periodicals,
- trade inscriptions,
- acknowledged (notarized) documents, and
- commercial paper and related documents.

Remember, however, that just because a document is properly authenticated does not mean that the document is admissible. It must satisfy all the conditions of admissibility.

Best Evidence Rule

At one time, the best evidence rule provided that, in trial, parties had to present the original of any document rather than a copy, unless the original was unavailable. Although the Federal Rules of Evidence do have a rule requiring the original document (Rule 1002), this rule is qualified and parties are often allowed to use copies rather than originals of documents. Unless there is a question regarding the genuineness of the document or unless introduction of a copy would be unfair, the original of the document is not required (Rule 1003). In addition, even when the genuineness is in issue, a copy might be introduced in some situations such as when the original is unavailable or has been destroyed (Rule 1004). As a litigation paralegal, you should take particular care to obtain and safeguard original documents.

Scientific Evidence and Expert Witnesses

Scientific evidence plays an important role in many lawsuits. For many years the test of admissibility was whether the evidence was based on established legal principles that were generally accepted within the scientific community. This test stemmed from a 1923 appellate case, *Frye v. United States*. In 1993, in *Daubert v. Merrell Dow Pharmaceuticals, Inc.*,

hearsay
A statement made out of court used to prove the truth of what was said.

the United States Supreme Court interpreted Federal Rule of Evidence 702 and established a different test for the admissibility of scientific evidence, stating:

> "General acceptance" is not a necessary precondition to the admissibility of scientific evidence under the Federal Rules of Evidence, but the Rules of Evidence—especially Rule 702—do assign to the trial judge the task of ensuring that an expert's testimony both rests on a reliable foundation and is relevant to the task at hand. Pertinent evidence based on scientifically valid principles will satisfy those demands.

Rule 702 allows an expert to testify as to scientific evidence when:

(a) the expert's scientific, technical, or other specialized knowledge will help the trier of fact to understand the evidence or to determine a fact in issue;
(b) the testimony is based on sufficient facts or data;
(c) the testimony is the product of reliable principles and methods; and
(d) the expert has reliably applied the principles and methods to the facts of the case.

Before allowing an expert to present scientific evidence, the trial court may hold a prior hearing to determine if the requirements of Rule 702 are met.

Hearsay Rule

One of the most involved rules of evidence is the hearsay rule. **Hearsay** is generally defined as an out-of-court statement introduced in court and offered to prove the truth of the statement made. It is generally a statement made by someone other than the person actually testifying in court. Hearsay includes documents as well as oral statements. For example, if the attorney in the *Saldivar* case tried to introduce a written statement from a witness obtained through the investigative process, that written statement would be hearsay (and in this case probably inadmissible).

The hearsay rules are complex but basically provide that a hearsay statement is not admissible as evidence unless it meets one of the stated exceptions to the rule. The hearsay rule and its numerous exceptions are found in Rules 801–807 of the Federal Rules of Evidence.

The underlying principle in attempting to exclude hearsay is to further the underlying role of evidence—to ensure truthful testimony at trial. In the courtroom, the attorneys for all parties have the opportunity to examine and cross-examine. Hearsay testimony does not afford that opportunity and creates an atmosphere of unfairness. On the other hand, the various exceptions to the hearsay rule include situations where truthfulness is likely to be present.

Exceptions to Hearsay

Rules 803 and 804 of the Federal Rules of Evidence list the exceptions to the hearsay rule. You should be careful not to assume that a statement is automatically admissible because it fits an exception to the hearsay rule. Testimony must still comply with the other rules of evidence discussed earlier in this chapter, including relevancy. Some of the more frequently encountered exceptions to hearsay include the following:

1. Excited utterance—Rule 803(2). Because of the excitement, the person making the statement is presumed to have had no time to fabricate the statement. Consider the following example. A police officer is called to a domestic disturbance. Upon arriving

at the residence, the officer hears a gunshot and rushes into the residence, where he sees Harry lying on the ground, bleeding profusely. When Harry sees the officer, he exclaims, "Wanda tried to kill me!" If Wanda is prosecuted for attempted murder, the police officer can testify as to what Harry told him because, even though it is hearsay, it is an excited utterance.

2. Existing mental, emotional, or physical condition (state of mind)—Rule 803(3). Statements that show the declarant's state of mind, emotion, or physical condition are admissible. This includes statements that show intent, plan, motive, mental feeling, or pain.

3. Statements made for the purpose of medical diagnosis or treatment—Rule 803(4). Patients seeking treatment from a doctor are presumed to be more likely to tell the doctor the truth to obtain appropriate treatment.

4. Business records—Rule 803(6). Records kept in the course of regular business activity generally fall within this exception, under the theory that businesses require accurate records for their operations.

5. Unavailability of person who made statement—Rule 804. Under some circumstances, certain types of hearsay are admissible if the person who made the statement is unavailable for trial. A witness is considered unavailable for trial only for the following reasons: death or illness, assertion of a privilege and refusal to testify, or inability of the court to secure the presence of that person at trial. Under these circumstances, if the witness had given prior testimony either at a hearing or a deposition, that prior testimony is admissible if the party against whom the testimony is offered had the opportunity to question the witness. As a paralegal, you should be aware that the attorney cannot unilaterally decide to use a witness's deposition in lieu of subpoenaing the witness to testify. The deposition is hearsay and therefore not admissible unless the witness is unavailable or all parties agree that it may be used.

6. Statements against interest—Rule 804(b)(3). When a person has made a statement against his or her legal, business, or financial interests, that statement is presumed to be true because it is assumed that the person would have no reason to make up detrimental statements against himself or herself.

One of the important elements of the definition of hearsay is that the out-of-court statement is used to prove the truth of the statement made. Therefore, if the out-of-court statement is used for another purpose, it may be admissible. The most common example of this is a written statement of a witness. If introduced to prove the truth of the statement, it is hearsay. However, if the witness testifies at trial and gives testimony that conflicts with the written statement, the out-of-court statement can be used to impeach the credibility of the witness. Consider the following. Sheppard witnesses an automobile accident between Hart and Mobley. Shortly after the accident Sheppard is interviewed by a paralegal in the law firm representing Hart. After the interview Sheppard signs a written statement indicating that Mobley ran a red light. If an attorney for Hart tried to admit that written statement at trial in an effort to prove that Mobley did in fact run the red light, the statement would be hearsay. (It was made out of court and is used to prove the truth of the statement.) However, if Sheppard testifies at trial, and denies that Mobley ran a red light, the attorney for Hart can use the statement to impeach Mobley's credibility, showing that at some point he told a different story.

Privileged Communications

Rule 501 of the Federal Rules of Evidence delegates to the courts and state legislatures the responsibility of developing rules for evidence protected by privilege. However, Rule 502 deals with situations in which inadvertent disclosure is made of material protected by the attorney–client or work product privileges. Rule 502 is a result of many of the problems that occur during discovery of electronically stored information. The paralegal is charged with the responsibility of helping the attorney ensure that protected information or evidence is not disclosed during litigation. Chapters 8 through 13 discuss at length the privileges that may be asserted during the discovery process, including attorney–client, husband–wife, physician–patient, and work product privileges.

State Rules of Evidence

In the *Saldivar* case, you would need to look at your state's statutes to determine the pertinent rules of evidence. Often the state will publish a compilation of all of its rules, including rules of civil procedure, appellate procedure, and so on.

Additional Resources Relating to Evidence

There are several excellent commentaries and treatises on the subject of evidence, including *Wigmore on Evidence* and *McCormick on Evidence.* Check a law library to locate additional information on evidence.

See Exhibit 4-13 for a list of some of the Federal Rules of Evidence.

EXHIBIT 4-13 Some Important Federal Rules of Evidence

Rule 102	Federal Rules of Evidence should be interpreted to secure fairness and avoid unnecessary delay and expense.
Rules 401–403	Relevant evidence is that which tends to prove a fact; to be admissible, evidence must be relevant; relevant evidence may be inadmissible if a judge decides the probative value is outweighed by unfair prejudice or undue delay.
Rules 404–406	Evidence of character is generally not admissible, but evidence to establish a habit may be admissible.
Rule 501	Delegates to states the responsibility of defining evidentiary privileges.
Rule 702	Sets out the requirements for scientific evidence and expert witness testimony
Rules 802–807	Definition of hearsay; hearsay is inadmissible unless it falls within one of numerous exceptions, which include excited utterances, state of mind, statements made for purpose of medical diagnosis or treatment, business records, unavailability of witness, and statement against interest.
Rules 901 & 902	In addition to other requirements, documentary evidence must be properly authenticated.
Rules 1002–1004	Best Evidence Rule; explains when an original of a document is required and when a copy can be used.

METHODS FOR LOCATING AND PRESERVING EVIDENCE

Coworkers and other fact witnesses are essential to Mr. Saldivar's case. However, testimony from witnesses is only one kind of evidence that can be used to prove a case. Written documents, photographs, and items of personal property are often introduced as evidence at trial to prove the facts of the case. In the situation described in the Commentary, evidence such as photographs, architectural drawings and building permits related to the warehouse, medical records of Mr. Saldivar, Environmental Protection Agency reports or citations, and plant safety programs are all critical. Your attorney may ask that you take responsibility for locating and organizing all available evidence.

Documents relating to your client, such as his medical bills or records and his employment records, are usually easy to obtain. If you have an authorization for the release of this information signed by the client, you can obtain these documents by sending a copy of that release to the appropriate person or business. For other types of evidence, a telephone call or letter may suffice; if it does not, a subpoena and deposition may be required. Moreover, any evidence in the possession or control of a defendant will have to be obtained through the proper discovery process. These methods are discussed in detail in subsequent chapters.

See Exhibit 4-14 for a checklist of sources of evidence in a typical personal injury case.

Court Records—PACER

An important method for locating evidence is checking court records. If any of the parties have been involved in similar cases, court records might reveal this. For example, if a plaintiff has filed prior lawsuits for similar injuries, this could be important to the case.

EXHIBIT 4-14 Sources of Evidence in a Personal Injury Case

Police Reports—Local, county, or state police and Department of Motor Vehicles

Automobile Ownership—Department of Motor Vehicles

Insurance Coverage—State Department of Insurance and Department of Motor Vehicles

Weather Reports—U.S. Weather Bureau

Fire Reports—Fire marshal

Aviation Records (on accidents or safety standards)—Federal Aviation Administration

Property Ownership or Taxes—Local tax assessor's office and State Department of Revenue

Birth and Death Records—Bureau of Vital Statistics and local coroner's office

Medical Treatment—Doctor, hospital, ambulance company, X-ray firm, and physical therapist

Personal Data—Registrar of Voters, criss-cross directories, U.S. Post Office, Social Security office, county court records (including judgments and/or liens, criminal, marriage, and divorce), and the Internet

Newspaper or Publicity—Local newspapers and television stations, archives of local library, and the Internet

Likewise, if a defendant has been sued previously this might also be important. While an attorney may not be able to refer to prior lawsuits at trial, knowledge about these can lead to other admissible evidence.

Court records are generally public records and therefore accessible to the public. Today, many courts include some or all of their court documents on their Web sites. The federal courts have a central system through which individuals can access federal court documents. The system is known as PACER, Public Access to Court Electronic Records. This system allows the public to electronically *access* case information concerning cases filed in federal courts. Generally this includes the identities of the parties, the attorneys, and a list of documents filed by the court. In many cases, use of the PACER system allows the user to see actual documents filed in the case by the attorneys (e.g., complaints, answers, and motions). Additional information about this system can be found at <http://www.pacer.gov>.

Evidence Control and Retrieval

You have assembled evidence to help substantiate Mr. Saldivar's claim. This evidence includes old photographs and building permits related to the warehouse, and copies of Mr. Saldivar's X-rays. To avoid charges by the opposition that the evidence has been tampered with or replaced, each piece of evidence should be tracked from its receipt by your law firm until its final introduction as a trial exhibit. Evidence should be marked to indicate its source, date of acquisition, and storage location. An **evidence log** will enable you to maintain an accurate record of the evidence, including any transfer of custody. Each time the evidence is removed from its storage location, the removal should be documented on the evidence log. Exhibit 4-15 shows a suggested form for an evidence log.

Complex litigation sometimes presents extra challenges for evidence control and production. Cases often involve hundreds or thousands of documents and may have many attorneys, located in different cities, working on the same case. A paralegal coordinating

EXHIBIT 4-15 Evidence Log

STYLE OF CASE: _____

EVIDENCE: _____

DATE ACQUIRED: _____ ACQUIRED BY:_____

MANNER BY WHICH ACQUIRED: _____

_____

PARTICULAR IDENTIFYING MARKS: _____

LOCATIONS OF EVIDENCE: _____

EVIDENCE CUSTODIAN: _____

CHAIN OF EVIDENCE CUSTODY:

RELEASED TO   DATE   PURPOSE OF RELEASE

_____

_____

_____

_____

such a case must be concerned with how to store the documents, where to store the documents, and how to make them available to multiple attorneys who may be geographically separated. One solution is to scan the documents, convert them to electronic format, and store them on a secure Internet site (the "cloud").

Another concern is that documents be organized in such a way that they can be easily retrieved when the opposing side requests specific documents during the discovery process. (Discovery is covered in subsequent chapters in this text.) A common practice has been to create a searchable database with relevant fields or features. Features, or database fields, might describe the date of creation, the author, or the subject matter. Because the database is easily searchable, documents meeting certain criteria can be easily identified. For example, if an attorney were looking for all documents written between certain dates, he or she would search the field of the database containing the date of creation. This field would identify all documents created within the specified time frame. The documents could then be retrieved. This process is sometimes referred to as document coding.

Preservation of Evidence

The method for preserving evidence varies, depending on the nature of the evidence. Photographs tend to fade or be damaged by handling. X-rays require a special folder for preservation. An original $300,000 note may be maintained in the firm's vault, with a copy of the note retained in an envelope labeled with the location of the original.

Some forms of evidence do not lend themselves to storage in the law firm during lengthy litigation because of their size or daily use on a job site. Photographs of these exhibits may be taken and retained in the client's file for use in preparing the case for trial, at which time the original piece of evidence may be introduced.

Ensuring that evidence is preserved in its original form may be one of your responsibilities. Because of the varied nature of the evidence in Mr. Saldivar's case, in-depth research on preserving the evidence could be required.

Litigation Holds

To manage the storage of both print and electronic information, many businesses have document retention policies. At regular intervals older documents are destroyed. Paper documents may be shredded, and electronic documents deleted. In some instances, however, documents scheduled for destruction might be potential evidence in a lawsuit. When litigation becomes reasonably probable, the attorney for any company is obligated to instruct the company to preserve relevant documents. This is known as a litigation hold. Serious consequences follow if relevant documents are destroyed. This subject is discussed in subsequent chapters.

EXPERT WITNESSES

In a case involving technical or medical issues, **expert witnesses** are often necessary. Experts can perform several functions in a case. They can be hired in an advisory capacity to explain the technical aspects of the case to the attorney. More often, they are hired to be

expert witness
A person who possesses special knowledge on a topic because of education and/or experience. An expert witness is allowed to give opinion testimony concerning facts within his or her expertise.

witnesses during the trial. Before individuals are allowed to testify as experts, they must be qualified by the court to do so. In qualifying experts, the court looks at their education, skill, and experience in that field. If an individual is qualified as an expert, at trial this individual can explain and simplify complicated technical issues for the judge or jury. For example, a jury might have difficulty understanding the mechanical functions of a tire manufacturing plant or the significance of a lung X-ray. Expert witnesses may translate the technical language to easily understood language through photographs, charts, or models. Also, expert witnesses, unlike lay witnesses, are allowed to testify about their expert opinions regarding matters within their expertise. For example, in the *Saldivar* case, a proper expert could testify that in his opinion materials to which Mr. Saldivar was exposed at work caused mesothelioma.

The decision to hire an expert witness is made by the supervising attorney. However, you may be asked to locate an expert. Suggested sources for locating potential experts include:

- professional organizations,
- published court records of experts,
- other attorneys in your office,
- colleges or universities,
- professional journals,
- attorneys who have handled similar litigation, and
- the Internet.

If the expert has testified in prior cases, you might wish to talk to the attorney who tried the case to get an evaluation of the expert's ability as a witness. The demeanor of an expert witness can be even more important than that of a lay witness. Although the expert's professional credentials are important, his or her ability to explain matters to a judge or jury in a simple and clear manner, without appearing condescending, is just as important.

Once you have located an expert, you must keep certain practical considerations in mind. An expert's time is very valuable, and use of that time by your law firm can be expensive. Most experts charge the firm not only for the time they spend testifying in court, but also for any time spent in talking to the attorneys (or paralegals). Any interview of an expert must be carefully orchestrated to maximize the expert's time. Preparation in advance of the interview will obviate the need for a lengthy interview process. Know ahead of time what areas should be covered and make notes. Also, if the expert is local, arranging the interview to take place at the expert's place of business can save time and therefore expense.

One pitfall to avoid in securing an expert witness is the "professional testifying expert." An excessive number of court appearances can have a negative impact on the jury, especially if that expert has always testified for the plaintiff or for the defendant. An expert whose testimony has been balanced will be more effective.

Before deciding to use a particular expert, you should review the expert's résumé and determine whether he or she has testified in prior cases. If he or she has qualified as an expert in prior cases, he or she is likely to be qualified by the court in your case. You should also review all prior cases to make sure that he or she has not given testimony that would contradict the testimony he or she expects to give in your case.

FINDING IT on the Internet

The Internet provides numerous sources to help litigation paralegals with the matters discussed in this chapter. The Federal Rules of Evidence can be found at **<http://www.law.cornell.edu>** (click on "Federal Rules"). They can also be found through **<http://www.uscourts.gov>** (click on "Rules and Policies," then on "Federal Rules of Practice and Procedure" then on "Current Rules of Practice and Procedure"). When accessing the federal rules through the Internet, make certain that you have accessed the current version. Older versions are posted in PDF format.

Experts can be located through numerous sources on the Internet, including **<http://www.expert4law .org>**" and **<http://www.medicalexperts.com/>** Information about expert witnesses can also be found at **<http://law.lexisnexis.com/infopro/zimmermans/>**

a. Access the Web site for the National Library of Medicine (**<http://www.nlm.nih.gov>**). Locate information about asbestos and write a memo summarizing findings that would be relevant to the *Saldivar* case described at the beginning of this chapter.

b. Using any of the above sites, or a general search engine, locate information about experts who might be helpful to the *Saldivar* case. Make a list of experts and their areas of expertise.

c. Access the Web site for the Environmental Protection Agency (EPA) (**<http://www.epa.gov>**). Using the search feature on the EPA page, find information about asbestos. Write a brief memo summarizing information that might be helpful to the *Saldivar* case.

Your responsibilities in the area of expert witnesses may include locating an expert, coordinating the interview of the expert witness with the attorney, taking notes during an interview, reviewing the qualifications of the expert, reviewing prior testimony of the expert, and, if the expert is located some distance away, handling hotel and air travel reservations.

SUMMARY

- A client interview establishes the foundation for the relationship between the client and the law firm. The paralegal is often involved in several different aspects of this procedure. Paralegal responsibilities might include researching potential causes of action or defenses prior to the interview, scheduling the interview, developing an interview questionnaire, gathering forms and documents for client signature, taking notes during the interview, and producing a summary of the interview. During and after the initial interview, a paralegal should always maintain a professional demeanor.

- Locating witnesses who have knowledge of the facts of the case is an essential part of the litigation process and is often a paralegal function. Likewise, locating the defendant in the action is a task often assigned to paralegals. Various sources exist to help the paralegal find witnesses or elusive defendants. Some of those sources include the client, the Internet, accident reports, and official records.

- When interviewing fact witnesses, a paralegal should always be properly identified. The paralegal should always be courteous and consider the convenience of the witness. Tape-recorded interviews are preferred, but if the witness objects, a written statement or notes can be used. A questionnaire should be prepared before the interview, and care should be taken during the interview itself to avoid leading questions. After the interview, the paralegal should prepare a typewritten statement for signature by the witness. During the interview, the paralegal should observe and make note of the witness's demeanor.

- Rules of evidence dictate what facts, documents, and other evidence will be allowed at trial. In federal court, these rules are found in the Federal Rules of Evidence. To be admissible, evidence must be relevant—that is, tending to prove a fact that is important to the case—and not otherwise objectionable. Evidence is objectionable if its probative value is outweighed by undue prejudice or consumption of time; if it is documentary evidence and has not been properly authenticated; if it violates the best evidence rule; if it violates the hearsay rule and is not subject to one of the many exceptions; or if it is a privileged communication.

- Paralegals are often involved in locating, preserving, and organizing evidence in a civil case. Evidence includes documents or other items that tend to prove the facts of the case. Items of evidence relating to the client can often be obtained by a simple request accompanied by a signed release from the client. In other situations, formal discovery methods must be utilized. After evidence is obtained, proper care must be taken to control and preserve the evidence for trial. To avoid charges that evidence has been altered, the chain of possession of the evidence must be verified.

- Expert witnesses are often essential in a case. They are able to explain technical matters to a judge or jury and can offer their professional opinions regarding issues in the case. Paralegals are sometimes asked to locate experts, coordinate interviews between the expert and the attorney, take notes during the interview, review the qualifications and prior testimony of the expert, and handle hotel and air travel reservations.

KEY TERMS

agent for service of process	evidence log	presumption
authorization	expert witness	release
character evidence	habit	relevant evidence
circumstantial evidence	hearsay	representation letter
demeanor	judicial notice	retainer agreement
direct evidence	leading question	
electronically stored information (ESI)	medical diary	

REVIEW QUESTIONS

1. What are the paralegal's responsibilities in preparing for the client interview?
2. What are the steps in setting up a client interview?
3. What types of questions should be included in a client interview questionnaire?
4. What forms might be needed during the client interview for client signature?
5. Describe the demeanor that a paralegal should maintain during and after the initial interview.
6. What are some possible sources for locating fact witnesses or elusive defendants?
7. Describe the various objections to admissibility of evidence.
8. What are the methods for locating, controlling, and preserving evidence?
9. What is the importance of the expert witness?
10. What is the paralegal's role in retaining an expert witness?

CHAPTER EXERCISES

Where necessary, check with your instructor prior to starting any of these exercises.

1. Review the Commentary at the opening of this chapter and draft questions for your attorney to ask at the initial interview.
2. Assume that you are to interview one of Arturo Saldivar's former coworkers. Draft a questionnaire to be used during the interview.
3. You have been asked to assist the attorney in finding an expert witness to help establish that Saldivar's work environment contributed to the mesothelioma. Identify and locate places in your general area where you might find such an expert.
4. When you review the *Saldivar* file (Commentary), you find the following items. Discuss whether they are admissible pieces of evidence and, if so, how they could be authenticated. If there are any hearsay problems, be sure to include that in your analysis.
   a. old photographs of the warehouse
   b. a letter from Peter Wayans, president of Greenwood Properties, Inc., apologizing to Saldivar for his company's involvement in his illness
   c. a letter from Greenwood's insurance company stating that they were handling the claim
   d. a recorded statement from Joseph Polizo, a coworker of Saldivar
   e. a deposition of Joseph Polizo
   f. copies of Saldivar's medical bills
   g. copies of Saldivar's medical records
   h. a report from the EPA detailing the hazards of exposure to asbestos
5. What types of demonstrative evidence might be created for trial in the *Saldivar* case?

CHAPTER PROJECT

For this project you need to work with another student in the class. One of you should assume the role of a former coworker of Arturo Saldivar, while the other assumes the role of a paralegal working in the firm representing Mr. Saldivar. The "paralegal" is to conduct a tape-recorded interview of the coworker. After the interview is recorded, both students should prepare a typewritten statement of the interview.

THE *BENNETT* CASE
Assignment for Chapter 4:

1. Prepare a list and description of the types and sources of evidence you might expect to find in the *Bennett* case. (Review Exhibit 4-14 for an example.)
2. Draft a questionnaire for the initial interview of Alice Bennett.
3. List the type of documents you would want to obtain from your client, Alice Bennett.

THE *DOUGLASS FINANCIAL SERVICES, INC.* CASE
Assignment for Chapter 4:

1. Gretchen Reily, the attorney for Douglass Financial Services, has scheduled an interview of one of Portman's coworkers. Prepare a list of interview questions for this witness.
2. List the types of demonstrative evidence Douglass Financial Services might use at trial. Describe your role as a paralegal in obtaining or creating this type of evidence.

The Complaint

CHAPTER OUTLINE

THE *HENDRICKS* CASE

Your attorney has just given you a file containing the preliminary investigative reports and notes concerning new clients Margaret and Paul Hendricks. After reviewing the various documents in the file, and after discussing the matter with your attorney, you learn the following facts. While vacationing in Nevada, the Hendrickses, residents of the state of California, attended a sales presentation regarding vacation property located in Idaho. During the sales presentation, which was conducted by May Forrester, a real estate agent with Hearth & Home Real Estate Company, the Hendrickses were shown numerous color slides of the vacation property, all depicting large, level lots surrounding a man-made lake. The lots were owned by Paradise Found, Inc., an Idaho corporation. The couple was told during the presentation that the lots were ready for building. The lots were offered for the price of $100,000 and only two lots remained unsold—and the realtor expected these to go quickly. Swayed by the sales presentation, the Hendrickses purchased a lot without personally visiting the site. They paid cash and received a deed. Shortly thereafter they visited the property in Idaho, only to find that the lot they owned was nothing like the photos they had seen. The lake was completely dry, no building had occurred, and in fact a great deal of preparation would have to be done before any building could begin. There were no utilities, sewers, or roads. The Hendrickses immediately contacted the realtor, May Forrester, the company she works for, Hearth & Home Real Estate Company, and the seller of the property, Paradise Found, Inc. The sellers refused to return the Hendrickses' money. The file also indicates that Hearth & Home Real Estate Company is a partnership owned by Harry and Harvey Rice. Your attorney is anxious to initiate a lawsuit in this matter and asked you to prepare a complaint for his review, naming all proper parties and containing all possible causes of action.

Chapter 4 introduced the methods for obtaining information necessary to pursue a lawsuit. After that information is obtained, the next step in the litigation process is the preparation and filing of the initial pleadings. After reading this chapter, you should be able to:

- define the term *pleadings*.
- describe, in general, the contents of a complaint.
- discuss the various considerations in determining and identifying parties to the lawsuit.
- analyze the various allegations found in a complaint.
- explain the types of relief that can be requested in a complaint.
- draft a complaint.
- explain the process of filing a complaint.
- define a summons.
- list the different methods of serving a complaint.
- describe the procedure for amending a complaint.

THE NATURE AND PURPOSE OF PLEADINGS

After completing the preliminary investigation, interviews, and research, the attorney determines whether to pursue the case. If the decision is made to proceed, the litigation process formally begins and each party files pleadings in court. **Pleadings** are the various documents filed in a court proceeding that define the nature of the dispute between the parties. Not all documents filed with the court are pleadings. The term *pleading* technically refers only to papers that contain statements, or **allegations**, describing the contentions and defenses of the parties to the lawsuit.

Unless a defendant defaults, both the plaintiff and the defendant file pleadings with the court:

- The plaintiff files the first pleading, a complaint (or sometimes a petition), stating the basis for the lawsuit.
- The defendant files an answer (or sometimes a response), responding to the complaint.
- If appropriate, the defendant also files related claims against the plaintiff, other defendants, or third parties.
- If necessary, the plaintiff, codefendants, or third parties reply or respond to a defendant's claims.

All of these documents contain either contentions or defenses of the parties. (Chapter 6 discusses the various pleadings filed by a defendant.) The pleadings set the framework for all of the steps and proceedings that follow. If an issue is not raised in the pleadings, the parties may be prevented from bringing it up at trial. Although pleadings relate to contentions of the parties, these documents are always prepared by the law firm representing the party. As a paralegal in a litigation firm, one of your duties might include drafting these documents. You might also be asked to review pleadings prepared by the opposing side.

The content and format of the various pleadings are largely controlled by the appropriate statutory law or rules of court. Cases filed in federal court are governed primarily by the Federal Rules of Civil Procedure. Cases filed in a state court are governed by the laws of the state. In addition to state rules, many county or area courts have their own individual rules, known as local rules of court. Within the federal court system, various district courts also have local rules. Local rules can differ from one court to another, even if the courts are located in the same state. Before preparing or filing any pleading, therefore, you must check all local rules. In spite of the numerous technical rules that govern pleadings, most courts take a liberal attitude in reviewing or judging the sufficiency of the documents. Courts usually prefer that the parties resolve their disputes on the merits of the case rather than on some technical rule regarding the format of a document.

THE ELEMENTS AND FORMAT OF A COMPLAINT

Generally, to start court proceedings, a plaintiff prepares and files a complaint, or a petition. In the complaint the plaintiff states the basis for the lawsuit. The complaint does the following:

1. identifies the plaintiffs and defendants in the lawsuit, and describes their status and capacity to sue and be sued,

pleadings
Documents that describe the claims and defenses of a lawsuit, including the complaint and the answer to the complaint.

allegation
A contention or claim made within a pleading, regarding a fact that the party intends to prove at trial.

caption
The heading found in all pleadings, usually identifying the court, the parties, the nature of the pleading, and the docket number.

prayer
The part of the pleading (usually at the end) where the party asks the court to either grant or deny some relief.

subscription
A signature at the end of a document.

verification (verify)
Statement at the end of a document and under penalty of perjury that the contents of the document are true.

2. contains a statement showing that the court in which it is filed has proper jurisdiction and venue,

3. describes the factual basis for the lawsuit, and

4. requests or demands some relief from the court.

The complaint itself usually follows a set format with the following parts:

1. The **caption**—the part of the complaint that identifies the court in which the complaint is filed, the names of the plaintiffs and defendants, and the title of the document.

2. The allegations (or cause of action)—a description of the parties, statements showing proper jurisdiction and venue, the factual basis for the lawsuit, and a description of the loss or damages incurred.

3. The **prayer** or "wherefore" clause—a request for some relief or remedy from the court.

4. The **subscription**—the signature of the attorney filing the document and the date. The subscription also includes the address and e-mail address of the attorney.

See Exhibit 5-1 for an example of a simple complaint.

Some complaints also contain a **verification**, which is a statement signed under penalty of perjury by the plaintiff that the contents of the complaint are true. A verification is required for certain kinds of complaints.

Many complaints are much more involved than the one shown in Exhibit 5-1. For example, there may be multiple plaintiffs and defendants, and these parties may be individuals or business entities, possibly using a fictitious name. Some complaints contain several causes of action based on complicated factual situations. Before you begin to draft any complaint you should analyze your case, determine the purpose of your pleading, and outline the general content of your document. Specifically you should know:

- who will be named as parties and how they will be named,
- how you will show that jurisdiction and venue are proper,
- the type of claims or causes of action that will be included in the complaint, and
- the type of relief you are demanding.

Only after you have done this preliminary analysis should you begin to actually draft the complaint.

IDENTIFYING AND DESCRIBING THE PARTIES

The parties to the lawsuit are identified in the caption by their names, indicating whether they are plaintiff or defendant. In the body of the complaint, the parties are described in more detail.

Normally identifying the plaintiff and defendant in the caption is relatively simple. At times, however, problems arise. As a paralegal involved in preparing or drafting a complaint, you should be aware of some of these problem areas.

EXHIBIT 5-1 Example of a Simple Complaint

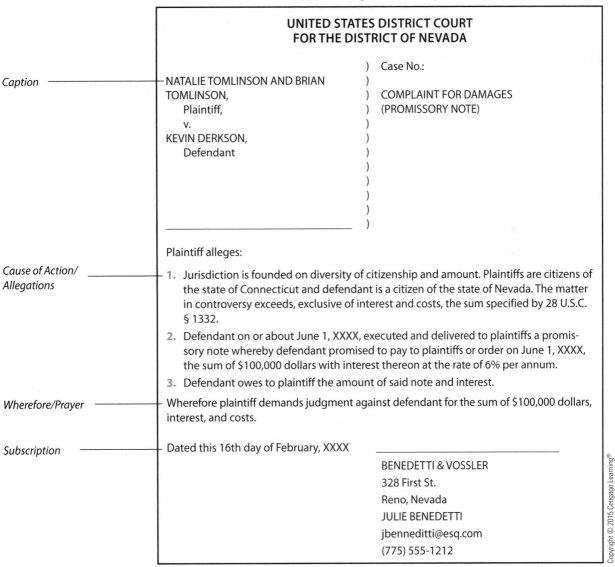

Caption

**UNITED STATES DISTRICT COURT
FOR THE DISTRICT OF NEVADA**

NATALIE TOMLINSON AND BRIAN TOMLINSON,
    Plaintiff,
    v.
KEVIN DERKSON,
    Defendant
	)
	)
	)
	)
	)
	)
	)
	)
	)
	)
	)
	)
	)
		Case No.:
		
		COMPLAINT FOR DAMAGES
		(PROMISSORY NOTE)

Plaintiff alleges:

Cause of Action/ Allegations

1. Jurisdiction is founded on diversity of citizenship and amount. Plaintiffs are citizens of the state of Connecticut and defendant is a citizen of the state of Nevada. The matter in controversy exceeds, exclusive of interest and costs, the sum specified by 28 U.S.C. § 1332.

2. Defendant on or about June 1, XXXX, executed and delivered to plaintiffs a promissory note whereby defendant promised to pay to plaintiffs or order on June 1, XXXX, the sum of $100,000 dollars with interest thereon at the rate of 6% per annum.

3. Defendant owes to plaintiff the amount of said note and interest.

Wherefore/Prayer

Wherefore plaintiff demands judgment against defendant for the sum of $100,000 dollars, interest, and costs.

Subscription

Dated this 16th day of February, XXXX

_____

BENEDETTI & VOSSLER
328 First St.
Reno, Nevada
JULIE BENEDETTI
jbenneditti@esq.com
(775) 555-1212

Real Party in Interest

The plaintiff in any lawsuit should be the one who is entitled to the relief sought in the complaint. This party is known as the **real party in interest**. In most cases, parties do not file lawsuits unless they have personally suffered some loss. However, at times a special relationship exists that creates a different situation. For example, an executor may want to sue on behalf of an estate, a trustee may sue on behalf of a trust, or a collection agency may

real party in interest
The person who is entitled to the relief requested in a complaint, even though not named as a plaintiff.

capacity
Having the legal ability to do something such as initiating a lawsuit.

guardian ad litem
A person who is appointed by the court to represent a party in a lawsuit, where the party lacks the capacity to file the action; guardians ad litem are usually appointed for minors or those who are mentally incapacitated.

wish to sue on a debt assigned to it for collection. In such cases, is the plaintiff the executor or the estate, the trustee or the trust, the collection agency or the creditor? Under Rule 17a of the Federal Rules of Civil Procedure, the executor, the trustee, and even the collection agency could be named as plaintiffs in the lawsuit even though they are not suing on their own behalf. However, if the action is in state court, appropriate state laws should always be checked.

Status

The *status* of a party refers to the type of entity that describes the party. Most commonly a party to a lawsuit is an individual, a corporation, a partnership or other unincorporated business, or a government agency. Unless a party is simply an individual, the status of the party is usually described both in the caption and in a separate allegation within the body of the complaint. For example, in the situation described in the Commentary to this chapter, if the Hendrickses were to sue the seller of the property, the seller would be identified in the caption as follows:

Example

	)
	)
v.	)
	)
PARADISE FOUND, INC., an Idaho	)
Corporation,	)
Defendant	)
	)

In addition, within the body of the complaint you would include a paragraph describing that status, such as the following:

Example

1. Defendant, PARADISE FOUND, INC., is and was at all times herein mentioned a corporation duly organized and existing under the laws of the state of Idaho.

Capacity

Minors and Incompetents

The parties named in the complaint must have **capacity**, or the legal right, to sue or be sued. Competent, adult individuals generally have the right to sue or be sued. However, children or incompetent adults do not have the capacity to pursue their own lawsuits. Unless a general guardian or conservator has already been appointed, the court will appoint a special person, referred to as a **guardian ad litem**, to pursue the case on behalf of the minor or incompetent. In many jurisdictions, even the parents of a child cannot file a lawsuit on their child's behalf unless they are appointed as guardians by the court. A guardian ad litem is usually appointed at the request of the parent or guardian. The person wishing to be appointed files a motion or a petition with the court prior to filing any lawsuit, asking to be named as guardian ad litem. The complaint in such a case has the same caption as the petition or motion for the appointment of the guardian. The following is an example of how the parties would be designated in such a case.

Example

MARY SMITH, a minor, by GEORGE SMITH, her guardian ad litem, Plaintiff	))))
v.	))
DEF CORPORATION, a California Corporation, Defendant	))))

AUTOMATED LITIGATION SUPPORT
Electronic Filing

SCENARIO

Your attorney is ready to file suit on behalf of the Hendrickses and asks you to prepare a draft of the complaint for fraud and negligent misrepresentation for his review. The attorney gives you the office file containing his detailed notes from interviews with the Hendrickses. He also gives you several letters written by the defendant that need to be attached to the complaint as exhibits. He reminds you to look at the rules of court and make sure that your complaint meets all of the requirements. Additionally, you are told that this complaint is to be electronically filed and this must be done before the end of the week.

PROBLEM

You have a great deal to do and very little time in which to do it. You must look in form books to find a form for a complaint for fraud and negligent misrepresentation. Using that form and the facts of your case, you must then prepare a written complaint that complies with all of the rules of court, including the rules for e-filing. The complaint is to be filed in a federal district court located in a different state. You have the original letters to be attached to the complaint, but you have only hard copies of these. On top of everything, you have never e-filed in a federal court. How do you complete this assignment on time?

SOLUTION

When faced with a complicated task, such as this one, you should begin by listing the individual activities you must complete. (If you are using case management software, a "to-do" list would be helpful.) In this case, that list might look like this:

1. Locate and review local rules for the court in which the complaint is to be filed.
2. Identify all document requirements and e-filing procedures.
3. Verify that the settings on your word processor are consistent with the court rules for documents to be filed.
4. Convert the document to a PDF format so that it can be e-filed.
5. Review the procedures for e-filing.
6. Convert the hard copies of the exhibits to electronic copies so that they can be e-filed.

Before the Internet age, locating local rules of court was often difficult, especially if the court was located at a distance. Today most, if not all, courts have Web sites and post the local rules of court on the site. When you access the Web site for the court in which your complaint is to be filed, you find that the local rules of court contain very specific requirements for documents to be filed. You find technical rules regarding margins, footers, type size, and spacing as well as rules that affect case title, attorneys' names and addresses, and exhibits. You also find information for e-filing. You can now format your complaint so it meets these requirements. Preparing a pleading for e-filing requires an additional step. Your complaint must be saved in a portable document format (PDF). Later versions of Microsoft Word or Corel's WordPerfect allow you to save a document in this format. Software programs such as Adobe Acrobat also enable you to do this. Because you are attaching exhibits to the complaint (i.e., copies of original letters), these will need to be scanned before they can be electronically sent to the court. Your office copier is able to scan the document. Learning how to e-file in a federal court may seem like a daunting task, especially since you do not have much time to do this. However, the local rules of court advise you to check the PACER Web site for detailed information. When you check this site you see that several training videos are available to help you learn the process. These videos take you step-by-step through the e-filing process. When you finish watching these, you are confident that you can successfully complete your assignment. Many legal tasks are simplified by the use of computers. Some tasks, such as electronically filing a document, cannot be done without automation.

Although children or incompetents cannot sue in their own names, they can generally be named as defendants in the complaint. However, after they are served with the complaint, they may be entitled to have a guardian appointed to represent their interests. Again, local law should be reviewed to determine whether appointment of a guardian ad litem for a defendant is necessary and, if so, how it is accomplished.

Corporations and Other Business Entities   A corporation is a "person" for legal purposes, including lawsuits. As such it has capacity to sue or be sued in the corporate name. In fact, if a corporation is a plaintiff or a defendant in a lawsuit, it must be identified by the corporate name rather than the name of the directors, officers, or shareholders. Exceptions do occur, however, in the case of corporate defendants. If the corporation fails to act like a corporation—not keeping corporate minutes, not holding meetings, failing to keep corporate assets separate from personal assets, and so on—then the individuals behind the corporation can be sued individually. This is known as *piercing the corporate veil*. The directors, officers, or shareholders of a corporation will also be named individually as defendants if they have personally done something wrong.

Business entities other than corporations may be treated differently. An unincorporated association, such as a partnership, does not have legal existence separate and apart from the partners. It is proper, therefore, for such an organization to sue and be sued in the name of its individual members. Some jurisdictions allow a partnership to be sued either in the names of the individual partners or in the partnership name. Suing a partnership in the partnership name alone is not always a wise choice, however, because state laws may adversely affect the plaintiff's ability to collect any judgment. In a general partnership, the individual partners are personally liable for partnership debts. However, if the individual partners are not named in the complaint, state law may limit collection of any judgment to partnership assets, protecting the non-partnership assets of the individual partners. When suing a partnership or other unincorporated business entity, it is common to list both the partners' names and the business name, as in the following example:

Example

```
                                          )
                                          )
                                          )
         v.                               )
HARRY RICE and HARVEY RICE,               )
A partnership, doing business as          )
Hearth & Home Real Estate Co.,            )
         Defendants                       )
                                          )
```

Governmental Agencies   There is no question about the right of a government entity to sue on a claim. However, because of the common law doctrine of sovereign immunity (the king could not be sued), many jurisdictions have laws that limit and regulate the circumstances under which a government entity can be sued. Appropriate statutes must be checked to see if the claim is one for which the offending government agency can be sued. Even when a statute permits the government to be sued, laws may require that claims be filed with the government agency before actually filing a lawsuit. (See Chapter 3.) If a claim is required, the complaint should state that this was done.

Parties and Fictitious Names

Parties Using Fictitious Names   Many businesses do not use their true names in the operation of their businesses. Individuals, either operating alone or with others, often choose to do business under a name that has more business appeal than their real names. At times, even corporations do business under a name other than the real corporate name. If a plaintiff uses a fictitious name in his business, a lawsuit should identify the plaintiff's true name. The plaintiff may indicate that he is doing business under another name. The plaintiff is then identified as follows:

Example

```
MARTIN REDSHAW, doing business as        )
Marty's Diner,                           )
         Plaintiff                       )
                                         )
         v.                              )
                                         )
                                         )
                                         )
```

fictitiously named
defendants
Defendants in a lawsuit who
are not identified by their
correct names; usually refers
to the practice in some state
courts of including several
"Does" as defendants to provide
for discovery of additional
defendants after the statute of
limitations has run.

permissive joinder
A concept allowing multiple
parties to be joined in one
lawsuit as plaintiffs or defendants
as long as there is some common
question of fact or law.

compulsory joinder
A party who should be included
or named in a lawsuit; in federal
court, Federal Rule of Procedure
19 sets out the criteria for
compulsory joinder of parties.

If the plaintiff is doing business under a fictitious name, before the lawsuit is filed you should verify that the plaintiff has complied with all local laws regarding such usage. Some states, for example, require that fictitious name statements be filed, and failure to do so can affect the right of a party to sue.

When the defendant is doing business under a fictitious name, the true name of the party may be unknown to you when you are preparing the complaint. Your state may have various records that can be checked, but these are not always complete or accurate. Therefore, the defendant must initially be identified in the complaint by the fictitious name. When the true name of the defendant or defendants is determined, the complaint can be amended.

Fictitious Defendants   Not to be confused with parties who use a fictitious name in business is a concept known as **fictitiously named defendants**, a procedure that is allowed in some jurisdictions. This term usually refers to defendants whose very identity is unknown. They are usually identified as "Does." In jurisdictions that allow this use, "Does" are commonly named as defendants in complaints to protect against a new defendant being discovered after the statute of limitations has run. This allows the attorney to argue that the complaint was filed against the newly discovered defendant within the statute of limitations; he was just referred to by an incorrect name. The attorney then tries to amend the complaint to "correct" the name. "Does" are not generally used in federal court. Instead, Rule 15 of the Federal Rules of Civil Procedure allows plaintiffs to name a newly discovered defendant even after the statute of limitations has run, as long as the new party received notice that the lawsuit had been filed within the time allowed for service, would not be unduly prejudiced, and knew that but for a mistake, he or she would have been named as a party in the original lawsuit. In such a case, the date of filing against the new party "relates back" to the original filing date.

Joining Multiple Parties

Many lawsuits involve disputes with multiple plaintiffs and/or defendants. The rules concerning joinder of multiple parties can be extremely involved and confusing. However, joinder of parties usually falls into two categories: joinder that is allowed but not required, known as **permissive joinder**; and joinder that is required, or **compulsory joinder**. Before drafting any complaint with multiple parties, you may need to review these rules. For example, in the *Hendricks* case described in the Commentary, you need to know whether the Hendrickses can sue the realtor, the company for which she works, and the seller all in the same lawsuit. This is determined by the rules of joinder, which are usually found in the appropriate state laws (or Rules 19–21 of the Federal Rules of Civil Procedure, if the case is in federal court).

The rules regarding permissive joinder, joinder of parties that is allowed but not required, are very liberal. Parties are permitted to be joined together in a complaint as plaintiffs or defendants as long as there is some common question of law or fact and the claim arises out of the same occurrence or series of occurrences. Of course, you would not name someone as a plaintiff in a complaint unless your law firm represented that party.

Whether certain parties *must* be joined in the same complaint is a more difficult issue. Generally, if the court cannot resolve the case without the presence of a party, then joinder of the party is required. For example, suppose that title to a certain piece of real property is in question, and four different individuals are claiming ownership. If one of those parties files a lawsuit to determine ownership (known as a *quiet title action*), he must name the other three claimants as defendants. The court cannot determine ownership unless all four parties appear before the court. When parties are required to be joined in the lawsuit, they are sometimes referred to as **indispensable parties**.

Even when it seems that joinder of certain parties is essential to the case, if jurisdiction over one of the parties is impossible to obtain, the court may allow the matter to proceed without that party being named. These cases obviously present complicated legal issues that must be thoroughly researched before you prepare the complaint.

Class Actions

At times the number of potential plaintiffs in an action becomes too numerous to be practical. When this happens, a class action can result. Class actions present complex questions for the attorneys and for the court. The related law and procedures are complicated and beyond the scope of this chapter. However, a brief overview is presented.

A **class action** occurs when one or more parties who share a claim with a multitude of others file a lawsuit in their own names and also claim to represent numerous others in a similar situation. The claim must be based on similar issues. To maintain a class action, the party filing the lawsuit must first ask the court to certify the case as a class action. Unless the court grants such an order, the case does not proceed. After the court certifies the action as a class action it determines how members of the class should receive notice. Rule 23 mandates that this notice must be the "best notice that is practical." Generally the court also orders that all class members who can be identified should get individual notice. The federal judiciary provides sample forms for the notices that should be served. These can be viewed on the Web site for the federal judiciary at <www.fjc.gov> (link to "Class Action Notices Page" for sample forms).

Complying with the notice requirements can be an overwhelming and expensive task. If your firm is involved in a class action, as a litigation paralegal you may be asked to take responsibility for this part of the litigation. Included in the notice to all potential members of the class is usually an explanation that any potential class member can request in writing that he or she be excluded from the class. If a member does not request exclusion, that class member will be bound by any judgment in the case.

Class actions permit cases to be brought when the amount of damages suffered by each plaintiff is minimal but the total damages suffered by all is substantial. In such a case it is not practical for parties to maintain their own individual lawsuits. The cost of litigation would outweigh any benefit. By joining together, the class of injured parties is able to minimize expenses and justify the litigation.

Every jurisdiction has its own rules, found in statutes and cases, regarding class action lawsuits. These rules usually deal with such matters as who can file, who is entitled to notice of the action, how that notice is to be given, and who must bear the cost of notice. Rule 23 of the Federal Rules of Civil Procedure governs class actions in federal court. Rule 23 allows a class action when all the following conditions are met:

- the class is so numerous that joinder of all members is impracticable,
- there are questions of law or fact common to the class,
- the claims or defenses of the representative parties are typical of the claims or defenses of the class, *and*
- the representative parties will fairly and adequately protect the interests of the class.

indispensable party
A person who must be joined in the lawsuit and whose absence makes it impossible for a court to render a judgment.

class action
A lawsuit brought by a limited number of parties on behalf of themselves and other persons with the same or similar issues.

interpleader

A type of action in which a party deposits money or property in the court because, although the party clearly owes money or the return of property, the parties to whom it is owed is unclear; after the property is deposited, the court determines its proper distribution.

Rule 23 also requires one of the following for maintaining a class action:

- individual lawsuits might produce the possibility of inconsistent decisions *or*
- the decision in one case might unfairly prejudice another case *or*
- the party opposing the class has acted in a way that is generally applicable to all members of the class *or*
- common questions of law or fact predominate over individual questions of law or fact.

In recent years, the Supreme Court has placed limits on the ability of plaintiffs to bring class action lawsuits. Additional information about class action lawsuits can be found on the Web site for the federal judicial center (<www.fjc.gov>). By reviewing the publications and searching by subject for class action litigation you find several manuals and articles related to this subject.

Interpleader

A special type of action or complaint, known as **interpleader**, also involves questions of joinder of parties. *Interpleader* refers to a type of action in which several different parties claim ownership to a fund or property that is in the control of another.

Example

An insurance company provides liability coverage to an airline with a policy limit of $1 billion. A plane crashes, and the heirs of the victims file claims with the airline and the insurance company in excess of $10 billion. Liability is clear, and the insurance company determines at the outset that it will have to pay the policy limits.

In this situation, even though the insurance company acknowledges that it will have to pay the insurance policy limits, the question of how the insurance proceeds are to be distributed remains. The insurance company does not want to unilaterally make this decision because it could be sued if the claimants did not agree with the distribution. The appropriate action, therefore, is for the insurance company to ask the court to decide how the funds should be disbursed. This is accomplished by filing an action in interpleader with the court, naming all of the claimants as defendants. The insurance company can then deposit the policy limits with the court and withdraw from the action, leaving the claimants to fight over the money. (Refer to Exhibit 5-4 in the chapter and read the form entitled Complaint for Interpleader and Declaratory Relief.)

ALLEGING JURISDICTION AND VENUE

The complaint must contain some allegation showing that the lawsuit is filed in the proper court. This involves questions of both jurisdiction and venue. In federal court, these allegations are usually very specific. In showing jurisdiction, the plaintiff states why the action is filed in federal court, giving a citation to the appropriate United States Code section. The Appendix to the Federal Rules of Civil Procedure contains sample allegations regarding federal jurisdiction (see Exhibit 5-2).

In state courts, jurisdiction is determined by state law. It is not always necessary to make an express statement that jurisdiction is proper in state court. Such a conclusion

EXHIBIT 5-2 Sample Allegations Regarding Federal Jurisdiction

a. (*For diversity-of-citizenship jurisdiction.*) The plaintiff is [a citizen of *Michigan*] [a corporation incorporated under the laws of *Michigan* with its principal place of business in *Michigan*]. The defendant is [a citizen of *New York*] [a corporation incorporated under the laws of *New York* with its principal place of business in *New York*]. The amount in controversy, without interest and costs, exceeds the sum or value specified by 28 U.S.C. § 1332.

b. (*For federal-question jurisdiction.*) This action arises under [the United States Constitution, *specify the article or amendment and the section*] [a United States treaty *specify*] [a federal statute, ___ U.S.C. § ___].

c. (*For a claim in the admiralty or maritime jurisdiction.*) This is a case of admiralty or maritime jurisdiction. (*To invoke admiralty status under Rule 9(h) use the following:* This is an admiralty or maritime claim within the meaning of Rule 9(h).)

EXHIBIT 5-3 Sample Venue Allegations

At all times herein mentioned, defendant was and now is a resident of the County of _____, State of _____.

or

The County of _____ is the proper county in which to bring and maintain this action by virtue of the fact that defendant, ABC Corporation, has its principal executive offices located therein.

or

The County of _____ is the proper county in which to bring and maintain this action by virtue of the fact that the real property, which is the subject of this action, is located in said county.

will usually follow from all of the facts alleged in the complaint. In some states, however, different trial courts have different types of jurisdiction. For example, some state trial courts are empowered to hear civil cases only when the amount in dispute is less than a set amount of money. Within the complaint and in the prayer, or demand for relief, it should be shown that the amount claimed is within the jurisdiction of the court in which the case is filed.

In federal or state courts, venue can be determined by a number of factors. The most common factor is the residence of the defendant. Proper venue can be shown in the complaint by an allegation that one of the defendants resides in the district in which the action is filed. Venue is also proper in the place where the cause of action arose. Therefore, another common way of establishing venue is by alleging that the cause of action arose in the district in which the action is filed. However, there are many different ways to establish venue, depending on the nature of the case (review Chapter 2). See Exhibit 5-3 for examples of allegations showing venue.

PLEADING THE CAUSE OF ACTION

Although the complaint or petition usually follows legal technicalities, it is primarily a document that shows the factual basis for the lawsuit. It does not contain any discussion or analysis of legal theories. However, when reviewing the facts that are alleged in the complaint, the defendant's attorney and the court should be able to see a legal basis for the lawsuit, even though the legal basis need not be expressly stated. How detailed this factual description must be depends on the jurisdiction in which the lawsuit is filed. You may recall from Chapter 3 that before deciding to file any lawsuit an attorney must determine that a party has a cause of action, that is, facts showing that the plaintiff is entitled to a legal remedy. In some jurisdictions the complaint must contain factual allegations or statements that support each element of the cause of action. Because this method of pleading is based on a New York law known as the "Field Code," these jurisdictions are sometimes known as *code pleading* jurisdictions. Other jurisdictions, including the federal courts, have a less stringent requirement. For most types of cases, the complaint must contain sufficient facts to put the defendant on notice as to why he is being sued, but it is not essential that each element of the cause of action be supported by factual allegations. This method of pleading is known as *notice pleading*.

Even in notice pleading jurisdictions, some types of cases demand more detailed facts within the complaint. Rule 9 of the Federal Rules of Civil Procedure, for example, requires that allegations of fraud or mistake be stated with particularity. Furthermore, even though the Federal Rules allow fairly general and nonspecific pleading, more particular allegations are allowed. The use of more detailed allegations in a complaint may affect later discovery and disclosure rights and obligations (discussed in Chapter 8) and should be carefully considered.

Although differences exist in the technical requirements between code pleading jurisdictions and notice pleading jurisdictions, a complaint that is sufficient under code pleading rules is generally sufficient under notice pleading rules. The important thing to remember is that both types of pleading require that facts, and not legal theories, be alleged.

The Federal Rules of Civil Procedure contain an Appendix of Forms, including several that can be used as a basis for various causes of action (see Exhibit 5-4). Remember, however, that these forms would be only a part of a complaint. For a complete document you would add a caption, the proper language showing jurisdiction, appropriate paragraphs showing status and capacity of the parties, as well as venue and any other relevant allegations. (Although the Federal Rules do not require that status and capacity be specifically stated, they often are.) Compare Exhibit 5-1, a complete complaint, with the form for a Complaint to Recover a Sum Certain found in Exhibit 5-4.

Alleging Multiple Claims

Often a plaintiff has more than one potential claim against the defendant. Again, consider the *Hendricks* case described in the opening Commentary. If the plaintiffs can prove their realtor knew that the slides of the property were forgeries and that the property was not suitable for

EXHIBIT 5-4 Allegations for Various Complaints (Federal Rules Appendix)

COMPLAINT TO RECOVER A SUM CERTAIN

(Caption—See Form 1.*)

1. (Statement of Jurisdiction—See Form 7.*)

   (Use one or more of the following as appropriate and include a demand for judgment.)

   (a) *On a Promissory Note*

2. On *date*, the defendant executed and delivered a note promising to pay the plaintiff on *date* the sum of $ _____ with interest at the rate of _____ percent. A copy of the note [is attached as Exhibit A] [is summarized as follows: _____.]

3. The defendant has not paid the amount owed.

   (b) *On an Account*

2. The defendant owes the plaintiff $_____ according to the account set out in Exhibit A.

   (c) *For Goods Sold and Delivered*

2. The defendant owes the plaintiff $_____ for goods sold and delivered by the plaintiff to the defendant from *date* to *date*.

   (d) *For Money Lent*

2. The defendant owes the plaintiff $ _____ for money lent by the plaintiff to the defendant on *date*.

   (e) *For Money Paid by Mistake*

2. The defendant owes the plaintiff $ _____ for money paid by mistake to the defendant on *date* under these circumstances: *describe with particularity in accordance with Rule 9(b).*

   (f) *For Money Had and Received*

2. The defendant owes the plaintiff $ _____ for money that was received from *name* on *date* to be paid by the defendant to the plaintiff.

Demand for Judgment
Therefore, the plaintiff demands judgment against the defendant for $ _____, plus interest and costs.

(Date and sign – See Form 2.*)

COMPLAINT FOR NEGLIGENCE

(Caption—See Form 1.)

1. (Statement of Jurisdiction—See Form 7.)
2. On *date*, at *place*, the defendant negligently drove a motor vehicle against the plaintiff.
3. As a result, the plaintiff was physically injured, lost wages or income, suffered physical and mental pain, and incurred medical expenses of $_____.

Therefore, the plaintiff demands judgment against the defendant for $ _____, plus costs.

(Date and sign—See Form 2).

COMPLAINT FOR SPECIFIC PERFORMANCE OF A CONTRACT TO CONVEY LAND

(Caption—See Form 1.)

1. (Statement of Jurisdiction—See Form 7.)
2. On *date*, the parties agreed to the contract [attached as Exhibit A] [summarize the contract].
3. As agreed, the plaintiff tendered the purchase price and requested a conveyance of the land, but the defendant refused to accept the money or make a conveyance.
4. The plaintiff now offers to pay the purchase price.

Source: http://www.uscourts.gov/uscourts/RulesAndPolicies/rules/2010%20Rules/Civil%20Procedure.pdf

EXHIBIT 5-4 Allegations for Various Complaints (Federal Rules Appendix) (*continued*)

Therefore, the plaintiff demands that:

(a) the defendant be required to specifically perform the agreement and pay damages of $ _____, plus interest and costs, or

(b) if specific performance is not ordered, the defendant be required to pay damages of $ _____, plus interest and costs.

(Date and sign—See Form 2.)

COMPLAINT FOR PATENT INFRINGEMENT

(Caption—See Form 1.)

1. (Statement of Jurisdiction—See Form 7.)
2. On *date*, United States Letters Patent No. ___ were issued to the plaintiff for an invention in an *electric motor*. The plaintiff owned the patent throughout the period of the defendant's infringing acts and still owns the patent.
3. The defendant has infringed and is still infringing the Letters Patent by making, selling, and using *electric motors* that embody the patented invention, and the defendant will continue to do so unless enjoined by this court.
4. The plaintiff has complied with the statutory requirement of placing a notice of the Letters Patent on all *electric motors* it manufactures and sells and has given the defendant written notice of the infringement.

Therefore, the plaintiff demands:

(a) a preliminary and final injunction against the continuing infringement;

(b) an accounting for damages; and

(c) interest and costs.

(Date and sign—See Form 2.)

COMPLAINT FOR COPYRIGHT INFRINGEMENT AND UNFAIR COMPETITION

(Caption—See Form 1.)

1. (Statement of Jurisdiction—See Form 7.)
2. Before *date*, the plaintiff, a United States citizen, wrote a book entitled _____.
3. The book is an original work that may be copyrighted under United States law. A copy of the book is attached as Exhibit A.
4. Between *date* and *date*, the plaintiff applied to the copyright office and received a certificate of registration dated _____ and identified as *date, class, number*.
5. Since *date*, the plaintiff has either published or licensed for publication all copies of the book in compliance with the copyright laws and has remained the sole owner of the copyright.
6. After the copyright was issued, the defendant infringed the copyright by publishing and selling a book entitled _____, which was copied largely from the plaintiff's book. A copy of the defendant's book is attached as Exhibit B.
7. The plaintiff has notified the defendant in writing of the infringement.
8. The defendant continues to infringe the copyright by continuing to publish and sell the infringing book in violation of the copyright, and further has engaged in unfair trade practices and unfair competition in connection with its publication and sale of the infringing book, thus causing irreparable damage.

EXHIBIT 5-4 Allegations for Various Complaints (Federal Rules Appendix) (*continued*)

Therefore, the plaintiff demands that:

(a) until this case is decided the defendant and the defendant's agents be enjoined from disposing of any copies of the defendant's book by sale or otherwise;

(b) the defendant account for and pay as damages to the plaintiff all profits and advantages gained from unfair trade practices and unfair competition in selling the defendant's book, and all profits and advantages gained from infringing the plaintiff's copyright (but no less than the statutory minimum);

(c) the defendant deliver for impoundment all copies of the book in the defendant's possession or control and deliver for destruction all infringing copies and all plates, molds, and other materials for making infringing copies;

(d) the defendant pay the plaintiff interest, costs, and reasonable attorney's fees; and the plaintiff be awarded any other just relief.

(Date and sign—See Form 2.)

COMPLAINT FOR INTERPLEADER AND DECLARATORY RELIEF

(Caption—See Form 1.)

1. (Statement of Jurisdiction—See Form 7.)
2. On *date*, the plaintiff issued a life insurance policy on the life of *name* with *name* as the named beneficiary.
3. As a condition for keeping the policy in force, the policy required payment of a premium during the first year and then annually.
4. The premium due on *date* was never paid, and the policy lapsed after that date.
5. On *date*, after the policy had lapsed, both the insured and the named beneficiary died in an automobile collision.
6. Defendant *name* claims to be the beneficiary in place of *name* and has filed a claim to be paid the policy's full amount.
7. The other two defendants are representatives of the deceased persons' estates. Each defendant has filed a claim on behalf of each estate to receive payment of the policy's full amount.
8. If the policy was in force at the time of death, the plaintiff is in doubt about who should be paid.

Therefore, the plaintiff demands that:

(a) each defendant be restrained from commencing any action against the plaintiff on the policy;

(b) a judgment be entered that no defendant is entitled to the proceeds of the policy or any part of it, but if the court determines that the policy was in effect at the time of the insured's death, that the defendants be required to interplead and settle among themselves their rights to the proceeds, and that the plaintiff be discharged from all liability except to the defendant determined to be entitled to the proceeds; and

(c) the plaintiff recover its costs.

(Date and sign—See Form 2.)

* The Appendix of Forms to the Federal Rules of Civil Procedures also contains sample forms for common features and allegations for complaints.

count
Separate claims stated in one complaint.

specific performance
A court order requiring a person to fulfill his or her promises in a contract.

building and lied to them about it, they have a claim for fraud or intentional misrepresentation. Such a claim, if proven, would entitle the plaintiffs to punitive damages in addition to their out-of-pocket losses. However, proving that a misrepresentation was intentional is sometimes difficult, and the plaintiff's attorney may wish to have a claim for negligent misrepresentation as well, in the event that the defendant's intent cannot be adequately shown. Proving negligent misrepresentation would entitle the plaintiffs to their actual losses but would not allow an award of punitive damages. This is an alternative claim, which can be stated in the complaint. Normally, this claim would be set out in a second cause of action, sometimes referred to as a **count**, separate from the first cause of action or first count for fraud. In the *Hendricks* case, other causes of action may also be possible. For example, the Hendrickses might simply wish to disaffirm the contract (rescind it) and get their money back (restitution). Additionally, because the Hendrickses did not have their own real estate agent, the facts might indicate that May Forrester was acting in a dual capacity, representing both Paradise Found, Inc. and the Hendrickses. As such, May Forrester would be in a special fiduciary relationship with the Hendrickses, a relationship that she abused. This could result in another claim.

A complaint may contain any number of causes of action or counts. Whenever a cause of action arises out of the same general factual situation, the rules of pleading usually allow them to be joined in the same complaint.

Determining whether the defendant's conduct toward the plaintiff results in more than one claim or cause of action can be very difficult. As a general rule, if the claims provide different remedies or are proven by different facts or evidence in the case, they should probably be separated into distinct causes of action. However, because the rules for interpreting pleadings are so liberal, if two or more claims are combined into one cause of action, the court could either allow the pleading to stand as written or allow it to be amended.

A question sometimes arises when a complaint contains two inconsistent causes of action.

Example

Bryant signs a contract with Yates to buy a house for $200,000. Before the time for the deal to close, Yates informs Bryant that he has changed his mind and will not sell. As of the date of sale, the value of the house had increased to $220,000. Bryant now has a choice. Does he want the house, or should he make Yates pay for any damages that he incurred because he did not get the house (the damages being the difference between the purchase price and the fair market value at the time and place of sale)? If he gets the house at the original contract price, he will not suffer any monetary damage.

Asking for both **specific performance** of the contract and for damages because it was not performed are inconsistent. The rules of pleading usually allow the plaintiff to allege causes of action that are inconsistent. However, the plaintiff will not get a judgment on both of them.

Multiple Parties and Causes of Action

We have already seen that a complaint may contain multiple plaintiffs or defendants. When this occurs, questions arise about whether the parties should be joined within the same cause of action, or whether separate causes of action are required. No absolute rules govern this situation, and the rules of pleading in most jurisdictions are liberal enough to allow almost any method of handling this situation. However, some guidelines are commonly followed.

Multiple plaintiffs should be joined within the same cause of action if they have a joint claim or if they are suing for the same damages or remedy. For example, in the factual situation described in the Commentary, both Margaret and Paul Hendricks are suing for the same thing—the damages that they sustained in buying the lot. Note that they are not each suing for one-half of the damages. They are suing together for the total damages. Therefore, they should be joined in the same cause of action.

When the plaintiffs are suing for something different, however, their claims should be in separate causes of action. For example, suppose that Herbert and Wanda Sepulveda, husband and wife, are both injured in the same automobile accident and wish to sue the driver of the other vehicle. In such a case they are suing for different things. He is suing for his injuries, and she is suing for her injuries. They would, therefore, have two separate causes of action. However, the two causes of action would be in one complaint. When there are multiple plaintiffs and defendants, it is not necessary that they all be parties to each of the causes of action. Again, when there is some common factual or legal basis among the various causes of action, they can be joined in one complaint.

REQUEST FOR DAMAGES OR OTHER RELIEF

Every complaint or petition filed in an action contains a demand for relief from the court, often called a *prayer*. Courts have the power to grant two different types of relief, money damages and equitable relief. Money damages are the award of money to the plaintiff as compensation for some loss. Equitable relief, in contrast, involves the court's ordering the defendant to do something or to stop doing something other than simply paying money damages. In some state jurisdictions, only certain courts have the power to grant equitable relief. Before preparing and filing any complaint requesting this type of relief, be sure to check jurisdictional power of the court.

Money Damages

Probably the most common relief sought in a civil lawsuit is money damages. The primary purpose of damages in a civil suit is to compensate plaintiffs for a loss they have sustained. These damages are known as **compensatory damages**. Compensatory damages may be referred to by other names. For example, in personal injury cases compensatory damages are categorized as either special damages or general damages. *Special damages* are actual out-of-pocket expenses incurred by the plaintiff, such as doctor bills and lost earnings. *General damages* are not out-of-pocket expenses; instead they are such things as pain and suffering, loss of use of a limb, or disfigurement caused by a scar. Even though general damages do not reimburse the plaintiff for an economic expense, they do compensate the plaintiff for some loss. In some jurisdictions an uninjured spouse has a separate claim for money damages for loss of consortium. Damages for loss of consortium are intended to compensate a person who suffers the loss of companionship and comfort of a spouse who was injured because of the wrongdoing of another. In a few jurisdictions, parents can also claim loss of consortium resulting from injury to a child.

compensatory damages
An award of money damages that compensates the plaintiff for actual loss, including pain and suffering.

punitive or exemplary damages
Damages that punish a defendant for intentional or malicious conduct that causes injury.

equitable relief
A judicial remedy other than money damages, such as specific performance of a contract or an injunction.

rescission
To "undo" or abrogate a contract.

restitution
Returning property to the original owner where fairness requires that it be done.

declaratory relief
A court order defining or explaining the rights and obligations of parties under some contract or other document.

quiet title action
A legal proceeding to determine ownership of real property.

injunction
A court order requiring a party to take some action or to stop some conduct.

Although money damages in most civil cases are compensatory in nature, sometimes a plaintiff is entitled to recover **punitive or exemplary damages**. These are meant to punish the defendant and are awarded only when the defendant has committed some extremely offensive act. Such damages are not favored by the courts and come under careful scrutiny by the appellate courts. The U.S. Supreme Court has also held that punitive damages are subject to limitations. Nevertheless, they are allowed in some cases.

In the course of any lawsuit, the parties inevitably incur substantial expenses, or costs. These include such items as filing fees, process server fees, deposition fees, and expert witness fees. Costs are not included in computing the plaintiff's damages. However, if the plaintiff wins her lawsuit, she will generally be awarded certain costs in addition to the actual damages. However, should the defendant win the case, he will generally be awarded his costs from the plaintiff. Items included in these recoverable costs are usually determined by a specific statute. One element that is usually not included in the list of recoverable costs is the attorney fee in the case. Unless the lawsuit is based on a contract that specifically provides for the payment of attorney fees in the event of a legal dispute, or unless there is some special law governing the situation, parties are expected to pay their own attorney fees.

Equitable Relief

Some legal disputes cannot be settled by an award of money damages.

Example

Friedman sells Brockland his business. As part of the sales agreement, Friedman agrees not to open a competing business within a 50-mile radius for a period of two years. However, two months after the sale, Friedman opens a competing business across the street from Brockland. As a result, Brockland's business income substantially decreases. Although money damages might compensate Brockland for his past loss, if Friedman continues in business, Brockland will continue to lose money, the exact amount of which would be difficult to calculate. Brockland would therefore prefer that the court order Friedman to close down his competing business. Such an order would be a kind of relief known as **equitable relief**.

Lawsuits in which equitable relief is sought are known as *actions in equity*, whereas lawsuits in which money damages are sought are known as *actions at law*. A complaint may combine a request for equitable relief and money damages.

The types of equitable relief that can be ordered by a court of equitable jurisdiction are varied. Some of the more common types of equitable relief follow:

- specific performance—an order requiring a party to perform a contract
- **rescission**—an order rescinding or voiding a contract
- **restitution**—an order to return money or property, usually paid in connection with a contract that was subsequently rescinded
- **declaratory relief**—a court order defining or explaining the rights and obligations of parties under some contract or other document

- **quiet title action**—an order clarifying ownership of real property
- **injunction**—an order requiring a party to stop doing something

Refer to Exhibit 5-4 for examples of complaints based on some of these types of equitable relief. Along with the award of equitable relief, the court generally awards the prevailing party her costs of suit, just as it would with actions for money damages.

Provisional Remedies

A substantial time often elapses between the filing of a complaint and the actual trial in a case. Therefore, when injunctive relief is the primary object of a lawsuit, the plaintiff frequently requests some provisional remedy from the court as soon as a complaint is filed. Provisional remedies include a temporary restraining order and a preliminary injunction. A **temporary restraining order (TRO)** usually compels the defendant to stop certain conduct immediately. These are granted without any formal hearing, based primarily on affidavits or declarations (written statements under penalty of perjury) submitted to the court. Because the courts are hesitant to grant any orders without giving all sides the opportunity for a full hearing, TROs remain in effect for a very short time, usually until a hearing can be scheduled in court. As soon as possible, then, a hearing is scheduled at which both sides have the opportunity to argue for or against the restraining order remaining in effect until the time of trial. This hearing is not a full trial of all the issues. Should the court decide to keep the restraining order in effect, it will issue a **preliminary injunction**, an order that remains in effect until the trial, at which time the injunction would become permanent if the plaintiff proves his case. In federal courts, TROs and preliminary injunctions are governed by Rule 65 of the Federal Rules of Civil Procedure. The procedures that a party must follow to obtain these provisional remedies are similar to the procedures followed in motion practice and are discussed in more detail in Chapter 7.

DRAFTING THE COMPLAINT

Once you identify the parties to the lawsuit, determine the causes of action, and decide on the appropriate remedy, you are prepared to start drafting the complaint for your attorney's review. Before actually writing the document, however, be sure to check any local court rules regarding technical requirements for the pleading. Is a certain type or size of paper required? Does the size of print matter? Is there a special format that must be followed? Many courts have special rules regarding these and other details. See Exhibit 5-5 for an example of a local rule of court regarding pleading formalities. Also, to save time in drafting the complaint, you should check form books (or a form file, if one is kept in the office) for a sample complaint that deals with a similar factual situation. Even the most experienced litigation attorneys and paralegals follow forms whenever possible. If a case is to be filed in federal court, *American Jurisprudence Pleading and Practice Forms Annotated*, a Thomson/West publication, can be helpful, as are the forms found in the Appendix of Forms to the Federal Rules of Civil Procedure.

In some jurisdictions, a complaint is prepared on numbered paper known as *pleading paper*. However, many jurisdictions have discontinued this practice. For an example of a complaint see Exhibit 5-6 and note the comments in the left margin of the exhibit.

temporary restraining order (TRO)
An order from the court requiring a person to act or refrain from acting in a certain way, issued for limited time until a full hearing on the matter can be scheduled.

preliminary injunction
A court order made prior to final judgment in the case, but after all parties have had the opportunity to present evicence, directing that a party take or refrain from some action until the trial in the case takes place.

EXHIBIT 5-5 Example of Local Rule of Court Regarding Pleadings

---

FORM OF PAPERS GENERALLY

Papers presented for filing shall be flat, unfolded, firmly bound together at the top, pre-punched with two (2) holes, centered two and three-quarters inch (2¾") apart and one-half inch (½") to five-eighths inch (⅝") from the top edge of the paper, and on eight and one-half inch by eleven inch (8½" × 11") paper. Except for exhibits, quotations, the caption, the title of the court, and the name of the case, lines of typewritten text shall be double-spaced, and except for the title page, shall begin at least one and one-half inch (1½") from the top of the page. All handwriting shall be legible and all typewriting shall be of a size which is either not more than ten (10) characters per linear inch; or, not less than twelve (12) points for proportional spaced fonts or equivalent. All quotations longer than one (1) sentence shall be indented. All pages of each pleading or other paper filed with the court (exclusive of exhibits) shall be numbered consecutively.
Local Rule of Civil Practice 10-1 of the U.S. District Court, District of Nevada

---

The Caption

As mentioned, the first part of any complaint or petition is known as the *caption*. The caption contains the name of the court in which the action is filed, the names of the plaintiffs and defendants, and the title of the document. In some jurisdictions, it also contains the name, address, and telephone number of the attorney and the client being represented. In other jurisdictions, the caption also contains the addresses of the plaintiff and defendant.

The Causes of Action

Below the caption is the body of the complaint, containing various jurisdictional and factual allegations that constitute the plaintiff's cause of action. These allegations are broken down into short, numbered paragraphs. As there is no absolute method for paragraphing, the use of form books or other sample complaints is very helpful in setting up this part of the complaint. In the absence of a form to follow, you can use normal paragraphing rules.

Even though there is no mandatory order in which paragraphing must be done, there are typically employed conventions:

1. In most cases you will see paragraphs on jurisdiction and venue first.
2. If any of the parties are businesses, either corporate or otherwise, allegations concerning their status or capacity then follow.
3. If there is more than one defendant in the lawsuit, it is standard to include an agency allegation. An *agency allegation* claims that one or more of the defendants were agents or employees of one or more of the other defendants and acting within the scope of that agency. Such an allegation refers to the substantive legal principle of vicarious liability or respondent superior, a concept that imposes liability on an employer for certain acts of its employees.
4. Following these standard allegations are various allegations describing the factual basis for the lawsuit and a description of the damages suffered.

EXHIBIT 5-6 Complaint

Title of court

**UNITED STATES DISTRICT COURT
FOR THE DISTRICT OF NEVADA**

Caption

MARGARET HENDRICKS and PAUL HENDRICKS,	)	
Plaintiffs,	)	No.
	)	
	)	COMPLAINT FOR FRAUD,
v.	)	NEGLIGENT MISREPRESENTATION
	)	And BREACH OF FIDUCIARY DUTY
MAY FORRESTER, an individual,	)	
HARRY RICE & HARVEY RICE,	)	
a partnership, doing business as	)	
HEARTH & HOME REAL ESTATE CO.,	)	JURY TRIAL DEMANDED
PARADISE FOUND, INC., a	)	
Corporation,	)	
Defendants	)	

Plaintiffs allege against each and every defendant:

Allegations of first cause of action

FIRST CAUSE OF ACTION
(Fraud)
Jurisdiction

Diversity of citizenship establishes jurisdiction

1. Plaintiffs are, and were at all times herein mentioned, domiciled in and citizens of the state of California. Defendants, MAY FORRESTER, HARRY RICE and HARVEY RICE are and were at all times herein mentioned, domiciled in and citizens of the state of Nevada. Defendant, PARADISE FOUND, INC., was and is now a corporation duly organized and existing under the laws of the state of Idaho, with its offices and principal place of business in the state of Idaho. This is a civil action involving, exclusive of interest and costs, a sum in excess of $75,000. Every issue of law and fact in this action is wholly between citizens of different states.

2. Plaintiffs are informed and believe and thereupon allege that Defendants, HARRY RICE AND HARVEY RICE, are a partnership doing business as HEARTH & HOME REAL ESTATE CO.

3. Plaintiffs are informed and believe and thereupon allege that Defendant, PARADISE FOUND, INC., is a corporation duly organized and existing under the laws of the state of Idaho.

4. Plaintiffs are now, and at all times mentioned in this complaint have been, residents of San Francisco County, California.

5. Plaintiffs are informed and believe and thereupon allege that at all times herein mentioned, each of the defendants was the agent and employee of each of the remaining defendants and in doing the things hereinafter alleged, was acting within the scope of said agency.

6. On or about June 1, _____, in the city of Reno, state of Nevada, defendant, MAY FORRESTER, made the following false and fraudulent representations to plaintiffs: Defendant represented that certain real property was ideal vacation property, that

EXHIBIT 5-6 Complaint (*continued*)

said property had been approved for and was suitable for building, that said property abutted a man-made lake, and that said property was worth at least $100,000.

7. The representations made by the defendant were false in that said real property has not been approved nor is it suitable for building, it is not adjacent to any body of water, and was and is valued at less than $5,000.

8. Defendant, at the time she made said representations, knew them to be false and made the statements with the intent to defraud and deceive plaintiffs and to induce them to purchase that certain real property described above.

9. Plaintiffs at the time the representations were made believed them to be true and had no reasons to believe that said representations were untrue. In reliance upon said representations, plaintiffs were induced to, and did purchase the above described real property. Had plaintiffs known the true facts they would not have taken such action.

10. By reason of the facts alleged, plaintiffs have been damaged in the sum of $100,000.

Allegations of second cause of action

SECOND CAUSE OF ACTION
(Negligent Misrepresentation)

Start by incorporating relevant paragraphs from first cause of action

11. Plaintiffs re-allege and incorporate by reference the allegations of paragraphs 1 through 7 above in their entirety.

12. At the time defendant, MAY FORRESTER, made said representations, she had no sufficient or reasonable ground for believing said representations to be true in that she, the defendant, did not have information and data sufficient to enable her to make a determination whether the representations were true. At the time of making the representations, defendant concealed from plaintiff her lack of information and data that prevented them from making a true evaluation of the facts.

13. At the time said representations were made, plaintiffs had no knowledge of their falsity, but, in fact, believed them to be true. Because of the fiduciary and confidential relationship which existed between defendant and plaintiffs, plaintiffs justifiably relied upon said representations.

14. Plaintiffs at the time the representations were made believed them to be true and had no reasons to believe that said representations were untrue. In reliance upon said representations, plaintiffs were induced to and did purchase the above described real property. Had plaintiffs known the true facts they would not have taken such action.

Restate damages

15. By reasons of the facts alleged, plaintiffs have been damaged in the sum of $100,000.

Allegations of third cause of action

THIRD CAUSE OF ACTION
(Breach of Fiduciary Duty)

Plaintiffs allege against defendant MAY FORRESTER:

16. Plaintiffs re-allege and incorporate by reference the allegations of paragraphs 1 through 15 above in their entirety.

17. Defendant, MAY FORRESTER, owed a fiduciary duty of loyalty, honesty, and confidentiality to plaintiffs by virtue of her status as their real estate broker.

18. The acts and omissions of defendant, MAY FORRESTER, as alleged above, constitute intentional breaches of her fiduciary duties to plaintiffs.

EXHIBIT 5-6 Complaint (*continued*)

Restate damages ———

19. As a direct and proximate result of defendant's breach of her fiduciary duties, plaintiffs have been damaged in the amount of $100,000.

20. Defendant's breach of fiduciary duties was willful, malicious, oppressive, and in conscious disregard of plaintiffs' rights. Accordingly, plaintiffs request punitive damages in the amount of $100,000.

WHEREFORE, plaintiffs pray for judgment against defendants as follows:

On the first cause of action:

Prayer or demand ———

1. For judgment in the sum of $100,000.
2. For costs of suit.
3. For such other relief as the court deems just.

On the second cause of action:

1. For judgment in the sum of $100,000.
2. For costs of suit.
3. For such other relief as the court deems just.

On the third cause of action (against defendant, MAY FORRESTER, only):

1. For compensatory damages in the sum of $100,000.
2. For punitive damages in the sum of $100,000.
3. For costs of suit.
4. For such other relief as the court deems just.

Subscription (In some states attorney information goes on first page of complaint.)

Dated: September 1, _____

By _____
Glenda Yee
Attorney at Law
246 Marshall Ave.
San Francisco, CA 96730
gyee@esq.com
(415) 555-2121

Pleading on Information and Belief   All statements contained in a complaint, or any pleading, should be true. However, at times a plaintiff is not certain about some facts that must be alleged in the complaint. For example, the plaintiff may not know for sure if the defendant business is a corporation or some other business entity, although the plaintiff believes that it is incorporated. In such cases, the proper way to plead the facts is on information and belief. Refer to Exhibit 5-6, paragraphs 2, 3, and 5 of the first cause of action. These allegations are made on information and belief.

Incorporating by Reference   Many complaints contain more than one cause of action. In such a case, each cause of action should be sufficient in itself to constitute a legally sufficient complaint. Because of this, it is often necessary to restate many of the same allegations that were alleged in prior causes of action. It is not necessary, however, to *expressly* restate those allegations. If something is being repeated, it can be referred to and incorporated by reference. Exhibit 5-6 contains three causes of action; see paragraph 11 for an illustration of a paragraph incorporating prior allegations.

Remember that not all parties to the complaint must be parties to all causes of action. However, each of those named in the caption must be a party to at least one cause of action within the complaint, and this includes "Doe" defendants when such defendants are allowed.

The Prayer

After the allegations in the complaint you find the prayer. The prayer is normally located at the end of all of the allegations. Even though the allegations in the complaint state that the plaintiff has incurred damages and is entitled to some relief, a specific request for these damages is made in the prayer. This is the part of the complaint in which the plaintiff asks the court for damages or other relief. It often begins with the words, "Wherefore, plaintiff prays as follows." When a complaint contains several causes of action, attorneys often include a request for damages for each of the causes of action. For example, the prayer might start, "Wherefore on the first cause of action plaintiff prays as follows." A separate prayer is then included for each cause of action.

The Subscription

Following the prayer is the date, signature, and address (including e-mail address and telephone number) of the attorney filing the complaint. Some jurisdictions also require that the attorney include a state bar number. This signature is called the *subscription*. In some jurisdictions the name, address, and telephone number of the attorney appear on the first page above the caption rather than at the end of the complaint. A signature or subscription is still required at the end of the prayer. Under Rule 11 of the Federal Rules of Civil Procedure, when an attorney signs a pleading in federal court, that attorney is making certain representations to the court. She is representing that the pleading is not being used for any improper purpose, that the contentions are warranted by law, and that the allegations have evidentiary support. If the court finds these representations to be false, it has the power to sanction the attorney. The prayer and signature are shown in Exhibit 5-6.

In the *Hendricks* case described in the Commentary, if the attorney for the Hendrickses decided to sue all of the parties for fraud and negligent misrepresentation, and May Forrester for breach of a fiduciary duty, the entire complaint would look as shown in Exhibit 5-6.

The Request for a Jury

In federal court and in some state courts, if the plaintiff is requesting a jury trial in the case, that request is often included in the complaint. In federal courts, under Rule 38(b) of the Federal Rules of Civil Procedure, such a demand must be made no later than 14 days after service of the last pleading.

EXHIBIT 5-7 Verification

I, Margaret Hendricks, am one of the plaintiffs in the above entitled action. I have read the foregoing complaint. The facts stated therein are within my knowledge and are true and correct, except those matters stated on information and belief, and, as to those, I believe them to be true and correct.

I declare under penalty of perjury under the laws of the state of Nevada that the foregoing is true and correct.

Executed this ___ day of September, ___, at San Francisco, California.

_____

Verifications

Also, in some jurisdictions certain complaints, such as those seeking injunctive relief or punitive damages, often are required to be verified, or sworn to, under penalty of perjury. This is usually done by the plaintiff rather than by the attorney. See Exhibit 5-7 for a sample verification.

Disclosure Statement by Nongovernmental Corporate Party

Also, if any plaintiff is a nongovernmental corporation, it must file a special disclosure statement required by Rule 7.1 of the Federal Rules of Civil Procedure. This statement identifies any parent corporation and any publicly held corporation that owns 10% or more of its stock or states that there is no such corporation. This disclosure statement is required to be filed by all nongovernmental parties at the time they file their first documents in court. Thus, if the defendant is a corporation, it must file a disclosure statement with its answer.

Exhibits

Occasionally it is desirable or even necessary to attach a copy of some document to the complaint. For example, if a complaint is based on a breach of contract, a copy of the contract might be attached to the complaint as an exhibit and referred to in the body of the complaint. In a lawsuit based on trademark or patent infringement, copies of the trademark or patent applications might be attached as exhibits. The Federal Rules allow exhibits to be attached but do not prescribe a way to do this. Many local courts, however, describe in detail how this is to be done. Exhibits are placed at the end of the complaint, following the signatures and declarations, and are labeled (e.g., Exhibit A). If there are several exhibits, the court might require an index to the exhibits.

Along with the complaint itself, many courts have a form cover sheet that must be filled out and accompany the complaint. See Exhibit 5-8 for a sample cover sheet from a federal court.

EXHIBIT 5-8 Civil Cover Sheet

JS 44   (Rev. 12/12) cand rev (1/15/13)

CIVIL COVER SHEET

The JS 44 civil cover sheet and the information contained herein neither replace nor supplement the filing and service of pleadings or other papers as required by law, except as provided by local rules of court. This form, approved by the Judicial Conference of the United States in September 1974, is required for the use of the Clerk of Court for the purpose of initiating the civil docket sheet. *(SEE INSTRUCTIONS ON NEXT PAGE OF THIS FORM.)*

I. (a) PLAINTIFFS

DEFENDANTS

(b) County of Residence of First Listed Plaintiff _____
(EXCEPT IN U.S. PLAINTIFF CASES)

County of Residence of First Listed Defendant _____
(IN U.S. PLAINTIFF CASES ONLY)
NOTE: IN LAND CONDEMNATION CASES, USE THE LOCATION OF
THE TRACT OF LAND INVOLVED.

(c) Attorneys *(Firm Name, Address, and Telephone Number)*

Attorneys *(If Known)*

II. BASIS OF JURISDICTION *(Place an "X" in One Box Only)*

☐ 1   U.S. Government
Plaintiff

☐ 3   Federal Question
(U.S. Government Not a Party)

☐ 2   U.S. Government
Defendant

☐ 4   Diversity
(Indicate Citizenship of Parties in Item III)

III. CITIZENSHIP OF PRINCIPAL PARTIES *(Place an "X" in One Box for Plaintiff*
(For Diversity Cases Only)   *and One Box for Defendant)*

	PTF	DEF		PTF	DEF
Citizen of This State	☐ 1	☐ 1	Incorporated *or* Principal Place of Business In This State	☐ 4	☐ 4
Citizen of Another State	☐ 2	☐ 2	Incorporated *and* Principal Place of Business In Another State	☐ 5	☐ 5
Citizen or Subject of a Foreign Country	☐ 3	☐ 3	Foreign Nation	☐ 6	☐ 6

IV. NATURE OF SUIT *(Place an "X" in One Box Only)*

CONTRACT	TORTS		FORFEITURE/PENALTY	BANKRUPTCY	OTHER STATUTES
☐ 110 Insurance	**PERSONAL INJURY**	**PERSONAL INJURY**	☐ 625 Drug Related Seizure of Property 21 USC 881	☐ 422 Appeal 28 USC 158	☐ 375 False Claims Act
☐ 120 Marine	☐ 310 Airplane	☐ 365 Personal Injury - Product Liability	☐ 690 Other	☐ 423 Withdrawal 28 USC 157	☐ 400 State Reapportionment
☐ 130 Miller Act	☐ 315 Airplane Product Liability	☐ 367 Health Care/			☐ 410 Antitrust
☐ 140 Negotiable Instrument	☐ 320 Assault, Libel & Slander	Pharmaceutical Personal Injury		**PROPERTY RIGHTS**	☐ 430 Banks and Banking
☐ 150 Recovery of Overpayment & Enforcement of Judgment	☐ 330 Federal Employers' Liability	Product Liability		☐ 820 Copyrights	☐ 450 Commerce
☐ 151 Medicare Act	☐ 340 Marine	☐ 368 Asbestos Personal Injury Product Liability		☐ 830 Patent	☐ 460 Deportation
☐ 152 Recovery of Defaulted Student Loans (Excludes Veterans)	☐ 345 Marine Product Liability	**PERSONAL PROPERTY**	**LABOR**	☐ 840 Trademark	☐ 470 Racketeer Influenced and Corrupt Organizations
☐ 153 Recovery of Overpayment of Veteran's Benefits	☐ 350 Motor Vehicle	☐ 370 Other Fraud	☐ 710 Fair Labor Standards Act	**SOCIAL SECURITY**	☐ 480 Consumer Credit
☐ 160 Stockholders' Suits	☐ 355 Motor Vehicle Product Liability	☐ 371 Truth in Lending	☐ 720 Labor/Management Relations	☐ 861 HIA (1395ff)	☐ 490 Cable/Sat TV
☐ 190 Other Contract	☐ 360 Other Personal Injury	☐ 380 Other Personal Property Damage	☐ 740 Railway Labor Act	☐ 862 Black Lung (923)	☐ 850 Securities/Commodities/ Exchange
☐ 195 Contract Product Liability	☐ 362 Personal Injury - Medical Malpractice	☐ 385 Property Damage Product Liability	☐ 751 Family and Medical Leave Act	☐ 863 DIWC/DIWW (405(g))	☐ 890 Other Statutory Actions
☐ 196 Franchise			☐ 790 Other Labor Litigation	☐ 864 SSID Title XVI	☐ 891 Agricultural Acts
			☐ 791 Employee Retirement Income Security Act	☐ 865 RSI (405(g))	☐ 893 Environmental Matters
REAL PROPERTY	**CIVIL RIGHTS**	**PRISONER PETITIONS**		**FEDERAL TAX SUITS**	☐ 895 Freedom of Information Act
☐ 210 Land Condemnation	☐ 440 Other Civil Rights	**Habeas Corpus:**		☐ 870 Taxes (U.S. Plaintiff or Defendant)	☐ 896 Arbitration
☐ 220 Foreclosure	☐ 441 Voting	☐ 463 Alien Detainee		☐ 871 IRS—Third Party 26 USC 7609	☐ 899 Administrative Procedure Act/Review or Appeal of Agency Decision
☐ 230 Rent Lease & Ejectment	☐ 442 Employment	☐ 510 Motions to Vacate Sentence			☐ 950 Constitutionality of State Statutes
☐ 240 Torts to Land	☐ 443 Housing/ Accommodations	☐ 530 General			
☐ 245 Tort Product Liability	☐ 445 Amer. w/Disabilities - Employment	☐ 535 Death Penalty	**IMMIGRATION**		
☐ 290 All Other Real Property	☐ 446 Amer. w/Disabilities - Other	**Other:**	☐ 462 Naturalization Application		
	☐ 448 Education	☐ 540 Mandamus & Other	☐ 465 Other Immigration Actions		
		☐ 550 Civil Rights			
		☐ 555 Prison Condition			
		☐ 560 Civil Detainee - Conditions of Confinement			

V. ORIGIN *(Place an "X" in One Box Only)*

☐ 1   Original Proceeding
☐ 2   Removed from State Court
☐ 3   Remanded from Appellate Court
☐ 4   Reinstated or Reopened
☐ 5   Transferred from Another District *(specify)*
☐ 6   Multidistrict Litigation

VI. CAUSE OF ACTION

Cite the U.S. Civil Statute under which you are filing *(Do not cite jurisdictional statutes unless diversity)*:

Brief description of cause:

VII. REQUESTED IN COMPLAINT:

☐ CHECK IF THIS IS A **CLASS ACTION**
UNDER RULE 23, F.R.Cv.P.

DEMAND $

CHECK YES only if demanded in complaint:
JURY DEMAND: ☐ Yes   ☐ No

VIII. RELATED CASE(S)
IF ANY   *(See instructions):*

JUDGE _____   DOCKET NUMBER _____

DATE _____   SIGNATURE OF ATTORNEY OF RECORD _____

IX. DIVISIONAL ASSIGNMENT (Civil L.R. 3-2)

(Place an "X" in One Box Only)   ☐ SAN FRANCISCO/OAKLAND   ☐ SAN JOSE   ☐ EUREKA

| Print | Save As... | Reset |

Source: http://www.cand.uscourts.gov/civilforms

EXHIBIT 5-8 Civil Cover Sheet (*continued*)

JS 44 Reverse (Rev. 12/12)

INSTRUCTIONS FOR ATTORNEYS COMPLETING CIVIL COVER SHEET FORM JS 44
Authority For Civil Cover Sheet

The JS 44 civil cover sheet and the information contained herein neither replaces nor supplements the filings and service of pleading or other papers as required by law, except as provided by local rules of court. This form, approved by the Judicial Conference of the United States in September 1974, is required for the use of the Clerk of Court for the purpose of initiating the civil docket sheet. Consequently, a civil cover sheet is submitted to the Clerk of Court for each civil complaint filed. The attorney filing a case should complete the form as follows:

I.   **(a) Plaintiffs-Defendants.** Enter names (last, first, middle initial) of plaintiff and defendant. If the plaintiff or defendant is a government agency, use only the full name or standard abbreviations. If the plaintiff or defendant is an official within a government agency, identify first the agency and then the official, giving both name and title.

(b) County of Residence. For each civil case filed, except U.S. plaintiff cases, enter the name of the county where the first listed plaintiff resides at the time of filing. In U.S. plaintiff cases, enter the name of the county in which the first listed defendant resides at the time of filing. (NOTE: In land condemnation cases, the county of residence of the "defendant" is the location of the tract of land involved.)

(c) Attorneys. Enter the firm name, address, telephone number, and attorney of record. If there are several attorneys, list them on an attachment, noting in this section "(see attachment)".

II.   **Jurisdiction.** The basis of jurisdiction is set forth under Rule 8(a), F.R.Cv.P., which requires that jurisdictions be shown in pleadings. Place an "X" in one of the boxes. If there is more than one basis of jurisdiction, precedence is given in the order shown below.
United States plaintiff. (1) Jurisdiction based on 28 U.S.C. 1345 and 1348. Suits by agencies and officers of the United States are included here.
United States defendant. (2) When the plaintiff is suing the United States, its officers or agencies, place an "X" in this box.
Federal question. (3) This refers to suits under 28 U.S.C. 1331, where jurisdiction arises under the Constitution of the United States, an amendment to the Constitution, an act of Congress or a treaty of the United States. In cases where the U.S. is a party, the U.S. plaintiff or defendant code takes precedence, and box 1 or 2 should be marked.
Diversity of citizenship. (4) This refers to suits under 28 U.S.C. 1332, where parties are citizens of different states. When Box 4 is checked, the citizenship of the different parties must be checked**. (See Section III below; NOTE: federal question actions take precedence over diversity cases.)**

III.   **Residence (citizenship) of Principal Parties.** This section of the JS 44 is to be completed if diversity of citizenship was indicated above. Mark this section for each principal party.

IV.   **Nature of Suit.** Place an "X" in the appropriate box. If the nature of suit cannot be determined, be sure the cause of action, in Section VI below, is sufficient to enable the deputy clerk or the statistical clerk(s) in the Administrative Office to determine the nature of suit. If the cause fits more than one nature of suit, select the most definitive.

V.   **Origin.** Place an "X" in one of the six boxes.
Original Proceedings. (1) Cases which originate in the United States district courts.
Removed from State Court. (2) Proceedings initiated in state courts may be removed to the district courts under Title 28 U.S.C., Section 1441. When the petition for removal is granted, check this box.
Remanded from Appellate Court. (3) Check this box for cases remanded to the district court for further action. Use the date of remand as the filing date.
Reinstated or Reopened. (4) Check this box for cases reinstated or reopened in the district court. Use the reopening date as the filing date.
Transferred from Another District. (5) For cases transferred under Title 28 U.S.C. Section 1404(a). Do not use this for within district transfers or multidistrict litigation transfers.
Multidistrict Litigation. (6) Check this box when a multidistrict case is transferred into the district under authority of Title 28 U.S.C. Section 1407. When this box is checked, do not check (5) above.

VI. Cause of Action. Report the civil statute directly related to the cause of action and give a brief description of the cause. **Do not cite jurisdictional statutes unless diversity.** Example: U.S. Civil Statute: 47 USC 553 Brief Description: Unauthorized reception of cable service

VII. Requested in Complaint. Class Action. Place an "X" in this box if you are filing a class action under Rule 23, F.R.Cv.P.
Demand. In this space enter the actual dollar amount being demanded or indicate other demand, such as a preliminary injunction.
Jury Demand. Check the appropriate box to indicate whether or not a jury is being demanded.

VIII. Related Cases. This section of the JS 44 is used to reference related pending cases, if any. If there are related pending cases, insert the docket numbers and the corresponding judge names for such cases.

Date and Attorney Signature. Date and sign the civil cover sheet.

filing
Presenting a paper to the court clerk to be included in the court file for the case.

docket number
A number assigned to a lawsuit by the court; each pleading or document filed in the action must bear this number.

FILING THE COMPLAINT

After the complaint has been prepared, reviewed by the attorney, and properly signed, it can be filed in the proper court (see Exhibit 5-9). **Filing** of a complaint means that the document is given to the court. The court, in turn, assigns a number, known as a **docket number**, to the case and starts a file that will contain all subsequent pleadings and other documents dealing with the case. All subsequent pleadings and papers filed in connection with the case must contain the docket number to ensure proper filing. When filing a complaint, the court usually requires a filing fee, which must be paid before the court will accept the document. Filing fees will be waived if the plaintiff can show financial hardship. Whenever you file a complaint with the court, you should retain copies of the complaint on which the docket number and date of filing are noted (usually two or three copies).

The traditional manner of filing complaints (as well as other pleadings and motions) involves delivery of the paper documents to the court. Delivery is made by the attorney or a member of his or her staff, by mail or, if the court allows, by fax. Today, many courts have procedures to allow for electronic filing; that is, delivery of the documents in electronic format through the Internet. Electronic filing is becoming common and in some courts even required. A litigation paralegal needs to be familiar with the process.

EXHIBIT 5-9 Complaint Checklist

COMPLAINT CHECKLIST

Before filing your complaint be sure that you have:

✓ reviewed all local rules to special format requirements
✓ included title of court
✓ properly identified and named the parties in the caption
✓ titled the complaint (i.e., Complaint for Damages)
✓ demanded a jury (if applicable)
✓ stated one or more **complete** causes of action, **each** containing (expressly or by incorporation by reference):
  • a statement of jurisdiction
  • identification of the status and capacity of the parties
  • a basis for a recognized claim
  • a description of the damages
✓ stated at least one cause of action against **each** defendant
✓ included a prayer or request for damages
✓ affixed the proper signature, and declarations
✓ attached any required cover sheets

ELECTRONIC FILING (E-FILING)

Federal Courts

Rule 5(d)(3) of the Federal Rules of Civil Procedure provides that "A court may, by local rule, allow papers to be filed, signed, or verified by electronic means that are consistent with any technical standards established by the Judicial Conference of the United States. A local rule may require electronic filing only if reasonable exceptions are allowed. A paper filed electronically in compliance with a local rule is a written paper for purposes of these rules."

To date almost every federal district court has adopted local rules regulating the process. Electronic filing in the federal court is dependent on two technology systems adopted by the federal court system: Public Access to Court Electronic Records (PACER) and Case Management and Electronic Case Files (CM/ECF).

Recall that PACER is a system whereby the public can electronically *access* case information concerning cases filed in a specified federal court. Use of the PACER system allows the user to retrieve information about court filings and see many actual documents filed in the case by the attorneys (e.g., complaints, answers, and motions); however, this system has no capabilities for attorneys to file documents in the court. To file papers in the federal courts, attorneys must use the court's case management system (CM/ECF).

Electronic filing provides many advantages to both the court and the attorneys. It allows the court to maintain an electronic file that is accessible through the Internet (using the PACER system for federal courts), documents are never "misplaced," and judges and attorneys can view documents at any time. In large complex cases with multiple parties and multiple pleadings, these are valuable features. Attorneys and paralegals are often faced with technical and practical considerations when e-filing documents. Fortunately, most courts provide detailed instructions, tutorials, and user guides to facilitate the process. Additional information and tutorial help can be found through the PACER Web site at <http://www.pacer.gov/cmecf/>.

Before attempting to electronically file a document several steps must be taken:

1. Read all local rules concerning the procedure. Local rules will inform you as to whether you are allowed to file a particular document electronically. Some courts do not allow the initial complaint to be e-filed and may have rules excluding certain types of cases from e-filing. In some instances local rules not only allow e-filing but also require it. A local rule may provide that individual judges have the right to determine whether cases assigned to them should be subject to e-filing. If so, you may find that once you file a paper copy of the complaint, you are ordered to submit an electronic copy to the court.

2. Make sure that your office has the computer hardware and software necessary to e-file. There are basic requirements for e-filing—a computer, a scanner, Internet access, and software that will convert your documents to a portable document format (PDF), which prevents anyone from making changes to the document.

3. Prior to actually filing, the attorney must register with both the PACER and CM/ECF systems. The attorney will be given a password that is required to log on to the e-filing system. You will not be allowed to e-file without this registration.

4. Prepare the documents to be e-filed according to court rules and convert them to a PDF. The federal courts require documents to be in a PDF format. (State courts may have different rules on this.) If you have attachments or exhibits for your document, they are usually scanned in.

5. Access the court Web site where the document is to be filed, and then log on to the system for e-filing. At this point you will be required to provide information about the document and case. Several screens will prompt you for information about the attorneys, the parties, and the nature of the documents. The courts have extensive lists describing labels to be assigned to documents. One of the more difficult aspects of e-filing is identifying the proper label or category of the documents to be filed.

6. If your document is successfully filed, you will receive an electronic receipt showing this fact.

One question that inevitably arises in the e-filing process is how to handle signature requirements. Attorney signatures are generally not required. Because the attorney has registered for PACER and CM/ECF and been given a special log-on password, the court considers use of that password to carry the same significance as a signature. If a signature of someone other than the attorney is required, many courts require the attorney to maintain the original paper document with the signature and to electronically file a conformed copy. A conformed copy often contains an indication on the signature line such as "s/" followed by the individual's name. This signifies that the original document contains an actual signature. Another consideration is payment of any filing fees. This is often done through credit cards.

When a document is e-filed, the attorneys realize one further advantage. Upon filing any document, the court often sends notice to all parties who have electronically appeared in the action. Because the parties can then access the document online, in many cases, no formal service is required for anyone who receives the electronic notice. Formal service is almost always required for a complaint, however, even if it is electronically filed. In such cases, defendants would not have already appeared and thus would not have received any electronic notice. See Exhibit 5-10.

State Courts

Like the federal courts, many state courts have implemented procedures for e-filing. State courts, however, do not use the federal CM/ECF system; each state has its own rules and procedures. For e-filing in state courts, some attorneys choose to use the services of third parties who handle the technical aspects of the process. To see links to state court rules on e-filing go to <http://www.americanbar.org/aba.html> and search for "electronic filing."

Even if you file documents electronically through the Internet, check local rules to find whether you also are required to send a paper "courtesy copy" of the document to the judge assigned to the case. Many courts require this.

EXHIBIT 5-10 PACER CM/ECF Web Site

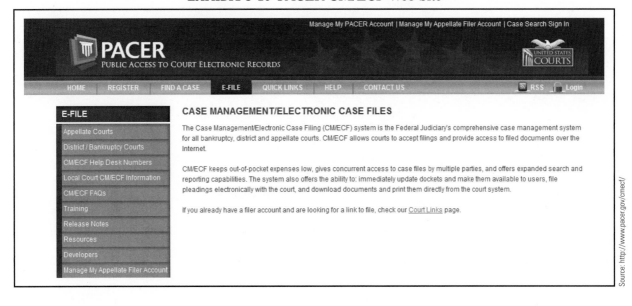

Source: http://www.pacer.gov/cmecf/

Source: http://www.pacer.gov/cmecf/

THE SUMMONS

At the time the complaint is filed, the court issues a summons. A **summons** is a form explaining that the defendant has been sued and should answer the complaint by a certain date. Issuance of the summons occurs when the clerk of the court affixes his or her signature to the form. It is expected that the attorney for the plaintiff will have the form filled out and will submit it to the clerk when the complaint is filed. The original summons is not filed with the court at this time; the plaintiff retains it until after the defendants have been served. At that time the original summons can be returned to the court for filing, along with evidence that the defendants have been served. In some courts, if the summons is not returned to the court within a certain time, the case can be dismissed. See Exhibit 5-11 for an example of a summons used in federal court.

summons
A form served with a complaint informing a person of a lawsuit against him or her, the time limit for responding to the lawsuit, and the consequences of failing to respond.

SERVING THE COMPLAINT

The defendant in any lawsuit is entitled to receive notice of the action. This is accomplished by service of process. A copy of the summons and a copy of the complaint must be delivered to the defendant. It is the plaintiff's responsibility, rather than the court's, to see that the defendant is properly served. As a litigation paralegal, one of your duties may be to arrange for service after the complaint has been filed.

All jurisdictions have rules regarding who can serve the papers, how they can be served, and time limits for service. For federal court, these rules are found in Rule 4 of the Federal Rules of Civil Procedure (see Exhibit 5-12A). Although there may be some differences from one jurisdiction to another, there are similar concepts. Generally, plaintiffs

EXHIBIT 5-11 Summons

AO 440 (Rev. 06/12) Summons in a Civil Action

UNITED STATES DISTRICT COURT

for the

_____ District of _____

	)	
	)	
	)	
	)	
Plaintiff(s)	)	
v.	)	Civil Action No.
	)	
	)	
	)	
	)	
Defendant(s)	)	

SUMMONS IN A CIVIL ACTION

To: *(Defendant's name and address)*

A lawsuit has been filed against you.

Within 21 days after service of this summons on you (not counting the day you received it) — or 60 days if you are the United States or a United States agency, or an officer or employee of the United States described in Fed. R. Civ. P. 12 (a)(2) or (3) — you must serve on the plaintiff an answer to the attached complaint or a motion under Rule 12 of the Federal Rules of Civil Procedure. The answer or motion must be served on the plaintiff or plaintiff's attorney, whose name and address are:

If you fail to respond, judgment by default will be entered against you for the relief demanded in the complaint. You also must file your answer or motion with the court.

CLERK OF COURT

Date: _____

_____
Signature of Clerk or Deputy Clerk

EXHIBIT 5-11 Summons (*continued*)

AO 440 (Rev. 06/12) Summons in a Civil Action (Page 2)

Civil Action No. _____

PROOF OF SERVICE
(This section should not be filed with the court unless required by Fed. R. Civ. P. 4 (l))

This summons for *(name of individual and title, if any)* _____

was received by me on *(date)* _____ .

❒ I personally served the summons on the individual at *(place)* _____

_____ on *(date)* _____ ; or

❒ I left the summons at the individual's residence or usual place of abode with *(name)* _____

_____ , a person of suitable age and discretion who resides there,

on *(date)* _____ , and mailed a copy to the individual's last known address; or

❒ I served the summons on *(name of individual)* _____ , who is

designated by law to accept service of process on behalf of *(name of organization)* _____

_____ on *(date)* _____ ; or

❒ I returned the summons unexecuted because _____ ; or

❒ Other *(specify):*

_____ .

My fees are $ _____ for travel and $ _____ for services, for a total of $ ___0.00___ .

I declare under penalty of perjury that this information is true.

Date: _____

_____
Server's signature

_____
Printed name and title

_____
Server's address

Additional information regarding attempted service, etc:

| Print | Save As... | | Reset |

EXHIBIT 5-12A Service under Rule 4 of the Federal Rules of Civil Procedure

SERVICE UNDER RULE 4 OF THE FEDERAL RULES OF CIVIL PROCEDURE

Under Rule 4 of the Federal Rules of Civil Procedure, the complaint and summons can be served by any of the following methods:

To serve an individual within the United States

1. Any manner authorized by the state in which the defendant is served.
2. Personal delivery of a copy to the defendant.
3. Leaving the papers with a person of suitable age at the defendant's dwelling.
4. Waiver of service by the defendant.

To serve an individual in a foreign country

1. Internationally agreed method (i.e., Hague Convention).
2. Manner prescribed by law of foreign country, provided service is reasonably calculated to give notice.
3. Unless prohibited by foreign country, either personal delivery of the papers to defendant or any form of mail requiring signed receipt.
4. As directed by court.
5. Waiver of service by defendant.

To serve a minor or incompetent

1. If the defendant is within the United States, in a like manner to that prescribed by the law of the state in which service is made.
2. If the defendant is outside the United States, as prescribed by the law of the foreign country.

To serve a corporation or association

1. Delivery of a copy to an officer, managing agent, or agent authorized by statute and mailing of a copy to the defendant if that statute so requires.
2. Waiver of service.

To serve the U.S. government and its agencies or officers

1. Delivery of a copy of the summons and complaint to the U.S. attorney, assistant U.S. attorney, or designated agent for the district in which the action is brought *and*
2. Mailing of a copy by registered or certified mail to the civil process clerk at the office of the U.S. attorney and sending of a copy to the Attorney General in Washington *and*
3. If the validity of any order of any federal officer or agency is involved, also by mailing of the papers to that officer or agency.
4. If a U.S. agency or officer is a named defendant, also sending of a copy of the papers to the agency or officer by registered or certified mail.

To serve a foreign government

1. Manner pursuant to 28 U.S.C. § 1608.

To serve a state or local government

1. Delivery of a copy to the chief executive officer or in any manner prescribed by the law of the state.

Source: http://www.uscourts.gov/uscourts/RulesAndPolicies/rules/2010%20Rules/Civil%20Procedure.pdf

EXHIBIT 5-12B Proof of Electronic Service

POS-050/EFS-050

ATTORNEY OR PARTY WITHOUT ATTORNEY *(Name, State Bar Number, and Address):*	*FOR COURT USE ONLY*
	To keep other people from seeing what you entered on your form, please press the Clear This Form button at the end of the form when finished.

TELEPHONE NO.:   FAX NO. *(Optional):*

E-MAIL ADDRESS *(Optional):*

ATTORNEY FOR *(Name):*

SUPERIOR COURT OF CALIFORNIA, COUNTY OF

STREET ADDRESS:

MAILING ADDRESS:

CITY AND ZIP CODE:

BRANCH NAME:

PLAINTIFF/PETITIONER:

DEFENDANT/RESPONDENT:

CASE NUMBER:

JUDICIAL OFFICER:

PROOF OF ELECTRONIC SERVICE

DEPT:

1. I am at least 18 years old and not a party to this action.

   a. My residence or business address is *(specify):*

   b. My electronic service address is *(specify):*

2. I electronically served the following documents *(exact titles):*

   ☐ The documents served are listed in an attachment *(Form POS-050(D)/EFS-050(D) may be used for this purpose.)*

3. I electronically served the documents listed in 2 as follows:

   a. Name of person served:

      On behalf of *(name or names of parties represented, if person served is an attorney):*

   b. Electronic service address of person served:

   c. On *(date):*

   d. At *(time):*

   ☐ The documents listed in item 2 were served electronically on the persons and in the manner described in an attachment. *(Form POS-050(P)/EFS-050(P) may be used for this purpose.)*

Date:

I declare under penalty of perjury under the laws of the State of California that the foregoing is true and correct.

▶

(TYPE OR PRINT NAME OF DECLARANT)   (SIGNATURE OF DECLARANT)

Page 1 of 1

Form Approved for Optional Use Judicial Council of California POS-050/EFS-050 [Rev.January 1, 2011]	**PROOF OF ELECTRONIC SERVICE** (Proof of Service/Electronic Filing and Service)	Cal.Rules of Court, rule 2.251 www.courts.ca.gov

For your protection and privacy, please press the Clear This Form button after you have printed the form.

Save This Form   Print This Form   Clear This Form

Source: http://www.courts.ca.gov/documents/efs050.pdf

*personal service of
process*
Notice of a lawsuit or other
proceeding that is given to a
party by personally delivering a
copy of the papers to that party.

proof of service
Written verification that papers
have been delivered to a party,
detailing when, where, and how
the papers were delivered.

cannot serve the papers themselves. Someone must do it for them. Various law enforcement agencies and personnel, such as the U.S. Marshal or a local sheriff, sometimes take responsibility for serving civil complaints. They may, however, charge the plaintiff a fee for doing this. In other instances, the complaint is served by a licensed process server, an individual licensed by the state to serve papers. In some cases, the complaint is served by any adult who is not a party to the action.

You must be concerned not only about who serves the complaint, but also with how it is served. A common method of service is **personal service of process**. In personal service, a copy of the summons and complaint are personally delivered to the defendant. Sometimes this is difficult, if not impossible. Some laws, such as Rule 4 of the Federal Rules of Civil Procedure, allow a copy of the summons and complaint to be left with a competent adult at the defendant's residence. Some states also allow the papers to be served by mail or in some cases by publication. When personal service cannot be accomplished, appropriate laws must be reviewed to determine alternatives.

If the defendant in the lawsuit is a corporation, service is usually accomplished by serving an officer of the corporation or by serving an individual whom the corporation has designated to accept service. As previously noted, this individual is known as the agent for service of process. The names and addresses of corporate officers or agents for service can usually be obtained from the secretary of state where the corporation is incorporated or does business.

Service on corporations or individuals located outside of the United States often presents special challenges. Rule 4 allows service in a number of different ways (see Exhibit 5-12a), including any method as directed by the court. In a 2013 case decided by the district court located in the Southern District of New York, the court authorized service through e-mail and Facebook, finding that these methods were likely to give actual notice to the defendants, who were located in India. The case was *FTC. v. PCCare247, Inc.* Service of individuals outside of the United states may also raise issues under treaties with foreign nations. Information about these treaties can be found on the Web site for the U.S. Department of State at <http://travel.state.gov/law/judicial /judicial_680.html>

In addition to the manner of service, you also need to be concerned about any time limits that may affect service. For example, in federal court the copy of the complaint and summons should be served within 120 days of the filing of the complaint. Failure to do so, without justification, can result in dismissal of the action. (See Rule 4[m] of the Federal Rules of Civil Procedure.) It is a good idea, therefore, to tickle or calendar the file to check for timely service. After service has been completed, the person serving the complaint must certify in writing when, where, and how service was accomplished. This is done in a document called a **proof of service**. A form for the proof of service will probably be found on the reverse side of the summons. See page 2 of Exhibit 5-11 for a copy of the form used in a federal court. The proof of service should then be filed with the court. See Exhibit 5-12B for form used for electronic service in a state court.

Waiver of Service

Under Rule 4 of the Federal Rules of Civil Procedure, a defendant is encouraged to waive formal service of process. The rule sets out a procedure to be followed to accomplish this.

The plaintiff sends by first-class mail the following documents: the complaint, a notice explaining the process of waiver and the consequences of failing to waive service, and a waiver form for the defendant to sign. The defendant then signs and returns the waiver-of-service form to the plaintiff's attorney within 30 days (or 60 days if the defendant is outside the country). Waiver of service is dependent on the defendant's agreement. If he fails to sign and return the written waiver form, then service must be accomplished in one of the more traditional methods. However, if the defendant refuses to waive service, the court can impose on that defendant the cost of subsequent service (see Exhibit 5-13 and Exhibit 5-14).

stipulation
An agreement between opposing lawyers in a lawsuit.

AMENDING THE COMPLAINT

Regardless of how carefully you draft a complaint, at times additions, deletions, or changes must be made. To do this you need to amend the complaint. Most jurisdictions view the rules of pleading very liberally. No court is interested in seeing a party lose a case because of some technical deficiency in the pleadings that could be easily corrected. As long as an amendment does not drastically alter the nature of the case, or cause any undue hardship to the defendant or delay in the case, it will probably be allowed. Rule 15 of the Federal Rules of Civil Procedure allows the plaintiff to amend the complaint once, as a matter of right, within 21 days after a responsive pleading or motion was filed. After that, the plaintiff needs either a stipulation from the other parties agreeing to the amendment or an order from the court. A **stipulation** *to amend the complaint* is a written agreement among all parties (signed by their attorneys) allowing the plaintiff to make certain changes in the complaint. It is generally filed in court along with the amended complaint. See Exhibit 5-15 for a sample stipulation to amend the complaint. If the plaintiff cannot obtain a stipulation, he must make a motion in court asking the court to allow the filing of the amended complaint.

To amend a complaint, appropriate changes are made to the original complaint, and a new complaint is prepared. It is entitled "First Amended Complaint." Other than the title, the format of the document is the same as that of the original complaint.

When a complaint is amended, the statute of limitations usually *relates back* to the original date of filing. In other words, a complaint can usually be amended even after the statute of limitations has expired. An exception to this rule sometimes occurs when the amendment seeks to add a new defendant, one who was not named in the original complaint. As mentioned, in jurisdictions that allow their usage, the use of fictitiously named defendants, "Does," avoids this problem. In such a case, when the complaint is amended, it is not to bring in a new defendant, but rather to correct the name of that defendant. In federal court, under Rule 15 of the Federal Rules of Civil Procedure, the amendment relates back to the original filing date only when the newly named party has received notice of the action within 120 days of its being filed, will not be prejudiced, and knew or should have known that but for a mistake he would have been sued in the original complaint.

After an amended complaint is filed with the court, it must be served. However, if the defendants have obtained an attorney to represent them, service can be accomplished by mailing a copy of the amended complaint to the attorney.

EXHIBIT 5-13 Notice of Lawsuit and Request for Waiver of Service of Summons

AO 398 (Rev. 01/09) Notice of a Lawsuit and Request to Waive Service of a Summons

UNITED STATES DISTRICT COURT
for the

_____

)
)
)
)
)
)

_____)
Plaintiff
v.

Defendant

Civil Action No.

NOTICE OF A LAWSUIT AND REQUEST TO WAIVE SERVICE OF A SUMMONS

To: _____

(Name of the defendant or - if the defendant is a corporation, partnership, or association - an officer or agent authorized to receive service)

Why are you getting this?

A lawsuit has been filed against you, or the entity you represent, in this court under the number shown above. A copy of the complaint is attached.

This is not a summons, or an official notice from the court. It is a request that, to avoid expenses, you waive formal service of a summons by signing and returning the enclosed waiver. To avoid these expenses, you must return the signed waiver within _____ days *(give at least 30 days, or at least 60 days if the defendant is outside any judicial district of the United States)* from the date shown below, which is the date this notice was sent. Two copies of the waiver form are enclosed, along with a stamped, self-addressed envelope or other prepaid means for returning one copy. You may keep the other copy.

What happens next?

If you return the signed waiver, I will file it with the court. The action will then proceed as if you had been served on the date the waiver is filed, but no summons will be served on you and you will have 60 days from the date this notice is sent (see the date below) to answer the complaint (or 90 days if this notice is sent to you outside any judicial district of the United States).

If you do not return the signed waiver within the time indicated, I will arrange to have the summons and complaint served on you. And I will ask the court to require you, or the entity you represent, to pay the expenses of making service.

Please read the enclosed statement about the duty to avoid unnecessary expenses.

I certify that this request is being sent to you on the date below.

Date: _____

_____
Signature of the attorney or unrepresented party

_____
Printed name

_____
Address

_____
E-mail address

_____
Telephone number

Source: http://www.uscourts.gov/uscourts/FormsAndFees/Forms/AO398.pdf

EXHIBIT 5-14 Waiver of Service of Summons

AO 399 (01/09) Waiver of the Service of Summons

UNITED STATES DISTRICT COURT
for the

_____)
              Plaintiff   )
                    v.   )   Civil Action No.
)
_____)
              Defendant   )

WAIVER OF THE SERVICE OF SUMMONS

To: _____
       (Name of the plaintiff's attorney or unrepresented plaintiff)

      I have received your request to waive service of a summons in this action along with a copy of the complaint, two copies of this waiver form, and a prepaid means of returning one signed copy of the form to you.

      I, or the entity I represent, agree to save the expense of serving a summons and complaint in this case.

      I understand that I, or the entity I represent, will keep all defenses or objections to the lawsuit, the court's jurisdiction, and the venue of the action, but that I waive any objections to the absence of a summons or of service.

      I also understand that I, or the entity I represent, must file and serve an answer or a motion under Rule 12 within 60 days from _____, the date when this request was sent (or 90 days if it was sent outside the United States). If I fail to do so, a default judgment will be entered against me or the entity I represent.

Date: _____

                                                     _____
                                                  Signature of the attorney or unrepresented party

_____   _____
   Printed name of party waiving service of summons   *Printed name*

                                                      _____
                                                     Address

                                                      _____
                                                   E-mail address

                                                      _____
                                                  Telephone number

Duty to Avoid Unnecessary Expenses of Serving a Summons

      Rule 4 of the Federal Rules of Civil Procedure requires certain defendants to cooperate in saving unnecessary expenses of serving a summons and complaint. A defendant who is located in the United States and who fails to return a signed waiver of service requested by a plaintiff located in the United States will be required to pay the expenses of service, unless the defendant shows good cause for the failure.

      "Good cause" does *not* include a belief that the lawsuit is groundless, or that it has been brought in an improper venue, or that the court has no jurisdiction over this matter or over the defendant or the defendant's property.

      If the waiver is signed and returned, you can still make these and all other defenses and objections, but you cannot object to the absence of a summons or of service.

      If you waive service, then you must, within the time specified on the waiver form, serve an answer or a motion under Rule 12 on the plaintiff and file a copy with the court. By signing and returning the waiver form, you are allowed more time to respond than if a summons had been served.

Source: http://www.uscourts.gov/uscourts/FormsAndFees/Forms/AO399.pdf

EXHIBIT 5-15 Stipulation for Filing Amended Complaint

(CAPTION)

	) NO.
	) STIPULATION FOR FILING
	) OF FIRST
	) AMENDMENT COMPLAINT
	)

_____

The undersigned hereby stipulates that plaintiff may file the attached First Amended Complaint in this action, and further acknowledge service of a copy.

_____

Attorney for Defendant

Copyright © 2015 Cengage Learning®

FINDING IT on the Internet

The paralegal in the *Hendricks* case had to prepare a complaint to be filed in a court in a distant jurisdiction. The Internet provides numerous sources that can help in such a case.

a. Review the *Hendricks* case found in the case Commentary. The plaintiffs chose to file in the District of Nevada. However, they could have filed elsewhere, including the District of Idaho. Using the site **<http://www.uscourts.gov>**, link to the home pages of each of these courts. Summarize the information that is available on these sites.

b. Electronic availability of court documents will make litigation practice more convenient for attorneys and paralegals, especially when dealing with distant courts. Do your local federal and state trial courts accept electronic filing? Access the Web sites for these courts and summarize any information concerning electronic filing. (Hint: The Web site for your local federal district court can be accessed through **<www.uscourts.gov>**.)

c. Wherever a lawsuit is filed, it always helps to see samples of similar complaints. Several sites contain copies of actual legal documents, including the U.S. Department of Justice, Civil Rights Division, **<http://www.justice.gov/crt/index.php>**. Access that site and search for "cases & briefs." You will find several legal documents, including complaints. Find and summarize one complaint from the Web site of the Department of Justice.

SUMMARY

- Pleadings are the documents filed in a court that define the nature of the dispute between the parties. The initial pleading filed in a lawsuit by the plaintiff is the complaint, or in some instances the petition. The complaint sets out the factual basis for the lawsuit. It is made up of a caption, which identifies the parties and the court; the body, which contains the factual allegations describing the dispute; the prayer, which is a request for relief; and the subscription, which consists of the signature, address, telephone number and e-mail of the plaintiff's attorney, and the date. Sometimes complaints are verified; that is, they contain the plaintiff's statement that the contents of the complaint are true under penalty of perjury.

- Before naming the various parties to the lawsuit, you must determine that the plaintiff is the real party in interest, identify and describe the status of the plaintiff and the defendant, and determine that the plaintiff and the defendant have the capacity to sue and be sued. A plaintiff is the real party in interest when he is the one entitled to the relief requested in the complaint. Status refers to the type of entity that describes the party, such as individual, corporate, or other business entity or government agency. Most competent adult individuals, corporations, and unincorporated associations have capacity to sue or be sued in their own names. However, minors and incompetent adults cannot sue on their own behalf, and a guardian ad litem must be appointed to represent their interests. A government entity can be sued only when allowed by law. Some jurisdictions allow the plaintiff to name fictitious defendants, or "Doe" defendants, in a lawsuit to provide for later-discovered defendants. All jurisdictions allow multiple plaintiffs and defendants to be joined in one lawsuit, as long as there is some common factual or legal question among them. When the number of potential plaintiffs in a lawsuit is too numerous to be practical, a class action may be filed as long as there are common issues. In a class action, certain named plaintiffs represent members of a class in a similar situation.

- The complaint must contain some allegation showing that the court in which the action is pending has proper jurisdiction and venue in the case.

- The body of the complaint, referred to as the cause of action or sometimes a count, contains allegations that describe the factual basis for the lawsuit. Some jurisdictions, known as code pleading jurisdictions, require that each element of the cause of action be supported by factual allegations. Other jurisdictions, known as notice pleading jurisdictions, only require that there be sufficient facts to put the defendant on notice as to why she is being sued. A complaint may contain multiple counts or causes of action, as well as multiple parties, as long as some common question exists.

- Every complaint or petition contains a prayer, which is a request for relief from the court. Courts can grant either money damages or equitable relief. Money damages are usually compensatory; that is, they compensate the plaintiff for a loss that he has sustained. In some cases, punitive damages are awarded. Punitive damages usually require some sort of extremely bad conduct on the part of the defendant. Equitable relief is varied, but includes orders such as specific performance, rescission, restitution, declaratory relief, and injunctions. Courts also have the power to grant provisional remedies such as a temporary restraining order or preliminary injunction pending the trial.

- Before drafting a complaint, you should check form books or forms files for complaints with similar factual situations. The physical appearance of the complaint is usually determined by the laws of the jurisdiction in which the complaint is filed. Local rules of courts also apply.

- After the complaint has been reviewed by the attorney and signed by the appropriate parties, it is filed in court. Filing involves giving the document to the court clerk with an appropriate filing fee. The court then assigns a docket number to the case. All subsequent papers filed in the case must bear this number. A complaint must be filed within the statute of limitations.

- Many courts now allow or require electronic filing. Electronic filing involves transmitting an electronic copy of the document to the court through the Internet. The federal courts use the system known as Case Management/Electronic Case Files (CM/ECF) to allow the filing. Local rules of court also control the procedures for e-filing.

- A summons is a form that explains to the defendant that he has been sued. It is issued by the court clerk at the time the complaint is filed. After the defendant is served, the summons is returned to the court.

- A copy of the complaint and a copy of the summons must be served on the defendant. Depending on the law of jurisdiction, these documents may be served by a U.S. Marshal, local sheriff, licensed process server, or any adult who is not a party to the action. Service can be accomplished in different ways. Personal service (delivering a copy of the documents personally to the defendant) is preferred in some jurisdictions. Under some circumstances, substituted service (leaving a copy of the documents at the defendant's home or business with another adult) is allowed. Some jurisdictions also permit service by mail or by publication. After the papers are served, the individual serving the papers fills out a proof of service that is later filed with the court. The Federal Rules encourage the defendant to waive formal service. However, the waiver process requires that the defendant be sent copies of all relevant papers.

- Additions, deletions, or changes to a complaint can be accomplished by amending the pleading. Amendments are allowed as a matter of right within 21 days of service of a responsive pleading or motion, but after that time an amendment requires either a stipulation from all parties or a court order. Unless an amendment adds new parties to the complaint, the statute of limitations relates back to the original date of filing the complaint.

KEY TERMS

allegation	guardian ad litem	quiet title action
capacity	indispensable party	real party in interest
caption	injunction	rescission
class action	interpleader	restitution
compensatory damages	permissive joinder	specific performance
compulsory joinder	personal service of process	stipulation
count	pleadings	subscription
declaratory relief	prayer	summons
docket number	preliminary injunction	temporary restraining
equitable relief	proof of service	order (TRO)
fictitiously named defendants	punitive or exemplary	verification
filing	damages	

REVIEW QUESTIONS

1. What is the purpose of pleadings?
2. What matters are generally contained in a complaint?
3. What factors should be reviewed before determining who will be named as parties to a lawsuit?
4. What is the difference between notice pleading and code pleading?
5. What are the types of remedies that may be requested from a court?
6. What are the steps in drafting a complaint?
7. How are complaints filed?
8. What is a summons?
9. How is service of process accomplished?
10. What is the procedure for amending a complaint?

CHAPTER EXERCISES

Where necessary, check with your instructor prior to starting any of these exercises.

1. Review the laws of your state and find all state laws dealing with the initial pleadings in a lawsuit. Check with your local courts to see if any local rules of court in your area regulate any aspect of the initial pleading. Local rules of court are often found on the Internet home page for the court.
2. Review the sample complaints found in this chapter. Do they meet the legal requirements in your state? If not, what would you have to change?
3. Locate a set of form books that provide sample forms for use in the courts of your state. Find a form for a complaint or petition for fraud and negligent misrepresentation. How does it compare with the sample complaint in this chapter?
4. Review the complaint found in Exhibit 5-6. Identify by number the paragraphs that show
   a. venue
   b. damages
   c. the existence of the doctrine of respondent superior
5. Review the case Commentary, the complaint in Exhibit 5-6, and Rule 4 of the Federal Rules of Civil Procedure outlined in Exhibit 5-12. How could Paradise Found, Inc. be served?
6. Assume that you are ready to file the complaint found in Exhibit 5-6. Because the court is located some distance away, you will be mailing the complaint and the summons to the court for filing. Draft a cover letter to the clerk of the court telling the clerk what documents are enclosed and what you want the court to do with the documents.
7. Assume that shortly after you filed the complaint, you discovered that Hearth and Home is a corporation rather than a partnership. It is incorporated in Nevada and this is its principal place of business. Prepare an amended complaint (Exhibit 5-6) that reflects this change.
8. Access the PACER Web site at <http://www.pacer.gov/> and from the home page access the PACER video tutorials by linking to the tab for "Training" and then selecting

the "Electronic Training Modules for District Court." Select the video tutorial "Filing a Complaint." Go through the tutorial and answer the following questions:

a. What tab is initially selected to start the e-filing process?

b. One of the steps in the e-filing process is to select the "party filing" from a drop down menu. How is the list organized?

c. How is the complaint identified?

d. What are the payment options for the filing fee?

CHAPTER PROJECT

Consider the following factual situation: Lowell Orloff, while shopping in a local department store, The Wear House, tripped and fell on a piece of torn carpeting. Lowell suffered severe injuries, including a broken leg. Lowell incurred medical bills in excess of $5,000 and was off work for three weeks, losing earnings in the amount of $6,000. Lowell is married to Barbara Orloff. The Wear House is a corporation incorporated under the laws of your state. The correct corporate name is A & B Corporation. Using form books from your state, prepare a complaint on behalf of Lowell Orloff against The Wear House based on their negligent maintenance of their premises.

THE *BENNETT* CASE
Assignment for Chapter 5

1. **Drafting a Complaint** Your supervising attorney is now ready to file a lawsuit on behalf of Bennett. You are to prepare a draft of the complaint. Check the Bennett research file (Appendix B) for a form to use in your preparation. The facts of the *Bennett* case will require you to make additions and changes to this form, however. Also, because this form was designed for a state action, you will have to add a paragraph establishing federal court jurisdiction. For further examples of employment discrimination complaints, review the Web site for the Civil Rights Division of the U.S. Department of Justice at <http://www.justice.gov/crt/index.php> (link to "Cases and Matters" and then to "Employment Litigation Cases").

2. **Serving the Complaint** After the complaint is filed, you will be responsible for serving the complaint on defendant Rikards-Harley. Your records indicate that this is a corporation. You have located a process server to serve the documents but you need to prepare specific instructions for the process server as to what documents need to be served, who to serve, and how to serve the papers. Write instructions to the process server with this information.

THE *DOUGLASS FINANCIAL SERVICES INC.* CASE
Assignment for Chapter 5: Drafting a Complaint

For the purposes of this assignment assume that you work for the firm representing the plaintiff, Jessica Hewitt. Draft a complaint against Creative Catering, Portman, and Douglass Financial Services Inc. for filing in your local state trial court. Be sure to follow all local rules of court. (A sample form for drafting the complaint is found in the Hewitt file in Appendix B.)

Responses to
the Complaint

CHAPTER OUTLINE

THE *GRANGER* CASE

Your supervising attorney has given you the file of a new client who was recently named as a defendant in a lawsuit for personal injury damages. Included in the file are the attorney's notes and copies of a summons and complaint. (See Exhibit 6-1 for a copy of the complaint.) After reading the file and discussing the case with the attorney, you learn that the client, Linda Granger, owns a flower shop and had employed Wesley Linstrom to make deliveries. Deliveries were made in a van owned by Granger. According to your client, last year Linstrom was involved in an automobile accident that is the subject of this lawsuit. The morning of the accident, Linstrom took the van without Granger's knowledge and drove several hundred miles to visit his girlfriend. In the past your client had allowed Linstrom to use the van for some personal errands. However, these always involved very short distances, and he always asked ahead of time. The client also stated that Linstrom told her that the accident happened when the driver of the other vehicle stopped suddenly for no reason and he, Linstrom, was unable to stop because the brakes on the van failed. The file indicates that your client was served with a copy of the summons and complaint 15 days ago. Your attorney has requested that, after reviewing the file, you prepare responsive pleadings for review.

Chapter 5 introduced the procedures for preparing, filing, and serving the complaint. The next step in the litigation process involves the response to that pleading. After completing this chapter, you should be able to:

- list the possible responses to the complaint.
- describe the time limitations for these responses, along with methods for changing these limitations.
- distinguish a general denial from a specific denial.
- explain the importance of pleading affirmative defenses.
- describe the general format of an answer.
- explain the procedure for serving and filing an answer.
- explain the process for amending a responsive pleading.
- define a counterclaim, cross-claim, and third-party complaint.
- identify and describe methods of raising legal challenges to the complaint.
- describe results of a failure to file any response to the complaint.

RESPONDING TO THE COMPLAINT

After the complaint is filed and served, the next step in the litigation process is up to the defendants. At this point defendants have various options; they can contest the lawsuit, negotiate a settlement with the plaintiff, or do nothing at all. If the defendants challenge the lawsuit, they can do so on two bases. They can either contest the facts of the case or challenge the action on some legal basis. For example, in the factual situation described in the opening Commentary, defendant Granger might deny that at the time of the accident Linstrom was acting as her employee, or she might deny that his negligence caused the

EXHIBIT 6-1 Complaint

UNITED STATES DISTRICT COURT
FOR THE NORTHERN DISTRICT OF CALIFORNIA

GORDON SHEFFIELD and AMY SHEFFIELD, Plaintiffs,	)))))	Civil No. 12345 COMPLAINT FOR NEGLIGENCE
v.	))	
WESLEY LINSTROM and LINDA GRANGER, Defendants.	)))	

_____

Plaintiff GORDON SHEFFIELD alleges:

JURISDICTION

1. Plaintiff is, and was at all times herein mentioned, domiciled in and a citizen of the state of California. Defendants and each of them are, and were at all times herein mentioned, domiciled in and a citizen of the state of Oregon. This is a civil action involving, exclusive of interest and costs, a sum in excess of $75,000. Every issue of law and fact in this action is wholly between citizens of different states.

FIRST COUNT

2. At all times herein mentioned, plaintiff was and now is a resident of the judicial district in which this action is filed.

3 At all times herein mentioned, defendant, LINDA GRANGER, was the owner of a certain motor vehicle, Oregon license number 123 XYZ.

4. At all times herein mentioned, defendant, WESLEY LINSTROM, was operating said motor vehicle with the permission and consent of defendant, LINDA GRANGER.

5. At all times herein mentioned, defendant, WESLEY LINSTROM, was the agent, employee, and servant of defendant, LINDA GRANGER, and at all times was acting within the course and scope of said agency and employment.

6. On May 1, _____, on a public highway called Market Street in San Francisco, California, defendant, WESLEY LINSTROM, negligently and carelessly drove the above-mentioned motor vehicle, Oregon license 123 XYZ, causing it to collide with another vehicle driven by plaintiff, who was also traveling on said highway.

7. As a result plaintiff was severely injured, having had his leg and arm broken and having suffered other bruises, contusions, and muscle strain. Also as a result plaintiff was prevented from transacting his business, suffered and continues to suffer great pain of body and mind, and incurred expenses for medical attention and hospitalization in the sum of ten thousand dollars ($10,000.00) and will continue to incur such expenses in an amount yet undetermined.

EXHIBIT 6-1 Complaint (*continued*)

SECOND COUNT

Plaintiff, AMY SHEFFIELD, alleges against defendants and each of them as follows:

8. Plaintiff realleges and incorporates by reference the allegations of paragraphs 1 through 5 above in their entirety.

9. On May 1, _____, plaintiff was a passenger in a vehicle being driven by co-plaintiff, GORDON SHEFFIELD, on a public highway called Market Street in San Francisco, California. At said time and place, defendant, WESLEY LINSTROM, negligently and carelessly drove a motor vehicle, Oregon license 123 XYZ, causing it to collide with the vehicle in which plaintiff, AMY SHEFFIELD, was a passenger.

10. As a result plaintiff was severely injured, having had her back broken and having suffered other bruises, contusions, and muscle strain. Also as a result plaintiff was prevented from transacting her business, suffered and continues to suffer great pain of body and mind, and incurred expenses for medical attention and hospitalization in the sum of fifteen thousand dollars ($15,000.00) and will continue to incur such expenses in an amount yet undetermined.

    Wherefore plaintiff, GORDON SHEFFIELD, demands judgment against defendants and each of them in the sum of $100,000.00 and costs.

    Wherefore plaintiff, AMY SHEFFIELD, demands judgment against defendants and each of them in the sum of $150,000.00 and costs.

Dated: April 30, _____

                                            _____

                                            TERRY ALVAREZ
                                            ALVAREZ & COE
                                            100 Market Street
                                            San Francisco, California 94101
                                            talvarez@esq.com
                                            (415) 555-1212
                                            Attorney for Plaintiffs

---

accident. In such a case she would be contesting the facts of the case. Alternatively, she might claim that she was not properly served with the complaint and summons and that therefore the action should be dismissed. She might also claim that the court lacks personal jurisdiction because she has had no contacts with the state of California. These would be legal challenges to the action (see Exhibit 6-2). In federal court every defense to the complaint can be asserted in the answer. However, certain defenses, such as lack of jurisdiction or venue, improper service, failure to state a proper claim or improper joinder of parties, may also be asserted by motion. In state court, some defenses must be asserted by motion or special pleadings.

Time Limits

If the defendants choose to contest the action, they must act within certain time limitations. If the case is filed in state court, the time limit is fixed by the state law. In federal court, under Rule 12, the time in which to respond is normally 21 days unless the

EXHIBIT 6-2 Defendant's Options

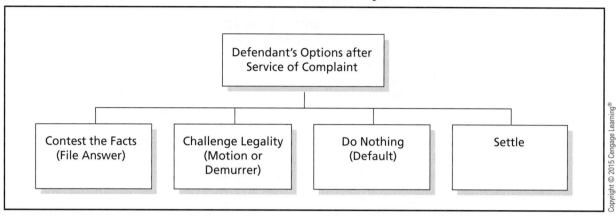

defendant waived service under Rule 4. If service was waived, the defendant has 60 days after the request for waiver was sent (or 90 days if the request for waiver was sent to a defendant out of the United States). Special rules also apply if the defendant is the U.S. government, a federal agency, or a federal employee. In such instances the time to respond is 60 days.

Frequently, as in the *Granger* case, a substantial part of this time has elapsed before the defendant locates and retains an attorney. As a result, once an attorney is retained, only a few days may remain for the attorney to evaluate the case, consider the possibility of an early settlement, or prepare a proper response to the complaint or petition. In most cases, the time in which to respond can be extended or enlarged, either by obtaining a stipulation from the plaintiff's attorney (which may have to be approved by the court, depending on the laws of the jurisdiction) or by making a motion, or formal request from the court, for such an order.

Stipulations Enlarging Time

A stipulation enlarging time to respond is an agreement between the attorneys in an action by which the defendant's attorney has additional time to respond. In federal court this agreement or stipulation must be approved by the court, but in some state courts it need not be. If the stipulation is subject to court approval, it should follow the same formalities required of the pleadings and bear the caption and docket number of the case. See Exhibit 6-3 for an example of such a stipulation.

If the stipulation does not require court approval, a letter between the attorneys confirming their agreement will suffice. The letter need not be filed in court, so it does not require a caption or docket number. Because you might be asked to write such a letter or prepare a formal stipulation for court approval, you should be aware of some possible problems that can arise. When preparing the stipulation, do not state that the agreement is for an extension of time in which to "answer." Rather, state that the agreement is for an extension of time in which to "answer or otherwise respond." Plaintiff's attorneys have been known to complain or object when, having given a defendant an extension of time in which to

EXHIBIT 6-3 Stipulation and Order Enlarging Time to Respond

UNITED STATES DISTRICT COURT
FOR THE NORTHERN DISTRICT OF CALIFORNIA

GORDON SHEFFIELD and AMY SHEFFIELD, Plaintiffs,	)))))	Civil No. 12345 STIPULATION AND ORDER FOR ENLARGEMENT OF TIME
v.	))	
WESLEY LINSTROM and LINDA GRANGER, Defendants.	)))	

IT IS STIPULATED by plaintiffs and defendant, LINDA GRANGER, through their respective counsel, that the time within which defendant, LINDA GRANGER, may have to respond to the complaint shall be, subject to approval by the court, extended to and including _____, _____ or such other date as the court may order.

There have been no previous stipulations or orders.

Dated _____, _____   _____

TERRY ALVAREZ
ALVAREZ & COE
100 Market Street
San Francisco, California 94101
talvarez@esq.com
(415) 555-1212
Attorney for Plaintiffs

_____

TAYLOR MARTIN
15 Plaza de Oro
Sacramento, California 94813
tmartin@esq.com
(916) 555-1212
Attorney for Defendant, Linda Granger

ORDER

Pursuant to the above stipulation filed herein, and good cause appearing, IT IS SO ORDERED.

Dated _____, _____   _____
                                                          Judge, District Court

"answer," they were served with a motion to dismiss or some other kind of legal challenge to the complaint. Although most courts refuse to sanction this type of narrow interpretation of the term *answer*, you can avoid any problem by making the agreement clear.

Another problem arises when the attorneys agree to an **open stipulation**. Most agreements for extensions or enlargements of time are for a definite amount of time. Sometimes, however, especially if attorneys are seriously discussing settlement, the extension of time will be open-ended. In such a case, the parties stipulate that the defendant need not answer until she is given notice by the plaintiff. This is referred to as an open stipulation. If such an agreement exists, be careful to tickle or calendar the case for review so that it is not forgotten. This is particularly important if your firm represents the plaintiff.

Motions to Extend or Enlarge Time

If the defendant's attorney needs more time to respond, and the plaintiff's attorney is unwilling to agree, an extension of time can be requested from the court. This is done by making a motion with the court. As mentioned, a motion is a formal request of the court for some kind of order. The details of motion practice are discussed in Chapter 7, but a motion to extend or enlarge time is usually made by filing papers with the court explaining the request and the reasons for it, serving these papers on the other attorneys in the action, and then possibly appearing in court for a short hearing on the motion.

TYPES OF ANSWERS

An answer is a pleading that challenges the plaintiff's right to the relief requested in the complaint. Normally this is done by contesting all or some of the facts alleged in the complaint, or by asserting other defenses. Answers are prepared using one of three main formats: the general denial, the specific denial, or the qualified denial.

General Denial

The substance of a **general denial** consists of one paragraph or allegation, in which the defendant denies all of the allegations contained in the complaint. Exhibit 6-5 found later in this chapter is an example of a general denial. In federal court, general denials are proper when the defendant denies all of the factual contentions of the complaint, including the allegations of subject matter jurisdiction, personal jurisdiction, and venue. However, an alternative method of challenging jurisdiction or venue exists and is more commonly used. These matters, along with certain other defenses, can be raised by a motion to dismiss the action. This method is discussed later in this chapter.

Many state jurisdictions follow the same procedures that apply in federal court, but some states treat general denials differently. In some courts general denials cannot be used if the complaint has been verified. Also, in some courts the use of a general denial is insufficient to raise certain legal defenses, such as lack of personal jurisdiction. Such a defense must be raised by motion. In fact, filing an answer of any kind might constitute a waiver of this defense.

open stipulation
An agreement between parties or their attorneys that a defendant need not answer a complaint within the time directed by law and need not answer until specifically notified by the plaintiff to do so.

general denial
A type of answer in which all of the allegations of the complaint are denied.

specific denial
A type of answer in which the defendant specifically replies to each of the contentions alleged in the complaint.

qualified denial
A type of answer denying all of the allegations of the complaint except those that are specifically admitted.

affirmative defense
Facts alleged by a defendant in an answer, which if proven, defeat plaintiff's claim, even if plaintiff can prove all the elements of his cause of action.

Specific Denial

A **specific denial** is an answer in which the defendant specifically replies to each contention or paragraph alleged in the complaint. The defendant replies to the various contentions by

- admitting all or part of the allegation or paragraph,
- denying all or part of the allegation or paragraph, or
- denying all or part of the allegation or paragraph on information and belief.

Admitting Allegations   Most complaints contain some allegations that are uncontested. For example, a defendant in a lawsuit might agree that the court has jurisdiction to hear the case even though that defendant is challenging the plaintiff's right to recover any damages. Allegations or contentions to which the defendant agrees are *admitted* in the answer. An admission of an allegation can be explicit in the answer or it can be implied by silence. If an allegation is not specifically denied, it is deemed to be admitted. Therefore, in drafting an answer, you must always use care not to ignore any allegation, unless you want to admit it.

Denying on Information and Belief   Occasionally, a defendant is not certain about an allegation, or does not have sufficient knowledge of the facts. Just as the plaintiff is allowed to plead facts on information and belief, so also is the defendant allowed to deny allegations in the same manner. Denials based on information and belief should be used only when the pleader honestly lacks firsthand knowledge of the true facts. If the truth or falsity of facts is within the knowledge of the defendant, the defendant is obliged to express this knowledge. Likewise, if the defendant can easily obtain the information regarding the truth or falsity of an allegation, he is obligated to do so.

Exhibit 6-6 found later in this chapter is an example of a specific denial.

Qualified Denial

A **qualified denial** is a combination of specific and general responses. In a qualified denial, the answering defendant expressly admits or denies certain allegations, then generally denies everything else.

Affirmative Defenses

An **affirmative defense** is a fact or circumstance that defeats the plaintiff's claim, even if the plaintiff can prove every contention alleged in the complaint.

Example

Assume that the plaintiff filed a lawsuit for breach of contract, alleging that the plaintiff loaned the defendant $75,000, and that when the loan was due the defendant refused to pay, and that the defendant continues to refuse to pay. Normally, if the plaintiff proves these allegations at trial, the plaintiff prevails and obtains a judgment for the amount of the unpaid loan. However, if the defendant alleges and proves that she filed bankruptcy and that this debt was discharged in bankruptcy, the plaintiff will lose the case. The fact that the debt was discharged in bankruptcy is an affirmative defense and operates to defeat the plaintiff's claim.

True affirmative defenses must be alleged in the answer or they are generally deemed waived. Thus, in the situation just described, the defendant must specifically allege in the answer that the debt was discharged in bankruptcy. If the defendant simply denies that the money is owed, this is insufficient, and the plaintiff would still get a judgment.

Whether a matter is an affirmative defense is a question of substantive law. Some matters, such as expiration of the statute of limitations, operate as affirmative defenses in all kinds of cases. However, other affirmative defenses vary depending on the area of substantive law involved. What constitutes affirmative defenses in contract cases may be very different from what constitutes affirmative defenses in tort cases. Researching the substantive law of the case may be necessary to determine what affirmative defenses exist in a particular situation.

AUTOMATED LITIGATION SUPPORT

Document Collaboration

SCENARIO

Your firm has been retained to represent Linda Granger who was sued for damages. She was served with a copy of the complaint and summons a few weeks prior. Your attorney gave you a copy of the complaint and asked you to prepare an answer for her review. The answer must be filed in five days. You have prepared several answers for complaints and know that you can do this within that time frame. However, your attorney also tells you that she will be away from the office for several days.

PROBLEM

As a conscientious paralegal you know that your work should be reviewed by an attorney. E-mail communication offers one way to transfer documents back and forth. However, your attorney's e-mail was "hacked" recently and she is very reluctant to send any client documents using e-mail. You also know that the answer should be signed by the attorney. How do you handle these issues and still file the answer on time?

SOLUTION

There are ways other than e-mail for parties to share and collaborate on documents. In addition to saving your documents on your computer, you can save and store documents on the "cloud." When you do this, your document is saved on a server available through the Internet. A popular service that allows you to do this is Dropbox. The program is downloaded to computers (or mobile devices) of the parties desiring to share documents. With proper passwords and access information different individuals can then retrieve, edit, and resave the document. Another popular way of sharing documents is Google Docs. Using this program, you save your documents online and can then share and edit them with other individuals. Using either of these programs, your attorney can review and, if necessary, edit your work and return it to you almost instantaneously.

Obtaining the physical signature of your attorney on the answer to be filed could be more difficult. She would need to have a final copy of the answer and use some sort of express delivery service to send it to you. Fortunately, the court in which your case is filed accepts electronic filing. When you check the local rules of court you find the following notice: "Per Civil Local Rule 5.1, all documents submitted under the attorney's login and password are automatically considered signed by that attorney, so the login and password are considered the attorney's 'electronic signature.'" You also see the following notice on the court's Web site: "an attorney may provide his/her login information to a staff member and authorize that staff member to e-file the attorney's court documents."

A partial list of affirmative defenses is found in Rule 8(c) of the Federal Rules of Civil Procedure. This list includes the following:

Affirmative Defenses Applicable to Contract Disputes

accord and satisfaction
duress
estoppel
failure of consideration
fraud
illegality
payment
release
statute of frauds
waiver

Affirmative Defenses Applicable to Tort Cases

assumption of the risk
contributory negligence
injury by fellow servant

Affirmative Defenses Applicable to All Cases

arbitration and award
laches
res judicata
statute of limitations

If any of these defenses is claimed in an action in federal court, it must be specifically alleged in the answer as an affirmative defense. Failure to do so could result in the defense being waived. This list, however, is not all-inclusive. Other affirmative defenses exist under different areas of substantive laws. See Exhibit 6-6 later in the chapter for examples of affirmative defenses in an answer.

DRAFTING THE ANSWER

An answer is a pleading that is filed in court. As such, it follows the same general format as the complaint. It contains a caption, body or allegations, prayer or "wherefore" clause, and signature. In some jurisdictions, it is prepared on pleading paper (paper that is numbered along the left side). Before drafting an answer, you might want to consult a form book, just as you do in drafting a complaint. Also, before actually beginning to draft the answer, review the entire complaint. It is often helpful to make a copy of the complaint and next to each paragraph make a note as to how you plan to respond to the allegations in the paragraph. This will help ensure that you do not inadvertently neglect to respond to an important allegation.

Caption

The caption for an answer is similar to the caption for the complaint. The names of the plaintiff and defendant are listed just as they are on the complaint. The document is titled ("Answer to Complaint"), and the docket number, which appears on the complaint, is included. The caption for an answer that would be prepared by your law firm on behalf of Granger would look as shown in Exhibit 6-4.

EXHIBIT 6-4 Caption for Answer to Complaint

**UNITED STATES DISTRICT COURT
FOR THE NORTHERN DISTRICT OF CALIFORNIA**

GORDON SHEFFIELD and AMY	)	Civil No. 12345
SHEFFIELD,	)	ANSWER TO COMPLAINT
Plaintiffs,	)	
	)	
	)	
v.	)	
	)	
WESLEY LINSTROM and LINDA	)	
GRANGER,	)	
Defendants.	)	

When several plaintiffs or defendants are named in a complaint, subsequent pleadings can contain a shortened form of their names. The caption contains the last name of the first listed plaintiff and the last name of the first listed defendant, with an indication that there are additional parties. The Latin phrase "et al." is used. Thus, the caption in Exhibit 6-4 could read

SHEFFIELD, et al.,
Plaintiffs,
v.
LINSTROM, et al.,
Defendants.

The term "et al." is Latin for "and others."

If the plaintiff demanded a jury, that demand appears in the caption of the complaint. It is not necessary that the defendant repeat this. However, if the plaintiff has not requested a jury, and the defense wants one, a jury demand should appear in the caption of the answer.

Body

The content of the answer depends on whether it is a specific, general, or qualified denial. A general denial contains only one paragraph, as described previously. See Exhibit 6-5 for an example of a general denial.

A specific denial is more detailed. However, only a few different paragraphs or allegations are generally used in an answer. Those responses generally fall into one of the following categories:

1. Defendants deny all the allegations or statements in a specifically named paragraph or paragraphs in the complaint.
2. Defendants deny having sufficient knowledge or belief to respond to the allegations or statements in a specifically named paragraph or paragraphs in the complaint.

EXHIBIT 6-5 General Denial

**UNITED STATES DISTRICT COURT
FOR THE NORTHERN DISTRICT OF CALIFORNIA**

GORDON SHEFFIELD and AMY   )   Civil No. 12345   —————   *Caption has same party*
SHEFFIELD,   )   ANSWER TO COMPLAINT   *names and docket number as*
     Plaintiffs,   )   *complaint*
)
)
     v.   )
)
WESLEY LINSTROM and LINDA   )
GRANGER,   )
     Defendants.   )

_____

Defendant, LINDA GRANGER, answers as follows: —————   *Introductory paragraph*
                                                          names answering defendant
Defendant denies each and every allegation of plaintiffs' complaint.

Wherefore defendant prays:

1. That the court enter judgment dismissing the complaint;
2. That defendant be awarded costs incurred herein; and
3. That defendant be awarded such other and further relief as the court may deem just.

Dated _____, _____

                              _____

                              TAYLOR MARTIN
                              15 Plaza de Oro
                              Sacramento, California 94813
                              tmartin@esq.com
                              (916) 555-1212
                              Attorney for Defendant, Linda Granger —— *Identify the specific answering*
                                                                      defendant

---

3. Defendants admit all the allegations or statements in a specifically named paragraph or paragraphs in the complaint.
4. Defendants admit some of the allegations or statements in a specifically named paragraph but deny other allegations in the same paragraph.

   The following are examples of paragraphs used in answers.

Example: Denial of all allegations of one or more paragraphs:

1. Defendant denies each and every allegation of Paragraphs 1, 2, and 3 of the complaint.

(Note that in the example above, the defendant is denying all of the allegations of three separate paragraphs in the complaint.)

Examples: Denial of information and belief:

2. Defendant denies having sufficient knowledge or information to form a belief as to the allegations contained in Paragraph 4 of the complaint, *or*

3. Defendant denies having sufficient knowledge or information to form a belief as to the allegations contained in Paragraph 4 of the complaint, and thereupon denies said allegations.

(Note that Paragraph 2 does not contain an express denial of the allegations of the complaint. The Federal Rules provide that when a defendant states that she lacks information and belief about an allegation, this will be deemed to be a denial. Some attorneys, however, prefer to expressly deny the allegations, and some jurisdictions require it.)

Example: Admission of allegation:

4. Defendant admits the allegations contained in Paragraph 5 of the complaint.

Example: Admission in part; denial in part:

5. Answering Paragraph 6 of the complaint, defendant admits that an automobile collision occurred between plaintiff and defendant but denies each and every other allegation contained in said paragraph.

Example: Qualified denial:

6. Defendant admits the allegations of Paragraphs 1, 2, and 3 of the complaint and denies each and every other allegation of plaintiff's complaint.

Answering a Multicount Complaint   In a complaint containing more than one count or cause of action, it is common to find a paragraph incorporating paragraphs from previous counts. (See Exhibit 6-1, Paragraph 8.) Responding to this paragraph sometimes presents difficulties, especially when some of the incorporated paragraphs have been admitted and some denied. The following is an example of a response that can be used:

Example: Incorporating by reference:

7. In answer to Paragraph 8 of Count Two of the complaint, wherein plaintiff incorporates by reference certain paragraphs of Count One of the complaint, defendant admits, denies, and alleges to the same effect and in the same manner as she admitted, denied, and alleged to those specific paragraphs previously in this answer.

In answering a complaint with more than one count or cause of action, questions sometimes arise regarding the format of the answer. Should each cause of action or count be answered separately in the answer, or can an allegation in the answer contain replies to allegations in the various counts? It is purely a matter of preference and can be done either way. For example, in the *Granger* case, if Granger were to deny Paragraphs 4, 5, 6, 7, 9, and 10 of the complaint, the body of the answer could be set up in one of two ways:

Example: Multicount answer:

Answer to Count 1

1. Defendant denies each and every allegation contained in Paragraphs 4, 5, 6, and 7 of plaintiff's complaint.

Answer to Count 2

2. Defendant denies each and every allegation contained in Paragraphs 9 and 10 of plaintiff's complaint.

Alternatively, the denial in the answer could be as follows:

Example: Multicount answer:

1. Defendant denies each and every allegation contained in Paragraphs 4, 5, 6, 7, 9, and 10 of plaintiff's complaint.

Affirmative Defenses   Whether a defendant files a general denial or a specific denial, affirmative defenses might apply. The substantive law of the case and the facts determine whether an affirmative defense exists. For example, suppose that in the factual situation described in the *Granger* case your client's records indicate that the accident occurred on April 29 instead of May 1. Because personal injury actions of this sort have a two-year statute of limitations in California, she would assert the expiration of the statute of limitations as an affirmative defense. The defendant might also assert the negligence of plaintiff, Gordon Sheffield, as an affirmative defense. In drafting the answer, affirmative defenses follow the paragraphs denying or admitting the allegations in the complaint. In an answer to a multicount complaint, affirmative defenses can be placed at the end of the answers to each count or at the end of answers to all of the counts (as is shown in Exhibit 6-6).

Prayer and Signature

The body of the answer is followed by a simple prayer, or "wherefore" clause, the date, and the signature of the attorney. In some courts, including federal court, the signature of the attorney is followed by the attorney's address, including e-mail address and telephone number. (In other jurisdictions this information is found on the first page of the document, above the title of the court.) The prayer usually requests that the plaintiffs be allowed no recovery. The date, signature, and address follow the same format as the complaint.

In its entirety, an answer prepared on behalf of Linda Granger to the complaint described in the Commentary would look as shown in Exhibit 6-6.

EXHIBIT 6-6

UNITED STATES DISTRICT COURT
FOR THE NORTHERN DISTRICT OF CALIFORNIA

GORDON SHEFFIELD and AMY SHEFFIELD, Plaintiffs,	)))))	Civil No. 12345 ANSWER TO COMPLAINT
v.	)))	
WESLEY LINSTROM and LINDA GRANGER, Defendants.	)))	

Answer to First Count

Defendant, LINDA GRANGER, answers as follows:

1. Defendant admits the allegations of Paragraphs 1, 2, and 3 of the complaint.
2. Defendant denies each and every allegation of Paragraphs 4, 5, 6, and 7 of the complaint.

Answer to Second Count

3. In answer to Paragraph 8 of Count Two of the complaint, wherein plaintiff incorporates by reference certain paragraphs of Count One of the complaint, defendant admits, denies, and alleges to the same effect and in the same manner as she admitted, denied, and alleged to those specific paragraphs previously in this answer.
4. In answer to Paragraph 9 of Count Two of the complaint, defendant admits that plaintiff, AMY SHEFFIELD, was a passenger in a vehicle being driven by co-plaintiff, GORDON SHEFFIELD, but denies each and every other allegation contained in said paragraph.
5. Defendant denies each and every allegation contained in Paragraph 10 of the complaint.

First Affirmative Defense

As and for an affirmative defense, defendant alleges that plaintiffs' right to maintain this action is barred by the statute of limitations in that more than two years have now elapsed between the date plaintiffs' alleged cause of action arose and the date plaintiffs filed their complaint.

Second Affirmative Defense

As and for a separate affirmative defense, defendant alleges that plaintiffs were themselves negligent, in that plaintiff, GORDON SHEFFIELD, failed to use ordinary care in the operation of his motor vehicle and failed to keep a proper lookout for other vehicles, and that both plaintiffs, GORDON SHEFFIELD and AMY SHEFFIELD, failed to exercise ordinary care, in that neither wore a seat belt. Defendant further alleges that said negligence contributed in whole or in part to any injuries which may have resulted.

EXHIBIT 6-6 (*Continued*)

Wherefore defendant prays:

1. That the court enter judgment dismissing the complaint;
2. That defendant be awarded costs incurred herein; and
3. That defendant be awarded such other and further relief as the court may deem just.

Dated _____, _____

_____
TAYLOR MARTIN
15 Plaza de Oro
Sacramento, California 94813
tmartin@esq.com
(916) 555-1212
Attorney for Defendant, Linda Granger

Verification

In federal court, complaints are not generally verified, that is, there is no express statement that the contents are true under penalty of perjury. In some state jurisdictions, however, plaintiffs are permitted to verify a complaint at any time. If the complaint is verified, usually the defendant cannot use a general denial and, furthermore, must verify the answer.

Service and Filing

After the answer is prepared, it must be served on the plaintiff or the plaintiff's attorney, and it must be filed in court. The procedures followed for accomplishing service and filing depend on whether the answer is subject to electronic filing. If an answer is not filed electronically, then prior to filing the answer with the court the following is done:

1. a copy of the answer is served on plaintiff's attorney, and
2. a copy of the answer is served on the attorney for any other codefendant who has previously responded to the complaint.

(If a plaintiff or codefendant does not have an attorney, then the party is served.)

An answer can be served personally, by first-class mail, or by fax or electronically if the plaintiff's attorney agrees. A certificate of service (sometimes called a proof of service) showing who was served, how the answer was served, and by whom it was served must be prepared. The original certificate of service should be affixed to the original answer and sent to the court for filing. A filing fee is often required for filing an answer. See Exhibit 6-7 for an example of a certificate of service by mail.

Electronic filing of answers in federal court uses the same process as electronic filing of complaints. The court's CM/ECF system is used. When the attorney for the answering defendant files electronically, generally the court automatically sends a notice

EXHIBIT 6-7 Certificate of Mailing

I, Taylor Martin, Attorney for defendant Linda Granger, do certify that a copy of the attached Answer was served on Terry Alvarez, Attorney for plaintiffs, by enclosing a true and correct copy in an envelope addressed to Terry Alvarez, 100 Market Street, San Francisco, California 94101, postage prepaid, and depositing the same in the United States mail at Sacramento, California, on _____.

_____

TAYLOR MARTIN
15 Plaza de Oro
Sacramento, California 94813
tmartin@esq.com
(916) 555-1212
Attorney for Defendant, Linda Granger

EXHIBIT 6-8 Answer Checklist

ANSWER CHECKLIST

Before filing the answer be sure that you have:

✓ Reviewed local rules for special format requirements
✓ Reviewed the complaint and determined how each paragraph will be answered
✓ Copied the caption, especially the docket number, correctly
✓ Included a demand for jury if plaintiff has not and you want a jury
✓ Included responses to each paragraph in the complaint unless they are admitted
✓ Included relevant affirmative defenses
✓ Affixed a proper signature
✓ Served a copy of the answer on plaintiff's attorney (unless not required by e-filing rules)
✓ Attached a copy of a certificate of service to the answer

to all other parties in the case that the answer was filed. Because electronically filed documents are usually accessible to the parties through the Internet and because the court notifies all parties that the answer was filed, some local courts do not require service of the answer. Local rules should always be reviewed prior to filing electronically. See Exhibit 6-8.

Amending

Most courts have liberal rules regarding the amendment of any pleading, including an answer. Under federal rules, a party can amend an answer any time within 21 days after it is served. If more than 21 days have elapsed, the answer can be amended only with permission of the court or by written consent of the adverse party.

counterclaim

In a civil lawsuit, a claim for some relief made by a defendant against the plaintiff.

cross-claim

In a civil lawsuit, a claim made by one defendant against another related to the plaintiff's claims.

third-party complaint

A complaint brought by a defendant in a lawsuit, based on the claims in that lawsuit, against someone not named in the original lawsuit.

compulsory counterclaim

A defendant's claim against a plaintiff that must be brought in the lawsuit or is forever barred; one that is based on the same subject or transaction as the original claim.

COUNTERCLAIMS, CROSS-CLAIMS, AND THIRD-PARTY COMPLAINTS

At times, defendants themselves have a claim and are entitled to some relief from the court. They may be asserting this claim against the plaintiff, a codefendant, or a third party (someone who is not a party to the original action). In federal court, defendants assert a claim against a plaintiff in a **counterclaim**, and against a codefendant in a **cross-claim**. When the claim is against a new party, a **third-party complaint** is prepared and filed. Counterclaims and cross-claims are included with the answer. Third-party complaints are pleadings that are separate from the answer. See Exhibit 6-9 for an outline of how defendant Linda Granger would handle various claims she might have.

Claims by a defendant resemble the complaint filed by the plaintiff. Numbered paragraphs describe the factual basis for the claim. For third-party complaints, the jurisdictional basis of the court must also be stated.

In some state jurisdictions, the format and the names of the pleading differ. For example, in some states, any claim a defendant asserts is a separate pleading known as a cross-complaint. This pleading is used to assert a claim against a plaintiff, codefendant, or third party.

Counterclaims

If a defendant has a claim against the plaintiff arising out of the same transaction as described in the complaint, that claim must usually be asserted in a counterclaim or the right to make a claim is lost. For example, if Granger claims that the plaintiff, Gordon Sheffield, caused the accident, and she wanted to pursue a claim against him for the damage to her vehicle, she would need to do this in a counterclaim. Moreover, because such a claim must be asserted or be deemed waived, the counterclaim need not satisfy the court's jurisdictional requirements. The fact that the court has jurisdiction over the plaintiff's claim is sufficient. Counterclaims that must be asserted or lost are known as **compulsory counterclaims**. A compulsory counterclaim that is not included as part of the answer is thereafter barred. Exceptions occur when the assertion of the claim involves bringing in third parties over whom the court cannot acquire jurisdiction, or when the defendant's claim has already been asserted in another action. Of course, if a defendant fails to assert a compulsory counterclaim in the answer, under proper circumstances the responsive pleading can be amended to add the counterclaim.

EXHIBIT 6-9 *Sheffield v. Linstrom and Granger*, Claims by Granger

Granger v. Sheffield	Defendant asserts claim against plaintiff	Counterclaim
Granger v. Linstrom	Defendant asserts claim against codefendant	Cross-Claim
Granger v. Brakefast	Defendant asserts claim against a new party	Third-Party Action

Copyright © 2015 Cengage Learning®

EXHIBIT 6-10 Comparison of Compulsory and Permissive Counterclaims

Compulsory counterclaims	Claim by defendant based on same transaction as described in complaint	The claim need not satisfy a separate jurisdictional basis to be heard by the court	The claim may be lost if not included with answer
Permissive counterclaims	Claim by defendant based on different facts from those alleged in complaint	The claim must satisfy a separate jurisdictional basis to be heard by the court	The claim can be raised in a separate action

Because it saves a great deal of court time, the courts encourage the parties to resolve all of their disputes in one action. Consequently, if a defendant has a claim against the plaintiff that did not arise out of the factual situation described in the complaint, she can still assert that claim as a counterclaim. Such a counterclaim is a **permissive counterclaim**. Unlike compulsory counterclaims, permissive counterclaims must satisfy the court's jurisdictional requirements. As a rule, claims forming the basis for a permissive counterclaim are not lost if they are not made as part of the answer. See Exhibit 6-10.

Because all counterclaims are part of the answer, they are served in the same manner as the answer. Exhibit 6-11 shows an example of an answer and counterclaim.

Cross-Claims

A cross-claim, a claim by one defendant against another, is allowed whenever the claim arises out of the same transaction or occurrence that is the subject matter of the complaint. For example, again in the factual situation described in the Commentary, if Granger believes that the accident was Linstrom's fault, she could file a cross-claim against him. Her claim might be twofold. First, she might be claiming damages for any destruction to her van caused by his negligence. Second, she might be claiming total reimbursement or **indemnification** for any judgment against her in the complaint. (Under the substantive law of torts, an employer is liable to third parties for injuries caused by the negligence of its employees while they are in the course and scope of their employment. However, the employer has a claim against the employee for reimbursement or indemnification.) Cross-claims often involve claims for indemnification. Related to the concept of indemnification is **contribution**, or partial reimbursement. For example, suppose that the accident was caused by Linstrom's negligent driving and Granger's negligence in maintaining the brakes on the van. Both Linstrom and Granger would have a possible claim for contribution. See Exhibit 6-12 for an example of a cross-claim.

permissive counterclaim
A defendant's claim against a plaintiff that a defendant is allowed, but not required to make; one that is not necessarily related to the plaintiff's claim.

indemnification
A concept allowing a defendant who has paid a judgment to seek reimbursement from another more culpable party, usually where the defendant seeking indemnification has done nothing wrong, but is nevertheless liable or where the parties have an agreement that one party will indemnify the other.

contribution
The right of a person who has paid an entire debt (or judgment) to be reimbursed a proportionate share of the judgment from another person who is also responsible for the debt.

EXHIBIT 6-11 Answer and Counterclaim

UNITED STATES DISTRICT COURT
FOR THE NORTHERN DISTRICT OF CALIFORNIA

GORDON SHEFFIELD and AMY SHEFFIELD,	))	Civil No. 12345
Plaintiffs,	)	ANSWER AND
	)	COUNTERCLAIM
	)	
v.	))	
	)	
WESLEY LINSTROM and LINDA GRANGER,	))	
Defendants.	)	

Answer to First Count

Defendant, LINDA GRANGER, answers as follows:

1. Defendant admits the allegations of Paragraphs 1, 2, and 3 of the complaint.
2. Defendant denies each and every allegation of Paragraphs 4, 5, 6, and 7 of the complaint.

Answer to Second Count

3. In answer to Paragraph 8 of Count Two of the complaint, wherein plaintiff incorporates by reference certain paragraphs of Count One of the complaint, defendant admits, denies, and alleges to the same effect and in the same manner as she admitted, denied, and alleged to those specific paragraphs previously in this answer.
4. In answer to Paragraph 9 of Count Two of the complaint, defendant admits that plaintiff, AMY SHEFFIELD, was a passenger in a vehicle being driven by co-plaintiff, GORDON SHEFFIELD, but denies each and every other allegation contained in said paragraph.
5. Defendant denies each and every allegation contained in Paragraph 10 of the complaint.

First Affirmative Defense

As and for an affirmative defense, defendant alleges that plaintiffs' right to maintain this action is barred by the statute of limitations, in that more than two years have now elapsed between the date plaintiffs' alleged cause of action arose and the date plaintiffs filed their complaint.

Second Affirmative Defense

As and for a separate affirmative defense, defendant alleges that plaintiffs were themselves negligent, in that plaintiff, GORDON SHEFFIELD, failed to use ordinary care in the operation of his motor vehicle, and failed to keep a proper lookout for other vehicles, and that both plaintiffs, GORDON SHEFFIELD and AMY SHEFFIELD, failed to exercise ordinary care, in that neither wore a seat belt. Defendant further alleges that said negligence contributed in whole or in part to any injuries which may have resulted.

EXHIBIT 6-11 Answer and Counterclaim (*Continued*)

Counterclaim

As a counterclaim against plaintiff, GORDON SHEFFIELD, defendant alleges:

1. On or about April 29,_____, in a public highway called Market Street in San Francisco, California, plaintiff, GORDON SHEFFIELD, negligently drove a motor vehicle, causing it to collide with another motor vehicle, owned by defendant, LINDA GRANGER.

2. That the motor vehicle driven by GORDON SHEFFIELD was owned jointly by plaintiffs, GORDON SHEFFIELD and AMY SHEFFIELD, and that at all times herein mentioned was driven and operated by GORDON SHEFFIELD with the knowledge and consent of plaintiff AMY SHEFFIELD.

3. As a result of plaintiff's negligence, defendant's motor vehicle was damaged, and defendant has incurred expenses in the amount of $5,000 to repair said vehicle.

4. Also as a result of said motor vehicle collision, co-plaintiff, AMY SHEFFIELD, has commenced a tort action against defendant for the recovery of $150,000, her alleged damages resulting from the collision. Defendant alleges that should judgment be assessed against defendant in favor of plaintiff, AMY SHEFFIELD, that defendant, LINDA GRANGER, is entitled to recover from plaintiff, GORDON SHEFFIELD, all or part of said judgment.

Wherefore defendant prays:

1. That the court enter judgment dismissing the complaint;
2. That defendant have judgment against plaintiff, GORDON SHEFFIELD in the amount of $5,000;
3. That defendant have judgment against plaintiff, GORDON SHEFFIELD in an amount equal to any judgment in favor of plaintiff, AMY SHEFFIELD;
4. That defendant be awarded costs incurred herein;
5. That defendant be awarded such other and further relief as the court may deem just.

Dated _____, _____

TAYLOR MARTIN
15 Plaza de Oro
Sacramento, California 94813
tmartin@esq.com
(916) 555-1212
Attorney for Defendant, Linda Granger

Because cross-claims are part of the answer, they are served in the same manner as the answer.

Third-Party Complaints

A defendant in a lawsuit may claim that some third party—that is, someone not named in the original complaint—is responsible, in whole or in part, for the damages claimed in the complaint. In the *Granger* case, facts suggest that the accident occurred because the brakes failed and Linstrom was unable to stop. Suppose that Granger had the brakes on

EXHIBIT 6-12 Answer and Cross-Claim

UNITED STATES DISTRICT COURT
FOR THE NORTHERN DISTRICT OF CALIFORNIA

GORDON SHEFFIELD and AMY SHEFFIELD, Plaintiffs,	)))))	Civil No. 12345 ANSWER AND CROSS-CLAIM
v.	))	
WESLEY LINSTROM and LINDA GRANGER, Defendants.	)))	

Answer to First Count

Defendant, LINDA GRANGER, answers as follows:

1. Defendant admits the allegations of Paragraphs 1, 2, and 3 of the complaint.
2. Defendant denies each and every allegation of Paragraphs 4, 5, 6, and 7 of the complaint.

Answer to Second Count

3. In answer to Paragraph 8 of Count Two of the complaint, wherein plaintiff incorporates by reference certain paragraphs of Count One of the complaint, defendant admits, denies, and alleges to the same effect and in the same manner as she admitted, denied, and alleged to those specific paragraphs previously in this answer.
4. In answer to Paragraph 9 of Count Two of the complaint, defendant admits that plaintiff, AMY SHEFFIELD, was a passenger in a vehicle being driven by co-plaintiff, GORDON SHEFFIELD, but denies each and every other allegation contained in said paragraph.
5. Defendant denies each and every allegation contained in Paragraph 10 of the complaint.

First Affirmative Defense

As and for an affirmative defense, defendant alleges that plaintiffs' right to maintain this action is barred by the statute of limitations, in that more than two years have now elapsed between the date plaintiffs' alleged cause of action arose and the date plaintiffs filed their complaint.

Second Affirmative Defense

As and for a separate affirmative defense, defendant alleges that plaintiffs were themselves negligent, in that plaintiff, GORDON SHEFFIELD, failed to use ordinary care in the operation of his motor vehicle, and failed to keep a proper lookout for other vehicles, and that both plaintiffs, GORDON SHEFFIELD and AMY SHEFFIELD, failed to exercise ordinary care, in that neither wore a seat belt. Defendant further alleges that said negligence contributed in whole or in part to any injuries that may have resulted.

EXHIBIT 6-12 Answer and Cross-Claim (*Continued*)

Cross-Claim

As a cross-claim against defendant, WESLEY LINSTROM, hereinafter referred to as cross-defendant, defendant and cross-claimant, hereinafter referred to as cross-claimant, alleges:

1. On or about April 29,___, on a public highway called Market Street in San Francisco, California, cross-defendant, WESLEY LINSTROM, without the knowledge or permission of cross-claimant, LINDA GRANGER, negligently drove a motor vehicle, owned by cross-claimant, LINDA GRANGER, causing it to collide with another motor vehicle.

2. As a result of cross-defendant's negligence, cross-claimant's motor vehicle was damaged, and defendant has incurred expenses in the amount of $5,000 to repair said vehicle.

3. Also as a result of said motor vehicle collision, plaintiffs, GORDON SHEFFIELD and AMY SHEFFIELD, have commenced a tort action against cross-claimant for the recovery of $250,000, their alleged damages resulting from the collision. Cross-claimant alleges that should judgment be assessed against her in favor of plaintiff, AMY SHEFFIELD, that cross-claimant, LINDA GRANGER, is entitled to recover from cross-defendant the amount of said judgment.

Wherefore defendant and cross-claimant prays:

1. That the court enter judgment dismissing the complaint;

2. The cross-claimant have judgment against cross-defendant, WESLEY LINSTROM, in the amount of $5,000;

3. That defendant have judgment against cross-defendant in an amount equal to any judgment in favor of plaintiff, AMY SHEFFIELD;

4. That defendant be awarded costs incurred herein;

5. That defendant be awarded such other and further relief as the court may deem just.

Dated _____, _____

                                     _____

                                     TAYLOR MARTIN
                                     15 Plaza de Oro
                                     Sacramento, California 94813
                                     tmartin@esq.com
                                     (916) 555-1212
                                     Attorney for Defendant, Linda Granger

---

the van checked two days before the accident and was told that the brakes were in perfect condition. Under such circumstances, she might feel that the auto repair service should be responsible for any damages. She could, therefore, bring the auto repair service into the action by filing and serving it with a third-party complaint.

A third-party complaint, unlike the cross-claim and counterclaim, is a separate pleading. Because it is a claim for relief, it resembles the complaint. The main difference is in the caption, which changes to reflect the fact that a third-party complaint is being filed. The defendant filing the third-party complaint is known as the "defendant and third-party plaintiff." The person against whom the claim is asserted is known as the "third-party defendant." A third-party complaint against the auto repair service would look as shown in Exhibit 6-13.

EXHIBIT 6-13 Third-Party Complaint

UNITED STATES DISTRICT COURT
FOR THE NORTHERN DISTRICT OF CALIFORNIA

GORDON SHEFFIELD and AMY SHEFFIELD, Plaintiffs,	)))
	)
v.	))
WESLEY LINSTROM, Defendants	))

LINDA GRANGER,
  Defendant and
  Third-Party Plaintiff,
	)
	)
	)

	)
v.	))
BRAKEFAST, Inc. Third-Party Defendant.	))

Civil No. 12345

Third-Party Complaint

Linda Granger, Third-Party Plaintiff, alleges:

1. Plaintiffs, GORDON SHEFFIELD and AMY SHEFFIELD, have filed against defendant, LINDA GRANGER, a complaint, a copy of which is hereto attached as "Exhibit A."

2. At all times herein mentioned, third-party defendant was an automotive garage engaged in the business of servicing and repairing automobiles, including brake systems.

3. On or about April 25,_____, third-party plaintiff took her automobile, Oregon license XYZ 123, to third-party defendant's automotive garage for the specific purpose of having the brakes checked and serviced.

4. On or about April 25,_____, third-party defendant negligently and carelessly checked, serviced, and inspected said brakes and negligently and carelessly advised third-party plaintiff that said brakes were in good condition.

5. On or about April 29,_____, the brakes on said automobile failed, causing the vehicle to collide with another motor vehicle driven by plaintiff, GORDON SHEFFIELD.

6. As a result of said collision, plaintiffs have filed the complaint attached as Exhibit A claiming damages from third-party plaintiff.

7. Any damages claimed by plaintiff are a direct and proximate result of the negligence of third-party defendant, and should any damages be assessed against third-party plaintiff, she is entitled to judgment against third-party defendant in the same amount.

EXHIBIT 6-13 Third-Party Complaint (*Continued*)

8. Wherefore third-party plaintiff demands judgment against third-party defendant for all sums that may be adjudged against defendant, LINDA GRANGER, in favor of plaintiffs, GORDON SHEFFIELD and AMY SHEFFIELD.

Dated _____, _____

TAYLOR MARTIN
15 Plaza de Oro
Sacramento, California 94813
tmartin@esq.com
(916) 555-1212
Attorney for Defendant and
   Third-Party Plaintiff,
Linda Granger

reply
In federal practice, a pleading in response to an answer sometimes required of a plaintiff.

Under the Federal Rules of Civil Procedure, a defendant has the right to file a third-party complaint within 14 days of filing the answer. If the third-party complaint is filed within this time, no permission of the court is required. To file a third-party action after that time, permission from the court is required. This is obtained by making a motion in court. At the time the third-party complaint is filed, a new summons must be issued, directed to the third-party defendant. See Exhibit 6-14 for a sample of such a summons.

A third-party complaint and summons must be served in the same way that a complaint is served.

Replies and Answers

In some instances, plaintiffs are allowed or even required to respond to allegations in an answer, especially if there is an affirmative defense. Such a response is called a **reply**. Responses must also be made to allegations contained in counterclaims, cross-claims, and third-party complaints. In federal court these are called answers and do not differ from an answer to the complaint. In some jurisdictions the response to a counterclaim is called a reply. Under the Federal Rules of Civil Procedure, all responses are due 21 days after service of the pleading containing the claim.

Amending

Counterclaims, cross-claims, and third-party complaints can be amended once within 21 days of service. Otherwise, court permission or the agreement of adverse parties is needed.

LEGAL CHALLENGES TO THE COMPLAINT

The primary purpose of an answer is to challenge the factual basis for the plaintiff's claim. However, not all defenses or challenges to a complaint deal with the truth or falsity of the factual allegations. Sometimes challenges are on a more technical, legal basis. For example, the

EXHIBIT 6-14 Third-Party Summons

AO 441 (Rev. 07/10) Summons on Third-Party Complaint

UNITED STATES DISTRICT COURT
for the

_____ District of _____

_____ *Plaintiff* v. _____ *Defendant, Third-party plaintiff* v. _____ *Third-party defendant*	))) Civil Action No.))))

SUMMONS ON A THIRD-PARTY COMPLAINT

To: *(Third-party defendant's name and address)*

A lawsuit has been filed against defendant _____ , who as third-party plaintiff is making this claim against you to pay part or all of what the defendant may owe to the plaintiff _____ .

Within 21 days after service of this summons on you (not counting the day you received it) — or 60 days if you are the United States or a United States agency, or an officer or employee of the United States described in Fed. R. Civ. P. 12 (a)(2) or (3) — you must serve on the plaintiff and on the defendant an answer to the attached complaint or a motion under Rule 12 of the Federal Rules of Civil Procedure. The answer or motion must be served on the defendant or defendant's attorney, whose name and address are:

It must also be served on the plaintiff or plaintiff's attorney, whose name and address are:

If you fail to respond, judgment by default will be entered against you for the relief demanded in the third-party complaint. You also must file the answer or motion with the court and serve it on any other parties.

A copy of the plaintiff's complaint is also attached. You may – but are not required to – respond to it.

Date: _____

CLERK OF COURT

_____
Signature of Clerk or Deputy Clerk

EXHIBIT 6-14 Third-Party Summons (*Continued*)

AO 441 (Rev. 07/10) Summons on Third-Party Complaint (Page 2)

Civil Action No.

PROOF OF SERVICE
(This section should not be filed with the court unless required by Fed. R. Civ. P. 4 (l))

This summons for *(name of individual and title, if any)* _____

was received by me on *(date)* _____ .

❏ I personally served the summons on the individual at *(place)* _____

_____ on *(date)* _____ ; or

❏ I left the summons at the individual's residence or usual place of abode with *(name)* _____

_____ , a person of suitable age and discretion who resides there,

on *(date)* _____ , and mailed a copy to the individual's last known address; or

❏ I served the summons on *(name of individual)* _____ , who is

designated by law to accept service of process on behalf of *(name of organization)* _____

_____ on *(date)* _____ ; or

❏ I returned the summons unexecuted because _____ ; or

❏ Other *(specify):* _____

_____ .

My fees are $ _____ for travel and $ _____ for services, for a total of $ 0.00   .

I declare under penalty of perjury that this information is true.

Date: _____

_____
Server's signature

_____
Printed name and title

_____
Server's address

Additional information regarding attempted service, etc:

| Print | Save As... | Add Attachment | Reset |

demurrer

A legal pleading in some state jurisdictions that attacks the validity of another pleading (usually a complaint) in that on its face, the pleading does not state facts that satisfy the requirements of the pleading.

motion to dismiss

A party's request that the court strike or terminate the case prior to any judgment.

defendant might challenge the court's authority to hear the case (jurisdiction), or the defendant might claim that she was not properly served with the complaint. Some jurisdictions, including federal court, allow this type of defense to be raised either in the answer or in a motion. Other jurisdictions require that certain defenses be raised in a special pleading, sometimes known as a **demurrer**.

The Appendix of Forms to the Federal Rules of Civil Procedure provides an example of how to raise certain technical defenses in an answer. See Exhibit 6-15.

In federal court, many legal challenges to the action are raised by the defendant in a motion to dismiss the case. (Procedures and forms for making or opposing motions are discussed in Chapter 7.) A **motion to dismiss** is a request that the court immediately terminate the action without granting the plaintiff any of the relief that was requested in the complaint. Legal challenges or defenses that can be raised in a motion to dismiss under Rule 12 of the Federal Rules of Civil Procedure include:

1. lack of subject matter jurisdiction,
2. lack of personal jurisdiction,

EXHIBIT 6-15 Answer Raising Rule 12(b) Defenses

UNITED STATES DISTRICT COURT
for the

<_____> **DISTRICT OF** <_____>

<Name(s) of plaintiff(s)>,	)	
	)	
Plaintiff(s)	)	
	)	
v.	)	
	)	Civil Action No. <Number>
<Name(s) of defendant(s)>,	)	
	)	
Defendant(s)	)	
	)	

ANSWER PRESENTING DEFENSES UNDER RULE 12(b)

Responding to Allegations in the Complaint

1. Defendant admits the allegations in paragraphs <_____>.
2. Defendant lacks knowledge or information sufficient to form a belief about the truth of the allegations in paragraphs <_____>.
3. Defendant admits <identify part of the allegation> in paragraph <_____> and denies or lacks knowledge or information sufficient to form a belief about the truth of the rest of the paragraph.

Failure to State a Claim

4. The complaint fails to state a claim upon which relief can be granted.

Failure to Join a Required Party

5. If there is a debt, it is owed jointly by the defendant and <Name>, who is a citizen of <_____>. This person can be made a party without depriving this court of jurisdiction over the existing parties.

EXHIBIT 6-15 Answer Raising Rule 12(b) Defenses (*Continued*)

Affirmative Defense—Statute of Limitations

6. The plaintiff's claim is barred by the statute of limitations because it arose more than <_____> years before this action was commenced.

Counterclaim

7. <Set forth any counterclaim in the same way a claim is pleaded in a complaint. Include a further statement of jurisdiction if needed.>

Cross-claim

8. <Set forth a cross-claim against a coparty in the same way a claim is pleaded in a complaint. Include a further statement of jurisdiction if needed.>

Date: <Date>   <Signature of the attorney or unrepresented party>

_____

<Printed name>
<Address>
<E-mail address>
<Telephone number>

---

3. improper venue,

4. insufficiency of process,

5. insufficiency of service of process,

6. failure to state a claim upon which relief can be granted, and

7. failure to join a party under Rule 19 (an indispensable party).

The defenses of lack of subject matter jurisdiction, failure to state a claim, or failure to join a party can be raised by the defendant at any time, even after all the pleadings have been filed. The other defenses must be raised in an answer or motion or they are waived.

If the defendant makes a motion to dismiss, she must do so before filing an answer and within the time permitted to answer. Whether these defenses are raised by motion or by the answer, if a party requests it, the court will usually hold a hearing prior to trial to determine the validity of the defense. If the motion to dismiss is denied, the court generally requires that the defendant file an answer within 14 days. An alternative method of challenging service of the complaint or personal jurisdiction is the motion to quash service of summons.

Another response to a complaint that is allowed in federal court is the **motion for a more definite statement**. If the complaint (or cross-claim, counterclaim, or third-party complaint) is so vague or ambiguous that the opposing party cannot reasonably be required to frame a responsive pleading, that party may petition the court to order the claimant to revise the pleading.

In some state jurisdictions another type of pleading, known as a demurrer, is used to challenge the legal sufficiency of the complaint. The grounds for a demurrer are similar to those for a motion to dismiss the case. When a demurrer is filed, the court usually holds a hearing to determine the issues that have been raised. If the demurrer is sustained, either the case is dismissed or the plaintiff is given the opportunity to amend the complaint. If the demurrer is overruled, the defendant is given a short time in which to file an answer.

motion for a more definite statement
A motion made in response to a complaint in which the defendant challenges the clarity or specificity of the complaint.

affidavit
A written statement sworn to under penalty of perjury before a notary or other person permitted by law to administer an oath.

FAILURE TO ANSWER

If a party fails to answer a pleading to which a response is required (i.e., the defendant fails to answer the complaint, or the plaintiff fails to respond to a counterclaim), then a judgment by default may follow. In most jurisdictions, including federal court, obtaining a judgment is a two-step process. First, the plaintiff or the plaintiff's attorney files with the court an **affidavit**—a statement under penalty of perjury, sworn to before a notary—verifying that the opposing party has defaulted (not responded) and

EXHIBIT 6-16 Affidavit in Support of Entry of Default

**UNITED STATES DISTRICT COURT
FOR THE NORTHERN DISTRICT OF CALIFORNIA**

GORDON SHEFFIELD and AMY SHEFFIELD,	)	Civil No. 12345
Plaintiffs,	)	
	)	AFFIDAVIT AND REQUEST
	)	
	)	TO ENTER DEFAULT
v.	)	
	)	
WESLEY LINSTROM and LINDA GRANGER,	)	
	)	
Defendants.	)	

_____

State of California

County of San Francisco

I, Terry Alvarez, being duly sworn say:

1. I am the attorney for plaintiffs in the above action.
2. A copy of the summons and complaint was served on defendant on May 15, _____, and the return of service of John Smith, United States Marshal, is on file in this action.
3. Defendant, Wesley Linstrom, has not answered or otherwise appeared in this action, and the time within which defendant may appear has expired.

_____

TERRY ALVAREZ
ALVAREZ & COE
100 Market Street
San Francisco, California 94101
talvarez@esq.com
(415) 555-1212
Attorney for Plaintiffs

Subscribed and sworn to before me on June 20, _____

_____

EXHIBIT 6-16 Affidavit in Support of Entry of Default (*Continued*)

> Request to Clerk to Enter Default
>
> To: Clerk
>
> Defendant, Wesley Linstrom, having failed to answer or otherwise appear in the above-entitled action, and the time for appearance having expired, you are requested to enter his default pursuant to Rule 55(a) of the Federal Rules of Civil Procedure.
>
> Dated June 20,_____
>
> _____
>
> TERRY ALVAREZ
> ALVAREZ & COE
> 100 Market Street
> San Francisco, California 94101
> talvarez@esq.com
> (415) 555-1212
> Attorney for Plaintiffs

requesting that the clerk enter that party's default. **Entry of default** is not the same as a default judgment. Entry of default means that the failure to respond had been noted in the court's file. See Exhibit 6-16 for an example of the request to enter default and accompanying affidavit. After the default has been entered, the claimant can apply for a default judgment.

entry of default
Action by a court clerk noting that the defendant has failed to file a proper response to the complaint.

To obtain a default judgment, the plaintiff must prove the claim. This can be done at a brief court hearing where evidence is presented to a judge. In lieu of a court hearing, many jurisdictions allow the plaintiff to submit affidavits to substantiate the claim. The laws of the jurisdiction determine the exact procedure that is followed, although generally a default judgment cannot be obtained if the defendant is a minor, incompetent, or in the military service. In federal court, the plaintiff may also request a hearing before a jury to determine the amount of damages.

Setting Aside Defaults

Courts usually permit parties against whom a default judgment was entered to petition the court to set it aside by making a motion to set aside the default judgment. The most common grounds for making and granting such a motion are that the judgment was entered through mistake, inadvertence, surprise, or excusable neglect. This type of motion usually must be made within certain time limits after the judgment was obtained. For example, Rule 60 of the Federal Rules of Civil Procedure provides that the motion must be made within a reasonable time of the judgment having been rendered (but not to exceed one year). Default judgments can also be set aside, without a motion, if the plaintiff will stipulate or agree to do so.

FINDING IT on the Internet

Local rules of court often specify requirements for obtaining an extension of time in which to respond to a complaint. Check your local courts for such rules. Your state court can be located through **<http://www.ncsc.org/>** (The National Center for State Courts). On the homepage search for "browse by state." Your local federal court can be located through **<http://pacer.psc.uscourts.gov/lookup.html>**, a site that allows you to search by your county or state.

    a. Summarize any local state court rules on this point.

    b. Summarize any local federal court rules on this point.

In the *Granger* case described in the Commentary, one area of concern might be the value of the Granger van, especially if it suffered extensive damage. The popular Kelley Blue Book for determining vehicle value is online at **<http://www.kbb.com>**. Assume that the Granger van is a 2006 Dodge Caravan Cargo, with V6 3.3 liter engine, automatic transmission, four-wheel drive, and standard equipment. It has 58,000 miles. Access the Kelley Blue Book site and

    a. determine the trade-in value of the van in your zip code area.

    b. determine the private party sale value of the van in your zip code area.

SUMMARY

- Defendants must respond to the complaint within certain time limitations. These time limitations are controlled by the laws of the jurisdiction in which the matter is pending. In federal court, depending on how service occurs, the defendant generally has 21 or 60 days from the date of service of the complaint in which to respond. Time limitations to respond can be enlarged or extended, either by stipulation or agreement of the parties or by obtaining a court order. In some jurisdictions a stipulation to extend the time must be approved by the court.

- An answer is a pleading that challenges the plaintiff's claim for relief. An answer can consist of either a general denial, a qualified denial, or a specific denial. A general denial contests all of the allegations contained in the complaint. In some jurisdictions a general denial cannot be used if the complaint has been verified. A qualified denial specifically admits or denies certain allegations, then denies everything else. A specific denial contains specific responses to each allegation contained in the complaint. An answer might also contain affirmative defenses. Affirmative defenses are facts or circumstances that operate to defeat the plaintiff's claim even if all of the contentions of the complaint are proved. Affirmative defenses are often matters of substantive law and therefore vary according to the nature of the case.

- An answer is a pleading and as such follows the same general format as the complaint or petition in the case. It contains a caption that states the names of the plaintiffs and the defendants, the title of the court, the docket number, and the title of the document (answer). The body of the answer contains numbered paragraphs in which the defendant responds to the allegations of the complaint, followed by affirmative defenses, if they exist. The answer concludes with a prayer and the signature and address of the attorney filing the document. The answer is served on the plaintiff or her attorney and filed in court. Service can be accomplished by mailing a copy of the answer to the attorney, or to the plaintiff if unrepresented. An answer can usually be amended. In federal court a party may amend an answer anytime within 21 days after it is served, as long as the case has not been placed on the trial calendar. After 21 days, court permission or a stipulation is required.

- The defendant in any action has the right to make a claim for relief. In general she may make any claim that she has against the plaintiff, whether it is related to the claim stated in the complaint or not. She may make a claim against a codefendant or a third person (not a party to the original action) if the claim stems from the circumstance or transaction described in the complaint. The names of the documents in which defendants assert their claim may differ from one jurisdiction to another. In federal court, a claim against the plaintiff is known as a counterclaim. A claim against a codefendant is known as a cross-claim, and a claim against a third person is known as a third-party complaint.

- In addition to being contested on the factual allegations, lawsuits can be challenged on technical legal grounds (such as lack of jurisdiction, expiration of the statute of limitations, or insufficiency of service of process). Legal challenges are often raised in some manner other than the answer. In federal court, even though legal challenges can be asserted in an answer, a motion to dismiss the action or a motion to quash service of summons can be an alternative. A motion for a more definite statement is also a possible response when the complaint is so vague or ambiguous that the opposing party cannot reasonably respond. Some jurisdictions have a pleading known as a demurrer that also operates to challenge the complaint on technical legal grounds.

- If a party fails to answer the complaint, the plaintiff can request that the defendant's default be entered in the court record and that a default judgment be granted in the plaintiff's favor. A court hearing may be required before the court will grant a judgment.

KEY TERMS

affidavit	entry of default	permissive counterclaim
affirmative defense	general denial	qualified denial
compulsory counterclaim	indemnification	reply
contribution	motion for a more definite	specific denial
counterclaim	statement	third-party complaint
cross-claim	motion to dismiss	
demurrer	open stipulation	

REVIEW QUESTIONS

1. What kinds of responses can the defendant make to the complaint?
2. What time limitations apply to these responses? Can these time limitations be changed? If so, how?
3. What is the difference between a general denial, a qualified denial, and a specific denial?
4. What is an affirmative defense, and why is it important?
5. What is the general format of an answer?
6. What are the procedures for serving and filing an answer?
7. How are responsive pleadings amended?
8. What are counterclaims, cross-claims, and third-party complaints?
9. What are the different ways in which a defendant can challenge legal deficiencies with the initial pleading or process?
10. What happens if the defendant fails to file a timely response to the initial pleading?

CHAPTER EXERCISES

Where necessary, check with your instructor prior to starting any of these exercises.

1. Review the laws of your state. How much time does a defendant have to respond to the complaint? Must a stipulation to enlarge or extend that time be approved by the court?
2. Review the laws of your state that deal with responses to the complaint. What responsive pleadings are allowed? What responsive motions are permitted?
3. Review the Commentary at the beginning of this chapter. If the action were filed in your state court, and Granger were to file a claim against Linstrom, the Sheffields, and Brakefast, Inc., how would she do so?
4. Use a legal dictionary to define and/or explain the various affirmative defenses listed in this chapter.
5. Review the case Commentary and the Complaint for Fraud, Negligent Misrepresentation, and Breach of Fiduciary Duty found in Chapter 5. Which, if any, of the affirmative defenses mentioned in Chapter 6 might apply? Explain your answer. Do the same for the case Commentaries found at the beginning of Chapters 13 and 4.
6. Make a copy of the summons found in Exhibit 6-14. Fill out the summons based on the complaint found in Exhibit 6-13.

CHAPTER PROJECT

Review the complaint found in Chapter 5 (Exhibit 5-6). Assume that your law firm represents May Forrester and that you have been requested to draft an answer and cross-claim on her behalf. You have been given the following facts: May Forrester was indeed a real estate agent working for Hearth & Home and did make a sales presentation to the Hendrickses.

Prior to the sales presentation, she was given facts and photos regarding the property by one of her employers, Harry Rice. Rice told her that he had visited the property and had taken the photographs himself. During the sales presentation, she only repeated what she had been told. Furthermore, she had worked for Hearth & Home Real Estate for three years and had no reason to doubt her employer. Draft an appropriate answer and cross-claim.

THE *BENNETT* CASE
Assignment for Chapter 6: Responding to Defense Requests

Assume that your office was contacted by the counsel who was recently retained to represent defendant Rikards-Hayley. The answer is due to be filed in four days, and they need more time to prepare their response. They would also like to enter into an agreement that all further papers can be served either by e-mail or by fax. Your supervising attorney has agreed to give the defense a 20-day extension for the answer. The attorney is also agreeable to electronic service of documents so long as the defense also agrees to that. You are to draft a proposed stipulation addressing these two matters.

THE *DOUGLASS FINANCIAL SERVICES INC.* CASE
Assignment for Chapter 6: Drafting an Answer and Cross-Claim and Third-Party Complaint

Your supervising attorney tells you that she was recently contacted by your client, Douglass Financial Services, Inc. and was advised that the company was just served with a copy of a complaint filed by Jessica Hewitt. The complaint names both Evan Portman and Douglass Financial as defendants in the lawsuit and it is filed in the local state court. Your attorney does not have a copy of the complaint yet, but she tells you that when she spoke with the client's representative he provided her with all the details of the complaint. Because time is short, your supervisor has asked you to prepare a draft of an answer and cross-claim. The answer will consist of a general denial and one affirmative defense. The affirmative defense is that the plaintiff's negligence contributed to the accident. She also wants you to prepare an appropriate cross-action against Evan Portman for reimbursement of any amounts Douglass Financial is required to pay. She also wants you to prepare a third-party complaint against the caterer. (See Exhibit 6-12 in the chapter.)

CHAPTER OUTLINE

THE *PYRAMID COMPUTER* CASE

Your firm has just been retained by Pyramid Computer Corporation, a manufacturer of tablet computers, to represent it in a lawsuit. A complaint, naming Pyramid Computer Corporation as defendant, was filed in federal court in the state of Massachusetts. The complaint bases federal court jurisdiction on diversity of citizenship, alleging that plaintiff is a citizen of Massachusetts and that defendant, Pyramid Computer Corporation, is a citizen of Delaware. The president of Pyramid Computer Corporation, however, states that although Pyramid Computer is incorporated in Delaware, it has its headquarters and conducts most of its business in Massachusetts. Your supervising attorney has told you that because a corporation is a citizen both of the state of incorporation and the state where the principal place of business is located, she believes that diversity does not exist and that, therefore, the federal court does not have subject matter jurisdiction. She has asked you to draft a motion to dismiss the action on that basis.

Chapter 6 introduced the various responses to complaints. Some of those responses are presented to the court in the form of a motion. After completing this chapter, you should be able to:

- define a motion.
- explain the procedure for making a motion.
- explain the procedure for opposing a motion.
- draft motion documents such as a motion, notice of hearing, and affidavit.
- explain the role of the paralegal in setting motions for hearing.
- explain the method for obtaining orders after hearings on the motion.
- define the term *sanctions* and explain their use in motion practice.
- identify some common pretrial motions.
- explain the procedure for making motions during trial.
- identify some common posttrial motions.
- explain the procedures for obtaining preliminary injunctions and temporary restraining orders.

MOTIONS GENERALLY

During the course of litigation, questions or problems regarding the case inevitably arise. Sometimes these questions or problems involve practical, procedural issues. For example, in the case mentioned in the Commentary to this chapter, the attorney representing Pyramid Computer might not be able to adequately research the law and prepare responsive documents within 21 days of serving the client. As explained in Chapter 6, this problem is easy to solve. The attorney asks for and usually receives more time to respond. Other times these problems involve more complicated and substantial legal issues. For example, in the

movant
Party in a lawsuit who makes a motion.

Pyramid Computer case, the defense attorney believes that diversity of jurisdiction is lacking and that, therefore, the federal court is not the proper forum for the case. This issue is more complicated, and the parties have a substantial disagreement regarding the facts and the law. Here the plaintiff's attorney is not likely to agree to dismiss the case. If the attorneys cannot resolve the problems by themselves, a court order is required to settle the issue. The application for such a court order is a motion. Some motions relate to procedural problems with a case, such as motions for an extension of time in which to respond to a complaint. However, motions can also relate to more substantial evidentiary issues in the case, such as motions for summary judgment (described later in the chapter). The court orders resulting from these motions may actually dispose of the entire case. For example, if a motion for summary judgment is granted, judgment is entered in favor of one party without further court proceedings, and the action in the trial court will end.

Except for motions made during the trial, motions must be written, filed in court, and served on the opposing attorneys (or parties, if not represented). If the motion is contested, the opposing attorneys also file papers opposing the motion. Often the written documents are followed by a brief court hearing before the judge rules on the motion. Although they are not considered to be pleadings, motions do resemble pleadings in appearance. The documents filed in a motion follow the same formalities required of pleadings and contain the same caption as the pleadings. As a paralegal, you might be asked to research the law governing the particular motion involved or prepare the written documents that are filed in court. You also might be requested to contact the court to set the motion for a hearing.

PREPARING, SERVING, AND RESPONDING

Many different types of motions are possible. Some motions are specifically described by statutes, which explain the procedures and time limits for making such motions. Other motions may be only briefly described, if at all. Regardless of any special procedures that may apply to some motions, certain procedures are common to all motions.

Preparation of the Written Papers

The party making the motion, known as the **movant** or *moving party*, begins by preparing written papers for service and filing. These papers follow the same general format as pleadings. The written papers filed in making a motion usually include these documents:

- the motion,
- the notice of hearing on the motion,
- affidavits in support of the motion, and
- a memorandum of points and authorities in support of the motion.

In motion practice, the term *motion* is used in two different contexts. On one hand, it refers to the whole process of making a request for an order from the court. On the other hand, it also refers to one of the documents filed in support of that request.

The document titled "motion" describes the nature of the specific motion, the grounds for the motion, and the relief requested. A motion that might be made on behalf

CHAPTER 7 MOTION PRACTICE

EXHIBIT 7-1 Motion to Dismiss

UNITED STATES DISTRICT COURT
DISTRICT OF MASSACHUSETTS

JOHN JONES,
  Plaintiff,
 	
    v.
 	
PYRAMID COMPUTER CORPORATION,
  Defendant.
	)
	)
	) Civil No. 123456
	)
	) MOTION TO DISMISS UNDER RULE 12(b)
	) FOR LACK OF JURISDICTION
	)
	)
	)
	)
	)

PYRAMID COMPUTER CORPORATION, by PAT RIVAS, its attorney, moves the court to dismiss the complaint on file on the following grounds: the complaint in this action alleges that this action is filed in federal court because it involves a dispute between citizens of different states; however, the court lacks subject matter jurisdiction as alleged in the complaint, in that plaintiff and defendant are citizens of the same state, as is more clearly stated in the affidavit of Owen Young, hereto annexed as Exhibit A.

A Memorandum of Points and Authorities in support of this motion is served and filed with this motion.

Dated August 1, _____

                                        _____
                                        PAT RIVAS
                                        Attorney for Defendant
                                        769 Lewis Street
                                        Boston, Massachusetts 02113
                                        privas@esq.com
                                        (402) 555-1212

---

of Pyramid Computer Corporation to dismiss the complaint filed against it is shown in Exhibit 7-1. Note that in Exhibit 7-1 the document describes

1. the nature of the motion—it is a motion to dismiss;
2. the grounds for the motion—the court lacks subject matter jurisdiction because the parties are citizens of the same state; and
3. the relief requested—a request that the court dismiss the case.

The **notice of hearing on the motion** is a simple paper stating the place and location of the court hearing. It might look as shown in Exhibit 7-2.

Many courts allow the motion and the notice of hearing to be combined into one document.

Motions are commonly supported by affidavits. An affidavit is a statement, under penalty of perjury, sworn to before a notary or other person authorized to administer an oath. An

notice of hearing on the motion

The part of a written motion that describes the nature of the motion being made and tells when and where a hearing on the motion will occur.

EXHIBIT 7-2 Notice of Motion

UNITED STATES DISTRICT COURT
DISTRICT OF MASSACHUSETTS

JOHN JONES, 　Plaintiff,	))) Civil No. 123456)
v.	)) Notice of Motion to Dismiss Under Rule 12(b)) for Lack of Subject Matter Jurisdiction)
PYRAMID COMPUTER CORPORATION, 　Defendant.	))))

_____

To: Lane Borman, Attorney for Plaintiff,

Please take notice, that the undersigned will bring the above motion on for hearing before this Court at Room _____, United States Court House, _____, City of Boston on the _____ day of _____, at 10 o'clock a.m. of that day or as soon thereafter as counsel can be heard.

_____

PAT RIVAS
Attorney for Defendant
769 Lewis Street
Boston, Massachusetts 02113
privas@esq.com
(402) 555-1212

---

declaration

A statement under penalty of perjury that certain facts are true or believed to be true.

affidavit usually describes the factual basis for making the motion and is made by a person having personal knowledge of those facts. It can be the statement of the attorney, a party, or a third person. Even though it may be the statement of a party or a witness, the attorney or paralegal normally prepares the document based on what the individual tells them. An affidavit serves the same purpose as testimony from a party or witness and is used in lieu of that testimony. As such, an affidavit should be written in the first person and should contain detailed facts. An affidavit in support of the motion described in the Commentary might look as shown in Exhibit 7-3.

In some courts, a **declaration** is used in lieu of an affidavit. Like the affidavit, a declaration is a statement under penalty of perjury, but it is not sworn to before a notary.

In drafting an affidavit or declaration, the following general format should be followed:

1. The affidavit or declaration is usually, although not always, written in the first person. Even though it may be signed by a party or a witness, it is written by the attorney or paralegal.

2. The first paragraph should describe the affiant (person making the affidavit) or declarant and describe the person's relationship to the case. For example, is the affiant the plaintiff, an employee of the plaintiff, an attorney for a party, or does the affiant have some other relationship to the case?

EXHIBIT 7-3 Affidavit in Support of Motion

UNITED STATES DISTRICT COURT
DISTRICT OF MASSACHUSETTS

JOHN JONES, Plaintiff,	))) Civil No. 123456)
v.	)) Affidavit of Owen) Young in Support of) Motion to Dismiss)
PYRAMID COMPUTER CORPORATION, Defendant.	)))

I, Owen Young, being first duly sworn, depose and say:

1. I am the president of PYRAMID COMPUTER CORPORATION, the defendant in this action, and am acquainted with the facts in this case, and have personal knowledge of the matter set forth in this affidavit.
2. I make this affidavit in support of the motion to dismiss the action.
3. I held the office of president of PYRAMID COMPUTER CORPORATION at all times mentioned in the complaint filed in this action.
4. At all times mentioned in the complaint, PYRAMID COMPUTER CORPORATION has been incorporated under the laws of the state of Delaware.
5. At all times mentioned in the complaint, PYRAMID COMPUTER CORPORATION has had its principal place of business in the state of Massachusetts. The corporation maintains four sales offices throughout the state of Massachusetts, maintains its primary bank account in the state of Massachusetts, and keeps copies of all corporate records within the state of Massachusetts. Business conducted within the state of Massachusetts accounts for more than 75% of the total income of said corporation.

_____
Owen Young

Subscribed and sworn to before me on _____, _____

_____

3. The affiant should state whether the affidavit is made in support of or in opposition to the motion and describe the general nature of the motion.
4. The affiant then states the facts supporting of or opposing the motion. This may be done in several short paragraphs. If not obvious from the facts, the affiant should include a brief statement that he or she knows the facts to be true based on his or her own knowledge.

*memorandum of points
and authorities*
A legal argument in the form of
an explanation and analysis of
the law that applies to the case.

ex parte
A legal proceeding in which only
one party needs to be present.

order shortening time
A ruling from the court, often
in connection with motions,
allowing a moving party to
give less notice of a hearing on
a motion than is required by
statute.

*proof of service
(certificate of service)*
Verification that a a copy of
a pleading, motion, or other
document has been served to
another party or attorney.

Along with a supporting affidavit, most attorneys also support a motion with a **memorandum of points and authorities**. In some courts this is required. A memorandum of points and authorities is a legal argument in the form of a discussion or analysis of the law (statutes, cases, or constitutional provisions) that applies to the case. If you are asked to help prepare a memorandum of points and authorities, you must research the law that governs the case. Some courts also require that the moving party submit a proposed order for the court to sign at the hearing.

Although the general requirements for motion practice are found in the Federal Rules of Civil Procedure or appropriate state laws, the area of motion practice is often the subject of local rules of court, in both federal and state courts. Before preparing any motion, it is imperative that you review all of the laws regulating motion practice in the particular court in which the action is filed. Rule 7 of the Federal Rules of Civil Procedure governs motions in general. Many local courts have additional rules. Usually local rules related to general motion practice also have some variation of the number 7 (i.e., 7.1, 7.2 etc.). Specific motions are governed by other Federal Rules as well as other local rules.

Service and Filing

The motion and supporting papers must be served on the other parties to the action and filed with the court. Service of motions is similar to service of an answer (by mail, by fax, electronically, or personally). Some courts also require that a separate copy of all papers be sent directly to the judge hearing the motion. This is referred to as a "chambers copy." All jurisdictions impose a time requirement for the service of motions. Under the Federal Rules of Civil Procedure, unless changed by a specific statute or court order, the written motion and notice of hearing must be served not later than 14 days before the time set for the hearing. If service is by mail, fax, or electronic means, you must allow an additional three days. Service of motions is governed by Rule 6. Time requirements for filing motions can be changed by court order or by local court rule. You must be careful to check local rules of court regarding this time limit. State courts may have different time requirements, and even some federal courts have local rules that have substantially changed this notice requirement.

Should a situation arise making it impossible or impractical to comply with the time requirement imposed by statute or local rule, the courts allow the parties to request that the time be shortened. In a sense, this request is in itself a motion. Courts generally treat this as an **ex parte** motion, meaning that no prior notice need be given nor any court hearing scheduled. If the court grants this request, it is often referred to as an **order shortening time**. The order shortening time is then served on the opposing party with the notice of hearing on the motion and the other moving papers. Service of a motion is usually accomplished by mailing, faxing, or electronically sending copies of the moving papers to the opposing attorneys. Proof of service of the moving papers is in the form of an affidavit or declaration by the person serving the papers and is sometimes known as a **proof of service** or **certificate of service**. The certificate should indicate how service was conducted. The certificate of service should be filed in court prior to the hearing. See Exhibit 7-4 for an example of a certificate of service for use in federal courts. See the checklist in Exhibit 7-5.

EXHIBIT 7-4 Certificate of Service

CERTIFICATE OF SERVICE

I certify that on _____ the foregoing document was served on all parties or their counsel of record through the CM/ECF system if they are registered users or, if they are not, by serving a true and correct copy at the addresses listed below:

_____

_____

_____

Signature _____   Date _____

EXHIBIT 7-5 Motion Checklist: Moving Party

MOTION CHECKLIST

If you are the *moving party*, be sure that you have:

✓ Reviewed all local rules for time limits and other requirements
✓ Checked possible hearing dates with opposing counsel
✓ Called the court to obtain a date for a hearing
✓ Prepared the proper documents
  • Notice of Motion
  • Motion
  • Affidavits or Declarations
  • Memorandum of Points and Authorities
  • Other documents required by the specific motion
  • Certificate of Mailing
  • Proposed Order
✓ Served all documents on all other parties to the action
✓ Filed the original documents (and chamber's copy if required) in court
✓ Calendared the date for hearing for the attorney
✓ Reviewed responding papers when received and determined if reply needed
✓ Checked for tentative ruling on motion where applicable

Responding to Motions

To oppose a motion, an attorney commonly serves and files papers in opposition. These usually consist of affidavits in opposition to the motion and a memorandum of points and authorities in opposition to the motion. These affidavits and the memorandum have the same technical requirements as do the moving papers. For most motions in federal court, opposing affidavits must be served not later than seven days before the hearing. You

EXHIBIT 7-6 Motion Checklist: Responding Party

MOTION CHECKLIST

If you are the *responding party*, be sure that you have:

✓ Calendared the hearing date
✓ Reviewed all local rules for time limits and other requirements
✓ Reviewed the moving party's papers
✓ Prepared proper papers
- Opposing Affidavits or Declarations
- Opposing Memorandum of Points and Authorities
- Other documents required by the specific motion
- Certificate of Mailing
- Proposed Order

✓ Served all documents on all other parties to the action
✓ Filed the original documents (and chamber's copy if required) in court
✓ Calendared the date for hearing for the attorney
✓ Checked for tentative ruling on motion where applicable

---

must also consult local rules to determine how many copies should be filed and whether a proposed order is required. Refer to the checklist in Exhibit 7-6. Again, the time limits vary depending on the state or local rules. In some courts, the moving party is given the opportunity to reply in writing to the opposing papers. As a litigation paralegal, you might be involved in drafting these documents for the attorney's review.

COURT PROCEDURES INVOLVING MOTIONS

In addition to written documents, motions often involve court hearings. The attorneys for the moving and responding parties appear before a judge and present oral arguments in support of or in opposition to the motion. The judge considers the written documents and the oral arguments and then makes a decision. After the judge rules on the motion, a written order, reflecting that ruling, must be submitted to the judge for signature. Many courts today allow attorneys to make a "telephone" appearance for motions. This involves telephone conference calls between the judge and the various attorneys. This can save substantial time. Local rules of court control this procedure, although many courts use a service known as CourtCall (<www.courtcall.com>), which facilitates the conference call.

Hearings

Because a hearing on the motion is a court appearance, it must be handled by the attorney. However, as a litigation paralegal, you might have some responsibilities in scheduling the hearing. Different courts have different methods of scheduling motion hearings. In some courts motions are heard at set times and in set departments (sometimes referred to as "law

---

AUTOMATED LITIGATION SUPPORT

E-mail and Hidden Data

SCENARIO

You have prepared the documents for the motion to dismiss in the *Pyramid Computer* case. Your attorney tells you that the motion is to be served electronically (by e-mail) on the other attorney, although it will not be e-filed with the court. She explains that even though the complaint was not e-filed, the plaintiff's attorney has agreed to electronic service for all papers. Included in the documents for the motion to dismiss is the affidavit of your client. You prepared several preliminary drafts of this document and made numerous changes and corrections to the information contained in it.

PROBLEM

You are not concerned about the mechanics of e-mailing the documents; you have done this several times before. However, you are concerned that the plaintiff's attorney might have the capability of accessing hidden metadata in the document, including comments and changes that were made to the affidavit before you produced the final draft. Some of this information is confidential and may harm your case. It might also be a violation of your ethical duties to the client. How do you protect against this?

SOLUTION

Documents prepared by normal word processing often contain hidden information or metadata that you do not want to share. When several drafts of a document are prepared and reviewed by different individuals, the final document may contain a record of comments and changes that were made to the document. Properties of the document (such as who created it, the date of creation, and the latest revision date) may also be retrievable. If you are e-mailing a document, such as an affidavit, you do not want an opposing party to access this information. Fortunately, there are ways to remove this hidden information (sometimes referred to as "metadata scrubbing"). For example, Microsoft Office contains a feature called Document Inspector that will also remove hidden data. To access this feature in Word 2013 click on "File" then "Info." The Document Inspector feature appears allowing you to inspect and protect the document. For earlier versions of Word, use the "help" feature to find out information about the Document Inspector. WordPerfect has a similar feature, "Save Without Metadata." However you choose to save the document without hidden metadata, always save a copy of your original document. Sometimes in removing hidden data, needed information is also deleted.

---

and motion"). In other courts you might have to specifically arrange a time with the judge hearing the motion. This is done through the judge's clerk. Scheduling the motion may require that you call the court, talk to the clerk handling the motion calendar, and arrange for a convenient date. Alternatively, a court might allow you to schedule a date through the court's Web site without talking to a court clerk. Be sure to check your attorney's calendar for conflicts. It is also advisable to call the opposing attorneys prior to doing this to schedule the hearing at a time that is convenient for all parties. This eliminates the need for continuing the hearing date. When setting a motion for hearing, be sure that you allow sufficient time for service of the moving papers. Also be sure to check state rules regarding service by mail, fax, or electronic means. State rules may change time limits.

Tentative Rulings

Because all moving and responding papers must be filed several days before the scheduled hearing, the judge has the opportunity to review the papers and consider the merits of the motion prior to the time for a hearing on the motion. Many judges feel that the brief

order

A judge's ruling in response to a motion.

oral arguments that take place at the hearing are no more than a repetition of information already in the documents. In an effort to save court time and avoid unnecessary hearings, some courts have adopted the practice of making a tentative ruling prior to the date of the hearing, usually a day or two prior to the hearing. Attorneys (or their paralegals) can then call the court and discover how the judge intends to rule on the motion. In some cases, this information is posted on the Internet. If the attorneys insist, they are still entitled to appear at the scheduled hearing.

Orders after Motions

After the motion is heard, the judge makes a ruling, called an **order**. Most courts require that the prevailing party prepare the written order for the judge's signature. As a litigation paralegal, you might be asked to do this. (Some courts have local rules that require the moving party to submit a proposed order with the moving papers.) Sometimes a judge's ruling on a case is not a simple grant or denial of the motion. Orders can be very involved. If you are asked to prepare an order after a hearing, be sure you know exactly what must be included in the order. The attorney may give you her notes from the hearing, or may simply tell you what to include in the order. In either case, be sure you understand the notes or directions before drafting the order. Exhibit 7-7 shows an example of an order.

EXHIBIT 7-7 Order after Motion

UNITED STATES DISTRICT COURT
DISTRICT OF MASSACHUSETTS

JOHN JONES,   )
  Plaintiff,   )
)   Civil No. 123456
)
  v.   )   Order
)
)
PYRAMID COMPUTER CORPORATION,   )
  Defendant.   )
)

_____

    This action was heard on _____, on the motion of defendant, PYRAMID COMPUTER CORPORATION, for an order dismissing this action. Pat Rivas appeared as counsel for defendant, in support of the motion, and Lane Borman appeared as counsel for plaintiff in opposition thereto. It appears to the court that defendant is a citizen of the same state as plaintiff and that therefore this court lacks subject matter jurisdiction. Therefore,

    IT IS ORDERED that the complaint filed herein on _____, _____, be and it is hereby dismissed.

    Dated _____   _____
                                      Judge, District Court

Sanctions

All courts demand that motions be made or opposed in good faith. To prevent unnecessary or frivolous motions, courts have the power to punish an attorney who abuses the motion process. This punishment often is an award of attorney fees to the opposing side. In some cases, if the court finds the behavior particularly unreasonable or unjustified, the court may find a party or attorney in contempt of court. If a party fails to comply with an order issued after a motion, the court may impose additional sanctions. In some extreme cases the court may even strike the pleadings of one who fails to comply with a court order, making it possible for the other side to win without trial. Should the court grant an order disposing of the case, that order would be immediately appealable.

motion for a more definite statement
A motion made in response to a complaint in which the defendant challenges the clarity or specificity of the complaint.

motion to strike
A request made to the court to delete part or all of a pleading; can also refer to a request made during trial to delete testimony.

SPECIFIC MOTIONS

As mentioned earlier, there are many different kinds of motions. The more common motions mentioned in the Federal Rules of Civil Procedure and seen in many state jurisdictions are described here.

Pretrial Motions

Motions can be made at any time during the litigation process. Consequently, they deal with all aspects of litigation. Pretrial motions deal with issues or problems that arise before the trial occurs. Most often, these motions deal with requests that are ancillary to the primary relief requested in the complaint. These requests or motions often relate to the pleadings, the jurisdiction and venue of the court, and the discovery process. However, some pretrial motions deal with substantive issues that may affect the very right to trial.

Motion to Dismiss   A motion to dismiss the action is a request that the court terminate the lawsuit immediately, without a hearing on the merits of the plaintiff's claim. A motion to dismiss is often made in lieu of an answer, and if granted eliminates the need for an answer. Such a motion can be made for several reasons. In federal proceedings, a motion to dismiss the case is proper when the court lacks subject matter or personal jurisdiction, when venue is improper, when process (the summons) or service of process is insufficient, when the complaint fails to state a claim upon which relief can be granted, or when a necessary party has not been joined (Rule 12 of the Federal Rules).

Motion for a More Definite Statement   If a complaint (or other claim for relief) is so vague and ambiguous that it cannot be understood and responded to, the party required to respond may make a **motion for a more definite statement**. Such a motion is intended to require the claimant to clarify the allegations and make them more intelligible. The moving party is expected to point out the defects in the complaint and explain what details must be added to the claim (Rule 12[e] of the Federal Rules).

Motion to Strike   A **motion to strike** is a request that the court delete portions of a pleading that are insufficient, redundant, immaterial, or scandalous (Rule 12[f] of the Federal Rules).

motion to amend
A request by one party to the court to allow a change in a pleading.

motion for judgment on the pleadings
A motion claiming that the allegations in the pleadings are such that no controversial issues remain and that judgment can be entered for only one party.

motion for change of venue
A request from a party that the court transfer the case to a another geographical location.

motion to quash the return of the service
Motion made by a defendant who claims that he was improperly served with the summons and complaint.

motion to compel
A request by one party to the court for an order requiring the other side to comply with a discovery request.

motion for a protective order
A motion made during discovery asking the court to limit a discovery request.

Motion to Amend   As discussed in previous chapters, all pleadings can be amended. Under some circumstances, pleadings can be amended as a matter of right without the necessity of a court order. If a court order is required, the party wishing to amend a pleading must make a **motion to amend**. The courts are very liberal in allowing parties to amend pleadings and grant such motions unless the amended pleading would unfairly prejudice the other party (Rule 15 of the Federal Rules).

Motion for Judgment on the Pleadings   After all pleadings have been filed in an action, any party may make a **motion for judgment on the pleadings**. The moving party in such a motion claims that the allegations in the pleadings are such that no contested issues remain and judgment can be entered for only one party. For example, if the defendant were to admit all of the allegations in the complaint, no disputed issue would remain. The pleadings themselves indicate that the plaintiff is entitled to judgment (Rule 12[c] of the Federal Rules).

Motion for Change of Venue   If an action is commenced in the wrong judicial district, a party can request that the court transfer the case to a proper court by making a **motion for change of venue**. Also, in cases where venue is proper in more than one district, a party can request a change of venue to another proper district for the convenience of parties and witnesses or in the interest of justice (28 U.S.C. § 1404).

Motion to Quash Return of Service   If the defendant claims that he was improperly served with the summons and complaint, he can make a **motion to quash the return of the service** (or motion to quash service of summons). A defendant is improperly served if the manner of service is not in accordance with the appropriate statute or if the defendant is not subject to the personal jurisdiction of the court. When such a motion is granted, service is negated. If the defect in service was in the manner of service, the defendant can be served again. However, if the court does not have personal jurisdiction over the defendant, the action cannot proceed in that court. If the plaintiff wants to pursue the case, he will have to begin the process again, this time in a court that does have personal jurisdiction over the defendant (Rules 4 and 12 of the Federal Rules).

Discovery Motions   An essential part of the litigation process is discovery, a legal process by which parties of the lawsuit are able to discover facts relevant to the case. Much of discovery involves requiring the opposing side to reveal relevant facts or provide pertinent documents. Problems often arise regarding exactly what has to be revealed or provided. If one party refuses to provide information to another, the party requesting the information can make a **motion to compel** the requested discovery. If the motion is granted, the court will order the party to comply with the discovery request and impose some sort of penalty or sanctions if the party refuses. If the court finds that the initial refusal to comply with discovery request was unreasonable, it can also impose sanctions for that initial refusal. Sanctions are usually in the form of attorney fees awarded to the moving party. Likewise, if the court finds that the motion to compel was not made in good faith, it can impose sanctions on the moving party. A second type of discovery motion is a **motion for a protective order**, which is a request that the court limit the other party's right to discovery (Rule 37 of the Federal Rules).

Motion for Summary Judgment

One of the most important motions in litigation is the **motion for summary judgment**. In a motion for summary judgment, one party asks the court to order that judgment be entered as a matter of law, without the necessity of trial, because there are no real disputes regarding material facts. When parties file pleadings, they sometimes make allegations hoping, and even believing, that they will be able to prove them. However, as the parties prepare for trial, it sometimes becomes evident that problems exist. Before a case goes to trial, parties have the opportunity, either through investigation or formal discovery, to uncover and evaluate the evidence that will be introduced by both sides during trial. At this point, one side may determine that the opposition really has no valid admissible evidence to support their contentions. In other words, in spite of what the parties claimed in their pleadings, no evidence supports their facts. Because the purpose of trial is to resolve factual disputes, there is no need for trial.

Motions for summary judgment can be made either by plaintiffs or by defendants. For plaintiffs to prevail in such a motion, they must show that the facts supporting each element of their cause of action are undisputed. For defendants to defeat plaintiffs' motions, they must show the court that either there is a dispute regarding a material fact related to the cause of action, or that there are facts that support an affirmative defense. For defendants to make a successful motion for summary judgment, they need to show only that the plaintiff cannot prove any one of the elements of the cause of action, or that the existence of an affirmative defense is undisputed. For example, suppose that in the situation described in the case Commentary, Jones is a manufacturer and distributor of video processors for tablet computers and that Pyramid Computer manufactures the computers. Assume that Jones has sued Pyramid Computer for $100,000 for video processors that were shipped to Pyramid Computer. Jones claims that no part of the $100,000 was paid. Jones makes a motion for summary judgment, supported by an affidavit and documents, establishing the following:

1. Jones and Pyramid Computer entered into a written contract whereby Pyramid Computer was to purchase video processors from Jones at agreed prices.
2. Pursuant to a written purchase order, Jones delivered the video processors to Pyramid Computer at an agreed price of $100,000.
3. Pyramid Computer received the video processors and signed a receipt for the goods.
4. Pyramid Computer failed to make any payment toward the $100,000 even though repeated requests have been made.

Jones has thus supported each element of a cause of action for breach of contract with factual evidence. Unless Pyramid Computer can show that there is a dispute as to a material fact (or that an affirmative defense exists), a motion for summary judgment would be proper. However, suppose that Pyramid Computer submitted an affidavit stating that it never received the processors. It claims that the signed receipt was for a different order. In such a case, a dispute regarding a material fact exists, and the court would deny the motion for summary judgment.

When making a motion for summary judgment, the parties often present their evidence to the court in the form of affidavits. This can also be done by submitting depositions, answers to interrogatories, or answers to requests for admissions. (Depositions, interrogatories, and requests for admissions are methods of discovery and are discussed in

motion for summary judgment
A motion requesting that judgment be entered immediately because there is no genuine dispute as to any material fact in the case and the movant is entitled to judgment as a matter of law.

motion for sanctions
A request to the court from one
party that penalties be imposed
on the other party for violating
the provisions of Rule 11 of the
Federal Rules of Civil Procedure.

subsequent chapters.) Along with these documents, the moving party also submits a memorandum of points and authorities. In most cases, a party opposing a motion for summary judgment will present the court with opposing papers supported by affidavits, depositions, answers to interrogatories, or answers to request for admissions. The opposing party also files a legal memorandum. All affidavits filed in support of or opposition to a motion for summary judgment must show that the persons making the affidavits are competent to testify to the matters stated within the affidavits, that the matters are within their personal knowledge, and that if they were testifying in court the statements would be admissible as evidence.

In addition to the normal moving papers (notice of motion, motion, affidavits, legal memorandum), many courts require the parties to submit a separate statement detailing the uncontested facts and showing how and where each fact is established (i.e., in an affidavit or in a deposition, including the page and line numbers). Responding parties must then submit a statement of contested facts, again showing their support for claiming that the facts are in dispute. In ruling on a motion for summary judgment, the court scrutinizes the various papers to see if a factual dispute does exist. At this point the court does not weigh the evidence or resolve a factual dispute. If a legitimate and genuine factual dispute exists, the motion must be denied, even if one side has overwhelming evidence.

A motion for summary judgment need not be directed to all of the issues in the case. A party can request a partial summary judgment or a summary judgment on certain issues in the case. For example, in a personal injury case there may be no factual dispute about liability, but a dispute may exist as to the amount of damages to which the plaintiff is entitled. If such a summary judgment is rendered, a trial is held to decide the remaining issues.

In making a motion for summary judgment, you must be careful to check the appropriate statute for time requirements. There are generally limits on how soon after commencement of the action this type of motion can be made. Notice requirements for such a motion may differ from other motions. Because of the complexity of summary judgment motions, some courts require extended notice of any hearing. It is also very important to check local rules regarding summary judgment motions.

Motion for Sanctions   The Federal Rules of Civil Procedure prohibit attorneys from filing documents in court that are frivolous or that contain contentions or allegations that are not supported by the evidence. If an attorney violates this rule, the opposing side has a right to make a **motion for sanctions**, which is a request for penalties for violating the provisions of Rule 11 of the Federal Rules. The court can also act on its own initiative. The sanctions can include an order to pay a penalty to the court or an order to pay the other side's reasonable attorney fees and costs incurred because of the violation. In addition, the court can impose nonmonetary sanctions, such as striking pleadings. Although similar sanctions can be imposed as a result of discovery violations, this section does not apply to discovery motions (Rule 11 of the Federal Rules).

Trial Motions

At the beginning of a trial, before any evidence is introduced, attorneys sometimes need to resolve questions or issues regarding matters of trial procedure. These often involve questions regarding the admissibility of certain kinds of evidence. For example, in a wrongful death case, the defendant may anticipate that the plaintiff's attorney will try to introduce photographs of the decedent that are graphic and inflammatory. The defendant might feel that these photos are too prejudicial and should be excluded from evidence. The defense attorney would therefore request that the court order that the evidence is inadmissible. This type of request or motion is made at the time of trial, but before evidence is actually presented. If it is a jury trial, it is important that these motions not be made in front of the jury. Motions such as this, made at the commencement of trial, are often referred to as **motions in limine**. Because all parties are present in court, no prior notice need be given, nor do the motions have to be in writing (although attorneys sometimes submit a memorandum of points and authorities in support of their position).

Motions made during the course of the trial itself also differ from pretrial motions. Trial motions are often made in immediate response to testimony or other evidence that is offered in the trial. Obviously, there is no opportunity to prepare written papers. Because all sides are already present in court, no need for prior notice of the motion arises. Sometimes, however, the attorneys do know ahead of time that they are going to make a particular motion. One such motion is a **motion for judgment as a matter of law** under Rule 50 of the Federal Rules of Civil Procedure. This motion is made in jury trials and, if granted, results in the judge entering a judgment without allowing the jury to consider the evidence. The basis for this motion is that the party against whom judgment is entered has not introduced sufficient evidence for a reasonable jury to find in his favor. This motion can be made at any time during the trial as long as the party against whom judgment is sought has fully presented its evidence. In some state courts, a *motion for a directed verdict*, rather than a motion for judgment as a matter of law, is used. In a motion for a directed verdict, the moving party is asking the judge to tell the jury how it must decide a case. The basis for such a motion is the same as for a motion for judgment as a matter of law. Motions for directed verdicts are usually made at the end of the trial, after all the evidence has been introduced. Although the attorney can make these motions without a written motion or notice, the attorney may want to present the judge with a memorandum of points and authorities to support the motion. As a litigation paralegal, you might be asked to help research the law and prepare such a memorandum.

Posttrial Motions

Motions made after the trial has occurred often are directed at the judgment that the trial court has rendered. However, a posttrial motion may also relate to the assessment of costs against the party who lost the case.

Motion for Judgment as a Matter of Law
As described earlier, a motion for judgment as a matter of law can be made in a jury trial at any time before the case is submitted to the jury. Sometimes judges are reluctant to grant such motions because they feel that the jury should be given the opportunity to decide the case. If the judge does not grant such a motion, it can be renewed by the party after the jury decides the case, should it return an unfavorable verdict. In some state courts, when this motion is made after trial, a **motion for judgment notwithstanding the verdict** is used rather than the motion for judgment as a matter of law (Rule 50 of the Federal Rules).

motions in limine
A request made to the court to delete part or all of a pleading; can also refer to a request made during trial to delete testimony.

motion for judgment as a matter of law
A motion made during or after a trial in which one party asks the judge to rule in his or her favor because the other side has produced no evidence upon which a judgment can be based; the motion cannot be made until the party against whom the motion is made has introduced all of its evidence.

motion for judgment notwithstanding the verdict
A motion made in some state courts after a jury verdict; a request from one party that the judge reverse the jury's verdict against that party and enter a different judgment in that party's favor.

motion for a new trial
A motion made after a trial requesting that the judge set aside the verdict or judgment and grant a new trial to the parties.

motion to tax costs
A motion made after a trial challenging the costs of suit that are claimed by the prevailing party.

motion for relief from a judgment or order
A request to the court by one party that the court relieve a party from any judgment, order, or proceeding.

Motion for a New Trial

The party who loses in a civil trial has the right to appeal that decision to a higher court. However, the appellate process is lengthy and costly. Prior to any appeal, that party also has the opportunity to request that the trial court itself set aside the verdict or judgment and grant a new trial by making a **motion for a new trial**. Such a request or motion is normally heard by the judge who presided over the trial. This motion is proper in both jury trials and court trials (trials in front of a judge only). Grounds for such a motion might include jury impropriety, mistake in law, or newly discovered evidence.

Normally, very strict time limits control when this kind of motion can be made. The Federal Rules of Civil Procedure allow a party 28 days after entry of judgment to serve such a motion. If you are assisting an attorney in preparing this motion, pay close attention to statutory time restraints and be careful that all papers are promptly filed and served (Rule 59 of the Federal Rules).

Motion to Tax Costs

The prevailing party in a lawsuit is usually entitled to recover his costs in addition to the judgment. Costs include expenses such as filing fees and service fees incurred as part of litigation. The amount of the costs is usually presented to the court in written form when the trial is over (sometimes referred to as a *cost bill*). If the other party challenges any or all of these costs, that party does so by filing a motion with the court, known as a **motion to tax costs**. As in all posttrial motions, timing of the motion is critical (Rule 54 of the Federal Rules).

Motions for Relief from Judgment or Order

In Chapter 6 we discussed the fact that, under Rule 60 of the Federal Rules of Civil Procedure, a default judgment could be set aside by the court upon a showing that the judgment was entered because of the mistake, inadvertence, surprise, excusable neglect, or fraud of the party or the party's legal representative. Under Rule 60, the court has the power to set aside any judgment, order, or proceeding for the same reason. A request of the court by one party to do this is a **motion for relief from a judgment or order**. Depending on the law of the jurisdiction, additional grounds for the granting of relief may exist. For example, Rule 60 of the Federal Rules of Civil Procedure provides as follows:

> On motion and upon such terms as are just, the court may relieve a party or a party's legal representative from a final judgment, order, or proceeding for the following reasons: (1) mistake, inadvertence, surprise, or excusable neglect; (2) newly discovered evidence which by due diligence could not have been discovered in time to move for a new trial under Rule 59(b); (3) fraud (whether heretofore denominated intrinsic or extrinsic); (4) the judgment is void; (5) the judgment has been satisfied, released, or discharged, or a prior judgment upon which it is based has been reversed or otherwise vacated, or it is no longer equitable that the judgment should have prospective application; or (6) any other reason that justifies relief.

Motions for relief are generally required to be filed within a reasonable time, although the term *reasonable* is not defined. Usually, maximum time limits do exist for the filing of such motions.

In granting or denying a motion for relief, especially on the grounds of mistake or excusable neglect, the court has the right to exercise a great deal of discretion. If you are drafting affidavits for this type of motion, you should be as detailed as possible in explaining the reasons for making the motion.

PRELIMINARY INJUNCTIONS AND TEMPORARY RESTRAINING ORDERS

Chapter 5 described temporary restraining orders and preliminary injunctions. These provisional remedies are sometimes granted before trial and are usually requested in conjunction with lawsuits that seek permanent injunctions. In federal court, the procedures for obtaining preliminary injunctions and temporary restraining orders are found in Rule 65 of the Federal Rules of Civil Procedure. Various local rules of court also control the procedures. Although these remedies are not normally considered to be motions, the method of obtaining these special equitable remedies is similar to motion practice.

A request for a preliminary injunction closely resembles a formal noticed motion. After a complaint is filed, the party requesting the preliminary injunction files papers in court requesting a preliminary injunction and setting the matter for a court hearing. This request is normally supported by affidavits setting forth the factual basis for the request. In lieu of affidavits, a verified complaint may be used. A memorandum of points and authorities is also usually filed. These papers must be served on the opposing party. A court hearing to determine whether to grant the preliminary injunction then takes place.

A temporary restraining order (TRO), which is granted only when a court finds that some immediate and irreparable harm will result without it, more closely resembles an ex parte motion and usually precedes a preliminary injunction. The request for a TRO resembles a motion in that it asks the court for an order. Like a motion, it also may be supported by affidavits and a memorandum of points and authorities. This order may be requested and granted at the time that the complaint itself is filed. Furthermore, although the requesting party must appear before a judge, a full hearing, such as the one that takes place in a request for a preliminary injunction, rarely occurs. Although the courts strongly encourage the requesting party to give prior notice to the other side that a TRO is being requested, the court can issue a TRO without written or oral notice to the adverse party. When notice is given, it is usually done in an informal manner. It may even be a telephone call made a few hours prior to the request. Rule 65 of the Federal Rules of Civil Procedure allows the court to grant a TRO without any notice if facts show that the restraining order is needed to avoid immediate and irreparable injury and the applicant's attorney certifies to the court in writing what efforts (if any) have been made to notify the adverse party and the reasons supporting the claim that notice should not be required. If a TRO is granted without notice, it must be followed as soon as possible by a hearing on a preliminary injunction, for which notice to the adverse party is required. The court will usually require that all of the moving papers for the preliminary injunction be filed prior to granting the TRO. The TRO expires not later than 14 days after it is issued.

FINDING IT on the Internet

Motion practice is often governed by local rules of court, which are usually found on a court's home page.

a. Assume that the motion in the *Pyramid Computer* case described in the Commentary has been filed in the federal district court for your area. Review the local rules of court that would apply to the motion to dismiss being made in that case. Be sure to include any rules regarding notice requirements. Write a brief memo describing your findings. You can link to any district court through the Judiciary home page at **<http://www.uscourts.gov/links.html>**.

b. Also check the court's home page to see if judges post tentative rulings in motions. If so, summarize the proposed rulings in at least three cases.

c. Telephone conferencing is a convenient way for attorneys and courts to handle uncomplicated matters. Most courts require that a third party be responsible for handling the actual conference call. One such company is CourtCall LLC. Review their Web site at **<http://www.courtcall.com>** to read more about telephone conferencing as a substitute for a court appearance.

SUMMARY

- The application for a court order is known as a motion. Motions are a common occurrence during the course of any litigation and can take place before, during, or after trial. Except for motions made during the trial, motions are generally in writing, filed in court, and served on the opposing attorneys in the case. Even though motions are not pleadings, they are prepared in the same general format as pleadings.

- The general procedure for making a motion involves serving and filing various documents with the court. These include the motion, which describes the nature of the request and the basis for it; the notice of motion, which states the date, time, and place of any hearing on the motion; affidavits in support of the motion; a memorandum of points and authorities; and a certificate of service showing all parties were served. Affidavits are statements made under oath before a notary. These statements are used in lieu of testimony. A memorandum of points and authorities is a discussion and analysis of the law controlling the case. A party wishing to oppose a motion does so by filing and serving affidavits and memoranda of points and authorities in opposition to the motion.

- Many motions involve court hearings. Scheduling the motion with the court is often a job for a paralegal. When setting a motion for hearing, care must be taken to allow enough time to give proper notice of the hearing to all parties. After the motion is heard, the judge's ruling is put in writing in a document known as an order. An order is normally prepared by the prevailing party. Some courts require that proposed orders be submitted with the moving papers. To prevent unnecessary or frivolous motions, courts have the power to punish attorneys who abuse the motion process. This punishment, known as sanctions, is usually in the form of attorney fees but can also be a finding of contempt of court.

- Motions can be categorized as pretrial, trial, or posttrial. Pretrial motions include motions that are related to the pleadings, such as a motion to dismiss, motion for a more definite statement, motion to strike, motion for judgment on the pleadings, motion for change of venue, motion to quash return of service, and motion to amend. Pretrial motions also include discovery motions, motions for summary judgment, and motions for sanctions. Trial motions differ from other motions in that they usually do not have to be in writing. Because all parties are already in court, no prior notice is required. Nevertheless, attorneys sometimes like to present memoranda of points and authorities in support of trial motions. One common trial motion is the motion for judgment as a matter of law. Motions made after trial include motions for judgment as a matter of law, motion for new trial, motion to tax costs, and motion to set aside a judgment.

- Requests for preliminary injunctions and temporary restraining orders closely resemble motions. They are requests for court orders in a pending case. The requests for these orders are made in writing and are supported by affidavits or verified complaints and memoranda of points and authorities. Preliminary injunctions require formal notice to the opposing side and involve a court hearing. Like ex parte motions, temporary restraining orders do not always require notice, and a court hearing may involve the appearance of the moving party only.

KEY TERMS

declaration	motion for judgment notwithstanding the verdict	motion to compel
ex parte		motion to quash the return of the service
memorandum of points and authorities	motion for judgment on the pleadings	motion to strike
motion for a more definite statement	motion for relief from a judgment or order	motion to tax costs
motion for a new trial	motion for sanctions	movant
motion for a protective order	motion for summary judgment	notice of hearing on the motion
motion for change of venue	motion in limine	order
motion for judgment as a matter of law	motion to amend	order shortening time
		proof of service (certificate of service)

REVIEW QUESTIONS

1. What is a motion?
2. What is the procedure for making a motion?
3. What is the procedure for opposing a motion?
4. What is an affidavit?

5. What role does the paralegal have in setting motions for hearing?

6. Describe the method for obtaining orders after a hearing on the motion.

7. What are sanctions and how are they used in motion practice?

8. What are some common pretrial motions?

9. How do trial motions differ from other motions?

10. What are some common posttrial motions?

CHAPTER EXERCISES

Where necessary, check with your instructor prior to starting any of these exercises.

1. Check your state laws regarding general motion practice. What forms must be filed to make a motion? What forms are generally filed in opposition to a motion? What are the time limits for giving notice of a motion? Are there any time limits for filing papers in opposition to a motion?

2. Determine whether the federal district court in your area has any local rules regarding motion practice. If so, review those rules. Are there any special procedures or time requirements that must be followed?

3. Determine whether the state court of general jurisdiction in your area has local rules regarding motion practice. If so, review those rules. Are there any special procedures or time requirements that must be followed?

4. Review the case Commentary at the beginning of the chapter. Assume that Jones filed a complaint against Pyramid Computer for $100,000 for video processors that Jones sold and delivered to Pyramid Computer, the amount becoming due on May 1, 2010. Analyze the following situations. What motion or motions would be appropriate? Explain your answers.

   a. Assume that Pyramid Computer filed an answer admitting all of the allegations of the complaint but asserting as an affirmative defense the following: "In recent months defendant Pyramid Computer Corporation has suffered severe financial setbacks and has been unable to meet its financial obligations. On or about May 1, 2010, defendants offered to pay plaintiff the sum of $1,000 per month toward the obligation described in the complaint; however, plaintiff refused and continues to refuse such compromise." There is no dispute regarding Pyramid Computer's financial situation or its offer to settle.

   b. Assume that Pyramid Computer filed a general denial to Jones's complaint. During the discovery process, the deposition of the president of Pyramid Computer Corporation was taken. During the deposition, the president admitted that Pyramid Computer and Jones had a written agreement regarding the sale and purchase of video processors, that Pyramid Computer received the goods that were the subject of this lawsuit, and that payment was not made because of Pyramid Computer's financial situation.

   c. Assume that Pyramid Computer filed an answer to the complaint admitting all of the allegations of the complaint but asserting as a defense the fact that Pyramid Computer has filed bankruptcy. Pyramid Computer has in fact had its debts discharged in bankruptcy.

d. Assume that Pyramid Computer files an answer containing denials of all of the substantive allegations of the complaint. Pyramid Computer adds a paragraph to the answer stating that "Jones should be precluded from maintaining any action in court because he is a dishonest, disreputable businessman who cheats everyone he deals with."

CHAPTER PROJECT

Review the factual situation described in the opening Commentary. Assume that the president of Pyramid Computer, Owen Young, relates that the complaint and summons were handed to Barbara Dexter, a sales representative in the New York office of the company. Ms. Dexter has no position with the company other than as a salaried employee. This is the only copy of the summons and complaint that were served upon Pyramid Computer. Your supervising attorney wants to challenge this service as not being in accordance with Rule 4 of the Federal Rules of Civil Procedure. Prepare the appropriate motion, notice of hearing, and affidavits for the attorney's review.

THE *BENNETT* CASE
Assignment for Chapter 7: Motion to Amend Complaint

The plaintiff's original complaint contained causes of action for discrimination and infliction of emotional distress. After interviewing several witnesses and reviewing various documents, the plaintiff's attorney has concluded that a cause of action for breach of contract also exists. The defendant will not stipulate to plaintiff amending the complaint. Therefore, you have been asked to prepare a motion to amend the complaint. Review Rules 7 and 15 of the Federal Rules of Civil Procedure, found in Appendix B, and then prepare a motion to amend the complaint.

THE *DOUGLASS FINANCIAL INC.* CASE
Assignment for Chapter 7: Assisting with Motion for a More Definite Statement

Your attorney is preparing to make a motion for a more definite statement. She wants you to check your local state court Web site for the following:

- any local rules on motion practice,
- what judges are hearing motions, and
- if a date for the hearing can be obtained online,
- whether your attorney can appear at the hearing through a telephone call.

Prepare a memo to your attorney addressing her questions.

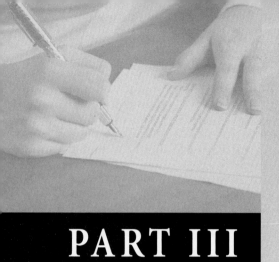

PART III

Discovery

CHAPTER 8

Overview of the Discovery Process

CHAPTER OUTLINE

THE *LUIS RAPHAEL* CASE

This morning your supervising attorney called you into her office to familiarize you with the details of a new case that you will be handling for her. Your firm has been retained to represent Dr. Luis Raphael, an archaeology professor at Jonas Halbert Northern University (JHNU), located in Portland, Maine. Dr. Raphael has been accused of improperly supervising the work of Victor Phipps, a research assistant who is alleged to have falsified evidence in various articles that resulted in the funding of several National Science Foundation (NSF) grants. Raphael supervises several research fellows at JHNU who are involved in multiple research projects, most of which are funded by NSF grants. The problem in the present case began several months ago when Raphael submitted an abstract to a prestigious journal allegedly based on evidence obtained at a recent archaeological dig in the Middle East. When the evidence was questioned by several referees, Phipps could not produce the evidence needed to support his claim. Rather than suspend Phipps at that time, Raphael permitted him to continue working on several additional projects all involving NSF money. After a six-month study of Phipps's work, JHNU discovered numerous problems with his publications, including the falsification and the fabrication of evidence. Phipps was dismissed from JHNU, but not before the NSF instituted the current lawsuit to recover the funds that had been obtained fraudulently by Phipps. As Phipps's supervisor, Raphael has been named as a defendant in the suit and has retained your supervising attorney to represent him separately from JHNU. The next step is the discovery process.

In previous chapters, you had the opportunity to explore the steps involved in the litigation process. In this chapter you will be introduced to another critical part of the litigation process—discovery. After completing this chapter, you should be able to:

- define discovery.
- identify the five major methods of discovery.
- outline the factors involved in choosing discovery methods.
- describe the ethical considerations involved in the discovery process.
- determine the types of evidence that can be obtained during discovery.
- differentiate among the attorney–client privilege, the work product privilege, the common interest privilege, and the Fifth Amendment privilege against self-incrimination.
- discuss the purpose of the confidentiality agreement and protective orders.
- indicate the objectives of quick peek and clawback agreements.
- indicate the types of disclosures that must be made by the parties under Rule 26 of the Federal Rules of Civil Procedures.
- indicate the content of a discovery plan as required under Rule 26 of the Federal Rules of Civil Procedure.
- discuss the need for voluntary cooperation in the discovery process.
- relate the process used to compel compliance with discovery and the sanctions that result from noncompliance.

discovery
The procedure that the parties
to a lawsuit follow in order
to uncover the facts that
are involved in the suit. The
system involves an exchange
of information among the
parties using certain established
discovery techniques including
depositions, interrogatories,
requests for real evidence,
requests for physical and mental
examinations, and requests for
admissions.

THE NATURE OF DISCOVERY

Discovery is the legal process by which the parties to a lawsuit search for facts relevant to a particular case. Most people who have not been involved in litigation are surprised to learn that all the parties involved in a lawsuit have the opportunity to gather all the facts relevant to that lawsuit before the case even reaches trial. Accustomed as they are to the surprise witness produced at the last minute by a wide variety of fictional lawyers, most people believe that the attorney who wins a case is the one who traps her opponent by concealing crucial evidence until the last possible second. The truth is almost exactly opposite to this fiction. Pretrial discovery is allowed because the law supports the principle that lawsuits should be decided on the facts and on the legal merits of the case, not on the ability of one attorney to conceal evidence or ambush the other attorney with surprise witnesses. In this chapter, you will explore the objectives of discovery, some preliminary considerations in the discovery process, and some ethical considerations in discovery. The discovery stage is very important not only because it reveals the facts in a suit but also because it helps shape the direction of the case. The results of an effectively conducted discovery process may encourage your attorney to proceed with the case. However, those results may also indicate that a settlement or a voluntary dismissal is in order.

Developments Concerning Discovery

The courts have long encouraged parties to cooperate with one another in the discovery process in order to promote full disclosure of relevant facts before trial. Regrettably, attorneys often ignore the spirit of this law and engage in behavior that, although not a technical violation of the law, defeats the purpose of discovery. The Federal Rules of Civil Procedure are designed to facilitate discovery and discourage any attempt to circumvent its true purpose. In particular, Rule 26 of the Federal Rules requires the parties to disclose certain information to the other party without the necessity of formal discovery requests. The rules also limit the formal discovery methods that are available.

Electronically Stored Information

The discovery process has changed over the last few years as judges, attorneys, and paralegals have adjusted to computer technology. Although this chapter will concentrate on the many problems associated with the entry of electronics into the law, we must not overlook the many benefits that have emerged with the computer revolution. These benefits include the ability to maintain close communication links among attorneys, paralegals, clients, witnesses, and experts; the power to instantaneously access cases, statutes, regulations, and pleadings on laptops, mobile phones, and tablets; and the capacity to gather, catalogue, and store hundreds of files on devices that can be carried in an attorney's briefcase or a paralegal's backpack. As we move through this chapter we should remember the words of that Elizabethan prophet, Francis Bacon, who said quite unapologetically that science and technology must be dedicated to the "endowment of human life with new inventions and riches."[1]

At the dawn of the 21st century, most legal professionals were content to treat electronic data in much the same way that they treated paper documents. They simply revised the scope of terms like "data compilations" and "documents" to include this new form of evidence. Business, they believed, could go on as usual. Experience has shown this position was based on wishful thinking. Computerized data, which is now referred to in the Federal Rules of Civil Procedure as **electronically stored information**, or ESI, had to be covered by special rules because this new form of evidence requires lawyers, paralegals, judges, and the even the parties involved in contemporary lawsuits to be more aware of the need to act in a manner that is timely, thorough, and prompt.[2] One problem is that electronically stored evidence multiplies so rapidly and is configured in so many different formats that even the most skilled practitioner can get lost trying to compile a basic discovery plan. Other problems arise because computers duplicate and preserve much of the data filed in their memories, yet they do not always have a consistent and predictable method for keeping track of that data. Additional problems arise when practitioners fail to search ESI adequately and thus retrieve and produce ESI that should have been protected by one of the many privileges provided by the law.[3] The Federal Rules of Civil Procedure have been amended to deal with the problems caused by the proliferation of ESI. Most of these amendments have had an impact on the nature and conduct of discovery.[4]

Paralegals, perhaps more than anyone else in the legal profession, must become as familiar as possible with these new amendments because the task of organizing and tracking ESI often becomes the responsibility of the paralegal. Fortunately, as many as 30 state court systems have added ESI amendments to their rules that closely parallel the 2006 ESI amendments to the Federal Rules of Civil Procedure.[5] This is good news for paralegals on two fronts. First, the fact that so many states have adopted the federal rules testifies to the effectiveness of those rules. Second, from a very practical perspective, the similarities that exist among federal and state rules greatly reduce a paralegal's learning curve when moving between the two court systems. Of course, the federal and state rules are rarely identical and some states have developed rules that are peculiar to their own jurisdictions, and so the paralegal cannot ignore the need to learn state rules. Moreover, a number of states have still elected to avoid the entire issue and are yet to make any rules that address ESI.[6]

The Objectives of Discovery

As noted, one of the primary objectives of discovery is to prevent one of the parties from winning the lawsuit by surprise or trickery. Another goal is to determine the truth or falsity of the alleged facts that form the basis of the lawsuit. A third objective of discovery is to examine the facts and weigh the advisability of proceeding with the case or settling early. Frequently, a case that looks promising in the opening stages loses its viability as more facts come to light. For example, in the *Raphael* case, if your supervising attorney uncovers evidence that Dr. Raphael helped Phipps to falsify some of the evidence used in his articles, she may decide to immediately settle the case with the NSF. In contrast, early discovery may reveal that your client's case is so strong that there is no need to proceed to trial. In such a situation, your attorney will file a summary judgment motion. For instance, in the *Raphael* case, your supervising attorney may discover that another administrator at JHNU rather than Dr. Raphael made the decision to retain Phipps despite Raphael's advice to dismiss him. In such a situation, the facts and the law would clearly support Raphael, and a summary judgment motion would appear to be appropriate. A fourth objective of discovery is to preserve testimony that might be lost should a witness disappear or become

electronically stored information (ESI)
Electronically stored information encompasses all computer-generated records such as those found in app records, backup tapes, blogs, "cookies," databases, data-processing cards, digital recorders, documented image technology, embedded chips, e-mail messages, metadata, fax machines, financial data, GPS tracking records, home computers, input data, Internet use records, instant messages, music files, PDAs, photos, scanners, smartphones, statistical data, system and network data, tablets, text messages, Web-based bulletin-board postings, Web-based discussions, widget records, wireless reading devices (WRDs), word-processed documents, videos, and voice mail, among others.

incapacitated or should records be lost or destroyed. Finally, some discovery methods can be used to impeach the credibility of a witness should that witness offer testimony at trial that contradicts his or her earlier statements made during discovery.

Preliminary Decisions Regarding Discovery

Conducting all discovery, but especially conducting the discovery of ESI, is difficult and complicated but not impossible. During the preliminary stages in a case, an attorney must decide which discovery techniques are best suited to the lawsuit. In making these decisions, the attorney must consider the cost and the amount of time involved.

Informal Discovery   The fact that formal discovery is an important part of the pretrial process does not mean that the informal process of uncovering information and evidence can be overlooked. Often a great deal of information can be gathered before the formal discovery process begins. In fact, the more information that can be collected at this time, the more efficient and economical the actual discovery process will become. For instance, it is often advisable for the attorney or the paralegal to visit any physical scene that is critical to the lawsuit. Thus, in the *Raphael* case, your attorney may decide to visit the offices and laboratories at the university to observe the environment in which Raphael and Phipps worked and to determine what additional witnesses might be available to testify about the operation of the department and the relationship between the two principal subjects of the lawsuit. At that time, the attorney or the paralegal may also want to call on witnesses to see whether they can provide any additional information about the case.

Web sites and databases can be explored at this stage in the informal discovery process too. For example, in the *Raphael* case, your supervising attorney may decide to gather information about the filing, accounting, and reporting systems used at JHNU to track NSF funds and to examine any computerized systems used to preserve evidence as it is used in the writing of journal abstracts and grant proposals. The paralegal's role can be very important during the informal stage of discovery because he or she can do much of the legwork involved in the process, thus saving time for the supervising attorney who can handle other matters that require her presence.

Discovery Strategies   Despite the changes in the Federal Rules of Civil Procedure and the new focus on ESI, some attorneys still overlook the importance of drawing up an effective discovery strategy before launching into the actual discovery process. This failure is unfortunate because it often means that the attorney and her paralegal are placed on the defensive rather than the offensive side of the litigation process. Instead of moving forward at a measured and controlled pace, she is caught reacting to what the other side has already done. As a consequence, the attorney loses control over the discovery process and spends far too much time patching up errors that could have been avoided had a strategic approach been developed during the earliest stages of the lawsuit. The key to success in developing a discovery strategy is to have a set routine that can be used as a pattern or a model in any case. Such a routine would involve a checklist of things that must be done before the discovery process begins. A good portion of this can be completed during the informal discovery process. However, some of it cannot be done until formal discovery begins. One of the first steps in the discovery strategy is to evaluate some of the new electronic discovery tools available to practitioners today. Another initial step involves identifying the type of ESI that is discoverable, as well as identifying those individuals who are responsible for the opponent's computer system. Your supervising attorney will most likely evaluate which of the traditional discovery methods would be best in each case.

Electronic Discovery Tools   **Electronic discovery**, **e-discovery**, and **digital discovery** are all terms used to describe the discovery of electronically stored information (ESI). No matter what it is called, however, e-discovery has become an inescapable part of the routine in most law firms today. Personal computers, which store data, create forms, and send e-mail, are as common in law firms today as the typewriter was in the past. Moreover, the use of audio- and videotaping as well as telephone, Web, and videoconferencing is becoming commonplace in firms across the country. In addition, many law firms now take advantage of the convenient and economical resources available on the Internet. E-discovery involves the use of a wide variety of electronic resources to conduct discovery. The use of electronic resources can make the paralegal's work more efficient and economical or more expensive and time consuming. Consequently, electronic discovery tools must be used properly when your attorney draws up her discovery plan.

As we investigate each discovery technique in the chapters that follow, we will consider the available electronic versions of these techniques. For instance, in Chapter 9 on depositions, we will examine not only the use of traditional in-person depositions, but also the application of electronic techniques such as web conferencing to conduct long-distance depositions in ways that are efficient and economical, and in Chapter 10 on interrogatories, we will look at the use of interrogatories as an aid in structuring the discovery of electronic evidence. Nevertheless, at this stage in the discovery process your supervising attorney may want to consider the use of some electronic discovery devices to conduct informal discovery.

The advent of e-discovery means that attorneys and paralegals must remain current with all amendments to the Federal Rules of Civil Procedure concerning discovery and ESI. Accordingly, we find that (1) the rules now require attorneys to develop discovery plans, including ESI issues, early in the litigation process; (2) the rules have been changed to deal specifically with forms of ESI production; (3) the rules now handle special problems involving matters of privilege; (4) the rules have been changed to facilitate the discovery of hard-to-find ESI and to apportion the money spent on such activities; (5) the rules now hand out sanctions against those who do not cooperate with discovery but limit those sanctions when the loss of ESI is unavoidable; and (6) the rules now adjust several time limits involved in discovery so that each time period is a multiple of seven in order to accommodate the realities of the working week.

The rules that were amended to accomplish these goals include Civil Rules 16, 26, 27, 32, 33, 34, 37, and 45 and Rules 502 and 702 of the Federal Rules of Evidence. As we continue in this chapter and those that follow, we will cover each of these rules and, at that time and place, explain the nature and the effect of each amendment.

e-discovery (also electronic discovery and digital discovery)
A series of techniques and tools that involve the use of a wide variety of electronic resources to conduct discovery of electronically stored information in an efficient and economical way.

webchat (webinar, online chat, online workshop)
An online process that permits individuals at separate locations to meet via the Internet using personal computers, smartphones, or tablets.

Web conference
An electronic conference setup that permits individuals at separate locations to meet online via the Internet.

webcam
A video camera that is connected to a computer by a USB port or other cable connector that facilitates the transmission of real-time images to a personal computer.

videoconference
An electronic conference setup that permits several individuals at separate locations to discuss the planning of the case.

deposition
An out-of-court question and answer session under oath, conducted in advance of a lawsuit as a part of the discovery process.

interrogatories
Written questions requiring written answers under oath and directed to a party, in which another party seeks information related to the litigation.

request for the production of documents, electronically stored information (ESI), and tangible things, or entry upon land for inspection and other purposes
A request that a party or other individual involved in a lawsuit provide specific documents or other physical evidence to the party making the request.

Web Conferences   One e-discovery tool that your supervising attorney might want to consider during informal discovery is the Web conference (sometimes referred to as a **webchat**, a **webinar**, an **online chat**, or an **online workshop**). A **Web conference** permits individuals at separate locations to meet online via the Internet using personal computers. As long as the appropriate software has been downloaded to each computer and provided that each computer is also equipped with a **webcam**, several people can talk together while viewing one another on a split screen on their monitors. The Web conference can involve preliminary discussions among attorneys and clients and may include expert witnesses, thus reducing travel expenses. A **videoconference** represents another way to permit several individuals at widely separated geographical locations to discuss the planning of the case. (*Note*: Today, most recordings are made using digital equipment, rather than video cameras, videotapes, and VHS cassettes, all of which have become nearly obsolete. Nevertheless, terms like "video," "taping," and "tapes" to refer to the recording process are likely to stay in the vocabulary of the legal profession for some time to come, despite their technical inaccuracy. This habit is not unlike the continued use of a word such as "typing," which is inaccurate but which is still used instinctively by most people. Consequently, we will continue to use those "taping" terms here.) The video setup often still requires the use of television cameras, microphones, monitors, and a speaker system at each location. However, in some cases, long-distance conferences can be conducted using only handheld mobile devices.

Choice of Discovery Methods   An attorney has five methods of discovery from which to choose: the deposition; interrogatories; a request for the production of documents, ESI, and tangible things or entry upon land for inspection and other purposes; a request for physical or mental examinations; and a request for admission. In federal court, the discovery process is regulated by Rule 16, Rules 26 through 37, and Rule 45 of the Federal Rules of Civil Procedure (see Exhibit 8-1) as well as Rules 502 and 702 of the Federal Rules of Evidence. Rule 16 authorizes the court to issue a scheduling order that, among other things, limits the time that the parties have to finish the discovery process. The amendments to the rule make it clear that this order can include any arrangements that the parties have made regarding the revelation or the discovery of ESI, as well as any promises regarding assertions of privilege or protection. Rule 26 sets out the general provisions concerning discovery. Rules 27 through 36 explain the various discovery techniques that can be used by litigants in federal court. The final rule, Rule 37, outlines the sanctions that are available when a party does not cooperate with discovery. A **deposition** is an out-of-court question and answer session under oath, conducted in advance of a lawsuit as a part of the discovery process. Depositions are regulated by Rules 27 through 32 of the Federal Rules of Civil Procedure. **Interrogatories** are written questions requiring written answers under oath and directed to a party, in which another party seeks information related to the litigation. Interrogatories are governed by Rule 33 of the Federal Rules. A **request for the production of documents, electronically stored information (ESI), and tangible things, or entry upon land for inspection and other purposes,** which is covered by Rule 34, is a request that a party or other individual involved in a lawsuit provide specific documents, ESI, or other physical evidence to the party making the request. As the name implies, this request may also involve a request to enter land to

EXHIBIT 8-1 Federal Rules of Civil Procedure

RULE 16 PRETRIAL CONFERENCES; SCHEDULING; MANAGEMENT

Rule 16 has been amended to make sure that the court is notified in advance that it will have to consider how to deal with the ESI involved in the case. It also includes an early warning to the court that the case may involve claims of privilege.

RULE 26 DUTY TO DISCLOSE; GENERAL PROVISIONS GOVERNING DISCOVERY

Rule 26 covers general provisions of discovery, including the duty to disclose certain information. It sets out the scope of discovery as well as its limits. It also covers protective orders, timing and sequence of discovery, supplementation of discovery, planning for discovery, and the effect of signing discovery requests, responses, and objections.

RULE 27 DEPOSITIONS TO PERPETUATE TESTIMONY

Rule 27 allows the perpetuation of testimony even though an action cannot be presently brought to court, or when an appeal is pending.

RULE 28 PERSONS BEFORE WHOM DEPOSITIONS MAY BE TAKEN

Rule 28 specifies that a deposition must be taken before an officer authorized to administer oaths and take testimony. The rule also outlines the persons before whom a deposition can be taken in a foreign country. The rule eliminates persons who are related to or employees of the parties or the attorneys, as well as persons who have a financial interest in the action.

RULE 29 STIPULATIONS REGARDING DISCOVERY PROCEDURE

Rule 29 allows the parties to an action to modify in writing the discovery procedures outlined in the rules.

RULE 30 DEPOSITIONS BY ORAL EXAMINATION

Rule 30 explains when depositions can be taken, notice requirements, examination and cross-examination, oath requirements, objections, motions to terminate or limit examination, failure to attend or failure to serve a subpoena, and exhibits, among other things.

RULE 31 DEPOSITIONS UPON WRITTEN QUESTIONS

Rule 31 discusses the service of depositions upon written questions, as well as the notice requirements, among other things.

RULE 32 USE OF DEPOSITIONS IN COURT PROCEEDINGS

Rule 32 outlines the circumstances under which a deposition can be used in court. For example, a deposition can be used to contradict or impeach the testimony of a witness. A deposition can also be used if the witness is dead, is located farther than 100 miles from the place of the trial or hearing, or is unable to testify because of age, illness, infirmity, or imprisonment. Also, the deposition will be allowed if the party who wants to introduce the deposition has been unable to make the witness attend the trial by subpoena.

RULE 33 INTERROGATORIES TO PARTIES

Rule 33 explains the procedure for using interrogatories, the allowable scope of the interrogatories, and the use of interrogatories at trial. The rule also indicates when business records can be produced in lieu of answering interrogatories.

RULE 34 PRODUCING DOCUMENTS, ELECTRONICALLY STORED INFORMATION, AND TANGIBLE THINGS, OR ENTERING ONTO LAND FOR INSPECTION AND OTHER PURPOSES

Rule 34 explains the scope of this discovery device as well as the process for its use. The rule specifies that this request can be made of nonparties.

RULE 35 PHYSICAL AND MENTAL EXAMINATIONS OF PERSONS

Rule 35 explains when a physical and/or mental examination can be ordered. It also explains the disposition of the report of the examining physician.

EXHIBIT 8-1 Federal Rules of Civil Procedure (*continued*)

RULE 36	**REQUESTS FOR ADMISSION**
	Rule 36 outlines the procedure for requesting admissions. It also explains the effects of an admission.
RULE 37	**FAILURE TO MAKE DISCLOSURE OR COOPERATE IN DISCOVERY; SANCTIONS**
	Rule 37 presents the procedure for filing a motion for an order compelling discovery. It also details the negative consequences of failing to comply with such an order, among other things.
RULE 45	**SUBPOENA**
	Rule 45 was changed to add ESI to the list of types of evidence that can be the subject of subpoena. The new rule also states that the subpoena is permitted to indicate the form of ESI to be used by the party responding to the subpoena.

request for a physical or mental examination

A request made by one party to another party in that lawsuit to undergo a physical or mental examination provided that the examination involves a condition that is at issue in the pending action.

request for admission

A request made by a party to another party in that lawsuit to admit to the truthfulness of a fact or the genuineness of a piece of evidence.

computer

During the planning stage, it is important to remember that the term computer includes desktop PCs, laptops, notebooks, mobile phones, personal digital assistants (PDAs), digital recorders, GPS units, smartphones, scanners, fax machines, tablets, wireless reading devices (WRDs), and home computers that are part of a network. This is true whether the device is owned by the employer or the employee, if the employer is involved in the lawsuit and if work-related ESI has been programmed into the device.

inspect that land to gain facts related to the lawsuit. A **request for a physical or mental examination** asks a party to undergo a physical or mental examination provided that the examination involves a condition at issue in the pending action. A **request for admission** asks a party to admit the truth of certain facts or the genuineness of a document so that these issues do not have to be proven at trial. An attorney must consider both the expense and the time available when choosing from among these methods. Requests for physical and mental examinations and for admissions are regulated by Rule 35 and Rule 36, respectively. Rule 45 outlines provisions regarding subpoenas. The new amendments to this rule add ESI to the list of evidence that can be contained within a subpoena. The new rule also asserts that subpoenas may indicate the form of ESI to be used by the party answering the subpoena. Rule 502 of the Federal Rules of Evidence protects the attorney–client privilege and the work product privilege, while Rule 702 covers the use of expert witnesses.

Discovery and ESI   During the initial discovery strategy, your attorney must make certain that she considers not only techniques for recovering ESI, but also the types of ESI that are discoverable and the individuals who are responsible for that data. Discoverable ESI falls into three categories: (1) types of ESI based on the configuration of the computer system, (2) types of ESI based on the nature of the evidence itself, and (3) types of ESI based on its storage status.

Your supervising attorney must remember that her client may have to furnish this information to the opposing party, which means that she will have to develop a discovery plan that includes all three categories of ESI, as well as the people responsible for managing that ESI.

The first type of ESI that should be included in a preliminary discovery plan is the configuration of the opposing party's computer system. This involves an understanding of the number and types of computers that are used in the party's ordinary business routine. During the planning stage, it is important to remember that the term **computer** includes desktop PCs, laptops, notebooks, mobile phones, personal digital assistants (PDAs), digital recorders, GPS units, smartphones, tablet computers, scanners, fax machines, wireless reading devices (WRDs), home computers that are part of a network, as well as apps and widgets that are located on mobile phones. It would also be helpful to know about any network systems that are located within the party's operation, as well as the number and location of all workstations and all network servers.

Another difficulty associated with the configuration of a party's computer system is the problem of ownership. Recently, it has become more and more acceptable, and in some firms even required, for staff members to use their own tablets, smartphones, and laptops at work. The trend has developed because people are so accustomed to their own machines that they are more efficient when they use the same devices on the job that they use in their personal lives. The trend makes sense and was probably inevitable as computerized devices became more compact, more user-friendly, more mobile, and more interchangeable. Companies generally handle this development in one of two ways. Some firms prefer to distribute employer-owned devices that include separate areas for the employee's personal use. Other companies permit employees to bring their own devices into the workplace. These devices are then programmed by the company's information technology (IT) department with secure work areas for e-mail, employee forms, and other work-related files.[7] Whichever tactic is used, questions can arise during litigation as to whether such devices can legitimately be included in a discovery request. The well-prepared attorney will assume that the answer to this question is "yes" and will plan accordingly. This assumption makes sense because the opposing party will want to see all relevant work-related data regardless of who owns the device used to make or store that data. While the opposing party will generally focus on work-related data rather than personal Twitter accounts and gaming apps, such apps might be used to impeach the credibility or the reputation of a particular witness. Whatever the case, the wise attorney will develop a discovery plan that protects her own client while allowing her to search for vital ESI within the devices used by her opponent's employees, regardless of who owns those devices.

The second type of ESI that must be included in the discovery plan is based on the nature of the evidence itself. The nature of the evidence can be expressed in two ways, as substance and as entity (or object). Substance is the information contained within the documents. When most attorneys consider the process of collecting relevant computer data they inevitably focus on substance. This tendency is, of course, only natural. When an attorney thinks about a filing a plan to retrieve paper memos, letters, and reports, she is concerned with what those memos, letters, and reports say, not with the desk they are piled on. Electronic data is different. With electronic data, the entity is itself an important source of information. Thus, when creating a discovery plan, your attorney must also consider looking at the ESI as an entity. This strategy, which is called, "exploratory social network analysis,"[8] involves searching for such things as the author, the people to whom the data was sent, the number of times it was accessed, copied, sent, received, altered, forwarded, and so on. Such things as the length of time spent on certain Web sites or the names of people who are part of certain communication cliques can reconstruct the communication patterns at a client's or at an opponent's place of business. These communication patterns or "social networks," can identify the key players in an activity that lies at the heart of a lawsuit.[9] Looking at ESI as an entity requires that your supervising attorney examine all relevant computer-generated records. This is a big task because such records are found in e-mail files, databases, Internet records, intranet or portal records, cell phone call records, calendaring programs, GPS logs, and all other relevant data files created by spreadsheets, word processing, or any analogous program. Another way to think about ESI as an

metadata
Computer data about data, including such things as a tracking record that shows how the data was compiled, who compiled it, what it was used for, where it is stored, and so on.

active data
Computer-generated records within a computer system that are in current use.

inactive data
Computer-generated records within a computer system that are relatively up-to-date but are not used on a routine basis.

backup data
Computer-generated records within a computer system that are stored as a precautionary measure.

extant data
Computer-generated records within a computer system that are hidden in the system, generally because they have been deleted.

residual data
Fragments of data that may be left over on a computer's hard drive.

legacy data
Data that was initially recorded on what is now an outmoded media format such as a floppy disk.

ephemeral data
Data that was created to self-destruct after a short period of time.

paper data
ESI that has been reduced to a hard copy for filing purposes as a safeguard against the loss of that data caused by the breakdown of the computer system.

artifact is to consider it as a type of metadata. **Metadata** is data about data and includes such things as descriptive metadata, archival metadata, administrative metadata, structural metadata, intellectual property rights management metadata, preservation metadata, and so on.[10]

The third type of evidence is based on the storage status of the data. Data can be considered to be **active data**, **inactive data**, **backup data**, **extant data**, **residual data**, **legacy data**, **ephemeral data**, or **paper data**. Data is considered active if it is in current use, and inactive if it is relatively up-to-date but is not used on a routine basis. In contrast, backup data is information stored as a precautionary measure. Extant data is information that is hidden in the system, generally because it has been deleted. Fragments of data left over on hard drives are referred to as residual data. Legacy data is data that may be hidden simply because it was originally recorded on what is now an outdated media format such as a floppy disk or a CD. Ephemeral data is data that was created to self-destruct after a short period of time, say in about 10 seconds or so. Unfortunately (or fortunately depending on whether your attorney is trying to protect or obtain the data) even ephemeral data can be retrieved by a really savvy IT specialist. Paper data includes any e-data that has been reduced to a hard copy for filing purposes or data that was never entered into an electronic format to begin with. (Yes, such data still exists and should not be overlooked as a source of evidence or even as a way of cleverly disguising vital evidence if your opponent happens to be obsessed with ESI, which happens today, more than you might think. See Exhibit 8-2.)

ESI Personnel   As one of the first steps in the discovery process, your supervising attorney must identify those individuals who are responsible for her own client's computer system, as well as those responsible for the opposing party's system. The individuals responsible for a company's or an institution's computer system generally include not only top executives but also middle-level managers and administrative assistants. Remember to include all in-house and independent IT experts who have shaped and maintained the system. Your supervising attorney should consider using interrogatories to uncover both the identities of the relevant personnel and the types of ESI available. The interrogatories can then be used to guide the choice of those individuals who will undergo depositions. This information can also guide document-production requests.

Characteristics of ESI   The proliferation of ESI in business and government has led to some critical changes in the strategies used to request, retrieve, hold, and protect ESI. Recent court decisions and the latest amendments to the Federal Rules of Civil Procedure, as well as the rules of many state courts, most of which mirror the federal rules to some extent, require that attorneys take proactive measures as early as possible in a lawsuit to make sure they do not violate their legal, ethical, and professional duties in the pursuit and protection of ESI. These proactive measures are necessary because ESI has some unique characteristics that many attorneys overlook.

First, ESI is voluminous. In a pre–ESI era lawsuit, your supervising attorney would have dealt with thousands of pages of paper documents. Today, that same attorney must handle hundreds of thousands of pages of e-mail correspondence, spreadsheets, databases, backup tapes, voice mail, text messages, Internet use records, instant messages, Web-based

EXHIBIT 8-2 Changes to the Federal Rules of Civil Procedure Affecting Discovery

RULE 16(b)(3)(B)	Adds ESI to the discovery report that goes to the court.
RULE 26(a)(1)(A)	States that a list of those who have access to discoverable evidence and the subject matter of that evidence (including ESI) must be provided to other parties without waiting for a request for such information.
RULE 26(a)(1)(A)(ii)	Incorporates ESI as one type of information that must be provided to other parties without waiting for a request.
RULE 26(b)(2)(B)	Creates two tiers of ESI: (1) the first is reasonably discoverable ESI and the second is (2) ESI that cannot be discovered without undue burden or cost.
RULE 26(b)(5)(A) and (B); RULE 26(f)(3)(D)	Covers new privilege and protection issues created by the voluminous nature of ESI. Provides for the creation of clawback agreements.
RULE 26(f)(1)	Demands that the parties have a meet-and-confer conference at least 21 days before a scheduling conference is held or a scheduling order is due.
RULE 27(a)(2)	A new amendment to the rule extends the time limit for service of notice from 20 to 21 days.
RULE 32(a)(5)(A)	A new amendment alters the time limit for a short notice deposition from 11 to 14 days. the rule now reads, "a deposition must not be used against a party who, having received less than 14 days' notice of deposition, promptly moved for a protective order."
RULE 32(d)(3)(C)	A new amendment extends the time limit for objections to written questions from five to seven days.
RULE 33(d)	Makes it clear that ESI is to be treated as a regular business record in relation to interrogatories. Consequently, the data requester may have to inspect the ESI and may have to get into the data retriever's computer system to ensure that the data requester has the same access to the ESI as the data retriever.
RULE 34(b)	Deals with the form in which ESI is to be handled and delivered from the ESI retriever to the ESI requester.
RULE 37(e)	Provides a good-faith exception for the loss of ESI caused by the "routine, good-faith operation of an electronic information system."
RULE 45	Adds ESI to the list of types of evidence that can be the subject of subpoena.

discussions, Web-based bulletin-board postings, tweets, blogs, photos, Instagrams, pop-ups, Internet search histories, statistical data, GPS logs, and so on. To make matters even worse, as noted previously, ESI includes not only the data itself but also a level of metadata that records "data about the data."[11]

Second, the discovery of ESI is difficult because it is stored in an assortment of formats and can, therefore, be delivered in those different formats, some of which may not be compatible with the requesting party's computer system. Although the use of different formats will not eliminate ESI from the discovery process, it can lead to costly delays. Third, unlike paper data, which can only be destroyed by the intervention of an individual, some ESI is routinely deleted by the computer system itself to make room for new data. Thus, a party may inadvertently erase relevant evidence simply by allowing a company's routine deletion procedures to continue unabated, despite pending litigation.[12] On the other hand, and this is the fourth point, most bits of ESI never really go away despite the fact that a system reports the deletion of that information. Therefore, an attorney should never announce that a certain report, a particular spreadsheet, or a series of e-mail correspondence has been erased unless she has already checked with IT personnel to make certain that the ESI is really gone for good. This advice is especially important when a client uses social network apps, such as Snapchat, that are designed to remove all transmitted data, especially photos, within a very short time. Despite assurances of privacy, app providers do not guarantee that all data is erased, and app users can never be certain that their pictures have not been photographed quickly by the receiver using a camera or a second mobile.[13] Moreover, a really talented and resourceful IT expert can probably find a way to retrieve even the most protected data.

Third, the discovery of ESI is complicated because technology changes with great speed. Rapid change creates hidden and unexpected ways to generate, store, erase, and retrieve ESI, catching even the most conscientious practitioner by surprise. For example, in today's workplace desktops and BlackBerrys are being replaced by laptops, smartphones, and tablets, all of which are more practical, more portable, and more accessible than their rapidly fading predecessors.[14] Some of the newest tablets are equipped with devices that permit the user to take notes and create documents with a high-tech stylus that can be used with the ease of a real pen and that, thus, eliminates many of the problems that have been associated with such devices in the past.[15] Consequently, modern attorneys must remember to include such devices in discovery requests. Moreover, and more to the point, attorneys must also remember that their own clients must be warned that the data stored on such devices can be used as evidence.

Fourth, many practitioners are now exploiting the huge amount of ESI that is stored on mobile applications (apps) and widgets. Many people use apps to record video images, to participate in games, to take photographs, to play tunes, to read e-books, and to count calories. However, many "app addicts" do not realize that, as they habitually access their ever-present apps, the app platform providers are collecting, storing, sharing, and distributing ESI about the users in ways that far exceed the data collected on desktops and other more conventional electronic devices.[16] This revelation is good news for ESI requesters, who can find ESI that was previously unavailable, but bad news for ESI retrievers, who suddenly discover that their clients have unknowingly accumulated volumes of damaging evidence on their innocent-looking mobile phones. Apps record and store sensitive ESI such as text messages, e-mail messages, photos, and videos. Other bits of sensitive ESI include phone logs, contact lists, date book information, bill payment histories, credit histories, health data, medical data, dental information, app use records, and Web-browsing logs. Some users may even discover that their every move has been recorded and stored by their GPS and WiFi geo-locator apps.[17]

Predictive Coding Protocols

These four ESI problems, volume, diversity, change, and storage, have inspired some experts to design new data retrieval techniques, not all of which are welcome by the courts or by everyone within the legal community. One technique that has been accepted by several courts is a data mining and retrieval process called the predictive coding protocol. **Predictive coding** uses a digital cataloging process to examine a range of documents in order to adjust a search algorithm so that the computer will know what to look for as it examines a larger field of documents to determine which of those documents are discoverable. The program then conducts a second, more extensive inspection of all the documents based on the new algorithm to reduce the storehouse of documents to a much more manageable number that clearly fits the pattern outlined in the algorithm. This shortened pile of documents can then be examined, studied, and collated by "flesh and blood" attorneys who produce the discoverable documents in response to the discovery request.[18]

ESI and the Litigation Hold Strategy

Despite the complexity, the uncertainty, and the multiplicity that surrounds ESI, a resourceful attorney can learn to avoid costly and time-consuming ESI discovery mistakes. For instance, one of the first steps when litigation threatens would be for an attorney to order her client to establish a **litigation hold** on the routine handling of all ESI. A litigation hold tells the client's employees and associates to stop deleting all ESI. It is best to order a litigation hold as early as possible in the litigation process and to repeat the order in writing often to make certain that all members of the client's firm take the message seriously.[19] The litigation hold process can be made more efficient by installing a case management software package that can be used to quickly initiate a legal hold in response to pending litigation. The software can be used to place e-mail boxes and other ESI into virtual folders for storage to await discovery and trial.[20] Recent case law has also made it clear that an attorney cannot simply issue and reissue the written litigation hold order and let it go at that. Instead, he or she must also take the initiative in discovering and separating "bad actors" who might be tempted to hide, alter, or delete vital evidence including especially ESI.[21] To emphasize the serious nature of the preservation process, an attorney would do well to remind her client and her associates that the responsibility to preserve evidence is a duty that is owed to the court, rather than to the other parties in the lawsuit.[22] Moreover, a smart attorney will also expressly remind all opposing parties of their preservation duty in the lawsuit by sending those parties a **spoliation letter**. The spoliation message can be sent as an e-mail or as a paper document.

ESI and the Litigation Response Team

As a second step, your supervising attorney should talk to every member of the client's firm who is likely to be named as a party in the lawsuit and to all those who have access to discoverable information.[23] During these discussions, she can reinforce the importance of the litigation hold, emphasize the need to be careful with all ESI, and find out all that she can about the client's computer system. As a third step, your supervising attorney should issue a directive that tells all workers to keep duplicates of everything in their electronic files. If possible, your supervisory counsel should take control of those duplicates. If this is not possible, then the backup material should be set aside and kept at the client's office in a secure place. This step will necessitate conversations with members of the client's IT department, who will be able to determine how best to preserve all necessary ESI.[24] Finally, your supervising attorney should set up

predictive coding
A strategy by which a computer program uses a digital cataloging process to examine a sampling of documents in order to adjust its search algorithm so that the computer will know what to look for as it determines which documents are relevant and which are not.

litigation hold
An order issued by an attorney to a client telling that client's employees and associates to stop the routine handling of all ESI, especially as that routine involves the deletion of ESI.

spoliation letter
A letter sent by an attorney to all opposing parties in a lawsuit placing those parties on notice that they should make an affirmative effort to preserve all ESI related to the case.

litigation response team
A group of highly trained individuals who are charged with the job of learning all there is to know about the client's ESI system, including all backup, retrieval, formatting, deletion procedures, and so on.

social media
Sites that include a wide variety of communication and networking spots, such as Facebook, LinkedIn, StumbleUpon, Twitter, YouTube, Pinterest, WordPress, Snapchat, and MySpace, on which individuals record their thoughts, beliefs, events, photos, videos, and texts with great regularity.

chain of custody
A precise record of who received, handled, evaluated, and safeguarded the evidence in a legal proceeding.

evidence in a legal proceeding
Relevant and admissible testimony, ESI documents, photographs, records, reports, objects, and other tangible items used by a party in a legal procedure to demonstrate the veracity of the party's claims to the finder of fact in the case.

e-forensics (computer forensics, cyber-forensics)
A strategy that employs certain processes to retrieve, examine, analyze, and authenticate ESI.

privilege
A protection afforded by the law to prevent or limit the discovery of evidence created within a setting such as that provided by the attorney–client or the physician–patient relationship.

a **litigation response team**. A litigation response team is a group of highly trained individuals who are charged with the job of learning all there is to know about the client's ESI system, including all backup, retrieval, formatting, deletion procedures, and so on.[25]

ESI and Social Media   One of the most important jobs of the litigation response team is to educate the client about unexpected ESI pitfalls. One of these unanticipated danger areas today is the proliferation of social media sites. **Social media** sites include a wide variety of communication and networking spots such as Facebook, LinkedIn, Twitter, YouTube, and MySpace, among many others. The litigation team must make certain that everyone involved in the lawsuit understands that information posted on such sites might be discoverable. The good news here is that, during discovery, your attorney will be able to mine the social media sites of the opposing party as she searches for relevant, admissible evidence. The bad news is that the other side will conduct the same kind of mining operation into her client's sites. Of course, your attorney might also take this opportunity to examine her client's social media sites, in case there is evidence on those sites that can somehow help build her client's case.[26]

ESI and Computer Forensics   One of the jobs of the litigation response team is to preserve the **chain of custody** for ESI. The chain of custody is a precise record of who received, handled, evaluated, and safeguarded the **evidence in a legal proceeding**. The object of creating a chain of custody is to guarantee the authenticity of the evidence by ensuing that no one has a chance to tamper with that evidence in anyway.[27] Until recently, the chain of custody process was important only within the criminal system. Now, however, with the increased importance of ESI in civil litigation, preserving the integrity of the chain of custody has become essential. As is the case with most issues involving ESI, the attorney in a case should defer to the IT experts in the chain of evidence process. Moreover, it is best to engage an outside firm that is well versed in computer forensics.[28] Computer forensics, also known as **e-forensics** or cyber-forensics, is a strategy that employs certain processes to retrieve, examine, analyze, and authenticate ESI. The process uses the chain of custody strategy to make certain that computer use and computer records are not altered, destroyed, or hidden. E-forensics is especially critical when the ESI in a case is related to exploring the residual data, rebuilding records that track computer use, and determining the technical characteristics of ESI. The processes involved in e-forensics require highly specialized skills that are not within the expertise of most IT staff members.[29]

ESI and Litigation Privileges   Another job for the litigation response team is to conduct a search of all paper documents and all ESI that has been retrieved in order to identify all privileged documents. A **privilege** is a protection afforded by the law to prevent or limit the discovery of evidence created within a setting such as that provided by the attorney–client or the physician–patient relationship. This has become one of the most difficult and expensive areas of discovery because ESI inevitably involves endless amounts of intricate, repetitive, disorganized, and complicated data.[30]

Even before the new rules went into effect, the courts recognized that attorneys could no longer conduct discovery as if ESI did not exist. For this reason, some courts issued serious sanctions against attorneys who did not properly deal with the unique problems created by ESI. For instance, in *Metropolitan Opera Assoc., Inc. v. Local 100, Hotel Employees &*

Restaurant Employees International Union, 212 F.R.D 178 (S.D.N.Y. 2003), the court issued a default judgment against the defendant as a sanction for improper discovery. The judge issued the sanction because the attorneys:

> (1) never gave adequate instructions to their clients about the clients' overall discovery obligation, [including] what constitutes a "document" ... ; (2) knew the Union to have no document retention or filing systems and yet never implemented a systematic procedure for document production or for retention of documents, including electronic documents; (3) delegated document production to a layperson who ... was not instructed by counsel that a document included a draft or other nonidentical copy, a computer file and an e-mail; ... and (5) ... failed to ask important witnesses for documents until the night before their depositions and, instead, made repeated, baseless representations that all documents had been produced.

In another case, the court stopped short of issuing a default judgment, but did bar the party responsible for deleting the relevant ESI from producing any evidence at trial concerning the deleted material. Nor would that party be permitted to cross-examine the other party's witnesses in relation to the missing evidence. The court also ordered the party responsible for the deletion to pay all attorney fees and any costs resulting from the motion regarding the deletion.[31]

Expense of Discovery   Discovery can be a very expensive proposition for all sides in a lawsuit. However, some techniques are more expensive than others. For instance, having a party sit for an oral deposition is considerably more expensive than sending a set of interrogatories to that party. The oral deposition would necessitate paying a court reporter to administer the oath and to transcribe the question-and-answer period. Oral depositions also involve more of an attorney's time, as the attorney must be physically present to interrogate the party. In contrast, the interrogatories would simply involve determining the questions to ask, or word processing those questions, mailing them to the party, and reviewing the answers when returned.

Amount of Time   If time is a more critical element than money, the attorney might make an entirely different decision in choosing a method of discovery. Under the pressure of time, having the party sit for a deposition would be much more advantageous than sending interrogatories and waiting for written responses. In addition, the Federal Rules of Civil Procedure allow parties at least 30 days to respond to a set of interrogatories and most states allow similar lengths of time. Moreover, although a court can easily shorten a time limit, the same court might also extend that time, causing further delay. The parties can also agree to extend or shorten the time as long as any agreement to do so is put in written form.

Ethical Considerations in Discovery

As noted earlier, the primary objective of discovery is to ensure that lawsuits are decided on the facts and the legal merits of the case rather than on surprise or trickery. For such an objective to be met, however, all parties must treat the discovery process with the highest ethical regard. It is unethical for an attorney to prevent another party from obtaining evidence or to destroy evidence before the other party can see it. For example, in the *Raphael* case from this chapter's Commentary, it would be unethical for your attorney to destroy a letter, memo, voice-mail recording, video or digital recording, computer printout, fax,

scope of discovery
The amount and type of evidence that can be sought during the discovery process.

text, IM, spreadsheet, or e-mail record that indicates that Dr. Raphael knew that Phipps had fabricated and falsified evidence in the writing of his abstracts and grant proposals. Similarly, it is a violation of ethical principles to falsify evidence or to help someone else falsify evidence. It is also unethical for an attorney to make a discovery request that is unwarranted or to request much more information than is really necessary for the case. Naturally, because the paralegal's activities are actually an extension of the attorney's, she is also bound by these same ethical principles.

THE EXTENT OF ALLOWABLE DISCOVERY

The Federal Rules of Civil Procedure limit discovery to information that will support the claims or defenses of the parties to the litigation. Most states impose similar limitations. Nevertheless, the extent of the discovery process is quite broad—broader, in fact, than the extent to which evidence can be introduced in a case once it has reached the trial stage. There are, however, several limits on the discovery process, including the attorney–client privilege, the work product privilege, the common interest privilege, the Fifth Amendment privilege against self-incrimination, controlled access to expert testimony, confidentiality agreements, and protective orders.

The Scope of Discovery

The **scope of discovery** refers to the amount and type of evidence that can be sought during the discovery process. The scope of discovery is vast compared to that which can be introduced at trial. Nevertheless, the evidence sought during discovery must be relevant to the claims or defenses in the case. Evidence is considered relevant if it tends to prove or to disprove facts that are necessary to determine the final outcome of the case. However, under Rule 26 of the Federal Rules of Civil Procedure, the evidence sought during discovery need not be admissible at the time of the trial, as long as it is reasonably calculated to lead to the discovery of evidence that will be admissible at trial. For example, most hearsay evidence is not admissible at trial. This ban against hearsay evidence means that in most situations a witness at trial cannot testify about the truth of what she heard someone else say. For example, in the *Raphael* case, it would be hearsay to try to prove that Phipps falsified the evidence used in a grant proposal by allowing Dr. Nina Bauer to testify that Dr. Anthony O'Bryan told her of this. However, the statement by Dr. Bauer would be within the scope of discovery because it could lead to admissible evidence, namely, the testimony of Dr. O'Bryan who actually saw Phipps falsify the data in the proposal.

Recent ESI Amendments
One of the primary reasons the Federal Rules were amended was to deal with difficulties caused by the amount of ESI in business and government today. Rule 26(a)(1)(A) compels the parties in a lawsuit to update one another promptly about those individuals who possess discoverable evidence. Today this list of individuals will likely include the names of employees in the client's IT department.

Following this example, Rule 26(a)(1)(A) directs that the parties in a lawsuit, without waiting for a request or a court order, provide one another with copies of all discoverable information, or at least a description of that information, including ESI. This, however, does not mean that all requests for ESI will evaporate. Parties will still find themselves on the sending and receiving end of ESI requests. For this reason it is good to distinguish between the party asking for and obtaining the data, the **ESI requester**, and the party from whom the data is asked and obtained, the **ESI retriever**.[32]

The Federal Rules have altered some of the time periods involved in discovery in order to parallel the counting provisions established in Rule 6 of the Federal Rules of Civil Procedure, which demand that all days be counted in determining time limits, even Saturdays, Sundays, and legal holidays. To ensure that most time limits will end on a weekday, discovery time limits are now listed in multiples of seven. For example, Rule 27(a)(2) was amended to extend the time limit for service of notice from 20 to 21 days before the hearing date. Similarly, Rule 32(a)(5) was changed, altering the time period that protects those who challenge the deposition itself and those who object to the location of the deposition. The time limit was extended from 11 to 14 days. The rule now reads, "A deposition must not be used against a party who, having received less than 14 days' notice of the deposition, promptly moved for a protective order under Rule 26(c)(1)(B) requesting that it not be taken or be taken at a different time or place—and this motion was still pending when the deposition was taken." Finally, Rule 32(d)(3)(C) was altered to lengthen the time period for objections to written questions from five to seven days.

Two Levels of ESI   Rule 26(b)(2)(B) creates two levels of ESI. The first level of ESI includes information that is reasonably available. **Reasonably accessible ESI** includes data that can be retrieved without unwarranted difficulty and without unfair cost. Reasonably accessible data must be surrendered to the other party without waiting for an order from the court and without waiting for a request from the other party.[33] The second level of ESI is information that is not reasonably available. Data is classified as **not reasonably accessible ESI** if retrieving that data would require unfair cost or unwarranted difficulties in the retrieval process. Rule 26(b)(2)(B) says that if the ESI requester asks for a motion to compel the discovery of second-level evidence, or if the ESI retriever asks for a protective order to shield that evidence, the ESI retriever must demonstrate to the court that the evidence is "not reasonably accessible because of undue burden or cost."

However, to succeed in any attempt to protect this type of evidence, the ESI retriever can no longer simply state that such a difficulty exists. Instead, when the expense in recovering the ESI is overly burdensome to the retriever, that retriever must demonstrate the existence of that burden to the court's satisfaction. In addition, the ESI retriever must also show that the materials sought are neither legal documents nor business related records. Also ESI retrievers cannot follow an expensive retention policy and then "innocently" assert that it would be "unduly burdensome" to produce the data requested. Finally, and perhaps most importantly, none of this will relieve any party of his or her underlying preservation duty. Such duties continue to bind parties in common law and in statutory law.[34] The ESI retriever may still be compelled to deliver the information, if the other party demonstrates to the court's satisfaction that there is a good reason for the information to be produced.[35]

Labeling ESI as inaccessible is a tricky proposition because some ESI that appears to be deleted and, therefore, reasonably inaccessible, may actually be accessible by knowledgeable IT experts.[36] ESI retrievers must also remember that, even if the ESI really is difficult to retrieve, they may still be responsible for protecting that evidence either under statutory law or according to common law principles.[37] Because the problems surrounding this issue

ESI requester
The party in a lawsuit who requests data, including ESI, from the other party.

ESI retriever
The party to a lawsuit from whom data, including ESI, is requested during the discovery stage.

reasonably accessible ESI
ESI that can be retrieved without unwarranted difficulty and without unfair cost.

not reasonably accessible ESI
ESI that cannot be retrieved without unwarranted difficulty or without unfair cost

cloud storage

A way for an institution to preserve ESI by eliminating the need to store the ESI on hard drives and flash drives and passing that responsibility to a third party, the ESI or data center.

ESI center

A third party in a cloud storage agreement that is paid to receive, organize, and store data and to make it available to the ESI or data owner.

ESI owner
(ESI depositor)

The owner of ESI in a cloud storage agreement.

are so novel and so uncertain, expect your supervising attorney to encourage her client to make an agreement about these matters with the other parties as soon as practical.

Cloud Storage, ESI Owners, and ESI Centers   Perhaps the most perplexing task facing an ESI producer today is where to store the vast amount of data that emerges from the process of working with a computer. One increasingly popular strategy is to involve the cloud storage process. **Cloud storage** is a technique for depositing and protecting ESI, which circumvents the need to store data on hard drives and flash drives and passes that responsibility on to a third party, the **ESI center**. The ESI center receives, organizes, and stores the ESI on a distant database, making the data available to the **ESI owner** (aka the **ESI depositor**) through the Internet. Of course, the cloud storage process is not without difficulties. Ownership problems occur, for example, when the ESI owner undergoes a transition such as bankruptcy that places the rights to the ESI in question. Such problems can be avoided if the parties draw up an initial agreement outlining what to do when such contingencies occur. ESI owners might also be uneasy about the dependability of an ESI center. To minimize such fears the ESI owner can insist upon an agreement that permits the owner to access the data at any time and under any circumstances within the limits of the ESI center's capabilities. Security may also cause concern for the ESI owner who wants assurances that any ESI situated in a cloud will be safe from prying eyes. The safety of the ESI can generally be enhanced with various encryption techniques, a list of authorized users, and an authentication process. It is also best to use an ESI center with redundancy services that permit the ESI to be stored on several servers with separate power sources, thus promising the preservation of stored ESI should the center be victimized by a thief, a hacker, or a power failure.[38]

ESI Protection and Retrieval on the International Scene   American businesses and organizations who have branches, plants, stores, factories, offices, and subsidiaries in foreign countries cannot transfer data to those foreign locations and then argue that the data is beyond their control.[39] Similarly, alien corporations with American subsidiaries may find that they must cooperate with American rules of discovery despite legal conflicts with the law of their own nations. The courts have little patience with alien companies that take advantage of the American socioeconomic system and the American legal system and then use foreign privacy laws to protect critical evidence. This position is especially apparent when the courts must deal with American companies operating subsidiaries in the European Union (EU) or with European corporations operating American subsidiaries. The conflict is caused by the EU's Data Protection Directive that prevents European companies from sharing ESI with countries, such as the United States, which do not provide the same level of security for the ESI as afforded by the EU.[40]

Consequently, American companies dealing with European corporations must convince those alien corporations that they, the American companies, will grant the same level of protection to ESI as that guaranteed by the EU Data Protection Directive. This process was given official status when, in 2000, the EU agreed to permit European companies to deal with American companies and transmit protected ESI to those American companies as long as the Americans follow established safeguards.[41] These safeguards, which are known as the Safe Harbor Principles, and which are enforced by the U.S. Department of Commerce, include (1) Notice—People subject to ESI collection and transfer must be notified about the process by the ESI collector, must be told the objectives of the collection process, and must have a chance to communicate questions or concerns about the ESI collected and about how to restrict the communication and treatment of that ESI; (2) Choice—People who are subject to the collection and transfer of ESI must be empowered to stop the process if they so choose; (3) Continuing protection—When ESI is sent to third parties those third parties must also give the same degree of protection to that ESI as guaranteed by the EU Directive, the Safe Harbor principles, or an equivalent privacy policy; (4) Access—People subjected to the ESI collection process must have the ability to see, challenge, alter, and erase mistaken ESI if necessary; (5) Security—The party taking the ESI must do what it can to protect the ESI from elimination, misapplication, and unapproved entry, as well as from unauthorized release, improper changes, and unapproved deletions; (6) Data Integrity—Only relevant, comprehensive, correct, and up-to-date ESI can be subject to the collection process; and (7) Enforcement—A way to uphold these rules must be in place, including a way to verify compliance and to punish those who do not comply.[42] None of this will prevent a court from ordering a corporation to deliver ESI during discovery. The use of a safe harbor protection may, however, demonstrate that a corporation's undue burden argument is made in good faith. A company that wants to comply with the Department of Commerce's Safe Harbor provisions can do so voluntarily by notifying the Department in writing of its intent to do so. The corporation must also renew this notice annually in writing. While following the Safe Harbor principles is not required by law, once a company declares its intent to adhere to the principles, the failure to do so may be actionable by the Federal Trade Commission or the Department of Transportation under federal statutes prohibiting unfair and deceptive practices. Authorized state agencies may also seek enforcement of the provisions under the appropriate state laws that prohibit unfair and deceptive practices.

Motions to Compel and Protective Orders   Whenever a dispute over the question of whether a party must produce evidence during discovery cannot be resolved in an informal manner, the evidence requester can ask for a motion to compel discovery, and the evidence retriever can ask for a protective order. Ironically, to demonstrate the validity of either request, the retriever may be forced to produce part of the ESI to show that it really does involve unreasonable difficulties. Short of this drastic step, the ESI retriever may have to let the ESI requester inspect the ESI retriever's computer system or, at the very least, to interview the ESI retriever's IT personnel.[43]

The ESI retriever has the responsibility of showing that the information sought by the ESI requester is not reasonably available, given the difficulties and the expense involved in retrieving the evidence sought by the ESI requester. In contrast, the ESI requester has the job of demonstrating that the evidence is so essential to the case that obtaining the evidence outweighs the expense and the difficulties involved.[44]

Two factors play into this decision. The first factor is that the decision to require a party to obtain difficult-to-access data is not just a matter of difficulty and expense. The court may consider other factors such as other sources of evidence available to the requester, speculation about the nature of the as yet undiscovered evidence, and the critical nature of questions that are related to the undiscovered evidence, among others.[45] The second factor that must be considered is that certain restrictions have been placed on this process by Rule 26(b)(2)(C):

attorney–client privilege
A privilege that belongs to the client in an attorney–client relationship that requires the attorney to treat all information revealed to him or her, or to anyone employed by the attorney, as confidential. Because the privilege belongs to the client rather than to the attorney, only the client can give permission for the revelation of such confidential matters.

(C) *When Required.* On motion or on its own, the court must limit the frequency or extent of discovery otherwise allowed by these rules or by local rule if it determines that: (i) the discovery sought is unreasonably cumulative or duplicative, or can be obtained from some other source that is more convenient, less burdensome, or less expensive; (ii) the party seeking discovery has had ample opportunity to obtain the information by discovery in the action; or (iii) the burden or expense of the proposed discovery outweighs its likely benefit, considering the needs of the case, the amount in controversy, the parties' resources, the importance of the issues at stake in the action, and the importance of the discovery in resolving the issues.

Limits on Discovery

Even though the scope of discovery is very extensive, it is not without limitations. Discovery, including matters that must be disclosed under Rule 26, is limited by several privileges. These include the attorney–client privilege, the work product privilege, the common interest privilege, the medical privilege, the confessor–penitent privilege, and the Fifth Amendment privilege against self-incrimination. Limits are also placed on access to expert testimony. In addition, the parties can initiate confidentiality agreements or ask the court to issue protective orders.

Attorney–Client Privilege   The **attorney–client privilege** prevents the forced disclosure of written or oral communications between an attorney and a client or a prospective client. For a communication to be protected by the privilege, it must be made between the client and the attorney or the attorney's subordinate. This means that the privilege extends to communications made to the paralegal when the paralegal is acting as an agent of the attorney. The communication also must be made within the context of the attorney–client relationship. In other words, information revealed while seeking legal advice would be protected by the privilege, but statements made at a social gathering during polite conversation would not. The privilege belongs to the client, not the attorney. For example, in the *Raphael* case, if Dr. Raphael has no objection to the revelation of the contents of a discussion he had with your supervising attorney, then the attorney could not assert the privilege herself. Certainly, she could advise Dr. Raphael to assert the privilege. However, the client, Dr. Raphael makes the final decision.

The attorney–client privilege may be lost or waived by the client if the client does not intend the communication to be confidential, discloses the communication to others, or refuses to assert the privilege. Also, if a third party who is not related to the client is present during an attorney–client discussion, the privilege has been waived by the client. Naturally, such a waiver would not occur if the third party who is present is another attorney in the firm, a paralegal employed by the firm, or a legal secretary who works for the attorney. Thus, if you were asked to be present during a meeting between your supervising attorney and Dr. Raphael, he would not have waived his attorney–client privilege.

The fact that many law firms today are involved in multi-jurisdictional (MJD) cases increases the danger of inadvertently losing the protection granted by the attorney–client privilege. The threat arises because significant differences exist in the way that the law is practiced in the United States and how it is practiced in other countries. These differences can involve (1) an attorney's status, (2) the nature of a waiver, and (3) the loyalty of an attorney. The status of an attorney in the United States is rarely, if ever, at issue. In the United

States, terms such as *attorney, lawyer,* and *legal counsel* are used consistently from state to state to refer to an individual admitted to the bar and thus legally empowered to practice law. This consistency is not necessarily followed in foreign jurisdictions. Thus, in Europe, for instance, an individual who is identified as "in-house counsel" or as the "in-house lawyer" may not be an attorney at all but may, instead, be a layperson, who has been taught to run a corporation's legal department. Communicating with this "in-house lawyer" about a case may cause the protection of the attorney–client privilege to evaporate.[46]

Similarly, in some foreign jurisdictions the waiver of the privilege is handled differently than it is in the United States. In some foreign jurisdictions, for instance, a client is permitted to waive the privilege in one instance without surrendering the entire scope of the privilege. This stipulation is not followed in the United States where, under the traditional rule, a single instance of waiver will eliminate the entire privilege.[47] Finally, the question of an attorney's loyalty may become a problem in MJD cases. In the United States loyalty is rarely an issue. It is clear that an attorney must, above all, be loyal to his or her client. This level of loyalty is not always the norm in foreign jurisdictions. For instance, until a short time ago, attorneys in China were, first and foremost, governmental agents. An American attorney working with an attorney in China on an MJD case, who did not realize that his or her colleague owed an uncompromising loyalty to the state, could innocently reveal something that would unintentionally destroy the attorney–client privilege.[48]

The unintentional waiver of the attorney–client privilege in an MJD case is only one situation in which an inadvertent waiver may occur. In a large and complex case, privileged documents may be frequently disclosed accidentally. The chance that an attorney will involuntarily waive the privilege seems to rise exponentially as the use of ESI increases. The sheer volume of ESI makes it impossible for any attorney to know what is contained in every document sent to the other side in a discovery process. Such disclosures can have extremely serious results. To avoid this problem, it is possible to enter an agreement with opposing counsel that the inadvertent production or disclosure of privileged information will not result in waiver of the privilege. This agreement may be incorporated in the protective order discussed later in this chapter.

Work Product Privilege

The **work product privilege**, which is also referred to as the **litigation privilege**, prevents the opposing party in a lawsuit from using the discovery process to obtain letters, memos, documents, records, and other tangible items that have been produced in anticipation of litigation or that have been prepared for the trial itself. If, for instance, in the *Raphael* case, your attorney were to take notes during her interview with Dr. Raphael, those notes would be considered work product and would, therefore, be protected by the litigation privilege.

One problem with the work product privilege is determining which documents actually were prepared in anticipation of litigation. For example, in most hospitals it is common practice for health care professionals to make out "incident reports" when an error has been made. Thus, a nurse who accidentally gives a patient the wrong medication would have to fill out one of these reports. If the patient became ill as a result of that error and litigation resulted, the hospital attorney would argue that the incident report was prepared in anticipation of litigation, whereas the patient's attorney would maintain that it was not. The judge would determine whether the incident report is covered by the work product privilege.

work product privilege (the litigation privilege)
A privilege that protects any information prepared by an attorney in a lawsuit if that information is prepared by the attorney or anyone employed by the attorney in anticipation of litigation or to present at trial.

Another problem with the work product privilege is that it is not an absolute privilege. Under Rule 26(b)(3) of the Federal Rules, the litigation privilege may be overridden by showing that the party seeking discovery has a substantial need for the documents or materials for the preparation of her case and that she cannot, without undue hardship, obtain the equivalent of that material by any other means. Most courts continue to provide protection for the portion of work product that consists of "mental impressions, conclusions, opinions, or legal theories of a party's attorney or other representatives concerning the litigation."

A third problem with the litigation privilege can surface in MJD cases. In some foreign jurisdictions, especially in Europe, the work product privilege may extend only until the end of the present case. This limit can cause problems for the unwary American attorney who is involved in a related case with the same clients. Consequently, it is always wise to double check on the duration and the nature of the coverage of the litigation privilege in every jurisdiction in which your supervising attorney is involved.[49]

Amendments to the Federal Rules of Civil Procedure have also clarified the work product privilege in relation to expert testimony. Under the old rule, when an expert prepared a draft opinion for an attorney in anticipation of trial, that draft was subject to discovery. The same would have been true when such drafts were communicated using e-mail or fax machines. The danger of having such drafts subject to discovery led attorneys and experts to engage in convoluted, complicated, and expensive schemes to guarantee that such drafts were not discoverable. Some law firms even went so far as to hire two different experts, one to render advice and one to actually appear in court. The objective here was to gain information from the advising expert while preserving the protection for the attesting consultant.[50] In the alternative, an attorney might also seek to shield such drafts and other preliminary messages by obtaining protection agreements or court ordered protection declarations. All of these measures involved time-consuming and expensive procedures, which was exactly what the new rules were supposed to prevent. Consequently, under recent amendments to Rule 26, the drafts drawn up by experts are now clearly shielded under the work product privilege.[51]

Federal Rules of Evidence—Rule 502

The extensive use of ESI today sometimes contributes to the accidental waiver of the attorney–client privilege or the work product privilege (or both), as well as the disclosure of privileged material covered under either or both of the two protections. Recall that, under the traditional rule, the loss of the privilege in a single incident generally means the loss of the privilege for all evidence related to the topic of the released and unprotected item. The strict parameters of the traditional rule led many attorneys into an inefficient and costly campaign designed to scrutinize every scrap of evidence in a case. Then, in a classic case of "overkill," the attorney would throw the blanket of protection over every piece of evidence imaginable, even those with only an outside chance of actually needing the protection requested.[52]

To combat this situation, Congress added Rule 502 to the Federal Rules of Evidence. Under Rule 502(b), the *unintentional* release of evidence protected by either the attorney–client privilege or the work product privilege will not be considered an overall waiver, provided that the initial disclosure was genuinely accidental, and resulted despite the fact that the holder of the privilege "took reasonable steps" to protect the evidence. Additionally, the holder of the privilege or protection must have made a reasonable attempt to correct the mistaken disclosure. This attempt must include the use of Rule 26(b)(5)(B) of the Federal Rules of Civil Procedure, which outlines what parties are supposed to do when they discover that privileged information has been accidentally released.

The new rule also covers the *intentional* waiver of either the attorney–client or work product privilege. According to Rule 502(a), such a waiver will affect the communication or the work produced intentionally waived and any additional communications or products involving the same subject matter, provided that, in fairness, the two items can be connected to one another. In addition, this type of waiver applies to both federal and state cases. Rule 502(c) also notes that, in a state case, if a disclosure is not subject to a state court order, then, "the disclosure does not operate as a waiver in a federal proceeding if the disclosure: (1) would not be a waiver under this rule if it had been made in a federal proceeding; or (2) is not a waiver under the law of the state where the disclosure occurred."

Rule 502(d) adds a further safeguard by providing that, when the privilege or protection is preserved under a court order in one federal court, it will be preserved by that order in any other federal court or in any state court. Rule 502(e) notes that an agreement related to a disclosure in federal court can be made binding on third parties, if the court so orders. Rule 502(f) adds the following provision: "Notwithstanding Rules 101 and 1101, this rule applies to state proceedings and to federal court-annexed and court-mandated arbitration proceedings, in the circumstances set out in the rule. And notwithstanding Rule 501, this rule applies even if state law provides the rule of decision."

Rule 502(g) defines "attorney–client privilege" and "work product protection." The rule states that the phrase "'attorney–client privilege' means the protection that applicable law provides for confidential attorney–client communications." Similarly, it states that the term "'work-product privilege' means the protection that applicable law provides for tangible material (or its intangible equivalent) prepared in anticipation of litigation or for trial." There is every reason to believe that terms such as *communications* and *tangible material* include ESI.

Finally, in a very generous interpretation of Rule 502 (b), recent case law has indicated that the federal courts have the power to order the parties in a lawsuit to engage in a protective agreement, such as a claw back or a quick peek agreement, even when one or more of the parties has refused to do so. In other words, the court can order the revelation of documents protected under the attorney–client privilege or the work product privilege while, at the same time, ruling that the revelation of those documents does not represent the waiver of the entire privilege. Whether this wide interpretation of Rule 502 (b) will be followed by other courts in the future is problematic at this time.[53]

Common Interest Privilege

The **common interest privilege** is designed to protect any communication that takes place between attorneys for different clients when those clients share a common interest. The privilege actually preserves the attorney–client privilege and the work product privilege when information is exchanged among attorneys whose clients share such a common interest. The privilege protects oral statements, written notes, and printed memos that pass among such attorneys. The privilege can be invoked by attorneys representing either plaintiffs or defendants and can be asserted in both civil and criminal procedures. As a paralegal, your communication with another attorney or with the client of another attorney would also be protected if that client shared a common interest with the client represented by your attorney.

common interest privilege
The rule that protects any communication that takes place between attorneys for different clients when those clients share a common interest.

medical privilege (physician–patient privilege)
The medical privilege exists between a patient and a medical practitioner and is designed to protect the patient's confidential communication with the practitioner. The privilege covers communications made between the patient and physicians, psychiatrists, podiatrists, psychologists, and dentists.

confessor–penitent privilege (clerical privilege)
A privilege designed to protect the confidentiality of any communication between an individual and his or her confessor when the relationship involves the spiritual support of the penitent. The privilege belongs to the penitent rather than the confessor. However, the law also protects the confessor who has taken a religious oath not to reveal the content of such counseling sessions.

In order to succeed in raising the privilege of common interest, attorneys must demonstrate that the communication occurred because of an actual or a probable legal or other adversarial process. In addition, the attorney must show that his client does indeed share a common interest with the clients represented by the other attorneys involved in the action. For example, in the *Raphael* case, if Dr. Raphael, Mr. Phipps, and Jonas Halbert Northern University were to be represented by different attorneys, those attorneys could use the privilege to protect any communication made between them while planning a common defense for their clients. Finally, the communication must be made in a way that preserves the privileged nature of its content in relation to any adverse parties.

Medical Privilege   The **medical privilege** is designed to protect the patient rather than the medical practitioner. Although common law rules did not recognize the privilege, it is now a firmly established principle that is acknowledged in most jurisdictions. The medical privilege is designed to encourage patients to be candid with certain health care professionals, generally those who are charged with the primary care of the patient. Although the privilege is usually called the medical privilege, in some jurisdictions it is still referred to as the **physician–patient privilege**. Nevertheless, whatever name is applied to the privilege, it generally protects not only physicians but also psychiatrists, podiatrists, psychologists, and dentists. The privilege applies only if the relationship is a valid one for purposes of diagnosis, treatment, and/or care, and if the consultation in question was sought voluntarily. Thus, the privilege does not exist if the plaintiff in a lawsuit has been required to submit to a physical or mental examination as a part of the discovery process.

Confessor–Penitent Privilege   Any communication between a clergy member and an individual is protected by the **confessor–penitent privilege** when the relationship involves the spiritual support of the penitent. Although, strictly speaking, the privilege belongs to the penitent rather than the clergy member and thus the penitent can give up the privilege, the law protects a clergy member who has taken a religious oath not to reveal the content of such counseling sessions. This is probably why some jurisdictions refer to the privilege as the **clerical privilege**. It is clear that the privilege covers spiritual transgressions and concerns that the penitent has revealed to his or her confessor. However, some jurisdictions limit the privilege to cover only matters associated with such a confession, whereas others expand it to include any confidential counseling session. Because of the differences among various courts, paralegals must check the status of this privilege in their jurisdiction.

Protection of Expert Testimony   Expert testimony is frequently indispensable in a lawsuit. In the *Raphael* case, for example, the jury would have a difficult time determining whether the abstracts and grant proposals written by Phipps include fabricated or falsified evidence without the use of expert testimony. Under Rule 26(a)(2) of the Federal Rules of Civil Procedure, parties are required to disclose the name of any expert who will testify at trial. Along with the name, information relating to the expert's opinion, report, and qualifications also must be provided. This information must be disclosed without the necessity of a formal discovery request. If the expert witness is to be compensated for his or her testimony or for a study undertaken for the case, that must be revealed, as well as a list of other cases in which the witness has served as an expert, either by deposition or at trial, within the previous four years.

Federal Rules of Evidence—Rule 702

Up until a short time ago, many attorneys still attempted to examine ESI manually. Today, the enormous amount of ESI stored in even the most average-size computer has rendered manual searches extremely difficult. Many attorneys now use computerized searches in order to locate relevant, responsive documents that are not privileged. One such strategy is the *keyword search*. Despite all the safeguards used to protect privileged documents, because of the vast amount of ESI housed in the memory of a computer system, at times, some privileged material may be inadvertently obtained by the opposing side.[54]

When the ESI retriever realizes the error and demands a return of the material, the ESI receiver will frequently argue that the privilege was waived when the ESI retriever voluntarily released the ESI. If the ESI retriever files a motion demanding a return of the alleged privileged material, the judge must examine the search technique used by the ESI retriever to determine whether the material was released voluntarily or accidentally. The courts have decided that any evidence that is offered to defend or to critique such a search must be supplied by an expert. This means that evidence must meet the requirements of Rule 702 of the Federal Rules of Evidence.[55]

Rule 702 says that whenever "scientific, technical, or other specialized knowledge" will help the judge or the jury to comprehend the nature of the evidence or to establish a fact that has been questioned in the case, then an expert witness may be called to testify as long as:

> (1) the testimony is based on sufficient facts or data, (2) the testimony is the product of reliable principles and methods, and (3) the witness has reliably applied the principles and methods to the facts of the case.

These requirements are not difficult to meet as long as the expert IT specialist is properly prepared by your supervising attorney. Finally, remember that, despite the increased emphasis on electronically controlled search techniques, manual searches of ESI, while difficult, are not yet obsolete and that, under the right circumstances, the courts will still allow such searches.[56]

The Fifth Amendment Privilege against Self-Incrimination

The Fifth Amendment to the U.S. Constitution states that "No person ... shall be compelled in a criminal case to be a witness against himself." This Constitutional right is referred to as the Fifth Amendment **privilege against self-incrimination**. Because the privilege is specifically aimed at self-testimony in a criminal case, it is usually not available as a privilege in a civil lawsuit if the only object of the suit is to seek compensatory damages. Some courts have held, however, that if a civil lawsuit seeks to protect the public, the privilege may be successfully invoked. For example, if a civil suit is brought by a private party under federal antitrust law, the privilege may be successfully raised. This is because the purpose of antitrust law, like the purpose of criminal law, is to protect the public at large. Antitrust laws protect the public by imposing triple damages and thus discouraging antitrust activity. Furthermore, if a government agency is the plaintiff in the suit, it is possible to invoke the Fifth Amendment privilege because such agencies are, by definition, designed to protect the public interests. For example, in the *Raphael* case, since the case was brought by the NSF to protect the

privilege against self-incrimination
A privilege granted by the Fifth Amendment to the Constitution that prevents a criminal defendant from being forced to testify against himself or herself, but which can, under certain circumstances, be used in a civil case.

public's interest in the legitimate spending of federal tax dollars, your supervising attorney may be able to successfully argue that Dr. Raphael is protected by the Fifth Amendment Privilege against self-incrimination. Moreover, a suit involving a government agency such as the NSF as the plaintiff is very similar in character to a criminal prosecution, which is also brought by the government. Similarly, if a witness, such as Dr. Raphael, could demonstrate that responding to a particular discovery request could expose him to a potential criminal prosecution, then the privilege may be successfully invoked.

Confidentiality Agreements and Protective Orders

Often, a lawsuit will involve matters that one party wants to keep as secret as possible. For instance, in a trade secrets case, the owner of the trade secret would want to protect that secret by limiting the people who would have access to the secret, or the circumstances under which it is to be revealed. For example, in the *Raphael* case, since the lawsuit involves research performed under the auspices of Jonas Halbert Northern University, the institution may wish to protect certain innovative research techniques or new state-of-the-art research equipment by limiting access to that information to a few select individuals. Such limitations can be imposed voluntarily through a **confidentiality agreement** or by court decree through a **protective order**. Confidentiality agreements and protective orders cover a wide spectrum. Some agreements and orders completely prevent all discovery of the secret material. Others designate a particular place and time for revelation of the protected information. Still others might indicate that only certain named parties can be present when the confidential matter is revealed. It is even possible for the agreement or order to stipulate that the information will be enclosed in sealed envelopes to be opened only at the judge's direction. Documents that fall into the category of "confidential" should be stamped with this designation prior to their production or disclosure to the other side. Protective orders are permitted under Rule 26(c) of the Federal Rules of Civil Procedure. It is within the power of the court to cancel or alter a protective order should the need arise to do so. Exhibit 8-3 shows a sample protective order.

Claims of Privilege and ESI

ESI presents a problem because of its quantity, its complexity, and the relative inexperience among attorneys who must deal with this new form of evidence. These two things—quantity and complexity—may lead to the inadvertent revelation of protected or privileged information.[57] Rules 26(b)(5)(A), 26(b)(5)(B), 26(f)(3), and 34(b) deal with this problem. First, Rule 26(b)(5)(A) declares that when a party decides it is not going to turnover privileged evidence, that party must expressly inform the other party of the claim. The claim must indicate the evidence withheld in enough detail that the other party can do a proper assessment of the situation.

According to Rule 26(b)(5)(B), as soon as a party discovers that privileged information has been accidentally sent to another party, the first party must inform the other party of its discovery. The party with the information must then return the privileged information, destroy it, or at least hold on to it until the court can determine whether the claim of privilege is genuine. The party with the now sealed evidence can present it to the court for a ruling as to whether it rates the claimed privilege. If that party has given the information to a third party, the information must be recovered. When the information has been returned to the first party, that party must hold the information until the court decides whether it is actually privileged.[58]

EXHIBIT 8-3 Sample protective order

IN THE UNITED STATES DISTRICT COURT

NATIONAL SCIENCE FOUNDATION, et al., Plaintiffs	))))	Civil No. 16 C 2748 PROTECTIVE ORDER
v.	))))	
JONAS HALBERT NORTHERN UNIVERSITY, et al., Defendants.	))))	

PURSUANT to Rule 26(c) of the Federal Rules of Civil Procedure, and stipulation of the parties, IT IS HEREBY ORDERED as follows:

1. This Protective Order (the "Order") shall govern all documents and other products of discovery obtained by the Plaintiff or Defendant, all information derived therefrom and all copies, excerpts, or summaries thereof, including but not limited to, documents produced pursuant to Rule 33(c) or Rule 34 of the Federal Rules of Civil Procedure, answers to requests for admissions, answers to interrogatories, documents subpoenaed in connection with depositions, and deposition transcripts (referred to collectively herein as Discovery Material). Any motions, briefs, or other filings incorporating Discovery Material are also governed by this Order.

2. All Discovery Material shall be treated as confidential, both during the pendency of and subsequent to the termination of this action. Discovery Material will be used solely for the purpose of this action and not for any other purpose. No Discovery Material will be disclosed to anyone except in accordance with the terms of this Order.

3. Disclosure of Discovery Material shall be made only to attorneys of record for parties in the litigation; in-house counsel for the parties; persons employed by the law firms of the attorneys retained by the parties whose assistance is required by said attorneys in the preparation for trial of this case; expert witnesses and consultants who are retained by the parties in connection with this proceeding. Counsel for the party making disclosure to any of the aforementioned individuals shall first obtain the written agreement of any such individual to whom disclosure is made to be bound by the terms of this Order. This requirement may be satisfied by obtaining the signed acknowledgment on a copy of this Order that he or she has read the Order and understands its provisions.

4. Counsel for the parties making disclosure of Discovery Material to a party shall first obtain written agreement from the party producing said Discovery Material. Written agreement shall be obtained from any such party to whom Discovery Material is disclosed to be bound by the terms of the Order. This requirement may be satisfied by obtaining a signed acknowledgment on a copy of this Order that he or she has read the Order and understands its provisions.

5. Discovery Material shall be conspicuously marked by the producing party or witness "Confidential—Subject to Protective Order of the United States District Court."

EXHIBIT 8-3 Sample protective order (*Continued*)

6. In the event a party inadvertently produces for inspection privileged or potentially privileged documents, such production shall not constitute waiver of the attorney–client privilege, the work product privilege, or any other privilege with respect to the document or portion thereof, or with respect to any other document or testimony relating thereto. In the event that a document that is privileged, in whole or in part, is inadvertently produced, the party claiming privilege shall promptly identify each document being withheld as privileged, and the inspecting party shall forthwith return such document or documents.

7. Within thirty (30) days after the termination of this action, all confidential information, and copies thereof, including but not limited to any notes or other recording made hereof, shall be returned to counsel for the party who initially produced such documents.

8. Nothing in this Order shall prevent any party or nonparty from seeking a modification of this Order or from objecting to discovery which it believes to be otherwise improper.

DATED this _____ day of _____, 20_____
SIGNED BY: U.S. MAGISTRATE

APPROVED AS TO FORM AND CONTENT BY:
(ALL COUNSEL OF RECORD)

---

quick peek agreement
An agreement that allows the data retriever to give evidence to the data requester for a preliminary assessment while still preserving all privileges associated with that evidence.

clawback agreement
An agreement, sometimes called a nonwaiver agreement that allows the parties to agree that privileges can be asserted after evidence has been sent to the other party if the data retriever discovers that it has accidentally included privileged information in the evidence sent to the data requester.

Rule 26(f)(3) goes a step further by encouraging the parties to discuss the format that will be used for the delivery of ESI. Rule 26(f)(3) also implicitly connects to Rule 34(b)(1)(C), covering requests for real evidence, which permits the ESI requester to specify the format in which ESI must be delivered. Should the ESI requester forgo that opportunity, under Rule 34(b)(2)(D) the ESI retriever is allowed to indicate the format that will be used. Moreover, Rule 34(b)(2)(E) give the ESI retriever a choice of formats. The rules says that the retriever may produce the ESI either the form used in its everyday business operation or in a form that can be easily used by the other party.[59]

Quick Peek and Clawback Agreements   Under the Federal Rules, two types of agreements minimize the risk of the accidental disclosure of privileged information: the quick peek agreement and the clawback agreement. A **quick peek agreement** allows the ESI retriever to give unexamined evidence to the ESI requester for a preliminary assessment while still preserving all privileges associated with that evidence.[60] The ESI requester can then indicate which parts of the evidence the requester would prefer to examine in detail. The ESI retriever will then look exclusively at the ESI designated by the ESI requester and either turn it over or make any claims of privilege it deems appropriate.[61] The quick peek agreement is a risky proposition because it grants the opposing party access to evidence that should have remained protected. As we shall see in a moment, Rule 502 of the Federal Rules of Evidence helps make the practice, just a bit safer. Still even Rule 502 cannot erase the insight gained by the opposing party which has had access to evidence that should have been shielded. For this reason, the quick peek agreement is not very effective and is thus largely disfavored.[62]

Clawback agreements, which are authorized under Rule 26(f)(3) and which are sometimes called nonwaiver agreements, allow the parties to agree that privileges can be asserted after evidence has been sent to the other party if the ESI retriever discovers that it has accidentally included privileged information in the evidence sent to the requester. Clawback agreements were authorized because the complicated nature of ESI makes the inadvertent revelation of privileged information more likely than it ever was when most evidence was in paper form.[63]

Clawback agreements are not fool proof, however. Rule 502 (b) of the Federal Rules of Evidence states that claims of privilege can be asserted after the mistaken transfer of protected evidence only if (1) the waiver really was unintended, (2) the party asserting the privilege took reasonable precautions to prevent the disclosure, and (3) as soon as the party asserting the privilege realized its mistake, that party took immediate steps to correct the mistake. Of course, just how these limits are interpreted is up to the discretion of the court.[64]

Disadvantages and Advantages to Clawback Agreements

The fundamental disadvantage associated with clawback agreements is that they run counter to the general policy of discovery. Discovery is supposed to be open, liberal, efficient, economical, easy to manage, and as free from unwarranted protection measures as possible.[65] In contrast, clawback agreements allow the parties to delay the discovery process, to assert a privilege after that privilege has been waived, and to release evidence without making a properly attentive search of that evidence. The net effect of a clawback agreement may, therefore, be to slow down the discovery process. Moreover, some legal experts argue, rather convincingly, that substantive law still controls any clawback or nonwaiver agreement reached by the parties.[66]

The main advantage to the clawback agreement has been provided by Rule 502 to the Federal Rules of Evidence. Rule 502 seems to have made all nonwaiver agreements including clawback agreements controlling whenever they are part of an order issued by a federal court. The rule also attempts to make these agreements enforceable in state courts. The future of clawback agreements under Rule 502 depends on whether the federal courts have the constitutional authority to control the state courts in this manner.[67]

DUTY OF MUTUAL DISCLOSURE UNDER RULE 26

As noted previously, Rule 26 of the Federal Rules of Civil Procedure now requires that the parties confer early in the proceeding. More importantly, the rule provides for mutual disclosure. **Disclosure** requires that the parties exchange certain information without the necessity of a formal discovery request. These disclosures occur at three different times in the course of litigation. Early in the case, the parties are required to exchange information identifying potential witnesses, documentary evidence and tangible evidence (including ESI), evidence of damages, and copies of insurance policies. Later in the case (no later than 90 days before trial), the parties must exchange information about expert witnesses who will testify at trial. However, if the expert testimony is to be used simply to challenge evidence that was introduced by another party related to the same topic, that time period is shortened to 30 days after the original revelation of that evidence. Shortly before trial

disclosure
The process of revealing some information that was previously unknown or difficult to comprehend.

pretrial conference
A conference that is designed to make the process of conducting a lawsuit as efficient, simple, economical, and fair as possible. The process may involve a simplification of the pleadings, a limitation on the witnesses to be called at trial, a narrowing of the issues to be considered at trial, a simplification of the discovery process, and so on.

(no later than 30 days before trial), the parties must exchange information about evidence they intend to use at trial.

The Discovery Conference

To facilitate discovery, the Federal Rules of Civil Procedure have generally required that the parties get together to discuss matters related to discovery as soon as possible in the litigation process. However, Rule 26(f) mandates that the preconference "meet-and-confer" session be conducted no later than 21 days before a scheduling conference is held or a scheduling order is due under Rule 16(b). When discovery was limited to depositions, interrogatories, and requests for paper documents, some trial attorneys, many of whom work well under pressure, postponed any preparatory work for the meet-and-confer session until the very last minute. Such "11th-hour" preparation steps are no longer advisable. Attorneys who wait for the meet-and-confer session to prepare for the discovery negotiations probably will find themselves bewildered by the complexities of their own client's computer system, to say nothing of the computer system of the opposing party. This is true because, as noted earlier, the rules now require that the discovery plan involve a discussion of ESI, including the format used for the delivery of ESI and the negotiation of clawback agreements. Rule 26(f)(3) states that a discovery plan should include:

1. any changes made in timing, form, or requirements for mutual disclosures;
2. subjects on which discovery is needed, a completion date for discovery, whether discovery should be conducted in phases, and whether discovery should be limited or focused upon particular issues;
3. those concerns that might involve the revelation or the discovery of electronically stored information (ESI), including its format for production;
4. those matters that might involve allegations of privilege or protection of information as material prepared for trial, including agreements allowing the assertion of such demands after the evidence has been delivered (aka clawback or nonwaiver agreements), and whether the court will be asked to add the agreement to an order;
5. what changes should be made in normal limitations on discovery; and
6. any orders that should be entered by the court.

Within 14 days of the Rule 26 conference, the parties are to file a written report outlining their plan.

The Pretrial Conference under Rule 16   Rule 16 of the Federal Rules of Civil Procedure allows the court to direct the parties to come to the court to consider various pretrial matters, including the discovery process. Such a meeting is called a **pretrial conference**. Often such a conference takes place after the court has received a discovery plan from the parties. Under Rule 26(f), the court may also be permitted to waive the written report required under Rule 26, provided the parties agree to file an oral report at the conference held under Rule 16. The court reviews the plan and discusses the matter with the attorneys, and then it issues orders concerning any aspect of discovery or disclosure, including scheduling time limits in which to complete discovery.

Mutual Disclosures

Initial Disclosures   Under Rule 26(a)(1)(A), without waiting for a discovery request, the parties should exchange the following information within 14 days of their meet-and-confer session:

1. name and, if known, address and telephone number of anyone likely to have discoverable information relevant to the disputed facts in the case, identifying the nature of that information;

2. a copy of, or a description by category and location of, all documents, data compilations, electronically stored information (ESI), and tangible things in the possession, custody, or control of the party;

3. a computation of damages claimed by the disclosing party, making available for copying or inspection any supporting documentation or other evidentiary material; and

4. any insurance agreement that may satisfy part or all of any judgment in the case must be available for copying and inspection.

As noted previously, the central change in Rule 26(a)(1)(A)–(D) is the addition of electronically stored information (ESI) to the list of mutual disclosures.

Excluded Categories   Rule 26(a)(1)(B) excludes certain types of proceedings from these initial discovery disclosure requirements. These exclusions include the following:

1. any action for review on an administrative record;

2. a forfeiture action in rem arising from a federal statute;

3. a petition for habeas corpus or any other proceeding to challenge a criminal conviction or sentence;

4. an action brought without an attorney by a person in the custody of the United States, a state, or a state subdivision;

5. an action to enforce or quash an administrative summons or subpoena;

6. an action by the United States to recover benefit payments;

7. an action by the United States to collect on a student loan guaranteed by the United States;

8. a proceeding ancillary to proceedings in another court; and

9. an action to enforce an arbitration award.

These proceedings have been explicitly excluded from the initial discovery disclosure requirements outlined in Rule 26, primarily because in many, perhaps most, situations these proceedings involve a minimum amount of discovery.

Disclosure of Expert Testimony   Before trial, the parties must disclose to one another the identity of any person who may be called to testify at trial as an expert witness. As noted above, this disclosure should be made at least 90 days before the trial date, unless the evidence is intended solely to contradict or rebut evidence of another expert. In such a situation, the disclosure should be made within 30 days after the disclosure made by the other party. Along with the identity of the expert, a copy of a written report prepared and signed by the witness should be supplied. This report should contain the following information:

1. statement of all opinions to be expressed and the basis for all opinions;
2. facts or data considered by the witness in forming opinions;
3. any exhibits to be used as a summary of or support for opinions;
4. qualifications of the witness, including a list of all publications authored by the witness within the preceding 10 years;
5. a list of any other cases in which the witness has testified as an expert at trial or by deposition within the preceding four years; and
6. a declaration of the compensation to be paid for the study and the testimony in the case.

Rule 26 was recently amended to protect the work product privilege as it relates to expert witnesses. Under the old rule, experts were required to reveal any "data or other information" that they used in writing reports, preparing testimony, or developing the opinion that they planned to deliver in court. This clause was frequently interpreted by the courts to permit the discovery of any communication that passed between an expert and an attorney, including a draft copy of any report written by the expert and sent to the attorney, thus clearly threatening the protection provided by the work product privilege. The new rule indicates that the only material that the expert must reveal in discovery is that which relates to "the facts or data considered by the witness" in creating his or her opinion (see #2 above).

This limitation does not mean that an expert's work in formulating an expert opinion is completely closed to discovery. On the contrary, the rule still requires that the expert provide (a) information about his or her compensation, (b) details on the information used to develop his or her testimony, and (c) any presumptions or suppositions about the case that the attorney might have given to the expert, if the expert's opinion came from those presumptions and or suppositions.[68] Also, under Rule 26 (a)(2)(C), when the expert witness is not obligated to provide a written report, that witness must still disclose "(i) the subject matter on which the witness is expected to present evidence under Federal Rule of Evidence 702, 703, or 705; and (ii) a summary of the facts and opinions to which the witness is expected to testify."

Unfortunately, the new amendments to Rule 26 have not eliminated all of the disclosure problems associated with expert witnesses. The disclosure requirements listed under Rule 26 can also cause difficulties in cases involving large amounts of ESI that must be accessed by IT personnel. Up until a short time ago, most attorneys would not have considered work done by their own IT employees as the work of experts. Recent federal cases, however, have demonstrated that this may have been an erroneous assumption. Recall, as noted earlier, that the prevailing opinion among the federal courts appears to be that any evidence offered to defend or to critique a computerized search for ESI must be supplied by an expert.[69]

Pretrial Disclosures   Unless otherwise ordered by the court, various evidentiary matters must be disclosed at least 30 days before trial. These matters include the following:

1. name and, if not previously provided, address and telephone number of each witness, stating whether the party actually expects to call the person as a witness or whether the witness will be called only if needed;

2. designation of those witnesses whose testimony is expected to be presented by means of a deposition and a transcript of the pertinent portions of the deposition testimony; and

3. an identification of each document or other exhibit, separately identifying those which the party expects to offer and those which the party may offer if the need arises.

Any objection to the admissibility of deposition testimony or admissibility of documents or other exhibits must be made within 14 days of service of the pretrial disclosures by the other party. Any objections not made may be deemed waived.

Duty to Supplement

Under Rule 26(e) all disclosures are required to be supplemented if the disclosing party later acquires information under the following circumstances:

1. if the party learns that in some material respect the information disclosed is incomplete or incorrect, and if the additional or corrective information has not otherwise been made known to the other parties during the discovery process or in writing; or

2. when the court has so ordered.

COOPERATING WITH DISCOVERY

It is to everyone's benefit for the discovery process to run as smoothly as possible. For this reason, most parties cooperate freely with discovery requests. However, there are times when parties refuse to cooperate. The rules of civil procedure provide methods for compelling discovery and sanctions for those who refuse to cooperate.

Voluntary Cooperation

Most of the time, attorneys involved in litigation will find that the other attorney and the other party cooperate with the discovery process. Parties cooperate generally for several reasons, all of which are based on enlightened self-interest. First, under the principle of reciprocity, each side knows that any attempt to disrupt the discovery process may result in a similar attempt by the other side. Second, each side knows that the court disapproves of any attempt to interfere with discovery. Finally, the Federal Rules of Civil Procedure provide severe sanctions for those parties who refuse to obey discovery orders made by the court. For these reasons, if one side resists the discovery process or any part of that process, the other side should make inquiries about the reason for such resistance. Often such problems can be resolved informally. For example, a party may resist sitting for a deposition because it is scheduled at an inconvenient time or place. A minor problem like this can be solved by explaining the importance of the discovery process to the party and rescheduling the deposition for a more acceptable time and place.

AUTOMATED LITIGATION SUPPORT
Invisible ESI

SCENARIO

Your supervising attorney has called you into her office to discuss the *Raphael* case. She informs you that in addition to calling several officers and employees of Jonas Halbert Northern University in for depositions, she also intends to serve them with interrogatories and requests for production of documents. Her preliminary investigation indicates that there will be hundreds of thousands of documents hidden within the ESI of JHNU's computer system. She is concerned about keeping all of the information organized and accessible. She tells you about a recurring nightmare that she has had about losing a key case because she could not find the relevant ESI because it had been deleted from the opposing party's computer system. While she does not suspect the opposing attorney's motives, she is concerned that he will be so unfamiliar with the computer operating system of his own client that he will declare some key ESI as inaccessible when it is, in fact, hidden somewhere on the computer system. She is certain that she will ultimately recover the ESI, but she is concerned about the delay that such a search will cause.

PROBLEM

In a complex litigation matter where there is substantial discovery of voluminous ESI, how do you make certain that the opposing attorney does not overlook some key ESI because he or she believes that it is inaccessible because it has been deleted, was never saved, or was simply printed without being saved by the computer operator?

SOLUTION

Most companies, institutions, and law firms have IT departments to handle the complexities of today's computer systems. In a lawsuit such as the *Raphael* case in which there will be numerous requests for ESI, it is often a good idea to get a fast education from the members of your own IT department. One thing that the members of the IT department will know about is the existence of invisible ESI. Here are a few of the types of invisible ESI that your IT department may be able to help you find.

Deleted ESI Most computer users do not realize that deleted ESI is not as inaccessible as the term "deleted" would lead them to believe. In fact, material that has been deleted has merely been rendered invisible. The ESI, however, is still located on the hard drive of the computer system and can be retrieved by a good IT expert. The problem is that when a document request asks for all ESI of a certain type, say all e-mail correspondence, the opposing attorney may label such ESI inaccessible and, therefore, not discoverable because the writers of those e-mail letters cannot themselves retrieve the deleted correspondence.[72]

Unsaved ESI When personal computers first became popular, operators were responsible for saving their own documents. If they did not do so, the data would be lost if the computer was shut down, especially when the shutdown was unexpected, as might happen during a power failure. Today's computers do not have this drawback. Nevertheless, many computer operators do not realize this and, therefore, continue to hit the "save" key every minute or so. This is not a bad habit to have; however, it leads many people to believe that material that has not been deliberately saved by the operator is lost forever. This is not the case. Everything created on the computer is saved automatically, whether the operator deliberately saves it or not, and can be resurrected by a well-trained IT professional.[73]

Printed ESI When a computer operator orders some ESI to be printed, the computer will transfer that ESI to an area known as the spool file from which it is printed. After the printing is completed, however, the ESI stays within the spool file. An attorney unfamiliar with this operation will label such ESI inaccessible and, thus, undiscoverable when, in fact, the ESI could be retrieved by an IT expert with the appropriate know-how.[74]

Ephemeral ESI Some social media enthusiasts have started using apps that are programmed to delete all data (commonly photos) within about 10 seconds of when the data is sent. It is important for you as the paralegal to understand that neither the app developers nor their providers nor promise unconditionally that the data will actually be erased. So remember, even a photo sent using an app like Snapchat might be retrieved by a really talented and resourceful IT expert. If you find yourself in such a situation, seek out that IT specialist and tell him or her what your supervising attorney needs in relation to the allegedly deleted ESI in question. Knowing that ESI, which has been deleted, not saved, or merely printed, may still be accessible can save an enormous amount of time, expense, and worry during the discovery process. Ultimately, it also may mean the margin between victory and defeat. If your firm does not have an in-house IT department to help educate you and your supervising attorney, you might try to locate one of the many litigation support firms that are becoming more and more knowledgeable about the details of ESI and its role in the modern lawsuit.

FINDING IT on the Internet

The Federal Rules of Civil Procedure have recently been extensively revised. Most of the amendments were added in an attempt to deal with the problems created by the proliferation of ESI, especially as that ESI relates to discovery. The Internet can be a great source of information about those rule changes. For example, the *E-Commerce Times* publishes a regular stream of articles dealing with IT management issues. The *E-Commerce Times* can be accessed at **<http://www.ecommercetimes.com>**. A recent issue of the *E-Commerce Times* featured a story entitled "The Stunning Impact of E-Discovery on IT."

Another good Internet source that can be used to keep up-to-date on recent developments in e-discovery, ESI, and the amendments to the Federal Rules that were written to deal with those developments is an online newsletter entitled *Law Technology News*. *Law Technology News* can be accessed at **<http://www.law.com/>**, and it can lead you to the top stories of the day dealing with legal technology issues. A recent issue of the *Law Technology News* (LTN) featured a story entitled, "Delaware Court Changes Discovery Schedule." Once you have registered with LTN, you can receive daily e-mails (and sometimes several times each day) that will keep you current on developments that relate to all aspects of ESI law. Moreover, if you have e-mail sent to your smartphone, you will never be without the latest news relating to computers and the law (unless you forget to charge your phone).

The American Bar Association (ABA) has had a long-term presence on the Internet. The ABA regularly publishes a cyberspace magazine called the *ABA Journal,* which highlights current issues of interest to practicing attorneys. The *ABA Journal* can be accessed at **<http://www.abajournal.com>**. Once on the site you can select "Topics," find the heading "Legal Technology," and identify recent stories on e-discovery along with many related issues. For example, one recent article of interest to the paralegal is entitled "Law Blogger Predicts 'Massive Rise' in Videoconferencing."

The Web site of the Administrative Office of the U.S. Courts can be accessed at **<http://www .uscourts.gov>**. The Web site contains a number of interesting features, including the most recent news releases from the federal courts and articles from *Third Branch News*, the court's newsletter. (Note the court recently changed the title of the newsletter from *The Third Branch* to *Third Branch News*. However, previous issues of *The Third Branch* are still accessible on the court's Web site.)

a. Conduct a search for recent news articles concerning the impact of ESI or the new amendments to the discovery rules, and, when you find an interesting feature, write a report on the essence of that article.

b. Access *Third Branch News* and find an article that interests you under the heading *Latest News* and write a report on the substance of that article.

c. Consider subscribing to *Third Branch News* by exploring the terms listed under the very logical heading of "Subscribe to Third Branch News."

Involuntary Cooperation

Despite the inclination toward cooperation, there are times when parties may feel that they have legitimate reasons for resisting discovery. In such cases, the parties must turn to the court for a resolution of the differences.

Orders to Compel Discovery If one of the parties to a lawsuit refuses to comply with a discovery request, the other party must move to force compliance. Under Rule 37 of the Federal Rules of Civil Procedure, the party seeking cooperation must file a motion with the court asking the judge to compel discovery. The judge will then decide whether to grant the motion. It is possible for the noncomplying party to have a legally sufficient reason for denying the discovery request. For example, in this chapter's *Raphael* case, Jonas Halbert Northern University might argue that a request for a list of all grants written by all research fellows over the last five years falls outside the scope of discovery; that is, the list is not relevant to the claims or defenses of a party, and such a list could not lead to admissible evidence. If the objection is valid, the judge will deny the motion to compel discovery. If the objection is not valid, however, the judge will grant the motion and issue an order compelling cooperation with the discovery process. In the case of JHNU's objection, the judge would likely see the objection as valid and would, therefore, deny the motion to compel JHNU's cooperation. Any motion to compel discovery, disclosure, or amend a previous response must be accompanied by a certification that the moving party has in good faith conferred or attempted to confer with the other party in an attempt to resolve the matter without court action.

Rule 37 ESI Amendment A recent amendment has been added to Rule 37 to protect parties who lose ESI because of routine computer operations. The amendment, which is often referred to as the "good-faith" amendment, states that the court cannot enact sanctions against a party if that party cannot produce ESI because that ESI has been eliminated because of standard computer procedures.[70] For example, if, prior to the threat of litigation, a company's computer system had been programmed to automatically delete e-mail records after a certain time period, the party cannot be sanctioned for the loss of those e-mail records. On the other hand, the party must make a genuine attempt to retrieve the ESI even if it has been deleted because, as we have seen, computers have a way of preserving data that appears to be erased. Moreover, a litigant cannot take advantage of a standard computer procedure that it knows will delete certain information if the computer is not reprogrammed. On the other hand, the litigant can show good-faith by proactively disabling any programs that automatically erase data. This is why, at the first sign of a pending lawsuit, your supervising attorney will advise a client to initiate an immediate litigation hold on all ESI.[71] Moreover, litigants must understand that, while the good faith provision will protect them against sanctions for lost data, it will not eliminate any extra work or extra expense that might be needed to reprogram their system to eliminate the automatic deletion process or to recover evidence that has already been lost when the program was still operational. Thus, if ESI is deleted because of standard computer procedures, a litigant may still have to pay for any additional depositions that might be needed to uncover the actual content of that ESI.

Sanctions against Noncomplying Parties If, after an order compelling cooperation is issued, a party still refuses to comply, the court can levy certain sanctions against the noncomplying party. Under Rule 37 of the Federal Rules of Civil Procedure, the sanctions include, but are not limited to, a dismissal of the action; the granting of a default judgment; the granting of reasonable expenses, including attorney fees, caused by the failure to cooperate; and a contempt-of-court ruling against the noncomplying party. Sanctions are permitted against either the attorney or the client, or both. This possibility should be considered when drafting a discovery plan. Discovery is an effective and necessary litigation tool. Abuse of discovery results in a protracted and complicated lawsuit.

SUMMARY

- Discovery is the legal process by which the parties to a lawsuit search for facts relevant to a particular case. The primary objective of discovery is to prevent one of the parties from winning the lawsuit by surprise or trickery. An attorney has five methods of discovery from which to choose: the deposition, interrogatories, a request for the production of documents, a request for physical or mental examinations, and a request for admission. An attorney must take into consideration the expense involved and the time available in choosing from among these five methods. Ethical considerations also play a part in conducting discovery. Attorneys must be aware of the new amendments to the Federal Rules of Civil Procedure that deal with the effective handling of electronically stored information (ESI) during discovery.

- The information sought during discovery must be relevant to the subject matter of the case and, at the very least, reasonably calculated to lead to evidence that can be introduced at trial. There are several limits to the discovery process, including the attorney–client privilege, the work product privilege, the common interest privilege, the medical privilege, the confessor–penitent privilege, limited access to expert testimony, the Fifth Amendment privilege against self-incrimination, confidentiality agreements, and protective orders. The new rules also allow the parties to protect themselves from the inadvertent disclosure of privileged information that may occur because of the vast quantity of ESI. Two forms of protection are the quick peek agreement and the clawback agreement. So far, Rule 502 of the Federal Rules of Evidence has strengthened the effectiveness of all nonwaiver agreements including clawback agreements.

- Rule 26 of the Federal Rules of Civil Procedure requires parties to mutually disclose certain relevant information without the necessity of a formal discovery request. This information includes names, addresses, and telephone numbers of persons who have relevant information about disputed facts; a description and location of documents and electronically stored information (ESI); a list of all damages; and a copy of any insurance policies covering the claim. Before trial, parties must also disclose names, qualifications, opinions, and compensation of expert witnesses who will testify in the case. Additionally, before trial, each side must disclose the identity of persons who will or may be called as witnesses or whose depositions may be used, and a list of all exhibits to be introduced at trial. Furthermore, prior to conducting any discovery, the parties must meet and prepare a discovery plan, which includes the handling of ESI.

- Most of the time, attorneys involved in litigation cooperate with one another during discovery. Those who do not may be compelled by the court to cooperate. The new rules limit sanctions against parties who fail to produce ESI during discovery when the loss of that ESI is unavoidable because of the standard operation of that party's computer system.

KEY TERMS

active data
attorney–client privilege
backup data
chain of custody
clawback agreement
clerical privilege
cloud storage
common interest privilege
computer
computer forensics
confessor–penitent privilege
confidentiality agreement
cyber-forensics
deposition
digital discovery
disclosure
discovery
e-discovery
e-forensics
electronic discovery
electronically stored
   information (ESI)
ephemeral data
ESI center
ESI depositor

ESI owner
ESI requester
ESI retriever
evidence in a legal
   proceeding
extant data
inactive data
interrogatories
legacy data
litigation hold
litigation privilege
litigation response team
medical privilege
metadata
not reasonably accessible
   ESI
online chat
online workshop
paper data
physician–patient privilege
predictive coding
pretrial conference
privilege
privilege against self-
   incrimination

protective order
quick peek agreement
reasonably accessible
   ESI
request for a physical or
   mental examination
request for admission
request for the production
   of documents,
   electronically stored
   information (ESI),
   and tangible things,
   or entry upon land for
   inspection and other
   purposes
residual data
scope of discovery
social media
spoliation letter
videoconference
webcam
webchat
Web conference
webinar
work product privilege

REVIEW QUESTIONS

1. What is discovery?
2. What are the five major methods of discovery?
3. What factors must be considered when choosing among discovery methods?
4. What five unethical practices are involved in the discovery process?
5. What types of evidence can be legally obtained during the discovery process?
6. What are the differences among the attorney–client privilege, the work product privilege, the common interest privilege, and the Fifth Amendment privilege against self-incrimination?
7. What is the purpose of confidentiality agreements and protective orders?
8. What is the purpose of quick peek and clawback agreements?
9. What types of disclosures must be made by the parties under Rule 26 of the Federal Rules?
10. What are the contents of a discovery plan as required under Rule 26 of the Federal Rules?

11. Why is voluntary cooperation necessary for the discovery process?

12. What consequences can result from a refusal to cooperate with an order compelling discovery?

CHAPTER EXERCISES

Where necessary, check with your instructor prior to starting any of these exercises.

1. Obtain a copy of the pertinent Federal Rules and a copy of the rules of your state governing discovery by checking out your firm's law library or accessing them online. Compare the two sets of rules and note any important differences.

2. Research your state's rules on the attorney–client privilege by accessing the most recent cases and articles that you can find online. Prepare a summary of those rules properly documented by those online sources. Do the same for the rules governing the work product privilege and the common interest privilege.

3. Find a set of sample forms online for use in the courts of your state. Review the forms for a confidentiality agreement and a protective order. List and explain the different options that are available for drafting these documents.

4. Check the local rules of court for the federal district court in your area by accessing them online. Does Rule 26 apply?

5. Analyze the following situation and, using your understanding of the discovery rules as explained in this chapter, determine which of the following items in the *Raphael* case would qualify as initial disclosures and which, under Rule 26 of the Federal Rules, would have to be provided to the National Science Foundation without waiting for a discovery request:

   a. a copy of a list of all of the abstracts and grant proposals written by Phipps over the last 18 months and in the possession of or under the control of Dr. Raphael;

   b. a set of notes written by your supervising attorney during the initial interview with Dr. Raphael;

   c. a series of e-mails that passed between Dr. Raphael and Phipps regarding the possible suspension of Phipps and the later results of those discussions;

   d. the names, addresses, e-mail addresses, mobile numbers, and office telephone numbers of the research fellows supervised by Dr. Raphael over the last 18 months; and

   e. a video of a practice session during which Dr. Raphael was questioned by an attorney in your law firm.

   In each situation, explain why the item in question should or should not be classified as an initial disclosure.

CHAPTER PROJECT

Review the details of the *Raphael* case. Draft a letter to Dr. Raphael in which you explain the different types of privileges that may be available to limit the discovery process as it relates to his case. Explain to Dr. Raphael why each privilege would or would not be applicable in his case.

THE *BENNETT* CASE
Assignment for Chapter 8: Discovery Plan

Now that all the pleadings in the *Bennett* case have been filed, your supervising attorney will be meeting with the attorney for the defendants pursuant to Rule 26 of the Federal Rules to develop a mutual discovery plan. The Federal Rules require the parties to identify the subjects on which discovery is needed. You have been asked to review the file and make a list of specific subjects or topics on which discovery is needed. You have also been asked to identify which discovery methods (deposition, interrogatories, etc.) should be used to obtain the needed information.

THE *DOUGLASS FINANCIAL SERVICES INC.* CASE
Assignment for Chapter 8: Identifying ESI

The case is about to proceed to the discovery phase. Your supervising attorney tells you that your client, Douglass Financial, Inc., will be subjected to numerous requests for ESI. Your attorney asks you to contact an individual who works in IT for your client and become familiar with how Douglass Financial utilizes technology to create and store data. Prepare a list of questions to ask when you contact the IT employee.

ENDNOTES

1. Sir Francis Bacon quoted by Neil Postman in *Technopoly: The Surrender of Culture to Technology* (New York Vintage Books, 1992), 35.

2. Lee H. Rosenthal, "An Overview of the E-Discovery Rules Amendments After December 1, 2006," *116 Yale L.J. Pocket Part* 167(2006) retrieved on August 29, 2013 from <http://yalelawjournal.org/index2.php? option=com_content&task=view&id=8 1&pop=1&page=0&Itemid=14>.

3. Donald A. Wochna, "Electronic Data, Electronic Searching, and Inadvertent Production of Privileged Data: A Perfect Storm, Why Attorneys Are Being Forced to Recognize That Searching Electronically-Stored Information Is an Expert Function," *Ohio State Bar Association: 2010 Annual Convention* (May 5–7, 2010): 1.3.

4. Rosenthal, "An Overview of the E-Discovery Rules Amendments," 1–2; Carolyn Southerland, "Ignorance of IT Minutiae No Excuse for Litigators: New Rules Mean They'll Need Serious Expertise on Scary Technical Details," *The National Law Journal* (July 17, 2006): 54–55.

5. David Canfield, "An Overview of the State E-Discovery Rules: Some States Line Up with the Federal Rules while Others Blaze Their Own Trails," *Inside Counsel* (March 15, 2012), retrieved on January 4, 2013 from <http://www.insidecounsel.com>, para. 3. The states that have adopted the 2006 Federal Rules regarding E-Discovery as of March 2012, include Alabama, Alaska, Arizona, Arkansas, California, Connecticut, Indiana, Iowa, Kansas, Louisiana, Maine, Maryland, Michigan, Minnesota, Montana, Nebraska, New Hampshire, New Jersey, New Mexico, North Carolina, North Dakota, Ohio, Oklahoma, South Carolina, Tennessee, Utah, Vermont, Virginia, Wisconsin, and Wyoming. See also Thomas Allman, "E-Discovery in Federal and State Courts after the 2006 Federal Amendments," *Bucklin Organization Research* (January 2012), retrieved on January 4, 2013 from <http://www.bucklin.org/research/index.htm>, 2.

6. The states that have made no attempt to amend their rules to include the handling of e-evidence and e-discovery include Colorado, Georgia, Hawaii, Kentucky, Missouri, Nevada, Oregon, Rhode Island, South Dakota, and West Virginia. The remaining states have either developed their own rules or are in the process of deciding how to deal with ESI. See: "State Court Rules and Statutes Regarding ESI," *Kroll Ontrac* (March 2012), retrieved on January 5, 2013, from <http://www.krollontrack.com/>, 1.

7. Dennis Kennedy, "Does Your Firm Have a Bring-Your-Own-Device Policy?" *ABA Journal* (January 1, 2013), retrieved on January 11, 2013 from <http://www.abajournal.com/>.

8. Donald A. Wochna, "Electronic Searching and Expert Function Data Analytics Are Making Computers and Networks the Best Witnesses," *Ohio State Bar Association: 2010 Annual Convention* (May 5–7, 2010): 1.23.

9. Wochna, "Making Computers and Networks the Best Witnesses," 1.21–1.23.

10. National Information Standards Organization, *Understanding Metadata*. Bethesda, MD: National Information Standards Organization Press, 2004, retrieved on June 16, 2010 from <http://www.niso.org>, 1.

11. David K. Isom, "Electronic Discovery Primer for Judges," *Federal Courts Law Review* 1 (February 2005), retrieved on February 15, 2007 from <http://fclr.org/fclr/articles /html/2005/fedctslrev1.pdf>.

12. Rosenthal, "An Overview of the E-Discovery Rules Amendments," 1; Southerland, "Ignorance of IT Minutiae No Excuse for Litigators," 54–55.

13. Nick Bilton, "Disruptions: Indiscreet Photos, Glimpsed Then Gone," *The New York Times* (May 6, 2012): 1–3, retrieved on January 16, 2013 from <http://query.nytimes .com/gst/fullpage.html?res=9904E6DF173AF934A35756C0A9649D8B63&ref=nic kbilton>, 1–2. The article issues a similar warning to those mobile users who send text messages using apps, such as Tigertext, that promise to erase sensitive text messages.

14. Alan Cohen, "Times They Are Sure A'Changing," *Law Technology News* (December 1, 2012), retrieved on January 11, 2013 from <http://www.law.com/jsp/lawtechnologynews /PubArticleLTN.jsp? id=1202585467397&Discovery_on_the_Go>.

15. William Caraher, "Tablet Wars," *Law Technology News* (October 10, 2012), retrieved on January 11, 2013 from <http://www.law.com/jsp/lawtechnologynews/PubArticleLTN .jsp?id=1202575027157&Could_Microsoft_Win_the_Tablet_Wars>.

16. Kamala D. Harris, *Privacy on the Go: Recommendations for the Mobile Ecosystem*, California Department of Justice (January 2013), 3–8. *Privacy on the Go* is a set of privacy guidelines for app producers, providers, and users. See also: Kamala D. Harris, "Attorney General Kamala D. Harris Issues Guidance on How Mobile Apps Can Better Protect Consumer Privacy," *State of California Department of Justice* (January 10, 2013), retrieved on January 14, 2013 from <http://oag.ca.gov/news/press-releases /attorney-general-kamala-d-harris-issues-guidance-how-mobile-apps-can-better>.

17. Harris, *Privacy on the Go*, 3–8.

18. Richard Acello, "Beyond Prediction: Technology-Assisted Review Enters the Lexicon," *ABA Journal* (August 1, 2012), retrieved on January 11, 2012 from <http://www .Abajournal.com>, 1. See also: "Revolutionary Predictive Coding: Predict, Code, Process," *Recommind* (2012), retrieved on January 11, 2013 from <http://www.recommind.com /predictive-coding>.

19. *Zubulake v. UBS Warburg*, 02 CIV. 1243 (SAS), (S.D.N.Y. July 20, 2004), 24 and 30.

20. Evan Koblentz, "Microsoft Office 2013 Bolsters E-Discovery," *Law Technology News* (July 17, 2012), retrieved on January 12, 2013 from <http://www.law.com/jsp/lawtechnologynews/PubArticleLTN.jsp?id=1202563210396>.

21. Chris Bright and Brad Harris, "Rimkus v. Cammarata: Another Great Reason Organizations Need an Effective Legal Hold Process," *Legal Hold Pro Tracker* (February 2010), retrieved on September 19, 2010 from <http://www.legalholdpro.com/Blog/2010/2/25/rimkus-v-cammarata-another-great-reason-organizations-need-an-effective-legal-hold-process>; see also *Rimkus Consulting Group, Inc. v. Nickie G. Cammarata, et al.* 07-cv-00405 (S.D. TX) (February 9, 2010) and *Pension Committee of the University of Montreal Pension Plan v. Banc of America Securities, LLC*, No. 05 Civ. 9016, 2010 WL 184312 (S.D.N.Y. January 15, 2010).

22. Allman, "E-Discovery in Federal and State Courts," 8. Allman cites one case in particular that supports this position: *Victor Stanley v. Creative Pipe*, 269 F.D.R. 497 (D. Md. 2010). In another article, Allman notes that a report issued by the Conference Committee on Rules of Practice and Procedure of the Judicial Conference of the United States states that the duty to preserve can emerge from statutory law, common law, administrative regulations, or an order issued by the court in a particular case. See: Thomas Y. Allman, "The Impact of the Proposed Federal E-Discovery Rules," 12 Rich. J.L. & Tech. 13(2006).

23. *Zubulake*, 30

24. *Zubulake*, 31.

25. Leigh Jones, "E-Discovery Zero Hour Approaching: Attorneys Warily Prepare for Changes," *The National Law Journal* (August 21, 2006): 10.

26. Peter Vogel, "How To Understand Social Media Evidence," *Law Technology News* (January 2, 2013), retrieved on January 11, 2013 from <http://www.law.com/jsp/lawtechnologynews/PubArticleLTN.jsp?id=1202582974936&How_to_Understand_Social_Media_Evidence>.

27. "Preserving Chain of Custody in E-discovery," *Discovery Services Fact Sheet*, LexisNexis, retrieved on June 15, 2010 from <http://www.lexisnexis.com/applieddiscovery/lawlibrary/whitePapers/ADI_FS_ChainOfCustody.pdf>, 1.

28. Christy Burke, "Examining E-Discovery Chain of Custody," *LTN Law Technology News* (2010), retrieved on June 7, 2010 from <http://www.law.com/jsp/lawtechnologynews/PubArticleLTN.jsp?id=900005494089&Examining_EDiscovery_Chain_of_Custody>, 2.

29. Ralph Losey, "Computer Forensics: Sherlock Holmes in the 21 Century," *Florida Law Firm.Com*, retrieved on June 15, 2010 from <http://floridalawfirm.com/forensics.html>, 3; see also *The Sedona Principles: Best Practices, Recommendations & Principles for Addressing Electronic Document Production*, Appendix A: Glossary, 51.

30. Wochna, "A Perfect Storm," 1.3.

31. *McCargo v, Texas Roadhouse, Inc.* 050211 CODC, 09-cv-02889-WYD-KMT (May 2, 2011). Although this case involved deleted videotapes, the ruling of the court is based on principles that clearly relate to ESI.

32. In her article, "Ignorance of IT Minutiae No Excuse for Litigators: New Rules Mean They'll Need Serious Expertise on Scary Technical Details," *The National Law Journal* (July 17, 2006): 53–55, Carolyn Southerland uses the terms *data requester* and *data producer*, rather than *ESI requester* and *ESI retriever*. Both phrases are appropriate.

33. Jones, "E-Discovery Zero Hour Approaching," 10.

34. Timothy J. Carroll and Bruce A. Radke, "Federal Rules of Civil Procedure Concerning E-Discovery Impact," *Business Management*, GDS Publishing Ltd. (2010), retrieved on June 7, 2010 from <http://www.busmanagement.com/article/Federal-Rules-of-Civil-Procedure-Concerning-E-Discovery-Impact/>, 1–2.

35. Jones, "E-Discovery Zero Hour Approaching," 10.

36. Donald A. Wochna, "The Cutting Edge: Request for Production of Documents Can Be a Technology Trap," *Cleveland Bar Journal* (September 2004): 37.

37. "Amendments to the Federal Rules of Civil Procedure," Committee Note on Federal Rule 26, *Committee on Rules of Practice and Procedure of the Judicial Conference of the United States*, retrieved on April 2, 2008 from <http://www.uscourts.gov/uscourts/RulesAndPolicies/rules/EDiscovery_w_Notes.pdf>, 14.

38. Jonathan Strickland, "How Cloud Storage Work," *How Stuff Works* (2008), retrieved on January 11, 2013 from <http://computer.howstuffworks.com>, 1, 4.

39. Carroll and Radke, "Federal Rules of Civil Procedure Concerning E-Discovery Impact," 2.

40. Ibid., 2–4.

41. Ibid., 3; see also Chris Connolly, "The US Safe Harbor—Fact or Fiction?" *Galexia Pty, Ltd.* (December 2, 2008), retrieved on June 17, 2010 from <http://www.galexia.com>, 4.

42. U.S. Department of Commerce, "Safe Harbor Overview," *Export.Gov*, retrieved on January 7, 2013 from <http://export.gov/safeharbor/>, 1–2.

43. Committee Note, 15.

44. Jones, "E-Discovery Zero Hour Approaching," 10; Rosenthal, "An Overview of the E-Discovery Rules Amendments," 3; Committee Note, 15-16.

45. Isom, "Electronic Discovery Primer for Judges," 14–15; Committee Note, 16–17.

46. William D. Manson, "Multi-Jurisdictional Issues for the In-House Legal Department," *Ohio State Bar Association: 2010 Annual Convention* (May 5–7, 2010): 3.1–3.11.

47. Manson, "Multi-Jurisdictional Issues for the In-House Legal Department," 3.8.

48. Ibid., 3.10.

49. Ibid., 3.9.

50. David J. Lender and Keven F. Meade, "Amendments to Expert Witness Discovery Under Federal Rule 26," *Weil, Gotshaf, and Manges* (February 8, 2011), para. 5, retrieved on January 3 2013 from <http://www.weil.com>.

51. "Litigation Update: Amended Federal Rules of Civil Procedure Extend Work Product Privilege to Draft Expert Reports and Other Communications," *Thompson Hine Litigation Update* (December 2010), retrieved on January 7, 2013 from <http://www.thompsonhine.com/publications/publication2201.html>

52. David M. Greenwald, Robert R. Stauffer, and Erin R. Schrantz, "New Federal Rule of Evidence 502: A Tool for Minimizing the Cost of Discovery," *Bloomberg Finance L.P.* (2009), retrieved on September 13, 2010 from <http://jenner.com/system/assets/publications/1929/original/Bloomberg_Greenwald_Stauffer_Schrantz.pdf?1314985571>, 1.

53. H. Christopher Boehning and Daniel J. Toal, "Federal E-Discovery: Broad Federal Court Powers Under Evidence Rule 502 (d)," *New York Law Journal: Technology Today*, Vol. 245, no. 64 (April 2, 2011), 1–2.

54. Wochna, "A Perfect Storm," 1.1–1.5.

55. Wochna, "A Perfect Storm," 1.5–1.17; see also *United States v. Albert Ganier*, Case No. 05-6350 (6th Cir. Ct. App.) November 15, 2006, and *Victor Stanley Inc. v. Creative Pipe, Inc., et al.*, Civil Action No. MJG-06-2662, D. Md. May 29, 2008. The *Ganier* court justified the requirement of expert testimony by explaining that configuring a keyword search requires an understanding of the uncertainties and the unusual shifts in the meaning of the language. The *Victor Stanley* court defended the expert witness stipulation by noting that the complicated process used in developing a keyword search requires an IT expert.

56. Mark S. Sidoti, Wendy R. Stein, and Verne A. Pedro, "Challenging 'Manual' ESI Collections," *The National Law Journal* (April 9, 2009), reprinted in *LTN Law Technology News*, retrieved on June 22, 2010 from <http://www.law.com/jsp/lawtechnologynews/PubArticleLTN.jsp?id=1202446756984&Challenging_Manual_ESI_Collections__>,; see also *Ford Motor Co. v. Edgewood Properties, Inc.* 257 F.R.D. 418 (D.N.J. 2009).

57. Rosenthal, "An Overview of the E-Discovery Rules Amendments," 2.

58. Ibid. 4.

59. Ibid.; Southerland, "Ignorance of IT Minutiae No Excuse for Litigators," S4–S5. See also: FRCP 26(f)(3), 34(b)(1)(C), 34(b)(2)(D) and 34(b)(2)(E).

60. Richard A. Schneider, Matthew S. Harman, and Robert B. Friedman (King & Spalding LLP), "The New Federal E-Discovery Rules: An Expository Narrative," *The Metropolitan Corporate Counsel* (2007) retrieved on April 2, 2008, from <http://www.metrocorpcounsel.com/articles/7974/new-federal-e-discovery-rules-expository-narrative>, 4.

61. Ibid.

62. "New Rule 502 Standardizes Law on Waiver, Seeks to Control Privilege Review Costs," *Faegre and Benson* (January 2009), retrieved on September 18, 2010 from <http://www.faegrebd.com/showarticle.aspx?Show=8607#x0003E>, 1–3.

63. Andrew Rhys Davies, "A Shield That Doesn't Protect: Courts Are Reluctant to Recognize the Deals Intended to Prevent Accidental Waiver of Privilege," *The National Law Journal* (July 17, 2006): S1; Jones, "E-Discovery Zero Hour Approaching," 10.

64. For a case upholding the clawback agreement under Federal Evidence Rule 502 see: *Board of Trustees, Sheet Metal Workers' National Pension Fund v. Palladium Equity Partners, Llc*, 722 F. Supp. 2d 845 (E.D. MI 2010). For the opposite ruling see: *Inhalation Plastics, Inc., v. Medex Cardio-Pulmonary, Inc.*, Civil Action No. 2:07-CV-116 (S.D. Ohio August 28, 2012).

65. Rhys Davies, "A Shield That Doesn't Protect," S1.

66. Ibid., S9 and S11; Southerland, "Ignorance of IT Minutiae No Excuse for Litigators," S4.

67. "New Rule 502 Standardizes Law on Waiver, Seeks to Control Privilege Review Costs," 1.

68. "Significant Changes to Federal Rules of Civil Procedure Will Protect Drafts of Experts from Discovery," *Duane Morris, LLP: Alerts and Updates* (2010), retrieved on August 29, 2013 from <http://www.duanemorris.com/alerts/FRCP_Rule_26_expert_witness_3735.html>.

69. Wochna, "A Perfect Storm," 1.1–1.17.

70. Rosenthal, "An Overview of the E-Discovery Rules Amendments," 5.

71. Ibid.; *Zubulake*, 24 and 30.

72. Wochna, "The Cutting Edge," 26.

73. Ibid.

74. Ibid.

CHAPTER 9 Depositions

CHAPTER OUTLINE

COMMENTARY

THE *FLANNIGAN* CASE

You are on your way to the conference room at your law firm to meet with your supervising attorney to review the facts in a case the firm will be handling. The client is a young man named Spencer Flannigan. Mr. Flannigan made a special trip from Rhode Island to Vermont to take advantage of the new state-of-the-art computerized diagnostic lab at the Lassiter Central Clinic of Vermont (LCCV). Unfortunately, Mr. Flannigan was injured during what should have been a routine diagnostic radiological procedure at the new lab. As a part of this diagnostic procedure, Dr. Bethany Randall, a radiologist and one of the defendants in the case, was scheduled to inject Mr. Flannigan with a contrast medium. A contrast medium is a dye that helps the radiologist visualize the patient's internal organs. The facts indicate that Mr. Flannigan had an allergic reaction to the contrast medium and almost expired in the Radiology Department at LCCV. At this point in the discovery process, a deposition has been planned for today. The person answering questions during the deposition will be Jonathan Harbinger, a certified radiologic technologist at LCCV. Harbinger is not a party to the action. Instead, he is a witness who was working in the LCCV Radiology Department at the time of the incident in question. Harbinger is expected to testify about certain irregularities in Dr. Randall's procedures on the day of Mr. Flannigan's test. Your supervising attorney asks you to organize the litigation file, summarize all previous discovery, and draft a deposition outline. The assignment is the beginning of your participation in taking an oral deposition.

OBJECTIVES

Chapter 8 introduced the discovery process. The deposition is an important discovery tool. After reading Chapter 9, you should be able to:

- define deposition.
- contrast the use of the traditional oral deposition with the use of the e-deposition.
- explain the amendments to the notice of intent to take an oral deposition.
- outline the responsibilities of the paralegal in preparing for an oral deposition.
- relate the duties a paralegal might perform during an oral deposition.
- discuss the paralegal's role in making transcript arrangements.
- explain the different types of deposition summaries.
- determine the advantages and disadvantages of taking a deposition upon written questions.

THE DEPOSITION

deposition
A deposition is an out-of-court question-and-answer session under oath, conducted as part of the discovery process before the trial is scheduled to begin.

A **deposition** is an out-of-court question-and-answer session under oath, conducted as part of the discovery process before the trial is scheduled to begin. It is one of the most important and widely used pretrial discovery tools. The use of depositions in federal court is regulated by Rules 27 through 32 of the Federal Rules of Civil Procedure. Under Rule 26 (d), depositions may not be taken before the meet-and-confer session authorized under Rule 26 (f). The purpose of the deposition is to uncover and explore all facts known by a party to the lawsuit or by a nonparty witness involved in the lawsuit. A party or nonparty witness who is questioned during a deposition is called a **deponent**. Under Rule 26 of the Federal Rules, the scope of testimony during discovery is much broader than the scope of testimony during trial. During a deposition the attorney is empowered to ask any question involving admissible evidence, and any question that could reasonably lead to the discovery of admissible evidence. The three types of depositions are the traditional oral deposition, the electronic or e-deposition, and the deposition upon written questions.

TRADITIONAL AND ELECTRONIC DEPOSITIONS

A **traditional oral deposition** involves the actual presence of the deponent who responds aloud to the questions asked by an attorney. A traditional oral deposition may be held in the attorney's office, at the courthouse, or at some other convenient location, such as a hotel room or a conference room often provided by one of the many legal support companies that specialize in assisting law firms in handling depositions. An **electronic deposition** (or **e-deposition**) is a deposition that is recorded by the use of a laptop, a smartphone, a tablet, a digital camcorder, or some other electronic device, thus allowing the participants involved in the deposition to be located at separate sites, often hundreds or even thousands of miles apart. Still, from a legal perspective, the e-deposition differs from the traditional oral deposition only in the means used to conduct and record the deposition. Of course, from a practical point of view, attorneys and paralegals must take additional steps to prepare for a successful e-deposition. Even so, whichever technique is used, Rule 30 of the Federal Rules of Civil Procedure regulates both traditional and e-depositions.

Traditional Oral Depositions

Rule 30 (d) (1) states that one deposition can take no more than a single day and a maximum of seven hours. The rule was written based on the assumption that the most cost-effective and time-efficient depositions are conducted at a single sitting—allowing, of course, for sensible, convenient breaks. The rule also permits the parties to make other arrangements on their own if, for whatever reason, that becomes preferable. Moreover, the rule recognizes that certain unexpected situations, such as emergency health problems, weather emergencies, terror attacks, or sudden power failures, might interrupt a deposition, thus requiring that it be continued on another day. Nothing in the rule prevents the court from shortening all the depositions in a particular case or the deposition of a specific witness if the judge determines that such measures are warranted. The court can also make changes in the single-day requirement if a change is appropriate in a given case.

Your supervising attorney may be involved in an oral deposition in one of two ways. First, he or she may ask questions of the opposing party or a nonparty witness. In this situation, your supervising attorney is said to be *taking the deposition* and can be referred to as the *deposition sponsor*. If, in contrast, your attorney's client is being questioned, then your supervising attorney will be present at the deposition to protect the best interests of that client. In this role, your supervising attorney is said to be *defending the deposition* and can also be identified as the *deposition defender*. Another individual who is generally present

deponent
An individual who responds to questions during a deposition.

traditional oral deposition
A deposition that involves the actual presence of the deponent who responds aloud to the questions asked by an attorney.

electronic deposition (e-deposition)
A deposition that is recorded by the use of a laptop, a smartphone, a tablet, or some other electronic device, thus allowing the participants involved in the deposition to be located at separate sites, often hundreds or even thousands of miles apart.

court reporter
An individual who records word for word the testimony of sworn witnesses in court or at depositions and who may be required to compose a written transcript of that testimony.

transcript
A typed, electronic, or word-processed copy of the testimony of a witness produced by a court reporter following the oral testimony of the witness at trial or at a deposition; an official record of the proceedings of a court.

electronic transcript (e-transcript)
An electronic transcript or an e-transcript is a word-for-word account of a proceeding that is handled electronically

at a deposition is the **court reporter** or *certified shorthand* reporter. The court reporter places the deponent under oath, takes a word-for-word account of the proceeding and, if required, produces a written or an electronic copy of the deposition. This copy of the deposition is called a **transcript**. When the transcript is handled electronically it is known as an **electronic transcript** or an **e-transcript**.

Under Rule 30 (b) (3) (A) the party taking a deposition may specify the means by which the deposition will be taken. The options available for taking a deposition stated in the rule include audio recording, audiovisual recording, and stenographic recording. Despite the antiquated and somewhat quaint language used in the rule, there is every reason to believe that any state-of-the art recording technique, including a digital recording, will meet the rule's requirements. These techniques would include smartphones, tablets, and any other e-device that might be in use now or in the near future. Regardless of the technique used to take the deposition, the party taking that deposition pays for the recording. One the other hand, Rule 30 (b) (3) (B) does permit a party, with prior notice, to designate another method of recording the deponent's testimony in addition to the method specified by the party taking the deposition. The supplemental recording is made at the expense of the party arranging for that additional method. Moreover, under Rule 26 (c) (1) (E), the court can grant a motion identifying the individuals who are permitted to be present during the deposition. To obtain an order excluding a person, the party or the person sitting for the deposition must file a motion with the court seeking the exclusion and stating that the movant attempted to resolve the exclusion issue before seeking the court's intervention.

Advantages of the Traditional Oral Deposition

One major advantage of the traditional oral deposition is that it gives the attorney taking the deposition the opportunity to see how well (or how poorly) a witness or the opposing party will perform on the witness stand. This insight may help the attorney determine how best to handle the party or witness should he or she actually testify at trial. For example, should the deponent appear unsure about certain aspects of the testimony, the attorney could be prepared to convince the jury at trial that the witness is unreliable. In contrast, an attorney defending a deposition can see how well the client reacts to questions under pressure. This knowledge will enable the attorney to help the client improve his or her performance when that client must testify in court.

For example, in the *Flannigan* case, your supervising attorney may elect to take the deposition of Dr. Randall. In her initial deposition, the doctor may try to explain some of her actions by saying that she did not feel well at the time of Mr. Flannigan's diagnostic test. If Dr. Randall changes her testimony at trial, your attorney can use these alterations to demonstrate to the jury that Dr. Randall's testimony is unreliable. Moreover, when the deponent is a party, a statement that he or she makes during the deposition can be taken as an admission if the statement contradicts what the deponent says during the trial. Also under Rule 801 (d) (1) (A) of the Federal Rules of Evidence, prior statements made by a witness during a deposition are not hearsay and can, therefore, be used to show the truth of the prior statement if that prior statement contradicts what the witness says at trial, just as long as the witness can be cross-examined.

Another advantage of a deposition is that it can be used to preserve the testimony of a witness who might be unavailable to testify at trial. In fact, historically, the preservation of evidence for trial was the primary motivation for permitting depositions to be used in the first place. However, today, under Rule 32 (a) (4), in order to permit the use of a deposition at trial, the court must be convinced that the witness is dead, ill, infirm, aged, imprisoned, out of the country, more than 100 miles away from the court, or has been unresponsive to a subpoena. As is often the case, an escape provision also permits the court to accept a deposition if an unusual situation makes the appearance of the witness at trial undesirable.

Disadvantages of the Traditional Oral Deposition

The primary disadvantages of traditional oral depositions are that they are expensive and time consuming. Frequently, such depositions must be taken at times and places that disrupt the regular office routine and that add costs to the bottom line. Moreover, from a planning and a strategic perspective, an oral deposition allows each attorney to gain insight into the other attorney's case and strategy. The oral deposition also allows deponents to rehearse their testimony before the trial. Unfortunately, such rehearsals often destroy spontaneity and damage the authenticity of the testimony.

Electronic Depositions

A wide variety of electronic recording devices and procedures are now available to attorneys that were not available to their counterparts in days gone by. Presently, one of the most widely used electronic recording devices is the digital camcorder. However, today most laptops, smartphones, and tablets permit participation in real-time streaming video depositions. Attorneys taking depositions can use such recorders as a part of their tactical package before trial. Certainly, your supervising attorney should record the testimony of all vital witnesses if those witnesses might be absent at the time of trial because of severe illness, impending death, or the possibility of an extensive absence from the jurisdiction, as might occur, for example, in time of war when the deponent is a member of the armed forces, the diplomatic corps, the intelligence community, the Red Cross, a private paramilitary or security organization, or the international news media. Although a copy of the deposition can be read into the record at trial, the recording of the deponent often has a more dramatic effect, provided the recording process is handled effectively.

Attorneys are also becoming more comfortable with training and rehearsal opportunities offered by electronic recording and communication devices. For instance, an attorney can now purchase prepackaged DVDs that show deponents how to be effective witnesses. The prepackaged DVDs can help deponents prepare for their own depositions by giving them tips and explaining how to act during a deposition. Moreover, many of these packages can be bought and viewed directly online without having to bother with the purchase of a DVD. Attorneys defending depositions can use digital recorders and a wide range of additional electronic devices to record their own clients during deposition rehearsals. The clients can then play back their testimony, watch their own performance, and then make appropriate adjustments during the actual deposition or during their testimony at trial.

As noted above, Rule 30 (b) (4) of the Federal Rules of Civil Procedure now includes a provision not only for telephone depositions but also for depositions conducted by any "other remote means." Most courts recognize that this provision indicates that the deposition can be carried out by any electronic device available to the participants. Thus, electronic depositions can be carried on from laptop to laptop, cell phone to cell phone, and so on. In addition, most smartphone users have equipped their devices with apps that permit live simultaneous video phoning, regardless of whether the other party is using a laptop, smartphone, or tablet, or some other device.

Advantages of the Electronic Deposition

The electronic deposition is very popular because it saves time and money by reducing or eliminating the travel involved in a traditional oral deposition, which requires the physical presence of all the participants in the same location. Electronic depositions can be supplemented by an e-transcript that is synchronized with video imagery. The e-deposition can also be augmented by a chat room, permitting those who are watching the deposition to "talk" in private to the attorney asking the questions. Moreover, the messages can be saved for later access. When the e-deposition has been completed, the e-transcript remains online and available to everyone involved in the case. While e-depositions are vulnerable to electronic interruptions and unauthorized listeners who might hack into the transmission of the session, electronic depositions are still cost-effective, especially if the deposition is time sensitive, if the deponent is located at a great distance, or if it is necessary to depose several different experts in a single case because of the technical, scientific, or medical complexities of that case.

Disadvantages of the Electronic Deposition

The main downside of an e-deposition is that it can be difficult to evaluate the appearance and the demeanor of the deponent because of electronic distortion and time delays that often occur during such communication sessions. Moreover, as noted previously, there is also the possibility of electronic difficulties or of unauthorized listeners hacking into the transmission during the deposition. Even so, the technique is useful when the deponent lives outside the jurisdiction, is a minor witness, or will be asked only a few questions. During this type of deposition, the deponent and the questioning attorney may be at two locations. The court reporter who records the deposition is permitted to be with the deponent being questioned or with the questioning attorney.

While Rule 30 of the Federal Rules clearly permits the use of any "other remote means" in federal court, the same is not necessarily true for all state courts. As we have seen, some states have not yet amended their rules to deal with the basics of e-discovery, let alone permitted electronic depositions as a matter of course. For this reason, your supervising attorney must make certain your state rules permit such depositions. Moreover, in those jurisdictions where the use of e-depositions is relatively new, your supervising attorney should also double check with the judge or the clerk to determine the accepted procedure for administering a proper oath to the witness.

Another disadvantage if the e-deposition is that it requires extra preparation by both the attorney and the paralegal. For instance, before beginning the e-deposition someone must check to make certain that everyone is present at both ends of the connection, and that the witness, the attorneys, and the court reporter can hear and be heard properly. It is also advisable to conduct a trial run to make sure that all the equipment is operating correctly and that the deposition is actually being recorded. At this time, all modifications must be made to make certain that the equipment is producing a high quality recording. When the deposition opens, the attorney taking the deposition must name all of the participants in the deposition and must identify all pertinent aspects of the case and of the deposition itself, including such key details as the date, the time, the parties, the docket number, the location of all participants, and the location of the court reporter. This same information should also be repeated at the end of the recording, just to make certain that none of the information is lost. At the opening, the attorney taking the deposition should also make absolutely certain that every participant knows about and agrees to both the taping and the preservation of the testimony.[1] The attorneys and the court reporter then carry on the question-and-answer period just as if the deposition were being conducted according to the traditional oral format.

THE PARALEGAL'S ROLE BEFORE THE ORAL DEPOSITION

As noted above, you will likely be required to assist your supervising attorney in preparation of both traditional and electronic depositions. Because you will be handling the procedural details of the deposition, the attorney will be free to concentrate on developing the substantive legal issues to be explored during the deposition. In the preparation for a deposition, you may be asked to handle the notice and subpoena requirements. You may also be asked to prepare questions.

Amendments to the Notice Requirements

Professional courtesy dictates that the attorney taking the deposition (AKA the deposition sponsor) should contact the defending attorney (AKA the deposition defender) to schedule mutually acceptable dates and times for taking the depositions of the defending attorney's clients. This requirement is necessary regardless of whether the deposition will be conducted in a traditional or an electronic format. Sometimes securing a mutually acceptable date is a difficult process. Also, at times, obtaining an agreement on the format for the deposition is also problematic. Because of their different strategic concerns in planning their cases, the two attorneys may have conflicting preferences as to which attorney should take depositions first, where they should be taken, and what format should be utilized. Such conflicting strategic concerns are usually resolved by the attorneys themselves through friendly compromise.

The party or witness may also resist the prospect of having to sit for a deposition, either because he or she is apprehensive about the process itself or because he or she sees the deposition as providing assistance to the opposition. The potential deponent may feel that the deposition is an inconvenient and unnecessary burden that infringes on work, leisure, or family time. In such cases, the defending attorney must allay the apprehensions of the client. Nevertheless, the attorney taking the deposition should be flexible in scheduling a date and a time that is convenient for the party or the witness.

The Federal Rules and the rules of many other jurisdictions require that formal notice of a deposition be given to the deponent and to each party. The length of time between the date that notice is required and the date of the deposition will be determined by the

notice of intent to take oral deposition
A notice spelling out the date, time, and place of a planned deposition. The notice will also indicate the name and address of the intended deponent as well as the identity of the attorney who will ask the questions during the deposition.

subpoena
A written order issued by a court or an administrative agency commanding the presence of a person in order for that person to give testimony in an official proceeding. The word *subpoena* is an abbreviated form of the Latin term *subpoena ad testificandum.*

jurisdiction in which the case is being heard. The Federal Rules of Civil Procedure have been amended to ensure that the rules of discovery are coordinated with the time-counting technique set up by Federal Rule 6. Under the amended rule, all days, including Saturdays, Sundays, and legal holidays, must be included in any count used to calculate a time limit. To make sure that most time limits end on a weekday, discovery time periods have been altered to include only multiples of seven. For example, Federal Rule 27 (a) (2), which covers notice and service for deposition hearings, extends the time limit from 20 to 21 days before the hearing date.

Similarly, Federal Rule 32 (a) (5) alters the time period that protects people who challenge a deposition itself or who protest the location of the deposition. This time limit was changed from 11 to 14 days. The rule now states, "A deposition must not be used against a party who, having received less than 14 days' notice of the deposition, promptly moved for a protective order under Rule 26 (c) (1) (B) requesting that it not be taken or be taken at a different time or place—and this motion was still pending when the deposition was taken." Finally, Rule 32 (d) (3) (C) has been altered to extend the time limit for objections to written questions from five to seven days.

Once an agreement on the deposition date has been reached, you may be asked to arrange for preparation and service of a **notice of intent to take oral deposition** (see Exhibit 9-1). This notice sets out the date, the time, the name and address of the person whose deposition is to be taken, and the means by which the testimony is to be recorded. Under Rule 30 (b) (3) of the Federal Rules, the means of recording can include any of the electronic techniques previously mentioned. Thus, the notice must indicate if the deposition is to be a traditional oral deposition or an electronic deposition. Rule 30 (b) (3) also makes it clear that the party taking an e-deposition is responsible for bearing the cost of any e-discovery technique used.

Documents may also be obtained from a party to the litigation by serving a request for that party to bring those documents to the deposition. Rule 30 (b) (2) of the Federal Rules of Civil Procedure allows for this process. However, the procedures of Rule 34, on production of documents, must also be followed whenever this is done. Thus, the specific documents or the categories of documents to be produced must be included in the deposition notice of attachment. For example, in the *Flannigan* case, your supervising attorney will want to see Mr. Flannigan's medical chart, his admission record, the pharmacy's record, any report filed by personnel in the LCCV Radiology Department, and all incident reports filed by clinic personnel. In preparing a notice of deposition for Dr. Randall, you might ask her to produce all documents related to the case to which she has access.

A request for records and documents at the time of a deposition is not, however, always the best way to handle discovery. If an attorney must wait to see the requested documents until the deposition, he may have to spend precious time reviewing the documents as the deposition proceeds. Moreover, subsequent examination of the documents often reveals information about which the deponent should have been questioned. This problem may necessitate the scheduling of another deposition.

Subpoena Requirement

When the attorney taking the deposition is requesting a nonparty witness to testify, securing the deponent's presence will be necessary. The legal means for securing the presence of such a witness is a subpoena. A **subpoena** is an official document issued by the clerk

EXHIBIT 9-1 Notice of Intent to Take Oral Deposition

UNITED STATES DISTRICT COURT FOR THE DISTRICT OF VERMONT

Spencer Flannigan,	)
	) Case No. 16-2248
Plaintiff,	)
	) NOTICE OF INTENT TO TAKE
	) ORAL DEPOSITION
v.	)
Lassiter Central Clinic of Vermont, et al.,	)
	)
	)
Defendants.	)
	)
	)
	)

To: Perry Kemelman, Attorney for Defendant,

PLEASE TAKE NOTICE that pursuant to Rule 30 of the Federal Rules of Civil Procedure, Robert Henderson will take the oral deposition of Jonathan Harbinger before a notary public on January 9, 2017, at 1 p.m. and thereafter from day to day until completed, at the law offices of Hysell, Hodges, and Henderson 361 Slate Avenue, Southfield, Vermont 80664.

Testimony will be recorded by stenograph and videotape.

Respectfully submitted,

_____

Robert Henderson
Attorney for Plaintiff

CERTIFICATE OF SERVICE

I hereby certify that a true and correct copy of the foregoing Notice of Intent to take Oral Deposition has been furnished to counsel of record on this the first day of December, 2016.

_____

of court commanding a person to be present at a deposition. To obtain a subpoena for a deponent in a federal lawsuit, you must provide a copy of the notice to take deposition to the clerk in the district where the deposition is to be taken. In state court, the state rules of civil procedures must be checked to determine who may serve a subpoena. In most states, a subpoena may be served by a sheriff, a bailiff, or any person who is not a party and who is 18 years of age or older. Your attorney may even request that you serve the subpoena.

subpoena duces tecum
A written order issued by a court or an administrative agency commanding the presence of a person in order for that person to give testimony and to surrender the evidence that is enumerated in the subpoena. Generally, such evidence takes the form of documents, records, letters, memos, and so on.

In addition to the court costs incurred for a subpoena, the deponent may also have to be reimbursed for his or her attendance at the deposition. For example, the witness may be entitled to reimbursement for mileage and meals. These costs would be in addition to the mandatory witness reimbursement fee provided by many states. Prior to obtaining the subpoena, check with the clerk of court to determine all of the fees involved in the process. Make certain that a check in the correct amount is furnished to the clerk issuing the subpoena. A nonparty witness can be subpoenaed to produce documents at his deposition according to Rules 30 and 45 of the Federal Rules of Civil Procedure. This can be accomplished by serving the nonparty witness with a **subpoena *duces tecum***. The subpoena *duces tecum* will contain a specific listing of the documents that the nonparty witness must produce at his deposition.

For example, in the *Flannigan* case, your supervising attorney may want Harbinger to produce all documents related to the case to which he has access. He might also ask him to produce a copy of the Lassiter Central Clinic's policy and procedure manual and any memos, notices, e-mails, pdf's, or other additional electronic attachments that explain and describe those procedures that are to be used in the LCCV Radiology Department. Records of any in-service training, continuing education courses, webinars, other online or distance classes or workshops, and any additional postgraduate work on the subject would also be helpful in this case.

Recent Amendments to Rule 45 Subpoena

Several of the consequences that have developed from the proliferation of ESI in litigation are found in the amendments to Rule 45, which covers subpoena practice in the federal courts. One of the interesting things about Rule 45 is that it repeats just about every other amendment that has been added to the rules in relation to ESI and applies those amendments to the practice of issuing a subpoena. Thus, in one sense, a study of Rule 45 constitutes a review of the ESI amendments to the other rules. For instance, as is true of Rules 33 and 34, Rule 45 (a) (1) (C) adds ESI to the list of evidence that can be requested by a subpoena. Similarly, Rule 45 (a) (1) (D) states that ESI can be copied, tested, sampled, or inspected. As is true of other new amendments, Rule 45 also asserts that the subpoena can indicate the format in which ESI is to be transmitted by the witness who is subject to that subpoena.

Moreover, Rule 45 (d) (1) (B) notes that whenever the format is not specified, then the ESI is to be produced in the format in which the ESI is usually kept or in some other reasonable format. Rule 45 (d) (1) (C) assures the witness that identical ESI does not have to be transmitted in more than one format. Rule 45 (d) (1) (D) makes it clear that the witness will not be compelled to produce ESI if the production of such evidence creates an undue burden or an unreasonable cost. In addition, the same section of Rule 45 specifies that the parties producing the evidence have the burden of demonstrating the extra cost or the unreasonable burden, and that, even if they meet that burden, the court may still order the production of that evidence, if there is no other way to obtain that evidence and it is necessary to the development of a party's case. Finally, Rule 45 (d) (2) makes provisions for the protection of privileged evidence.

Preparation for the Deposition

Once the deposition has been scheduled and notice has been given to the potential deponent, preparation for the deposition begins. The nature of the preparation process depends on whether your supervising attorney will be taking or defending the deposition and whether the deposition will be a traditional or an e-deposition. If your supervising attorney is taking the deposition, he or she will prepare to question the opposing party or a non-party witness. If he or she is defending the deposition, he or she will prepare his or her own client to answer questions posed by the opposing attorney.

Preparation for Taking the Deposition

If your attorney is preparing to take a deposition, you must perform a variety of tasks designed not only to gather background information, but also to plan the actual deposition. In gathering background information, you will be required to review documents related to the deponent, to develop a history of events as they involve the deponent, and to summarize prior discovery pertaining to the deponent. In planning the deposition, you may be called upon to prepare a deposition outline and to plan the questions that your attorney will ask the deponent. During this step you may also be asked to prepare any exhibits that may be used during the deposition.

For example, in this chapter's *Flannigan* case, you might be asked to compile Mr. Flannigan's statements, medical bills, and medical history prior to Harbinger's deposition. You may also be asked to arrange for the hiring of a court reporter to place the deponent under oath, to record the question-and-answer session, and to provide the necessary transcripts. If the deposition is to be recorded, you may be asked to set up and test the recording equipment before the session. If the deposition is to be part of a videoconference, the paralegal may assist in setting up the needed equipment.

The site of the deposition will also have to be arranged. In determining how far a deponent can be required to travel to a deposition, Rule 45 of the Federal Rules of Civil Procedure must be consulted. This rule states that, if a person who is not a party or an officer of a party has been issued a subpoena to appear for a deposition that is to be held more than 100 miles from the person's residence, place of employment, or place of transacting business, that person may file a motion with the court to quash or modify the subpoena. On the other hand, if the party who arranged the deposition can convince the court of the substantial need for the deponent's testimony or that material cannot be otherwise obtained without undue hardship, the court may require the deponent to travel more than 100 miles provided that the deponent is reasonably compensated for the inconvenience. (See Chapter 2 for a discussion of the place of the district courts in the structure of the federal court system.)

Residents of the district can be subpoenaed to appear at a deposition in the county where they reside, work, or transact business. The rule, however, does allow the court to choose another location that would be convenient to the deponent. A resident of another federal court district can be required to attend a deposition in the county where he or she is subpoenaed. Again, the rule allows the court to set some other convenient location. As far as the actual physical setting of the deposition, there are no rules. The deposition may be held at the attorney's office, at the courthouse, or at some neutral site, such as a hotel meeting room or a conference room provided by one of the many support firms that specialize in helping attorneys conduct both traditional and electronic depositions.

As noted previously, electronic depositions also take a few extra but essential preparation steps. These steps begin on the day of the e-deposition and include checking

overbroad
A request made during discovery that is so wide-ranging and inclusive that it asks for more evidence than could ever be useful to the other party in the lawsuit.

duplicative
A request made during discovery that replicates a request that was made at some previous time during the lawsuit.

to make certain that everyone is present at both ends of the connection, verifying that everyone in attendance can hear and be heard, ensuring that the equipment is operating correctly, and confirming that the deposition is actually being recorded. It is often helpful for you to conduct a test run to accomplish these tasks. As the deposition begins, you might want to remind your supervising attorney to name all of the participants in the deposition and to disclose all noteworthy aspects of the case, including date, time, parties, docket number, location of all participants, and location of the court reporter. If necessary, you might also remind your supervising attorney to make certain that everyone involved in the e-deposition agrees to taping and preserving the testimony.[2]

Preparation for Defending the Deposition   Should your client be asked to appear for a deposition, you may want to consult with your supervising attorney to determine whether any preliminary objections should be raised. For example, if your client has been asked to bring documents, records, letters, memos, ESI, or any other form of physical evidence to the deposition, your attorney may, depending on the circumstances, decide that certain objections are in order. As noted in Chapter 8, such objections can be based on the attorney–client privilege, the work product privilege, the common interest privilege, the Fifth Amendment privilege against self-incrimination, the medical privilege, or the confessor-penitent privilege.

A party or a nonparty witness who is asked to produce documents at the deposition may also object on the grounds that the request is **overbroad**. Such an objection claims that the request seeks more information than could ever be useful to the other party in the lawsuit. Another additional objection that can be raised is that the request is **duplicative**. This objection means that the other party has asked for the same information a number of different times in a number of different ways.

Once the preliminary discussion concerning objections is complete, you will need to prepare the client for the deposition. This preparation will require an initial conference with the client. At the conference, your supervising attorney explains the deposition process to the client and reviews anticipated areas of questioning. Usually such a conference should be scheduled prior to the day of the deposition. Such an early meeting will give the attorney time to react should the client be unable to produce a needed document or the required ESI, or should the client's planned testimony appear to contradict the testimony of a party or another witness. If your supervising attorney prefers extensive deposition planning, he or she may want to prepare an outline predicting the strategy of the opponent. You may be called upon to write a plan that anticipates the opposing attorney's questions. You may also be asked to organize any documents the witness has been asked to produce.

Often the preparation of the deponent must go beyond simply determining the subject matter of the question-and-answer period. Sometimes the witness must be coached on how to act during the deposition. For example, it may be necessary to help the deponent develop his technique by being encouraged to restate all questions, to answer questions carefully, and to ask for the clarification of ambiguous or puzzling questions. This advice should be heeded especially if the opposing attorney is asking deliberately misleading or intentionally confusing questions, or if that attorney is soliciting irrelevant or unnecessary information, which can often happen in such depositions. Deponents should also be cautioned never to volunteer any information not specifically sought by the interrogator.

Also remind the deponent to observe the 5 C's of good testimony. First, the deponent should appear *confident* as he or she answers the questions. Second, the deponent should answer all questions in a *clear* and *convincing* way. Next, each deponent can ensure accuracy by making certain that all answers are *correct*. Finally, all deponents can guarantee authenticity by answering in a *candid* and genuine way. Sometimes it is necessary to deal with an anxious or fearful deponent. Often, having the deponent view a DVD or a downloaded version of another deposition will allay his or her anxiety. Such DVDs and downloaded deposition models can reassure the deponent that the deposition procedure is an ordinary, uncomplicated process that happens on a routine basis in such lawsuits.

In the case of an electronic deposition, you may also need to counsel the deponent on certain details that are unique to an electronic setup. For example, while dress is important in any deposition, and while the deponent always needs to be advised about what to wear to make a good impression, the electronic deposition adds additional concerns peculiar to that format. For instance, generally dark clothing works best in broadcast situations, whereas gray sport coats, pinstripe suits, polka dot dresses, and loud patterned, plaid or flowered shirts, ties, skirts, blouses, and scarves do not. Similarly, when the deponent plans to use a set of visuals as evidence to supplement his or her oral testimony, you will have to determine just how well the images are transmitted to the other end of the setup. You should also make certain that distracting objects such as water glasses, coffee cups, soda bottles, paper files, keys, pens and pencils, good luck charms, and open law books are removed from within camera range. The backdrop behind the deponent should also be free of visual distractions. Annoying movement caused by swivel chairs and recliners, or irritating noises coming through an open window, from the office next door, from the hallway, or from the witness's own jewelry must also be eliminated, and so on.[3]

In addition, many attorneys today conduct mock depositions. A **mock deposition** is a practice session designed to help the party or witness prepare for the questioning process. Such a preparation session helps a client or witness to know what to expect when his or her deposition is taken. This rehearsal not only relaxes the client but also helps him or her recall the events about which he or she will be questioned in the real deposition. In the mock deposition, the client will be questioned by your supervising attorney or by another attorney in the firm. The format of the mock deposition should closely follow that of an actual deposition. You may be asked to evaluate the effectiveness of the client during the mock deposition. In such an evaluation, the following questions should be considered: Is the client believable? Does the client answer questions completely? Does the client volunteer information not called for in the question? Many law firms provide a checklist for potential deponents that explains the procedure and outlines pitfalls to avoid. See the checklist in Exhibit 9-2.

mock deposition

A practice session that attempts to duplicate the question-and-answer period that will occur during a real deposition. The objective of a mock deposition is to help the party or witness rehearse for an upcoming deposition.

EXHIBIT 9-2 Witness Checklist for Deposition Testimony

1. Dress neatly but conservatively.
2. Listen to the question carefully. Take your time in answering.
3. Answer each question aloud. Avoid head nodding and shaking.
4. Answer the question asked, not the question you wish had been asked.
5. Do not volunteer information.
6. Be courteous, but not overly friendly.
7. Do not be argumentative. Do not lose your temper.
8. Do not interrupt the attorney's question.
9. If you do not understand the question, ask that it be repeated or explained.
10. Listen carefully to any rephrasing of your answer. Correct any inaccurate rephrasing.
11. If you need to review a document to answer a question, request permission to do so.
12. If you do not know the answer to the question, say so. Do not guess or estimate. "I don't recall" is an acceptable answer.
13. Do not look at your attorney for help in answering a question.
14. Do not be distracted by objections made by your attorney.
15. If your attorney advises you not to answer a question, follow that advice.

THE PARALEGAL'S ROLE DURING THE ORAL DEPOSITION

Notice of the deposition has been given, and preparation for the deposition is complete. Deposition time has arrived. Your job at the deposition will vary, based on your experience, the complexity of the case, and the attorney's division of responsibilities. Your duties will also vary depending on whether your supervising attorney is taking or defending the deposition. In either case, you will most likely be asked to take notes and evaluate the witness. However, the focus of the note-taking and evaluating will depend on whether your supervising attorney is taking or defending the deposition. You may also be called upon to control or produce documents and exhibits, depending upon your attorney's role in the deposition.

Note-Taking

One of the most critical functions at the deposition is taking notes. Your note-taking will free your supervising attorney to concentrate on the questions and the topics covered. If your supervising attorney is taking the deposition, follow the deposition outline to make certain all questions are asked. Also, make certain the deponent answers each question. Use your notes to call incomplete or inconsistent answers to your supervising attorney's attention. If your supervising attorney is defending the deposition, chart what facts the other attorney tends to focus on as he or she questions your client. Moreover, try to determine whether the attorney's questioning pattern reveals his or her legal strategy in the case. Also, remember that the attorney is allowed to object to any question that he or she feels violates one of the privileges or principles discussed earlier in this chapter and in Chapter 8. Make certain that you accurately document these objections.

Witness Evaluation

You may be asked to assist in evaluating the effectiveness of a witness. If your supervising attorney is taking the deposition, look for weaknesses in the deponent's testimony. The following questions should be addressed:

1. Has the deponent contradicted himself or herself?
2. Has the testimony by the deponent contradicted the testimony of other witnesses?
3. Does the deponent's testimony seem incomplete or vague?
4. Does the deponent seem hesitant, nervous, or secretive about aspects of his or her testimony?
5. How often does the deponent refer to notes or documents to answer questions?
6. Is the deponent intimidated or rattled by your attorney?
7. How often does the deponent say that he does not remember certain facts?
8. How accurate, authentic, and convincing are the visual aids used by the deponent?
9. How often does the deponent seem distracted or confused about his or her testimony?
10. Does the deponent tire easily, requiring multiple breaks during the deposition?

Your evaluation will help the attorney determine how to use the deponent's testimony and how to treat the deponent should he or she be called to testify at trial. For example, in the *Flannigan* case, your observations might reveal that Mr. Harbinger's description of the events surrounding Mr. Flannigan's examination differs in minor but significant ways from the account given by Dr. Randall. This information will help your attorney prepare for the examination of both Mr. Harbinger and Dr. Randall at trial.

If your supervising attorney is defending the deposition, your evaluation will be aimed at helping the witness improve his testimony. In this situation, the following questions should always be addressed:

1. Is the deponent *confident*, *clear*, *convincing*, *correct*, and *candid*? (Remember the 5 C's?)
2. Does the deponent take his or her time answering questions?
3. Does the deponent volunteer information unnecessarily?
4. Is the deponent argumentative or overly friendly?
5. Does the deponent answer questions aloud, or does he rely on nodding and shaking?
6. Are the visual aids used by the deponent visible, readable, and understandable?
7. Is the deponent's present testimony consistent with his or her past testimony?
8. Is the deponent's testimony consistent with the testimony of other witnesses?
9. Does the deponent seem to misapprehend the limits of the privileges that apply to him or her?
10. Does the deponent seem glib or overly serious in his or her attitude toward the process?

Your evaluation will help your supervising attorney review his or her client's testimony as he or she plans the strategy that will be used at trial. In this chapter's *Flannigan* case, for instance, your evaluation of Mr. Flannigan's deposition might help your supervising attorney decide that the client must conduct a detailed and thorough review of the deposition before the trial to prevent any contradictions on the witness stand.

THE PARALEGAL'S ROLE AFTER THE ORAL DEPOSITION

Your responsibilities in the deposition do not end with the final question. Post-deposition tasks include assuming responsibility for the transcript and for the preparation of a deposition summary. These tasks will require that you familiarize yourself with the various types of deposition summaries that are available. If problems arise, the paralegal may also be involved in drafting and defending motions.

Transcript Arrangements

Both the attorney taking the deposition and the attorney defending the deposition may need to see a transcript. To obtain copies of the transcript, you must contact the court reporter to find out when the transcript will be ready. Many reporters will provide a copy of the deposition on a disc or a flash drive that facilitates summaries or even allows for the use of deposition-summary software. Naturally, whether the reporter provides you with a disc, flash drive, or a paper copy of the deposition, you will be charged for the service. The reporter might also e-mail the deposition transcript to you as an attachment. Rarely will you be charged for such a routine courtesy. However, if your supervising attorney needs to see a copy immediately, the court reporter will probably charge an additional fee for having to speed up the process. You must also arrange for the appropriate number of copies, handle billing for the court reporter's services, and secure an appropriate date and place for delivery.

When you receive the deposition from the court reporter, make copies and distribute them to your supervising attorney and to anyone your attorney has identified as a proper recipient. The deposition should be reviewed for errors or significant omissions before it is summarized. This process will move more quickly if you compare the transcript with your deposition notes. You should also check the spelling of all unusual legal, technical, scientific, and medical terms, as well as the names of all the parties, witnesses, and attorneys involved in the process. The procedure for review of the deposition and signature by the deponent has been simplified by an amendment to Rule 30 of the Federal Rules of Civil Procedure. The review and the signature are required only if they are requested by the deponent or a party before the deposition has been concluded. The deponent has 30 days to sign and make any changes to the transcript after notice that the transcript or recording is available.

It is important to recall that e-depositions can be supplemented by an e-transcript that is synchronized with the video imagery on the computer screen. Moreover, after completion of the e-deposition, the e-transcript is preserved online and is thus accessible to anyone authorized to read it. In addition, both types of e-depositions are enhanced by a chat room feature that authorizes those observing the e-deposition to "speak" to the attorney asking the questions. Significantly, the chat room messages, like the e-transcript, can be saved for later access. None of this necessarily eliminates the need for a paper transcript of the e-deposition. In fact, it is wise to remember that some people still do not comprehend the text of an e-document completely until they read it on paper. Consequently, it is unwise to place too much faith in e-copies of e-depositions, at least to the exclusion of paper copies of such documents. Moreover, it may be necessary to have paper copies of e-depositions available at the time of the trial. Rule 30 (f) (1) requires that depositions be sent to the attorney who set up the deposition in the first place but does not require a filing with the court. This change was made to parallel Rule 5 (d) of the Federal Rules of Civil Procedure, which expressly forbids the filing of depositions until such time as the deposition is actually used in the proceeding or until the court orders that the filing take place.

The Deposition Summary

The **deposition summary** is a written abridgement of a deposition that condenses the question-and-answer period down to a concisely written, understandable account. A properly written deposition summary can organize selected topics or subject matter into an orderly arrangement. Once the testimony has been arranged in the deposition summary according to a particular plan, inconsistent and unreliable testimony may become evident. A well-drawn summary could also point out missing pieces of evidence that might lead your attorney to conduct further discovery.

Presummary Considerations   Before writing your deposition summary, determine when your supervising attorney needs it. Determine the format to be used, the amount of detail required, and the issues or testimony the attorney wants pinpointed. Find out whether the attorney prefers a paraphrased summary or one that includes direct quotes from the deponent. Also, make certain you know whether the attorney wants you to write in phrases or complete sentences. Finally, determine which type of deposition summary the attorney wants you to use.

Types of Deposition Summaries   Basically, you have three types of deposition summaries from which to choose: the page-line deposition summary, the topical deposition summary, and the chronological deposition summary. The **page-line deposition summary** records the information in the order in which it was actually presented during the deposition process (see Exhibit 9-3). Such a summary is helpful when the attorney

deposition summary
A written abridgement of a deposition that condenses the question-and-answer period to a concisely written, understandable account.

page-line deposition summary
A written abridgement of a deposition that records the information produced by the deposition in the order in which it was actually presented during the deposition process.

EXHIBIT 9-3 Page-Line Deposition Summary

PAGE-LINE DEPOSITION SUMMARY			
Page	Line	Topic	Summary
7	9	Test	Patient Flannigan was scheduled for an intravenous polygram.
16	1–14	Antidote	The antidote had to be retrieved from the pharmacy.

AUTOMATED LITIGATION SUPPORT

Full Text Searching

SCENARIO

It is the day of the Flannigan trial. Dr. Randall has just been examined by Perry Kemelman, the attorney for Lassiter Central Clinic of Vermont (LCCV). Dr. Randall has testified that on the day of the Flannigan examination she had eight hours of sleep prior to the session and was in perfect health. Your supervising attorney recalls that at some time during Dr. Randall's deposition, she said that she had just finished an eight-hour shift when she was called back to LCCV to cover the second shift because the physician scheduled for that shift had been involved in an accident. Your attorney also recalls that at another point in the deposition, Dr. Randall had tried to explain some of her behavior by saying that she felt "flu-like symptoms accompanied by some dizziness." Unfortunately, your supervising attorney cannot recall exactly where in the deposition these remarks were made. Your supervising attorney is granted a half-hour recess before beginning the cross-examination of Dr. Randall.

PROBLEM

Your attorney wants you to locate the discrepancies in Dr. Randall's deposition. You have less than 30 minutes to search through a 157-page deposition. Conventional techniques prove useless. Your chronological summary provides no help. Paging through the deposition is too time consuming. The clock is ticking. Precious seconds are being lost. What can you do to save your client's case?

SOLUTION

One of the features of litigation support software described in a prior chapter is the ability to conduct a full-text search of depositions and other documents.

The program works like this: At the deposition, the court reporter transcribes verbatim the testimony of the witness. The court reporter gives the transcript to the attorneys on a disc. The disc is then loaded into the litigation software. Recent developments in software for court reporters allow the court reporter and attorney to link their computers so that the court reporter's transcript is immediately fed into the attorney's computer. The attorney has an instantaneous record of the oral proceedings. New enhancements to litigation support software incorporate this feature so that it is not even necessary to obtain a copy of the transcript on disc (assuming that the computers for the court reporter and attorney are adequately equipped).

Once the transcript is loaded into the litigation support software, you can search the deposition for key words or phrases and locate any references by Dr. Randall as to her physical condition. This is only one way in which this software can be used in connection with depositions. Software, such as the popular summation programs, allows you to annotate or make notes to the transcript (printing these notes allows you to summarize the deposition electronically), to create and search databases of evidentiary documents, to search transcripts and document databases simultaneously (if a document is referred to in a deposition, it can be called up immediately and viewed), to perform searches of transcripts and document databases by date or by issue to create a case profile, and to print numerous reports. Some software will allow you to integrate and search recorded depositions. The features of this type of software, as well as the number of different products, are continually developing.

---

topical deposition summary
A written abridgement of a deposition that records the information produced by the deposition according to certain designated topics.

is uncertain about just how to use the deponent's testimony. The page-line summary allows the attorney to review the testimony quickly and to focus on areas that he wants to explore further. The **topical deposition summary** records the information produced by the deposition according to certain designated topics (see Exhibit 9-4). Such a deposition is useful when the attorney knows what areas he needs to concentrate on in planning his legal strategy. Finally, the **chronological deposition summary** records the information produced by the deposition based on a specified temporal sequence (see Exhibit 9-5). Such a summary is needed when the chronology of events is of critical importance to the case.

EXHIBIT 9-4 Topical Deposition Summary

Topic	Page	Summary
TOPICAL DEPOSITION SUMMARY		
Education	2	He received an associate's degree from Providence County Community College (PTriC).
Employment Experience	2	Harbinger was employed by Lassiter Central Clinic of Vermont 6/5/12 as a radiologic technologist.
Certification	2	He became a certified radiologic technologist in 2013.
Patient's Chart	11	Mercer identifies contents of Flannigan's chart.
Patient's Condition	16	Flannigan suffers cardiac arrest.

Copyright © 2015 Cengage Learning®

EXHIBIT 9-5 Chronological Deposition Summary

Date	Event	Page
CHRONOLOGICAL DEPOSITION SUMMARY		
2012	Graduated from PTriC	1
2012	Employed at LCCV	3
2013	Certified as R.T.	2

Copyright © 2015 Cengage Learning®

The type of summary that you use in a case will depend not only on the facts involved but also on the legal issues that your supervising attorney wants to emphasize. For instance, in the *Flannigan* case, your attorney may be primarily interested in demonstrating that Dr. Randall was negligent in the procedure that she followed in administering the contrast medium. Therefore, your supervising attorney would be interested in tracing the steps followed by Dr. Randall. In such a case, the chronological summary would be most helpful.

THE DEPOSITION UPON WRITTEN QUESTIONS

A **deposition upon written questions** is a deposition before a court reporter that consists of oral responses by the deponent to written questions. Although the deponent is physically present at this type of deposition, the attorney who prepared the questions is not. Instead, he or she has submitted the written questions prior to the deposition. Rule 31 of the Federal Rules of Civil Procedure regulates the use of this type of deposition. Rule 31

chronological deposition summary
A written abridgement of a deposition that records the information produced by the deposition based on a specified temporal sequence.

deposition upon written questions
A deposition before a court reporter that consists of oral responses by the deponent to written questions.

incorporates the Rule 30 amendment limit on number of depositions, deposing the same witness twice, or taking a deposition before the time set by Rule 26(d). The time for serving written questions is set under Rule 31:

cross questions—within 14 days after notice and written questions are served

redirect questions—within 7 days after service of cross questions

recross questions—within 7 days after service of redirect questions

The court does have the authority to alter these time limits if there is a good reason to do so. Depositions upon written questions are easy and inexpensive. They are used primarily to obtain business records and testimony from a minor witness whose oral deposition

FINDING IT on the Internet

Law Technology News (LTN) maintains a Web site at **<http://www.law.com/jsp/lawtechnologynews/index.jsp>**. Access the Web site and see if you can find an article on technology and depositions. Alternatively, look for a general article that discusses some aspect of ESI and the discovery process. You might want to concentrate on searching for an article on one of the unique trends in certain aspects of the technology revolution in litigation such as cyberinsurance, privacy expectations in relation to GPS technology, and cybersecurity priorities.

The federal courts have developed an education and resource center called the Federal Judicial Center (FJC). The FJC, which was instituted by Congress in 1967, conducts research on the operation of the federal courts. In addition, the FJC runs a Web site that houses a list of publications and videos available through the Center. Access the Web site at **<http://www.fjc.gov>** and find a publication or a video that relates to depositions and/or ESI.

The Web site of the Administrative Office of the U.S. Courts can be accessed at **<http://www.uscourts.gov>**. The Web site contains a number of interesting features, including *The Third Branch News*, the court's newsletter.

a. Access *The Third Branch News* and find an article that involves the Federal Rules governing the deposition process. Write a report on the essence of that article.

b. Access *The Third Branch News* and find an article that involves ESI. Write a report that reflects the issues discussed in that article.

You can subscribe to *The Third Branch News* by entering your e-mail address in the appropriate spot on the Web site or by using your preferred social media account: *Facebook*, *Yahoo*, or *Google*.

K&L Gates, LLP, is a private firm that offers a cost-effective way to manage e-discovery issues. In keeping with this, the K&L Gates Web site hosts a blog entitled "Electronic Discovery Law." Access the blog at **<http://www.ediscoverylaw.com>** and list some recent developments in e-discovery law.

One of the most important cases in recent years involving electronically stored information is the case of *Zubulake v. UBS Warburg*. Several opinions issued by the court in *Zubulake* have had a great effect on the disposition of ESI during electronic discovery. Conduct a search on the Internet for the *Zubulake* case, find an appropriate article or essay on the case, and write a report that explains and analyzes its content. State whether you agree or disagree with the position adopted in the article, and explain your rationale in detail.

could be very expensive because of the witness's distant location. Although this type of deposition is inexpensive, it does have certain disadvantages. For example, because the questions are written in advance, there is no way to ask follow-up questions based on the witness's answers. Similarly, there is no opportunity to observe the witness during the deposition.

Your supervising attorney may request that you prepare the **notice of intent to take deposition upon written questions**. This notice is similar to the notice of intent to take oral deposition. It spells out the date, time, and place of a planned deposition upon written questions. The notice will also indicate the name and address of the intended deponent as well as the identity of the officer who will attend the deposition. A subpoena must accompany any such notice served upon a nonparty to the lawsuit.

An additional responsibility you may be asked to assume is the drafting of the written questions. To draft these questions, you should first review the pleadings and previous discovery. Determine the areas of examination to be included in the questions, draft the questions, and furnish them to your supervising attorney for review and revisions. Once your supervising attorney's changes have been made, incorporate those changes into your draft questions and arrange the written questions in final order.

notice of intent to take deposition upon written questions
A notice spelling out the date, time, and place of a planned deposition upon written questions. The notice will also indicate the name and address of the intended deponent as well as the identity of the officer who will attend the deposition. A subpoena must accompany any such notice served upon a nonparty to the lawsuit.

SUMMARY

- A deposition is the written or oral testimony of a witness or party given under oath outside the courtroom. A person questioned during a deposition is a deponent. The scope of testimony during a deposition is much broader than the scope of testimony during trial.

- A traditional oral deposition involves the actual presence of the deponent who responds aloud to the questions asked by an attorney. A traditional oral deposition may be held in the attorney's office, at the courthouse, or at some other convenient location, such as a hotel room or a conference room often provided by one of the many legal support companies that specialize in assisting law firms in handling depositions. An electronic deposition is a deposition that is recorded by the use of a laptop, a smartphone, a tablet, a digital camcorder, or some other electronic device, thus allowing the participants involved in the deposition to be located at separate sites, often hundreds or even thousands of miles apart. Whichever technique is used, Rule 30 of the Federal Rules of Civil Procedure regulates both traditional and e-depositions.

- The role of the paralegal in the preparation for the deposition is quite broad. The paralegal may be asked to arrange for the preparation and service of a notice of intent to take an oral deposition. The paralegal may also be asked to obtain subpoenas for several deponents. Finally, the paralegal may be called upon to help prepare for the deposition. The exact nature of this preparation will depend upon whether the attorney is taking or defending the deposition.

- During the actual deposition, the paralegal may be asked to take notes. The paralegal may also be asked to evaluate the effectiveness of the deponent.

- After the deposition, the paralegal may have to obtain a transcript of the deponent's testimony. The paralegal may also have to write a deposition summary. There are three types of deposition summaries: the page-line deposition summary, the topical deposition summary, and the chronological deposition summary.

- A deposition upon written questions is a discovery tool that requires the deponent to answer written questions orally in the presence of a court reporter.

KEY TERMS

chronological deposition
   summary
court reporter
deponent
deposition
deposition summary
deposition upon written
   questions
duplicative
e-deposition

e-transcript
electronic deposition
electronic transcript
mock deposition
notice of intent to take
   deposition upon written
   questions
notice of intent to take oral
   deposition
overbroad

page-line deposition
   summary
subpoena
subpoena *duces tecum*
topical deposition
   summary
traditional oral deposition
transcript

REVIEW QUESTIONS

1. What is a deposition?
2. What are the advantages and the disadvantages of the traditional oral deposition?
3. What are the advantages and the disadvantages of the electronic deposition?
4. What is a notice of intent to take an oral deposition?
5. What responsibilities does a paralegal have in preparing for a deposition?
6. What responsibilities does a paralegal have during an oral deposition?
7. What is the paralegal's role in arranging for a transcript?
8. What are the three types of deposition summaries?
9. What are the advantages and the disadvantages of taking a deposition upon written questions?

CHAPTER EXERCISES

Where necessary, check with your instructor prior to starting any of these exercises.

1. Review the laws of your state and find all state laws that deal with depositions. Check your local court rules to see if any local rules of court in your area regulate who may be present during the taking of a deposition. Also check local rules to see who may be present to record the questions and answers to a deposition.

2. Contact your local bar association. Try to find out how many local attorneys are using prerecorded DVDs or downloaded sessions to instruct clients on how to conduct themselves during a deposition. Also find out if any local attorneys are using digital camcorders or other recording devices to help clients rehearse for their own depositions.

3. Analyze the following situation. Jonathan Harbinger, a certified radiologic technologist, was to be a witness in the case of *Spencer Flannigan v. Lassiter Central Clinic of Vermont*. Attorney Robert Henderson was charged with the responsibility of conducting Harbinger's deposition. After the completion of Harbinger's deposition, a transcript was produced (see Appendix A). Read the transcript of the deposition and create one of the following: a chronological deposition summary, a page-line deposition summary, or a topical deposition summary. Use your own judgment in deciding which of the three types of depositions would best help your attorney's client in this case.

CHAPTER PROJECT

Review the *Flannigan* case in the opening Commentary. Recall that your supervising attorney will be conducting the deposition of Jonathan Harbinger, the certified radiologic technologist. Draft a checklist for evaluating Harbinger.

THE *BENNET* CASE
Assignment for Chapter 9: Preliminary Research

Your supervisory attorney wants to take the deposition of Martha Yee, a former employee of defendant and coworker of Bennett. Prepare the notice of deposition for the defense attorney and subpoena for Ms. Yee.

THE *DOUGLASS FINANCIAL SERVICES INC.* CASE
Assignment for Chapter 9: Setting up a Videotape Deposition

Your attorney wants to depose both the plaintiff and the codefendant in the case. The attorney also wants to videotape the depositions. Check your state laws and forms and prepare the documents necessary to set up these depositions.

ENDNOTES

1 Cassandra Tribe, "How to Do a Phone Deposition," *eHow* (n.d.), retrieved on February 2, 2013, from <http://www.ehow.com/print/how_6509521_do-phone-deposition.html>.

2 Ibid.

3 Ken Adams, "Video Depositions: Tips for Boosting Quality," *Sunbelt Blog: Sunbelt Reporting and Litigation Services* (September 24, 2012), retrieved on February 12, 2012 from <http://www.sunbeltreporting.com/sunbelt-blog/bid/90800/Video-Depositions-Tips-for-Boosting-Quality#emart -form-anchor>.

Interrogatories

CHAPTER OUTLINE

THE *FAIRNESS FOR ALL BLOG.COM* CASE

Early last spring, James Gilbert learned that he was the subject of a blog posted on a Web site known as the Fairness for All Blog.com (FFABlog.com) operated by Jenna Hamilton and Kenneth Kaufmann. FFABlog.com invites bloggers to report cases of fraud or negligence committed by business firms. The troublesome blog that concerns Gilbert was posted by a professional blogger named Wade Greenwood. Writers like Greenwood are paid by William Watson, the owner of Dismay, Disclose, Disrupt, Inc. (TriD, Inc.), a California watchdog firm, to blog at FFABlog.com and similar sites in order to harass corporations that do less than admirable work, at least by Watson's standards. Greenwood's latest blog claims that Gilbert, the owner and operator of an Ohio firm named Dimensional Accounting, Ltd. (DA), failed to follow generally accepted accounting standards (GAAS) as established by the Financial Accounting Standards Board and mandated by the American Institute of Certified Public Accountants, resulting in over $5 million in combined losses for a variety of DA's clients. Gilbert argues that the blog is entirely false and has asked your firm to represent him in a defamation and disparagement case against Greenwood, the blogger; his employers, TriD and Watson, as well as the Web site, FFABlog.com, and its owners and operators, Kaufmann and Hamilton. Preliminary negotiations yielded no positive results and so the complaint has been filed in federal court based on a jurisdictional claim of diversity. All parties have been served and discovery is underway. Your supervising attorney has asked you to draft a set of interrogatories to be answered by Greenwood, a second set to be answered by Watson, and a final set to be answered by Kaufmann and Hamilton at FFA. The goal is to compile additional information about the sources of Greenwood's blog, about the hiring and research procedures used at TriD, and about the editing standards in place at FFA. You will also assist in preparing answers to a set of interrogatories sent to your client by TriD.

The preceding chapters gave you an overview of the discovery process and introduced you to the tools of discovery, especially the deposition. Interrogatories are another effective discovery device. After reading this chapter, you should be able to:

- define interrogatories.
- explain the various purposes of interrogatories.
- list the advantages and disadvantages of using interrogatories.
- explain the rules regarding ESI and interrogatories.
- describe the specific types of interrogatories.
- identify the types of topics covered in a set of interrogatories leading to a document-production request for ESI.
- explain the options available when a party refuses to answer an interrogatory.
- outline the duty to supplement interrogatory answers.
- describe when it would be appropriate to produce business records, including ESI, instead of a written interrogatory response.
- explain the form of the interrogatory answer.
- outline the objections that can be raised to interrogatories.

INTERROGATORIES

Interrogatories are written questions submitted by one party in a lawsuit to another party in that suit. The responding party must answer these questions in writing and under oath. Rule 33 of the Federal Rules of Civil Procedure regulates the use of interrogatories in federal court. As noted earlier in Chapter 8, many states have adopted civil rules that closely follow the Federal Rules. Still, you must always check for variations in state and local rules governing the use of interrogatories. This warning is especially appropriate when handling ESI because not all states address that issue in the same way. The interrogatories must be answered by the party upon whom they are served. In the case of partnerships, government agencies, institutions, and corporations, such as TriD and FFA, the answers are given by officers and agents of those organizations. For example, in the *Fairness for All Blog.com* case, if an interrogatory asked about the blogging standards used at TriD, the answers could be given by any company officer or agent with that knowledge. Interrogatories should not be served until the parties have initially conferred as required under Rule 26 of the Federal Rules. Once served, the answering party has 30 days to respond. Unlike depositions, interrogatories cannot be served on nonparty witnesses involved in the lawsuit. Rule 33 of the Federal Rules of Civil Procedure provides for an alternative to answering interrogatories in writing. A responding party may identify specific documents in which information might be found that would answer the question. The responding party must also pull the information together, identify the particular document that answers the question, and give the other party the opportunity to review those documents. The rules also permit a responding party to offer ESI as an alternative to answering an interrogatory.

Scope and Number of Interrogatories

The type and the amount of evidence that can be sought by discovery is much broader than that which could be produced at the trial. Rule 33 (a) (2) of the Federal Rules incorporates Rule 26 (b) to make it clear that the broad scope of discovery authorized by Rule 26 applies to interrogatories. Rule 33 (a) (2) states that: "(a)n interrogatory may relate to any matter that can be inquired into under Rule 26 (b)." Later Rule 33 (c) adds that "(a)n answer to an interrogatory may be used to the extent allowed by the Federal Rules of Evidence." All the interrogatories sent to a party at one time constitute a set. Multiple sets of interrogatories, however, can be served on the parties to a lawsuit. Within each set, each interrogatory is numbered for convenient reference. The Federal Rules require sequential numbering throughout all sets. For example, in the *Fairness for All Blog.com* case, if the first set of interrogatories contained 20 interrogatories, the second set would begin with number 21. Because parties are automatically entitled to receive information through mutual disclosures under Rule 26, they are allowed to ask no more than 25 interrogatories (including discrete subparts). Of course, the parties can increase the number of interrogatories by written agreement or with the court's permission. Most states also limit the number of interrogatories that can be asked of a party, although the permitted number of interrogatories varies from state to state. The state of Ohio, for example, authorizes the use of 40 interrogatories but allows the parties to ask the court for leave to increase that number, when necessary.

Purposes of Interrogatories

Interrogatories obtain information about the facts in a case and supplement any information that was disclosed under Rule 26 of the Federal Rules of Civil Procedure. Interrogatories may also be used to determine the party's contentions and to identify specific individuals or documents that support those contentions. Not all state courts have rules comparable to Rule 26 or require automatic mutual disclosures. In such jurisdictions, interrogatories are commonly used to obtain the information that is exchanged under Rule 26 in the federal courts. That information might include the identity and location of both lay and expert witnesses that the other party intends to call at trial, as well as a description and location of any relevant documents. Properly drafted interrogatories can narrow the issues and facts in preparation for trial. Also, like the deposition, interrogatories can impeach witnesses during the trial. Finally, interrogatories may facilitate settlement of the case.

Advantages of Interrogatories

Interrogatories offer substantial advantages over other discovery methods. First of all, they are simple, inexpensive, and efficient. For instance, because a party responds to interrogatories at her own pace, interrogatories avoid the logistical problems associated with scheduling depositions. Second, interrogatories are more thorough than depositions because interrogatories must be answered and verified by the party. Moreover, the responding party also has the duty to provide the identity of the person who has custody of a document or of ESI if the party does not have it. Finally, interrogatories enhance other discovery techniques. For example, interrogatories may determine the identities of future deponents. They may also reveal documents that should be included in a subsequent request for production of documents.

Disadvantages of Interrogatories

Like the other discovery devices, interrogatories are not without their disadvantages. The first disadvantage is that they are limited to the parties to a lawsuit. Consequently, the use of interrogatories may not eliminate the need to take depositions at a later date. In fact, the use of interrogatories does not even eliminate the need to take the deposition of a party. Second, interrogatories lack spontaneity, because a party responding to a set of interrogatories has time to draft narrow, self-serving answers. In addition, the answers are often edited by the attorney or the paralegal before they are finalized and delivered. Moreover, because the answers are written, they do not allow for immediate follow-up questions. Certainly, follow-up questions can be drafted and submitted, but this strategy does not eliminate the possibility of further self-serving answers. Another disadvantage is that interrogatories may help the opposing attorney by motivating her to begin the preparation of her case earlier than she might ordinarily be inclined to proceed. In line with this, interrogatories can also alert the opposition to the direction of your case. In spite of these disadvantages, interrogatories are an effective discovery device.

INTERROGATORIES AND ESI

Federal Rule 33 (d) allows a party who is answering a set of interrogatories to incorporate business records as part of the responses to that set of questions. This provision also recognizes the pervasive presence of ESI by noting that, when a party is inclined to respond to an interrogatory by offering business records, those records may now consist of ESI.[1]

The Use of ESI to Respond to Interrogatories

Frequently, it will be quite convenient for the ESI retriever to go directly to the computer to produce the requested records. Nevertheless, the retriever must be wary of this process because the rule requires the ESI retriever to help the ESI requester to find the records that actually provide the needed answer to the interrogatories in question. Does this mean allowing the requester entrance the retriever's computer network? The answer here appears to be "yes."[2] Should this be a concern, it is probably best for the retriever to skip the business records option and just come out with an answer to the question in a straight forward way.[3]

The Downside of Electronically Stored Information

Again, the threshold question is whether the ESI retriever has provided the ESI requester with enough information to allow the requester to access the ESI as effortlessly as the retriever. To make sure the requester has easy access to the evidence, the ESI retriever might have to provide its own tech support to the ESI requester, if the ESI retriever would need that same tech support to capture the ESI himself or herself.[5]

Such steps can increase the cost of retrieval and inspection. It also may be difficult to figure out who should pay the cost and what that cost might involve. For instance, what if the data retriever's information technology (IT) staff must be paid overtime? Who bears that cost? What if the interrogator's tech team must be trained on the ESI retriever's system? Who pays for the extra training? What if the ESI requester or the ESI retriever must purchase additional hardware or software, or hire additional support staff to access one system or the other? Who is responsible for that expenditure?[6] What if a judge orders the ESI retriever to abstain from a linear document review and, instead, use a computer or technology assisted review (TAR) such as predictive coding?[7]

In general, the cost of discovery is carried out by the party charged with retrieving the evidence. However, when ESI is involved the courts are often willing to alter this rule. This course of action was taken, for instance, in the case of *Zubulake v. UBS Warburg*. In that landmark case, the court shifted *part* of the cost of discovery involving inaccessible ESI to the plaintiff. The **Zubulake proportionality test** is an analytical process that provides the court with seven factors for determining who should pay how much in a search for ESI. Those factors include (1) the specificity of the request; (2) the accessibility of the ESI from other locations; (3) the complete cost of the production balanced against the amount in controversy; (4) the capacity of each party to pay production costs; (5) the significance of the questions at issue in the case; (6) the complete cost of securing the evidence weighed against the ability of each side to pay; and (7) the proportional benefit of securing the evidence in question. In the *Zubulake* case, after weighing these seven factors, the court decided to split the expenses between the parties, ordering the ESI requester to pay one-fourth of the cost for the additional request.[8]

To deal with some of the confusion over these points, the American Bar Association has provided guidelines for determining how the courts will allocate the cost of discovery and how they will resolve motions to compel discovery or for protective orders. These guidelines include:

1. the real cost of discovery compared to the amount in controversy;
2. the importance of and the benefits to be derived from the data;
3. the convenience of obtaining the data from other locations;
4. the risk of violating any privileges associated with the data;

Zubulake proportionality test
An analytical process that provides the court with seven factors for determining who should pay how much in a search for ESI.

bring-your-own-device
(BYOD) policy
The practice of permitting, and
sometimes even expecting,
employees to use their own
smartphones or tablets on the job.

company-owned,
personally enabled
(COPE) device policy
The practice of providing
employees with business-owned
handheld e-devices, such as
smartphones and tablets, that
include separate apps for the
employee's personal use.

5. the difficult nature of the case itself;

6. the possibility of revealing trade secrets or other confidential matters;

7. the burden placed upon the data retriever;

8. the extent of the question or request;

9. the extent to which the cost can be limited;

10. the technique used to store that data;

11. the deletion of the data and the motive for that deletion; and

12. the available resources of each party.[9]

The bottom line is that the simplicity of just delivering the ESI may be eclipsed by the risk of giving the other side more information than was intended. Accordingly, a party is usually better off just answering the question instead of risking the disclosure of privileged or damaging evidence.[10]

In addition to the issue of cost, the question of privileged material also arises when one litigant is allowed to access to the other litigant's ESI network.[11] Although the safe harbor and clawback provisions are designed to protect such ESI, the courts are not necessarily bound by such agreements and may overturn them if they suspect the party seeking protection was negligent in guarding or recovering the ESI after discovering its unintended revelation. Besides, even when a clawback agreement is honored by the court, it cannot prevent the insight and the information picked up by the opposing party who has seen the other party's material.[12]

Another problem affecting the use of ESI in response to interrogatories involves the practice of permitting employees to use their own smartphones or tablets on the job. This trend is referred to as the **bring-your-own-device (BYOD) policy**. Companies that have adopted a BYOD policy will allow employees to bring their own devices into the workplace. These devices are then programmed by the company's IT department with secure work areas for e-mail, employee forms, texts, tweets, and other work-related correspondence. Some companies take a less radical approach that involves having the company provide employees with business-owned devices that include separate apps for the employee's personal use. This second practice is referred to as **COPE** which stands for the use of **company-owned, personally enabled devices**.[13] Because of this trend, your supervising attorney must now remember that, whenever her client answers an interrogatory by offering business records, that response will have to include ESI, whether the client likes it or not. This step does not cause a problem unless those business records include e-mails, texts, and tweets that are stored on employee-owned or operated smartphones and tablets. If that is the case, then, when the time comes to produce business records, the judge *may* order the party to turn in all smartphones and tablets used to send or receive e-mails, texts, and tweets, regardless of who actually owns the phone or the tablet.[14]

DRAFTING INTERROGATORIES

The drafting of interrogatories is one of the most important jobs that you may have during the litigation process because properly drafted interrogatories not only provide information themselves but also indicate the need to use other discovery devices. Your role in drafting interrogatories may later be expanded to include drafting a motion to compel the other party to respond to some of the interrogatories that have not been properly answered. You may also be responsible for reviewing the other party's response.

Preliminary Steps in Drafting Interrogatories

Before you can draft an effective set of interrogatories, you must familiarize yourself with the facts of the case. To do this properly, review the pleadings, the correspondence file, the attorney's notes, the research notebook, and the information provided in the initial and subsequent mutual discovery disclosures. Your review should be as active as possible. Take notes as you review the material and consider the types of questions you will want to ask the other party. In the *Fairness for All Blog.com* case, for example, as a paralegal for the firm representing the plaintiff, you will want to ask executives at TriD, Inc., the procedures they follow when they recruit, hire, and pay freelance bloggers. Other questions may involve the policies and procedures they follow as they fact check, review, edit, and post these blogs. Upon termination of the preliminary review, you will be ready to draft the interrogatories.

Form and Content of Interrogatories

Consult the appropriate state or federal court rules to determine the form required to draft interrogatories in your jurisdiction. In most jurisdictions, interrogatories contain a title, introductory paragraph, definitions, instructions, specific interrogatories, a signature, and a certificate of service. Acknowledging that most interrogatories are word processed, many, perhaps even most, law firms today send those interrogatories electronically and expect a new document to be generated incorporating the questions and the answers. In many states, however, the rules still insist that a printed copy be served on the answering party and require that all time periods for response be calculated based on receipt of the paper copy. This discrepancy can cause problems when the electronic copy is not sent promptly or when a computer glitch, such as a difference in the software used by each firm, delays the responding party's ability to use the electronic copy. Generally, however, a prompt request to the court for a time extension based on this type of problem will remove this obstacle.[15]

Title of the Interrogatories and Introductory Paragraph

Discovery involves the production of a variety of pleadings, motions, and requests. For this reason, the Federal Rules of Civil Procedure require that all documents carry an appropriate title. This procedure allows participants in the action to identify any document just by glancing at its title. The title of the interrogatories should identify the party serving the interrogatories, the party receiving the interrogatories, and the number of the set of interrogatories:

Example

Defendant—Dismay, Disclose, and Disrupt, Inc.
First Set of Interrogatories
to Plaintiff James Gilbert

Even though the Federal Rules do not require an introductory paragraph, tradition dictates including an introductory paragraph immediately after the caption of the case and the title of the interrogatories. Usually this paragraph identifies the recipient of the interrogatories and indicates that an answer is required within a specified period of time. The introductory paragraph should state the appropriate federal or state rule under which the interrogatories are presented. Finally, the introduction may set forth the number of interrogatories permitted and the statutory requirements for supplemental answers. Exhibit 10-1 shows an example of the introductory paragraph.

Definitions   The definition section should be distinct so that the responding party can locate it easily. The heading "definitions" should be placed in the center of the page in boldfaced lettering. Definitions can be used to clear up discrepancies among words that have several meanings and to establish the meaning of a word that is used frequently throughout the interrogatories. For example, in the *Fairness for All Blog.com* case, the word *blog* may be repeated several dozen times. To avoid confusion, the definition section of the interrogatories might establish the definition in the following way, " 'blog' refers to the May 4, 2015, posting on Fairness for All Blog.com, the subjects of which were the plaintiff, James Gilbert, and his firm, Dimension Accounting, LLC." The definition section also conserves space and shortens the questions by eliminating the need to repeat the meaning of a word that appears throughout the interrogatories. Finally, properly drafted definitions can enlarge the number of questions asked by defining a word to include several subtopics. For example, as indicated in Exhibit 10-2, the words *identify* and *identity*, when effectively defined, can result in an abundance of information about the people and the documents involved in a case.

Instructions   The proper use of a set of well-drawn instructions can prevent confusion and help the party preparing the interrogatories to obtain the needed information. When drafting the instructions, be sure to include instructions for any desired action by the other party. Also make certain to offer the opposing party the opportunity to attach documents, including ESI, instead of answering an interrogatory. This approach will save time and avoid the need to file a request for production of documents.

It is also important, when drafting the instructions, to consider the time period that the interrogatories will cover. Your request should seek not only information about the incident that gave rise to the lawsuit but also information about past conduct, conditions, and activities. For example, in the *Fairness for All Blog.com* case, if the posting took place on May 4, 2015, your instructions should indicate that the applicable time period for the answers to the questions will extend from May 4, 2014, to the date the defendant

EXHIBIT 10-1 Introductory Paragraphs for Interrogatories

Pursuant to Rule _____, _____ Rules of Civil Procedure, you are to answer the interrogatories hereinafter set forth, separately, fully, in writing, and under oath. You should deliver a true copy of your answer to the undersigned attorney within 30 days after the date of service of these interrogatories.

EXHIBIT 10-2 Definitions

DEFINITIONS

1. To "identify" a document or state the "identity of" a document shall mean to state with respect thereto:
   a. The identity of the person who prepared it;
   b. The identity of the person who signed it or over whose signature it was or is issued;
   c. The identity of each person to whom it was addressed or distributed;
   d. The nature and substance of the document with sufficient particularity to enable it to be identified;
   e. The date, if any, which the document bears; and
   f. The present location of the document, including the identity of its custodian or custodians; or in lieu thereof, attach a copy of said document to your response to these interrogatories.

2. To "identify" or to state the "identity of" a person shall mean with respect thereto:
   a. The person's full name;
   b. The person's title and business or professional affiliation, if any, as of the time to which the answer relates; and
   c. The person's present title and business or professional and residence addresses.

actually answers the interrogatories. This will allow you to detect any existing procedures as well as changes in the procedures used at TriD, Inc. to hire and regulate the work of freelance bloggers. Drafting these instructions must be done with care, however. The inquiry must be comprehensive enough to discover relevant information, yet narrow enough to avoid an objection from the ESI provider that the request is overbroad and burdensome.

Another topic often included in the instructions is the duty to supplement answers when additional information is received or when the content of any previous answer has changed. However, it is important to note that not all states recognize this duty to supplement. Furthermore, the Federal Rules [especially Rule 26 (e)] only require supplementation when ordered by the court or when a party learns that the response was materially incomplete or incorrect and the correct information has not otherwise been made known during the discovery. The instructions also should explain how to deal with any objections that the responding party has to the interrogatories. For example, should the responding party object to part of a question, she should be instructed to answer any other part of that question that is not objectionable. A special instruction may be used to inquire about any information withheld under a claim of the attorney–client privilege, the work product privilege, or the common interest privilege.

Because the instruction section of the interrogatories is a crucial part of this document, that heading should be centered and placed in boldfaced type. Some law firms combine definitions and instructions, so check on the accepted procedure in your office. Exhibit 10-3 contains examples of the instructions that you might incorporate in the interrogatories directed to the plaintiff in the *Fairness for All Blog.com* case.

EXHIBIT 10-3 Instructions

INSTRUCTIONS

A. You are required by Rule _____ of the _____ Rules of Civil Procedure to:

 1. Answer fully and factually each of the interrogatories hereinafter set out.

 2. Furnish all information called for by said interrogatory.

 3. Sign your response.

 4. Swear to your response.

 5. Serve same upon the undersigned attorney within thirty (30) days after the date of service of these interrogatories. You are further instructed:

B. Every interrogatory herein shall be deemed a continuing interrogatory, and you are to supplement your answers promptly if and when you obtain relevant information in addition to, or in any way inconsistent with, your initial answer to any interrogatory.

C. If you object to, or otherwise decline to answer, any portion of an interrogatory, provide all information called for in that portion of the interrogatory to which you do not object or which you do not decline to answer. If you object to an interrogatory on the grounds that to provide an answer would constitute an undue burden, provide such requested information as can be supplied without undertaking an undue burden. For those portions of any interrogatory to which you object or otherwise decline to answer, state the reason for such objection or declination.

D. The applicable period of time, unless otherwise provided, shall be from _____ to the date of answering these interrogatories.

E. If any answer is refused in whole or in part, on the basis of a claim of privilege or exemption, state the following:

 1. the nature of the privilege or exemption claimed;

 2. the general nature of the matter withheld (e.g., substance of conversation of the withheld information, name of originator);

 3. name(s) of person(s) to whom the information has been imparted; and

 4. the extent, if any, to which the information will be provided subject to the privilege or exemption.

Specific Interrogatories   Interrogatories come in a variety of types. These types include interrogatories that identify people, interrogatories that establish facts or lead to the discovery of facts, interrogatories that identify documents, and interrogatories that identify contentions. The number of specific questions allowed under the Federal Rules is 25. Care must be taken in drafting questions because "discrete" subparts are counted separately. Obviously this is so that attorneys do not defeat the 25-question limit by drafting compound questions with multiple subparts.

1. **Interrogatories that identify people.** The identities of the people who are involved in the lawsuit are very important. As part of the initial mutual discovery, you should receive the names of persons who are likely to have discoverable knowledge relevant to the disputed facts that are stated with particularity in the pleadings. However, you

may still wish to ask some specific questions about individuals. You also may be in a jurisdiction that does not provide for any mutual disclosure. For example, in the *Fairness for All Blog.com* case, you may need to determine the identities of any employees involved in hiring and reviewing the work of freelance bloggers. You also may need to identify previous employees and other bloggers who work for or who have worked for TriD, Inc. In addition, it would be helpful to uncover the identities of individuals who have direct knowledge of the operational decisions made at TriD, Inc., by Kaufmann and Hamilton in relation to Gilbert and Dimensional Accounting, Inc., to determine whether they had any actual knowledge of the false nature of the claims posted on the anti-Gilbert blog.

Another area of questions about people concerns the identities of all persons who have given statements to the other party's attorney. For example, has the opposing attorney taken statements from witnesses, accountants, auditors, bloggers, employees of TriD, Inc., and so on? Once you receive this information, you will be able to schedule any depositions that your attorney decides are necessary. You also will be able to draft any document-production requests that appear appropriate. Finally, in some jurisdictions, interrogatories can be used to identify the *expert witnesses* that the opposition intends to call at trial as witnesses. The courts recently expanded the definition of "expert" to include the IT specialist who conducts a search of either party's computer system. This means that your interrogatories can also be used to identify those IT specialists. Exhibit 10-4 gives an example of this type of interrogatory. It is important to note that such an interrogatory can be asked only about an expert who will be called to testify at trial. If an expert will not be called to testify, this information is not discoverable. It is protected by the work product privilege.

2. **Interrogatories to establish facts.** Some interrogatories will seek the facts surrounding the allegations in the pleadings. These questions should always be aimed at the most recent pleading filed by the opposition. Thus, if the plaintiff has filed an amended complaint, that amended complaint becomes the target of the fact-finding interrogatories, rather than the original complaint. Fact-finding interrogatories should cover the who, what, when, where, why, and how of the allegations. This is known as seeking the "five Ws and an H."

3. **Interrogatories that identify documents.** Although mutual discovery may have revealed the existence of some documents, you should also ask specific questions regarding those documents. Interrogatories directed at uncovering documents may seek information about medical reports, medical bills, earning statements, and income tax returns. Such questions also may seek to discover any statements made in connection with the accident. Pleadings and prior discovery are additional documents that interrogatories may investigate.

4. **Interrogatories that identify contentions.** Rule 33 (a) (2) of the Federal Rules of Civil Procedure states that an interrogatory need not be objectionable simply if "it asks for an opinion or contention that relates to fact or the application of law to fact." This is a crucial part of the interrogatories because it requires the disclosure of not only the contention but also the basis for that contention. For example, in the *Fairness for All Blog.com* case, the interrogatories sent to your client may seek the following contention.

EXHIBIT 10-4 Expert Witness Interrogatory

State the name, business address, title, and qualifications of each and every person whom you intend to or may call as an expert witness during the trial of this case. With respect to each such expert, state the following information:

a. Describe in detail the subject matter about which the expert is expected to testify;

b. Each and every mental impression and opinion held by the expert with respect to this lawsuit and all facts known by the expert (regardless of when the actual knowledge was acquired) that relate to or form the basis of such mental impressions and opinions;

c. The style, case number, and court of each and every case in which such expert has previously provided expert testimony, whether by deposition or at trial;

d. List and describe completely all facts provided to the expert witness for use in connection with the expert's analysis of all or any portion of the issues in this case. For any such facts that are in document form, you may instead attach a copy of such document to your response to these interrogatories; and

e. If the expert has submitted a report, please recite verbatim all contents thereof or, if you prefer, a copy of same may be attached to your response to these interrogatories.

Example

1. Do you contend that the owners and operators and employees of Defendant, TriD, Inc., had actual knowledge of those statements that you allege to be false as they appeared in the blog of May 4, 2015?

2. If so, please state all facts upon which you base your contention.

3. If your answer to question number 1 is yes, please identify every person who has knowledge or information relating to those facts.

4. If your answer to question number 1 is yes, please state whether any statements have been given by persons you identified in question number 3 above.

5. If your answer to question number 1 is yes, please identify any document or other evidence that you believe supports your contention.

The answers to these questions may not be obvious early in the lawsuit. Therefore, these types of questions are of greater value in a set of interrogatories filed toward the end of the discovery process. In fact, under Federal Rule 33 (a) (2) the court may order that this type of "interrogatory need not be answered until designated discovery is complete, or until a pretrial conference or some other time."

ESI and E-Interrogatories   One of the most effective ways for an attorney involved in a complicated lawsuit to obtain information about his opponent's computer records is by filing interrogatories aimed at determining the nature of those records. The most efficient way to gather ESI is to first send interrogatories, the answers to which can then guide the attorney's document-production requests. As is true of traditional interrogatories, the initial step in fashioning the e-interrogatories is to define all terms. The interrogatories that then follow should fall under several categories. First, the interrogatories should ask about the actual nature of the party's computer system. Such questions would attempt to determine the number and types of computers that are operating in the party's daily routine. This is not as simple as it seems on the surface. Sometimes certain computers may escape detection. This is why it would be helpful to make certain that the interrogatories specify that the term *computer* includes the mainframe, desktop PCs, laptops, iPods, iPads, mobile phones, smartphones, GPS devices, digital camcorders, personal digital assistants (PDAs), tablets, and home computers that are part of a network. It is also wise to remember that many employees retain the habit of filing paper copies of all e-documents, even those e-files that have been deleted from their computer system. In fact, some employers require the retention of paper copies as a precaution against a computer system failure.

Another set of questions attempts to determine the configuration of any network systems that are involved in the party's operation. Such questions should also identify the number and location of all workstations and all network servers. It is also important to ask about any upgrades that have occurred, any equipment changes, any reformatting, and any policies that involve the elimination of data. As noted above, these requests must also include questions about whether employees use their own personal e-devices, especially smartphones and tablets, that have been programmed by the employer's IT department with secure work areas for company e-mail, texts, tweets, and other work-related correspondence. In fact, it is best to ask outright if a company has either BYOD or a COPE policy in place. Closely related to these policies are those that mandate the preservation of certain records or any backup processes in use for the saving of data. Another set of questions should be specifically aimed at acquiring an understanding of the party's e-mail system. It is also important to obtain the names and a list of responsibilities of all individuals who are in any way involved in maintaining or servicing the party's computer system. This may include the identities of both in-house and outside IT experts, as well as administrative assistants, interns, and temps who work or have worked with IT experts.

Forms of Electronically Stored Information   When writing interrogatories, it is essential to remember the diverse nature of ESI. Recall that ESI includes all computer-generated records, including animations, anti-theft systems and databases, archives, audio discs, audio networks, audio records, audio systems, audio tapes, backup tapes, blogs, calculators, calendars, cartridges, chatrooms, contacts, "cookies," credit cards and records, databases, data-processing cards, debit cards, debit records, deleted data, digital cameras, digital photographs, discs, documented image technology, drafts (e-mail, texts, etc.) drives, embedded chips, e-mail attachments, e-mail messages, e-mail software, event data recorders (in vehicles), e-vites, external hard drives, fax machines, financial data, flash drives, global positioning systems, graphics, handheld wireless devices, hardware, images, input data, instant messages, Internet service providers, Internet use records, intranets, keyloggers, laptops, legacy data, medical devices and records, memory sticks and flash cards, metadata, mobile phones, mobile phone memory, music files, networks, notepads, pagers, personal computers, PDAs, printers, radio frequency identification tags or chips (RFIDs), removable discs, search histories, security cameras and other security and surveillance devices, servers, smartphones, software, spreadsheet data, spreadsheets, spyware

metadata mining
The process of searching
metadata for evidence.

databases, statistical data, system and network data, tablets, tapes, texts, to-do lists, toll
road cards, travel drives, tweets, video discs, videotapes, voicemail, Web-based bulletin-
board postings, Web-based discussions, word-processed documents, and voice mail. Once
more, make certain to include in the request ESI stored on any e-devices, such as smartphones and tablets, that may be the party's personal property but that have been programmed by the employer's IT department with secure work areas for company e-mail,
texts, tweets, and other work-related correspondence. When interrogatories involving ESI
are compiled, your supervising attorney must be careful to ensure that all forms of data are
included in the questions.[16]

Metadata and Metadata Mining

It is essential to understand that ESI also in-
cludes metadata. Metadata involves ESI that records data about data and, therefore, is
an essential component of electronic data. Metadata includes such things as a tracking
record that shows the technique used to compile the data, who compiled the data, how
they used the data, where they stored the data, and so on.[17] Metadata describes the data
itself by indicating its size, name, nature, and content as well as changes that have been
made to the data as it was developed. Metadata can also include invisible data that is
preserved in a wide variety of software programs. These programs include spreadsheets,
e-mail records, printing records, databases, and word-processing records. When a document is sent electronically, rather than delivered in paper form, the invisible metadata
goes along with that document. Consequently, the recipient can access the metadata
and discover a wide range of things that the sender did not intend to reveal.[18] This
means that your supervising attorney might be able to access the metadata and, as a result, uncover additional information that was hidden within that data, thus enhancing
the discovery process.

On the other hand, some people believe that searching metadata for evidence, a process referred to as **metadata mining**, is at the very least unprofessional and perhaps even
unethical and illegal. Those who oppose metadata mining suggest that because metadata
is hidden ESI and because ESI retrievers are often unaware that, along with the requested
ESI, they are retrieving and sending information about alterations, insertions, removals,
corrections, extensions, notations, enhancements, criticisms, authorship, and attachments,
the practice amounts to electronic theft. A savvy attorney can use metadata mining software to locate privileged information by recovering e-mail messages sent to and from opposing counsel.[19] Still, it is difficult to see how parties who deliberately remove metadata
from ESI are not culpable for failing to preserve evidence, one of the most fundamental
duties of those involved in litigation.[20] This warning is especially true today because the
courts have consistently viewed the duty to preserve ESI as a paramount responsibility in
a lawsuit. As we have seen, the courts have repeatedly held that the duty to preserve is so
critical that it emerges at that moment in time when a party has a credible reason to believe
that a lawsuit is on the horizon.[21]

Interrogatories and Rescued ESI

Another set of questions might attempt to deter-
mine whether some of the ESI that is in the possession of the ESI retriever might be retrievable although it appears to have been permanently deleted. Such interrogatories should ask
about those IT experts who might understand the intricacies of the computer system to
such a degree that they can retrieve even apparently irretrievable ESI. As noted previously,

this tactic may involve obtaining a list of those individuals who function as both internal and external information technology experts, in addition to interns, adjunct employees, trainees, paralegals, work study students, retirees, temps, and administrative assistants who might have similar experience, education, and expertise. Moreover, even before the advent of the current amendments to the Federal Rules of Civil Procedure, the courts were willing to acknowledge that even deleted ESI is a legitimate target of discovery.[22] Therefore, this valuable source of evidence ought not to be ignored.

Summary Paragraph   No matter how careful you are in drafting interrogatories, you will not cover all the information you will need to help your client in the lawsuit. A summary paragraph can be used to request any information that may be relevant to the suit. Such a summary question might read, "Do you have any additional information relevant to the subject of the lawsuit that has not been previously covered in your foregoing answers to these interrogatories? If so, please state that information." There are problems, however, with using this type of summary question. Although there is no harm in asking such a question, the responding party may object on the grounds that it is either over-broad or vague.

Signature and Certificate of Service   At the end of the specific questions, a signature line for the attorney and the firm's address should be included. Following the signature block, a certificate of service sets out the date, type of service, and to whom service of the interrogatories was made. Interrogatories are not filed in the federal court. You should consult your state and local rules to determine whether filing is necessary in your jurisdiction. Exhibit 10-5 is a checklist for the paralegal's use in drafting interrogatories.

Motion to Compel

Usually the party responding to the interrogatories will cooperate fully. If there are objections to certain questions, such objections can frequently be resolved on an informal basis. However, there are times when the other party does not cooperate. The motion to compel can help remedy this situation. Once the opposing party's answers are received, you should promptly read each answer, review the objections, and note any answer that is incomplete, unclear, evasive, or nonresponsive. Your supervising attorney will be required to communicate with the other attorney and make a good faith effort to resolve any problem (Rule 37 of the Federal Rules of Civil Procedure). However, if agreement cannot be reached between the parties, you may be asked to draft a motion to compel.

Rule 37 of the Federal Rules of Civil Procedure allows for the filing of a motion to compel the uncooperative party to respond to the interrogatories. The motion must contain a declaration from the attorney for the moving party stating that a good faith effort to resolve the matter was made. Sanctions are available under Rule 37 if the responding party fails to answer the interrogatories properly and completely. Normally the courts are reluctant to grant sanctions unless efforts have been made by the parties to resolve the problem. Recall also that Rule 37 protects parties who lose ESI because of routine computer operations. This safe harbor provision asserts that the court cannot place a penalty on a party if that party cannot retrieve ESI that was deleted following the standard operating procedures of a computer system.

EXHIBIT 10-5 Tips for Drafting Interrogatories

1. Read the documents—correspondence, pleadings, statements, documents produced, and so on.
2. Understand what the attorney wishes to accomplish with this particular set of interrogatories.
3. Read the pertinent court rules to determine such items as format and number of interrogatories permitted.
4. Consult form interrogatories.
5. Draft preliminary portions of request: title of document, introductory paragraph, and definitions and instructions, including time covered, continuing nature of interrogatories, procedure to be followed for objections, and permission for the party to provide a document instead of describing same.
6. Draft interrogatories that are directed to your facts and issues. Remember to identify facts and expert witnesses and documents that form the basis for the party's allegations or defenses. Include interrogatories that ask for legal and factual contentions.
7. Keep the interrogatories simple.
8. Organize interrogatories into categories.
9. Make certain the interrogatories ask the who, what, when, why, where, and how questions.
10. Request all facts relied upon in the last pleading filed.
11. Interrogatories should not be excessive in length or number.
12. Read the interrogatories for possible objections. Revise to avoid objections, if possible.
13. Proofread carefully prior to submitting to attorney for review, signature, and execution of certificate of service.
14. Arrange for service and filing, if necessary.
15. Calendar the answer date and follow up for same.
16. Consult with the attorney regarding the possibility of filing a motion to compel.

DRAFTING ANSWERS TO INTERROGATORIES

Like all other forms of discovery, responding to interrogatories requires patient and careful planning. Because your client is responsible for answering the questions, it is essential that he be contacted immediately upon the receipt of a set of interrogatories. Working with the client, you can then determine how much time is needed to respond, how each question should be answered, which questions must be supplemented, which questions are best answered with business records, and which questions require objections.

Determining Time Limits

As soon as your office receives a set of interrogatories, you should contact the client and forward a copy of those interrogatories to him. Remember that the deadline for responding is normally 30 days after the interrogatories were received. Remember also that, in some states at least, the time to respond begins to run when the paper copy of the interrogatories has been served. For this reason, it is best to get into the habit of contacting parties immediately upon service rather than waiting for the more convenient and efficient e-copy to arrive. Most interrogatories cannot be answered quickly. Therefore, you will have to consult with the client to determine whether the time allowed is realistic. If you and the client conclude that more time is required, your supervising attorney will have to negotiate an extension of that time period. It is important to take care of this immediately, because in some jurisdictions the failure to respond on time may waive the right to object to any interrogatory for which a proper objection might have been made in a timely fashion. Exhibit 10-6 is a checklist for use in drafting interrogatory answers.

engrossed (or engrossment or engrossing)
The process of creating the final form of a document just before that document is used in a formal setting.

Answering the Interrogatories

Interrogatories directed to an individual must be answered by that individual in writing under oath. Interrogatories addressed to a corporation may be answered by any officer, agent, or employee who has the requested information. In the *Fairness for All Blog.com* case, for instance, any TriD, Inc. employee who has information about the hiring procedures could answer interrogatories on that issue.

Form of the Answers   The client is responsible for answering the interrogatories. The client normally supplies the information to the attorney or the paralegal, who drafts the actual answers. Each interrogatory must be answered separately, in writing. In some jurisdictions, answers must be **engrossed** by restating the interrogatory to be

EXHIBIT 10-6 Checklist for Drafting Interrogatory Answers

1. Calendar deadline for answering interrogatories. Place several interim reminders into the system.
2. Send a copy of the interrogatories to the client and schedule a meeting to begin working on the answers.
3. Make another copy of interrogatories. Put one interrogatory on a page for drafting purposes. Place a copy of each interrogatory into a file. Any information or documents received that relate to that interrogatory should also be placed in the file.
4. Note on the individual interrogatories the names of individuals who might have the information to answer the interrogatory and the location of that information.
5. Review pleadings file for any previous answers to avoid contradictions.
6. Review possible objections to interrogatories.
7. Draft interrogatory answers after information is received from the client.
8. Review draft interrogatories with client and attorney. Arrange for signing, filing, if necessary, and service of interrogatories.
9. Remember to update interrogatory answers.

answered. The form of the answer must duplicate the interrogatory. For example, if the interrogatory contains six subparts, the answer contains six subparts. Some states, notably California, do not require that answers be engrossed. No rule requires answers to be complete sentences. Your supervising attorney decides matters of writing style.

Producing Business Records   The federal rules also permit a responding party to answer an interrogatory by referencing the business records in which the answer can be found. Rule 33(d) states that if the most effective way to grasp an answer is to examine, compile, or summarize a party's business records, then as long as burden in obtaining the answer is not increased for either party, the records can be used as an answer. The responding party can answer by indicating the records that must be examined and by giving the other party a chance to duplicate, collect, or summarize the records. As noted at length, this rule also applies to business records that are preserved as ESI.

Content of the Answers   A party answering the interrogatories has a duty to make a reasonable investigation to obtain all information requested. Interrogatory answers must be straightforward and complete. On some occasions, however, you may need to qualify a response or indicate that the answer is unknown at the time. If the answer is unknown at the response time, you may state that fact and supplement the answers later if so required. If you do not answer a question because of lack of sufficient information, you must include the reason for failing to answer. If the answer to an interrogatory has been given in a previous response, you may refer to that prior response. All hearsay information should be designated accordingly. This can be done by beginning the answer with a qualifying statement such as, "I have no personal knowledge, but have been informed by . . . " A qualified response such as, "Upon information and belief . . . " should be adopted if you are not sure of your information or source.

You should disclose as little harmful information as possible. However, you must never deliberately conceal information that is requested in an interrogatory. Your supervising attorney's role is to place the client in the best possible light in each answer *without either distorting or misrepresenting the facts.* One word of caution is appropriate here. Interrogatory answers are admissible only against the interest of the responding party. This means that you cannot use your client's answers to prove the facts in your case. However, because your client was under oath, the opposition may use the answers to impeach the testimony of your client. Naturally, not all interrogatories can be used in this fashion. Some interrogatories ask for relevant but inadmissible information.

Fulfilling the Duty to Supplement

Federal and state rules may vary on the duty of a party to supplement interrogatory answers. In federal court, the following situations require that interrogatory answers be supplemented:

1. If a party learns that the response given was in some material respect incomplete or incorrect and the additional or corrective information has not otherwise been made known; or
2. By order of the court or by agreement of the parties.

Because the duty to supplement interrogatory answers is a statutory requirement, your supervising attorney will determine when updated answers are needed. However, you can assist in supplementing answers by maintaining a file on any interrogatories that might have to be updated.

Objecting to Interrogatories

Objections to interrogatories may be served with the answers or in a separate pleading. As might be expected, the same objections that are available in response to the other discovery devices are available in response to interrogatories. Rule 26 (g) (1) and Rule 33 (b) (5) of the Federal Rules of Civil Procedure require that objections be signed by the attorney. As noted in previous chapters, the grounds for such objections include arguing that the answer to a particular question would provide information that is protected by the attorney–client privilege or the work product privilege. You may also argue that an interrogatory is irrelevant, overbroad, vague, or unintelligible. Another objection is that the interrogatories are unduly burdensome. If a question is objectionable in part only, it must be answered to the extent that it is not objectionable. You should not object to the whole question if part of it is proper.

The Attorney–Client, the Work Product, and the Common Interest Privileges
Recall that the attorney–client privilege seeks to protect any and all types of communication between the attorney and the client. In the same way, the work product privilege protects letters, notes, memos, documents, records, e-mails, text messages, and other items that are prepared by an attorney in anticipation of a lawsuit. The common interest privilege protects any communication that takes place between attorneys for different clients when those clients share a common interest. Should an interrogatory ask for information that would violate these privileges, an objection can be raised. According to Rule 26 (b) (5) of the Federal Rules of Civil Procedure, if an attorney objects to a question based on privilege, the objection must include a description of the nature of the documents, communications, or things not produced or disclosed in a manner that, without revealing the information, will enable the other party to assess the applicability of the privilege or protection.

Federal Rules of Evidence—Rule 502
Rule 502 of the Federal Rules of Evidence states that the accidental disclosure of evidence protected by either the attorney–client privilege or the work product privilege will not be a complete waiver, provided the disclosure was unintentional and occurred despite attempts to protect the evidence. Additionally, the holder of the privilege must make a reasonable attempt to recover the evidence. This attempt must include the use of Rule 26 (b) (5) (B) of the Federal Rules of Civil Procedure which outlines the procedure to follow when privileged information is released accidentally.

The new rule also covers the intentional waiver of either the attorney–client privilege or the work product privilege. According to Rule 502(a), such a waiver will affect only the communication or the work product intentionally waived and only those additional communications or work products that involve the same subject matter, provided that, in

unduly burdensome
A set of interrogatories made during discovery that is so complex and detailed that it will require the party answering the interrogatories to spend excessive time, effort, and expense, and which will result in a burden on that party that far exceeds any benefit gained by the opposing party.

fairness, the two can be connected to one another. Moreover, these limitations will apply to both federal and state cases.

The Medical and the Confessor–Penitent Privileges

Recall that the medical privilege that exists between a patient and a physician (psychiatrist, psychologist, dentist, and podiatrist) is designed to protect the patient's confidential communication with medical professionals. Similarly, the confessor–penitent privilege protects the confidentiality of any communication between a person and confessor. This privilege belongs to the penitent, but the law also protects a confessor who has taken a religious oath not to reveal the content of such communications.

Inadmissible and Irrelevant Evidence

The scope of discovery is much broader than the scope of evidence that can be presented at trial. Still, even the search for evidence during discovery has its limits. Any interrogatory must be reasonably calculated to lead to admissible evidence. If the answer to an interrogatory cannot be reasonably calculated to lead to admissible evidence, you may object to it. Also, should an interrogatory ask for information that is irrelevant to the subject matter of the lawsuit, you may object on that basis.

Overbroad, Vague, and Unintelligible Interrogatories

An overbroad interrogatory is one that is not narrowly defined and is, therefore, difficult, if not impossible, to answer. A vague interrogatory is one that does not clarify exactly what information is sought. An unintelligible interrogatory is one that cannot be understood. All provide appropriate grounds for an objection.

Unduly Burdensome Objections

The exact definition of an **unduly burdensome** set of interrogatories is elusive. Generally the courts ask the following questions to determine whether a set of interrogatories is unduly burdensome:

1. Will an inordinate amount of time be required to answer the questions?
2. Will the expense incurred in locating the answers be excessive?
3. Does the question seek information for which there is no compelling requirement?
4. Will the burden placed on the responding party exceed the benefit gained by the requesting party?
5. Has the information already been revealed during other steps in the discovery process?

The more of these questions to which the court can say yes, the more likely it is that the interrogatories will be found to be unduly burdensome.

Confidentiality Agreements and Protective Orders

Often a lawsuit involves matters that one party wants to keep confidential. For example, one party may have a trade secret that requires protection or a customer list that must be kept classified. Such limitations can be imposed voluntarily through a confidentiality agreement or by a court decree through a protective order. Interrogatories that seek information covered by a protective order or a confidentiality agreement should be answered in accordance with the terms of the order or agreement.

AUTOMATED LITIGATION SUPPORT

Casemaker

SCENARIO

Your supervising attorney has asked you to review the answers written by your client, Mr. Gilbert, in response to the interrogatories sent to him by TriD, Inc. The attorney would like the answers reviewed and back on her desk by the end of the work day. You are about to begin working on the project when she calls you into her office and tells you that she has just received word that one of the defendants, Fairness for All Blog.com, has refused to answer any of the interrogatories sent to them, and that the owners of FFABlog.com plan to file a summary judgment motion to dismiss the case on the grounds that blog owners are protected from defamation lawsuits because they are not to be considered "publishers" under provisions in the Communications Decency Act of 1996. Your attorney wants both the text of the statute and a Florida case that is almost exactly on point with the present case. Unfortunately, she does not remember the name of the case, nor any of the parties involved in that case. You are now under serious pressure. To make matters just a tiny bit worse, one of the other paralegals in your firm has called in sick. Your fellow paralegal was working on the answers to another set of interrogatories in another case that your attorney needs by 1 p.m. She asks that you review not only the answers to interrogatories drafted by Mr. Gilbert but also the ones on which the absent paralegal was working. However, she emphasizes that she wants the applicable section of the Communications Decency Act and the Florida case on her desk ASAP.

PROBLEM

It would be very time consuming to run across the street to the court house (or even to move from your office to the firm's law library) in order to comb through the United States Code (USC) to find the correct section of the Communications Decency Act and to find the Florida case that your attorney requires immediately. Is there any shortcut you can take that will allow you to find this information and have it readily available for your attorney within the allotted time without having to leave the comfort and the security of your desk?

SOLUTION

Of course you could use one of the corporate-owned and operated search engines to find the information that your attorney has requested if your firm subscribes to one of these services. However, another time-saving and very inexpensive search engine may be provided by the Bar Association in your state. For example, the Ohio State Bar Association has compiled a powerful search engine designated *Casemaker* that can help you find the material that you need. *Casemaker* is available not only to members of the Ohio State Bar Association but also to subscribers in most other states. To use *Casemaker* you must first access the Ohio State Bar Association's Web site and click on the *Casemaker* icon. Once into the *Casemaker* site, you will see a list of portals for Federal and State Materials. Clicking on State Materials will give you a list of states that participate in the Web site. If you click on "Florida" and then on "case law," you will be able to search for the missing case by using *key words* such as "defamation" and "internet." This search will provide you with a list of cases, one of which is *Giordano v. Romeo*, 76 So.3d. 1100 (Fla. App. 3 Dist. 2011), which turns out to be the case that your attorney needs. Now you can move back to the *Casemaker* site, click on "Federal Materials," and search the United States Code using the law's short title, The Communications Decency Act. Following the simple pull-down instructions will lead you to 47 U.S.C. 230 which reads, "No provider or user of an interactive computer service shall be treated as the publisher or speaker of any information provided by another information content provider." Once you have taken the case and the code section to your supervising attorney, you can get back to the task of reviewing the client's answers to the interrogatories.

ETHICAL CONCERNS

Once you return to your office your conscience begins to trouble you. You wonder why your attorney did not know about the prohibition built into the federal law at 47 U.S.C. 230. You also wonder why she suddenly "remembered" an obscure Florida case that just happens to be exactly on point. To ease your conscience more than anything else, you review the entire case file. This doesn't help. In fact, you find the file equally disturbing because in the file you find an agreement entitled, "General Release." The release states that the client will not hold the law firm liable for any potential malpractice claims against the firm. As you read the release you become concerned about its ethical legitimacy. Are there any speedy steps that you can take to explore the ethical nature of your attorney's failure to take 47 U.S.C. 230 into consideration and about the ethical nature of the "General Release"?

SOLUTION

Once again *Casemaker* can serve as a quick and efficient research tool. You can move right back into the

Casemaker Web site and click on "All Content." There you will find an entry for "Ethical Opinions." Clicking on that heading will give you a list of states that have ethical opinions filed with the Web site. Those states include Alaska, California, Connecticut, Hawaii, Indiana, Kansas, Massachusetts, Mississippi, New Hampshire, Ohio, Oregon, Rhode Island, Utah, and Washington. You can now conduct a key word or an issues search (or both) in the files of your state as you attempt to solve your ethical dilemma.

in camera

A hearing or other proceeding that is held in the judge's private chambers out of the sight and hearing of any spectators; in private; in chambers.

Burden of Proof   The party objecting to an interrogatory has the burden to prove the validity of the objection. Thus, the specific and particular grounds for the objection must be explained. The amount of detail required to sustain an objection in a hearing varies, depending on the nature of the objection. An objection based on privileged information or work product may be resolved by the judge's inspection of the documents **in camera**, a private viewing by the judge to determine the validity of the objection.

FINDING IT on the internet

American Legal Net, Inc. (ALNI) is a private firm that keeps a detailed, extensive database of more than 60,000 legal forms that cover all jurisdictions in the United States. The database includes not only forms used in the courts but also those used by governmental agencies. Access the American Legal Net Web site at **<http://www.alncorp .com/>** and click on "Products." Once you enter that site you will find a portal named **eDockets**. Report on what the **eDockets** software provides and determine how helpful it might be to a paralegal on the job.

The U. S. Supreme Court maintains a Web site at **<http://www.supremecourt.gov>**. Access the site and locate the Court's recent decisions on the right-hand side of the Court's home page. Locate the five most recent cases decided by the U.S. Supreme Court and report on the subject of each case.

The Web site of the Institute for the Advancement of the American Legal System (IAALS) at the Sturm College of Law of the University of Denver can be accessed at **<http://iaals.du.edu/>**. Access the site and navigate to the heading "News Spotlight." Click on the highlighted law-related story and report on that story. Next navigate to the heading "Denver Law News." You will find several recent stories involving law students and law professors at the Sturm College of Law. Click on one and report on the content of that story. As part of that report consider whether the activity involving the Denver students and faculty members might be something that students and faculty at your institution might adopt as well.

Reread the facts in the case at the opening of this chapter. Then reread the Automated Litigation Support feature explained earlier. Now follow the steps as suggested in the Automated Litigation Support feature and locate the case of *Giordano v. Romeo*, 76 So.3d. 1100 (Fla. App. 3 Dist. 2011). Read the case and write a report that explains and analyzes its content. State as part of your conclusion, whether the case demonstrates that the defendant, Fairness for All Blog.com (FFABlog.com), should never have been included in the lawsuit from the outset.

SUMMARY

- Interrogatories are written questions submitted by one party to another party. The responding party must answer these questions in writing and under oath. Rule 33 of the Federal Rules of Civil Procedure regulates the use of interrogatories in federal courts. Answers sought by interrogatories must be relevant to the pending lawsuit. However, those answers need not be admissible at the time of the trial, as long as they are reasonably calculated to lead to the discovery of evidence that can be submitted at trial. The primary purpose of interrogatories is to obtain information on the basic facts in a case, including any other people who may be involved in the lawsuit. Interrogatories also may be used to determine the party's contentions and to locate relevant documents. A set of interrogatories may disclose the identities of both lay and expert witnesses that the other party intends to call to the stand at trial. Interrogatories offer substantial advantages over other discovery methods. However, they also have distinct disadvantages.

- One of the primary methods for an attorney to obtain information about the opposing party's ESI is by filing interrogatories designed to uncover the nature and extent of that ESI. The most proficient way to compile ESI is to send interrogatories, the answers to which will determine the attorney's document-production requests. The interrogatories should include several topics: (1) the actual nature of the party's computer system; (2) the configuration of any networks; (3) information on any upgrades, equipment changes, and reformatting; (4) the details of any policies that mandate the preservation or elimination of certain records; (5) information concerning any backup processes in use to save data; (6) a description of the party's e-mail system; and (7) the names and responsibilities of all IT experts, their assistants, and interns involved in maintaining or servicing the party's computer system.

- Most jurisdictions require a title, introductory paragraph, definitions, instructions, specific interrogatories, a signature, and a certificate of service for interrogatories. Several types of interrogatories may be asked. Each of these is designed to elicit a different form of information related to the lawsuit. These special interrogatories include interrogatories that identify people, interrogatories that establish facts or lead to the discovery of facts, interrogatories that identify documents, and interrogatories that identify contentions.

- Because the client is responsible for answering the questions, he must be contacted immediately upon the receipt of a set of interrogatories. Working with the client, the paralegal can then determine how much time is needed to respond, how each question should be answered, which questions must be supplemented, and which questions are best answered with business records.

KEY TERMS

bring-your-own-device (BYOD) policy

company-owned, personally enabled (COPE) device policy

engrossed

in camera

metadata mining

unduly burdensome

Zubulake proportionality test

REVIEW QUESTIONS

1. What are interrogatories?
2. What are the purposes of filing interrogatories on the opposing party?
3. What are the advantages and disadvantages of using interrogatories?
4. What are the rules regarding interrogatories and ESI?
5. What are the specific types of interrogatories that can be asked?
6. What types of topics would have to be covered in any set of interrogatories designed to pave the way for a document-production request in relation to ESI?
7. What options are available to the requesting party should the responding party refuse to answer an interrogatory?
8. When is it necessary for the responding party to supplement an answer to an interrogatory?
9. When is it appropriate to produce business records as a response to interrogatories?
10. What form should answers to interrogatories take?
11. What objections to interrogatories can be raised by the responding party?

CHAPTER EXERCISES

Where necessary, check with your instructor prior to starting any of these exercises.

1. Review your state's rules relating to interrogatories. Check local court rules to see whether there are any restrictions on the number of interrogatories and/or the number of sets of interrogatories that can be filed in a lawsuit.
2. Prepare a chart of the objections to interrogatories that are permitted in the federal and state courts in your area.
3. Analyze the following situation and determine the proper response:
    a. Suppose that in the *Fairness for All Blog.com* case, your supervising attorney has asked you to draft a set of interrogatories to be sent to TriD, Inc., the object of which is to lay the foundation for a later document-production request related to all ESI stored in the corporation's computer system. One set of interrogatories would have to attempt to determine the number and types of computers that are in operation as a part of the corporation's daily routine. How would you phrase the interrogatories to ensure that no computers escape consideration?

b. Another set of questions would attempt to determine the configuration of the corporation's e-mail system. What questions would you consider asking about the e-mail system?

c. Another set of questions would aim to obtain the names and a list of responsibilities of all individuals who are in any way involved in maintaining or servicing the corporation's computer system and any network systems that are a part of the corporation's operation. List the types of individuals who would have to be included in this question.

d. Another set of questions would have to deal with the computer records themselves. What types of questions would you have to ask about these records?

CHAPTER PROJECT

In your state's form book, locate a sample set of interrogatories for a case involving the type of incident that occurred in the *Fairness for All Blog.com* case. Draft a set of interrogatories to the defendant corporation, in which you request all information relating to the allegedly defamatory blog. Also, if appropriate in your state, request information relating to the identity of all experts who will be called to testify at trial. Remember that IT specialists may have to be included among these experts. Include questions on the subject matter about which each expert will testify, all opinions that each expert has on the matter, the case number and court of each case in which each expert has testified, and all facts provided to each expert witness for use in analysis of the case. Also, request a copy of any reports the expert witnesses have prepared in connection with the case.

THE *BENNETT* CASE
Assignment for Chapter 10: Drafting Interrogatories

Your supervising attorney is interested in identifying all parties who worked for Bennett while she was acting manager as well as all parties who were involved in the hiring process of the permanent training manager. Your attorney is also interested in identifying all documents, including all ESI, that might contain relevant information. Prepare a set of interrogatories to be sent to the defendant requesting this information, as well as other relevant information.

THE *DOUGLASS FINANCIAL SERVICES INC.* CASE
Assignment for Chapter 10: Interrogatories in State Court

Your supervising attorney is preparing to send interrogatories to the plaintiff and your supervising attorney wants to check your state law regarding the following: (a) When can interrogatories be served, (b) how long will the plaintiff have to respond, and (c) is there a limit as to how many interrogatories can be served? Check your state law and prepare a short memorandum to the attorney addressing these questions.

ENDNOTES

1. Laurie Carl G. Roberts, "The 2006 Discovery Amendments to the Federal Rules of Civil Procedure," *Law Practice Today: The American Bar Association* (August 2006), retrieved on September 6, 2013 from <http://apps.americanbar.org/lpm/lpt/articles/tch08061.shtml>, 2–3.

2. Ibid.

3. Ibid.

4. Ibid.

5. "Amendments to the Federal Rules of Civil Procedure," Committee Note on Federal Rule 33, Committee on Rules of Practice and Procedure of the Judicial Conference of the United States, retrieved on April 2, 2008 from <http://www.uscourts.gov/uscourts/RulesAndPolicies/rules/EDiscovery_w_Notes.pdf>, 28; Roberts, "The 2006 Discovery Amendments," 3.

6. Kenneth J. Withers, "Electronically Stored Information: The December 2006 Amendments to the Federal Rules of Civil Procedure," *The Northwestern Journal of Technology and Intellectual Property* (Spring 2006), retrieved on January 26, 2007 from <http://scholarlycommons.law.northwestern.edu/njtip/vol4/iss2/3>, 43.

7. *Monique Da Silva Moore, et al. v. Publicis Groupe & MSL Group*, 11 Civ. 1279 (S.D.N.Y. Feb. 24, 2012).

8. *Zubulake v. UBS Warburg*, 216 F.R.D. 280 (S.D.N.Y. 2003).

9. *Electronic Discovery Task Force Report 103 B—Amendments to the Civil Discovery Standards* (revised as of 6/04), quoted in R. Bryan Nace, "Law Practice in the Electronic Age: Discovery in an Electronic Age," *The Ohio State Bar Association: 2006 Annual Convention* (May 3–5, 2006): 3.12.

10. Roberts, "The 2006 Discovery Amendments," 3; Committee Note, 28–29.

11. Withers, "Electronically Stored Information," 43.

12. Judy Branham, "New Rule 502 Standardizes Law on Waiver, Seeks to Control Privilege Review Costs," *Faegre and Benson* (January 2009), retrieved on September 18, 2010 from <http://www.faegre.com/8607>, 1–3.

13. Dennis Kennedy, "Does Your Firm Have a Bring-Your-Own-Device Policy?" *ABA Journal* (January 1, 2012), retrieved on January 11, 2012 from <http://www.abajournal.com/>, 1.

14. *EEOC v. The Original Honeybaked Ham Company of Georgia, Inc.*, No. 11-cv-02560-MSK-MEH (D. Colo. Nov. 7, 2012). While the The *Honeybaked Ham* case did not involve company-owned or programmed smartphones or tablets, it did involve social media communication. As a result, the court's ruling can easily be applied to such devices because such devices are generally the ones that are used most often to transmit social media messages , and thus, the door has been clearly been opened to similar rulings. Cecil Lynn, "New York, New York: Manhattan-Based Jurists Are the First to Enthusiastically Embrace Predictive Coding in Federal and State Courts," *E-Discovery Showcase: Law Technology News* (February 2013), retrieved on January 11, 2013 from <www.lawtechnologynews.com>, 61.

15. For a detailed explanation of this issue and suggestions on how such disputes can be handled see the Staff Notes to Rule 34 in the *Ohio Rules of Civil Procedure*.

16. David K. Isom, "Electronic Discovery Primer for Judges," *Federal Courts Law Review* (2005), retrieved on September 6, 2013 from <http://fclr.org/fclr/articles/html/2005 /fedctslrev1.pdf>, 15–17.

17. Lee H. Rosenthal, "Metadata and Issues Relating to the Form of Production," *The Pocket Part: A Companion to the Yale Law Journal* (December 4, 2006), retrieved on September 6, 2013 from <http://yalelawjournal.org/the-yale-law-journal-pocket-part /procedure/metadata-and-issues-relating-to-the-form-of-production/>.

18. Nace, "Law Practice in the Electronic Age," 3.4–3.5. For more information on metadata see David Hart and Hugh Phillips, "Metadata Primer—A 'How To' Guide on Metadata Implementation," *National States Geographic Information Counsel* (June 10, 1998), retrieved on January 29, 2007 from <http://www.lic.wisc.edu/metadata/metaprim.htm>. For an article that sees metadata simply as a method of cataloguing information, see Marty Lucas, "Demystifying Metadata," *Mappa Mundi Magazine* (2002), retrieved on January 29, 2007 from <http://mappa.mundi.net/trip-m/metadata/>.

19. Gary Blankenship, "What's in your Document? Board Says It's Unethical to Mine Hidden Data from e-Texts," *Florida Bar News* (January 1, 2006), retrieved on February 15, 2007 from <http://yalelawjournal.org/the-yale-law-journal-pocket-part/procedure /metadata-and-issues-relating-to-the-form-of-production/>, 1.

20. See *Kucala Enterprises, Ltd. v. Auto Wax Co.*, N.D. Ill., No. 02 C 1403 (May 23, 2003).

21. *Zubulake v. UBS Warburg*, 216 F.R.D. 280 (S.D.N.Y. 2003). See also: Lynn, "New York, New York," 61.

22. *See Simon Prop. Group LP v. mySimon*, 194 F.D.R. 639, 640 (S.D. Ind. 2000); see also *Dodge, Warren & Peters, Ins. Servs. v. Riley*, 130 Cal. Rptr. 2d 385 (Cal. Ct. App. 2003). Referenced in Nace, "Law Practice in the Electronic Age," 3.15. See also Marcia Coyle, " 'Metadata' Mining Vexes Lawyers, Bars: Invisible Document Data a Big Problem," *The National Law Journal* (February 18, 2008): 1, 22.

CHAPTER 11 Physical and Mental Examinations

CHAPTER OUTLINE

THE *PEACEKEEPER SECURITY* CASE

Your supervising attorney has just informed you about a case that she has been working on for several days. Her client is an older gentleman named Dr. Theodore A. Kavanaugh, an Iowa resident and a molecular biologist, who was in Omaha at a scientific conference hosted by the Unisave Institute for Human Genetics and Molecular Research. While at the conference and on the premises of the Unisave Institute, Dr. Kavanaugh was embroiled in a demonstration conducted by a group of activists protesting the institute's research program. Dr. Kavanaugh was riding in an armored van that was part of a convoy of vehicles owned and operated by Peacekeeper Security, Inc., the institute's protection agency. As the convoy entered the institute's parking garage, it was attacked by protestors representing a political group called the Osborne Planetary Treaty for Instituting Management of Artificial Life (OPTIMAL). As OPTIMAL protestors swarmed over the vehicles, the driver of Kavanaugh's van lost sight of the garage entrance ramp and crashed into a brick wall at the end of the ramp. Dr. Kavanaugh, who was injured in the collision, has brought a lawsuit against Peacekeeper Security, the Unisave Institute, and OPTIMAL, as well as several employees working for each group. As expected, one of the defendants, Peacekeeper Security, has demanded that Dr. Kavanaugh undergo a medical examination. Your supervising attorney is convinced that the Peacekeeper's attorney, Sandra Hobson, will argue that Dr. Kavanaugh's injuries are either imaginary or less serious than claimed. After reviewing Dr. Kavanaugh's version of the incident, your supervising attorney has concluded that Major Allan Hathaway, the Peacekeeper Security employee who was driving the armored van at the time of the incident, was not wearing his glasses the morning of the incident, something that would have prevented him from running the vehicle into the brick wall. This piece of evidence will help solidify your attorney's case against both Peacekeeper Security and Major Hathaway, and may even force them to settle. Your supervising attorney wants you to cooperate with Attorney Hobson in arranging the exam for Dr. Kavanaugh. On the other side of the ledger, she also wants you to arrange for an eye examination for Major Hathaway.

Chapters 8, 9, and 10 introduced two specialized types of discovery, depositions, and interrogatories. The request for physical or mental examination is another effective tool in the discovery process. After reading this chapter, you should be able to:

- define physical and mental examination.
- outline four types of cases in which the physical and mental examination may be used.
- explain the purposes for requesting a physical or mental examination.
- detail the procedure for obtaining a physical or mental examination if the parties cannot agree to the examination.
- define the concepts of "good cause" and "in controversy."
- relate the responsibilities a paralegal might perform in the physical and mental examination process.
- determine the possible consequences of a party's refusal to submit to a physical or mental examination.

THE PHYSICAL OR MENTAL EXAMINATION

A **physical or mental examination** is the examination that a *party* must undergo concerning a physical or mental condition at issue in a pending legal action. One party to a lawsuit can request that the other party undergo a physical or mental examination when that physical or mental condition is an important factor in a lawsuit. The request can be made even if the party who is to undergo the examination is a minor, in the custody of a parent, or a legally incapacitated person under the legal control of a guardian. Physical and mental examinations, by their very nature, will invade the privacy of the person undergoing the examination. For this reason, among others, this discovery tool is used only in certain types of narrowly defined cases.

Types of Cases Using Physical or Mental Examinations

Physical and mental examinations are often used in personal injury cases. In such cases, the physical or mental condition of a party can be very important in establishing the personal liability of the defendant or in determining the extent of the injuries suffered by the plaintiff. For example, in this chapter's *Peacekeeper Security* case, your supervising attorney has requested a physical examination to determine if Major Hathaway is nearsighted and whether he has difficulty seeing in darkened areas such as the inside of a parking garage. Because your supervising attorney has alleged that Major Hathaway's failure to wear his glasses contributed to the accident, and because Major Hathaway has stated that his eyesight is quite good, an eye examination would be in order. Moreover, Ms. Hobson, Major Hathaway's attorney, has asked Dr. Kavanaugh to undergo a physical examination to determine whether his injuries are as serious as he claims.

Personal injury cases are not the only types of lawsuits that involve physical and mental examinations. A physical exam might be used to provide evidence concerning the nature and the extent of the injuries in an industrial accident case. Such an examination may also be requested to determine the identity of the father of a child in a paternity suit or to establish whether a plaintiff is eligible for payments under the terms of a disability insurance policy. Whether an examination is requested often depends on the purpose that the attorneys have in mind when they are planning the legal strategy in a lawsuit.

Reasons for Allowing Physical and Mental Examinations

The law allows physical and mental examinations to establish the truth about the plaintiff's allegation of physical or mental injuries. For example, in the *Peacekeeper Security* case, if Dr. Kavanaugh says that he has a back strain as a result of the accident, the defendant may demand a physical examination to determine the validity of this claim. The possibility of a physical or a mental examination may also discourage plaintiffs who have filed lawsuits based on false or exaggerated claims. In fact, the very existence of this rule deters the filing of fraudulent or exaggerated lawsuits in the first place. Such examinations may also reveal inconsistencies between a plaintiff's complaints and the real nature of the injury. In the *Peacekeeper Security* case, for instance, Dr. Kavanaugh may complain of severe back pain. A physical examination could determine whether the pain is imaginary or is caused by a real injury.

FILING A MOTION FOR COMPULSORY EXAMINATION

compulsory examination
An examination that a party to a lawsuit has been ordered by the court to undergo concerning a physical or mental condition.

Most physical and mental examinations are scheduled by mutual agreement made by the attorneys for the parties. In such cases, this mutual agreement should be set out in a letter or formal stipulation filed with the court. If agreement cannot be reached, however, a formal motion for **compulsory examination** will be necessary. Such a motion must establish good cause for the requested physical or mental examination. Exhibit 11-1 is an example of a motion for compulsory examination.

EXHIBIT 11-1 Motion for a Physical Examination

UNITED STATES DISTRICT COURT FOR THE DISTRICT OF IOWA

THEODORE KAVANAUGH,)
    Plaintiff,) Case No. 17-61491
    v.) MOTION FOR PHYSICAL EXAMINATION
PEACEKEEPER SECURITY, INC.)
    Defendant, et al.)

TO THE HONORABLE JUDGE OF SAID COURT:

    COMES NOW Peacekeeper Security, Inc. and Allan Hathaway, the Defendants in the above cause, and file this Motion under Rule 35 of the Federal Rules of Civil Procedure, to require Theodore Kavanaugh, the Plaintiff in the above cause, to submit to a physical examination by Patrick Weber, M.D., at 602 Lauren Avenue, in the city of Iowa City, and respectfully show the Court as follows:

I.

    This is a case in which the Plaintiff alleges that he suffered permanent and disabling injuries as a result of a vehicle accident on May 20, 2016, at Unisave Institute for Human Genetics and Molecular Research in the city of Omaha in the state of Nebraska. The Plaintiff alleges that said accident was directly and proximately caused by the negligence of the Defendants.

II.

    Defendant denies the allegations made by the Plaintiff concerning his injuries and disabilities. Accordingly, the physical condition of the Plaintiff is in controversy.

III.

    Defendant has heretofore requested the Plaintiff to submit to a voluntary examination, and that request has been denied.

IV.

    Defendant requests that the Plaintiff be ordered by the Court to submit to an independent medical examination at the offices of Patrick Weber, M.D., at 602 Lauren Avenue, in the city of Iowa City, in this state, on March 25, 2017, at 2 p.m.

EXHIBIT 11-1 Motion for a Physical Examination (*continued*)

WHEREFORE, the Defendant herein prays that the court grant this Motion in all respects and award all other and further relief to which Defendant is justly entitled.

Respectfully submitted,

_____

Sara Hobson
Attorney for Defendant

CERTIFICATE OF SERVICE

I hereby certify that a true and correct copy of the foregoing Motion for Physical Examination has been furnished to counsel of record on this the seventh day of February, 2017.

_____

---

notice
A formal notification of intent; the knowledge of a particular set of facts; the formal acquisition of the knowledge of a fact or set of facts.

good cause
A legally acceptable reason for doing something or for refusing to do something.

The content of a motion requesting an order for a physical or a mental examination is outlined in Rule 35 (a) (2) of the Federal Rules of Civil Procedure. The party requesting the examination must give notice to the person to be examined and to all the other parties or their attorneys. **Notice** is a formal written notification to the person to be examined and to the other parties. The moving papers, which are filed with the court and which give notice to the other party and the examiner, must specify the time, place, manner, conditions, scope of the examination, and the name of the person conducting the examination. The motion must be specific. In the *Peacekeeper Security* case, for example, a broad request for Major Hathaway to undergo a physical examination would be too vague and probably would not be ordered by the court. To be acceptable the motion would have to ask for an eye test to determine whether Major Hathaway is nearsighted, has difficulty seeing in darkness, or has macular degeneration, all of which would be relevant to the case.

REQUIREMENTS FOR GRANTING THE MOTION FOR COMPULSORY EXAMINATION

Rule 35 of the Federal Rules of Civil Procedure gives the trial judge total discretion in determining whether the request for a physical or mental examination meets two essential requirements. These requirements are that there be "good cause" for the examination and that the nature of the condition be "in controversy."

Evidence of Good Cause

Because physical and mental examinations invade a person's privacy the courts define **good cause** very strictly. In general, the court will decide that good cause exists only if the same information cannot be found any other way. Still, good cause is an adaptable concept that varies based on the nature of the case and the type of examination requested. For example, in the *Peacekeeper Security* case, the physical condition of Dr. Kavanaugh is an important aspect of the case, and the need for an examination is obvious. This may not be true in other lawsuits, such as one involving the question of whether a person was mentally competent to enter a contract.

Condition in Controversy

Federal Rule 35 also requires that the physical or mental condition to be examined by the medical professional must be in controversy. To be **in controversy**, the condition to be examined must be at issue in the lawsuit. For example, a request for an order compelling Dr. Kavanaugh to submit to a DNA test would have nothing to do with his personal injury claim. Such a request would not be ordered. In contrast, in a paternity suit, a request for an order to compel a defendant to undergo a DNA match to determine whether he is the father of a child would be at the heart of the dispute; such a request would be granted. Similarly, a request for a mental examination would not be granted if neither mental nor emotional injuries have been alleged. However, if a plaintiff claims to be the victim of intentionally caused emotional distress, a mental examination would be appropriate. In the *Peacekeeper Security* case, because your supervising attorney intends to prove that Major Hathaway's poor eyesight contributed to the accident, and because Major Hathaway has denied having eye problems, the matter is in controversy. Similarly, the nature and the extent of Dr. Kavanaugh's injuries are also in controversy.

in controversy
In the case of any physical or mental examination, the prerequisite that states that the condition to be examined must be at issue in the lawsuit.

GRANTING A MOTION FOR COMPULSORY EXAMINATION

Federal Rule 35 gives the trial judge total discretion to decide if the party seeking a physical or mental examination has good cause for the request and whether the examination involves a condition in controversy. This discretion, however, does not mean that the moving party must prove his case on the merits as he would at a trial. Nor does this discretion automatically mean that a hearing will be held prior to entry of an order for the examination. In some cases a hearing may be required. In others, the judge may decide that these requirements have been met on the basis of an affidavit filed by the attorney or a physician who believes that the examination is vital to establishing the claims or defenses of the case.

If the court decides to grant the motion for compulsory examination, the judge will issue an order compelling the party to submit to the examination. Usually the party seeking the order includes a proposed order when filing the original motion. Exhibit 11-2 is a sample form of a proposed order for entry by the trial judge. The judge may or may not enter the proposed order as submitted. In fact, the judge could even change the number or type of examinations asked for in the motion. For example, in the *Peacekeeper Security* case, the judge might order several examinations of Dr. Kavanaugh to determine the nature and the extent of his injuries. The court also has the authority to order subsequent examinations if it feels the facts require further validation. In the *Peacekeeper Security* case, for example, part of Major Hathaway's defense may be that Dr. Kavanaugh's problems stem from a previous industrial accident and not from his collision in the institute's parking garage. In such a case, the judge might order several examinations to help validate or invalidate that defense.

EXHIBIT 11-2 Sample Form of a Proposed Order for
Entry by the Trial Judge

UNITED STATES DISTRICT COURT FOR THE DISTRICT OF IOWA

THEODORE KAVANAUGH,   )
)   Case No. 17-61491
    Plaintiff,   )
)   ORDER
    v.   )
)
PEACEKEEPER SECURITY, INC.   )
)
)
    Defendant, et al.   )
)

    This matter being heard on Defendant's Motion to compel the physical examination of Plaintiff, all parties having been given notice, and the court having heard arguments, it is hereby ordered that:

1. Plaintiff Theodore Kavanaugh be examined by Patrick Weber, M.D., at 602 Lauren Avenue, in the city of Iowa City in this state, on March 25, 2017, at 2 p.m. unless the Plaintiff and Dr. Weber mutually agree to an earlier date and time.

2. Plaintiff shall submit to such neurological examinations and tests as are necessary to diagnose and evaluate Plaintiff's back and legs, so that Dr. Weber can reach opinions and conclusions about the extent of any injuries, their origin, and prognosis.

3. Dr. Weber shall prepare a written report detailing his findings, test results, diagnosis, prognosis, and opinions along with any similar reports on the same conditions, and deliver it to Defendant's attorneys on or before March 25, 2017.

Signed this 14th day of February, 2017.

                                                _____
                                                JUDGE

THE PARALEGAL'S ROLE IN PHYSICAL AND MENTAL EXAMINATIONS

Your role as the paralegal in the request for a physical or mental examination will depend on which attorney has requested such an examination.

Arranging for the Examination of an Opposing Party

If your supervising attorney has requested an examination of an opposing party, you may be asked to schedule the examination. In such a situation, you should contact the opposing attorney immediately to ascertain if he or she has any objections to the examination. If the other party objects, you may be asked to draft the motion for compulsory physical exam and a proposed order, as shown in Exhibits 11-1 and 11-2, respectively.

Fortunately, however, most physical and mental examinations are voluntary. If your supervising attorney has requested the examination, it will normally be conducted by a physician of her choice, unless the party to be examined has a valid objection to that selection. This selection is not an absolute right, however. If the parties cannot agree on a physician, the court will make the selection. Check your local court rules to determine whether they include an approved list of impartial experts from which the examining physician must be selected. In any event, Rule 35 (a) (1) of the Federal Rules of Civil Procedure requires that the examiner be "suitably licensed or certified."

Convenience should be a major criterion in the selection. If the party to be examined lives in Iowa City, Iowa, and the party requesting the examination selects a physician at the Cleveland Clinic, the court could refuse to approve the physician selected. On the

---

AUTOMATED LITIGATION SUPPORT

The Administrative Database

SCENARIO

You have just been called into a meeting with your supervising attorney in the *Peacekeeper Security* case. She has just met Greg Stuart, a private investigator who has spent the last month compiling dossiers on all of the key members of the Osborne Planetary Treaty for Instituting the Management of Artificial Life (OPTIMAL). This was the group that was involved in the protest on the morning of May 20, 2015, the date of the incident in which Dr. Kavanaugh, your client, was injured. Your attorney wants to store all of this data for review later in the week. However, she is concerned that, because of several class action cases that her partners have taken on in the last few weeks, your firm's computer system, especially in relation to its storage capacity, is rapidly becoming obsolete. She and the other partners are considering the advisability of shifting to cloud computing as an alternate technique. She wants you to research the advisability of moving toward the use of a cloud computing system. She is especially concerned with the downside of the shift to the cloud and she wants you to play devil's advocate in this afternoon's meeting.

PROBLEM

You know very little about cloud computing and even less about the advantages and disadvantages of the system. You have only a few hours to prepare a presentation. You do not want to paint an unrealistic picture of the disadvantages of the system, especially if establishing such a system helps to lessen the workload on the firm's already overextended paralegal staff. On the other hand, if you do

not paint a realistic picture of the risks involved in the shift to the cloud, you may open the firm to liability. What do you do?

SOLUTION

The best place to begin your search is to jump on your favorite search engine and find a simple and straightforward definition of cloud computing, one that you can introduce to the firm's partners in a nonthreatening and helpful way. The next step would be to do a search for national firms that offer the cloud storage services What you will find is that some of the major computer companies on the planet such as Google, Microsoft, AT&T, and Amazon are involved in cloud computing. You can then go directly to their Web sites for detailed information on what they have to offer. However, remember that you have been assigned to play the devil's advocate in this presentation. To play this role successfully, you should find answers to each of the following key questions as you compile your research: (1) What type of security system does the cloud company offer to protect your ESI and that of your clients? (2) How much storage capacity does each cloud company provide? (3) What type of privacy guarantees does each company promise to provide? (3) To what extent does the company warrant the integrity of the data stored in their cloud? (4) What are the details of their service contract? (5) Which companies will ensure that your firm is in compliance with all relevant federal and state laws regarding the protection of sensitive and confidential ESI? Finally, make sure that you compare price tags from company to company. After all, this is one question that someone at that table is certain to ask.

other hand, the parties may be required to come to the city where the suit is filed for the physical or mental examination, even though they do not reside in that city. Assuming that everyone involved is agreeable up to this point, your next job would be to contact the physician or laboratory to discuss the purpose of the examination and the nature of the case. Arrangements for payment of the physician or laboratory should also be discussed at the time of the initial contact.

Following the examination, you should contact the physician or laboratory and request a copy of the report. Once you have received the report, review it with the attorney and, when the report has been approved, pay the physician or the laboratory. Remember also to add that amount to the client's ledger for billing. Your supervising attorney will direct when and where a copy of the medical report should be sent. Your supervising attorney may also ask you to review the medical report and prepare a summary by chronology of events or category of injury. The fact that you have received a written report from the physician who examined the opposing party does not affect your supervising attorney's ability to depose the examining physician. The examination under Rule 35 (b) (6) is not a substitute for discovery through a deposition or other available discovery tool.

Preparing the Client for an Examination

If opposing counsel has requested an examination of your client, you should notify the client immediately. Hopefully, your supervising attorney has already warned the client about this possibility. Still, the client may be apprehensive about the examination. Explaining the purpose and procedure should give the client some comfort. This explanation can be sent in a letter to the client setting out the details concerning the examination. Exhibit 11-3 is an example of such a letter to the client.

You may have to meet with the client before the examination to review the types of questions he can expect from the physician. Caution your client not to tell the examiner anything he has not talked about with his attorney. Also warn your client not to discuss the facts of the case with the examining physician. However, the client should be reminded to review all facets of his medical history, including the names of all doctors and hospitals that have treated him, the nature of the illness or injury, the names of medications including over-the-counter medications, and the dates of all illnesses, injuries, or hospitalizations. For example, in the *Peacekeeper Security* case, Dr. Kavanaugh should not discuss with the physician anything he has talked over with you or your supervising attorney about the suit he has filed against Peacekeeper Security and Major Hathaway. Nor should he discuss the incident itself. He should, however, be prepared to discuss his own medical history.

Furnishing the client with a medical summary sheet such as the one in Exhibit 11-4 will help him recall information that will be covered in the physical examination. However, the client probably should not take this summary into the examination room. Using such a written record to answer questions in the presence of the examiner may cast some doubt on your client's ability to independently recall his own medical history. Such a revelation may hurt your client's credibility, should it somehow come to the jury's attention at trial. Your client may ask that his own physician be present during the examination.

EXHIBIT 11-3 Sample Letter to Client Concerning Physical Examination

---

LYBARGER, PLOTTS, KASENBERG, AND PEARSALL

6225 St. Clair Avenue
Council Bluffs, Iowa 51503
March 5, 2017

Dr. Theodore A. Kavanaugh
433 East 310th Street
Iowa City, Iowa 51509

Dear Dr. Kavanaugh,

You may recall that attorney Lybarger mentioned in your initial visit to our office that the other side may request an examination by a physician of their choosing to confirm the existence and the extent of your injuries. Ms. Sara Hobson, the attorney of record for both Peacekeeper Security, Inc. and Allan Hathaway, two key defendants in the action, has requested such an examination.

The examination is tentatively scheduled for March 25, 2017, at 2:00 p.m. The examining physician is Dr. Patrick Weber. His office is located at 602 Lauren Avenue, Iowa City. Please be at his office several minutes prior to that time so that the examination can begin on schedule.

This examination will consist of an examination of your neck and back injuries as well as several diagnostic X-rays. The examination should last no longer than one hour.

Before the examination, you should review the medical recap sheet that you have prepared so that you may respond quickly and correctly to the physician's questions about prior illnesses, injuries, medication, etc.

Please cooperate with the physician, but do not volunteer any information not specifically requested. Do not exaggerate or minimize any medical problem about which you are asked.

Attorney Lybarger believes this examination will be beneficial in establishing the damages you have suffered to this date. If you have any questions about the examination, please let me know.

Thanks for your time.

Sincerely,

Savannah Hargis

_____
Paralegal

That request must be made through the opposing attorney. Permission for the examining physician is up to the trial judge. Some states—California, for example—also allow a paralegal to accompany the client.

Sanctions   Hopefully, your client will voluntarily submit to any necessary examination. However, if he refuses to submit to an examination, you should point out that such a refusal carries sanctions or penalties. These sanctions include an order striking all or parts of pleadings, staying the proceedings until the order for the examination is obeyed, entry of a default judgment against a defendant who refuses to submit to the examination, or the

EXHIBIT 11-4 Medical Summary Sheet

MEDICAL RECAP

PHYSICIANS:

Name	Date of Visit	Diagnosis/Treatment
Andrew Roberts Omaha General Hospital 5296 South View Blvd. Omaha, Nebraska (402) 555-1966	May 20, 2015	Broken leg Sprained back Concussion
Sam Gardner Iowa Central Clinic 2000 Prospect Avenue Iowa City, Iowa (712) 555-6333	May 28, 2015 to June 14, 2015	Treatment for above noted injuries
Sam Gardner Vilnius Street Clinic 1917 Vilnius Avenue, Suite 2 Iowa City, Iowa (712) 555-1924	June 27, 2015	Cast removed
Gary Kahn 1954 West Lynwood Street Council Bluffs, Iowa (712) 555-5293	June 30, 2015 to September 9, 2015	Physical therapy

PRESCRIPTIONS:

Name	Date	Drug Prescribed/Reason
Andrew Roberts Omaha General Hospital 5296 South View Blvd. Omaha, Nebraska (402) 555-1966	May 20, 2015	Tylenol w/Codeine Pain
Sam Gardner 1917 Vilnius Avenue Suite 2 Iowa City, Iowa (712) 555-1924	June 27, 2015	Vasotec/Hypertension

HOSPITALS/CLINICS:

Name	Date	Reason for Visit
Omaha General Hospital 5296 South View Blvd. Omaha, Nebraska (402) 555-1966	May 20, 2015	Treatment—injuries noted

EXHIBIT 11-4 Medical Summary Sheet (*continued*)

Iowa Central Clinic 2000 Prospect Avenue Iowa City, Iowa (712) 555-6333	May 28, 2015 to June 14, 2015	Treatment for above noted injuries
St. Cloud Medical Clinic 310 Claremont Street Iowa City, Iowa (712) 555-6225	June 30, 2015 to September 9, 2015	Physical therapy

LABORATORIES/DIAGNOSTIC SERVICES:

Name/Referring Physician	**Date**	**Service/Reason**
Alex Rogers Omaha General Hospital 5296 South View Blvd Omaha, Nebraska (802) 555-1966	May 20, 2015	Diagnostic X-rays

dismissal of a plaintiff's case if the plaintiff refuses to submit to the examination. Your client may also be ordered to pay the physician's fee if the client fails to appear for an appointment and it must be rescheduled.

Distributing the Medical Records Be very careful when asking for a copy of the physician's report or the laboratory test results after the examination of your client has been conducted. This is because the discovery provisions of Rule 35 of the Federal Rules of Civil Procedure are reciprocal. In other words, if you request a copy of the report on your client's examination, then the other side can request copies of all reports you have that deal with the same condition, regardless of when those reports were made. Because of this, ask your supervising attorney before you request a copy of the medical report on your client. Although the reports in your possession do not automatically have to be produced, your request allows the opposing counsel to gain access to them as requested. Your supervising attorney may not want to open that window. However, the rules of your state may allow opposing counsel access to your client's medical records regardless of any request on your part. This eventuality often materializes when your client is the plaintiff in a personal injury case. In such a situation you would want to request a copy of the report. Again, you should consult with your supervising attorney and check the rules of your particular state before making such a request.

Medical Reports and Electronically Stored Information The new amendments to the Federal Rules of Civil Procedure do not specifically describe the medical nature of the reports (except for a mention of blood groups) that are produced by medical personnel as the result of an examination authorized under Rule 35. Nevertheless, Rule 35 does describe such reports using language such as "examiner's report," "results of any test," "diagnoses," "conclusions," and "reports of all earlier examinations." As noted previously, Rule 35 also states that a party who has undergone an examination under Rule 35 and

FINDING IT on the Internet

The Florida Bar Association produces a publication appropriately named the *Florida Bar Journal* that prints articles on substantive law, policy issues, and procedural concerns of interest to practicing attorneys. The journal, which maintains an archive that extends back to 1997, can be accessed through the Florida Bar Association Web site at **<http://www.floridabar.org>**. Access the site and use the site map in the left margin to navigate to "Publications" and from there to the journal's home page, and conduct a search for articles on physical or mental examinations in litigation. Report on your findings.

The Legal Studies Division of the Washington Legal Foundation publishes cutting-edge articles in its Working Papers Series that focus on legal issues related to judicial activism, the basic principles of the free enterprise system, and the security of the United States. The papers are aimed at influencing the news media, policy makers, and other central players on the policy-making scene in Washington today. Access the Washington Legal Foundation site at **<http://www.wlf.org>** and navigate to "Publishing" on the top left of the home page. Find the heading "Become a WLF Author" and report on what the foundation tells you about becoming one of their authors.

Like the Florida Bar Association, the Massachusetts Bar Association publishes a journal on legal issues that concern lawyers today. The journal published by the Massachusetts Bar, named the *Massachusetts Law Review*, can be accessed at the MBA Web site at **<http://www.massbar.org>**. Access the site and navigate from "Publications" to the home page for the *Massachusetts Law Review*. Once you find the law review's home page conduct a search for articles on Rule 35 of the Massachusetts Rules of Civil Procedure. Report on what you find.

The American Medical Association (AMA) maintains a Web site at **<http://ama-assn.org>**. The AMA also produces a weekly publication called the *Journal of the AMA (JAMA)*. The journal has been published since 1883. Access the AMA site and conduct a preliminary search to see if the journal has published any recent articles on physical and mental examinations in litigation. Report on what you uncover.

The American Psychological Association also maintains a Web site at **<http://www.apa.org>**. Navigate to the site and find "Publications." Do a quick search for articles using the key words *psychology* and *litigation* and report your results.

who requests a copy of an examiner's report must produce, on request, a copy of all reports that deal with the same condition. Such reports will inevitably involve electronically stored information (ESI). This designation makes the delivery of such reports more difficult and more risky than the delivery of paper reports. Thus, if your client delivers a medical report to opposing counsel, he might inadvertently send along with that ESI, metadata that can be mined successfully by the opposition. This possibility makes it imperative that your client request a copy of the original report only if there is some compelling reason to do so.

The Genetic Information Nondiscrimination Act The Genetic Information Nondiscrimination Act provides protection against discrimination in employment and health insurance based on genetic information compiled by genetic testing, whatever the purpose of that testing.[1] Under provisions of the act, information that comes from genetic tests cannot be used by insurance companies to alter premiums or to change contributions for a group. In fact, the law goes so far as to prevent insurers from asking for such tests. The law does not, however, stop health care professionals from asking for such tests. Nor does the new law stop a group health plan from determining payments based on genetic information, although it does demand that the group plan limit their request to the smallest amount of information needed to make the decision.[2] Additionally, the law stops employers from using a person's genetic code to make detrimental employment-related decisions.[3] So far as can be known at this point in time, the law does not affect requests for physical examinations in litigation. However, the antidiscrimination provisions in the act prohibit adverse employment and insurance decisions based on genetic information regardless of the source of that information. This prohibition adds another reason for the paralegal to be careful about protecting the information gained from such tests in the litigation process.

SUMMARY

- A physical and mental examination is the examination of a party to a lawsuit to determine factual information about the physical or mental condition of that party. The request can be made even if the party is a minor, in the custody of a parent, or a legally incapacitated person under the control of a guardian. The examination is a tool used to establish the validity of allegations of mental or physical injuries.

- Most physical and mental examinations are scheduled by mutual agreement. If an agreement cannot be reached, however, a formal motion for a compulsory examination must be filed with the court.

- Rule 35 of the Federal Rules of Civil Procedure sets forth the conditions under which a motion for a physical or mental examination will be granted by the trial court. These requirements are that there be good cause for the examination and that the nature of the condition be in controversy.

- The trial judge has total discretion as to whether the party seeking a physical or mental examination has good cause for the request and whether the examination involves a condition in controversy. If the court decides to grant the motion for the examination, it will issue an order compelling the party to submit to the examination.

- The paralegal's role in the request for a physical or mental examination depends on whether the paralegal's attorney or the opposing attorney has requested the examination. The paralegal's role will also depend on whether the examination is proceeding by agreement or by a motion filed with the court.

KEY TERMS

compulsory examination	in controversy	physical or mental
good cause	notice	examination

REVIEW QUESTIONS

1. What is a physical and mental examination?

2. What are four types of cases in which a physical or mental examination might be requested?

3. What are four reasons the law allows one party to compel another party to submit to a physical or mental examination?

4. What is an example of a party "in the custody of" or "under the legal control of" another person?

5. What are the concepts of *good cause* and *in controversy* as they relate to the physical and mental examination?

6. What is the procedure for obtaining a physical or mental examination if the parties cannot agree to the examination?

7. What is the paralegal's role in arranging for the physical or mental examination of an opposing party?

8. What is the paralegal's role in preparing the client to undergo a physical or mental examination?

9. What are the considerations to be evaluated prior to requesting a copy of the examinee's medical report?

10. What are the possible consequences of a party's refusal to submit to a physical or mental examination ordered by the court?

CHAPTER EXERCISES

Where necessary, check with your instructor prior to starting any of these exercises.

1. Review the laws of your state and find all laws that deal with requests for physical and mental examinations. Find out whether any local court rules in your area regulate any aspect of the request for a physical or mental examination.

2. Find the form books in your law library that provide sample forms for use in drafting legal documents in your state. Find a sample motion for a physical examination and a sample proposed order compelling such an examination. How do they compare to the samples found in this chapter?

3. Analyze the following situation and decide on the proper response. Suppose in the *Peacekeeper Security* case that your supervising attorney's client, Dr. Kavanaugh, has announced that he will not show up for his scheduled appointment with Dr. Weber.

   a. What are the possible sanctions under the Federal Rules of Civil Procedure that Dr. Kavanaugh risks if he follows through on his threat? Explain.

   b. How would you dissuade Dr. Kavanaugh from going through with his threat to refuse to see Dr. Weber?

   c. Dr. Kavanaugh insists that his own physician be allowed to be present for his physical examination. Explain to Dr. Kavanaugh the circumstances that would allow this to occur.

d. Dr. Kavanaugh also insists that you be allowed to accompany him to the physical examination. Does your state permit a paralegal to accompany the client to a physical examination such as the one ordered for Dr. Kavanaugh?

CHAPTER PROJECT

Review the *Peacekeeper Security* case in the opening Commentary. Draft a checklist of duties that you might expect to assume in preparing Dr. Kavanaugh for his physical examination. Also draft an e-mail message to your supervising attorney exploring the issue of whether you should request a copy of Dr. Kavanaugh's examination results, in light of the laws of your state.

THE *BENNETT* CASE
Assignment for Chapter 11: Stipulation for Medical Exam

Because Bennett claimed in her complaint that she suffered both physically and mentally as a result of defendant's action, the defendant has requested that she submit to both a physical and a mental exam. Your supervising attorney has agreed to one examination to be conducted by Dr. Peter Ebert, a board-certified psychiatrist. The attorneys have also agreed that the doctor will not inquire into any events that occurred more than five years ago. The examination is scheduled for the 25th of next month. You have been asked to prepare a written stipulation reflecting this agreement.

THE *DOUGLASS FINANCIAL SERVICES INC.* CASE
Assignment for Chapter 11: Setting up a Medical Exam

Your attorney wants to set up a medical examination of the plaintiff. Dr. Marvin Macy, an orthopedist, has agreed to conduct the examination. The exam will consist of an examination of the neck and back of the plaintiff. Draft a letter to plaintiff's attorney requesting that the plaintiff voluntarily submit to such an examination. Anticipating plaintiff's agreement, a tentative appointment is scheduled for the 20th of next month at 11 a.m.

END NOTES

1. David J. Kovach, "GINA," *Ohio State Bar Association: 2010 Annual Convention* (May 5–7, 2010): 6.1–6.5.

2. "The Genetic Information Nondiscrimination Act," *Department of Health and Human Services* (April 6, 2009): 1. Retrieved on September 25, 2010 from <http://www.genome.gov>; "H.R. 493: Genetic Information Nondiscrimination Act of 2008," *Congressional Research Service*, 1. Retrieved on August 20, 2010 from <http://www.govtrack.us/congress/bills/110/hr493/text>.

3. Kovach, "GINA," 6.3–6.4.

CHAPTER 12 **Request for Documents**

THE *KELTEX* CASE

The Keltex Center for Advanced Technology (Keltex) entered a contract with the electronics firm of Netcore, Inc., headquartered in Grand Rapids, Michigan, to remodel its experimental electronics laboratory in Port Clinton, Ohio. The contract involved the installation of a new state-of-the-art computer system that would enable Keltex to handle innovative scientific and technological problems that are presently beyond the capabilities of two regional research institutions, the Advanced Physics Institute in Detroit and the Innovative Nanotechnology Research Complex in Cleveland. The plan is to give Keltex the capability of handling those problems so that the labs in Detroit and Cleveland do not have to farm those projects out to labs in China and the EU. During the initial contract negotiation session, Marcel Aspect, the executive director of Keltex, made certain that Alyendra Raveau, the chief engineer at Netcore, knew that the work at Keltex had to be completed by September 9, 2015, in order for Keltex to meet a contract deadline that it had with the Detroit Advanced Physics Institute. A long and complicated series of e-mails, texts, voice mails, memos, tweets, and faxes, were sent between Aspect and Raveau, as well as several drafts of the contract. When the new computer system was not operational by September 9, Keltex had to dismiss Netcore from the job and hire a second construction firm, Global Net, Ltd., to complete the job. The delay and the new contract cost Keltex $433,310. This led to further financial difficulties for Keltex, which lost the Advanced Physics contract. Raveau and Netcore have argued that no deadline was built into the contract and that September 9 was nothing more than an estimated completion date. Raveau also claims that Aspect received repeated updates from Raveau indicating that the September 9, 2015, timetable was unreasonable. Aspect, of course denies all of this. Keltex and Aspect have retained your firm to bring a suit against Netcore. Your supervising attorney wants you to help draft a document request that will allow her to obtain copies of any e-mails, texts, memos, tweets, contract drafts, faxes, and voice mails that were sent between Aspect and Raveau. She is especially concerned about losing the ESI stored in Netcore's computer system. She knows almost nothing about computers, and will rely on you for help in this matter.

Chapters 8, 9, 10, and 11 introduced you to depositions, interrogatories, and requests for physical and mental examinations. The next discovery technique is the request for documents. After reading this chapter, you should be able to:

- explain a request for production of documents.
- decide when a legal hold should be placed on the use of document and ESI.
- identify the different approaches to document requests.
- outline the three categories of ESI.
- explain how the various evidentiary privileges relate to document production.
- explain Rule 502 of the Federal Rules of Evidence.
- determine when confidentiality agreements or protective orders should be sought.
- explain what objections are available to prevent the production of documents.
- identify the duties of the paralegal in the production of documents.
- explain when a party can request an inspection of property or an on-site visit to obtain ESI.

request for documents
A request that a party or other individual involved in a lawsuit provide specific documents or other physical evidence to the party making the request for such documents or physical evidence.

THE REQUEST FOR DOCUMENTS

A **request for documents** is a request that a party or other individual involved in a lawsuit provide ESI, paper documents, or other physical evidence to the party making the request. Prior to the mutual disclosure amendments to Rule 26 of the Federal Rules of Civil Procedure, the majority of documents produced in a lawsuit were delivered through this formal request for documents. Because of this significant change in production methods, we will examine the process of document production through mutual disclosure.

Recent Developments Concerning Mutual Disclosure of Documents

Rule 26 (a) (1) (A) (ii) of the Federal Rules of Civil Procedure requires the mutual disclosure of the following information within 14 days (under Rule 26 (a) (1) (C)) after the initial conference between the parties: "a copy—or a description by category and location—of all documents, electronically stored information, and tangible things that the disclosing party has in its possession, custody, or control and may use to support its claims or defenses, unless the use would be solely for impeachment."

Mutual Disclosures and ESI

Federal Rule 26 (a) (1) (A) (ii) states that all electronically stored information (ESI) must be disclosed along with all paper documents and other tangible things as early as possible in the discovery process. This requirement encompasses all relevant items of ESI including those found in any electronic device, not just those that are commonly thought of as computers. Here are a few of these devices, some of which may have escaped your supervising attorney's notice because they include devices that many people do not think of when they hear the word *computer*: antitheft systems and databases, audio networks, audio systems, digital cameras, documented image technology, embedded chips, e-mail software, e-mail systems, event data recorders (in vehicles), external hard drives, fax machines, flash drives, global positioning systems, handheld wireless devices, hardware, iPods, iPads, landline phones, laptops, medical devices and records, memory sticks and flash cards, mobile phones, notebooks, pagers, personal computers, PDAs, printers, radio frequency identification tags or chips (RFIDs), security cameras and other security and surveillance devices, servers, servers at data centers (cloud storage centers), software, smartphones, spyware, tablets, toll road cards, travel drives, videodiscs, videotapes, and Web-based bulletin boards. To be on the safe side, all of these devices should be considered when examining the nature of ESI in your client's possession, custody, and control.[1]

Moreover, today it has become acceptable for employees to use their own tablets, smartphones, and laptops on the job. Some businesses distribute employer-owned devices that include separate areas for the employee's personal use, while others allow workers to bring their own devices into the workplace that are programmed by the firm's IT department with secure work areas for e-mail, employee forms, and other work-related files.[2] Whichever tactic is used, the methodical attorney will assume that her opponent's clients are engaged in this practice and will include the ESI stored on business-owned and personally owned e-devices in a document request. Moreover, she will also make sure that her clients realize that personal electronic devices may be included in any document request filed by the other party.

Alternative Methods of Requesting Documents

In federal court, as well as in many state courts, in addition to mutual disclosure and a Rule 34 request for production, the parties to a lawsuit can request documents and ESI at the deposition of a party, or they can use a subpoena duces tecum to compel a nonparty to produce documents and ESI at the time of a deposition. The use of interrogatories may also result in the production of documents and ESI.

Request for Documents at the Deposition of a Party
Documents may be obtained from a party by serving a request for that party to bring those documents to her deposition. Rule 30 (b) (2) of the Federal Rules of Civil Procedure allows this alternative. The specific documents or the categories of documents to be produced must be included in the deposition notice of attachment. Exhibit 12-1 is an example of this.

A request for documents at the deposition of a party is not always the most efficient way to handle document discovery. If an attorney must wait to see the requested documents until the deposition, she may have to spend precious time reviewing the documents as the deposition is in progress. Moreover, subsequent examination of the documents often reveals information about which the deponent should have been questioned. This may necessitate scheduling another deposition, which may or may not be allowed by the court.

If the request includes ESI, and today there are few reasons that it would not, the situation becomes more complicated because that ESI may have to be evaluated by IT experts using a computer system that may not be available at the deposition or by using a format that cannot be read by the computer that is at the deposition.

Subpoenas Duces Tecum for a Nonparty to Produce Documents
A nonparty can be subpoenaed to produce documents at a deposition, according to Rule 45 of the Federal Rules of Civil Procedure. The deposition notice served on the nonparty will contain a specific listing of the books, paper documents, electronically stored information, or tangible things to be produced. That list is repeated in the deposition subpoena served on a nonparty. As noted earlier in the book, Rule 45 has been amended to accommodate problems associated with ESI. However, this method of document and ESI production is still handicapped by the same shortcomings that plague the request for documents at the deposition of a party. If the attorney is viewing the paper documents or the ESI for the first time, she will waste valuable time at the deposition. In addition, the later review of the paper documents and the ESI may suggest the need to schedule another deposition. Again, the court may or may not be amenable to a second deposition.

Interrogatories and the Production of Documents
The use of a set of interrogatories sometimes results in the production of documents. Rule 33 (d) of the Federal Rules of Civil Procedure allows a party answering a set of interrogatories to produce business records, including ESI, if the examination of those records will provide the answer to an interrogatory.

EXHIBIT 12-1 Request for Production of Documents at Deposition of a Party

---

UNITED STATES DISTRICT COURT NORTHERN DISTRICT OF OHIO

THE KELTEX CENTER FOR ADVANCED TECHNOLOGY	)
Plaintiff,	)
	) Case No. 16 -77976
	) NOTICE OF TAKING
v.	) DEPOSITION UPON
	) ORAL EXAMINATION
	)
NETCORE, INC.,	)
Defendant.	)
	)
	)
	)

TO: Janine Waterson, Attorney of Record for Defendant, Netcore, Inc., in the above styled and numbered cause.

   Please take notice that the deposition of Sara Zizek, Chief Financial Officer of Netcore, Inc., whose address is 1652 Jeffries Drive, Grand Rapids, Michigan, will be taken upon oral examination on October 31, 2016, beginning at 9 a.m., and continuing from day to day until completed.

   The witness is requested to bring with her to the deposition those items in her custody or subject to her custody, care, or control, identified in Exhibit "A" attached hereto.

   You are hereby invited to attend and cross-examine.

                                  Respectfully submitted,

                         _____

                         Gina Stevens
                         Stevens, Jefferson, and Usalis
                         2229 Hamilton Avenue
                         Cleveland, Ohio 44119
                         Tel.: (216) 555-2121
                         Fax: (216) 555-2122
                         Attorneys for Plaintiff
                         Keltex Center for Advanced Technology

CERTIFICATE OF SERVICE

I hereby certify that a true and correct copy of the foregoing has been mailed by first class mail, postage prepaid to Janine Waterson 77 Superior Avenue, Cleveland, Ohio, 44118, on this 29th day of September, 2016.

_____

Interrogatories and ESI   Interrogatories are best used at an early stage in the discovery process to help your supervising attorney determine what documents are available for a later document production request. ESI is especially susceptible to this strategy because computer records can sometimes be difficult to identify, retrieve, and interpret. Thus, the interrogatories must include questions that focus on the nature of the party's computer system; the configuration of any network systems that are involved in the party's operation; the number and location of all workstations and all network servers; information on upgrades, equipment changes, and reformatting; details on any policies on the elimination of ESI; policies that mandate the preservation of certain records or any backup processes in use; information on the party's e-mail system; and a list of all individuals who are responsible for maintaining, upgrading, repairing, or servicing the party's computer system, including in-house and independent outside information technology (IT) experts. Other interrogatories should involve references to the same types of electronic systems included in the original Rule 26 disclosure list. When the case involves a business or an organization, the interrogatories should also determine whether the employer permits employees to use their own electronic devices on the job or whether the employer distributes dual purpose electronic devices that have both professional and personal functions. Once your supervising attorney has this information in hand, she will have a clearer idea of how to frame document requests and on-site visits to retrieve ESI.

Request for Documents to Parties   Despite these other techniques, the request for documents still remains the most efficient and effective way to obtain documents. A request for production should not be served until the parties have initially conferred as required under Rule 26. Once served, under Federal Rule 26 (a) (1) (D), the answering party has 30 days in which to respond. The court, however, may shorten or lengthen this time period. The opposing attorney's response to the request must indicate that her client will comply with the request or should indicate the grounds for any objection to the request. Exhibit 12-2 is an example of the opening paragraph in a request for documents.

According to Federal Rule 34 (b) (1) (A) the ESI requester must specify with "reasonable particularity" the general categories of documents or the particular documents that the other party wishes to inspect. The request should also specify a reasonable time, place, and manner of production. Naturally, the attorneys may alter these arrangements to make the production more convenient to all those involved in the process. The manner of production is also determined by negotiation and agreement between the attorneys. Sometimes the original documents will be required, whereas at other times copies will be sufficient. The Federal Rules of Civil Procedure do not limit the number of requests for production. Several requests may be needed in a complicated lawsuit involving many parties located across the country.

Recent amendments to Rule 34 also permit a party requesting ESI to specify the format in which it will be transmitted. As might be expected, the terms documents and ESI have a wide variety of meanings. Rule 34 (a) (1) (A) explicitly defines both **documents** and ESI as "any designated documents or electronically stored information—including writings, drawings, graphs, charts, photographs, sound recordings, images, and other data or data compilations—stored in any medium from which information can be obtained, either directly or, if necessary, after translation by the responding party into a reasonably usable form."

document
An artifact that contains written matter, such as words or figures, in the form of a message or record.

EXHIBIT 12-2 Introductory Paragraph for a Request for Documents

UNITED STATES DISTRICT COURT NORTHERN DISTRICT OF OHIO

THE KELTEX CENTER FOR ADVANCED TECHNOLOGY)
    Plaintiff,   )
)
)
    v.   )
)
)
 NETCORE, INC.   )
)
    Defendant.   )
)
 _____)
	Case No. 16-77976
	 REQUEST FOR DOCUMENTS

TO: Janine Waterson, Attorney of Record for Defendant, Netcore, Inc., in the above styled and numbered cause.

    Pursuant to Rule 34 of the Federal Rules of Civil Procedure, The Keltex Center for Advanced Technology, plaintiff in the above cause, requests that Netcore, Inc., defendant in the above cause, produce for inspection and copying by Keltex, within thirty days of service hereof or at such other time as may be agreed upon by counsel for the parties, originals or legible copies of the documents and electronically stored information in the formats specified below requested herein. You are also requested to serve upon plaintiff within thirty (30) days after service of this request a written response in accordance with Rule 34 of the Federal Rules of Civil Procedure.

The scope of the rule extends not only to documents and ESI in the actual custody of the party, but also to those documents and ESI under the "control" or in the custody of the party. This means that the ESI requester has the right to obtain documents and ESI that are actually in the possession of a third individual, such as the party's tax consultant or financial adviser. The rule also allows the ESI requester to inspect and copy those documents and ESI. Of course, determining who has actual control of the ESI and figuring out whether the person in possession of the material or the person who passed that material along actually owns the ESI or the documents is problematic at best.

Legal Holds and the Duty to Preserve Evidence Including ESI

Today, because businesses tend to delete ESI automatically, one of the attorney's first steps in a lawsuit must be to put a litigation hold on the routine handling of all of the client's ESI. Depending on local custom, a litigation hold might be called a hold order, a document hold, a data hold, a record hold, or a preservation order, among several others.[3] Whatever it may be called, however, a litigation hold has one primary function. It tells the client's employees and associates to preserve all ESI, even ESI that appears unrelated to the lawsuit. Such hold orders are necessary because many firms delete large amounts of data automatically (read "without human intervention" here) as an economic way of freeing storage space on their systems. Because of this, a preservation order must be issued as early as possible and must be repeated often and in writing to make sure that all members of the client's firm take the message seriously.[4] Moreover, as we shall see below, even this tactic may be insufficient in the modern world of e-litigation.

Managing the Litigation Hold Process

The litigation hold process can now be made more efficient by installing a case management software package that empowers managers to directly initiate a legal hold in response to pending litigation, without having to install additional software to do the job. The new organizing software package can place not only e-mail documents on hold to await discovery and trial, but also other ESI documents currently being stored in other virtual folders.[5] Some legal experts have also asserted in no uncertain terms that lawyers can no longer write a single litigation hold order and then assume that everyone will understand and comply. Rather the lawyer must step forward and ensure that any employees who may be inclined to go "rogue" are detected and stopped before they eliminate or disguise critical evidence, including ESI.[6] To make certain that clients comprehend the seriousness of these requirements, they should be reminded that the duty to preserve evidence is a responsibility that is owed to the court, not to the opposing parties.[7] Moreover, a smart attorney will also expressly remind all opposing parties of their preservation duty in the lawsuit by sending those parties a spoliation memo. The spoliation memo can be sent as an e-mail message or as a paper document.

Trigger Events and Adverse Inferences

Determining when to issue a litigation hold is not an easy task. Nevertheless, the courts have developed a few rules that make the task a bit easier. The most fundamental rule says that the duty to issue a litigation hold emerges as soon as the party knows, or should have known, that litigation is pending. Any set of circumstances that sparks this responsibility is a **trigger event**, although depending on local custom, it may also be called an opening episode, an instigating event, or a precipitating incident. Some triggering events are obvious, while others are harder to spot. One clear-cut triggering event is the letter, memo, e-mail, text, fax, voice mail, IM, or tweet that states, "We are going to sue you."[8] Other triggering events might include a notification of a missed payment, an inquiry into a corporation's hiring policies, or even the scheduling of an appointment for "preliminary discussions on a matter of mutual interest."

It is even possible for a firm to stumble into a self-induced trigger event. A **self-induced trigger event** is an incident or a discussion about litigation that occurs completely within the confines of an institution but that produces the need to issue a preservation order. A self-induced or self-initiated trigger event can occur, for instance, when executives speculate about the possibility of their firm being sued because of an incident with a customer, client, supplier, or employee. Despite these warning signs, the courts still use a reasonableness standard when determining whether a legitimate triggering event has occurred.[9] Nevertheless, the failure to preserve evidence can produce severe consequences up to and including the possibility of an adverse inference ruling.[10] An **adverse inference** is a ruling that declares that the jury may interpret any missing evidence against the interests of the party that failed to produce the evidence.

Preliminary Decisions Regarding Requests for Documents

In the *Keltex* case, your clients, Keltex and Aspect have elected to sue the firm of Netcore, Inc., which failed to finish updating its state-of-the-art computer system by the specified deadline. At this time, your supervising attorney will have to make some preliminary

trigger event
A trigger event is any set of circumstances that sparks the duty to issue a litigation hold.

self-induced trigger event
A self-induced trigger event is an incident or a discussion about litigation that occurs completely within the confines of an institution but that, nevertheless, still produces the need to issue a litigation hold.

adverse inference
An adverse inference is a ruling by a judge that declares that the jury may interpret any missing evidence against the interests of the party that failed to produce the evidence.

decisions regarding any requests for documents to be served on the defendant. Two crucial considerations are the timing of the request and the potential cost of production of the documents.

Timing of the Request   A formal request for document production should not be served before the parties have conferred as required under Rule 26. Given that limitation, your supervising attorney will still initiate a request for production of documents as soon as possible. Often this will mean drafting a request for production prior to scheduling the first deposition. This early production request will enable the use of documents and ESI produced in preparing deposition questions. On the other hand, in some cases it may be better to delay filing a request for documents until after depositions and interrogatories have been conducted. This decision is especially valid if the interrogatories may help determine how to draft an effective document request. As we've seen, in the case of ESI, interrogatories can help determine such things as the nature of the party's computer system, the type of data available, and the identities of all the people who are responsible for managing, maintaining, or servicing the party's computer system. After your supervising attorney has access to these facts, she will have a better idea about the nature of any document request or on-site visit that ought to be conducted to recover ESI.

Cost of the Production   Your attorney also will consider the cost of having the documents inspected and reproduced. It is also possible, even likely, that your client will have to pay the expenses involved in photocopying paper documents, duplicating video recordings, reproducing audio recordings, scanning paper documents, duplicating flash drives, or having duplicate DVDs, CDs, or photographs made, so your attorney must consider this factor carefully. Additional cost factors may be involved in the recovery of ESI. In order to assure the opposing party that his or her computer data will not be damaged, lost, or compromised during an on-site visit, it is sometimes necessary to hire an outside IT expert to conduct the details of the on-site examination and retrieval process. Such steps will, of course, add to the cost of document production. Therefore, you must inform the client of the extra cost that may be involved in the entire document production process including, especially, the additional cost of ESI production.

At this point in the discussion, we must issue a warning regarding the costs involved in gathering ESI. Traditionally the cost of the production of ESI is carried by the ESI producer, unless the judge intervenes because he or she has decided that "burden or the expense of the proposed discovery outweighs its likely benefit" Rule 26 (b) (2) (C) (iii). Recently some judges have been willing to review this practice. This new tendency on the part of some judges has been sparked by the unwillingness of many attorneys to become more aware of the complexities involved in the discovery of ESI. Some judges have decided to prod those attorneys into solving certain ESI problems by shifting the cost of ESI to the requesting party. These judges feel justified in shifting the costs because, in their view, any extra cost that results from an ill-advised ESI request should be borne by the party that made the ineffective and costly request in the first place.[11]

Approaches to Document Production

An attorney's approach to document production is based on two factors. First, when responding to a document request, the attorney must decide on the organizational approach that will best serve her purposes. Second, the attorney will have to determine the number of documents to be produced.

Organizing and Formatting Documents

Based on organization, a party producing evidence has a choice of three strategies. The documents may be produced (1) as they are kept in the usual course of business, (2) according to categories specified in the document request, or (3) as ESI.

Producing the documents as they are kept in the usual course of business requires less time and effort by the responding party. If an enormous amount of information is requested by the other party, this approach would be appropriate. However, do not make the mistake of thinking that the phrase "in the usual course of business" allows the responding party to shuffle the documents to hide pertinent information.[12]

Producing the documents according to the categories in the request requires additional time and effort for the responding party. Still, such an organizational effort can be managed if relatively few documents are requested. Naturally, the party initiating the request prefers this approach because it reduces the time and effort required to organize and analyze the documents. Moreover, the party producing the documents also may prefer this technique because it forces a review of all the requested documents, lessening the chance of inadvertently revealing privileged documents.

Producing the documents as ESI requires the ESI requester to specify the format used for the recovery and transmission of the data. Thus, if the ESI requester specifies a format, the ESI retriever must follow that format request. However, Federal Rule 34 does permit the ESI retriever to object to the format suggested by the ESI requester, provided that the retriever explains the objection in writing. If the ESI requester has not specified the ESI format to be used, the ESI retriever is permitted to transmit the ESI in the format in which it is regularly kept or in a reasonably useful format.

The Number of Documents

Based on the number of documents, the party responding to the request has three options available in producing the documents. These three options are (1) the warehouse approach, (2) the comprehensive approach, and (3) the limited approach. Each has its own particular advantages and disadvantages. In the *warehouse approach*, all documents, both relevant and irrelevant, are produced without any type of organization. The advantage for the producing party here is savings in the time and effort involved in organizing the documents. However, this approach does not relieve the attorneys and paralegals of the need to review the documents before releasing them. Also, by releasing all of the documents available to the party, some documents that appear irrelevant early in the litigation may later be discovered to be highly relevant. These apparently innocent documents could disclose information to which the requesting party is not entitled. Such a disclosure might assist the opposing party in preparing the case for trial.

In a *comprehensive approach*, all documents even remotely relevant are produced, even those not directly requested. This strategy is advantageous because it can save time and effort later. The underlying premise is that all of these documents will be requested sooner or later anyway. By releasing them now, the paralegal eliminates the need to repeat the process of combing through the files a second and possibly even a third time. Nevertheless, the comprehensive approach remains a risky strategy because the responding party may inadvertently release documents that the other party would never have requested and should never have seen because the distribution of those documents violates a privilege involving evidence that should have remained protected. A *limited production* is one in which only the documents requested are produced. The advantage here is the protection of relevant documents that the other party has yet to request. An attorney might elect this approach if the request is very limited in scope or if it is poorly drafted. However, the disadvantage is that later document searches may be necessary as subsequent requests are received.

The Volume of ESI   In most, perhaps all, cases, the amount of ESI available within a company, institution, or organization's computer system far exceeds the paper evidence available. This is often due to the fact that many documents that e-workers believe they have deleted still exist somewhere in the system either as inactive or extant data. For example, in the *Keltex* case, Alyendra Raveau, the chief engineer at Netcore, may believe that she has deleted all e-mail on her desktop PC, on her home computer, on her tablet, on her smartphone, and on her laptop involving the Keltex contract. However, if she did not tell the recipients of those e-mails to delete their versions or if she did not inform those who received copies of those e-mail documents to do the same, each of those e-mails will still be discoverable. In addition, even if all of the copies were deleted, extant copies may exist that a sufficiently clever IT expert will be able to retrieve.

Because of this problem, the extent to which ESI is concealed within a computer network is often a mystery even to the most well-informed member of an organization. Consequently, the targets of an early document production request should not be the type of data as much as the computers themselves (PCs, laptops, home computers, tablets, smartphones, and other mobile phones) of key individuals on the opposing side who might be privy to important evidentiary ESI. Still, such requests also should seek to examine e-mail files, flash drives, scanners, printers, CDs, network files, voice-mail files, computer tapes, fax machine records, backup data, servers, and extant data.

ESI AND THE DOCUMENT REQUEST

When your supervising attorney drafts a document production request under Rule 34 of the Federal Rules of Civil Procedure, she must be aware of the different types of ESI that exist within computer systems today. Discoverable ESI falls into three groups: (1) types of ESI based on the configuration of the computer system, (2) types of ESI based on the nature of the evidence itself, and (3) types of ESI based on its storage status. Your supervising attorney must be sure to consider all of these categories when preparing a Rule 34 document production request for ESI. As noted earlier, it is critical to include the people responsible for collecting, managing, storing, and communicating that ESI. It is also important to recall that paper copies of ESI may exist and should be included in a search for ESI. Remembering these points will make the search for ESI productive.

Document Production Requests and Computer Systems

The first type of ESI that must be considered in structuring a document production request would be evidence based on the configuration of the computer system itself. Your supervising attorney must be aware of the fact that most companies, institutions, organizations, and individuals store their data in more than one place. This involves an assessment of the types of computers that may be in operation in the party's ordinary, everyday routine. At this step, it is vital to recall that the phrase *computer system* incorporates such things as desktop PCs, laptops, mobile phones, fax machines, printers, scanners, servers, tablets, and home computers that are part of a network or that may be used as word-processing workstations or as storage for documents worked on away from the office, at home, on business trips, or even on vacation.

Also recall that, in many corporate and institutional settings today, employees use their own tablets, smartphones, and laptops at work and that many employers distribute employer-owned devices that include separate areas for the employee's personal use.[13] Whichever technique is used by a business or an organization, your supervising attorney must include the ESI stored on these personal devices in all her document requests. Sometimes the request must also include a confiscation order, demanding that such devices, even those owned by the employees themselves, be turned over with the documents requested. In addition, your attorney must make certain that her own clients know that personal electronic devices may be included in all document requests filed by the other party. Moreover, and perhaps more crucial here, it is especially important that she advise clients to include these devices in any legal hold order issued after a trigger event that signals the beginning of the ESI preservation process.

In addition, it would be helpful to know which employees at the opposing party's offices have access to the Internet and whether the opposing party's client has an intranet or portal system. Internet searches, intranet communications, and portal records may hold documents of importance to the lawsuit. Other computer systems that can harbor ESI and that are often overlooked by attorneys and paralegals alike involve the same type of electronic systems included in the original Rule 26 disclosure list and included in the interrogatories sent to the other party. Because of this, it would be wise to make certain that the definition and instruction section of the document production request specifies that any petition for ESI includes data stored in any computer operation.

Document Production Requests and the Nature of ESI

The second type of ESI that must be included in the discovery plan is based on the nature of the evidence itself. For instance, ESI generally includes all relevant computer-generated records including those found in e-mail files, printer files, voice-mail files, fax machine records, databases, calendaring programs, servers, and all other relevant data files created by spreadsheets, word processing, or any analogous program. E-mail can be a very profitable source of information in a lawsuit. The ease and efficiency of e-mail has made it one of the most popular means of communicating in business today. Many individuals use e-mail almost without thought. Moreover, they often have no reservations about sending e-mail messages that are blunt, informal, and even, at times, sarcastic. Lengthy detailed attachments are also sent via e-mail and can, therefore, be a source of critical evidence.

Much of this is due to the fact that in many workplaces, e-mail has replaced the telephone, the office intercom, the public address system, the paper memo, and even face-to-face meetings as the quickest way to reach coworkers. Much of it also is due, however, to the fact that many workers forget that their e-mail messages are not as fleeting as discussions by the coffee machine or in the employee lounge. For instance, the receiver of an e-mail message may retain a copy in his or her computer even though the sender has deleted it, and messages may be automatically preserved in the memory of the mainframe computer or in a remote server located at an outside data center. Some employees still

mobile applications (apps)

Mobile applications or apps are miniature dedicated programs downloaded to an e-device to provide a variety of services, such as game playing, calorie counting, music playing, photo editing, and so on.

app platform providers

An app platform provider is an organization, institution, or business, that creates and operates a mobile application.

make paper copies of all e-mails. Others routinely send blind copies to a list of managers, supervisors, and coworkers. This practice should not be overlooked in any document request for ESI. E-mail files might also be mined for dates to establish a chronology of critical events or as a way to determine who knew the pertinent facts and who had a role in the decision-making process.

Texting has become much more common today than it was even four or five years ago. Although texting is generally considered a leisure time activity for the sending of informal, personal messages, this does not prevent businesspeople from using it as part of their communication network. Also, many lawsuits may involve personal injury torts, property disputes, contract disagreements, and domestic problems that have nothing to do with business. For these reasons, it is a good idea for you and your attorney to remember that texting may be a good source of ESI.

Another overlooked source of ESI is the electronic data stored on mobile applications. **Mobile applications** or **apps** are miniature dedicated programs downloaded to an e-device to provide a variety of services. Mobile users can purchase apps to store videos, take photos, play games, read e-books, browse e-mags, surf the net, chat, play tunes, watch movies, list contacts, calculate sums, download articles, schedule appointments, store medical data, play voice mail, plan trips, check the weather, read e-mail, and even, in some cases, count calories. What many *app fanatics* do not understand is that as they routinely, perhaps even compulsively, access their favorite apps, the **app platform providers** are collecting, storing, sharing, and distributing ESI about the users in ways that goes beyond the ESI collected and stored on other devices, including laptops, tablets, PCs, and other more conventional electronic gadgets.[14] ESI requesters are blessed by the app revolution because they can uncover ESI that was formerly inaccessible. In contrast, ESI retrievers are cursed because they must deal with clients who may have unwittingly amassed reams of harmful evidence on their ever-present smartphones. Apps store sensitive ESI such as text messages, e-mail messages, photos, contacts, calendars, voice mails, books, maps, and videos. Other bits of sensitive ESI include phone logs, date book information, bill payment histories, credit histories, health data, medical data, dental information, app use and app download records, trip tickets, and Web-browsing logs. Some users may even discover that their every move has been recorded and stored by their GPS and WiFi geo-locator apps.[15]

By far the most overlooked, most revealing, most controversial, and least understood source of ESI is metadata. Metadata is data about data and, therefore, is a crucial element of ESI. Metadata frequently involves tracking records that log the person or persons who gathered the ESI, the technique used to compile the ESI, the goal of the compilation process, and so on.[16]

Metadata describes the data itself by indicating the identity of the person who wrote the original document, when that document was written, who had a hand in altering it, and the actual content and nature of those alterations.[17] Metadata frequently involves concealed ESI that is stockpiled in a wide range of software programs, including but not limited to spreadsheets, e-mail records, printing records, databases, and word-processing records.[18] As a result, your supervising attorney may want to access that metadata in order to uncover additional information that was hidden within that data, thus enhancing the discovery process. Naturally, this means that your supervising attorney ought to add metadata to any document request regarding ESI.

On the other hand, does the ESI retriever have to include metadata if the ESI requester has failed to mention it in a data request? The jury, or rather, the judge, is still out on that question. Some judicial experts argue that examining metadata for evidence, a practice labeled *metadata mining*, is unprofessional and unethical. These experts suggest that metadata mining can amount to an illegal intrusion into privileged information because often the ESI retriever is not even aware that sensitive material has been included in the ESI sent along to the data requester. Thus, it is possible for a well-informed attorney working for the data requester to use *metadata mining software* to uncover privileged information within the ESI metadata sent from the unsuspecting data retriever. For example, an e-mail response by a client to an e-mail request from his or her attorney for feedback on a matter related to the lawsuit would be privileged information. Yet, if those e-mails were attached to a document that was eventually sent to the other party's attorney, both e-mail messages might be recoverable by that opposing attorney as metadata, even if they had both been deleted before the main document was sent.[19]

Understanding this risk may lead some attorneys, especially those representing the ESI retriever, to use a software package of their own to remove the hidden metadata from the ESI before it is sent to the ESI requester. This might work in some courts. However, not every court supports this tactic. In fact, some judges have ruled that parties who deliberately remove metadata from ESI are culpable for failing to preserve evidence. This is a very serious matter because preserving evidence is one of the most basic responsibilities of those involved in the discovery process.[20]

ESI and Key Players in the Lawsuit   A request for documents should include the e-mail records of any key player in the lawsuit. For example, in the *Keltex* case, suppose that Sara Zizek the CFO of Netcore, sent an e-mail to Maria Masterson, another key member of the management team at Netcore, in which she casts doubt on the honesty of Raveau, the officer who negotiated the Keltex contract on behalf of Netcore. Even if Zizek has deleted the e-mail from her outbox, a copy may still exist in Masterson's inbox or it may be archived within the computer. It is also possible that Zizek sent a copy of the e-mail to another member of the firm or that Masterson forwarded it to someone else in the firm. Moreover, one of those two individuals may have created a paper copy of the e-mail for his or her files. An administrative assistant, an intern, a trainee, a temp worker, or the filing clerk may also have retained both e-copies and paper copies of such e-mail records. Therefore, these individuals should not be overlooked in a document request. Even though a record appears to have been expunged, that record may still exist somewhere and, rest assured, a clever IT expert will be able to find it.

ESI and IT Experts   Computer systems within the workplace have become so complex, so intricate, and so extensive that many businesses, organizations, and institutions have found that it is in their best interest to hire IT experts to direct their employees through the process of using their computer system to its best advantage. Rule 26(a) (1) (A) (i) of the Federal Rules of Civil Procedure requires the initial disclosure of the name, address, and telephone number of anyone likely to have discoverable information relevant to any claims or defenses in the case. Obviously, this includes the IT experts involved in maintaining the opposing party's computer system. At this time during the request for production of documents, your supervising attorney should make certain that the IT expert or experts of the opposing party are part of the request process. Certainly, IT experts may send and receive their own e-mails that may be discoverable and that may have a bearing on the case. However, they can also access the system and retrieve hidden e-mail messages that have been deleted by their senders and receivers or archived automatically by the system itself. In this capacity, they would qualify as agents of the opposing party who have "possession, custody, or control" of the ESI that your supervising attorney seeks to obtain. Remember that the administrative assistants, trainees, file clerks, temp workers, and interns who work with IT experts may routinely retain e-copies and paper copies of all such files. Therefore, always include such personnel in your supervising attorney's document request.

ESI and Associated Individuals   Determining whether the opposing party's computer system is configured as an intranet system or as a portal network is a key step in the document request process. When a business or organization has installed an intranet system, only employees have access to the system. Thus, the persons who have "custody, control, or possession" of the ESI in that organization would be limited, for the most part, to employees. In contrast, an organization with a portal network has probably extended the access to people who are associated with the organization. In the case of a business, persons associated with the organization might include people outside of the organization, such as suppliers, customers, clients, consultants, subcontractors, and independent contractors. Therefore, your supervising attorney might need to determine how to include people associated with, but actually outside, the organization in the document production request.

Problems arise when privileged ESI is inadvertently obtained by the opposing side.[21] If the ESI retriever discovers the mistake but the ESI receiver refuses to return the privileged ESI, the ESI retriever should file a motion demanding the return of the privileged material. The judge will then examine the search technique used by the retriever to figure out whether the ESI was turned over voluntarily. To make this determination, the judge will examine the IT expert's search technique. The courts have ruled that any evidence offered to defend or critique the search must be given by an expert. Of course, this means that evidence must meet the parameters set up under Rule 702 of the Federal Rules of Evidence.[22]

Rule 702 says that whenever "(a) the expert's scientific, technical, or other specialized knowledge will help the trier of fact to understand the evidence or to determine a fact in issue," then an expert witness may be called to testify as long as, "(b) the testimony is based upon sufficient facts or data, (c) the testimony is the product of reliable principles and methods; and (d) the witness has reliably applied the principles and methods to the facts of the case."

These parameters can be met as long as the IT specialist has been adequately prepared by your supervising attorney.

Also remember that challenges to search techniques are not limited to questions of privilege. Sometimes after the ESI requester examines the evidence provided by the ESI retriever, the requester is not satisfied and will challenge the search technique used by the retriever. In these cases, the Rule 702 parameters should be followed to evaluate the search. Despite this emphasis on the electronic search techniques, however, the courts are not ready to abandon the manual search strategy. Following the lead provided by the second edition of the Sedona Principles, the assumption remains that the ESI retriever is the party who knows the most effective way to conduct a search of his or her own computer system.[23] On the other hand, the courts have also made it clear that whenever an ESI retriever does decide to use the traditional manual search strategy, that search must be closely supervised by the attorney in charge of the case. Moreover, those individuals who are charged with conducting the manual search process must be properly trained, must be supervised by management, and must communicate with the attorney in charge on a regular basis.[24]

Document Production Requests and Storage of ESI

The final category of ESI that must be included in the document production request is determined on the basis of its storage status within the opposing party's computer system. As we have seen, ESI includes active data, inactive data, backup data, extant data, residual data, legacy data, ephemeral data, and paper data. Data is considered active if it is of ongoing importance in the day-to-day operation of the business, institution, or organization. Data is termed inactive if it was produced and used recently but is no longer critical to the daily operation of the workplace. On the other hand, backup data is information that has somehow been preserved in the memory of the computer because of the chance that it may be needed in the future, in case the active files are deleted or destroyed accidentally by an operator's error or a computer malfunction. Such data may be captured on disc, tape, CD, flash drive, the computer's hard drive, or a server at a remote data center. Extant data is information hidden in the system, generally because it has been deleted. It usually takes an IT expert to dig out extant data that is present only in a residual form. Fragments of data left over on hard drives are referred to as residual data. Legacy data is data that may be hidden simply because it was originally recorded on what is now an outdated media format such as a floppy disk or a CD. Ephemeral data is data that was created to self-destruct after a short period of time, say in about 10 seconds or so (you know, like in the *Mission Impossible* films). Finally, paper data includes any ESI that has been transferred to paper and retained by an individual.

Because of the variety of storage techniques available, make certain that the definition and instruction section of the request specifies that any petition for ESI includes information that has been stored as active, inactive, backup, extant, residual, legacy, ephemeral, or paper data. In a document production request, remember that ESI may also be stored off-site. Workers often have off site home computers, laptops, smartphones, and tablets, on which ESI is stored. Also remember that ESI might be stored in digital cameras, fax machines, global positioning systems, pagers, printers, RFIDs, security systems, vehicle data recorders, and so on. Workers also may transport ESI home on CDs, discs, and flash drives or to a server located at a remote data center. Most often, an employee takes home data on a disc, CD, or flash drive for convenience. Sometimes, however, an employee may relocate a disc, CD, or flash drive, because it contains sensitive material; this would make that disc, CD, or flash drive very interesting to opposing counsel. Therefore, it is wise to include such discs, CDs, and flash drives in the document production request.

Cloud Storage, ESI Owners, and ESI Centers
Another newer and, therefore, often overlooked storage place for ESI is "in the cloud." **Cloud storage** is a strategy for delivering and preserving ESI which bypasses the need to place data on hard drives and flash drives and passes that task to a third party, an **ESI or data center**, which receives, organizes, and stores the ESI on a remote database, while making the data available to the ESI owner (aka the data owner or the ESI depositor) through the Internet. Since many

cloud storage
The cloud storage process is a strategy for preserving ESI which bypasses the need to place data on hard drives and flash drives and passes that task to a third party, an ESI or data center, that is remote and secure, but easily and quickly accessible to the data owner.

ESI or data center
An ESI or data center is a remote, secure facility designed to store and save electronic data for data owners who have quick and easy access to that data.

predictive coding
Predictive coding is a document
retrieval strategy that employs
a digital cataloging process that
involves several well-orchestrated
steps.

firms are now taking advantage of this relatively efficient and economical tactic, document discovery requests should always include a demand for all relevant ESI that might be stored in that off-shore cloud.[25]

The Chain of Custody and E-Forensics A chain of custody will keep track of people who receive, handle, evaluate, copy, transfer, and store the evidence in a lawsuit. The goal of the chain is to make certain no one tampers with the evidence.[26] The complexity and the amount of ESI makes the chain of custody process extremely important in civil cases. In establishing a chain of custody for the ESI, both ESI requesters and ESI retrievers should rely on IT professionals, preferably e-forensics experts.[27] E-forensics, electronic forensics, cyberforensics, or computer forensics, is a process that applies customized methods to retrieve, examine, analyze, and validate ESI. The chain of custody strategy is part of this process. E-forensics is especially important when ESI involves finding hidden data, reconstructing records that track computer use, and determining the scientific characteristics of ESI.[28] Just as a brief reminder, recall that the retrieval, cataloging, and preservation of this evidence, including the establishment of an effective chain of custody, is the responsibility of the litigation response team discussed in Chapter 8.[29]

The Expense Involved in the Retrieval of ESI

Because IT experts must often be hired to locate, recover, reformat, and interpret ESI, and because such operations frequently involve using special programs to retrieve the data, the expense of gathering ESI may begin to escalate over the outlay that would be involved in the retrieval of paper documents. In addition, because of the need to hire extra IT help and to obtain additional programs, your supervising attorney must be reminded to add extra time to the recovery process. In addition, you may have to help your attorney justify such requests and to anticipate any added expenses that may be incurred in the process. Finally, the possible creation of paper copies of ESI means that the expense associated with the request for and the retrieval of ESI does not always eliminate the expense of looking for paper files. In fact, in those cases that involve extensive backup paper files, the cost of the search may actually escalate.

Predictive Coding and the ESI Production Revolution

The four most troubling problems associated with the retrieval of ESI in a document request process are volume, diversity, change, and storage. These problems have motivated some computer technicians to construct new data retrieval systems, many of which can be used successfully by attorneys and paralegals to find their way through the maze of ESI. Perhaps the most effective technique in data mining and retrieval is predictive coding. **Predictive coding** is a document retrieval strategy that employs a digital cataloging process that involves several well-orchestrated steps. In the first step, the predictive coding program examines a wide range of documents in order to adjust its search algorithm so that the computer can determine what to look for as it studies an even larger set of ESI documents. This first step empowers the computer to focus on the characteristics of those documents that are relevant or can lead to relevant ESI records. In the second step, the predictive coding protocol directs a more in-depth inspection of all documents, based on those targeted characteristics. This second level search is based on an advanced algorithm that decreases the list of documents to a more manageable number that plainly fits the pattern established in the algorithm. In the third step, the smaller file of documents is then scanned and organized by "human" attorneys who produce the discoverable ESI documents to answer the discovery request.[30]

Despite the obvious advantages provided by predictive coding, not all professionals favor this approach. The battle is being waged between those attorneys, academics, and judges who support **technology assisted review** (TAR) protocols, such as predictive coding, and those who endorse a more traditional "hands-on" **linear document review** (LDR) process. The supporters of TAR point to the vast amount of ESI that can be examined by various TAR protocols that are not only time saving and economical, but also nearly error free. In short, TAR defenders, and among them are many sitting judges, argue that TAR works so well that those attorneys who do not implement some form of TAR in the near future may not be meeting the minimum competency level required of attorneys as they gather evidence during discovery. Those more skeptical about TAR argue not that LDR is a superior search method, but that the move to TAR, especially to predictive coding, has been made without a proper set of procedures, rules, and standards in place, by which to judge just how well the process actually works. Without these industry-wide rules and regulation, the argument goes, legal professionals will be forced to rely, somewhat blindly, on outside technical experts, something which the critics of TAR wish to avoid.[31]

PROTECTION OF DOCUMENTS

A party served with a request for documents has 30 days to respond to that request. The response must indicate either that the party will comply or that the party objects to the request or to part of the request. If an objection is made as to part of a request, inspection of the remaining parts must be permitted. Grounds for such objections include arguing that complying with the request will violate either the attorney–client privilege, the attorney work product privilege, or the common interest privilege. Other objections include that the request is overbroad, duplicative, or irrelevant. In addition, under the new amendments to Rule 34, an objection can be made to the ESI format demanded by the ESI requester. If none of these objections is appropriate, the documents and the ESI may still be kept private by using a confidentiality agreement or a protective order. The new rules also include the quick peek and clawback provisions for protecting ESI.

The Attorney–Client Privilege

The attorney–client privilege prevents the forced disclosure of communication between an attorney and a client. Like the other forms of discovery, a request for documents is limited by the attorney–client privilege. This extends to communications to or from both inside and outside counsel. At an early stage in the discovery process, the paralegal should draw up a list of all attorneys who represented the client in matters relevant to the lawsuit. The list will be used to identify documents, including ESI that should be withheld from the other party on the basis of the attorney–client privilege. Recall that the attorney–client privilege is waived if a document is disclosed to a third party. Care should be taken to limit access to these protected documents.

technology assisted review (TAR)
Technology assisted review is a technique used during the discovery phase of a lawsuit that involves compiling, accessing, examining, and assessing documents by employing a computer-run protocol such as predictive coding.

linear document review
Linear document review is a technique used during the discovery phase of a lawsuit that involves compiling, accessing, examining, and assessing documents, using a traditional hands-on, manual approach.

The Work Product Privilege

The work product privilege prevents the opposing party from obtaining, through discovery, letters, memos, documents, records, ESI, and other tangible items that have been produced in anticipation of litigation or that have been prepared for the trial itself. Because the work product privilege protects tangible evidence, it is especially applicable to a request for documents. Investigator's reports and materials prepared by expert consultants who will not testify at trial are examples of protected work product. Handwritten notes penned by the attorney during office visits or phone conversations with the client also are considered work product. Similarly, lists made by the client in response to a request by the attorney are protected. Whenever a law firm is involved in a multi-jurisdictional (MJD) case, the risk of accidentally losing the attorney–client privilege increases exponentially. The possibility arises because the law is practiced differently in foreign jurisdictions. These differences can involve (1) an attorney's status, (2) the nature of a waiver, and (3) the loyalty of an attorney. (See Chapter 8.)

Unlike the attorney–client privilege, the work product privilege is not an absolute privilege. Disclosure of some documents may be compelled if the party requesting production of the documents has a substantial need for the documents and cannot, without undue hardship, obtain the equivalent of the material by any other means. Calculating the time period when a document could be considered work product can be difficult. Is a document, including an e-mail message, a text message, an IM, a note on a smartphone, a voice mail, an entry on a tablet, or some other form of ESI, which was prepared by in-house counsel six months prior to the beginning of the lawsuit, protected by the work product privilege? What if the note is entered on the attorney's privately owned smartphone that is used by the attorney in a work setting. The answer is "yes," on both accounts as long as the message involves legal advice or discusses potential litigation. If, however, in-house counsel sends a memo or an e-mail on some general legal issue, that memo would probably not be protected by the privilege even if sent six weeks, six days, or six hours before the lawsuit is brought against the company. On the other hand, such a memo or e-mail would probably not hurt your client nor help your opposing counsel.

Federal Rules of Evidence—Rule 502

Under Rule 502 of the Federal Rules of Evidence, the *accidental* disclosure of evidence protected by either the attorney–client privilege or the work product privilege will not be a general waiver, as long as the disclosure really was accidental, and resulted despite the fact that the holder of the privilege tried to protect the evidence. Moreover, according to Rule 502 (a), the *intentional* waiver of either the attorney–client privilege or the work product privilege affects only the communication or the work product intentionally waived and only those additional communications or work products that involve the same subject matter, as long as it is clear that the two are related to one another. These limitations will apply to both federal and state cases. When the privilege or protection is preserved under a court order in one federal court, it will be preserved by that order in any other federal court or in any state court. Rule 502 (e) notes that an agreement related to a disclosure in federal court can be made binding on third parties, if the court so orders. Rule 502 is relatively new; therefore, it is best to check the text of the rule itself and to review the detailed coverage included in Chapter 8.

Additional Privileges

As noted in Chapter 8, the common interest privilege protects any communication among attorneys for different clients when those clients share a common interest. Other privileges that can be used to protect evidence include the medical privilege and the confessor–penitent privilege. The medical privilege was established to shield any sensitive information that passes between a patient and a medical practitioner. In like manner, the confessor–penitent privilege was formulated to guard the confidences disclosed by a penitent to a member of the clergy.

Overbroad and Duplicative Requests

A party who is responding to a request for documents may also object on the grounds that the request is overbroad. Such an objection would argue that the request is so wide ranging and inclusive that it asks for more evidence than could ever be useful to the other party in the lawsuit. In the *Keltex* case, for example, if Keltex requested all of the corporate minute books of Netcore, that firm's attorney would be justified in objecting on the ground that the request is overbroad.

Usually, such an objection is accompanied by an alternative suggestion. Thus, in response to the Keltex request, Netcore would refuse to produce all of the corporate minute books, but it would promise to produce any corporate minute books that expressly refer to the contract between Keltex and Netcore which would be relevant to the lawsuit. Another objection to a request for production of documents is that the request is duplicative. This objection argues that the other party has already asked for that information in another part of the request.

Inadmissible and Irrelevant Evidence

The scope of discovery is much broader than the scope of evidence that can be introduced at trial. Documents that would be inadmissible at trial can still be requested if those documents are reasonably calculated to lead to admissible evidence. However, documents that cannot reasonably be expected to lead to admissible evidence are not subject to discovery. Thus, the producing party may object to a request on those grounds. The producing party may also object on the ground that the documents sought are irrelevant to the lawsuit. Thus, in the *Keltex* case, Netcore might object to a request for its certificate of incorporation on the ground that the certificate is irrelevant to the lawsuit. In contrast, if the lawsuit involved allegations that Netcore was improperly incorporated, then a copy of the certificate of incorporation would be relevant, and no objection should be made.

Confidentiality Agreements and Protective Orders

The secrecy of documents may be difficult to preserve during discovery. In the *Keltex* case, for example, at least two law firms (one for Keltex and one for Netcore) would be working on the case. Both law firms will probably have several attorneys and paralegals involved in the suit. In addition, legal secretaries, word-processing personnel, copy center personnel, interns, trainees, temps, and receptionists, among many others, will have access to the documents. How can the privacy and secrecy of documents be preserved in this atmosphere?

One way to maintain privacy and secrecy is to have everyone who works on the case sign a confidentiality agreement. Another way is to seek a protective order from the court to limit the people who are allowed to see the document or the circumstances under which the contents of the document will be revealed.

Format Objections to Document Requests

Federal Rule 34 also permits the ESI requester to ask that the ESI retriever transmit the requested ESI in a particular format. The ESI retriever is then permitted, under the new amendments, to object to the format if the objection is explained and placed in writing. Such explanations might include that the format requested is not the format used by the ESI retriever in the day-to-day operation of the firm and, as such, is incompatible with its computer system and that translating the ESI into a compatible format would be too time consuming, too costly, or too difficult.

Inadvertent Production of Documents

Despite the most stringent safeguards, privileged documents are sometimes sent to the other party inadvertently. In complex litigation, parties often provide for this eventuality by an agreement to notify the other party of the accidental production of documents and request a return of all copies of the documents. Unfortunately, the parties to a lawsuit are not always cooperative. If a party in possession of inadvertently released documents refuses to return those documents, your supervising attorney will have to file a motion asking the court to compel the return of those documents. If, however, the documents were released as a result of your supervising attorney's negligence, the court may not be sympathetic and might very well refuse to grant your attorney's motion. Also recall that Rule 502 of the Federal Rules of Evidence will limit the damage that results from this inadvertent disclosure of privileged material.

Inadvertent Production of Electronically Stored Information

Even before the addition of Rule 502 to the Federal Rules of Evidence, the Federal Rules of Civil Procedure included provisions for the protection of evidence and for the preservation of the established privileges. Two of these provisions are the quick peek process and clawback agreements. The quick peek provision works like this. Under Rule 26 (b) (5) a party is permitted to hand over evidence that counsel has not yet examined without surrendering the right to assert claims of privilege in regard to that evidence.[32] Once the other party has that material in hand, it will review the data and send back notice of its intent to examine certain parts of that evidence. The original party can then narrow the focus of its review to determine whether a claim of privilege ought to be asserted regarding that material. The real benefit of the quick peek agreement is that it allows the data retriever to respond quickly to the data requester's demand without losing the protection of established privileges. As should be clear, however, both quick peek agreements and clawback arrangements require a huge amount of trust on the part of the data retriever. This single factor, more than any other, probably explains why many parties are reluctant to make such agreements in the first place, unless absolutely necessary.[33]

The goal of this procedure, which is admittedly fraught with peril, is to recognize that the vast amount of ESI makes it difficult, some argue impossible, for the ESI retriever to examine every last bit of ESI for privileged matter. If the ESI retriever were required to do this, as it was under the old rules, the litigation process would either grind to a halt or would proceed in a way that would effectively destroy the whole concept of privilege. Thus, the quick peek, dangerous as it is, streamlines what might be a tedious, expensive, and ultimately pointless process.

Rule 26(f) authorizes clawback agreements. Clawback agreements, which are often referred to as nonwaiver agreements, permit the litigants to agree that privileges can be asserted after evidence has been sent to the other party if the ESI retriever discovers that it has accidentally included privileged information in the evidence sent to the ESI requester. Once again, the amendments authorized clawback agreements because the vast quantity and complicated nature of ESI make the unintended delivery of privileged information more likely than it was when most information was printed on paper.[34]

REQUESTING THE PRODUCTION OF DOCUMENTS

Before you begin drafting a request, you should develop a working knowledge of the case. You can gain this understanding of the case by reviewing the pleadings binder, the correspondence file, the attorney's notes, and the research notebook. As you review these files, take notes of the possible types of documents or particular documents that are relevant to the case. In the *Keltex* case, for example, as a paralegal for the firm representing the Keltex Center for Advanced Technology, you might want to see Netcore's corporate minute books; any policy manuals followed by the firm's officers in negotiating contracts; all correspondence (paper, e-mail, and otherwise) between Keltex and all subcontractors; and all internal memos, e-mails, and reports involving the construction contract. Once you have done this initial research, you will be ready to draft the request. However, your responsibilities will not end with drafting the request. You may also need to draft a motion to compel the other party to produce the paper documents and the ESI, and you may be responsible for reviewing the documents once they are received.

Form and Content of the Request

Before drafting the request, you might locate sample requests for documents in form books, in the firm's word-processing form file or, if necessary, online. Of course, you will have to modify any form or sample request to fit the particular facts and issues in the case. Still, forms and samples can often be used for the basic areas of the request, such as the introductory paragraph and the definitions of terms. You also need to be familiar with the pertinent court rules involving discovery. Each court may have individual rules relating to the number of requests allowed, the time allowed for responding to requests, the manner of objecting to requests, and the availability of a motion to compel the production of the requested documents.

Title of the Document and Introductory Paragraph   Document production often involves many parties and several requests. Your draft request for the production of documents should identify the party making the request, the party receiving the request, and the number of the request:

Example

THE KELTEX CENTER FOR ADVANCED TECHNOLOGY'S

FIRST REQUEST FOR PRODUCTION OF DOCUMENTS

TO DEFENDANT NETCORE, INC.

Using this type of detailed title avoids confusion and eliminates the need to read the entire request to determine the parties involved. The introductory paragraph of your request should list the applicable federal or state authority and the time and place of the production.

Definitions   The definition section is a pivotal area of the request. The heading "definitions" should be placed in the center of the page in boldfaced lettering. This emphasis will direct the party answering the request to that section for clarification of any ambiguous terms. Having a separate section devoted solely to definitions avoids the need to include this information in the body of the request. Some of the terms that may be defined include *agreement*, *computers*, *ESI*, *document*, and *report*.

Instructions   Because the instruction section of the request is also crucial, its heading should be placed in the center of the page in boldfaced lettering. Some law firms combine the definition and instruction sections of the request, so make sure to check on your firm's procedure. The instruction section specifies the time period in which the documents should be produced. For example, in the *Keltex* case, the renovation deadline was September 9, 2015; the request should cover at least the period from September 9, 2014, to the date of the upcoming production of documents. This entire period should be included because the negotiations, correspondence, memos, and interim reports that preceded the final contract may be critical in litigating your client's case.

The instructions also may indicate whether the requesting party wants to see originals or copies of the documents. It is customary to ask for the identity of anyone who has any of the requested documents not in the custody, possession, or control of the party served with the request. The instructions should remind the responding party of the duty to supplement the production of documents with any documents found or created after the first production takes place. This can usually be done by labeling the request as a "continuing request." It is customary to remind the responding party to correct any errors uncovered after the original production of documents. The instructions will indicate the format that should be used by the ESI retriever for transmitting all requested ESI.

Documents Requested   Rule 34 of the Federal Rules of Civil Procedure states that a request for documents must specify with "reasonable particularity" the general categories of documents or the individual documents that the requesting party wishes to inspect. This requirement is accomplished in the section headed "Documents Requested." Generally, this section consists of a list of numbered paragraphs, each one specifying a document or a category of documents. Because the preceding paragraphs have explained the definitions and instructions, the job of listing the documents in this section has been considerably simplified. Exhibit 12-3 is an example of a request for production of documents that might be filed in the *Keltex* case.

EXHIBIT 12-3 Sample Request for Documents

UNITED STATES DISTRICT COURT NORTHERN DISTRICT OF OHIO

THE KELTEX CENTER FOR ADVANCED TECHNOLOGY Plaintiff,	))))	
	)	Case No. 16-77976
v.	)))	
NETCORE, INC., Defendant.	))))))	

PLAINTIFF THE KELTEX CENTER FOR ADVANCED TECHNOLOGY'S FIRST REQUEST FOR PRODUCTION OF DOCUMENTS TO DEFENDANT NETCORE, INC.

TO: Janine Waterson, Attorney of Record for Defendant, Netcore, Inc., in the above styled and numbered cause.

Pursuant to Rule 34 of the Federal Rules of Civil Procedure, The Keltex Center for Advanced Technology, plaintiff in the above cause, requests that Netcore, Inc., defendant in the above cause, produce for inspection and copying by Keltex, within thirty days of service hereof or at such other time as may be agreed upon by counsel for the parties, originals or legible copies of the documents requested herein. You are also requested to serve upon plaintiff within thirty (30) days after service of this request a written response in accordance with Rule 34 of the Federal Rules of Civil Procedure.

DEFINITIONS AND INSTRUCTIONS

1. Unless specified otherwise, documents requested herein include all those which were dated, written, rewritten, modified, sent, or received from September 9, 2014, to September 9, 2015.

2. The following definitions apply to this request:

    a. The term *agreement* means any document or oral statements that constitute or purport to be in whole or in part a contract, lease, or license, and includes all changes, amendments, covenants, alterations, modifications, interpretations, and drafts thereof, whether or not carried out.

    b. The term *computer* means any electronic device, regardless of whether said device is owned by the corporation or by an individual employee, so long as said device contains corporate business carried out by that employee in the regular course of his or her job duties, including but not limited to antitheft systems and databases, audio networks, audio systems, digital cameras, documented image technology, embedded chips, e-mail systems, e-mail software, event data recorders (in vehicles), external hard drives, fax machines, flash drives, global positioning systems, handheld wireless devices, hardware, iPods, landline phones, laptops, medical devices and records, memory sticks and flash cards, mobile phones, notebooks, pagers, personal computers, PDAs, printers, radio frequency identification tags or chips (RFIDs), security cameras and other security and surveillance devices, servers, smartphones, software, spyware, tablets, toll road cards, travel drives, video discs and videotapes, and Web-based bulletin boards.

EXHIBIT 12-3 Sample Request for Documents (*continued*)

c. The term *document* means any written, recorded, taped, typed, or word-processed material, whether produced, reproduced, filed, or stored on paper, cards, disks, tapes, belts, charts, films, cassettes, or any other medium, and shall include books, booklets, pamphlets, brochures, statements, speeches, memos, notebooks, agreements, appointment calendars, working papers, contracts, notations, records, telegrams, journals, diaries, or summaries, cash ledger books, checkbooks, corporate minute books, bank statements, stock transfer books, monthly statements, city tax returns, state tax returns, federal tax returns, and annual reports, and shall also include all drafts, originals, and copies.

d. The term *electronically stored information* means any animations, antitheft system and database records, archives, audio discs, audio records, audio tapes, backup tapes, blogs, cartridges, CDs, chat rooms, "cookies," credit cards and records, databases, data on external hard drives, data-processing cards, debit cards, debit records, deleted data, digital photographs, discs, drives, documented image technology, embedded chips, e-mail attachments, e-mail messages, e-mail software, event data records (in vehicles), fax machines data, financial data, flash drives, global positioning system data, graphics, handheld wireless device records, images, input data, instant messages, Internet use records, intranets, intranet use records, junk files, laptop data, legacy data, medical devices and records, memory sticks and flash cards, metadata, mobile phone memory, music files, networks, pagers, personal computers, PDAs, printer data, radio frequency identification tags or chips (RFIDs), removable discs, security camera and other security and surveillance device data, smartphones, software, spreadsheets, spyware databases, statistical data, spreadsheet data, system and network data, tablets, tapes, text messages, toll road card records, travel drives, video discs and videotapes, voice mail, Web-based bulletin-board postings, Web-based discussions, word-processed documents, and zipped files.

e. The term *report* means any written, recorded, taped, typed, or word-processed material, whether produced, reproduced, filed, or stored on paper, cards, disks, tapes, belts, charts, films, cassettes, or any other medium, and shall include books, booklets, pamphlets, brochures, statements, speeches, memos, notebooks, agreements, appointment calendars, working papers, contracts, notations, records, telegrams, journals, diaries, or summaries, cash ledger books, checkbooks, corporate minute books, bank statements, stock transfer books, monthly statements, city tax returns, state tax returns, federal tax returns, and annual reports, and shall also include all drafts, originals, and copies.

f. The term *defendants* means Netcore, Inc., including their directors, officers, employees, and agents.

g. The phrases *relate to* and *relating to* shall be construed to include "refer to," "summarize," "contain," "include," "mention," "explain," "discuss," "define," "describe," "point out," "comment on," or "remark."

h. The words *and* and *or* shall be interpreted in such a way as to bring within the scope of the specification all responses that otherwise might be interpreted as being outside its scope.

i. The term *each* shall be interpreted to include the word *every*, and the word *every* shall be interpreted to include the word *each*.

j. The word *any* shall be interpreted to include the word *all*, and the word *all* shall be interpreted to include the word *any*.

k. A plural noun will be interpreted to be a singular noun, and a singular noun will be interpreted as a plural noun, whenever needed to bring within the scope of the specification all responses that otherwise might be interpreted as being outside its scope.

3. Produce each and every document in its original file folder, cover, envelope, or jacket, and write on that folder, cover, envelope, or jacket the person or the corporate office, department, subdivision, or subsidiary for which, by which, and/or in which the file is maintained.

4. Should you be unable to produce any of the documents or ESI called for in this request, explain the reason that you cannot comply.

EXHIBIT 12-3 Sample Request for Documents (*continued*)

5. Should you be unable to produce any of the documents called for in this request, because such documents are no longer in your custody, control, or possession, please identify the document and the reason that you no longer have custody, control, or possession of said document or documents.

6. Should you be unable to produce any of the documents called for in this request, because such documents are no longer in your custody, control, or possession, please identify the document, and the person, department, subdivision, or subsidiary that does have custody, control, or possession of said document.

7. Should you wish to assert the attorney–client privilege, the work product privilege, or any other privilege as to any of the documents called for in this request, then as to each document subject to such privilege, please provide an identification of such document, including the name of the document, the date of the document, the type of document, the author of the document, the receiver of the document, the names of all people receiving copies of the document, the names of all people who saw the original document, and a summary of the subject of the document in sufficient detail to allow the court to determine the validity of the assertion of the privilege, should a motion to compel be filed.

8. Each paragraph in this request should be interpreted independently and not in relation to any other paragraph for the purpose of limiting the request.

9. This request is to be considered a continuing request requiring the defendant to supplement the production of document with any documents found or created after the first production takes place.

10. The defendant has the additional duty to correct any errors that are uncovered after the original production of documents takes place.

11. Any questions that may arise as to this request for documents may be directed by the counsel for the defendant to the undersigned representative of the plaintiff before the dates set for the production of the documents that are the subject matter of this request.

DOCUMENTS REQUESTED

1. All agreements, documents, electronically stored information, and reports that relate to the corporate organization of Netcore, Inc.

2. All agreements, documents, electronically stored information, and reports that Netcore, Inc. directed to or were received by Keltex.

3. All agreements, documents, electronically stored information, and reports that relate to contracts, proposed contracts, draft contracts, contemplated contracts, or offers of contracts that passed between Netcore, Inc. and The Keltex Center for Advanced Technology.

4. All agreements, documents, electronically stored information, and reports that constitute or relate to any and all communication between Netcore, Inc. and The Keltex Center for Advanced Technology.

5. All agreements, documents, electronically stored information, and reports that relate to timelines, deadlines, schedules, calendars, and planners involving the contract between Netcore, Inc. and The Keltex Center for Advanced Technology.

6. All agreements, documents, electronically stored information, and reports that constitute internal communication within Netcore, Inc.

7. All agreements, documents, electronically stored information, and reports that constitute internal communication within Netcore, Inc. that relate to The Keltex Center for Advanced Technology.

8. All agreements, documents, electronically stored information, and reports that relate to any and all communication between Netcore, Inc. and any and all subcontractors concerning The Keltex Center for Advanced Technology.

EXHIBIT 12-3 Sample Request for Documents (*continued*)

9. All agreements, documents, electronically stored information, and reports that relate to the audit conducted by Netcore, Inc. on the financial condition of Netcore, Inc.

10. All agreements, documents, electronically stored information, and reports that relate to the contract between Netcore, Inc. and The Keltex Center for Advanced Technology that are not covered by the prior requests herein.

Gina Stevens
Stevens, Jefferson, and Usalis
2229 Hamilton Avenue
Cleveland, Ohio 44119
Tel.: (216) 555-2121
Fax: (216) 555-2122
Attorneys for Plaintiff
Keltex Center for Advanced Technology

CERTIFICATE OF SERVICE

I hereby certify that a true and correct copy of the foregoing has been mailed by first class mail, postage prepaid to Janine Waterson 77 Superior Avenue, Cleveland, Ohio, 44118, on this 29th day of September, 2016.

Final Responsibility in Drafting the Request

Responsibility for the final review and signature of the request for documents rests with the attorney. Once the request has been signed, you will have to arrange for service on the other party or parties. Under the Federal Rules of Civil Procedure, a request for production of documents need not be filed with the court. However, some states and some local courts do have this filing requirement, so you should check your state and local rules on this matter. After the other party has been served with the request, place a reminder of the response due date in the firm's tickler or calendar system. If a timely response is not received, check with your supervising attorney to determine whether an extension of time has been granted. If an extension has not been granted, then it may be necessary to file a motion to compel.

Motion to Compel

Usually, all the parties in a lawsuit will be cooperative during the discovery process. Dates and times for the production of documents are negotiated and adhered to with great regularity. Even when a party objects to the production of a document on the ground that it is irrelevant, the document is often produced anyway. Similarly, objections on the ground that the request is overbroad often will be followed by a narrowed response. However, sometimes the other party refuses to cooperate or makes invalid objections to the request. For this situation, the law provides the motion to compel. Rule 37 of the Federal Rules of Civil Procedure allows a party to file a motion asking the court to compel the uncooperative party to produce the document requested for inspection.

As the paralegal, you may be asked to draft this motion. Again, in preparation for drafting this motion, review your firm's form books and document file or, if necessary, conduct an online search. Generally, however, your supervising attorney will avoid the motion to compel as much as possible. Such motions are not favored by the court and should be used only when your supervising attorney feels no other option remains.

Reviewing the Documents of the Opposing Party

Once the documents requested have been received in your office, you may be asked to review those documents, either alone or with an attorney. Naturally, knowledge of the facts, issues, and parties in the case is essential to a successful document review. However, you must also have an understanding of what your supervising attorney is looking for as you inspect and review the documents. Therefore, you should ask your attorney for guidance in reviewing the documents. For example, you ought to know which of the files must be read in-depth and which can be scanned. You might want to know if your supervising attorney is interested in a particular category of documents or in the documents produced by a particular individual.

Because reviewing a large volume of documents is a time-consuming and tedious task, you will want to try various techniques for expediting the job. One technique is to dictate file labels and a brief summary of the contents of each file. This strategy will help you review more documents over a shorter period of time. Another technique is to keep a record of the files that you have reviewed. This tactic will help you recall the precise location of documents that you have seen and consider crucial to the case. If you are dealing with original documents, your supervising attorney may want to have copies made of the more important documents. Your attorney will set the parameters for the documents that she will want you to copy. However, if you have any doubt about the value of a document to your case, designate the document for copying.

RESPONDING TO A REQUEST FOR DOCUMENTS

A document production is only as successful as the planning that precedes it. The first action you should take, once you have been served with a document request, is to determine whether the production date is realistic. Other important elements in the successful production process are categorizing the documents, involving the client, and organizing the documents.

Determining a Target Date

Whether the requested target date is feasible depends on the number of documents in your client's possession, the extent and the complexity of the ESI request, the number of people in the law firm who will assist in the production, and the availability of tech support for the retrieval and classification of ESI. Moreover, estimating the number of documents and the volume of ESI in a document production can be difficult. Often the first estimate will be revised a number of times, as you locate and review pertinent documents and as you begin to comprehend the vast quantity of the ESI in your client's possession or under his or her control. Nevertheless, you must make some initial assessment of the feasibility of meeting the deadline indicated in the request. Consulting with other paralegals who have been through several document productions and talking with IT personnel about the nature of the ESI request may help you evaluate the deadline.

Categorizing the Documents

You can make the task of documentation production easier if you divide the request into several general categories. For example, you might divide the request into the following categories:

Request 1	Contracts (including preliminary drafts)
Request 2	Correspondence (including all e-mail correspondence)
Request 3	Corporate Minutes, Bylaws, and Articles of Incorporation
Request 4	Material Lists
Request 5	Timetables

AUTOMATED LITIGATION SUPPORT

Predictive Coding

SCENARIO

You and your supervising attorney have received a document request from the defendant Netcore, Inc. The request covers all documents that are in any way related to present and past contracts between The Keltex Center for Advanced Research and Netcore, Inc. At first this does not sound all that difficult until you realize that to properly respond you will have to include all ESI related to the contract negotiations as well as the bidding process and all communication efforts that occurred before the contracts were entered, all communication efforts during the planning stages of the project, all communication efforts during negotiation process, all those that occurred during the execution of the contract, and even those that occurred after those contracts in relation to payment and nonpayment disputes. You also realize that the request for documents will include all e-mails, all calendar entries, all contract drafts, all word-processing drafts, all e-mails with subcontractors, all internal e-mails about Netcore, and so on. On top of that, looking back over the years, you also realize that Keltex and Netcore have been involved in hundreds of contracts, some of which include not only Keltex and Netcore, but also both with additional parties. This will mean combing through not only active data but also ephemeral, residual, and legacy data. Taking all of this into consideration you realize that there are hundreds of thousands maybe even millions of documents to comb through, just to locate those that are relevant and admissible, let alone those documents that will lead to admissible evidence. Just to complicate matters a tiny bit, your attorney adds that she wants the documents produced by noon tomorrow.

PROBLEM

Document production in massive and complex litigation is time consuming and cumbersome. Organizing thousands of documents for fast and accurate retrieval presents a challenge for you and your supervising attorney. After giving your attorney's orders some thought, you realize the immensity of the task you face. Hundreds of thousands (even millions) of documents are on your client's system. How are you going to sort through those electronic documents and narrow them to the ones required by the document request?

SOLUTION

Fortunately for you, your law firm recently introduced an automated litigation support program to help with the numerous litigation tasks. One feature of this program is a program called predictive coding. Predictive coding is a document retrieval strategy that employs a digital cataloging process that involves several well-orchestrated steps. In the first step, the predictive coding program examines a wide range of documents in order to adjust its search algorithm so that the computer can determine what to look for as it studies an even larger set of ESI documents. This first step empowers the computer to focus on documents that are relevant or can lead to relevant ESI records. In the second step, the predictive coding protocol directs a more in-depth inspection of those documents. This second level search is based on an advanced algorithm that decreases the list of documents to a more manageable number that plainly fits the pattern established in the algorithm. In the third step, the smaller file of documents is then scanned and organized by "human" attorneys, who produce the discoverable ESI documents in answer to the discovery request.

Once the general categories are developed, subcategories can be easily defined. These categories and subcategories will give your document search a controlling structure that will guide your work.

Involving the Client in Document Production

Although you have requested categories of the documents that you believe are responsive to the request, you must remember that only the client, and perhaps the client's IT assistant, knows what types and how many documents actually exist. Also remember that only the client can make the documents available to the law firm for production. Therefore, the client must be involved in the production of documents as early as possible. In fact, because the rules require early mutual disclosure, because ESI plays a huge role in most lawsuits today, and because a litigation hold must be placed on ESI immediately upon the discovery of a trigger event, you must involve the client, the client's staff, and the client's IT support group from the outset.

As noted earlier, the client must establish a litigation hold as soon as your supervising attorney detects even the slightest hint that a trigger event has occurred. Your attorney should talk to every member of the client's firm who has contact with or control over ESI so that they understand the crucial importance of maintaining that litigation hold.[35] Once your firm receives a copy of a document request, you must send a copy to the client immediately. In addition, make sure that you point out the date by which the production is to be made so that the client is aware that the process should not be delayed. Next, schedule a meeting with the client as soon as possible to plan the document production process.

Requirements Imposed by the Sarbanes–Oxley Act   One of the consequences that resulted from a high-profile case involving corporate corruption in recent years was the passage by Congress of the Sarbanes–Oxley Act. Sarbanes–Oxley created a series of criminal sanctions that can be levied against companies that deliberately distort their records in order to disguise their actual net worth. One of the major provisions in the act is directed primarily at preserving evidence for criminal investigations brought by the government. The main objective of these provisions is to prevent corporations and accounting firms from deliberately destroying evidence that can be used in a criminal prosecution. The act has, understandably, created numerous problems for modern corporations which tend to store most of their records in computer files, many of which are routinely erased because of the cost involved in storing such data in systems that have a limited carrying capacity. Despite the differences that exist between criminal and civil law, the development of a criminal law standard against destroying ESI, will likely be related to the traditional rules of discovery in civil cases in federal court which impose an affirmative duty to preserve evidence for the litigation process.[36]

Making Document Production a Joint Effort with the Client   Sometimes clients suggest that they conduct the document search without the aid of someone from the law firm. Several disadvantages argue against this approach. First, clients are often unaware of the attorney–client privilege, the work product privilege, and the common interest privilege and may, therefore, not recognize protected documents. Second, clients may fail to recognize the documents they actually *must* produce. Third, clients often do not comprehend the amount of time and effort involved in a document production. Finally, the client probably does not realize that sanctions can result if all the documents requested are not produced. Pointing out these disadvantages to your client should help convince the client to make document production a joint effort with the law firm. Your client may suggest hiring an independent contractor to conduct the document search. Although reputable firms can conduct such a search, your firm should never relinquish control over the process. The law firm should also conduct the document search without the help of the client, especially when ESI is involved. Your supervising attorney may, therefore, assign you the task of creating a liaison point with the client's IT department, with the administrative assistants, with the independent data center, if one is involved, and with any interns and temps who work directly with the client's computer system and with the client's ESI.

Selecting a Client's Representative for Document Production   The client should designate a representative to coordinate the document production with the legal team. The representative should be a member of the client's in-house legal department, if possible. Whatever the case, the person chosen should know about the client's business during the entire period of time covered by the document request. Because the client's representative must devote a significant amount of time to the document production project, clients often appoint junior executives who are new to the corporation. Such a move can be a mistake, not only because the junior executive will not be familiar with the entire case, but also because the other employees may refuse to cooperate with the "outsider." If you find yourself in this uncomfortable situation, seek the help of the client's in-house legal department to find a replacement. The replacement should be someone who is more familiar with the case and who will command the respect needed in such a sensitive operation. Remember that your supervising attorney may also want to establish a litigation response team charged with the task of learning all there is to know about the client's computer system and the ESI recorded on that system.

Organizing the Document Production

Organization is a key factor in conducting a successful document production. One effective way to organize is to gather all of the required documents in one central location. Exhibit 12-4 is a checklist you might follow to locate and gather in one location all the documents from your client's executive offices and branches. The checklist, however, is intended as a guide only. Planning strategy in a lawsuit is not like running an experiment in physics. No absolute principles of nature guide the operation of a lawsuit. The best that you can do is to develop a rough outline of those steps that have worked in the past and, therefore, might be helpful in the present for determining what will probably happen in the future. Unfortunately, no one can predict exactly what will happen in every lawsuit every time. Sometimes you just have to adjust to changing circumstances.

Controlling the Documents   Control is also an important factor in effective document production. You must be able to determine the location of any document among the thousands of documents that you will compile. For example, when your attorney asks for a one-page opinion that is part of a closing binder, you will be expected to locate the pertinent document quickly. Or if the client's chief financial officer needs to review the minutes of the board meeting at which the directors discussed the Netcore and Keltex contracts before the next board meeting, you must know exactly where that file is and make certain that the CFO has it on time for that meeting. Exhibit 12-4 includes steps that will help in the organization of the document production process. For ESI, your supervising attorney should already have taken control of all copies of all pertinent ESI files. If this did not happen as a part of the original litigation hold, it should be established now.

EXHIBIT 12-4 Checklist for Production of Client Documents and ESI

DOCUMENTS AND ESI CHECKLIST

1. At the first hint of litigation, establish a litigation hold on ESI deletion in the daily operation of the client's business.

2. Request a copy of the client's document-retention policy as well as the client's deletion procedure for ESI, including, especially, the deletion policy for e-mail files.

3. Meet with all of the employees who work for the client in any capacity that puts them in the custody or control of ESI in order to reinforce the critical nature of the litigation hold.

4. Establish a litigation response team to learn as much as possible about the client's computer system.

5. Request an organization chart to determine departments, employees, and computer systems where documents and ESI are located. Ask for a dedicated workroom for the litigation team, including telephones, a fax machine, office furniture, several computer terminals, and at least one printer.

6. Turn over all material required under the Rule 26 mutual disclosure provisions.

7. After a document request arrives, review the request and determine the time and the personnel that might be required to respond to the request.

8. Review the request for any documents or ESI that might be privileged.

9. Review the request to determine the data requester has specified the format to be used for the ESI.

10. If the data requester has specified a format for ESI, determine whether you should object to that format and, if so, why.

11. If the data requester has not specified the format to be used for transmitting ESI, determine the format that your client will use to transmit that ESI.

12. Consider the advisability of including metadata or, in the alternative, deleting metadata from the requested ESI before sending it to opposing counsel.

13. Forward the request for production to the client and ask that client representatives, including IT personnel, be named to assist in production, if this has not already been taken care of as a part of the establishment of the litigation response team.

14. For paper documents, determine whether the originals or copies will be produced.

15. Determine whether the documents will be produced as kept in the ordinary course of business or by document request number.

16. Determine whether only relevant documents will be produced or whether the production will be a "warehouse" production.

17. Meet with the client's representative to begin planning the collection and organization of the client's documents and ESI for production.

18. Search all of the pertinent files in the client's offices. Draw a map of each office or department to indicate the location and titles of files and filing cabinets and of relevant computer terminals and systems.

19. Search all pertinent computer systems or supervise IT personnel who can search the systems for you. Remember all the electronic devices that can be included within the term *computer*.

20. List all files removed on the document production log, and indicate the employee from whom documents were received, or the ESI file from which the data was retrieved, in addition to the date that the files and the ESI were received.

21. Request an index to the archived files to determine files that might pertain to the litigation. Order those files brought from the archives to the production site.

22. Search ESI archives to determine ESI files that might pertain to the lawsuit and save those files to a separate flash drive or disc.

23. For paper documents, number each box as it is brought into the work area. Place that number on the log and index files within the box, including source and date received. Create electronic files to accomplish the same goals for ESI, remembering to store the files on the flash drive or disc.

EXHIBIT 12-4 Checklist for Production of Client Documents and ESI

24. For paper documents, review the contents of each box of documents. Create new file folders labeled "Produce," "Non-produce," "Privileged/Work Product." Place a colored sticker or flag on each document about which there is a question. Ask the supervising attorney to review those documents immediately to determine the appropriate folder. In case of documents that require redaction, make a copy of the original before redaction, note the redaction at the top of the document, make a copy of the document with the redaction and place it in the "Produce" file; place the original and the original redacted copy in the "Non-produce" or the "Privilege/Work Product" folders, as applicable. For ESI, construct electronic files to accomplish the same goals and save to a flash drive or disc. Once again, consider the advisability of including metadata or, in the alternative, deleting metadata from the requested ESI before sending it to opposing counsel. Check precedent in your jurisdiction to determine the court's position on the deletion of metadata.

25. Remove the privileged paper documents from the workroom. Place all privileged ESI in special files and save the files to a flash drive or a disc. Once the attorney has reviewed the documents and determined that the privileged designation is correct, these documents may be numbered with a different numbering prefix from the documents to be produced. A notation should be made on the production log to indicate privileged documents, the original files from which they came, and their document numbers once they are assigned. For ESI, construct electronic files to accomplish the same goals and save to a flash drive or disc.

26. After the document review has been completed, all documents to be produced should be copied and numbered. The document number can indicate the source of the documents. For example, documents from defendant A begin with "1," from defendant B with "2," and from third-party defendants, "3."

27. Prepare a privilege list to attach to the response to the request for production.

28. Prepare the response to the request for production.

29. Create an index for the produced paper documents and for produced ESI.

30. Produce documents to the opposing party. The paralegal should remain in the production room at all times. Neither the opposing party nor its counsel should remove copies.

31. Copy documents and ESI that the opposing party designates for copying. Review the documents and ESI and notify your supervising attorney of the documents and ESI requested by opposing party. Forward the copies and a statement of the copying costs to the counsel for the opposing party. Make a notation on the production log of all copies received by the opposing party.

32. Return original documents to the client's office. Place a notation in the file that no documents are to be added or taken from this file because the matter is in litigation. Begin a new file with the same file label for all new correspondence and documents. In the event of a supplemental request for production, you may be able to avoid reviewing files previously reviewed.

33. Make additional copies of documents produced and organize in chronological, subject matter, or witness order for later deposition exhibit, trial exhibit, or general trial preparation use.

Copying and Printing the Documents   The decision of when to copy or print the documents must be made early in the document production process. With paper documents, it is generally not advisable to release original documents because the release of such documents can handicap the daily operation of the client's business. Also, when original paper documents are released, they may be lost. Finally, government regulations may prohibit the removal of some documents from the principal place of business.

Unfortunately, copying thousands of paper documents or printing reams of ESI documents can be expensive and time consuming. Therefore, the legal team should be aware of ways to reduce these expenses. For example, time and money can be saved by waiting until the opposing counsel designates the documents that are to be copied or printed. A disadvantage to this approach is that you may miss some documents that could be helpful to your client's case. Opposing counsel will have no interest in copying documents that support your client's position.

Scanning the Documents

Sometimes you should scan all paper documents so that those documents can be preserved electronically. The scanning process allows you to store the material without talking up extra space in the office or file room. Often when most of the evidentiary material is already in a computerized format, scanning the remaining paper documents keeps everything in the same electronic file. You will probably have a choice as to what format to use in the scanning process. When possible, use a format that will make the newly scanned files compatible with the ESI files.

Numbering the Documents

Numbering and control are synonymous. Without identifying numbers, organizing and controlling document production is almost impossible. A number assigned to a document during the production process should remain with the document throughout the lawsuit. The traditional technique for numbering the paper documents is the Bates numbering system. The **Bates numbering** system involves the numbering of documents in a lawsuit using a stamping machine. Recently, computer-generated numbers on peel-off labels have replaced the Bates numbering system. The new system is different, but the result is the same. Documents can be identified quickly and easily. Bates software can be used to label electronic documents. Alpha prefixes can be used to identify the source of a document. For instance, the plaintiff's documents might begin with "A," and the defendant's begin with "B." However, you should not act too quickly in numbering the documents. All privileged documents must be removed from production before numbering to avoid suspicious gaps in the numbering system. Exhibit 12-5 represents a sample **document production log** to assist you in organizing the documents for production.

You should also make out a **privilege log**, indicating all documents that are shielded by the attorney–client privilege, the work product privilege, the common interest privilege, the

Bates numbering
The numbering of documents in a lawsuit using a machine.

document production log
A method of keeping track of documents in a lawsuit by categorizing those documents based on source and file location. The document production log should indicate whether the documents have been excluded as privileged.

privilege log
A method of keeping track of documents that are shielded by the attorney–client privilege, the work product privilege, or the common interest privilege.

EXHIBIT 12-5 Document Production Log

STYLE OF CASE: _____ REVIEWER: _____ REVIEW DATE: _____						
BOX NO. _____ SOURCE _____						
FILE NAME	SOURCE	PRODUCED	NON-PRODUCE	PRIVILEGE	BATES NO.	DATE PRODUCED	OPPOSING PARTY TO WHOM PRODUCED

Copyright © 2015 Cengage Learning®

EXHIBIT 12-6 Privilege Log

BATES NO.	DATE	DOC. TYPE	AUTHOR	RECIPIENT COPIES	SUMMARY	TYPE PRIVILEGE

responsive documents
Documents that must be presented to a party in answer to a request from that party for the production of those documents.

nonresponsive documents
Documents that need not be presented to a party in answer to a request from that party for the production of those documents.

privileged documents
Documents that are shielded by the attorney–client privilege, the work product privilege, or the common interest privilege.

redaction
A procedure that involves removing information from a document before duplicating the document and turning the duplicate over to another party in a lawsuit in response to a request for production.

medical privilege, or any other privilege that might be available to your client. Exhibit 12-6 will help you compile such a log.

Reviewing, Labeling, and Filing Documents before Removal

A paralegal and an attorney should review all documents before they (the documents, not the paralegal and the attorney) are removed from the client's office. Sometimes one or more of the client's original files will contain documents that you must produce, other documents that you need not produce, and still others that are protected by privilege. The documents that you will have to produce are called **responsive documents**; the documents that you do not have to produce are called **nonresponsive documents**. The protected documents are called **privileged documents**.

To separate these documents, set up three duplicate files. Place copies of the documents to be produced in one of the folders and give it the same title as the client's original file. Place the nonresponsive documents in the second file and label it "nonresponsive" or "non-produce." The term *non-produce* is simply a synonym for nonresponsive. Place the privileged documents in the third file and label it "privileged." All privileged files should be removed from the area where the responsive documents are kept. This simple precaution will prevent them from being inadvertently sent to the other party. For ESI, create e-files that correspond to the categories listed above.

Sometimes a single document will contain information that you must produce and information that you need not produce. The same document also may include information that is protected by privilege. In such a case, cover the irrelevant or the protected information before making a photocopy. Place the notation "deletion" on the covered portion. This deletion process is referred to as **redaction**. Make two copies of the redacted page. Place one of the redacted copies in the file that is marked as the client's original file. Place the other redacted copy in the nonresponsive file or the privileged file, whichever is appropriate.

You can follow a similar process for ESI. Moreover, you may be able to alter the electronic files to hide the fact that privileged material has been deleted from the ESI. *However, you should definitely resist this temptation.* Remember that the general theme of discovery is to maintain a free flow of evidence in an efficient and economical manner, while preserving genuinely privileged information. Therefore, many judges will look at the process of doctoring ESI to hide the existence of privileged information as tampering with evidence.

ORGANIZING AND INDEXING THE DOCUMENTS AFTER PRODUCTION

As the paralegal, you will have several duties following production of your client's documents and review of the opposition's documents. Because thousands (and with ESI possibly hundreds of thousands) of documents are often involved in the litigation, control problems will be very serious. You can aid in establishing tight control over these documents by organizing and indexing them.

Organizing the Documents after Production

Before the mass of information in these documents can be used properly, the documents must be organized. Organizational plans vary from case to case. Some cases are hinged on chronological events. Documents in such cases are ordered by dates. Other cases may be broken down into several subject categories, and the documents would be organized by those subjects. In other cases you will be asked to organize the documents in anticipation of the upcoming depositions. In such a case, you will need to pull together all documents related to the testimony of each deponent to be called. The method of organization is less important than the fact that the documents are organized in a way that will help you instantly locate a document when asked to do so.

If the case is to be managed manually, without the aid of a computer (a rare but not nonexistent technique today), several copies of each document should be made. One set can be placed in chronological order, a second set in subject order, and a third set in deponent order. Keep the copies separate from the original numbered set and limit access to that original set. A missing original that is incorrectly numbered may disappear forever. The absence of that crucial document could have a severe impact on the case. Remember, control and organization are the keys to effective document management in any successful litigation.

In the case of ESI, backup files must also be kept, preferably on a disc or a flash drive, to guard against the loss of crucial electronic evidence. Moreover, today it is also possible to store the documents using the cloud storage process of stockpiling documents. Recall that cloud storage is a new tactic for preserving ESI that sidesteps the usual techniques for saving data on hard drives, flash drives, and on-site servers and delegating that job to the servers at a distant ESI center (aka data center). The ESI center collects, categorizes, and controls the ESI by placing it on a distant server, making the data available to the ESI or data owner (aka the ESI or data depositor) through the Internet.[37] The process is efficient and relatively safe, provided that the data center is dependable and has appropriate protection protocols in place. These two features, dependability and protection, are extremely important because almost all discovery data received by an attorney will be critical to the lawsuit, and must, thus, be both accessible and secure. This means that an attorney must take reasonable steps to make sure that all data that is stored in a "cloud" is not only protected (preferably by encryption, authorization, and authentication practices), but also available with little or no notice.[38] Still, despite the exotic nature of ESI, the paralegal can apply the same fundamental principles of organization that she used for paper files to establish a plan for ESI.

Indexing the Documents after Production

An index of the documents produced by all parties is critical to controlling the files throughout the lawsuit. This index can be limited to the document number, date, author, recipient, document type, and a brief summary of its content. If you place the document in word processing or on the firm's computer, a particular document can be located quickly by any of the identifying labels. The index is your final control measure. However, this does not mean that you should minimize its importance. It may be a difficult job at the outset of the lawsuit, but it is much less difficult than searching for a document by trial and error later in the case.

INSPECTION OF PROPERTY

The request for documents is directed only to documents. However, often a case involves tangible property, such as a piece of equipment or a parcel of real estate. Rule 34 of the Federal Rules of Civil Procedure provides a procedure through which the parties or their representatives can inspect property for the purposes of measuring, photographing, or testing.

Obtaining an Inspection

Normally, the demand for inspection is made informally by letter. Sometimes the demand may be transmitted by e-mail or fax. The letter, e-mail, or fax will also designate a date and place of inspection. If the date and time specified in the letter, e-mail, or fax are

FINDING IT on the Internet

The federal courts maintain a Web site at **<http://www.uscourts.gov>**. Access the site and click on the entry for "Forms & Fees." On that page, locate and click on "Court Forms by Number," then find the form used for the *Subpoena to Produce Documents, Information, and Objects or to Permit Inspection of Premises in a Civil Action*. Click on that entry and use the form to create an imaginary subpoena to be served on Sara Zizek, CFO of Netcore in the *Keltex* case at the beginning of this chapter.

The Catholic University of America maintains a Web site at **<http://www.cua.edu/>**. Access the site and navigate to "Academics." Click on "Academics" and find the home page for the Columbus School of Law. Click on "Academic Programs" and report on the core curriculum, practice areas, and practical training available at the law school.

All Business is a private firm that specializes in helping entrepreneurs start and operate their own businesses. Access their Web site at **<http://www.allbusiness.com>** and conduct a search using "document production" as your key words. Find an article on "document production" and summarize its contents.

Access Litigation Law Firms at **<http://www.litigationlawfirms.com>**. On their site, click on "FindLaw Answers." Conduct a search for "Legal Research-How To" and find an interesting subtopic. Report on the contents of that subtopic.

inconvenient for the other party, another time and place can be set. In some instances, the party who has custody or possession of the property in question is reluctant to allow the other parties access to the property. Rule 34 of the Federal Rules of Civil Procedure sets out the procedure by which a party may demand that the party with custody of the property relevant to the case shall produce the property for inspection. The court will usually grant the inspection if it determines that the inspection is calculated to lead to the discovery of evidence that will be admissible at trial. The procedure for gaining access to property in the possession of another party is simple. A **demand for inspection** must be prepared and served upon all parties in the litigation, even if it is directed only to the party that has custody of the property at issue. The property must be identified with reasonable particularity, and the demand must not be overly broad or vague. A demand for inspection may be made only upon the parties to the litigation.

demand for inspection
A discovery technique that involves a request to enter property to inspect that property to gain facts in relation to the lawsuit.

Responding to a Demand for Inspection

Under Rule 34, the respondent has 30 days to respond to the demand for inspection. The respondent may agree to the inspection, limit or place conditions on the inspection, or serve formal objections to the requests. Normally, inspections of land, buildings, or equipment must be timed so as not to interfere with the other party's normal use. If a test to be used on the property might destroy that property, the test may be conducted by an expert agreeable to both parties. A video recording may be made of the test.

ESI AND ON-SITE INSPECTIONS

Rule 34 of the Federal Rules of Civil Procedure authorizes on-site inspections in order for a party to enter premises that are held or overseen by a party to inspect and/ or record either an object located on the premises or an operation carried out therein. Clearly, this would include the computer system itself, as well as workstations, data storage facilities, and paper files of such ESI. The rule also specifies that the information must be inspected as it is preserved in the "usual course of business." There is very little doubt that in many, perhaps most, businesses, organizations, and institutions, the ordinary course of business involves the storage of data within an individual computer or within a computer system, as well as the paper copies of such ESI. As we shall see, the operation of the rule is made even more problematic because such requests also can be made of nonparties.

Reasons for the On-Site Inspection of a Computer System

If your supervising attorney intends to conduct such an inspection, she should have a legitimate reason for doing so. For example, often a party may have no idea how to retrieve computer data that was the subject of an initial document request. As strange as this may seem at first glance, we must remember that obtaining ESI is not always as simple as obtaining paper evidence that can easily be lifted from a briefcase, pulled out of a filing cabinet, taken off a tabletop, or removed from a desk drawer. This is especially true when the ESI requested is extant data that was deleted but is still hidden somewhere within the data stream of the computer system.

Other problems and concerns with the ESI produced or with the data collection process might motivate your supervising attorney to ask for an on-site inspection. For example, the issues in the lawsuit may not be associated with the actual data produced but with the operation of the entire computer system. Therefore, your attorney may require an on-site inspection by your firm's IT expert to track the daily computer operation of a party. Such an inspection might examine the handling of ESI to determine whether it is secure, controlled, and, above all, authentic. Moreover, such an inspection might reveal the routine procedure of making paper files of ESI, something that even the workers within the system may have overlooked, forgotten, or taken as a matter of course. Other questions may surface after an initial document request has been filed and responded to and your supervising attorney begins to suspect that not all of the ESI requested has been delivered, either because the request has not been properly honored, because some of the relevant ESI has been deleted, or because the routine paper storage of deleted ESI has been forgotten or ignored.

Procedures for the On-Site Inspection of a Computer System

The federal courts are extremely sensitive to the problems associated with permitting a party to enter the premises of another party in order to inspect the operation of a party's computer system. Part of this sensitivity arises because the courts realize that any on-site inspection is intrusive, expensive, and often threatens the integrity of the computer system itself as well as the very existence of its ESI. For example, in at least one case, the on-site inspection of a computer system for ESI resulted in an enormous amount of lost ESI from that system. The loss of the ESI was eventually traced directly to the careless actions of an IT expert from the opposing party who failed to follow proper protocols in the extraction of certain pieces of ESI. In addition, the inspection of a computer system often involves privacy issues associated not only with classified business and employment records but also with trade secrets and professional confidences. On-site inspection requests have been further complicated by the cloud storage system because the servers on which the ESI is saved will not be on the physical premises of the law firm.

For these reasons, the federal courts have, in a series of cases, developed a protocol for the handling of on-site inspections for ESI, whether that inspection calls for an examination of the operation of the computer system itself, or for the actual extraction of ESI from the system. This protocol must be followed when the federal courts have mandated the on-site inspection of a computer system. As we review the elements of this protocol, remember that the courts have several objectives in mind. First, they are attempting to preserve ESI that is relevant to the case. Second, they are attempting to keep the inconvenience, the intrusiveness, the danger, and the expense of the on-site visit to a minimum. Third, the courts are mindful of the need to respect sensitive material by ensuring the confidentiality and privacy of the records themselves and of trade secrets and professional confidences associated with that part of the business that is involved in the on-site inspection.

Goals of the On-Site Inspection Protocol for ESI

It is crucial to keep in mind the goals and objectives of the court's on-site ESI inspection protocol. These goals and objectives include the following: (1) to retrieve and preserve all ESI relevant to the case; (2) to regulate the extent of the production process so that unnecessary or repetitious ESI is not revealed or compromised in any way; (3) to minimize the inconvenience, intrusiveness, and expense of an on-site visit; (4) to preserve the privacy of certain business records; (5) to protect the privileged nature of trade secrets and professional confidences, and, above all, (6) to prevent the unnecessary and costly loss of ESI stored in a computer system.

Steps in the On-Site Inspection Protocol for ESI

To be effective, the protocol ought to include the following steps:

(a) Before the actual document production process is to begin, the individuals involved in the search will set procedural restrictions. These ought to include a list of the key players whose computer stations and records will be a part of the search and a list of the computer stations that will be subject to the search.

(b) It would be wise at this point to determine which party or parties will be responsible for covering the expense of the on-site production process.

(c) The parties should decide which party or parties will be accountable for the expense that might be involved in recovering any lost or destroyed ESI that results from the search.

(d) The parties ought to specify the status (active data, inactive data, backup data, extant data, residual data, legacy data, ephemeral data) of the ESI subject to the search.

(e) The parties should specify whether any backup paper copies of the ESI will be included in the on-site search.

(f) The individuals involved in the search should establish a time frame in which the ESI will be gathered.

(g) An independent, objective IT specialist will be retained to conduct the search for ESI. The independent IT specialist must be mutually agreeable to everyone involved in the search. Moreover, he or she will operate as an official court representative.

(h) Rather than handling the actual ESI, the IT specialist should make copies that are turned over to the owner of the ESI. The owner of the ESI will then examine the copy to preserve any confidential or private data.

(i) After all private and confidential data is expunged from the ESI, it is turned over to the party that filed the document request.

Preparing for an On-Site Inspection for ESI

It is very important for the party producing the ESI to prepare for an on-site visit of its computer operation system. Much of the anxiety, concern, and inconvenience that results from an on-site visit can be lessened if certain steps are taken to minimize the impact of such a search. Unfortunately, once a production request has been filed, it is often too late to avoid many of the troublesome aspects of the visit. Therefore, it is best to prepare for such a search as a part of the everyday process of doing business. To lessen the impact of a document production request for ESI at the time of a lawsuit, your supervising attorney might advise clients, in advance, to initiate some of the following suggestions:

a.1. Instruct workers, especially IT specialists, about the ever-present possibility of a lawsuit against the company, organization, or institution. This means making certain that they carefully store, catalog, and retain ESI so that it can be retrieved easily without damaging the system, losing data, or spending valuable downtime, should a document production request and an on-site investigation be called for during litigation.

a.2. Implement a plan that can be activated automatically to halt any routine deletion of ESI. This will minimize the loss of any crucial ESI and eliminate any suspicion that ESI has been deliberately destroyed to escape discovery.

a.3. Make certain that all IT specialists and their supervisors and assistants are prepared to deal with the rigors of discovery, but especially with the intrusive nature of an on-site inspection of computer operations.

a.4. Once there is even the smallest suggestion that the client might be involved in litigation, instigate a litigation hold to prevent the deletion of ESI.[39]

a.5. Visit the client's place of business as soon as possible to make certain that everyone at the firm appreciates the importance of maintaining the litigation hold.[40]

a.6. Establish a litigation response team of key personnel to learn all there is to know about the client's ESI system, including all backup, retrieval, formatting, deletion procedures, and so on.[41]

a.7. Once a document production and/or an on-site inspection request has been filed, hold sessions to educate the key players and IT specialists about the facts in the case and the types of ESI that could be considered discoverable.

a.8. After an on-site inspection request has been filed, advise key players and IT specialists about the protocol established by the courts for dealing with an on-site inspection. Make certain that they are fully acquainted with their individual roles and responsibilities in the operation of the protocol.

In Chapter 13 we will see that the federal court is preparing to offer a less costly and more effective alternative to this inspection process. The new amendments to Rule 34 may be welcomed by many practitioners, but especially those whose clients use a data center as part of a cloud storage protocol for preserving ESI. This is because any request to inspect the computer system of a client using a cloud storage protocol would require involving the data center in the process outlined above. It does not take great imagination to see how adding the data center owners and operators to the inspection process would complicate the steps in an inspection to such an extent the process might become almost unmanageable. To help alleviate such complications, under the new rule, the ESI retriever would be obligated to deliver the targeted ESI before the requested inspection date (or within a reasonable period of time related to that date).[42]

SUMMARY

- Five ways that documents can be obtained during discovery include a request for documents, mutual disclosure, a request for documents at the deposition of a party, a subpoena duces tecum for a nonparty to produce documents at the time of a deposition, and the option of producing business records as an answer to an interrogatory. A request for documents and ESI is a request by one party in a lawsuit to allow the first party access to documents that are relevant to the subject matter of the lawsuit. To make certain that no evidence is lost, once a trigger event occurs initiating lawsuit (or at least signaling its potentiality) the parties to that suit must institute a litigation hold which signals the preservation of all data from that moment forward. Two crucial preliminary considerations in a production request are the timing of the request and the potential cost of the production.

- When an attorney structures a Rule 34 document production request, he must be knowledgeable of the types of ESI available within a computer system. Discoverable ESI can appear within three groups: (1) types of ESI based on the configuration of the computer system, (2) types of ESI based on the nature of the evidence itself, and (3) types of ESI based on its storage status. An attorney must consider all of these categories when preparing a document production request. Moreover, to be doubly certain that all relevant evidence is retrieved, the attorneys on both sides of a lawsuit must remember that many employers today permit employees to use dual purpose e-devices that store both personal and business data. It is also essential to include the key players and IT specialists involved in collecting, managing, storing, and communicating that ESI. Because of the need to hire experts who frequently use special programs to retrieve ESI, the expense of ESI production is often greater than the expense involved in retrieving paper records. Consequently, an attorney seeking ESI must be prepared to verify the need for such data. In order to locate all relevant documents, attorneys and paralegals must also be ready to use technology assisted review techniques, such as predictive decoding, as well as linear document review.

- Not all documents requested must be produced. Some are protected by the attorney–client privilege, the work product privilege, or the common interest privilege. Other objections are that the request is overbroad, duplicative, or irrelevant. The new rules also permit a format-based objection for ESI. If none of these objections are available, the documents can still be protected by using a confidentiality agreement or a protective order.

- The paralegal often will be called on to draft the request for production of documents. The parts of the request include the title, the definitions, the instructions, and a list of documents requested. The paralegal may need to draft a motion to compel the other party to produce the documents requested. The paralegal may be required to review and organize the documents once they arrive.

- The paralegal will be involved in responding to a request for documents. The steps in this process include determining a realistic production date, categorizing the documents, involving the client, and organizing the documents.

- After document production by all parties, the paralegal may be required to organize the documents by various categories.

- The request for documents is directed only to documents and ESI. Often a case involves tangible property such as a piece of equipment or a parcel of real estate. The Federal Rules of Civil Procedure stipulate a procedure through which the parties or their representatives can inspect property for purposes of measuring, photographing, or testing.

- Because on-site inspections for ESI covered by Rule 34 are generally intrusive and expensive, the courts have been very careful to outline a detailed protocol that must be followed by the parties to a lawsuit. This protocol applies whether that inspection calls for an examination of the operation of the computer system itself, or for the actual extraction of ESI from the system. The court has several objectives in mind supporting the establishment of this protocol. They include (1) preserving ESI relevant to the case; (2) minimizing the inconvenience, intrusiveness, and expense of the on-site visit; (3) ensuring the confidentiality and privacy of records, trade secrets, and professional confidences; and (4) preventing the unnecessary loss of ESI from the inspected computer system. The federal courts are also now in the process of amending some of the rules of civil procedure. Some of these amendments may affect the inspection of a party's computer system.

KEY TERMS

adverse inference	document production log	privileged documents
app	ESI or data center	redaction
app platform provider	linear document review	request for documents
Bates numbering	mobile application	responsive documents
cloud storage	nonresponsive documents	self-induced trigger event
demand for inspection	predictive coding	technology assisted review
document	privilege log	trigger event

REVIEW QUESTIONS

1. What is a document request?
2. When should a legal hold be placed on the use of documents and ESI?
3. What are the different approaches to document requests?
4. What are the three categories of ESI?
5. How do the attorney–client privilege, the work product privilege, and the common interest privilege differ from one another?
6. What is Rule 502 of the Federal Rules of Evidence?
7. When should a confidentiality agreement or a protective order be sought?
8. What objections can be raised to a request for production of documents?
9. What are the duties of a paralegal in the preparation of a document request?
10. When can a party request an inspection of property or an on-site visit to obtain ESI?

CHAPTER EXERCISES

Where necessary, check with your instructor prior to starting any of these exercises.

1. Review the laws of your state and find all laws that deal with requests for the production of documents. Check your local court rules to see if any local rules supplement or alter the state laws.

2. Obtain sample forms from your firm's form book, online, or from your state civil rules book. Find a sample request for production of documents and compare it with the sample found in this chapter.

3. Review the laws of your state and find out whether your state allows the same objections to the request for documents as those outlined in this chapter.

4. Carefully consider each of the following documents and determine whether it should be a part of the documents and/or ESI requested from Netcore, Inc.

   a. A series of internal e-mails on the computer system in the offices of Netcore, Inc., detailing negotiations with The Keltex Center for Advanced Technology;

   b. ESI detailing the results of an earlier contract also negotiated by Netcore, Inc. with The Keltex Center for Advanced Technology;

   c. All stored metadata from the negotiations conducted by Netcore, Inc. with The Keltex Center for Advanced Technology;

   d. A series of e-mails between the members of the Netcore team that negotiated the contract with The Keltex Center for Advanced Technology;

   e. A series of e-mails from Keltex to Netcore reminding them of the Keltex contract and the need to meet the September 9 deadline.

CHAPTER PROJECT

Review the Commentary at the beginning of this chapter. Recall that your firm has been retained by The Keltex Center for Advanced Technology to bring a lawsuit against Netcore, Inc. for failing to meet the deadline in the construction contract. Review the sample request for production of documents in this chapter or the one that you located in your state's form book or online. Assume that the defendant, Netcore, Inc., has responded to the request for documents and has delivered the documents and the ESI that you asked for. Now, you and your staff face the task of organizing and indexing these documents and ESI. During the process, you and your IT assistant uncover an enormous amount of metadata hidden within the ESI documents detailing internal discussions at Netcore on the Keltex contract. A quick glance at the metadata reveals that it includes a record of the officers and lower-level employees at Netcore who had access to the contract and changes in the contract, including alterations in the contractual language related to the September 9 deadline. Draft an e-mail to your supervising attorney explaining the legal arguments for and against the next step in the process, which would be mining the metadata revealed in the ESI. Then ask your supervising attorney what would be the proper way to proceed.

THE *BENNETT* CASE
Assignment for Chapter 12: Drafting a Request for Production

The answers to interrogatories submitted by the defendant in the *Bennett* case indicated that the defendant has copies of e-mails between several parties relating to Ms. Bennett. These e-mails are archived on a tape backup. Your attorney would also like to inspect the hard drives of the computers used by Darren Blackwood and Martin Yardly. Draft a request for production and/or for an on-site inspection to obtain these.

THE *DOUGLASS FINANCIAL SERVICES INC.* CASE
Assignment for Chapter 12: Responding to a Request for Production

Your attorney tells you that your client, Douglass Financial, Inc., was served with a Request to Produce Documents with the following requests:

1. Personnel file of defendant Evan Portman.
2. All receipts for food and drinks from the office party of December 19.
3. Any and all documents related to the office party of December 19.
4. Any and all receipts for food and alcohol for the past five years.
5. List of names, addresses, and telephone numbers of all employees of defendant, Douglass Financial, Inc.

Your attorney has asked you to evaluate these requests and indicate if you should respond or object. If you think you should object please explain why.

END NOTES

1. David K. Isom, "Electronic Discovery Primer for Judges," *Federal Courts Law Review* (2005), retrieved on September 7, 2013 from <http://fclr.org/fclr/articles/html/2005/fedctslrev1.pdf>, 15–16.
2. Dennis Kennedy, "Does Your Firm Have a Bring-Your-Own-Device Policy?" *ABA Journal* (January 1, 2012), retrieved on January 11, 2012 from <http://www.abajoual.com>, 1. See also: Lauren Schwartzreich and Aaron Crews, "Investigation of Employee Smart Device Apps," *Law Technology News* (April 17, 2013), retrieved on September 7, 2013 from <http://www.law.com/jsp/lawtechnologynews/PubArticleLTN.jsp?id=1202596015218&Investigation_of_Employee_Smart_Device_Apps&slreturn=20130807083618>, 11.
3. John Isaza, "Legal Holds 101: Legal Holds, Requirements, and Notices," *GS Newsletter: Legal Holds and Trigger Events* (2007), retrieved on April 26, 2013 from <http://legalholdsblog.com/resources/>, 1.
4. *Zubulake v. UBS Warburg*, 02 CIV. 1243 (SAS), (S.D.N.Y. July 20, 2004), 24 and 30.
5. Evan Koblentz, "Microsoft Office 2013 Bolsters E-Discovery," *Law Technology News* (July 17, 2012), retrieved on September 7, 2013 January 12, 2013 from <http://www.law.com/jsp/lawtechnologynews/PubArticleLTN.jsp?id=1202563210396>, 1.

6. Brad Harris, "Rimkus v. Cammarata: Another Great Reason Organizations Need an Effective Legal Hold Process," *Legal Hold ProTracker* (February 2010), retrieved on September 19, 2010 from <https://www.legalholdpro.com/Blog/2010/2/25/rimkus-v-cammarata-another-great-reason-organizations-need-an-effective-legal-hold-process>, 2.

7. Thomas Y. Allman, "E-Discovery in Federal and State Courts After the 2008 Federal Amendments," *Kroll Ontrack Publications* (January 4, 2012), 8, retrieved on May 22, 2013 from <http://www.krollontrack.com/publications/2012>. Allman cites one case in particular that supports this position: *Victor Stanley v. Creative Pipe*, 269 F.D.R. 497 (D. Md. 2010). In another article, Allman cites several cases to demonstrate that the duty to preserve can emerge from statutory law, common law, or administrative regulations. See: Thomas Y. Allman, "The Impact of the Proposed Federal E-Discovery Rules," 12 Rich. J.L. & Tech. 13 (2006): 10–11.

8. Isaza, "Legal Holds 101," 2–3.

9. Isaza, "Legal Holds 101," 2–3. See also: *Doe v. Norwalk Community College*, 248 F.D.R. 372 (D. Conn 2007).

10. Harris, "Rimkus v. Cammarata," 1. See: *Pension Committee of the University of Montreal Pension Plan v. Banc of America Securities, LLC*, No. 05 Civ. 9016, 2010 WL 184312 (S.D.N.Y. Jan 15, 2010).

11. James C. Francis. "Judicial Modesty Not an Oxymoron—The Case for Jurist Restraint in the Electronic Age," *Law Technology News* (February 1, 2013), retrieved on April 27, 2013 from <http://www.law.com/jsp/lawtechnologynews/PubArticleLTN.jsp?id=1202585467525&Judicial_Modesty_Not_an_Oxymoron>, 27–29.

12. Note: The phrase "in the usual course of business" cannot be used to stonewall the legitimate collection of ESI. Thus, if a party deletes ESI routinely "in the usual course of business" the litigation hold must halt this practice.

13. Kennedy, "Does Your Firm Have a Bring-Your-Own-Device Policy?" 1.

14. Kamala D. Harris, *Privacy on the Go: Recommendations for the Mobile Ecosystem*, California Department of Justice (January 2013), 3–8. *Privacy on the Go* is a set of privacy guidelines for app producers, providers, and users. See also: Kamala D. Harris, "Attorney General Kamala D. Harris Issues Guidance on How Mobile Apps Can Better Protect Consumer Privacy," *State of California Department of Justice* (January 10, 2013), retrieved on January 14, 2013 from <http://oag.ca.gov/sites/all/files/agweb/pdfs/privacy/privacy_on_the_go.pdf>.

15. Harris, *Privacy on the Go*, 3–8.

16. Lee H. Rosenthal, "Metadata and Issues Relating to the Form of Production," *The Pocket Part: A Companion to the Yale Law Journal* (December 4, 2006), retrieved on January 26, 2007 from <http://yalelawjournal.org/the-yale-law-journal-pocket-part/procedure/metadata-and-issues-relating-to-the-form-of-production/>, 1.

17. Kenneth A. Bravo, "What General Practitioners Need to Know About Computer Law: Electronic Discovery: Not Just for the Million Dollar Case," *The Ohio State Bar Association: 2006 Annual Convention* (May 3–5, 2006): 1.2.

18. R. Bryan Nace, "Law Practice in the Electronic Age: Discovery in an Electronic Age," *The Ohio State Bar Association: 2006 Annual Convention* (May 3–5, 2006): 3.4–3.5.

19. Gary Blankenship, "What's in Your Document? Board Says It's Unethical to Mine Hidden Data from e-Texts," *Florida Bar News* (January 1, 2006), retrieved on

February 15, 2007 from <http://www.floridabar.org/DIVCOM/JN/jnnews01.nsf/8c 9f13012b96736985256aa900624829/c3f75b4e10e94f78852570e50051b23e>, 1.

20. See *Kucala Enterprises, Ltd. v. Auto Wax Co.,* 2003 WL 21230605 (N.D. ILL).

21. Donald A. Wochna, "Electronic Data, Electronic Searching, and Inadvertent Production of Privileged Data: A Perfect Storm, Why Attorneys Are Being Forced to Recognize That Searching Electronically-Stored Information Is an Expert Function," *Ohio State Bar Association: 2010 Annual Convention* (May 5–7, 2010): 1.1–1.17.

22. Wochna, "A Perfect Storm," 1.5–1.17. See also *Victor Stanley Inc. v. Creative Pipe, Inc., et al.*, Civil Action No. MJG-06-2662, D. Md. May 29, 2008.

23. Mark S. Sidoti, Wendy R. Stein, and Verne A Pedro, "Challenging 'Manual' ESI Collections," *The National Law Journal* (April 9, 2009). Reprinted in *LTN Law Technology News*, retrieved on September 7, 2013 from <http://www.law.com /jsp/lawtechnologynews/PubArticleLTN.jsp?id=1202446756984&Challengi ng_Manual_ESI_Collections__>.

    See also *Ford Motor Co. v. Edgewood Properties, Inc.* 257 F.R.D. 418 (D. N.J. 2009). Note: The Sedona Conference is a nonprofit institute that is committed to seeing that the law evolves to meet the challenges that face society today. Much of the work done by the institute is carried out by its working groups, each of which focuses on a key legal issue. After extensive research and discussion, each working group publishes a report intended to encourage the advancement of the law in that area. One such report, *The Sedona Principles: Best Practices, Recommendations and Principles for Addressing Electronic Document Production*, recommended that document retention and production follow 14 basic principles. *The Sedona Principles: Best Practices, Recommendations & Principles for Addressing Electronic Document Production*, Appendix E: Background on The Sedona Conference and Its Working Group Series (The Sedona Conference® Working Group Series July 2005 Version), retrieved on September 7, 2013 from <https://thesedonaconference.org/publications>.

24. Sidoti, Stein, and Pedro, "Challenging 'Manual' ESI Collections," 2. See also *Pension Comm. of the Univ. of Montreal Pension Plan v. Banc of America Sec. LLC*, No. 05 Civ. 9016, 2010 U.S. Dist. Lexis 4546, at *1 (S.D.N.D. Jan 15, 2010).

25. Jonathan Strickland, "How Cloud Storage Work," *How Stuff Works* (2008), retrieved on January 11, 2013 from <http://computer.howstuffworks.com>, 1–2.

26. "Preserving Chain of Custody in E-discovery," *Discovery Services Fact Sheet*, Lexis-Nexis, retrieved on June 15, 2010 from <http://www.lexisnexis.com/applieddiscovery /lawlibrary/whitePapers/ADI_FS_ChainOfCustody.pdf>.

27. Christy Burke, "Examining E-Discovery Chain of Custody," *LTN Law Technology News* (2010), retrieved on September 7, 2013 from <http://www.law.com/jsp/lawtechnologynews /PubArticleLTN.jsp?id=900005494089&Examining_EDiscovery_Chain_of_Custody>.

28. Ralph Losey, "Computer Forensics: Sherlock Holmes in the 21st Century," *Florida Law Firm.Com*, retrieved on June 15, 2010 from <http://floridalawfirm.com/foren-sics.html>, 3. See also *The Sedona Principles: Best Practices, Recommendations & Principles for Addressing Electronic Document Production*, Appendix A: Glossary, 57.

29. Leigh Jones, "E-Discovery Zero Hour Approaching: Attorneys Warily Prepare for Changes," *The National Law Journal* (August 21, 2006): 10.

30. Richard Acello, "Beyond Prediction: Technology-Assisted Review Enters the Lexicon,"*ABA Journal* (August 1, 2012), retrieved on January 11, 2012 from <http://www.abajournal.com>, 1.

31. Howard Reissner, "Too Fast, Too Soon? Are Predictive Coding Advocates Speeding Toward Trouble?" *Law Technology News* (February 1, 2013), retrieved on April 27, 2013 from <http://www.law.com/jsp/lawtechnologynews/PubArticleLTN.jsp?id=1202585467333&Too_Fast_Too_Soon>, 68.

32. Isom, "Electronic Discovery Primer for Judges," 19–20.

33. Richard A. Schneider, Matthew S. Harman, and Robert B. Friedman (King & Spalding LLP), "The New Federal E-Discovery Rules: An Expository Narrative," *The Metropolitan Corporate Counsel* (2008), retrieved on April 2, 2008 from <http://www.metrocorpcounsel.com/>, 2.

34. Andrew Rhys Davies, "A Shield That Doesn't Protect: Courts Are Reluctant to Recognize Deals Intended to Prevent Accidental Waiver of Privilege," *The National Law Journal* (July 17, 2006): S1.

35. *Zubulake*, 24 and 30.

36. Andrew J. Stanger, "Document Destruction after Enron: Interpreting the New Sarbanes–Oxley Obstruction Statutes," *Business Law Journal University of California, Davis, School of Law* (May 1, 2005), retrieved on September 7, 2013 from <http://blj.ucdavis.edu/archives/vol-5-no-2/Document-Destruction-after-Enron.html>, 1–5.

37. Strickland, "How Cloud Storage Work."

38. Strickland, "How Cloud Storage Work." See also: Barron K. Henley, "Legal Technology Tips, Tricks, Gadgets, and Websites," *The Ohio State Bar Association: 2013 Annual Convention* (May 8, 2013).

39. *Zubulake,* 24 and 30.

40. *Zubulake,* 30–31.

41. Jones, "E-Discovery Zero Hour Approaching," 10.

42. Henry Kelston, "Are We on the Cusp of Major Changes to E-Discovery Rules?" *Law Technology News* (17 April 2013), retrieved on September 7, 2013 from <http://www.law.com/jsp/lawtechnologynews/PubArticleLTN.jsp?id=1202596362366&Are_We_on_the_Cusp_of_Major_Changes_to_EDiscovery_Rules>.

CHAPTER 13 # Requests for Admission and the Future of Discovery

CHAPTER OUTLINE

THE *NEVINS* CASE

COMMENTARY

Your supervising attorney has been retained by Professor Martina Nevins, a symbologist, linguist, and translator, who believes she was wrongfully "downsized" when her services were terminated at the Wayne Institute of Language, Linguistics, and Semiotics (the Institute), where she was employed as a research specialist for two decades. Although Professor Nevins now lives in Maine, she has decided to file the case in Cleveland to take advantage of the new Discovery Protocols Pilot Project taking place in the Northern District of Ohio. Surprisingly, the new protocols have moved the case along so rapidly that your attorney is operating ahead of schedule. Under the new protocols he has already received most of the documents that he needs to move forward, including your client's employment contract, her personnel file, a copy of several complaints lodged against her, and a series of e-mails between your client and the HR department at the Institute. Located within this collection of data, your attorney has found several documents that might cause a problem in the future if the defense decides to deny their authenticity. Consequently, he has decided to take certain preemptive steps to ensure their legitimacy. In addition, he wants to establish the validity of several facts so those facts are not challenged at trial. As part of this effort, he has asked you to draft a request for admission. This request will be served on Dr. Anders Parshall, the executive director of the Institute. Your attorney has also received a request for admission from the law firm of Jacquet, Breinich, and Milner, which represents the Institute. Consequently, you must also contact Professor Nevins so she can help prepare a response. To comply with your attorney's request, you must research all relevant federal and local rules, as well as any rules that might be imbedded within the new Discovery Protocols. It also will be a good idea to examine the pleadings, the pertinent documents, and the rest of the evidence, including especially all ESI.

Now that the discovery process has been nearly completed, you may need to establish the truthfulness, accuracy, and genuineness of the evidence that you and your supervising attorney have compiled. You will also have to make certain (1) that you are up-to-date on all new Discovery Protocols that might affect your case, (2) that you are familiar with any pending amendments to the Civil Rules, and (3) that you have not overlooked any ESI issues that might impact your work on this case. After reading this chapter, you should be able to:

OBJECTIVES

- define request for admission.
- report on the purposes for filing a request for admission.
- explain the uses of the request for admission.
- list the advantages of the request for admission.
- identify the procedures involved in drafting a request for admission.
- explain the content of each section of a request for admission.
- differentiate among the responses and the objections to a request for admission.
- explore the history, goals, and progress of the new Discovery Protocols Pilot Project.
- explain the latest issues related to ESI and discovery.
- summarize the proposals for new amendments to the civil rules regarding discovery.

REQUESTS FOR ADMISSION AND THE FUTURE OF DISCOVERY

The request for admissions stands as the final weapon in your attorney's discovery arsenal. As such, it represents the last step in a contemporary discovery strategy. Nevertheless, the request for admissions is not the last part of our overall study of discovery. Before we move on to the next unit, we must also look at three items that are on the horizon for all attorneys and paralegals, but especially those involved in civil litigation. These three items are the new Discovery Protocols Pilot Project, the continuing impact of ESI on civil procedure, and the proposed amendments to the Federal Rules of Civil Procedure.

Requests for Admission

The request for admission is a petition filed by one party in a lawsuit on another party in that lawsuit asking the second party to admit to the truthfulness of some fact or opinion. A request may also ask the party to authenticate the genuineness of a document. According to Rule 36 of the Federal Rules of Civil Procedure, a request for admission may be served on any party in a lawsuit, but may not be served on a nonparty. Under Rule 26 (d), admissions cannot be served until the parties have conferred as mandated by Rule 26 (f). A party has 30 days to respond to a request. The Federal Rules still place no limit on the number of requests that can be filed. However, this open-ended self-determination may end soon. Recently, the Federal Court's Advisory Committee on Civil Rules proposed an amendment to Rule 36 that would limit the number of requests for admission to 25. Reportedly, this amendment would not alter the number of requests for an admission that certain documents are genuine. All other requests for admission, however, would be limited to 25.[1] When this book went to press, the rule had not yet been amended. However, since the amendments are on the drawing board, the wise paralegal will double-check for this change, and others like it, before drafting any additional admission requests in all upcoming cases. Moreover, since some states (California, for example) have already limited the number of requests that can be filed, it is always wise to check on the status of state and local rules.

The request for admission differs from all of the other discovery tools that we have examined thus far. In fact, some legal scholars would argue that the request for admission is not, strictly speaking, a discovery tool at all. This argument is based on the fact that the request for admission seeks a commitment regarding information that has already been discovered. Thus, the request does not, in itself, "discover" anything. Nevertheless, it is a very powerful tool that can be used to great advantage in the compilation of relevant and admissible evidence. For that reason alone, the humble request for admission deserves a place of respect in the hierarchy of discovery tools.

Purposes of Requests for Admission

The purpose of the request for admission is to simplify a lawsuit by reducing the number and nature of the points in controversy. The simplification of the points in controversy has a "ripple effect," limiting many of the other matters involved in the lawsuit. For example, the fewer points in controversy, the fewer witnesses are necessary should the case go to trial.

The fewer witnesses needed, the less money spent. These savings can be especially lucrative if the request eliminates the need to call expensive expert witnesses. Simplifying the points in controversy could also lead to an early settlement of the case. Claims and defenses that have no legal merit evaporate quickly under the scrutiny of a well-drafted request for admission. Finally, a carefully drafted request for admission can emphasize important factual information that is buried in volumes of documents, testimony, and ESI.

Uses of Requests for Admission

A request for admission can be used in three ways: (1) to authenticate the genuineness of individual documents, (2) to confirm the truthfulness of certain facts or opinions, and (3) to verify the proper application of the law. A single request for admission can fulfill all of these uses, if necessary.

Authenticating the Genuineness of Documents

One of the most widely recognized purposes of the request for admission is to authenticate the genuineness of a document. For example, in the *Nevins* case, it would be very helpful if Dr. Parshall, the executive director of the Institute, were to verify the genuineness of the letter of dismissal sent to Professor Nevins, the Institute's progressive disciplinary policy, the list of offenses for which an employee can be terminated, and the evaluation records of Professor Nevins. Obviously, such documents could be authenticated at trial, but only after handling a number of evidentiary arguments. These arguments can be eliminated with the filing of a request for admission, provided the admission is made, ordered by the court or, as we shall see below, undenied. Of course, an individual may admit to the genuineness of a document and still object to its admissibility. For example, in the *Nevins* case, Dr. Parshall may authenticate the document outlining progressive disciplinary procedures and the list of dischargeable offenses, but he may object to their relevance and admissibility in this case, although in this case, that objection would be quite a stretch. Moreover, a party who admits to the genuineness of a document does not at the same time admit to the truthfulness of the contents of the document. For instance, in the *Nevins* case, Professor Nevins might be asked to admit to the genuineness of a letter of dismissal for failing to follow the Institute's policies and procedures. In admitting to the genuineness of the letter, she is not admitting that any of the alleged violations are true.

Confirming the Truthfulness of Facts and Opinions

A request for admission can also be used to confirm the truthfulness of certain facts or opinions. In the *Nevins* case, for example, your supervising attorney may ask the executive director to authenticate the fact that he signed all of Nevins' employment evaluations and that each of those employment evaluations stated that she had done outstanding work for the Institute. These admissions, however, only authenticate the content of the evaluations and the fact that they were signed by Dr. Parshall. They do not admit anything about the quality of Professor Nevins' job performance. Thus, your supervising attorney might also ask Dr. Parshall to admit that Professor Nevins did outstanding work. Note the differences among these admissions. The admissions about the content and the signature authenticate facts, whereas the admission about the quality of Professor Nevins' job performance authenticates Dr. Parshall's opinion. Factual admissions are usually easier to obtain than those that state an opinion.

deemed admitted

A principle that holds that an undenied request for admission is treated as if it were admitted.

Admissions about the truthfulness of facts and opinions in response to a request for admission carry much more weight than an admission made using some other form of discovery. Anything that is admitted in a deposition, for example, can be altered or denied when the party takes the witness stand. Although this tactic weakens the credibility of the witness in the eyes of the judge and the jurors, the finders of fact must still weigh the alterations and denials against the rest of the witness's testimony. Such is not the case with an admission made in response to a request. Such an admission is taken as proven. Court permission is required for a party to withdraw an admission. Thus, such admissions can be very effective for the party obtaining them and very damaging to the party giving them.

Verifying the Proper Application of the Law

A request for admission can also combine the authentication of the facts in a case with the law that applies to those facts. For example, in the *Nevins* case, your supervising attorney may request Dr. Parshall to admit that Professor Nevins was employed by the Institute on a contractual basis and was, therefore, subject to the employee policy manual, including all provisions regarding dischargeable offenses and the progressive discipline. Such an admission would shorten the time necessary to demonstrate the legal status of Professor Nevins' employment. However, such an admission would not prove that she was wrongfully terminated because other issues, such as whether she committed a dischargeable offense, whether the disciplinary procedure was followed properly, and whether, in this situation, she was actually entitled to the policy's protection, must still be proven.

Advantages of Requests for Admission

The request for admission offers several advantages over other discovery devices. One principal advantage is that a request for admission cannot be ignored or overlooked. Under the **deemed admitted** rule, any *undenied* request for admission is treated as if it were admitted. Also, if the response to the request does not conform to the requirements of Rule 36 of the Federal Rules of Civil Procedure, the court may order that the fact has been admitted. For example, in the *Nevins* case, if Dr. Parshall's denial of the request to authenticate Professor Nevins' status as a contractual employee is not specific enough, the court may rule that he has admitted that she is a contractual employee. Similarly, if Dr. Parshall were to claim that he is unable to admit or deny that Professor Nevins performed her job well, and that claim is not detailed enough, the court may order that the matter has been admitted. In both of these examples, the court could, instead, order Parshall to file an amended response to the request. Many legal scholars argue that the deemed admitted rule is overly strict and unnecessarily harsh. Some states have responded to this criticism by altering or eliminating the rule entirely in state court. In California, for instance, nothing is deemed admitted unless the party requesting the admission files a motion to that effect. This strategy would seem to be the wiser process to adopt.

An advantage that the request for admission shares with interrogatories is that the parties cannot refuse to respond simply because they lack the information needed to make the response. Rather, they must make a reasonable attempt to obtain the missing information. Moreover, a party cannot refuse to cooperate merely because the other party could obtain the information another way. Furthermore, although a request for admission is usually made toward the end of the discovery process, such requests can be made at any time, even with the service of the summons and complaint. Thus, because a total knowledge of the facts is not a prerequisite for the request, it can be used as a learning tool. Finally, as noted earlier, the federal rules place no limit on the number of requests that can be filed. Again, a number of legal scholars, judges, and practicing attorneys believe that this type of open-ended process causes delays and costly setbacks. Moreover, as noted above, the Federal Court's Advisory Committee on Civil Rules has recognized this problem. Among a series of amendments to the rules now under consideration, Rule 36 will be altered to limit the number of requests to 25, although, as it is currently formulated, this amendment would not touch the request for an admission that a document is genuine.[2] Also remember that some states have already placed limits on the permissible number of requests for admission.

DRAFTING REQUESTS FOR ADMISSION

As a paralegal, you may be called upon to draft a request for admission. This responsibility is extremely important because, as we have seen previously, properly drafted requests can lead to an early settlement of the lawsuit. Consequently, great care must be taken in preparing for and actually drafting the request.

Preliminary Steps in Drafting Requests for Admission

Before drafting the request, you should do some preliminary work. First, discuss the matter with your supervising attorney so that you understand the goals and objectives of the request. Then make certain that you review all previous pleadings and important documents as you assemble the facts. Also, take some time to look over the applicable federal or state and local court rules so that you can accurately determine response deadlines and procedural details.

As a last stage before actually writing the request, list and organize the admission that the other party ought to make. For example, in the *Nevins* case, your attorney wants Dr. Parshall to admit that Professor Nevins was a contractual employee, that she was covered by the company's employment manual, and that her job performance was satisfactory. With these suggested admissions in hand, check with your attorney to make sure that you have not missed something. Remember you should always ask your attorney specific questions about form and content, rather than general and open-ended questions such as, "How does this look?" or "Is this alright?"

Form and Content of Requests for Admission

With your preliminary list of desired admissions in hand, locate a sample request in a form book, in your firm's word-processing file, or online. Naturally, no two situations are exactly the same, so you will have to modify the form to fit the facts of your particular case. Nevertheless, we can make some general statements about the title, the introductory paragraph, the definitions and instructions, and the request itself.

Title of the Request and the Introductory Paragraph

The title of your request should reflect the party making the request, the party receiving the request, and the number of the request:

Example

PLAINTIFF NEVINS' FIRST REQUEST FOR ADMISSIONS

TO DEFENDANTS ANDERS PARSHALL AND THE

WAYNE INSTITTUTE OF LANGUAGE, LINGUISTICS, AND SEMIOTICS

Make certain that you cite the appropriate court rules in the introductory paragraph. If you follow the actual language of the rule, you will avoid any possible misunderstanding. The introductory paragraph should also include a demand for written answers to the request within the applicable time limits. Exhibit 13–1 includes a typical introductory paragraph for the request.

Definitions

As in the request for production of documents covered in Chapter 12, the definition section of the request for admission may have a separate heading placed in the center of the page in boldfaced lettering. Terms that may be defined include such words as *document, ESI, letter, memorandum, metadata,* and *report,* among others.

Instructions

The heading "instructions" may also be placed in the center of the page in boldfaced letters. The instructions specify any procedures that should be followed in responding to the request. Often the request for admission is so complex that it is not possible to include a separate instructional paragraph at the beginning of the request. In such a case the instructions must be included with each category of documents examined and with the list of facts to be admitted. For instance, in the *Nevins* case, the introductory section leading to a request to authenticate the genuineness of certain documents may have to specify that Dr. Parshall must admit that the documents in question were written by employees of the Institute, that the documents were sent to the named recipients, that they were sent on the dates noted on the documents, and so on. In contrast, the instructions leading to the list of facts and opinions to be admitted may simply read that Dr. Parshall is to admit "that each of the following statements is true." (See Exhibit 13–1.)

Specific Requests

The request should be as simple as possible. The part of the request that lists the documents should be very specific as to the identity of each of those documents. List each document separately; combining documents can cause confusion and can open the request to objections. If possible, include any identifying dates or numbers found on the documents. Copies of the documents in the list must be gathered together and attached to the request with an appropriate identifying heading. For example, in the *Nevins* case, if you request the authentication of certain e-mails, texts, and IMs that passed between Dr. Parshall and the human resources director at the Wayne Institute, and the authentication of certain letters and faxes that passed between Dr. Parshall and Professor Nevins, you would include two separate lists, each with its own instructional paragraph. In turn, copies of the memos and letters would be attached to the request and labeled as such. The e-mails, texts, and IMs might be labeled "Appendix A" and the letters and faxes, "Appendix B."

EXHIBIT 13-1 Request for Admission

UNITED STATES DISTRICT COURT NORTHERN DISTRICT OF OHIO

MARTINA NEVINS,	)
	) Case No. 16-09916
Plaintiff	)
	) REQUEST FOR ADMISSION
v.	)
	)
ANDERS PARSHALL AND	)
THE WAYNE INSTITUTE	)
	)
	)
	)
Defendants.	)

_____

PLAINTIFF, Martina Nevins ("Nevins"), requests that the DEFENDANTS, Anders Parshall ("Parshall") and the Wayne Institute of Language, Linguistics, and Semiotics ("the Wayne Institute"), within thirty (30) days after the service of this request separately admit in writing, pursuant to Rule 36 of the Federal Rules of Civil Procedure and for the purposes of this action only, the truth of the following statements.

DEFINITIONS

1. The Wayne Institute of Language, Linguistics, and Semiotics (the Wayne Institute) will be taken to mean the non-profit think tank established under the laws of the state of Delaware with its principal place of business at 55 Public Square, Cleveland, Ohio, and all its officers, employees, agents, representatives, and others who act or appear to act on its behalf and in its stead.

2. "Officers" will be taken to mean all executives, directors, managers, agents, representatives, and others who act or appear to act on behalf of respondent, the Wayne Institute of Language, Linguistics, and Semiotics.

3. "Employees" will be taken to mean all workers, research workers, non-research workers, scientific professionals, linguists, translators, language experts, anthropologists, sociologists, psychologists, numerologists, symbologists, philosophers, mathematicians, technicians, and others who act or appear to act on behalf of respondent the Wayne Institute.

4. "Employee evaluation" will be taken to mean any and all evaluation tools, processes, forms, strategies, sessions, meetings, and any and all other activities taken to measure the effectiveness of an employee for purposes of advancement, promotion, salary, vacations, work space, continuing education opportunities, job assignment, and any other employment-related activity.

5. "Dismissal process" will be taken to mean any procedure, process, system, network, and/or activity used to determine an employee's tenure at the Wayne Institute.

6. "The Wayne Institute of Language, Linguistics, and Semiotics Handbook" will be taken to mean the employment handbook in both its paper and electronic forms used to set, determine, measure, and so on, employment-related activities at the Wayne Institute.

7. "Memo" is taken to mean any written internal or external communication sent and received between employees of the Wayne Institute whether reduced to paper form, maintained as electronic copy, formatted as an e-mail message, formatted as a text message, or maintained in any other recorded format, including all forms of ESI.

8. "Letter" is taken to mean any written internal or external communication sent and received between employees of the Wayne Institute whether reduced to paper form, maintained as electronic copy, formatted as an e-mail message, formatted as a text message, or maintained in any other recorded format, including all forms of ESI.

EXHIBIT 13-1 Request for Admission (*continued*)

9. "Research report" is taken to mean any written internal or external communication sent and received between employees of the Wayne Institute whether reduced to paper form, maintained as electronic copy, formatted as an e-mail message, formatted as a text message, or maintained in any other recorded format, including all forms of ESI.

10. "Pay increase" is taken to mean any and all compensation increases at the Wayne Institute including salary increases, hourly wage increases, benefit package increases, bonuses, and any and all other similar increases in pay.

11. "Promotion" is taken to mean any and all employment-related decisions that affect an employment-related position at the Wayne Institute in relation to other employees whether related to changes in authority, duties, privileges, pay, benefits, and any and all other similar changes.

INSTRUCTIONS

1. These requests for admission must be answered under oath completely and fully in writing and must include any and all information, data, and ESI that is in your possession, control, custody, or care, or that is in the possession, control, custody, or care of any of your agents, attorneys, employees, consultants, assistants, associates, or anyone else who might be performing activities on your behalf.

2. Should you be unable or unwilling to respond truthfully to any of these requests, or any subdivision of any request, relate the specific grounds upon which you base your refusal.

3. Should you object to one of the following requests or any of their subdivisions, you must still respond to whatever part of the request for which you offer no objection.

4. Should you deny sufficient knowledge to admit or deny one of the requests or any subdivision of any request, relate the specific grounds upon which you base your denial and respond to whatever part of the request to which you offer no objection.

REQUESTS FOR ADMISSION

A. Admit that each of the following documents listed below, the best copies of which are attached as Appendix A,

1. is genuine and is a complete and accurate representation of the actual writing which the document purports to represent;

2. was prepared or sent by an officer or employee of the Wayne Institute during his or her employment with the Wayne Institute;

3. was directed to or concerned matters within the scope of the employment of said officer or employee of the Wayne Institute;

4. was written and sent on or about the date listed on the document;

5. was written on the basis of the officer's or employee's firsthand knowledge of the matter contained therein;

6. was written in the ordinary course of business of the Wayne Institute;

7. was kept as part of the routine employee evaluation process at the Wayne Institute:
   a. Nevins employee evaluation of September 9, 2014.
   b. Nevins employee evaluation of October 31, 2014.
   c. Nevins employee evaluation of January 19, 2015.
   d. Nevins employee evaluation of February 7, 2015.
   e. Nevins employee evaluation of March 17, 2015.
   f. Nevins employee evaluation of April 23, 2015.
   g. Memo of February 21, 2015.
   h. Memo of February 28, 2015.
   i. Memo of March 27, 2015.

EXHIBIT 13-1 Request for Admission (*continued*)

       j. Memo of April 1, 2015.

       k. Memo of August 19, 2015.

B. Admit that the best copy of each of the documents listed below and attached as Appendix B

    1. is genuine and is a complete and accurate representation of the actual writing which the document purports to represent;

    2. was prepared or sent by an officer or employee of the Wayne Institute during his or her employment with the Wayne Institute;

    3. was directed to or concerned matters within the scope of the employment of said officer or employee of the Wayne Institute;

    4. was written and sent on or about the date listed on the document;

    5. was written on the basis of the officer's or employee's firsthand knowledge of the matter contained therein;

    6. was written in the ordinary course of business of the Wayne Institute;

    7. was sent as part of the dismissal process involving Nevins:

       a. Letter of September 9, 2014.

       b. Letter of September 15, 2014.

       c. Letter of December 23, 2014.

       d. Letter of January 29, 2015.

       e. Letter of February 14, 2015.

       f. Letter of March 17, 2015.

       g. Letter of June 16, 2015.

       h. Letter of August 31, 2015.

C. Admit that the document entitled THE WAYNE INSTITUTE OF LANGUAGE, LINGUISTICS, AND SEMIOTICS' HANDBOOK, the best copy of which is attached as Appendix C,

    1. is genuine and is a complete and accurate representation of the actual writing that the document purports to represent;

    2. was distributed to all employees at the Wayne Institute between August 19, 2013, and September 19, 2013;

    3. was received by Nevins on August 19, 2013.

D. Admit that each of the following documents listed below, the best copies of which are attached as Appendix D,

    1. is genuine and is a complete and accurate representation of the actual writing that the document purports to represent;

    2. was prepared or sent by an officer or employee of the Wayne Institute during his or her employment with the Wayne Institute;

    3. was directed to or concerned matters within the scope of the employment of said officer or employee of the Wayne Institute;

    4. was written and sent on or about the date listed on the document;

    5. was written on the basis of the officer's or employee's firsthand knowledge of the matter contained therein;

    6. was written in the ordinary course of business of the Wayne Institute;

    7. was kept as part of the routine employee evaluation process at the Wayne Institute:

       a. Research report dated September 23, 2013.

       b. Research report dated October 19, 2013.

       c. Research report dated November 30, 2013.

       d. Research report dated March 28, 2014.

       e. Research report dated August 19, 2014.

EXHIBIT 13-1 Request for Admission (*continued*)

  f. Research report dated December 2, 2014.

  g. Research report dated December 15, 2014.

  h. Research report dated December 31, 2014.

E. Admit that each of the following documents listed below, the best copies of which are attached as Appendix E,

 1. is genuine and is a complete and accurate representation of the actual writing which the document purports to represent;

 2. was received by an officer or employee of the Wayne Institute during his or her employment with the Wayne Institute;

 3. was received within the scope of the employment of said officer or employee of the Wayne Institute;

 4. was received on or about the date listed on the document;

 5. was kept in the ordinary course of business of the Wayne Institute;

 6. was kept as part of the routine employee evaluation process at the Wayne Institute:

  a. Letter of September 12, 2013.

  b. Letter of September 20, 2013.

  c. Letter of December 27, 2013.

  d. Letter of January 1, 2014.

  e. Letter of February 18, 2014.

  f. Letter of March 27, 2014.

  g. Letter of June 19, 2014.

  h. Letter of September 2, 2014.

F. Admit that each of the following statements is true:

 1. The Wayne Institute is an incorporated nonprofit organization under the laws of the state of Delaware and has its principal place of business in Cleveland, Ohio.

 2. Nevins was discharged on or about September 9, 2014.

 3. Nevins received favorable employee evaluations from September of 2012 to September of 2014.

 4. Nevins received all scheduled pay increases between September of 2012 and September of 2014.

 5. Nevins received all scheduled promotions between September of 2012 and September of 2014.

DATED: Cleveland, Ohio
    March 27, 2016

          McCoy, Bauer, and Kennedy

          BY _____
          A member of the firm
          Attorneys for the Plaintiff
          Professor Martina Nevins
          17810 Windward Road
          Cleveland, Ohio 44119
          Tel.: (216) 555-4412
          Fax: (216) 555-4413

TO: Jacquet, Breinich, and Milner
   Attorneys for Defendant
   The Wayne Institute for Language, Linguistics, and Semiotics and Anders Parshall,
   Executive Director of the Wayne Institute
   433 East 310th Street
   Willowick, Ohio 44122

The part of the request that lists the facts and opinions to be admitted should be carefully worded. Each fact and opinion should be listed separately. All facts that are undisputed should be included in this list. By identifying and including those facts in the request, your supervising attorney will avoid having to argue those facts at the time of the trial. Also include facts that you know are true but that you might have a difficult time proving at trial. If you can get an admission now, you will save a lot of work later. However, you should be very careful to avoid topics that will elicit an appropriate objection from the other party.

judicial admission
A statement or other piece of evidence that has been admitted and that can, therefore, be introduced during the trial.

RESPONDING TO REQUESTS FOR ADMISSION

Make certain, when you receive a request for admission, that you determine that the target date is reasonable. Once you have established that the target date is reasonable, place a reminder of the due date on your supervising attorney's paper calendar, e-calendar, and white board calendar. If your attorney uses a smartphone or a tablet, make sure that the date has been added to the calendars on those devices too. If you have the responsibility of drafting the response, you should meet with the client to cover the alternatives available in responding to each request. You also should consider any objections that you might raise to the request.

Alternative Responses to Requests for Admission

Your response to the request must be filed on time. This step may mean that you must work quickly. However, because of the finality of an admission, you should never sacrifice care and accuracy for speed. Before beginning the drafting process, review the applicable court rules relating to the format and procedure. The alternatives available in a response are:

1. to admit,
2. to deny,
3. to refuse to either admit or deny, or
4. to object.

When you draft the response, first copy each statement to which you are responding, exactly as it appears on the original request. If a statement is true, you must respond by admitting that it is true. However, if reasonable doubt exists as to the truthfulness of a particular statement, you may deny it. A statement that has been admitted is called a judicial admission. A **judicial admission** is a statement or other piece of evidence that has been admitted and can, therefore, be introduced during the trial.

Any statement that is not truthful should be denied. However, you should resist the temptation to deny a statement on a technicality, such as a misspelled word or an obvious typographical error. If the error actually alters the substance of the statement, you may consider denying it. For example, in the *Nevins* case, if your client, Nevins, is mistakenly identified as Marina Nevis, rather that Martina Nevins, you probably would not be justified in denying the statement. If a statement listed her as Ms. Nevins or Miss Nevins, rather than Professor Nevins, you might be justified in denying the statement, because a legal question concerning her professional competence is at the center of the case. Such questions, however, are best discussed with your supervising attorney. Be careful in your denials because the other party may ask the court to compel your client to pay the cost of proving a matter that should not have been denied in the first place. Interestingly, even the losing party can make this request of the court.

Sometimes, when the deadline for a response is approaching, you may deny all requests and later amend your response, admitting only those requests that should have been admitted in the first place. This practice has its dangers, however. The chief danger is the deemed admitted rule. As we have seen, under this rule, unless a party delivers a written denial or a detailed reason why that party cannot admit or deny a statement, that statement is deemed admitted.

The third alternative is to refuse to either admit or deny a request. However, the Federal Rules of Civil Procedure do not allow you to do this unless you have made a reasonable inquiry into the subject. Moreover, a lack of personal knowledge is not a proper basis for refusing to respond unless the party has reason to doubt the credibility of the source of the information. Your response to the request for admission does not require verification in federal court. Still, because some state and local rules demand such verification, you should check on the proper procedure in your area.

Objections to Requests for Admission

Basically, you have the same objections available against a request for admission as you do in all the other discovery tools we have looked at so far. The grounds for such objections include responses that violate the attorney–client privilege, the work product privilege, the common interest privilege, the medical privilege, and the confessor–penitent privilege. Other objections are that the request is overbroad, irrelevant, or duplicative. You may also object on the ground that the statement is a compound request.

The Attorney–Client, Work Product, and Common Interest Privileges   As we have seen previously, the attorney–client privilege prevents the forced disclosure of communication between an attorney and a client. Similarly, the work product privilege protects letters, memos, documents, records, ESI, texts, IMs, blogs, voice mail messages, and other tangible items that have been prepared in anticipation of litigation. In addition, the common interest privilege protects any communication that takes place between attorneys for different clients when those clients share a common interest. If a request for admission would violate any of these privileges, you could lodge an appropriate objection on those grounds.

The Medical Privilege and the Confessor–Penitent Privilege   The medical privilege will protect all confidential communications between a medical practitioner and his or her patient. Similarly, the confessor–penitent privilege was designed to shield confidences that pass between a member of the clergy and a penitent. Unlike the medical privilege, however, the confessor–penitent privilege also safeguards a member of the clergy who has offered a religious oath not to reveal such disclosures.

Inadmissible and Irrelevant Evidence   You will recall that the scope of discovery is much broader than the scope of the evidence that can be introduced at trial. Later in this chapter you will learn that this rule may change in the near future. Nevertheless, right now

it remains the law, and must be treated as if it were an unchanging standard. Despite the broad scope, however, any discovery request must be reasonably calculated to lead to admissible evidence. Should a request for admission ask your client to respond to the truthfulness of a matter that could not be reasonably calculated to lead to admissible evidence, you may object on those grounds. Similarly, a request for admission must address a fact, opinion, or document that is relevant to the lawsuit. The request for admission must further the discovery process. If it does not, you may object.

Overbroad and Duplicative Requests

An overbroad request is one that is not narrowly defined. For instance, in the *Nevins* case, the lawsuit involves Professor Nevins' employment with the Institute. If the opposing party sought admissions regarding every employment evaluation ever filed on Professor Nevins, even those for part-time jobs when she was in high school, college, and graduate school, you could feel safe filing an objection that argues that the request is overbroad. Another objection is that the request is duplicative or repetitious. This objection argues that the request includes one item for admission that is repeated several times. Your duty extends to only one request. Often requests are varied slightly to elicit a different answer. You should object to every variation of the request.

Compound Requests

A **compound request** asks a party to admit in a single statement the truthfulness of two or more facts. The compound request makes a response tricky, if not impossible. Your objection should address the compound nature of the request and explain the difficulty that it presents in framing an accurate response. This objection may not, however, prevent the ultimate need to respond to the subject matter of the statement, as the opposing party can file an amended request.

compound request
A request made by a party in a lawsuit to another party in that lawsuit to admit in a single statement the truthfulness of two or more facts.

THE DISCOVERY PROTOCOLS PILOT PROJECT

As we have seen repeatedly, the entry of ESI into civil litigation has increased both the time and the expense associated with discovery. In an attempt to deal with these issues, the Judicial Conference Advisory Committee on Civil Rules (Advisory Committee) has initiated a new program that is designed to streamline the discovery process in employment cases brought into federal courts. The Advisory Committee designed and initiated a volunteer pilot program in several U. S. Districts Courts to test the effectiveness of the new protocols. The project resulted from recommendations in a report entitled the Joint Project Final Report which was issued by the American College of Trial Lawyers Task Force on Discovery and the IAALS.[3]

The Creation of the Pilot Project

The Joint Project Final Report led to a conference on civil litigation that was held at Duke University under the auspices of the Advisory Committee. The Duke University Conference determined that discovery would be more effective and more economical if the civil rules were tailor-made for various types of cases. A committee that included both defense and plaintiff attorneys met at the IAALS in Denver. Those meetings, as well as a series of lengthy conference calls followed by innumerable e-mails, resulted in the creation of the Discovery Protocols Pilot Project.[4]

AUTOMATED LITIGATION SUPPORT

The Federal Judicial Center and the IAALS

SCENARIO

Your supervising attorney has called you into his office to discuss the *Nevins* case. He indicates that he is concerned because all employment cases filed in the Northern District of Ohio must follow the new rules of the Discovery Protocols Pilot Project. Under those protocols he knows that he will have to produce an enormous amount of evidence by the end of the first 30 days after Wayne Institute has filed its first responsive plea. Your attorney is very familiar with the firm representing the Wayne Institute and so he knows that the responsive pleading will be filed within a few days. He also does not want to simply turn everything over to the defense because he is concerned about unwittingly violating certain privileges. Consequently, he wants to know if there is a special way to draft a protective order under the new protocols. He wants you to have a full report about the new employment law Discovery Protocols Pilot Project by noon today.

PROBLEM

The employment law Discovery Protocols Pilot Project is new to both you and your supervising attorney and within a few hours you must have a complete report on the history, the protocols, the orders issued by the Federal Judicial Center, and the documents that must be produced within those first 30 days. You also need to know what a protective order looks like under the protocols because your supervising attorney wants to be ready to draft one, if necessary.

SOLUTION

Your best bet in this case is to turn to the Internet and to access the Web site of the Federal Judicial Center. On the home page of that Web site you will find a link that is labeled "Publications and Video Catalogue." Click on that link and you will be shifted to a site search engine that will help you find the material needed. Conduct a key word search using "Protocol Pilot Project" as your terms. Set the search to cover all fields and all formats. As you conduct the search you will find three important results. The first result is a report entitled *Pilot Project Regarding Initial Discovery Protocols for Employment Cases Alleging Adverse Action, November 2011*. This report was issued by the Federal Judicial Center itself and contains the protocols which list the documents that must be produced within the first 30 days. If you look closely at the Table of Contents you will also find that the report includes a Model Protective Order that your supervising attorney can use as a template for any protective order that he may deem necessary in the *Nevins* case. The report comes in a downloadable pdf format so you should have no trouble reproducing it for your attorney. Fortunately, the report is only 15 pages long. You can also conduct a search using the Institute of the Advancement of the American Legal System (IAALS) as your key words. When you enter the IAALS Web site you will find a pull-down menu under the heading "Library." Once you are into the IAALS library, conduct a search for the Discovery Protocols Pilot Project. There you will find a report entitled *Final Report on the Joint Project of the ACTL Task Force on Discovery and IAALS*. This report also comes in a downloadable PDF format. It is broader than the report issued by the Federal Judicial Center and includes not only discovery but also a set of proposals regarding pleadings, experts, and judicial management. The report was issued by both the IAALS and the American College of Trial Lawyers (ACTL) Task Force on Discovery.

The protocols are based upon the assumption that discovery rules should be custom-made for certain types of cases. Employment law cases became the subject matter of the first pilot project because the federal docket is crowded with employment cases and because the necessary documents in such cases tend to be uniform regardless of the nature of the employment-related complaint. The participants in the project eventually settled on rules that would require, at the very beginning of a lawsuit, the automatic production of certain key documents that are essential to the case and that everyone knows will eventually be released anyway. The mandatory release of these key documents saves time and money because it prevents the hassle that generally occurs during the initial stages of discovery.[5]

In the *Nevins* case for example, the Institute will want to see all the communication records that Nevins has retained concerning the lawsuit and that she may present as evidence. Such communication records would include e-mails, IMs, voice mails, and so on, that might have passed between Nevins and her boss, Nevins and the human resources director, Nevins and Parshall, and so on. The defendants will also want to examine such items as Nevins' diaries, journals, and calendars, including e-calendars, especially those marked with comments the plaintiff made about the case; Nevins' most recent resume; any claims for unemployment benefits made by Nevins; a list of people with information about the case, and so on. Similarly, on the other side of the case, Nevins and your attorney will want to see all the Institute's documents related to Nevins' hiring and firing; her personnel file; her performance evaluations; all documents used by the people who made decisions regarding her employment; all documents related to any complaints filed against her; all documents related to any of the Institute's investigations of her work performance, and so on.

Experimental Discovery Protocols for Employment Cases

The success of this project depends on the assumption that these initial documents are essential to the case and the conviction that they would eventually be delivered to the other side anyway. The protocols establish the following rules. First, without being asked, within 30 days of the defendant's filing of an answer (or other responsive document) in response to the complaint, the plaintiff will automatically deliver (again that means without being asked) the following documents to the defendant:

1. All communications between the plaintiff and defendant about the facts in the case;
2. All complaints, charges, claims, and lawsuits by the plaintiff regarding those facts;
3. All documents related to the termination;
4. All documents setting out terms of employment;
5. All personal records (diaries, journals, blogs, Facebook and YouTube entries, and so on) made by the plaintiff regarding the case;
6. An up-to-date resume by the plaintiff;
7. All documents related to any claim for unemployment benefits made by the plaintiff;
8. All documents involving the plaintiff's contact with potential employers;
9. All documents involving the plaintiff's termination from other jobs;
10. Any other documents that the plaintiff plans to use to prove his/her case;
11. A list of people with information about the case;
12. A description of the categories of damages;
13. A statement of whether the plaintiff has applied for disability benefits.[6]

Second, within the same time frame as the plaintiff, again without being asked, the defendant will deliver to the plaintiff the following documents:

1. Any communication between the plaintiff and the defendant;
2. Any communication between the plaintiff's supervisor and the defendant;
3. All responses to any claims filed by the plaintiff;

4. Any documents concerned with the hiring or termination;

5. The plaintiff's personnel file;

6. The plaintiff's performance evaluations;

7. All documents used to make employment decisions;

8. All workplace policies and procedures;

9. Table of contents for the employer's employment manual;

10. All job descriptions for the plaintiff;

11. All documents that reveal the employees benefits and pay;

12. All agreements to waive a jury trial;

13. All documents related to complaints about and investigations of the plaintiff;

14. All documents relating to the plaintiff's filing for unemployment benefits;

15. All other documents that the defendant will use to support his or her case;

16. A list of the plaintiff's supervisors;

17. A list of people involved in the decision affecting the plaintiff in this case;

18. A list of people who have information about this case;

19. A statement of whether the plaintiff attempted to get disability payments.[7]

The Discovery Protocols Pilot Project is currently underway in the Southern District of New York, the Eastern District of Pennsylvania, the District of Arizona, the Northern District of Illinois; the Northern District of Ohio; the Southern District of Texas, the Northern District of California, and the Western District of Pennsylvania.[8]

EMERGING ETHICAL ISSUES AND THE ESI REVOLUTION

Our discussion on the request for admission has only briefly touched on the elusive and exotic topic of ESI. However, this lack of coverage can be excused in this chapter because ESI plays only a peripheral role in the admission request. Still, throughout this unit, we have learned that ESI has become a critical part of the discovery process. Consequently, before leaving our study of discovery entirely, we shall pause for a moment to look at some upcoming issues related to ESI and discovery. These issues include (1) the ethical duty that lawyers and paralegals have to keep current on developments in computer technology; (2) the ethical responsibility to preserve a client's confidential records when they are preserved in a cloud storage center; and (3) the ethical duty to create a technology plan for the law firm.

Ethical Responsibilities Related to ESI

Attorneys must always keep up-to-date on developments in the law. Formerly, this duty focused on changes in substantive law, including statutory law, case law, and administrative regulations. Thus, an attorney who fancied himself or herself an expert in criminal law would be expected to know whenever the legislature amends the criminal code, and what those new amendments are all about. Similarly the same attorney would be expected to know when the rules of criminal procedure change, what those changes include, how the court will operate under the new rules, and so on.[9]

FINDING IT on the Internet

The Cornell University Law School hosts a Legal Information Institute that enlists the help of attorneys, legal scholars, publishers, computer scientists, and government agencies to rewrite the law and to present legal issues in a format that is accessible to most everyone. Access the site at **<http://www.law.cornell.edu>** and navigate to the current subject by clicking first on "Federal Rules" and then on the "Federal Rules of Civil Procedure." Find Rule 36 and report on content of the Committee Notes that explain the 2007 Amendment to the rule.

U.S. Legal, Inc. hosts a Web site designed to assist consumers, small businesses, attorneys, corporations, and all others who are concerned about the law or who need legal information, products, or services. Access the site at **<http://uslegal.com>** and conduct a search for the "Site Map" of the section on Civil Procedure. Once you find the "Site Map," you will see an outline that covers every conceivable aspect of the Civil Rules. Find the discovery subsection and click on "Request for Admission." The first three paragraphs explain the nature of the request. Write a brief summary to explain the content of those three paragraphs.

Probono.net is a group that offers assistance and provides resources to people who need *pro bono* legal help. Access the site at **<http://www.probono.net>** and find the "National Sites" listing in the left-hand margin. Click on the menu and find the entry entitled "The Wage and Hour Clearinghouse." On that site, locate the banner at the top of the page and click on "Other Wage and Hour Resources." Look down the list and you will find the heading, "Work Place Fairness." Click on that link and see what resources might help Professor Nevins in her employment case against Dr. Anders Parshall and the Wayne Institute of Language, Linguistics, and Semiotics.

The University of Denver maintains a Web site for its Institute for the Advancement of the American Legal System at **<http://www.du.edu/legalinstitute>**. Access the site and click on "Library" at the top of the page. On the Library page click on "Publications," find the publication entitled, *Navigating the Hazards of E-Discovery: A Manual for Judges in State Courts Across the Nation*, and report on its content.

Litigation Law Firms hosts a Web site at **<http://www.litigationlawfirms.com>**. On the home page in the lower right-hand side, you will find the heading "Recent Articles." Click on that heading and you will see the subheading labeled, "Civil Litigation, Lawsuits, and Trials." Click on that subheading and you will find another heading that reads "More Information." Click on the additional subheading, "Preparing for a Lawsuit." Report on what you read there.

The Federal Civil Action Bulletin maintains a blog at **<http://federalcivilpracticebulletin.blogspot.com>**. Bloggers add comments to the site on a daily basis. Most of the blogs involve recent cases decided in the federal courts. Others involve journal and law review articles on topics of interest involving the federal courts. Access the site, and find a recent blog related to ***predictive coding***. Outline the content of the blog, and explain whether you agree or disagree with the position taken by the blogger.

Wikipedia, the free encyclopedia, can be accessed at **<http://www.wikipedia.org>**. Conduct a search for the subject "Discovery (law)." Access *one of the many articles on discovery* that you find there, read the article, and outline the critical points in that article.

Find Law publishes an online journal, *Modern Practice,* that focuses on technology, the law, and e-discovery. The journal is located at **<http://practice.findlaw.com>**. Access the Web site and, in the left-hand margin, you will find a feature entitled "Find Law Career Center." Under that heading you will find the "Paralegal" jobs subheading. Click on that subheading and report on at least five of the paralegal jobs now posted there.

Unfortunately, in today's world, attorneys and paralegals can no longer limit their attention to substantive and procedural law. In the age of the computer and the era of ESI, lawyers and paralegals are charged with the additional task of keeping abreast of changes in technology, especially as that technology relates to the running of a law office, the handling of clients, the delegating of law office tasks, and the impact of technology on discovery. The day is not far off—some legal experts argue that it has already arrived—when an attorney may be sanctioned by the courts and perhaps even brought before a disciplinary tribunal for failing to keep current on the latest developments in law-related technology.[10]

The Ethics of Cloud Storage

To understand more concretely how this emerging responsibility might play out, let's look at one issue in particular—the issue of cloud storage. Recall that cloud storage is a new technique for protecting ESI by circumventing the need to store data on delicate hard drives, limited flash drives, and huge expensive servers. The cloud storage technique transfers the job of securing ESI from the law firm to a third party, the ESI or data center. The ESI center receives, organizes, stores, and protects the ESI on a distant server, making the data available to the ESI owner (aka the ESI depositor or the data depositor) through the Internet.[11] So far so good. However, remember that almost all client data received by an attorney is privileged and, therefore, highly confidential. This realization means that an attorney must take reasonable steps to make sure that all confidential client data that is stored in a "cloud" is protected.[12]

The bad news about cloud storage is that any law firm using this technique is in danger of violating client confidentiality, and may even have done so already, without even knowing it. The good news is that those same law firms can follow several easy steps to minimize that risk. These steps are based on a very familiar legal standard, the standard of reasonableness. First, whenever a law firm has hired a data center, that law firm must inform the data center that it, the center, will be receiving confidential data. Once this fact has been established, the attorney and the paralegal should ask a series of question designed to gauge the safety and security of the data center's storage protocols.[13] Earlier in this unit back in Chapter 11, Physical and Mental Examinations, we covered this issue briefly in the Automated Litigation Support feature. The questions that we examined at that point in our study were aimed primarily at the practical issues related to cloud storage problems. Those questions included:

1. What type of security system does the cloud company offer to protect your ESI and that of your clients?
2. How much storage capacity does each cloud company provide?
3. What type of privacy guarantees does each company promise to provide?
4. To what extent does the company warrant the integrity of the data stored in their cloud?
5. What are the details of their service contract?
6. Which companies will ensure that your firm is in compliance with all relevant federal and state laws regarding the protection of sensitive and confidential ESI?

At this stage in our study of ESI and discovery, we must add 10 additional questions that are designed not only to flesh out the practical side of cloud storage, but also to explore the ethical layers of the cloud storage strategy. The new questions look like this:

1. Where is the "cloud" located?
2. Does the ESI center have an ESI recovery protocol?
3. Who has access to the ESI?
4. Is the ESI sent by the law firm mixed with the data of other customers?
5. Is the ESI encrypted?
6. Who can decrypt the ESI?
7. What happens when the center's security is breached?
8. Does the ESI center notify customers of a breach?
9. Can a client download his or her ESI?
10. Just how long has the ESI center been in business?[14]

Once the attorney and the paralegal have asked these questions and have received a satisfactory answer to each one, then they have made a reasonable effort to protect client confidentiality. Naturally, both the attorney and the paralegal should keep written records of this entire process—just in case.[15]

Positive Steps to Avoid ESI Pitfalls

Avoiding the pitfalls associated with the growth of ESI in relation to discovery is easier said than done. For one thing, little theory is available to guide practitioners in the evolution of technology. In his recent study on technological issues, *The Nature of Technology*, W. Brian Arthur of the Palo Alto Research Center has noted that, although we have an enormous amount of information about (1) the technological developments in computer science, (2) about the impact of technology on economics and culture, and (3) about the relationships that exist between technology and history, we do not yet understand how technological innovations arose in the past or when they will emerge in the future.[16] Arthur makes his point by coining an interesting turn of phrase when he writes that, we have no " '-ology' of technology."[17]

Although Arthur has overly romanticized the problem, he does make a valid point. Most of us do not really understand how these rapid technological changes appear. Nevertheless, those of us who operate law firms cannot wait for an "-ology" of technology to emerge. Attorneys and paralegals must proactively prepare for technological change. They cannot simply wait for technology to happen to them. If they simply sit back and wait, they may already be too far behind to catch up. In order to be proactive in this arena, law firms must develop a technology plan that includes several key steps.[18]

1. Make sure that all members of your firm are getting the most out of the equipment that they have. If a piece of equipment does not seem to work as it should, read the manual. If no manual was shipped with the equipment, access the manufacturer's Web site. You will find a manual there.
2. Do not wait for equipment to break down before replacing it. Phase in new equipment based on a preplanned schedule.

3. Do your research on the capabilities and the cost of new equipment.

4. Draw up a technology budget so you know how much you can spend and where those funds are coming from.

5. When you do purchase new equipment, assign learning and teaching tasks to specific members of the firm and schedule training sessions for the entire firm on those new devices.[19]

Although these last points on a technology plan do not directly relate to discovery, they are, nevertheless, a necessary part of the culture of technology that has become the reality of the modern legal practice. The more that you and your supervising attorney appreciate, understand, and take advantage of technology, the more successful the discovery process will be.

AMENDING DISCOVERY IN THE FEDERAL COURTS

One thing that you must get used to as a new paralegal in the modern law office is that the rules governing discovery are always changing. Gone are the good old days when an attorney and his paralegal could settle into a fixed routine dictated by a permanent set of discovery rules. With the skyrocketing cost of searching for ESI, the rapid increase in the number of civil suits filed each year, and the rising demand for a less expensive, more efficient legal process, the courts are in the regular business of constantly altering the rules.

The Federal Court's Advisory Committee on Civil Rules

Case in point—the Federal Court's Advisory Committee on Civil Rules has been hard at work recently revising and amending the rules of discovery. These changes in the rules are so recent that they may have even been added to the process while this edition of *Civil Litigation* was rolling off the presses. Specifically several significant changes have been proposed that will affect the discovery process. The rules that have been targeted for amendments include Federal Rules 26, 30, 31, 33, 34, and 37.

Streamlining the Discovery of ESI

One of the most radical changes in the rules will be the elimination of two sentences from Rule 26. The deletion of those sentences would significantly narrow the scope of discovery. Recall that today's standard states that discovery can include both evidence that is relevant and admissible *and* evidence that might *lead to* admissible evidence. The new standard would permit only the discovery of evidence that is admissible. Another change to Rule 26 would limit discovery to evidence that is "proportional to the needs of the case." While the exact nature of this change is ambiguous, it is clear that determining what is "proportional to the needs of the case" would become a duty of the parties that no longer requires the intervention of the court. Changes to Rules 30 and 31 would limit the number of depositions to five and would change the time period for an oral deposition from seven to six hours. Similarly, a change to Rule 33 would reduce the number of interrogatories from 25 to 15.[20]

As noted earlier in the chapter, the new amendments would also change Rule 36 by limiting the number of requests for admission to 25, although this change would not touch the request for an admission that a document is genuine. So, in the *Nevins* case, for example, under the proposed amendment, Dr. Parshall could receive only 25 general admission requests. In contrast, he might still be served with an unlimited number of requests asking him to admit to the genuineness of any documents that affect Professor Nevins' employment at the Institute.

The amendments to Federal Rule 34 deal with several problems that are unique to ESI. For example, often during ESI discovery, in response to a request for an inspection, ESI retrievers will offer to produce the ESI instead of permitting an inspection of their computer systems. When that happens, under the new rule, the ESI retriever must deliver that ESI before the requested inspection date (or within a reasonable time, thereof). The changes to Rule 34 also require that any objection to a document request be specifically worded to reveal if any ESI has been held back until the objection is resolved.[21]

Proposed New Sanctions for Spoliation

The changes to Rule 37 are designed to deal with spoliation. Under the amendments to Rule 37, two classes of sanctions have been created to deal with any party responsible for the destruction (spoliation) of ESI. The first class deals with accidental spoliation. **Accidental spoliation** occurs when ESI has been destroyed despite a reasonable attempt to forestall that spoliation. The sanctions against accidental spoliation include (1) allowing more discovery to offset the spoliation, (2) renewing the attempt to recover the missing ESI, and (3) paying for the other party's effort to retrieve the absent ESI. The second class deals with deliberate spoliation. **Deliberate spoliation** results from conduct that is "willful or in bad faith." The sanctions against deliberate spoliation include (1) a court order excluding all evidence that might have been used to counter the destroyed ESI; (2) an order that strikes a pleading completely; (3) an order that dismisses the action; and (4) an instruction allowing the jury to take an adverse inference from that destruction.[22]

accidental spoliation
The destruction of ESI that occurs when ESI is ruined despite a reasonable attempt to prevent that destruction.

deliberate spoliation
The destruction of ESI that results from conduct that is "willful or in bad faith."

SUMMARY

- A request for admission is a request filed by one party in a lawsuit on another party in that suit asking the second party to admit to the truthfulness of certain facts or opinions or to authenticate the genuineness of certain documents. The primary purpose of the request is to simplify the points in controversy. An admission made in response to a request for admission cannot be withdrawn without the court's permission. Any request that is not denied is deemed admitted.

- In preparing to draft a request for admission, the paralegal should discuss the matter with the supervising attorney, review all pleadings, and look over the applicable court rules. The actual request for admission will include the title, the introductory paragraph, the definitions and instructions, and the specific request. Copies of any documents involved in the request must be attached to the request.

- The alternatives available in responding to a request for admission are to admit, to deny, to refuse to either admit or deny, or to object. Grounds for objection include arguing that compliance with the request would violate the attorney–client privilege, the work product privilege, the medical privilege, or the confessor–penitent privilege. Other objections are that the request is overbroad, irrelevant, or duplicative. A final objection is that the statement is a compound request.

- The Judicial Conference Advisory Committee on Civil Rules has initiated a new program that is designed to streamline the discovery process in employment-related cases in federal court. The Protocols Pilot Project is currently in operation in six U.S. District Courts.

- The most pertinent ethical issues involving ESI today are (1) the ethical duty that lawyers and paralegals have to keep current on developments in computer technology; (2) the ethical responsibility to preserve a client's confidential records when they are preserved in a cloud storage center; and (3) the ethical duty to create a technology plan for the law firm.

- The Advisory Committee on Civil Rules is also currently in the process of revising and amending the rules of discovery. Specifically, several significant amendments will alter Federal Rules 26, 30, 31, 33, 34, and 37.

KEY TERMS

accidental spoliation	deemed admitted	judicial admission
compound request	deliberate spoliation	predictive coding

REVIEW QUESTIONS

1. What is a request for admission?
2. What is the principal purpose for filing a request for admission?
3. What advantages does the request for admission have over other discovery tools?
4. What preliminary steps should be taken before drafting a request for admission?
5. What are the parts of a request for admission?
6. What is the content of each part of a request for admission?
7. What are the possible responses to a request for admission?
8. What is the danger of not responding to a request for admission?
9. What are the possible objections to a request for admission?
10. What are the assumptions for starting the new Discovery Protocols Pilot Project?
11. What are the key ethical issues facing legal professionals using ESI today?
12. Why has the federal court decided to amend the Rules of Civil Procedure?

CHAPTER EXERCISES

Where necessary, check with your instructor prior to starting any of these exercises.

1. Review your state's rules relating to requests for admission. Prepare a summary of the differences between the Federal Rules and your state's rules. Also check your local court rules and do the same.

2. Prepare a summary of the amendments that are slated to occur to the Federal Rules of Civil Procedure, including Rules 26, 30, 31, 33, 34, and 37.

3. Create a list of the documents that must be turned over without request in an employment case under the new Discovery Protocols Pilot Project.

4. Prepare a chart of the objections to requests for admission that are permitted in the federal and state courts in your area.

5. In the *Nevins* case, your supervising attorney has received several requests for admissions involving records that were sent to the Wayne Institute during the required discovery production process mandated by the Discovery Protocols Project. Carefully consider each of the following requests and determine whether they should be admitted.

   a. A request for admission asking Professor Nevins to authenticate an electronic copy of her employment application showing her signature, under a statement that reads, "I, the undersigned, understand that, should I be employed by the Wayne Institute of Language, Linguistics, and Semiotics, my employment would be at-will, and that, in accordance with the laws of this state, I can be discharged at any time, for any reason, with or without notice. I further understand that no one, except the Executive Director of the Wayne Institute of Language, Linguistics, and Semiotics, has the authority to alter this at-will situation."

   b. A request for admission asking Professor Nevins to authenticate a photocopy of the last page of the Wayne Institute of Language, Linguistics, and Semiotics' policy and procedure manual, showing her signature under a statement which reads, "I, the undersigned, state that I have read and understood the contents of this employment manual. Moreover, I further state that I agree to abide by all rules, regulations, and procedures in said manual."

   c. A request for admission asking that Professor Nevins authenticate a letter that she sent to Dr. Parshall, the executive director of the Wayne Institute of Language, Linguistics, and Semiotics, complaining of her harsh treatment while employed at the hospital.

CHAPTER PROJECT

Review the Commentary at the beginning of this chapter. Recall that, in this case, your firm is representing Professor Nevins in an unjust dismissal lawsuit against her former employer, the Wayne Institute of Language, Linguistics, and Semiotics (the Wayne Institute). The other defendant is Dr. Anders Parshall, the executive director of the Wayne Institute of Language, Linguistics, and Semiotics. Locate a sample request for admissions in your state's form book or online. Draft a request for admission in which you request that Dr. Parshall admit that he signed all of Professor Nevins employee evaluation forms, that all of those forms indicate that she did an outstanding job for the company, that Professor Nevins was a contractual employee, and that she personally believed that her job performance was satisfactory. Also request that Dr. Parshall authenticate the attached document purporting to be the company's list of dischargeable offenses and its progressive disciplinary procedure. Also request that he authenticate the letter that he sent Professor Nevins announcing her termination and the internal memo that he sent to the company's human resources director informing the director of Nevins' dismissal.

THE *BENNETT* CASE
Assignment for Chapter 13: Answering a Request for Admission

Ms. Bennett has been served with a set of requests for admission concerning the following questions:

1. Do you admit that prior to being hired by Rikards-Hayley you had seen a psychologist for marital problems?
2. Do you admit that any of your current medical or psychological problems are due exclusively to marital problems you presently experience?
3. Do you admit that any of your current medical or psychological problems are in part due to marital problems you presently experience?
4. Do you admit that you tendered an oral resignation of your position with defendant?
5. Do you admit that all of the medical bills claimed in this lawsuit have been covered by insurance?

You have been asked to prepare a response to these questions. When you discussed the matter with Ms. Bennett, she told you that she did in fact have marital problems and that her husband had filed for divorce last week. She admitted to seeing a marriage counselor prior to her employment with defendant. However, she does not believe that any of this is relevant to the case. She assures you that all of her medical problems were caused by the defendant's actions. She does acknowledge that her bills have been paid by insurance. She also tells you that when she was terminated she replied, "You can't fire me. I quit." Prepare a draft of appropriate answers to requests for admission. Be sure to assert proper objections.

THE *DOUGLASS FINANCIAL SERVICES INC.* CASE
Assignment for Chapter 13: Request to Request for Admissions

Your attorney tells you that Douglass Financial, Inc., your client, was recently served with Requests for Admissions. Using a proper format for your state court, deny or object to each of the following requests for admissions sent by plaintiff to your client, Douglass Financial, Inc.:

A. Admit that each of the following statements is true:
   1. Defendant Evan Portman was in the course and scope of his employment with Douglass Financial Inc. when he consumed alcohol at an office party on December 19.
   2. When Evan Portman left the office party sponsored by Douglass Financial, Inc., he was in such an inebriated state that it was not safe for him to drive an automobile.

3. All employees of Douglass Financial, Inc. were required to attend the company's office party held on December 19.

4. The automobile accident that is the subject of this lawsuit was caused by the negligence of defendant Evan Portman.

5. Plaintiff, Jessica Hewitt, was not negligent in any matter contributing to the automobile accident that is the subject of this lawsuit.

END NOTES

1. Henry Kelston, "Are We on the Cusp of Major Changes to E-Discovery Rules?" *Law Technology News* (April 17, 2013), retrieved on May 7, 2013 from <http://www.law.com/jsp/lawtechnologynews/PubArticleLTN.jsp?id=1202596362366&Are_We_on_the_Cusp_of_Major_Changes_to_EDiscovery_Rules>, 1.

2. Ibid.

3. Robert A. Steinberg, "Historical Origins of the Initial Discovery Protocols Pilot Project for Employment Cases," *The Ohio State Bar Association: 2013 Annual Convention* (May 10, 2013): 55–56. See also: "Pilot Program Introduces Protocols for Employment Cases," *The Third Branch News* (February 2012).

4. Ibid.,58.

5. Ibid., 59–60.

6. *Pilot Project Regarding Initial Discovery Protocols for Employment Cases Alleging Adverse Action*, The Judicial Conference Advisory Committee on Civil Rules (November 2011): 6–7.

7. Ibid., 7-9.

8. Steinberg, "Historical Origins of the Initial Discovery Protocols Pilot Project for Employment Cases," 61.

9. Barron K. Henley, "Legal Technology Tips, Tricks, Gadgets, and Websites," *The Ohio State Bar Association: 2013 Annual Convention* (May 8–10, 2013); and Chad Burton, "The Future of the Profession," *The Ohio State Bar Association: 2013 Annual Convention* (May 8–10, 2013): 7. In fact, both Henley and Burton remind us that the American Bar Association has already altered its commentary to Model Rule 1.1 of the Model Rules of Ethics and Professional Responsibility, stating quite clearly that attorneys have no choice but to keep current with technological changes.

10. Henley, "Legal Technology Tips" and Burton, "The Future of the Profession," 7.

11. Jonathan Strickland, "How Cloud Storage Work," *How Stuff Works* (2008), retrieved on January 11, 2013 from <http://computer.howstuffworks.com>.

12. Henley, "Legal Technology Tips."

13. Ibid.

14. Ibid.

15. Ibid.

16. W. Brian Arthur, *The Nature of Technology: What It Is and How It Evolves* (New York: Free Press, 2009), 13–14.

17. Ibid., 14.

18. Henley, "Legal Technology Tips."

19. Ibid.

20. Kelston, "Are We on the Cusp of Major Changes to E-Discovery Rules?" 1.

21. Ibid.

22. Ibid., 1–2.

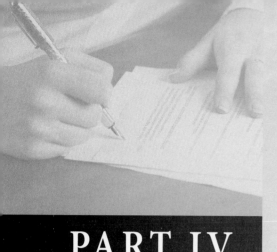

PART IV

Pretrial, Trial, and Posttrial

CHAPTER 14

Settlements, Dismissals, and Alternative Dispute Resolution

CHAPTER OUTLINE

THE *KOWALSKI* CASE

Clark Kowalski is a nuclear physicist employed by Americans for Environmental Safety (AES), an independent organization of individuals devoted to protecting the environment. The Cuyahoga Valley Nuclear Power Plant, located on the outskirts of Cleveland, Ohio, and owned and operated by the Everett-Stimson Power and Light Company, had retained Dr. Kowalski to inspect the power plant. The objective of the inspection was to reassure AES and the public that the plant was safe. Unfortunately, during the inspection tour, Dr. Kowalski was severely injured in an explosion. Shortly after the accident, a reporter asked Dr. Kowalski for an interview, during which Kowalski revealed some very damaging information about the plant's safety procedures. Shortly after the news story appeared, Dr. Kowalski decided to bring a lawsuit against Everett-Stimson. Because Everett-Stimson has filed a counterclaim against Dr. Kowalski for libel, your attorney thinks it would be a good idea to explore the possibility of settling some of these claims out of court. Accordingly, she asks you to organize the litigation file in preparation for a possible settlement. Depending on the outcome of the preliminary investigation, you may also be called upon to prepare a settlement summary, a settlement letter, or a settlement brochure. If a settlement is actually reached, you may be needed to assist your attorney with drafting a settlement agreement. This chapter covers the details surrounding the settlement process.

Part III introduced you to the discovery process. Like the discovery process, the settlement process is an integral part of any lawsuit. After reading this chapter, you should be able to:

- define settlement.
- identify the initial factors regarding settlement.
- describe the factors involved in a preliminary investigation in the settlement process.
- differentiate between a settlement summary and a settlement letter.
- relate the paralegal's duties in compiling a settlement brochure.
- outline the nature of a settlement agreement.
- explain the differences among general releases, partial releases, and mutual releases.
- discuss the nature of a stipulated dismissal.
- define the voluntary dismissal on notice.
- explain a court-ordered involuntary dismissal.
- discuss the nature of a consent decree.
- explain the need for a settlement proceeds statement.
- describe methods of alternative dispute resolution.

settlement
To come to an agreement about;
disposition of a lawsuit.

THE SETTLEMENT

A **settlement** is an agreement or a contract between parties that terminates their civil dispute. Many civil cases end in a settlement. Often settlement negotiations are conducted simultaneously with active preparation of the lawsuit. In fact, the preparation of the lawsuit may actually lead to the settlement. As the attorney gathers information about the suit, she may decide that a settlement is in the client's best interests. In such a case, the lawsuit is settled quickly. If, however, the attorney, with the client's concurrence, decides not to settle, no time has been lost in the litigation process. To be an effective paralegal, you must understand the factors in a settlement decision. It is also very helpful for you to know how to conduct a preliminary investigation.

Initial Factors Involved in the Settlement Decision

An attorney must consider a number of factors before deciding to settle a case. The two most obvious factors are time and money. Because the legal system is overburdened with a heavy case load, it is not uncommon for a court's calendar to be backed up for months. Some courts in large metropolitan areas have dockets that are backed up for years. This type of overcrowding may mean that a trial date cannot be set for months or even years after the original complaint has been filed. If your client cannot afford to wait that long for a judgment, then your attorney may elect to settle the case without going to trial.

Also recall that a lengthy and involved discovery procedure may be needed to gather the facts required to prove your client's case at trial. The more involved the discovery process, the more expensive the lawsuit becomes. For example, in the *Kowalski* case, discovery may be necessary to uncover not only the facts surrounding the explosion itself, but also the circumstances leading to the explosion. In addition, discovery will be needed to uncover whether the defendants had any knowledge of similar incidents involving the type of pump that exploded and harmed Dr. Kowalski. This will mean taking multiple depositions and serving interrogatories, requests for production of documents, requests for disclosure, and requests for admissions. Your client may have to undergo a physical examination, and your attorney will probably want to inspect the site of the explosion. All of this costs money, which will erode the value of any final judgment rendered by the court.

Another settlement factor may be the particular court's decisions in similar cases. In the *Kowalski* case, for example, you may find that the court recently rendered a judgment favorable to a utility company in a case with facts very similar to the facts in your case. In such a situation, it may be in your client's best interest to engage in settlement negotiations.

Finally, the subsequent tactics of the other party's attorney may motivate a client to seriously consider a settlement. Recall, for example, that the defendant, in responding to a lawsuit, may elect to file a counterclaim against the plaintiff. The legitimacy of the counterclaim and the degree to which the defendant may succeed in presenting that counterclaim would be critical factors to consider in making any settlement decision. In the *Kowalski* case, for instance, Everett-Stimson has filed a counterclaim for libel against Dr. Kowalski. Such an event may motivate your attorney to consider the possibility of settling the case without proceeding to trial.

Preliminary Investigative Work

Generally, a settlement offer originates with the plaintiff because the plaintiff's attorney is in the best position to assess the injuries to the client and can therefore set a reasonable figure as the basis for the settlement. Naturally, this means that some preliminary assessment work is in order. Usually this preliminary investigative work is the responsibility of the paralegal. During this stage, you will have to obtain a personal history of the client, a preliminary assessment of the client's present health, and the client's medical history. You may also be required to calculate the damages in the case. Additionally, you may be asked to assist your attorney with the probe of some collateral areas to get an accurate picture of the probability of your client prevailing should the case go to trial.

The Client's Personal History   One of the preliminary steps in the settlement investigation is to obtain an accurate personal and financial history of the client. This would include the client's family information, education, employment record, earnings records for several previous years, and religious, professional, and civic organization memberships. It might also be helpful to determine whether your client has any hobbies or participates in sports. For example, in the *Kowalski* case, it would help your attorney calculate damages if she knew that Dr. Kowalski was an avid tennis player prior to sustaining the injuries caused by the explosion in the power plant.

The Client's Present Health and Medical History   The client's medical history before and after the accident are key factors in the case. You will have to determine the nature and the extent of the injuries the client has suffered. You will also need to find out what treatment he has undergone and will be compelled to undergo in the future. It is helpful to know what diagnostic tests were performed on the client and what therapy, if any, was performed. Furthermore, your attorney will want to know whether the client was disfigured and whether he has suffered any temporary or permanent disability as a result of the accident. Do not overlook any psychiatric or psychological damage that may have resulted from the accident. It is advisable to have the client keep a medical diary on a daily or a weekly basis. Instruct the client to record any symptoms related to the accident and any medical visits to physicians, chiropractors, psychologists, and physical therapists. A video diary of a typical day in the life of your client would be very persuasive in settlement negotiations. You might be asked to work with a family member to prepare the video.

Calculating Damages   If, as the paralegal, you are asked to calculate the damages in the case, make sure to organize and review all checks, receipts, income tax returns, and paycheck stubs furnished by the client. This will ensure that you have presented a concise and accurate picture of the damages. Extreme care should be exercised in this calculation because damages are often a substantial part of any settlement agreement.

Investigating Collateral Matters   Before your attorney can make an informed decision regarding the potential of settlement, she must take into consideration certain collateral matters. *Collateral matters* are considerations that go beyond the facts and the merits of the case but that, nevertheless, have a definite impact on the decision to settle or to proceed with the suit. The attitude of the trial judge assigned to the case may play an

settlement summary
A summary of all essential information outlining the benefits of settling the case at an early stage in the litigation.

settlement letter
A detailed account of the information needed to determine the benefit of settling a case.

important part in the decision. In the *Kowalski* case, for example, if you learn that the trial judge tends to rule in favor of utility companies in tort suits of this nature, your attorney may decide that a settlement would be in your client's best interest.

Another collateral area to look at is the experience or inexperience of the opposing attorney. For example, in the *Kowalski* case, if you are dealing with an opposing attorney who has a strong record representing utility companies in this type of suit, your attorney will approach her with a different strategy than if the opposing attorney were inexperienced.

Recent statutes and court rulings involving this area of the law also must be researched to help your attorney determine if any recent trends in the law make it advisable to settle the suit. For example, in the *Kowalski* case, it would be essential for your attorney to know whether there have been any changes in the law of Ohio that would affect the outcome of your case. This information will be helpful to your attorney when she negotiates for a settlement with Everett-Stimson.

SETTLEMENT OFFER

As a paralegal, your talents may be used in a number of ways as your attorney prepares a settlement offer. Often the paralegal will be asked to draft a settlement summary, a settlement letter, or a settlement brochure. The complexity of the lawsuit and the amount of money involved will be primary factors in determining which of the three will be used in a given case.

Settlement Summary and Settlement Letter

Once the preliminary investigative work has been completed, the information should be organized into a useful report format. This report must convince the defendant that a settlement would be in its best interests. Depending on the situation, you may be charged with writing a settlement summary or a settlement letter. The objective of each is to persuade your opponent to agree to your settlement terms. The choice of which format to use is based on the complexity of the case and the amount of money involved. Drafting settlement summaries and settlement letters is an important part of the paralegal's role in the overall settlement process. The law firm's forms files and personal injury form books should be used to prepare the initial draft of a settlement summary or settlement letter.

Settlement Summary
Simple cases involving relatively small claims may be settled early, primarily because the cost of litigation outweighs the benefit of a long and expensive suit. In such a case a short settlement summary may be drafted by the paralegal. The **settlement summary** compiles all essential information outlining the benefits of settling the case at an early stage in the litigation. Settlement summaries are usually not much longer than one page. Exhibit 14-1 is an example of a settlement summary for the *Kowalski* case.

Settlement Letter
Cases that involve complex issues and an extensive list of damages may require the writing of a settlement letter. The **settlement letter** is a much more detailed account of the essential information needed to determine the benefit of settling a case.

EXHIBIT 14-1 Sample Settlement Summary

TO: Kowalski, Moldovan, and Zuer
     Attorneys for Defendant
     Vagran-Orrell Cybernetics, Inc. and Daniel Vagran, CEO of Vagran-Orrell
     17810 Brinkerhoff Blvd.
     Seattle, Washington

Kowalski v. Everett-Stimson Power and Light Company, et al.
Common Pleas Court
Cuyahoga County, Ohio
Case No. 12-CD-980

Settlement Summary

   On the morning of November 16, 2012, at approximately 11:45, the plaintiff, Dr. Clark Kowalski, acting as a representative of Americans for Environmental Safety, and plant technician Samuel Kirk were making an inspection of the cooling system at the Cuyahoga Valley Nuclear Power Plant. An incident report filed by Samuel Kirk indicates that Dr. Kowalski had followed all proper safety procedures as he conducted his inspection. The incident report filed by Mr. Kirk also indicates that at approximately 11:47 that morning, while he and Dr. Kowalski were preparing to complete their inspection, a nearby hydraulic pump malfunctioned, causing an explosion that threw both Dr. Kowalski and him to the floor. Dr. Kowalski had been facing Mr. Kirk, with his back to the pump, and thus took the full force of the explosion in the upper back. Dr. Kowalski has testified that at approximately 11:47 on the morning of November 16, 2012, he was struck in the back by an explosive force. Dr. Kowalski has stated that at no time was he in any way in contact with said pump.

   Dr. Kowalski may recover in tort law under two theories: (a) The defendants knew about the dangerous condition of the pump and negligently failed to remedy the situation or to warn Dr. Kowalski; and (b) the defendants should have known about the dangerous condition of the pump but did not because of a negligently conducted inspection.

   Dr. Kowalski suffered third-degree burns across the upper one-half of his back. He also received a broken arm and a broken wrist. Dr. Kowalski also suffered a minor concussion, a sprained neck, and received minor cuts and abrasions to his face and hands. He also lost three teeth and will require a series of corrective dental operations as well as restorative plastic surgery. The medical expenses incurred by Dr. Kowalski total $52,440. The plaintiff also intends to seek $235,000 in damages for pain and suffering, plus $500,000 in punitive damages under the theory that the defendants' conduct was intentional. The plaintiff has also incurred lost wages amounting to $8,000.

   The plaintiff is asking for a total of $795,440 in damages. Because of the climate of anti-utility, antinuclear sentiment prevalent in Ohio at the present time, it is anticipated that the jury will award the full amount. However, in the interest of a speedy and just end to the suit, the plaintiff is willing to settle for an award of $400,000. This represents just slightly more than one-half of the anticipated recovery should the matter go to trial. The plaintiff is also willing to negotiate a payment plan, provided that he can receive an immediate cash payment of the first $100,000.

   The settlement letter begins with a statement of the facts involved in the case and is written from the perspective of the defendant's potential liability. The letter also includes a detailed assessment of your client's injuries, medical history, present medical condition, and future medical prognosis. To be persuasive, the letter should reveal the plaintiff's legal theory or theories of recovery. The amount of money spent by your client because of his injuries should be included as well as the amount of any wages he has lost or anticipates losing because of those injuries. Finally, the settlement letter should present to the defendant a statement of the amount that your client is prepared to seek as a reasonable settlement. Exhibit 14-2 is an example of a settlement letter sent by Dr. Kowalski's attorney to the Everett-Stimson Power and Light Company.

EXHIBIT 14-2 Sample Settlement Letter

LAW OFFICE OF EDWARDS, BLAKE, FITZSIMMONS, AND MYLORIE

31753 EAST CLOVER AVENUE CLEVELAND, OHIO 44121

May 6, 2013

Ms. Charlene Bannister
Andrews, Bannister, Vilnius, and Friedman
The Billings Building, Suite 81989
2748 West Lexington Blvd.
Cleveland, Ohio 44117

RE: *Kowalski v. Everett-Stimson Power and Light Company, et al.*
Common Pleas Court
Cuyahoga County, Ohio
Case No. 12-CD-980

Dear Ms. Bannister:

In the interests of bringing the case of *Kowalski v. Everett-Stimson Power and Light Company, et al.* to a speedy and just conclusion, I have been authorized by my client, Dr. Clark Kowalski, to make the following settlement offer to your client. Please consult with your client, give this settlement offer all due consideration, and contact my office with your response within 14 days from the receipt of this letter.

Plaintiff's Background—Clark Kowalski was born on February 9, 1948, the first of seven children born to Mr. and Mrs. Vytautus Kowalski. The plaintiff attended St. Mary Magdalene Grade School in Willowick, Ohio; St. Joseph High School in Cleveland; John Carroll University in Cleveland; and Case Western Reserve University, also in Cleveland. He received his doctorate in nuclear physics from Case Western Reserve University in June of 1974. Dr. Kowalski has taught at a number of universities and colleges over the course of the last twenty years. He is an acknowledged expert in the field of nuclear physics, having no fewer than 30 scholarly articles to his credit. Prior to his accepting employment as nuclear physicist with Americans for Environmental Safety (AES), he directed the research department at the prestigious North Central Institute of Technology (NCIT).

Medical History—Dr. Kowalski's medical history is notable for its lack of incident. He suffered a knee injury while playing tennis at St. Joseph High School in 1966. Aside from that, he has a mild case of hypertension that is kept under control by the daily administration of the minimum dose of Vasotec. He has no previous history of head, back, or arm injuries. Before the accident he was, in fact, in good enough health to win the Cleveland-Akron-Toledo Tri-City Amateur Tennis Championship for three years in a row.

The Facts Surrounding the Accident—On the morning of November 16, 2012, at approximately 11:45, Dr. Kowalski was making an inspection of the cooling system at the Cuyahoga Valley Nuclear Power Plant. The inspection of the plant by an AES representative had been arranged by Everett-Stimson to reassure AES and the public that the plant was safe. The attached incident report filed by Samuel Kirk indicates that Dr. Kowalski had followed all proper safety procedures as he conducted his inspection. The incident report filed by Mr. Kirk also indicates that at approximately 11:47 that morning, while he and Dr. Kowalski were preparing to complete their inspection, a nearby hydraulic pump malfunctioned, causing an explosion that threw both Dr. Kowalski and him to the floor. Dr. Kowalski had been facing Mr. Kirk with his back to the pump and thus took the full force of the explosion in the upper back. Dr. Kowalski's position shielded Mr. Kirk from the force of the explosion.

Dr. Kowalski's deposition, a copy of which is attached, also indicates that at approximately 11:47 on the morning of November 16, 2012, he was struck in the back by an explosive force. Dr. Kowalski has stated that at no time was he in any contact with said pump. He has indicated that he was talking to Mr. Kirk as they were preparing to complete their

EXHIBIT 14-2 Sample Settlement Letter (*continued*)

inspection when he was suddenly thrown from his feet by a sudden hot blast. He was looking at Mr. Kirk at the time and had no warning that the pump was about to explode.

Theories of Recovery—Dr. Kowalski may recover in tort law under two theories:

a. The defendants knew about the dangerous condition of the pump and negligently failed to remedy the situation or to warn Dr. Kowalski.

b. The defendants should have known about the dangerous condition of the pump but did not because of a negligently conducted inspection.

The first theory will be proven by an examination of the accident records of the Everett-Stimson Power and Light Company, which will clearly indicate that identical explosions involving identical pumps taken from the same lot number occurred at two other nuclear power plants owned and operated by Everett-Stimson. Testimony from Dr. Kowalski, Mr. Kirk, and from Julius Angelitis, the director of the Cuyahoga Valley Nuclear Power Plant, will indicate that neither Dr. Kowalski nor Mr. Kirk was informed of the previous accidents, despite Mr. Angelitis's knowledge of the accidents and his knowledge that Dr. Kowalski and Mr. Kirk would be working in the vicinity of the suspect pump. Such a failure to warn of impending danger would amount to negligent conduct, making the company liable for Dr. Kowalski's resulting injuries.

The defendants may wish to argue that Mr. Angelitis did not inform Dr. Kowalski about the dangerous pump because a recent inspection had revealed that the pump was not flawed. The defendants may argue that because of this favorable inspection they did not know that harm to the plaintiff would occur. If this is the argument presented by the defendants, then the plaintiff will call upon his second theory. That theory suggests that the inspection performed by the defendants must necessarily have been conducted in a negligent manner. The plaintiff will submit evidence that will convince a jury that even a cursory examination of the pump would have revealed the same flaw in this pump which caused the other two pumps to explode. The plaintiff will submit further convincing evidence that will prove that this pump exploded in the same manner and as a result of the same flaw that caused the other two pumps to explode.

Injuries to the Plaintiff—The initial medical examination conducted by Dr. Wesley Forbes, the staff physician at Cuyahoga Valley, indicated that Dr. Kowalski suffered third-degree burns across the upper one-half of his back. Dr. Forbes's initial assessment also indicated that the plaintiff received a broken arm and a broken wrist. The plaintiff was airlifted to the Burn Unit at Cleveland Metropolitan General Hospital, where the diagnosis of his burns and broken bones was confirmed. Dr. Michelle Gonzales also found that Dr. Kowalski had suffered a minor concussion, a sprained neck, and had received minor cuts and abrasions on his face and hands. He also lost three teeth and will require a series of corrective dental operations as well as restorative plastic surgery. The reports issued by Dr. Forbes, Dr. Gonzales, and the dentist, Dr. Herman Kleinhenz, are attached.

Medical Expenses—The medical expenses incurred by Dr. Kowalski have been itemized on the attached forms. However, a general summary of those expenses includes the following items:

a. Medivac Transportation to Cleveland Metro	$1,000
b. Emergency Room Treatment	$2,300
c. One-Week Hospital Stay at Metro	$9,800
d. Orthopedic Treatment	$7,900
e. Burn Unit Treatment	$8,000
f. Radiology Department	$1,000
g. Dr. Kleinhenz's Examination	$1,500
h. Anticipated Oral Surgery	$2,400
i. Anticipated Cosmetic Surgery	$9,900
j. Anticipated Treatment	$8,640
TOTAL	$52,440

Further Damages—The plaintiff, Dr. Kowalski, also intends to seek $235,000 in damages for pain and suffering plus $500,000 in punitive damages. The plaintiff has also incurred lost wages amounting to $8,000.

EXHIBIT 14-2 Sample Settlement Letter (*continued*)

Proposed Settlement—The plaintiff is asking for a total of $795,440 in damages. Because of the climate of anti-utility, antinuclear sentiment prevalent in Ohio at the present time, it is anticipated that the jury will award the full amount. However, in the interest of a speedy and just end to the suit, the plaintiff is willing to settle for an immediate cash award of $400,000. This represents just slightly more than one-half of the anticipated recovery should the matter go to trial.

As counsel for the plaintiff, I urge you to take this settlement offer to your client in the spirit in which it is offered. I will look forward to your affirmative response.

Very truly yours,

_____

Terry A. Mylorie

TAM/skg
Enclosures
CC: Dr. Clark Kowalski with enclosures

settlement brochure
A summary of facts designed to get the other side to settle a case.

Settlement Brochure

The **settlement brochure** is a summary of facts designed to persuade the other side to settle a case. The objective and the basic content of a settlement summary, a settlement letter, and a settlement brochure are the same. They differ, however, in the amount of the material presented and in the format used. The settlement brochure tends to be more elaborate, in that it includes photographs, charts, graphs, newspaper articles, witness statements, medical reports, and the like. It is frequently made more striking by its use of multicolored graphs and charts. A settlement brochure can be a very persuasive settlement tool. However, it is also expensive and is thus used most effectively in lawsuits seeking fairly large settlements. The individual parts of a settlement brochure should include a statement of the facts, the client's personal history, the client's medical history and medical condition, the damages suffered by the client, and an evaluation of the case and statement of the settlement. Exhibit 14-3 is an example of a table of contents that might be used for a settlement brochure in the *Kowalski* case.

Statement of the Facts
Like the settlement letter, the settlement brochure begins with a *statement of the facts* involved in the case. Again, this statement of the facts must be written from the perspective of the defendant's potential liability. The use of newspaper articles and photographs can be an especially effective way of creating a vivid effect. Consider, for example, the dramatic impact in the *Kowalski* case of including in your settlement brochure a front-page news story of an accident at the Cuyahoga Valley Plant and color photographs of the accident site and the injuries to Dr. Kowalski. Such a package can be very sobering to the defendant, who realizes that these same photographs may be presented to jury members who live near the Cuyahoga Valley Plant.

Client's Personal History
The *client's personal history* should be included in the settlement brochure. To complete this section of the settlement brochure, you should review the preliminary investigative work that you did in the case. The personal history includes the client's family information, education, employment record, and religious, professional,

EXHIBIT 14-3 Table of Contents of Settlement Brochure

   I. Description of the Accident
      Witness Statements
      Photos of the Accident Scene
      Photos of the Plaintiff before the Accident
      Photos of the Plaintiff after the Accident
  II. Statement of the Facts
 III. Plaintiff's Personal History
  IV. Medical History of the Plaintiff
   V. Medical Condition of the Plaintiff
  VI. Medical Expenses
 VII. Evaluation of the Claim

and civic organization memberships. It might also be helpful to include information about your client's hobbies or participation in sports. As in the case of the facts, photographs can be used here. Photographs may be helpful later in calculating the damages that your attorney will seek on behalf of Dr. Kowalski.

Client's Medical History and Medical Condition

Like the settlement letter, the settlement brochure includes a detailed assessment of your client's *medical history and medical condition*. Again, this should include the injuries suffered by the client as well as any future medical prognosis. To be convincing, this section of the settlement brochure can include the hospital records and the reports filed by any physicians and therapists involved in the case, as well as the client's medical diary. Photographs of the plaintiff's injuries are a very effective supplement in this section of the brochure.

Damages, Evaluation, and Settlement

In a separate section devoted to **damages**, the amount of money spent by your client because of his injuries should be included as well as the amount of any wages he has lost or anticipates losing because of those injuries. All checks, receipts, income tax returns, and pay stubs furnished by the client must be organized and totaled to present a precise and accurate picture of the damages. Finally, the settlement brochure should include an *evaluation of the claim* and present to the defendant a *statement of the settlement* that your client believes is reasonable.

Settlement Conference

A **settlement conference** is a meeting of the parties to discuss settlement of the case. It might be part of the pretrial conference procedures under Rule 16 of the Federal Rules of Civil Procedure or it may arise after the pretrial conference. The court may order a settlement conference or a party may request such a conference.

The paralegal's role in preparing for the settlement conference mirrors preparation for the pretrial conference. Employ your organizational skills so that all materials needed for or during the settlement conference are readily available for the attorney's review.

---

damages
Money that a court orders paid to a person who has suffered damage (a loss or harm) by the person who caused the injury (the violation of the person's rights).

settlement conference
A meeting of the parties to discuss settlement of the case.

SETTLEMENT AGREEMENT AND RELEASE

If the parties reach an agreement based on the settlement offer, then it will be necessary to put the details of that settlement into a permanent written form. The complexity of the case and the settlement arrangement will determine whether the parties will use a settlement agreement or a release.

Settlement Agreements

A **settlement agreement** is actually a contract between the parties. As such, it must meet all the legal requirements of a contract. This means that it must involve the voluntary, mutual assent of the parties. It must include the give-and-take element of consideration. Also, to be legal and binding, the agreement must be made by parties with the capacity to contract.

Voluntary, Mutual Assent   Because a settlement agreement is a contract, it must be made with the voluntary, mutual assent of both parties. If the client is against the settlement, the attorney cannot agree to it no matter how lucrative and beneficial it may appear to be. In fact, the rules of ethical conduct that guide attorneys specify this limitation on the attorney's power to represent a client in settlement negotiations. Similarly, to be voluntary, the settlement agreement must not result from duress or undue influence. Threats of bodily harm or threats to property would constitute duress.

Consideration   Because the settlement agreement is a contract, it will not be valid unless each side gains something and each side gives up something. This exchange of values is called **consideration**. Money is the most common form of consideration. In the *Kowalski* case, for example, your attorney may decide to ask Everett-Stimson for a $400,000 settlement to compensate your client for the injuries he suffered as a result of the explosion of the hydraulic pump used in the Cuyahoga Valley Nuclear Power Plant. Money, however, is not the only form of consideration. A promise to act or not to act may also be consideration. In the *Kowalski* case, for example, the consideration offered by Dr. Kowalski is his agreement to drop the lawsuit. Once the settlement has been agreed to, it is binding even if Dr. Kowalski later finds out that he had no legal basis for bringing the suit against Everett-Stimson.

Capacity and Legality   In order for the settlement to be enforceable in court, it must be made by parties who have the legal capacity to enter into a contract. If one of the parties is a minor or under a mental disability, the parent or the guardian enters into the settlement agreement and obtains the court's approval on behalf of that party. Additionally, court approval is required for attorney fees and court costs incurred. Naturally, the terms of the settlement must not require either party to do something that is illegal.

High-Low Agreements   A **high-low agreement** is an agreement in which the parties agree that the outcome of the case will be no less than "X" dollars (the low) and no more than "Y" dollars (the high). Such agreements often are used in cases in which the damages are high and the liability is uncertain. For example, medical malpractice cases are expensive to litigate. In the event that a plaintiff is particularly sympathetic to jurors, the defendant might decide that a high-low settlement agreement is preferable to taking his chances with a jury verdict. If the verdict returned is in favor of the plaintiff and exceeds the "Y" dollars, the plaintiff will receive only the "Y" dollars. If the verdict is in favor of the defendant, and lower than "X" dollars, the plaintiff is still guaranteed the "X" dollars.

High-low agreements may be entered into before or during a trial, prior to the jury verdict. These agreements are viable in all types of cases. Court approval of a high-low agreement is required in cases involving minors to prevent the possibility of a reversal by a higher court. A guardian ad litem, a person who has the legal authority (and the corresponding duty) to care for the personal and property interest of a child or incapacitated person for the purposes of a legal procedure, will then be appointed to approve or disapprove the proposed high-low settlement agreement.

Loan Receipt Agreement   A **loan receipt agreement** is a contract between a claimant and a settling **tortfeasor** by which they agree that one of them will prosecute the claim against another tortfeasor. This type of agreement gives the claimant the opportunity to recover additional damages and the settling tortfeasor may get some money back by pursuing the claim. The settling party, or his liability insurer, agrees to "loan" the claimant a specified amount of money, and the claimant agrees not to pursue the claim against the settling tortfeasor. The parties then agree on an allocation of any recovery from the nonsettling tortfeasor. If the claimant recovers nothing from the nonsettling tortfeasor, the "loan" does not have to be repaid.

Loan receipt agreements are court approved and often provide the best strategy for potential settlement. Generally, such agreements are used only where the lender has paid most (or perhaps all) of the claimant's damages. Most jurisdictions have upheld the validity of this settlement vehicle. However, courts often require disclosure of the existence and terms of the loan receipt to the other defendants.

Mary Carter Agreements   A **Mary Carter agreement** (from the case *Booth v. Mary Carter Paint Co.,* 202 So. 2d 8 [Fla. Dist. Ct. App. 1967]) is a secret or semisecret agreement between the claimant and one or more, but not all, the tortfeasors. There are several elements to this type of agreement:

1. The settling defendant guarantees the plaintiff a minimum amount of money even if the plaintiff loses the case or recovers less than the guaranteed amount.
2. The settling defendant agrees to remain in the lawsuit until a judgment is reached or the claimant consents to its dismissal. Its payment to plaintiff is reduced if money is recovered by settlement or judgment from the other defendants.
3. Plaintiff agrees not to enforce any subsequent judgment against the settling defendant.
4. The agreement is confidential and disclosed only as required by the rules of the court.

A few jurisdictions (including Texas) prohibit the use of Mary Carter agreements. Other jurisdictions require safeguards on their use to balance the public policy promoting settlements with a possible distortion of the adversarial process. Some jurisdictions require disclosure of this "secret" agreement.

Form of the Settlement Agreement   The settlement agreement should specify the identities of the parties, the action that gave rise to the claim, the type and extent of the injuries caused, the consideration given for the settlement, the time and circumstances

loan receipt agreement
A contract between a claimant and settling tortfeasor by which they agree that one of them will prosecute the claim against another tortfeasor.

tortfeasor
A person who commits a tort (civil wrong) either intentionally or through negligence.

Mary Carter agreement
A secret or semisecret agreement between the claimant and one or more, but not all, the tortfeasors.

under which any and all payments will be made, and any special conditions that have been agreed to by the parties. If a dispute arises over any part of the agreement, a court will interpret the provision in question. In the event that the court finds that a term of the agreement is vague or ambiguous, it may seek additional testimony or evidence to determine the intent of the parties at the time they entered into the agreement. Exhibit 14-4 presents an example of a settlement agreement in the *Kowalski* case.

EXHIBIT 14-4 Sample Settlement Agreement

COURT OF COMMON PLEAS CUYAHOGA COUNTY STATE OF OHIO

CLARK KOWALSKI
  Plaintiff,   )
)
)
)
  v.   )
)
EVERETT-STIMSON POWER AND)
LIGHT COMPANY, et al.   )
  Defendants.   )
)
_____)
	Civil Action No. 12-CD-980
	SETTLEMENT AGREEMENT

THIS ACTION, Kowalski v. Everett-Stimson Power and Light Company, et al., Case No. 12-CD-980, was brought in the Common Pleas Court of Cuyahoga County, Ohio, by Clark Kowalski, hereinafter called "plaintiff," against Everett-Stimson Power and Light Company and Cuyahoga Valley Nuclear Power Plant, hereinafter called "defendants." The plaintiff brought this action to recover damages for injuries received in an explosion at the Cuyahoga Valley Nuclear Power plant, a facility owned and operated by the defendant. Subsequent to the filing of this action, the defendant in its answer filed a counterclaim against the plaintiff for libel relating to certain remarks made to a reporter for the *Cleveland Daily News*, and which appeared in that paper in a story dated December 20, 2012.

THIS AGREEMENT has been made and entered into at Cleveland, Ohio, this 6th day of July, 2013.

WITNESSETH

WHEREAS, the parties desire to settle and adjust all matters relating to this action, all property rights, all payments in the nature of damages, or other allowances that each might be entitled to, and

WHEREAS, each of the parties is fully advised as to the extent of the injuries, the value of the property, and the prospects of the other,

NOW, THEREFORE, in consideration of the mutual covenants and agreements herein contained, the parties hereby acknowledge and agree as follows:

a. The plaintiff agrees to accept the sum of Four Hundred Thousand Dollars ($400,000) in full satisfaction of all claims in the complaint filed against the defendant in Case No. 12-CD-980 in the Common Pleas Court of Cuyahoga County, Ohio.

b. The defendants agree to pay the plaintiff the sum of Four Hundred Thousand Dollars ($400,000) payable as follows: the sum of $100,000 payable in cash when the settlement agreement is final and signed, the sum of $300,000 payable over a seven-year period with 10 percent interest per annum, with the first payment of $4,000 beginning on the first day of the month following the signing and finalizing of this agreement and continuing at a rate of $4,000 per month on the first day of every month thereafter until paid in full.

c. The plaintiff agrees that there will be no prepayment penalty should the defendants decide to pay the balance early.

EXHIBIT 14-4 Sample Settlement Agreement (*continued*)

d. Contemporaneous with the signing of this agreement, the defendants shall execute a note payable to the order of the plaintiff, providing for the payment of the $400,000 as indicated above.

e. The parties agree that with the signing and execution of this agreement and of the aforementioned note, the parties shall cause the complaint in the action to be dismissed with prejudice.

f. The parties agree that with the signing and execution of this agreement and the aforementioned note, the parties shall cause the defendant's counterclaim in this action for libel to be dismissed with prejudice.

g. The plaintiff agrees that the payment of the sum of $400,000 is also in full satisfaction for all wrongful discharge claims that the plaintiff may have against the defendants.

h. The plaintiff shall sign and execute all releases prepared by the attorney for the defendants, provided that those releases are consistent with the provisions of this agreement.

i. The defendants are to pay court costs of the action.

It is further agreed that the foregoing provisions are in full settlement of all claims that either party might assert against the other.

IN WITNESS WHEREOF, the parties hereto have executed this agreement on the day and the year first above written.

SIGNED AND ACKNOWLEDGED
IN THE PRESENCE OF

_____   _____
                                          Clark Kowalski, Plaintiff

_____   _____
                                          President and CEO
                                          Everett-Stimson Power and Light Company

_____   _____
                                          Cuyahoga Valley Nuclear Power Plant

Covenant Not to Sue

A **covenant not to sue** is a type of settlement agreement in which the plaintiff agrees not to commence or maintain an action against the defendant, but does not release the defendant from liability arising from the incident. The nonsettling tortfeasor may bring a third-party action against the settling tortfeasor for contribution.

Releases

If the facts and the legal issues involved in the lawsuit are not overly complex, the parties may be satisfied to settle the case by using a release rather than a settlement agreement. Although a release is also a contract and, as such, accomplishes essentially the same thing as a settlement agreement, the release is simpler and shorter than the settlement agreement and, therefore, much more efficient. The two most common releases are the general release and the partial release. If both parties have agreed to release each other from any and all claims, then a mutual release is appropriate.

General Release   A **general release** is used for full and final settlements. In a general release, all possible claims against all possible persons who might be liable for the plaintiff's injuries are settled. This type of release is advantageous for the defendant because the

covenant not to sue
A type of settlement agreement in which the plaintiff agrees not to commence or maintain an action against the defendant, but does not release the defendant from liability arising from the incident.

general release
A document by which a claim or right is relinquished.

EXHIBIT 14-5 Sample General Release

COURT OF COMMON PLEAS CUYAHOGA COUNTY STATE OF OHIO

CLARK KOWALSKI)
  Plaintiff,)
)
)   Civil Action No. 12-CD-980
)   GENERAL RELEASE
)
v.)
)
EVERETT-STIMSON POWER AND)
LIGHT COMPANY, et al.)
  Defendants.)
)
)
_____)

Clark Kowalski, Plaintiff, in the above case, hereby releases the Defendants and all other persons, known or unknown, who may have contributed to the incident which forms the basis of this lawsuit, from all claims and demands for any act or matter whatsoever which may have arisen or may arise in the future.

    Signed and sealed this 6th day of July, 2013, at Cleveland, Ohio.

_____

---

partial release
The relinquishment of some claims and the retention of others by a party.

mutual release
An agreement by which each party relinquishes its claims against the other.

defendant can rest assured that the plaintiff will take no further action in relation to the subject matter of the lawsuit. In the *Kowalski* case, for example, a general release would cancel all claims that Dr. Kowalski has or may have relating to the explosion at the Cuyahoga Valley Nuclear Power Plant. Exhibit 14-5 is an example of a general release form that might be used in the *Kowalski* case.

Partial Release   In a complex lawsuit involving multiple claims, a party may elect to relinquish some claims while retaining others. In such a situation a **partial release** would be appropriate. This type of release is advantageous to the plaintiff because it preserves some of the grounds that he has for bringing a subsequent lawsuit against the defendant. However, the defendant also benefits because at least a portion of its potential liability has been eliminated. For example, in the *Kowalski* case, in addition to the negligence suit for the injuries suffered as a result of the explosion at the power plant, your client may have filed an invasion of privacy suit against Everett-Stimson for making illegal tapes of his private phone conversations. Should Dr. Kowalski decide to settle the negligence suit against Everett-Stimson while maintaining the invasion of privacy suit, he would use a partial release.

Mutual Release   If the defendant in a lawsuit has filed a counterclaim against the plaintiff, then both parties in the case may find themselves in the position of relinquishing part or all of their claims in the suit. If this is the case, then a mutual release would be used. In a **mutual release**, each party relinquishes its claims against the other party. This type of release benefits both parties because each of them can be assured that all potential liability in regard to this particular lawsuit has been eliminated. For example, in the *Kowalski* case,

Everett-Stimson filed a counterclaim against Dr. Kowalski for libel, claiming that he made false statements to a newspaper reporter about certain inadequate safety procedures followed at the plant. If both Dr. Kowalski and Everett-Stimson agree to release each other, they would use a mutual release.

Form of the Release   Regardless of the type of release needed in a given case, it should include the identities of the parties, the action that gave rise to the claim, the consideration given for the release, and a specifically worded explanation of the claim that has been relinquished. The release should be signed by all parties. As in the case of the settlement agreement, if the court finds that a term of the release is vague or ambiguous, it may seek additional testimony or evidence to determine the intent of the parties at the time that they negotiated the release.

DISMISSAL, CONSENT DECREE, AND DISTRIBUTION OF FUNDS

Once a lawsuit has been settled, an order for dismissal is drawn up. As an alternative to a dismissal, the parties may prefer to file a consent decree with the court. Finally, a statement outlining how the settlement funds will be distributed should be drawn up and delivered to the client.

Dismissals

There are three major types of dismissals: a stipulated dismissal, a voluntary dismissal on notice, and a court-ordered involuntary dismissal.

Stipulated Dismissal   The parties to a lawsuit may stipulate to a dismissal at any time and on any terms. A stipulated dismissal may be either with prejudice or without prejudice. A stipulated **dismissal with prejudice** means that the claim cannot be brought to court again at any time in the future. In contrast, a stipulated **dismissal without prejudice** means that the lawsuit can be brought at another time in any court that has jurisdiction to hear the case. If the parties fail to stipulate the form of the dismissal, the court presumes that the dismissal is without prejudice. In a stipulated dismissal, it is not necessary to state the terms and the conditions of the settlement. This type of dismissal avoids having to disclose, in public records, the amount of the settlement. It also preserves the confidentiality of the terms surrounding the settlement. Exhibit 14-6 is a stipulated dismissal.

Voluntary Dismissal on Notice   Rule 41 of the Federal Rules of Civil Procedure permits a plaintiff to voluntarily dismiss a claim without order of the court by filing a motion of dismissal "at any time before service by the adverse party of an answer or of a motion for summary judgment, whichever comes first." Although not required under the terms of Rule 41, the plaintiff should serve a copy of the dismissal upon the defendant. As in the case of the stipulated dismissal, this dismissal can be with prejudice or without prejudice. The presumption is that the dismissal is without prejudice unless the court order of dismissal specifically states that it is with prejudice. Exhibit 14-7 reflects a dismissal without prejudice.

dismissal with prejudice
A court order or judgment that ends a lawsuit. No further lawsuit may be brought by the same persons on the same subject.

dismissal without prejudice
A court order or judgment that ends a lawsuit. A further lawsuit may be brought by the same persons on the same subject.

EXHIBIT 14-6 Stipulated Order of Dismissal

COURT OF COMMON PLEAS CUYAHOGA COUNTY STATE OF OHIO

CLARK KOWALSKI	)
Plaintiff,	)
	) Civil Action No. 12-CD-980
v.	) STIPULATED ORDER OF
	) DISMISSAL
	)
EVERETT-STIMSON POWER AND	)
LIGHT COMPANY, et al.	)
Defendants.	)
	)
	)

On this 6th of July, 2013, it is stipulated between counsel for the Plaintiff and counsel for the Defendants that this action be dismissed without prejudice regarding all claims and counterclaims of the parties.

_____
Attorney for Plaintiff

_____
Attorney for Defendant
Everett-Stimson Power and Light Company

_____
Attorney for Defendant
Cuyahoga Valley Nuclear Power Plant

EXHIBIT 14-7 Voluntary Dismissal without Prejudice

COURT OF COMMON PLEAS CUYAHOGA COUNTY STATE OF OHIO

CLARK KOWALSKI	)
Plaintiff,	)
	) Civil Action No. 12-CD-980
v.	) VOLUNTARY DISMISSAL
	) WITHOUT PREJUDICE
	)
EVERETT-STIMSON POWER AND	)
LIGHT COMPANY, et al.	)
Defendants.	)
	)
	)

Having reviewed the Plaintiff's Motion for Voluntary Dismissal Without Prejudice in this action, it is hereby
ORDERED this 8th day of July, 2013, that this action be dismissed without prejudice regarding all claims of the parties.

_____

EXHIBIT 14-8 Court-Ordered Involuntary Dismissal

COURT OF COMMON PLEAS CUYAHOGA COUNTY STATE OF OHIO

CLARK KOWALSKI	)	
Plaintiff,	)	Civil Action No. 12-CD-980
v.	)	COURT-ORDERED
	)	INVOLUNTARY DISMISSAL
	)	
EVERETT-STIMSON POWER AND	)	
LIGHT COMPANY, et al.	)	
Defendants.	)	
	)	

    Upon consideration of the failure of the Plaintiff to timely prosecute this action, it is hereby
    ORDERED this 8th day of July, 2013, that the complaint filed in this action against the Defendants is hereby dismissed.

Court-Ordered Involuntary Dismissal   Rule 41(a)(2) of the Federal Rules of Civil Procedure renders to the court the authority to dismiss an action if a party has failed to proceed with an action or if the party has failed to comply with a court order, stating, "unless the order states otherwise, a dismissal under this paragraph 2 is without prejudice." For example, in the *Kowalski* case, if your client fails to comply with a court order compelling him to respond to repeated discovery requests from Everett-Stimson, the case may be dismissed by the court. In addition, the court may dismiss if the plaintiff's evidence is insufficient to establish liability against the defendant. Normally, it does not result in the court's entry of a judgment. Exhibit 14-8 gives an example of a court-ordered involuntary dismissal.

consent decree

A settlement of a lawsuit or prosecution in which a person or company agrees to take certain actions without admitting fault or guilt for the situation causing the lawsuit.

Consent Decree

As an alternative to a dismissal, the parties may elect to use a consent decree. A **consent decree** outlines the details of the settlement agreed upon by the parties. The parties file the decree with the court, requesting that the judge examine the agreement and either approve or disapprove the terms that they have set forth. Generally, the judge will have no hesitation in rendering approval. Once it has been approved by the court, the consent decree is just as effective as a judgment would have been had the case gone to trial. Unlike the terms of a stipulated dismissal, the settlement terms of a consent decree become a public record. Because of the official nature of the consent decree, should one of the parties violate the terms of a decree, that party may be held in contempt of court.

Distribution of Settlement Funds

Distribution of funds normally occurs when the stipulated dismissal is signed or when the court has approved of the consent decree. A settlement proceeds statement should be

summary bench trial
A trial before a judge rather than a jury in which evidence is introduced in a condensed manner.

early neutral evaluation
An ADR technique in which litigants meet with an outside neutral person who is an expert in the subject matter of the case. The evaluator provides a nonbinding evaluation of the merits and value of the case in an effort to facilitate settlement.

prepared, similar to a closing statement in a real estate transaction, to account for the receipt of all proceeds. Such an accounting avoids later problems or questions by a party as to the payment of any expense involved in the settlement.

ALTERNATIVE DISPUTE RESOLUTION

Although negotiated settlements are the most desirable way of resolving civil disputes, parties often lack the objectivity needed to reach reasonable compromises. In the past few years the legal community has adopted a number of different methods to help parties properly evaluate their cases for settlement purposes. Usually these procedures use the services of a neutral person or group of people who try to bring the parties to an agreement or who give the parties their independent evaluation of the case. These methods or procedures are collectively referred to as alternative dispute resolution (ADR). This process is facilitated by the active and early involvement of the paralegal in tasks that are quite similar to those required for trial preparation or settlement. The paralegal may be asked to research potential mediators or arbitrators, prepare a summary of the evidence in the case, which is similar to the preparation of a settlement package, draft documents for filing the ADR request, and ultimately, documents to be used at the ADR hearing.

The various methods of ADR have proved to be an effective means of resolving civil disputes. This has benefited not only the parties to a civil dispute but also the court system. ADR occurring during the course of litigation and required by the courts is referred to as court-related alternative dispute resolution. If court-related ADR does not produce a mutually agreeable result, the parties resume litigation.

In some instances, the parties, rather than the court, initiate ADR. They can do this prior to filing a lawsuit or even during the course of litigation. Furthermore, the parties can agree to be bound by any result, giving up their right to litigate. Of course, they also can agree that the ADR procedure will not be binding. ADR voluntarily undertaken by the parties is sometimes referred to as *private or voluntary alternative dispute resolution.*

Court-Related ADR

In 1990 Congress passed the Civil Justice Reform Act of 1990 (28 U.S.C. § 1). This statute required every federal district court to develop a plan to resolve civil disputes more smoothly and swiftly. To accomplish this goal, federal trial courts either require or encourage most litigants to attempt some method of ADR as provided for in the Alternative Dispute Resolution Act of 1998 before the case can be tried. Unless the parties agree otherwise, these ADR procedures are not binding on the parties. If either side is not satisfied with the suggested method of resolving the case, that party has the right to proceed to trial. The various methods of court-related ADR include early neutral evaluation, mediation, nonbinding arbitration, summary jury trials, and **summary bench trials**.

Early Neutral Evaluation   In **early neutral evaluation**, an ADR technique developed by the courts and led by the U.S. District Courts for the Southern and Northern Districts of California, litigants meet with an outside neutral person who is an expert in the subject matter of the case. The expert selected is likely to be an attorney. During this procedure,

AUTOMATED LITIGATION SUPPORT
Document Assembly

SCENARIO

At 1 p.m. on Friday, your attorney calls you into her office. She has just received a call from Charlene Bannister, the attorney for Everett-Stimson Power and Light Company. Apparently, Everett-Stimson has made a settlement offer of $400,000. Your attorney has already talked to Dr. Kowalski, who has given his permission to accept that offer. Your attorney is anxious to conclude the settlement before Ms. Bannister leaves for the Middle East on Monday morning.

PROBLEM

Your attorney is scheduled to return to the county courthouse on another matter at 1:30 p.m. She asks that you draft all settlement documents and deliver them to the courthouse during an anticipated recess at 3 p.m. so that she can review them. You will need to fax or e-mail the documents to Ms. Bannister for approval and put them in final form for execution of the settlement documents on Saturday morning. Drafting the lengthy, complicated settlement documents is time consuming. The time to complete the project is limited. How can

you accomplish this mammoth undertaking in less than two hours?

SOLUTION

Software available to law firms today includes programs that simplify drafting long, standardized legal documents. These programs work with word processors (particularly Word and WordPerfect) and are known as "document assembly" or "document generator" programs. This is often a questionnaire-predicated software package that asks targeted questions in order to assemble a document incorporating those answers into otherwise standard paragraphs. A document generator is similar to a building block. One answer determines the next question. The word-processing part of the program then takes all the applicable paragraphs to build the settlement agreement. The speed, accuracy, and completeness that can be obtained by using the document generator cannot be obtained with standard word-processing programs. A popular assembly program is Hot Docs. You can read more about this software product on their Web site at <www.hotdocs.com>.

the parties and their counsel exchange information and position statements. They can then make brief oral presentations to the evaluator. The evaluator provides a nonbinding evaluation of the merits and value of the case in an effort to facilitate settlement. All written and oral communication in connection with this type of proceeding is confidential, and the parties and their attorneys might be asked to sign a confidentiality agreement.

nonbinding arbitration
An adversarial hearing before a neutral party or arbitrator who listens to each side and then makes a decision (an award) regarding the dispute.

Mediation   Like early neutral evaluation, mediation is a nonbinding, confidential process in which a neutral mediator (usually an attorney) tries to facilitate settlement negotiations between the parties. Unlike an early neutral evaluator, the mediator does not give an opinion regarding the case, but rather attempts to strengthen the communication between the parties. The mediator also tries to get the parties to examine the strengths and weaknesses of their sides of the case.

Nonbinding Arbitration   **Nonbinding arbitration** is an adversarial hearing before a neutral party or arbitrator who listens to each side and then makes a decision (an *award*) regarding the dispute. The arbitrator is selected by the parties from a list of candidates provided by the court. Most cases have one arbitrator, but sometimes a case is heard by a three-person panel. Prior to the hearing, each party may submit written statements summarizing its case, identifying significant factual and legal issues, and listing proposed

summary jury trial
A trial in which the parties present their evidence before a six-person or eight-person jury which renders a nonbinding decision.

negotiation
A situation in which the parties discuss their problems with one another.

witnesses. At the arbitration hearing, each side puts on evidence. Based on the evidence, the arbitrator or arbitration panel makes an award or judgment. Either party can then reject the award and demand a trial in court. If neither party rejects the award, it becomes a final judgment in the case.

Summary Jury Trial

In a **summary jury trial**, the parties present their evidence before a six-person or eight-person jury, which renders a nonbinding decision. This format typically includes opening and closing statements by counsel for each party and a short narrative of each party's position. There is generally no live testimony in this proceeding. Because of the summary nature of the trial, the jury is given a limited amount of time in which to deliberate. Jury members are encouraged to come to a consensus, but if they cannot, their opinions and findings are relayed to the attorneys trying the case. A summary jury trial requires more time and expense than the other methods of ADR and thus is not favored, except in extraordinary cases.

Summary Bench Trial

A summary bench trial resembles a summary jury trial except that the case is tried before a judge rather than a jury. Again, evidence often is introduced in a condensed manner so as to avoid the lengthy process of an actual trial.

Private ADR

Parties often wish to avoid the court process in its entirety and look to ADR as a means to accomplish this. In many instances, the parties agree to be bound by alternative dispute resolution, although in some cases they do not. Methods of private ADR include negotiation, mediation, binding arbitration, minitrial, and private judging.

Negotiation

Probably the most common method of resolving disputes is negotiation. **Negotiation** involves the disputing parties' discussing their problems with one another. If an agreement is reached, then the negotiation results in a settlement. In most cases, negotiation starts before the parties file any lawsuit in court. If the parties are able to reach an agreement at an early stage in the negotiations, a lawsuit may never be filed. However, if the parties are unable to reach an early settlement, they often continue their informal negotiations even though one party has filed a lawsuit.

Mediation

Mediation voluntarily undertaken by the parties resembles mediation proceedings that are ordered by the court as part of its ADR procedures. The only difference is in the selection of the mediator. In private mediation, the mediator is selected without the assistance of the court. Parties generally tend to use mediation in a case in which they believe they can reach an agreement with the assistance of a neutral third party, or when there will be a relationship between the parties that continues after resolution of the conflict. Another positive factor in the choice of mediation to resolve a dispute is that it is available earlier than traditional litigation, in which a trial setting may be several years after the filing of a lawsuit. Inherent with the potential time saved by choosing mediation over litigation is the resulting money saved by the potentially shorter time period required to resolve a dispute. The American Arbitration Association Web site offers an online mediation process for disputes involving only two parties, where neither the claim nor the counterclaim exceeds $10,000. The total cost for the online mediation is $200, including the mediator's charge. Most online mediations are concluded within 30 days.

FINDING IT on the Internet

The American Arbitration Association maintains a Web site on the Internet at the following address: <**http://www.adr.org/**>. Access the Web site and review the types of information available at this site.

a. Access the site and click on the "Neutrals" tab for potential arbitrators for the *Kowalski* case discussed in this chapter. Review the credentials of the listed individuals to find an arbitrator with a background in environmental law.

b. As an alternative assignment, locate a "Demand for Arbitration" form on the American Arbitration Association's Web site and complete it, based on the facts of the *Kowalski* case.

Use the 'Lectric Law Library search engine entitled "Law Looker-Upper" at <**http://www.lectlaw.com /search.html**> to perform the assignments above. Write a report on the differences between information available on the subject of arbitration at these two sites.

Mediation Statement   A **mediation statement** is a statement of facts and legal argument for your case. It should contain information as to what you anticipate the opposing party believes its key supporting facts and legal arguments are, and why they are not supported by the evidence.

mediation statement
A statement of facts and legal argument for your case.

This position paper is intended to give the mediator some perspective on any settlement history. It should include information about any underlying personal or emotional issues. For example, assume that a family member of one party was formerly in a partnership with the other party, and the partnership ended on a sour note, financially and personally. That information might reflect a personal reason that one party will be reluctant to settle with the other, unless it is a settlement favorable to the party who perceives himself as having been hurt by the other party.

If there are written documents or pleadings that would be helpful to the mediator, attach them to your mediation statement. In addition, you should either highlight or summarize them to indicate their significance in your view of the case.

Binding Arbitration   A binding arbitration hearing resembles a nonbinding arbitration hearing. However, in addition to the binding nature of the decision, the preliminary steps in this procedure are substantially different. First, the parties must agree to binding arbitration. That is, the parties must agree to give up their right to sue and agree to accept the arbitrator's decision. This is often done before any dispute has arisen and is usually found in a written contract in a clause providing that "in the event of a dispute, the parties agree that it shall be resolved through arbitration." Such provisions are becoming common in business and commercial transactions. Arbitration clauses are also frequently found in automobile insurance policies under the uninsured motorist provisions. Also, many health care providers are asking their patients to sign such agreements.

A second difference between binding and nonbinding arbitration is the way the hearing is set up. In binding arbitration, one of the disputing parties usually requests in writing that the dispute be arbitrated. This writing may loosely resemble a complaint. Because the court is not a party to binding arbitration, the parties must formulate the details of the

baseball arbitration
Each side presents its evidence to the arbitrator, each party informs the arbitrator what one number it believes the award should be, and the arbitrator must choose one of those proposed awards, based on the evidence heard.

night baseball arbitration
The parties submit their proposals in confidence to the arbitrator after evidence is presented, the arbitrator then assigns a value to the case, and the parties agree to accept the high or low figure closest to the arbitrator's value.

med-arb
The dispute is mediated first, and if the dispute is not settled, the parties then move into the arbitration phase, which would generally be binding.

arbitration hearing, including selection of the arbitrator, on their own. For parties who are already disputing, this can be a major problem. Various organizations exist that can help the parties with this. One of the most popular is the American Arbitration Association, which has adopted a set of rules to be followed for maintaining the arbitration if the parties agree. Those rules are available at the American Arbitration Association's Web site, <http://www.adr.org/>. Once a binding arbitration award is made, it is usually final.

The paralegal should also be familiar with the Uniform Arbitration Act of 2000 (UAA), which has been adopted by a significant number of states. Check <http://www.law.cornell.edu/> to determine whether Ohio has adopted the Uniform Arbitration Act. Note any differences between the Federal Arbitration Act and the UAA.

High-Low Arbitration

Also known as *bracketed arbitration*, this is an arbitration in which the parties agree in advance on "high-low" parameters within which the arbitrator may render an award. An arbitrator may or may not be advised of the amounts of the parameters, or even the fact that the parameters exist.

Baseball Arbitration

In **baseball arbitration** (also known as *final offer arbitration*), after each side presents its evidence to the arbitrator, each party informs the arbitrator what one number it believes the award should be. The arbitrator must choose one of those proposed awards, based on the evidence heard. The arbitrator does not have the authority to select another figure. As reflected in the name, this concept originated in Major League Baseball when a club and player could not agree on a salary figure and under certain circumstances could submit their respective figures to a sole arbitrator who was bound to pick one of the submitted figures. This type of arbitration is attractive to companies or parties who have a long-term relationship, and who anticipate continuing that relationship.

Night Baseball Arbitration

In **night baseball arbitration**, the parties submit their proposals in confidence to the arbitrator, in a sealed envelope or otherwise, after evidence is presented. The arbitrator then assigns a value to the case, and the parties agree to accept the high or low figure closest to the arbitrator's value.

Med-Arb

In **med-arb**, the dispute is mediated first, and if the dispute is not settled, the parties move into the arbitration phase, which would generally be binding. This process offers two benefits—the opportunity for a negotiated resolution through mediation and the finality of arbitration.

Med-arb begins with a written agreement from both parties to participate in and be bound by the med-arb process through either a mediated or an arbitrated outcome. If the dispute is successfully mediated, it is then reduced to writing. If there is an impasse in the mediation, the mediator changes roles and becomes an arbitrator. Either at the end of the mediation or at an agreed later date, the arbitrator receives evidence from the parties and renders a binding arbitration decision. In some instances, the parties stipulate in advance that the arbitrator's decision cannot exceed the high-low parameters discussed previously.

A principal advantage of med-arb is that it reduces both the delay and the cost involved in retaining a second neutral person to resolve the dispute. Because the neutral person has conducted the mediation, he is better equipped to render a cost-effective, expeditious decision.

Arb-Med   A recent development in the world of ADR is the **arb-med**, in which an arbitrator is allowed to act as a mediator after hearing the arbitration. At the end of the arbitration, the arbitrator makes a binding decision that is memorialized, but not disclosed to the parties. The parties then mediate. If not successful in mediation, the arbitrator announces a decision and the parties are bound by the decision.

One difficulty inherent in the use of a hybrid type of mediation, either med-arb or arb-med, is the different approach and skills required for each. Not every mediator is qualified to be a good arbitrator, and the reverse is also true. Both parties need to have confidence that the individual they select for the mediation and/or arbitration process has the requisite skills for both.

Discovery in Arbitration   Arbitration is less costly, both in terms of money and time, because it normally has less extensive discovery than traditional litigation. However, virtually all institutional arbitration rules, such as the commercial rules of the American Arbitration Association (AAA) and the Federal Arbitration Act (FAA), permit sufficient discovery for purposes of a fair decision from the arbitrator or arbitrators.

The determining factor as to how extensive the discovery process will be in any arbitration is the arbitration agreement itself.

Discovery under the American Arbitration Association Rules   Discovery under the American Arbitration Association commercial rules is referred to as an "Exchange of Information" and is governed by Rule 21 of AAA. Parties or the arbitrator may request discovery, but the arbitrator must approve any requests by the parties.

The arbitrator may subpoena witnesses or documents at the request of a party, or independently. A "person who is authorized by law to subpoena witnesses or documents may sign a subpoena in an arbitration," under the AAA rules. In the case of an arbitration panel, the majority of the panel makes the decision on whether to issue a subpoena. The parties to the arbitration are responsible for preparing the subpoena, serving it, and having it enforced. Enforcement is governed by an appropriate court of competent jurisdiction.

Discovery under the Federal Arbitration Act   The FAA rules may apply to arbitration in the following instances:

1. The arbitration agreement specified such discovery.
2. If the contract did not specify the applicable law and the contract involved commerce and did not implicate one of the exclusions listed in FAA § 1.

Section 7 of the FAA governs discovery. It also permits arbitrators to punish those who fail to obey a discovery directive.

Minitrial   **Minitrials** are proceedings in which high-level executives of all the parties are brought together to hear a summary version of each other's case as presented by its lawyers and presided over by a neutral party (often a retired judge). The presentation is generally outside the courtroom. After hearing the evidence, the executives are encouraged to engage in settlement discussion. This is a nonbinding type of proceeding.

Private Judging   In recent years, especially in areas where the courts are very congested, parties have resorted to hiring their own private judge to try the case. A trial occurs in much the same way as it does in formal litigation. The major advantage to the

arb-med
An arbitrator is allowed to act as a mediator after hearing the arbitration.

minitrial
A proceeding in which high level executives of all the parties are brought together to hear a summary version of each other's case as presented by its lawyers and presided over by a neutral party (often a retired judge).

parties is that they are not restricted by the court calendar. Trial can be scheduled at a time convenient for the parties and the judge. In most instances, these private judges are retired trial and appellate court judges. The parties can agree to be bound by the judge's decision, excluding all rights of appeal, if they want to make the process completely final. Absent such an agreement, the parties have limited rights to appeal this judge's decision directly to the higher court.

SUMMARY

- A settlement is an agreement or a contract between parties that terminates their civil dispute. Most civil cases end in a settlement. The preliminary investigative work in the settlement process is often the responsibility of the paralegal, and it includes obtaining a personal history of the client, a preliminary assessment of the client's present health, and a medical history of the client. In addition, the paralegal may be required to calculate the damages in the case. The paralegal may also have to assist the attorney with some collateral areas to get an accurate picture of the probability of the client's prevailing should the case go all the way to trial.

- Once the preliminary investigative work has been completed, the information should be pulled together into a settlement report. This report must convince the defendant that a settlement would be in its best interests. Depending on the situation, the paralegal may be charged with writing a settlement summary, a settlement letter, or a settlement brochure.

- A settlement agreement is actually a contract between two or more parties. As such, it must meet all the legal requirements of a contract, including the voluntary mutual assent of the parties, the elements of consideration, legality, and capacity. If the facts and the legal issues involved in the lawsuit are not overly complex, the parties to the suit may be satisfied to settle the case by using a release rather than a settlement agreement. The two most common releases are the general release and the partial release. If both parties have agreed to release each other from any and all claims, a mutual release is appropriate.

- There are three major types of dismissals: a stipulated dismissal, a voluntary dismissal on notice, and a court-ordered involuntary dismissal. The parties to a lawsuit may stipulate to a dismissal at any time and on any terms. A stipulated dismissal may be either with prejudice or without prejudice. Rule 41 of the Federal Rules of Civil Procedure permits a plaintiff to voluntarily dismiss a claim without order of the court by filing a motion of dismissal. The court has the authority to dismiss an action if a party has failed to proceed with an action, if the party has failed to comply with a court order, or if the plaintiff's evidence is insufficient to establish liability against the defendant. As an alternative to a dismissal, the parties may elect to use a consent decree. A consent decree outlines the details of the settlement agreed upon by the parties. The parties file the decree with the court, requesting that the judge examine the agreement and either approve or disapprove the terms that they have set forth. When the stipulated dismissal is signed or when the court has approved the consent decree, a settlement proceeds statement should be prepared to account for the receipt of all proceeds.

- Alternative dispute resolution involves several different procedures used by parties to a civil dispute as a means of resolving their dispute without the necessity of trial. Such procedures can occur prior to or subsequent to any lawsuit being filed. Sometimes these procedures provide an exclusive remedy for the parties. Other times the procedures are only an attempt to avoid trial. ADR in connection with a pending case is often referred to as court-related ADR. ADR voluntarily undertaken by the parties is sometimes referred to as private or voluntary ADR. The various methods of court-related ADR include early neutral evaluation, mediation, nonbinding arbitration, summary jury trial, and summary bench trial. The methods of voluntary ADR include negotiation, mediation, arbitration, minitrial, and private judging.

KEY TERMS

arb-med	high-low agreement	partial release
baseball arbitration	loan receipt agreement	settlement
consent decree	Mary Carter agreement	settlement agreement
consideration	med-arb	summary bench trial
covenant not to sue	mediation statement	summary jury trial
damages	minitrial	settlement brochure
dismissal with prejudice	mutual release	settlement conference
dismissal without prejudice	negotiation	settlement letter
early neutral evaluation	night baseball arbitration	settlement summary
general release	nonbinding arbitration	tortfeasor

REVIEW QUESTIONS

1. What is a settlement?
2. What are some of the preliminary decisions surrounding settlement?
3. List areas that must be investigated before a settlement offer is made.
4. Describe the difference between a settlement summary and a settlement letter.
5. How does a settlement brochure differ from a settlement summary and a settlement letter?
6. What is a settlement agreement?
7. What is a release? What types of releases are available?
8. Describe the advantages of a stipulated dismissal.
9. When is a voluntary dismissal on notice allowed?
10. Under what circumstances can a court order an involuntary dismissal?
11. How does a consent decree differ from a stipulated dismissal?
12. What is a settlement proceeds statement?
13. Describe the various methods of court-related ADR.
14. Define the various methods of private or voluntary ADR.

CHAPTER EXERCISES

Where necessary, check with your instructor prior to starting any of these exercises.

1. Review the laws of your state and find all laws that deal with settlements. Check your local court rules to see if there are any specific rules of court in your area regulating settlements.

2. Prepare an interoffice memorandum in which you explain the preliminary investigative work that you would have to do in the *Kowalski* case.

3. Check with your local bar association to see if any ADR services exist in your area. If so, contact them and determine what services they provide.

4. Assume that Dr. Kowalski has decided to settle the negligence suit against Everett-Stimson while maintaining the invasion of privacy suit. Prepare a partial release to facilitate that partial settlement.

5. Assume that both Dr. Kowalski and Everett-Stimson agree to release each other from all claims in the Kowalski litigation. Prepare a mutual release to accomplish that settlement.

CHAPTER PROJECT

Review the *Kowalski* case in the opening Commentary. Recall that Dr. Kowalski has elected to sue the Cuyahoga Valley Nuclear Power Plant and its owner and operator, the Everett-Stimson Power and Light Company, for the injuries he sustained in the explosion of a hydraulic pump. Also recall that he is considering an additional lawsuit for invasion of privacy against Everett-Stimson. Note also that Everett-Stimson has brought a counterclaim against him for libel. Draft a memo in which you explore the factors to be taken into consideration in a decision regarding the possibility of a settlement offer.

THE *BENNETT* CASE
Assignment for Chapter 14: Drafting a Settlement Letter

Substantial evidence exists supporting Alice Bennett's claims. Your attorney now has copies of several employment evaluations that are all excellent. Several of her prior coworkers, including Martha Yee, confirm that she was a competent and efficient acting manager. None of them could understand why she was not hired permanently for the position. Her physician, Dr. Susan Bell, a board-certified psychiatrist, has written a report detailing the various physical and mental symptoms experienced by the plaintiff. The doctor attributes these to her work experience. To date her medical bills total $10,000. Bennett has been unemployed since she was terminated approximately 18 months ago. The doctor feels that she may be able to return to work in six months. In the meantime, she has no income. You have been asked to draft a letter to the defendant requesting settlement in the amount of $1 million. Before drafting the letter, review 42 U.S.C. § 2000e regarding Title VII claims as well as the complaint filed on Ms. Bennett's behalf.

THE *DOUGLASS FINANCIAL SERVICES INC.* CASE
Assignment for Chapter 14: Drafting a Mediation Statement or Brief

Your attorney advises you that the parties have agreed to go through voluntary mediation in an effort to settle the case. The mediation will not be binding, but the attorney wants to make a good faith effort to resolve the matter. You are asked to help the attorney prepare a mediation statement. The statement itself will have the following sections:

1. Statement of key facts
2. Statement of factual and legal issues
3. Legal arguments in favor of defendant, Douglass Financial, Inc.

The attorney will prepare the legal argument, but asks you to draft a statement of key facts and a statement of factual and legal issues. You are also asked to try to find a sample mediation statement or brief from your state.

CHAPTER OUTLINE

THE *DELGADO* CASE

You have been called into a meeting with your attorney to discuss the details of an upcoming trial. The trial involves your client, a certified public accountant named Joseph Delgado, who was injured in a fire last year while he was conducting an audit at the laboratories and main offices of BioMed Pharmaceuticals, Inc. The company has denied liability for Delgado's injuries by claiming that all maintenance and security work done in that building was performed by two independent companies, Diversified Security Solutions, Inc., and the Rawlings Maintenance Corporation. Although the trial date is three months away, your attorney is concerned about the heavy workload that she has in several other cases. Therefore, she requests that you immediately begin to assist in preparing the *Delgado* case for trial. Your responsibilities will include handling the litigation file organization, preparing a trial notebook, coordinating witness and exhibit preparation, and assisting in obtaining jury information.

In the first two parts of this book we explored the litigation process, the beginning of a lawsuit, the pleadings, and motion practice. In Part III you were introduced to the details of the discovery process. This preliminary work and the discovery process can produce volumes of documents as well as significant information about the facts in the case, all of which must be organized before trial.

This chapter introduces the preparations that must be made before the trial. After reading this chapter, you will be able to:

- explain the paralegal's role in organizing the litigation files and assisting with amending pleadings.
- describe the purpose and content of the trial notebook.
- outline the paralegal's role in assisting the attorney with preparing witnesses for trial.
- list the standards by which a proposed trial exhibit should be tested.
- explain the paralegal's participation in preparing trial briefs.
- determine the paralegal's logistical duties in preparing for trial.
- outline the paralegal's role in preparation for a focus group or mock trial.
- describe the paralegal's role in the jury process.
- discuss the paralegal's function at trial.

PRELIMINARY PREPARATION FOR TRIAL

The preparation for trial actually begins at the initial client interview. It is at this point that the attorney begins to develop the **theory of the case**, the plan for where you are going with the case and how you will shape the law and the facts to achieve your ultimate destination. The late great baseball player, Yogi Berra, has been credited with the quote, "If you don't know where you're going, when you get there, you'll be lost." That statement is especially true in the planning and execution of trial strategy. As a paralegal, you may be

theory of the case
the plan for where you are going with the case and how you will shape the law and the facts to achieve your ultimate destination.

involved in establishing the theory of the case. Perhaps when your attorney first assigned you to work on the case, she began by saying, "This case is about…." Many attorneys have difficulty articulating the theory of the case. They often equate the theory with a claim or defense. That is the beginning point. For example, in the *Bennett* case featured in this text, you might begin with the complaint in Appendix B. The theory should be succinct, credible, interesting, utilize common sense, and include the emotions of the client's case. Once you have developed the theory of the case, you are ready to identify witnesses and exhibits through which you can flesh out this theory.

proof chart

a list of the elements of the case that must be proved, witnesses to prove the various elements, exhibit/s that should be introduced to prove up the element, and any anticipated objection/s to the exhibit.

A **proof chart** is a list of the elements of the case that must be proved, witnesses to prove the element, the exhibit to be utilized, and any anticipated objection(s) to the exhibit. Completion of a proof chart enables the attorney or paralegal to determine any gaps in establishing their theory of the case. Exhibit 15-1 is an example of a proof chart.

Each of the processes and tasks that we have examined thus far in the text advances the prosecution or the defense of the case. Although most cases are settled or dismissed before reaching the trial stage, you must proceed on the assumption that eventually the

EXHIBIT 15-1 Proof Chart

ISSUE	WITNESS	EXHIBIT	OBJECTION

case will reach trial. Some preparation tasks may be performed several months in advance of trial, whereas others must be handled at the last minute.

Whatever the case, the client will prevail only if you and your attorney are thoroughly prepared for all eventualities. To insure the success of such preparation, the paralegal should develop a trial preparation checklist of all the tasks that must be performed before the trial and the time frame for completion of those tasks. Regular monitoring and updating of this checklist will ensure that the case is truly ready for the trial. Exhibit 15-2 is an example of a trial preparation checklist.

EXHIBIT 15-2 Trial Preparation Checklist

Three to Six Months Prior to Trial Date

1. Place the trial date on the law firm's docket system and on the individual calendars of the trial team. Reschedule any conflicts within the docket or individual calendars.
2. Schedule regular trial team meetings.
3. Review and docket all entries on a trial scheduling or case management order.
4. Review all discovery to determine whether any supplementation is required for witnesses or documents and coordinate any necessary supplementation.
5. Check with the attorney for additional depositions that should be scheduled.
6. Begin logistical planning, particularly if the trial is out of town. Contact hotels, conference centers, copy vendors, and so forth.
7. Coordinate technological requirements for the trial with the trial team and the firm's litigation support staff.
8. If exhibit enlargements, computer-generated exhibits, or models made to scale are required, begin the process of ensuring that these are under way in time for review well before the beginning of trial.
9. Review litigation files and organize.
10. Complete trial notebook.
11. Finalize trial logistics, including travel, hotels, conference rooms, and food arrangements.

Four to Six Weeks Prior to Trial

1. Review pleadings and check with the attorney regarding any amendments necessary. Assist with drafting to the extent requested by the attorney.
2. Begin the preparation of exhibit lists and witness lists.
3. Coordinate deposition designations with the trial team.
4. Assist with the drafting of the pretrial order, if requested by your attorney.
5. Assist with drafting pretrial and trial motions, including motions in limine and voir dire, if requested to do so by your attorney.
6. Coordinate mock jury or focus group.
7. Visit the courtroom, if possible, to review space available, placement of electronic equipment, and so forth.

Two to Three Weeks Prior to Trial

1. Contact the client and other witnesses regarding the trial schedule and logistics. Schedule meetings to prepare for their trial appearances.
2. Prepare trial subpoenas.
3. Conduct jury investigation if the jury pool data are available.
4. Continue the preparation of trial exhibits and trial notebook.

EXHIBIT 15-2 Trial Preparation Checklist (*continued*)

One Week Prior to Trial

1. Verify service of trial subpoenas.
2. Finalize logistics such as hotel rooms, travel arrangements, and transportation of trial materials to the courthouse.
3. Confirm arrangements for expedited or regular trial transcripts with the court reporter.
4. Assist with cite checking of trial brief.

One Day Prior to Trial

1. Conduct meetings with trial team and office support personnel who will be assisting at trial.
2. Review all trial exhibits and trial notebooks for accuracy and completeness.
3. Assist with final changes to motions and/or trial brief.
4. Check with the clerk's office regarding potential jury pool information, and prepare juror information sheets or summary sheets, as necessary.

---

pretrial conference

Meeting between the presiding judge and attorneys to facilitate both the preparation for and management of a trial. There may be two such conferences, one several weeks before the trial and the final pretrial conference immediately before trial.

Pretrial Conference

Rule 16(c) of the Federal Rules of Civil Procedure provides for a **pretrial conference**, a meeting between the presiding judge and attorneys, to facilitate both the preparation for and management of a trial. There may be two such conferences, one several weeks before the trial and the final pretrial conference immediately before trial. Pretrial conferences narrow and simplify the legal and fact issues of the case. The judge may ask for briefing on particularly difficult legal issues in the case. All uncontroverted facts will be included in the pretrial order entered by the court.

Stipulations for the handling of evidence is another topic of the pretrial conference. Parties may agree to the use of copies of records rather than originals. In addition, they may stipulate to the foundation of certain business records so that the custodian does not have to appear in court to identify the records.

The initiation of a summary judgment motion is often considered at the pretrial conference, if the judge or magistrate believes that an issue or the case as a whole may be disposed of through this means. Scheduling of oral argument for the summary judgment motion may also be handled at that time. During the pretrial conference, the judge may suggest Alternative Dispute Resolution (ADR), and increasingly more courts' rules now require the parties to undertake nonbinding ADR before the case may be tried. Rule 16(c)(2)(I) of the Federal Rules of Civil Procedure authorizes the presiding judge to encourage settlement negotiations. It is not unusual for a judge to attempt to mediate or to appoint a magistrate to mediate the case.

Litigation File Organization

One of the tasks in trial preparation that can be completed during the preliminary stages of litigation is the organization of the litigation files. Naturally, it is best if the files are kept current as the case develops. For example, each time a pleading is filed by either side it should immediately be placed in the pleadings binder. However, the hectic pace of most law firms will challenge even the most efficient paralegal. Consequently, not all litigation files are kept up to date. The setting of the trial date, however, signals the need to organize the litigation files. This will mean reviewing all the pleadings and motions that have been filed in the case. It will also necessitate locating all documents, records, deposition transcripts, interrogatories, and admissions generated during discovery. You may have to transcribe all witness interview notes that you have not yet examined. Reviewing the litigation files at an early stage will probably add a number of items to the to-do list on the trial preparation checklist (see Exhibit 15-2).

Amending the Pleadings

One problem that might surface during organization of the litigation files is the need to amend the pleadings in the case before expiration of the time to do so. According to Rule 15(a)(1) of the Federal Rules of Civil Procedure, once a case has been placed on the trial calendar, the pleadings in that case can be amended only with permission of the court or with the written consent of the opposing party. Fortunately, most state courts do not have this strict requirement. However, it is best to check local court rules to determine the procedure that must be followed should you find that a pleading in your case must be amended after the trial date has been set.

Motions at the Beginning of Trial

The paralegal may be asked to assist with drafting trial motions for inclusion in the trial notebook. A **motion in limine** is one of the first motions filed before or at the beginning of trial. "In limine" is defined as "at the threshold." Such motions are frequently used to prevent opposing counsel from introducing certain evidence at trial. Motions in limine often attempt to exclude an opponent's expert witness or an expert opinion. Success in this area can severely damage the opposition's case and possibility of success. For instance, your attorney might prepare a motion in limine to exclude one of the opposition's expert witnesses on the grounds that his only security experience has been in the area of residential property security services. She might argue that security requirements for a 40-building condominium development are not applicable to the demands of a multi-acre commercial park, such as the one which included the building in which your client was injured.

The Trial Notebook

The trial notebook, a vital part of any trial preparation, usually is the paralegal's responsibility. The **trial notebook** is a binder that contains, in complete or summary form, everything necessary to prosecute or defend a case. Preparation of the trial notebook, like the preparation of the trial itself, begins with the initial client interview. The contents and the organization of the trial notebook are determined by the individual preferences of the attorney or the paralegal. The form of the notebook is dictated by the type of case, the number of pleadings, the complexity of the legal issues, the number of exhibits and witnesses, and the anticipated length of the trial. However, most trial notebooks include the following basic sections: (1) information regarding the parties and the attorneys; (2) the pleadings, motions, and discovery responses; (3) information regarding the witnesses; (4) information regarding the expert witnesses; (5) document indices; (6) deposition summaries; (7) chronology; (8) the cast of characters; (9) legal research; (10) trial exhibits; (11) jury profiles and instructions; (12) the trial outline; (13) the attorney's notes; and (14) the "things to do" list. It is not unusual for a paralegal to maintain a hard copy of the trial notebook and a computerized version also. In those instances, caution must be taken to ensure that updates and deletions are made in both.

motion in limine
One of the first motions filed before or at the beginning of trial, frequently used to prevent opposing counsel from introducing certain evidence at trial.

trial notebook
A binder that contains, in complete or summary form, everything necessary to prosecute or defend a case.

curriculum vitae
A list of an expert's credentials, including each educational and professional credential, and a summary of publications and research projects.

Information Regarding the Parties and the Attorneys   The first entry in the trial notebook is a list of all the parties and attorneys involved in the lawsuit. This list can also function as a service list for pleadings. In addition to the names and addresses of the attorneys, the list should include the telephone numbers, fax numbers, and e-mail addresses of their law firms. Updating this list is extremely important. Each time a pleading is received, you should check to determine that the attorney's name, firm, address, and client represented are correct on your list of parties and attorneys. If you do not take this simple precaution, you may send a pleading to the wrong address or to an attorney who has withdrawn from a case. Such an error is not only embarrassing and costly, but it is also grounds for a potential malpractice action.

Pleadings, Motions, and Discovery Responses   In a simple case, a copy of all the pleadings, motions, and discovery responses would be filed in the trial notebook. However, in a complex case only pertinent pleadings, such as the complaint and the answer, would be placed in the notebook because of space limitations. Separate notebooks of motions and discovery responses should be prepared in advance of trial and updated with new filings.

Witnesses   This section should include a list of all witnesses, their telephone numbers, addresses, fax numbers, and e-mail addresses, and a copy of their trial subpoena, if one was issued. A copy of potential trial exhibits to be introduced through this witness should be placed within this section of the trial notebook. If possible, it also includes a summary of the factual areas that each witness is expected to cover in his testimony. Your attorney will benefit from an outline of the questions that the witnesses will be asked at trial. Exhibit 15-3 is an example of a witness list that contains the type of information that will help you locate a witness rapidly, either before or during the trial.

Expert Witnesses   At the beginning of this section, place a list of all expert witnesses that each side intends to call at trial. As in the case of the factual witnesses, include their addresses, telephone numbers, fax numbers, and e-mail addresses. Copies of each expert's curriculum vitae should also be included. A **curriculum vitae** lists the expert's professional credentials. The list will include each witness's educational and professional credentials, as well as a summary of his publications and research projects. If the witness has written any reports regarding the present case, they should be included in this section. You may want to include a list of any other cases in which the expert has testified and a list of all documents or other materials that the expert has reviewed for the case. Major components of this section are the potential questions that each expert will be asked at trial and a copy of potential trial exhibits to be used with the expert witnesses.

Document Index   In a simple case, the trial notebook may contain all documents that are produced in the case. However, in more complex cases, an index of all documents produced by each party should be sufficient. A comprehensive but clear document index will enable you to quickly yet unobtrusively locate a document during trial, when time and discretion are of the essence.

Deposition Summaries   A complex case may require a separate binder for the deposition summaries. You will recall from our discussion in Chapter 9 on depositions that a deposition summary is a written record that reduces many hours of testimony to a few

EXHIBIT 15-3 Witness List

NAME AND ADDRESS	TEL#	ROLE	SUBPOENA SERVED/ RETURNED
Mario Montalvo	542–4999	CEO of Diversified Security Solutions Finances and Organization of Diversified Security Solutions	3/8/13 3/15/13
Maria Mendez	756–9989	Secretary at Bio-Med Pharmaceuticals Witness to fire	3/15/13 3/19/13
Carl Loggia	756–9989	CPA at Bio-Med Pharmaceuticals Finances of Bio-Med	3/15/13 3/19/13
Lon Robertson	756–9989	Janitor at Diversified Security Solutions and Rawlings Maintenance Witness to fire	3/15/13 3/18/13
Sam Guzman	756–9989	CEO of Bio-Med Pharmaceuticals Organization Chart for Bio-Med Pharmaceuticals	3/15/13 3/25/13
Angie Guzman	756–9989	Treasurer of Bio-Med Pharmaceuticals Organization Chart for Bio-Med Pharmaceuticals Finances of Bio-Med Pharmaceuticals	3/15/13 3/25/13
Alex Rawlings	481–9997	CEO of Rawlings Maintenance Organization Chart for Rawlings Finances of Rawlings Vice-President of Bio-Med Pharmaceuticals Organization Chart for Bio-Med Pharmaceuticals Finances of Bio-Med Pharmaceuticals	3/15/13 3/25/13
Mercedes Herrera	481–9997	Treasurer of Rawlings Maintenance Organization Chart for Rawlings Finances of Rawlings Vice-President of Bio-Med Pharmaceuticals Organization Chart for Bio-Med Pharmaceuticals Finances of Bio-Med Pharmaceuticals	3/15/13 3/25/13
Rachel Friedman, M.D.	825–1409	Physician at Parkland County Hospital	3/15/13 3/18/13
Jay Kellerman, M.D.	825–1409	Physician at Parkland County Hospital	3/15/13 3/18/13
Abe Greenstein	825–3800	Professor at Auburn University	3/16/13 3/18/13

concisely drawn, easily read, and quickly understood pages. The three types of deposition summaries are the page-line deposition summary, the topical deposition summary, and the chronological summary. The page-line deposition summary covers testimony as it occurred in the deposition itself. The topical deposition summary organizes the material into specific subject areas. Finally, the chronological deposition summary organizes the testimony according to a particular time sequence. A complex case involving numerous depositions would require an index of these summaries. The index should be arranged in alphabetical order by the last name of each deponent.

Chronology   Another important tool in the trial notebook is the chronology—the listing of what happened, when it happened, where it happened, and who was involved. A properly constructed chronology includes information regarding the source of each fact. However, a chronology is more than a document index sorted by date. A chronology moves from the beginning of the case—the first client interview—and includes the most current information on the case up to the time of trial. Use database software, not word-processing software, to create your chronology. If your firm has a multiuser database, several trial team members can simultaneously enter, edit, or review the facts in the chronology. The most important benefit of a database-generated chronology is the ability to quickly make choices in what is to be printed from a voluminous chronology—perhaps facts dealing with a particular issue, witness, or time frame. When reviewing documents, depositions, and so forth for preparation of a chronology, list facts, not documents. For each fact, begin by entering the information reflected in Exhibit 15-4. Include both prospective facts and disputed facts in your chronology. You may not have a document source at the time of the entry, but that can be added when a document is subsequently produced or a deposition of a witness is taken. Certain facts in a chronology may not have an associated date. Use "N/A" in the date column. When the chronology is sorted, all facts for which a date is inappropriate will be sorted together.

In addition to some facts that have no associated date, many facts in your chronology may have an incomplete date. For example, the client has stated in his deposition that a meeting took place in March 2012 or that the decision to sell the company was made in "the fall of 2012." The entry is critical, and should be entered into the computer as 03/00/12. Such an entry is a reminder that further research is needed to establish the exact date of the meeting. A separate column might be added to the chronology form to indicate the disputed or undisputed status of each entry.

A chronology should include issues in addition to dates and facts. The majority of cases involve multiple and often complex issues. Apply the issues previously developed by your attorney to the chronology, perhaps through a column entitled "Related Issues." Creating a link between facts and issues in a chronology facilitates isolating facts relating only to a particular issue. From the issue list, develop the chronology to include facts currently known about an issue and a "wish list" of facts. This might include testimony that you "wish" you could obtain from a treating physician, accident witness, or other key players in a case. A chronology reflects important and trivial facts. An additional column in the chronology might be used to "rate" the significance of a fact to a case. As the trial approaches, you must review the chronology for completeness by checking key documents, pleadings, witness interviews, depositions, and exhibits to make certain that all dates from these sources have been placed in the chronology.

The Cast of Characters   The cast of characters is a roster of all key participants in the case. This list can be developed from witness interviews, documents, depositions, exhibits, and pleadings. As is true of the chronology, you must be careful to update the cast of characters as new information is received.

EXHIBIT 15-4 Chronology of the Case

DATE	EVENT	SOURCE	NOTES
4/25/05	Incorporation of Diversified Security Solutions, Inc.	Secretary of State's records/Delaware	Formed to provide security for Bio-Med Pharmaceuticals
4/26/05	Incorporation of Rawlings Maintenance	Secretary of State's records/Delaware	Formed to provide maintenance for Bio-Med Pharmaceuticals
4/29/05	Shareholders meetings for both Rawlings and Diversified Security Solutions cancelled	Carl Loggia	Initial indication that the two new corporations will not become separate entities
5/5/05	Bank accounts opened for Rawlings and Diversified Security Solutions	Carl Loggia	Both accounts undercapitalized
2/7/12	Semi-annual safety inspection of Bio-Med Pharmaceuticals performed jointly by employees of Rawlings and Diversified Security Solutions	Rawlings and Diversified Security Solutions records Lon Robertson	Inspection not carried out properly indicates negligence
2/7/12	Repairs performed on heating unit in storeroom	Lon Robertson	Indicates that repairs were done negligently
2/28/12	Delgado arrives at Bio-Med Pharmaceuticals for audit	Delgado, et al.	Indicates lawful presence
3/4/12	Date of fire	Delgado, et al.	Several people will testify as to the events surrounding the fire
3/4/12 to 5/11/12	Delgado's hospital stay	Hospital records Several physicians	Extent of injuries must be explained

Legal Research   This section of the trial notebook should contain copies of all cases that are on point with the legal issues involved in the present case. A case **on point** is one that has been decided in your jurisdiction and that involves both facts and legal principles that are so similar to the facts and principles in the present case that your attorney feels the court will be bound to follow the court's ruling in that earlier case. If the cases on point are numerous and lengthy, the paralegal should include a case summary and a citation to the case and maintain the actual cases in a separate, clearly marked cases binder.

on point

A law or prior case that directly applies to the facts of the present case.

Trial Exhibits   This section should include lists of plaintiff's and defendant's proposed trial exhibits, a normal requirement of the final pretrial conference. In addition, the paralegal should place a copy of each exhibit that her attorney plans to introduce into the notebook unless the number and size of the exhibits precludes such inclusion. In that case, the exhibits would be placed in separate trial exhibit binders. As an exhibit is introduced at trial, the paralegal notes the following on the trial exhibits list: the exhibit number; the party introducing the exhibit; the witness through whom the exhibit was introduced; whether there was any objection to the exhibit; and the court's ruling on the objection, either admitting or rejecting the exhibit. If an exhibit consists of an enlargement, photograph,

EXHIBIT 15-5 Juror Profile

Case Name: _____

Case Number: _____

Juror Name: _____ Juror No. _____

Age: _____ Sex: _____ Marital Status: _____

Cultural Background: _____ Religion: _____

Nationality: _____

Education: _____ Economic Status: _____

Physical Appearance: _____ Dress: _____

Body Language/Facial Expressions: _____

Behavioral Information (drinking, law enforcement background, etc.): _____

_____

_____

_____

Personality Characteristics: _____

Prior Jury Experience: _____

Litigation (Plaintiff or Defendant): _____

_____

Other Information: _____

_____

_____

_____

_____

_____

_____

_____

_____

_____

jury instructions
Directions given to the jury explaining the law that applies in the case and spelling out what must be proved and by whom. These instructions are given just before the jury is sent out to deliberate and return a verdict.

or medical model, for example, a hard copy of the exhibit should be included in the notebook, or an entry should be made to indicate what the exhibit is, and its location.

Juror Profiles and Instructions   This section of the trial notebook consists of two parts. The first part is a juror profile. The juror profile lists the characteristics of the ideal jury that you would like to assemble in the case. For example, you might want the jury to include persons with a certain background or with a certain level of education. Exhibit 15-5 is a sample that you might use to develop a profile of your ideal juror.

The second part of this section is the jury instructions. **Jury instructions** explain the legal principles that the jury must apply to the facts in the case in reaching the verdict. Jury instructions also outline the procedures that the jury members must follow as they attempt to reach a verdict. Although these will change during the course of the trial, drafting a proposed set of jury instructions and placing them in the trial notebook will save a substantial amount of time during the trial. A disc containing the proposed set of jury instructions should be included with trial materials to enable changes while the trial is in process. The ultimate responsibility for giving the jury instructions lies with the judge. However, attorneys are permitted to suggest the substance of those instructions to the judge and may object when they feel the judge has not properly instructed the jury. Attorneys who fail to object to jury instructions cannot raise the inaccuracy of the instructions as an issue on appeal.

Trial Outline   A trial outline is a chronological listing of the tasks that must be performed just prior to and during the trial. Such a chronological outline is a vital part of the trial notebook because it simplifies and organizes the tasks facing the paralegal and the attorney as the trial date approaches. For example, the paralegal may be asked to assist in drafting the questions to be used during voir dire. **Voir dire examination** is the process by which the jurors are questioned to determine any bias they might have that would affect their ability to be fair and impartial in the case. Allow space on the trial outline for annotations and changes.

Attorney's Notes   Blank pages should be inserted in this section of the trial notebook for the attorney's notes about witnesses, legal issues, or other general information to be used during the trial.

"Things to Do" List   In addition to the trial preparation checklist, you will discover tasks that must be performed in the case. You should make notes of these items as they arise, then transfer them to the trial calendar specifically developed for the case.

voir dire examination
The preliminary in-court questioning of a prospective witness (or juror) to determine competency (or suitability) to decide a case.

PREPARATION OF WITNESSES

As a paralegal, you will be instrumental in assisting your attorney with preparing the witnesses for trial. One task that you may have to perform is drafting and arranging for the service of subpoenas to certain witnesses. You may also be charged with communicating the details of the trial to the witnesses. Finally, you may be required to arrange and attend all witness preparation meetings.

Subpoena of Witnesses

You must consult with your attorney to determine whether any witnesses will require a subpoena. In some instances, attorneys prefer to subpoena only witnesses who are not considered "friendly." However, a friendly witness may request a subpoena to present to an employer as evidence that she has been ordered to appear and testify at trial.

Trial subpoenas require the same procedure as deposition subpoenas. You should review your state and local rules to determine whether there are any unusual requirements for subpoenas. In federal courts, the subpoena process is governed by Rule 45 of the Federal Rules of Civil Procedure. According to Rule 45, the clerk of court is responsible for issuing subpoenas. Attorneys can also issue subpoenas in federal court under Rule 45(3) of the Federal Rules of Civil Procedure. Exhibit 15-6 is an example of this type of subpoena.

EXHIBIT 15-6 Subpoena

AO88 (Rev. 12/07) Subpoena in a Civil Case

Issued by the
UNITED STATES DISTRICT COURT

SUBPOENA IN A CIVIL CASE

V.

Case Number:[1]

TO:

☐ YOU ARE COMMANDED to appear in the United States District court at the place, date, and time specified below to testify in the above case.

PLACE OF TESTIMONY	COURTROOM
	DATE AND TIME

☐ YOU ARE COMMANDED to appear at the place, date, and time specified below to testify at the taking of a deposition in the above case.

PLACE OF DEPOSITION	DATE AND TIME

☐ YOU ARE COMMANDED to produce and permit inspection and copying of the following documents or objects at the place, date, and time specified below (list documents or objects):

PLACE	DATE AND TIME

☐ YOU ARE COMMANDED to permit inspection of the following premises at the date and time specified below.

PREMISES	DATE AND TIME

    Any organization not a party to this suit that is subpoenaed for the taking of a deposition shall designate one or more officers, directors, or managing agents, or other persons who consent to testify on its behalf, and may set forth, for each person designated, the matters on which the person will testify. Federal Rule of Civil Procedure 30(b)(6).

ISSUING OFFICER'S SIGNATURE AND TITLE (INDICATE IF ATTORNEY FOR PLAINTIFF OR DEFENDANT)	DATE
ISSUING OFFICER'S NAME, ADDRESS AND PHONE NUMBER	

(See Federal Rule of Civil Procedure 45 (c), (d), and (e), on next page)

[1] If action is pending in district other than district of issuance, state district under case number.

EXHIBIT 15-6 Subpoena (*continued*)

AO88 (Rev. 12/07) Subpoena in a Civil Case (Page 2)

PROOF OF SERVICE

	DATE	PLACE
SERVED		

SERVED ON (PRINT NAME)	MANNER OF SERVICE

SERVED BY (PRINT NAME)	TITLE

DECLARATION OF SERVER

I declare under penalty of perjury under the laws of the United States of America that the foregoing information contained in the Proof of Service is true and correct.

Executed on _____
DATE

SIGNATURE OF SERVER

ADDRESS OF SERVER

Federal Rule of Civil Procedure 45 (c), (d), and (e), as amended on December 1, 2007:

(c) PROTECTING A PERSON SUBJECT TO A SUBPOENA.

(1) Avoiding Undue Burden or Expense; Sanctions. A party or attorney responsible for issuing and serving a subpoena must take reasonable steps to avoid imposing undue burden or expense on a person subject to the subpoena. The issuing court must enforce this duty and impose an appropriate sanction — which may include lost earnings and reasonable attorney's fees — on a party or attorney who fails to comply.

(2) Command to Produce Materials or Permit Inspection.

(A) Appearance Not Required. A person commanded to produce documents, electronically stored information, or tangible things, or to permit the inspection of premises, need not appear in person at the place of production or inspection unless also commanded to appear for a deposition, hearing, or trial.

(B) Objections. A person commanded to produce documents or tangible things or to permit inspection may serve on the party or attorney designated in the subpoena a written objection to inspecting, copying, testing or sampling any or all of the materials or to inspecting the premises — or to producing electronically stored information in the form or forms requested. The objection must be served before the earlier of the time specified for compliance or 14 days after the subpoena is served. If an objection is made, the following rules apply:

(i) At any time, on notice to the commanded person, the serving party may move the issuing court for an order compelling production or inspection.

(ii) These acts may be required only as directed in the order, and the order must protect a person who is neither a party nor a party's officer from significant expense resulting from compliance.

(3) Quashing or Modifying a Subpoena.

(A) When Required. On timely motion, the issuing court must quash or modify a subpoena that:

(i) fails to allow a reasonable time to comply;

(ii) requires a person who is neither a party nor a party's officer to travel more than 100 miles from where that person resides, is employed, or regularly transacts business in person — except that, subject to Rule 45(c)(3)(B)(iii), the person may be commanded to attend a trial by traveling from any such place within the state where the trial is held;

(iii) requires disclosure of privileged or other protected matter, if no exception or waiver applies; or

(iv) subjects a person to undue burden.

(B) When Permitted. To protect a person subject to or affected by a subpoena, the issuing court may, on motion, quash or modify the subpoena if it requires:

(i) disclosing a trade secret or other confidential research, development, or commercial information;

(ii) disclosing an unretained expert's opinion or information that does not describe specific occurrences in dispute and results from the expert's study that was not requested by a party; or

(iii) a person who is neither a party nor a party's officer to incur substantial expense to travel more than 100 miles to attend trial

(C) Specifying Conditions as an Alternative. In the circumstances described in Rule 45(c)(3)(B), the court may, instead of quashing or modifying a subpoena, order appearance or production under specified conditions if the serving party:

(i) shows a substantial need for the testimony or material that cannot be otherwise met without undue hardship; and

(ii) ensures that the subpoenaed person will be reasonably compensated.

(d) DUTIES IN RESPONDING TO A SUBPOENA.

(1) Producing Documents or Electronically Stored Information. These procedures apply to producing documents or electronically stored information:

(A) Documents. A person responding to a subpoena to produce documents must produce them as they are kept in the ordinary course of business or must organize and label them to correspond to the categories in the demand.

(B) Form for Producing Electronically Stored Information Not Specified. If a subpoena does not specify a form for producing electronically stored information, the person responding must produce it in a form or forms in which it is ordinarily maintained or in a reasonably usable form or forms.

(C) Electronically Stored Information Produced in Only One Form. The person responding need not produce the same electronically stored information in more than one form.

(D) Inaccessible Electronically Stored Information. The person responding need not provide discovery of electronically stored information from sources that the person identifies as not reasonably accessible because of undue burden or cost. On motion to compel discovery or for a protective order, the person responding must show that the information is not reasonably accessible because of undue burden or cost. If that showing is made, the court may nonetheless order discovery from such sources if the requesting party shows good cause, considering the limitations of Rule 26(b)(2)(C). The court may specify conditions for the discovery.

(2) Claiming Privilege or Protection.

(A) Information Withheld. A person withholding subpoenaed information under a claim that it is privileged or subject to protection as trial-preparation material must:

(i) expressly make the claim; and

(ii) describe the nature of the withheld documents, communications, or tangible things in a manner that, without revealing information itself privileged or protected, will enable the parties to assess the claim.

(B) Information Produced. If information produced in response to a subpoena is subject to a claim of privilege or of protection as trial-preparation material, the person making the claim may notify any party that received the information of the claim and the basis for it. After being notified, a party must promptly return, sequester, or destroy the specified information and any copies it has; must not use or disclose the information until the claim is resolved; must take reasonable steps to retrieve the information if the party disclosed it before being notified; and may promptly present the information to the court under seal for a determination of the claim. The person who produced the information must preserve the information until the claim is resolved.

(e) CONTEMPT.

The issuing court may hold in contempt a person who, having been served, fails without adequate excuse to obey the subpoena. A nonparty's failure to obey must be excused if the subpoena purports to require the nonparty to attend or produce at a place outside the limits of Rule 45(c)(3)(A)(ii).

In federal court under Rule 45, a federal marshal can serve a witness with a subpoena. However, the rule also states that any person who is 18 years of age or older can serve a subpoena. A trial subpoena must be personally served on the witness, and all mileage and witness fees required must be tendered to the witness.

Payment for only the first day's trial appearance fee plus round-trip mileage is tendered with the subpoena. The clerk of court will be able to supply the paralegal with the amount of that fee and mileage.

Subpoenas are valid for the date or dates reflected and for the remainder of the trial, unless the witness is dismissed prior to the end of the trial by either the party that subpoenaed the witness or the court. It is virtually impossible to know precisely when a witness's testimony will be required at trial. Thus, the appearance date on the subpoena should reflect the earliest possible time that a witness's presence in court might be necessary. The witness's schedule can be accommodated during the uncertain trial schedule by allowing the witness to remain at home or near a telephone to receive updates on the trial's progress.

The trial subpoena remains in effect through a continuance or postponement of trial. The one instance where a subpoena must be reissued is in the event of a change of venue.

A person who has been subpoenaed may challenge the subpoena on the basis that it is unreasonable, oppressive, or insufficient through a motion to quash, modify, or vacate.

Finally, the return-of-service information on the subpoena must be completed and filed with the court for the subpoena to be considered valid. An important paralegal responsibility is checking for the filed return prior to the time the witness is to testify. Failure to do so may result in a "no-show" witness and a major hole in your trial schedule.

Communicating with Witnesses

The preparation of a witness for trial is much more involved and generally much more critical than the preparation of the witness for the deposition. For this reason it is usually advantageous for the paralegal to work with the witnesses in the case from the time of the initial interview. This early involvement will build a relationship that facilitates communication and helps put the witnesses at ease while working with the paralegal.

As the paralegal, you may be asked to communicate with witnesses early in the trial preparation period about the basic details of the trial, including the date, the location, and the anticipated length of their testimony. The witnesses should be informed that they may have to meet with the attorney and the paralegal closer to the time of the trial. Remind the witnesses to review their deposition and/or affidavit at least once before the meeting.

Exhibit 15-7 is an example of a letter that transmits to a witness basic information about the trial and his role in the case. By signing the letter and agreeing to remain in touch with you for availability at trial, the witness may feel committed to whatever length of time is required for his testimony.

It is essential that the paralegal be able to reach witnesses to advise them of changes in the trial schedule. Also, the client and all the witnesses should be given a designated contact person at the law firm. Each morning and afternoon during the trial, the client and the witnesses should check with this person to make certain that there have been no changes in the schedule and order of witnesses.

EXHIBIT 15-7 Letter to Witness Regarding Trial

POPSON, PIERCE, RUEBER, AND BURKE
5200 International Boulevard, Suite 200
Brownsville, Texas 78586
March 4, 2013

Mr. Carl Loggia
Certified Public Accountant
4226 Superior Avenue
Montgomery, AL 36101

RE: *Delgado v. Bio-Med Pharmaceuticals, Inc.*

Dear Mr. Loggia:

The trial in the above-captioned case has been scheduled for March 18, 2013, at the Smith County Court House, in Courtroom Number 1, 7220 Main Street, Montgomery, Alabama 36101.

We would appreciate your keeping us informed of your location at all times because there may be a change in the trial starting date. If for any reason you will be unable to attend to testify during the period of March 18 to April 5, please let us know immediately.

By signing a copy of this letter at the space indicated below, you agree to comply with the terms of this letter.

Sincerely,

_____

Laura Burke
Attorney-at-Law

ACCEPTED AND AGREED TO
THIS _____ DAY OF _____, 20_____:

_____

Copyright © 2015 Cengage Learning®

Witness Preparation Meeting

Shortly before trial, your attorney will probably request that you arrange a meeting between each witness and your attorney. Before the meeting, you may be asked to collect all documents that refer to the witness. You should review the witness's deposition and note any areas that gave the witness difficulty or that may require further clarification. In addition, a review of other deponents' references to the witness is necessary. That review will include determining any discrepancies between the other deponents' testimony and the previous deposition testimony of the witness. You may be asked to assist the attorney with the preparation of an outline or actual questions that your attorney anticipates asking each witness during the trial. Make sure that you correlate the necessary trial exhibits with that outline. During the witness preparation meeting, your attorney will explain the trial process and what is expected of the witness during trial. Many attorneys conduct mock questioning sessions so that the witnesses will know exactly what questions will be asked during direct examination. Your attorney may request that you videotape this mock questioning session for evaluation of the witness's appearance and testimony prior to trial. Many of the

EXHIBIT 15-8 Witness Instructions for Trial Testimony

1. Arrive at the courthouse well in advance of your scheduled appearance time.
2. Wear appropriate courtroom attire; avoid flashy or unusual styles.
3. Do not discuss your impending testimony with friends or family.
4. Speak slowly, distinctly, and loud enough to be heard by the judge and jury.
5. Listen carefully to the question. Request clarification if the question is unclear.
6. Do not guess at the answer. "I don't know" or "I don't recall" are acceptable answers.
7. Allow sufficient time for your attorney's objection to the question before answering.
8. Follow your attorney's advice if your attorney instructs you not to answer.
9. Look at the attorney asking the question or at the jury, not at your attorney. Such glances may indicate that you are asking your attorney for guidance on answering the question.
10. Answer a question as briefly, but completely, as possible.
11. Avoid using the qualifiers "I think," "maybe," "I believe," or "I honestly."
12. When questioned about prior testimony or the contents of a document, request a copy to review prior to answering the question.
13. Be polite and respectful of the attorney asking the questions in both your answers and body language.
14. Do not argue with the questioning attorney.
15. If asked a general question such as, "Is there anything else?" your answer should be clear that your testimony is all that you recall at this time.
16. In response to a question about discussions with your attorney prior to testifying, answer truthfully. There is nothing wrong with a witness's meeting with his or her attorney prior to trial testimony.
17. Request a short recess for a water or bathroom break if you become tired, irritated, or confused with the line of questioning.
18. If you realize that a prior answer is incorrect, you should notify the judge as soon as possible that you want to correct earlier testimony.

guidelines for testifying in a deposition carry over to preparation for trial testimony. However, there are some significant differences. Exhibit 15-8 is an example of instructions for witnesses prior to testifying at trial.

PREPARATION OF TRIAL EXHIBITS AND BRIEFS

Often the paralegal is called upon to gather and organize the exhibits in a case. This responsibility may require obtaining enlarged exhibits or unusual graphics. Whatever they may be, it helps to know what to look for in the evaluation of those exhibits. It is also possible that the paralegal may be called upon to help conduct research for the trial brief.

Preparing Trial Exhibits

In some jurisdictions, court rules require that the parties exchange lists of all the trial exhibits before the trial. A major source of trial exhibits is the universe of deposition exhibits. Once you have established the documents or the materials that your attorney will introduce at trial, you may begin to prepare a trial exhibit log that will trace the trial exhibit's progress throughout the trial. It is important for the paralegal to know how to determine the effectiveness of a document that may be used as a trial exhibit.

Enlarged Exhibits and Unusual Graphics   It may be necessary for you to obtain enlarged exhibits or unusual graphics. For example, in the *Delgado* case, your attorney may request that you have Mr. Delgado's X-rays enlarged for the jurors to view during his testimony. In addition, many litigation support services offer models of various parts of the human anatomy, created to show the effects of certain types of injuries to various parts of the body. You should obtain printed copies of any charts or diagrams that will be used as exhibits. For instance, if you use a large chart to portray the extent of Mr. Delgado's medical expenses in this case, you should prepare a printed copy for the jury to take into the jury room when deliberations begin. Photographs should be reproduced by a photocopy machine. All of these exhibits must be secured several weeks in advance of the trial. Once your attorney has selected the exhibits that she plans to use, you should immediately locate companies that can produce effective trial exhibits.

Chronology of the Case as a Trial Exhibit   A chronology of the case, especially in a tort suit like the *Delgado* case, is an effective trial exhibit. You should review the litigation files, depositions, and documents and construct the critical events in the case. A color-coded, large trial board may be an effective way to present the chronology of the *Delgado* case, including the date of the accident, the days that Mr. Delgado was unable to work, the dates of all doctor visits and periods of hospitalization, the dates of all physical therapy treatments, and the date that he finally returned to work. Removable color magnets might also be used with this type of trial exhibit to focus on a particular type or length of treatment. Jurors can more easily assimilate a large amount of data if it is presented in an enlarged, color-coded, well-organized exhibit.

Evaluating Documents as Trial Exhibits   In most lawsuits the discovery process produces a mountain of documents. Not all of these documents, however, make effective trial exhibits. Consequently, it is crucial that the attorney and the paralegal ask the following questions to evaluate how effective a document will be as a trial exhibit:

1. Is the document relevant?
2. Is the document admissible?
3. Is the document necessary?
4. Does the document support the cause of action?
5. Is the document confusing?
6. Does the document contain repetitive information?
7. Will the document detract from the witness's testimony?
8. Does the document increase the effectiveness of the witness's testimony?
9. Is the document easy to read from the jury box and counsel table?
10. Is the document accurate?
11. Does the document have an attractive appearance?
12. Is the document clear?

trial brief
A document prepared by a lawyer to use at trial. It usually contains lists of witnesses, evidence, and citations as well as arguments to be presented.

13. Can a clear and readable copy of the document be made?

14. Can the procedural foundation be laid for introduction of the document at trial?

If the document meets these tests, it is marked as a trial exhibit and entered on the trial exhibit log. You should make copies of the exhibit and place those copies in manila folders. Label the files by trial exhibit number and by the name of the witness through whom the exhibit will be introduced. Make copies of each exhibit for all of the attorneys, a copy for the judge, a copy for the trial notebook, and at least two extra copies. Many courts require that a trial exhibit notebook for the exclusive use of the court be delivered to the court prior to the beginning of the trial.

Researching for the Trial Brief

If your jurisdiction requires filing a trial brief, you may be asked to assist with its preparation. A **trial brief** explains the legal issues involved in the case and the law that demonstrates the validity of the position your attorney has taken in relation to those issues. Exhibit 15-9 is an example of a trial brief.

EXHIBIT 15-9 Trial Brief

COUNTY COURT MONTGOMERY COUNTY STATE OF ALABAMA	
JOSEPH DELGADO Plaintiff,	) Civil Action) No. 12-71891)
v.	)) PLAINTIFF'S) TRIAL BRIEF
BIO-MED PHARMACEUTICALS, INC. et al., Defendants	))))

BACKGROUND

    This is a personal injury action arising out of a fire that occurred on March 4, 2012 at the headquarters of Defendant Bio-Med Pharmaceuticals, Inc., in Montgomery, Alabama. The fire started in a storeroom when a portable heating unit that had been recently repaired by Lon Robertson, an employee of Defendant Rawlings Maintenance Corporation, ignited. The fire rapidly spread to combustible chemicals that were left in the storeroom, causing a dangerous flame to envelop the fourth-floor offices. A safety inspection, conducted jointly on 2/7/12 by employees of Defendant Rawlings Maintenance Corporation and Defendant Diversified Security Solutions, Incorporated, failed to note the accumulation of dangerous, highly combustible chemicals in the storeroom.

    Plaintiff Joseph Delgado, a certified public accountant, hired as an independent contractor by Defendant Bio-Med Pharmaceuticals, Inc., was conducting an annual financial audit in an office adjacent to the storeroom at the time of the occurrence and was severely injured. Plaintiff sustained third-degree burns over his chest, hands, forearms, and legs, necessitating two full months of hospitalization and treatments.

Normally an employee cannot sue his or her employer.

An independent contractor has a different relationship with his or her employer and may bring a legal claim.

EXHIBIT 15-9 Trial Brief (*continued*)

LIABILITY OF DEFENDANTS

Plaintiff contends that both Defendant Rawlings Maintenance Corporation and Defendant Diversified Security Solutions, Incorporated, are subsidiaries that were formed, financed, and operated solely for the benefit of the parent corporation, Defendant Bio-Med Pharmaceuticals, Inc. Defendant Rawlings Maintenance Corporation was incorporated and provides maintenance and janitorial services strictly for the parent corporation. Likewise, Defendant Diversified Security Solutions, Incorporated, was created solely to provide security and protection services for the parent corporation and does no work for any other entity. Both subsidiaries were formed in a feeble attempt to shield the parent corporation from legal liability as a result of claims arising from the performance of faulty or negligent repair work and security services, as in the instant case.

The Defendant Bio-Med Pharmaceuticals, Inc. maintains that the inspection and repair work were carried out by employees of the security firm of Diversified Security Solutions, Incorporated, and the maintenance firm of Rawlings Maintenance Corporation, who were hired as independent contractors, thereby exonerating Defendant Bio-Med Pharmaceuticals, Inc. from any and all liability. Plaintiff denies this claim and will prove at the time of trial that both subsidiaries acted as mere empty shells and that they are corporations in name only, entitling Plaintiff to "pierce the corporate veil" and hold Defendant Bio-Med Pharmaceuticals, Inc. completely responsible for Plaintiff's injuries.

The injuries sustained by Plaintiff on the morning of March 4, 2012, were the direct result of the fire that broke out at the corporate headquarters of Defendant Bio-Med Pharmaceuticals, Inc. Said fire was caused by the negligence and carelessness of the Defendants Bio-Med Pharmaceuticals, Inc., Diversified Security Solutions, Incorporated, and Rawlings Maintenance Corporation, and their agents, servants, and/or employees. Defendant Bio-Med Pharmaceuticals, Inc. knew or should have known of the dangerous and defective conditions existing on its premises and warned the Plaintiff. Defendant Bio-Med Pharmaceuticals, Inc. was further negligent in that Defendant, its agents, servants, and/or employees failed to perform or negligently and carelessly performed safety inspections of the premises, and failed to detect or correct safety hazards that might endanger persons lawfully on the premises. In addition, Defendant, its agents, servants, and/or employees failed to repair or negligently and carelessly repaired the defective heating unit, creating a dangerous and hazardous condition that seriously and permanently injured and damaged the Plaintiff.

As the evidence clearly shows, neither Diversified Security Solutions, Incorporated, nor Rawlings Maintenance Corporation was an independent corporation. At all times from the date of their incorporation to the date of the fire that severely injured Plaintiff, both corporations were acting as a part of the overall operation of Bio-Med Pharmaceuticals, Inc. In fact, the sole purpose for incorporating the two entities was to protect the parent corporation from liability in two areas, maintenance and security. In the interests of justice, the court must pierce the corporate veil and reach Bio-Med Pharmaceuticals, Inc. as the parent corporation of both Diversified Security Solutions, Incorporated, and Rawlings Maintenance Corporation.

In the alternative, counsel for Plaintiff will demonstrate that, even if the corporate veil is not pierced and the court concludes that both subsidiaries are independent contractors, Bio-Med Pharmaceuticals, Inc., should still be held liable for the injuries suffered by Plaintiff. The duty of a landowner to maintain his or her property in a reasonably safe condition, the duty of proprietors to protect third parties from injury caused by inherently

Plaintiff demonstrates reasons to the court for holding parent corporation liable.

The subsidiary corporations are virtually assetless, making any judgment against them worthless.

Defendant tries to escape blame by looking to other defendants.

"Piercing the corporate veil" is a term used when the court is willing to look beyond the name of a corporation to assess damages and liability against the individual directors and officers, or to treat one corporation as one and the same as another corporation, such as when a parent/subsidiary relationship exists, and one corporation serves as a mere agent for the other corporation.

Plaintiff could also have brought a claim against the individual officers and directors of defendant Bio-Med Pharmaceuticals, Inc. under the theory of piercing the corporate veil.

EXHIBIT 15-9 Trial Brief (*continued*)

dangerous activities or conditions, and the duty of employers and suppliers to comply with all safety provisions of the Labor Code are all nondelegable duties.

When Bio-Med Pharmaceuticals, Inc., gave the maintenance and security responsibilities to its subsidiaries, it was attempting to sidestep these duties. The law in this state is quite clear on this matter. Such duties cannot be delegated. Therefore, despite the independent contractor status of Diversified Security Solutions, Incorporated, and Rawlings Maintenance Corporation, Bio-Med Pharmaceuticals, Inc., is still liable.

The facts will reveal at the time of trial that both Defendant Diversified Security Solutions, Incorporated, and Defendant Rawlings Maintenance Corporation are "alter egos" of Defendant Bio-Med Pharmaceuticals, Inc. In support, Plaintiff will offer the following:

a. The parent corporation incorporated both subsidiaries, neither of which has assets of its own.

b. The parent corporation shares common directors and officers with its subsidiaries.

c. The parent corporation, Defendant Bio-Med Pharmaceuticals, Inc., owns all stock and finances of both of its subsidiaries, which are grossly undercapitalized.

d. Neither subsidiary does business with any entity other than the parent corporation.

e. The directors and officers of both subsidiaries take all orders from the parent corporation and do not act in their corporations' own self-interests, nor do they follow any of the legal requirements for a corporation.

PLAINTIFF'S WITNESSES

WITNESSES *(not in order of appearance):*	TESTIMONY
a. Carl Loggia (CPA), former employee of Bio-Med Pharmaceuticals, Inc.	Neither Diversified Security Solutions, Incorporated, nor Rawlings Maintenance Corporation were ever intended to be anything other than a front for Bio-Med Pharmaceuticals, Inc., in the event of a lawsuit against Bio-Med Pharmaceuticals, Inc., for any injuries occurring at Bio-Med Pharmaceuticals, Inc.
b. Maria Mendez, secretary, employee of Bio-Med Pharmaceuticals, Inc.	Neither Diversified Security Solutions, Incorporated, nor Rawlings Maintenance Corporation were ever intended to be anything other than a front for Bio-Med Pharmaceuticals, Inc.
c. Lon Robertson, employee of Diversified Security Solutions, Incorporated, and Rawlings Maintenance Corporation	Safety and security inspection procedures used by Diversified Security Solutions Incorporated, and Rawlings Maintenance Corporation; will also testify about the repairs.
d. Rachel Friedman, M.D., physician at County Hospital	Extent of Mr. Delgado's injuries.
e. Jay Kellerman, M.D., physician at County Hospital	Extent of Mr. Delgado's injuries.

If the court applies the law to the facts of the case and draws a different conclusion, plaintiff is offering alternate theories of law for recovery.

EXHIBIT 15-9 Trial Brief (*continued*)

f. Yuri Vilnius, CEO of Diversified Security Solutions, Incorporated	Diversified Security Solutions, Incorporated, has always been treated as an extension of Bio-Med Pharmaceuticals, Inc.
g. Julius Vilnius, CEO of Bio-Med Pharmaceuticals, Inc.	Organization and operation of Bio-Med Pharmaceuticals, Inc.
h. Kay Vilnius, Treasurer of Bio-Med Pharmaceuticals, Inc.	Financial structure of Bio-Med Pharmaceuticals, Inc., Diversified Security Solutions, Incorporated, and Rawlings Maintenance Corporation.
i. Albert Vilnius, CEO of Rawlings Maintenance Corporation, Vice-President of Bio-Med Pharmaceuticals, Inc.	Relationship between Bio-Med Pharmaceuticals, Inc., and Rawlings Maintenance Corporation.
j. Vytautas Vilnius, Treasurer of Rawlings Maintenance Corporation, Vice-President of Bio-Med Pharmaceuticals, Inc.	Relationship between Bio-Med Pharmaceuticals, Inc., and Rawlings Maintenance Corporation.
k. Abe Greenstein, Professor at Auburn University	Lost wages and reduction in future earnings potential.

PLAINTIFF'S DAMAGES

The devastating effects of the fire upon Plaintiff is readily apparent. Joseph Delgado, who was 35 years old at the time of the occurrence, suffered third-degree burns over 30% of his body. Tragically, his arms were most damaged and will probably always be disabled. Plaintiff had numerous painful operations and procedures during his initial two-month hospitalization and will require many such operations and procedures in the future. Plaintiff's arms are covered with motion-restricting scars. Plaintiff will always suffer from limitation of motion, altered sensation, itching, and skin sensitivity. It is hoped that with continued physical therapy, Plaintiff will be able to resume working in some capacity.

The injured Plaintiff sustained the following:

Hospitalizations

County Hospital	3/4/12–5/11/12
County Hospital	5/30/12–6/2/12
County Hospital	6/15/12
County Hospital	10/4/12–10/6/12

Medical Expenses

County Hospital	$281,112
County Hospital	$3,402
County Hospital	$800
County Hospital	$1,654
Prescriptions	$3,488
Dr. Friedman	$35,000
Dr. Kellerman	$20,008
County Radiologists	$4,213
Physical Therapy Associates	$6,000

EXHIBIT 15-9 Trial Brief (*continued*)

APPLICABLE LAW

The line of cases supporting Plaintiff's claim for piercing the corporate veil is as follows:

Kwick Set Components, Inc. v. Davidson Industries, Inc., 411 So. 2d 134 (Ala. 1982). In this case the Supreme Court of Alabama pierced the corporate veil of Capital Components, Inc., a wholly owned subsidiary of Kwick Set Components, Inc. Davidson Industries, Inc., had sold goods to Capital Components, Inc., which then delivered them to Kwick Set Components, Inc. Kwick Set Components, Inc., used the goods. Kwick Set Components, Inc., never paid Capital Components, Inc., and Capital Components, Inc., never paid Davidson Industries, Inc. Subsequently, Capital Components, Inc., went out of business. When Davidson Industries, Inc., found out that Capital Components, Inc., had been a subsidiary of Kwick Set Components, Inc., and that all the goods sold to Capital Components, Inc., had gone directly to Kwick Set Components, Inc., without payment, Davidson Industries, Inc., asked the court to pierce the corporate veil and hold Kwick Set Components, Inc., liable. The court agreed for three reasons. First, Kwick Set Components, Inc., and Capital Components, Inc., had the same president and the same directors. Second, all goods used by Kwick Set Components, Inc., were purchased through Capital Components, Inc. Third, the entire purpose of Capital Components, Inc., had been to postpone or totally avoid payment for goods purchased through Capital Components, Inc. This demonstrates that Capital Components, Inc., had no corporate identity separate from Kwick Set Components, Inc. In conclusion, the court quoted an earlier case, *Forest Hill Corp. v. Latter & Blum Inc.,* 29 So. 2d 298 (Ala. 1947), in which the Supreme Court of Alabama said "the courts will not allow the corporate entity to successfully masquerade through its officers, stockholders, representatives, or associates so as to defeat the payment of its just obligations." *Id.* at 302.

Matrix-Churchill v. Springsteen, 461 So. 2d 782 (Ala. 1984). In this case the court restated and approved the standard it had established in the *Kwick Set* case.

Messick v. Moring, 514 So. 2d 892 (Ala. 1987). In this case the Supreme Court of Alabama outlined three elements that must be present in order to pierce the corporate veil. These elements are:

1. The dominant party must have complete control and domination of the subservient corporation's finances, policy, and business practices so that at the time of the attacked transaction, the subservient corporation had no separate mind, will, or existence of its own.

2. The control must have been misused by the dominant party. Although fraud or the violation of a statutory or other positive legal duty is misuse of control, when it is necessary to prevent injustice or inequitable circumstances, misuse of control will be presumed.

3. The misuse of control must proximately cause the harm complained of. *Id.* at 895.

Simmins v. Clark Equipment Corp., 554 So. 2d 398 (Ala. 1989). In this case the Supreme Court of Alabama approved of the factors and elements presented in the *Messick* case.

Cohen v. Williams, 318 So. 2d 279 (Ala. 1975). In this case the court held that the plaintiff need not prove that the defendant corporation engaged in fraud to convince the court to pierce the corporate veil. Rather, the court concluded that the court can pierce the corporate veil if it is convinced that upholding the separateness of the entities will cause an injustice. The court stated, "actual fraud is not necessarily a predicate for discarding the theory of separate corporate existence. It may also be discarded to prevent injustice or inequitable consequences." *Id.* at 281.

Woods v. Commercial Contractors, Inc., 384 So. 2d 1076 (Ala. 1980). In this case the court reaffirmed its position in *Cohen v. Williams,* stating that "the theory of corporate

EXHIBIT 15-9 Trial Brief (*continued*)

existence can properly be discarded, even in the absence of fraud, to prevent injustice or inequitable consequences." *Woods,* 384 So. 2d at 1079.

Barrett v. Odum, May & DeBuys, 453 So. 2d 729 (Ala. 1984). In this case the Supreme Court of Alabama reaffirmed the principle that corporate existence can be disregarded to prevent injustice even in the absence of fraud.

Deupree v. Ruffino, 505 So. 2d 1218 (Ala. 1987). In this case the Supreme Court of Alabama again reasserted that fraud is not a necessary element in a case involving an attempt to pierce the corporate veil.

United Steelworkers v. Connors Steel, 847 F.2d 707 (11th Cir. 1988). In this case the United States Court of Appeals for the Eleventh Circuit, in interpreting Alabama law, upheld the position that the corporate veil can be pierced to prevent inequity even without a showing of fraud.

In support of the doctrine of nondelegable duties are the following:

Dixie Stage Lines v. Anderson, 134 So. 23 (Ala. 1931). In this case the Supreme Court of Alabama set down the nondelegable duty exception to the rule that the proprietor is not liable for the negligent acts of an independent contractor. The court said, "a person is responsible for the manner of the performance of his nondelegable duties, though done by an independent contractor, and therefore, that one who by his contract or by law is due certain obligations to another cannot divest himself of liability for a negligent performance by reason of the employment of such contractor." *Id.* at 24.

Arlington Realty v. Lawson, 153 So. 425 (Ala. 1934). In this case the court states that landlords have a nondelegable duty to see that proper care is used in making repairs to their property.

Alabama Power Co. v. Pierre, 183 So. 665 (Ala. 1938). This case reiterates and approves the nondelegable duty exception laid down by the Supreme Court of Alabama in the *Dixie Stage Lines* case.

Knight v. Burns, Kirkley & Williams Construction Co., 331 So. 2d 651 (Ala. 1976). In this case the Supreme Court of Alabama cites with approval the nondelegable duty exception established in the *Dixie Stage Lines* case.

General Finance Corp. v. Smith, 505 So. 2d 1045 (Ala. 1987). In this case the court again upholds the nondelegable duty exception.

Boroughs v. Joiner, 337 So. 2d 340 (Ala. 1976). In this case the Supreme Court of Alabama specifically identifies the performance of inherently dangerous activities, such as the storing of combustible materials, as a nondelegable duty. In doing so the court quotes with favor the *Restatement (Second) of Torts* § 427 (1965), which states, "One who employs an independent contractor to do work involving a special danger to others which the employer knows or has reason to know to be inherent in or normal to the work, or which he contemplates or has reason to contemplate when making the contract, is subject to liability or physical harm caused to such others by the contractor's failure to take reasonable precautions against such danger." *Id.* at 342.

Laura Burke, Trial Attorney
Attorney for the Plaintiff
Popson, Pierce, Rueber, and Burke
Attorneys at Law
5293 St. Clair Avenue
Montgomery, Alabama 36101
(205) 725-8788
[facsimile number]

cite check
Verifying the accuracy and proper form of all the citations in a document.

Your role in preparation of the trial brief may consist of legal and factual research. For example, your attorney may request that you locate specific testimony from a particular witness's deposition. You may also be asked to determine the validity of the cases cited in the brief. This task is known as a **cite check**.

The paralegal is often responsible for coordinating the preparation and filing of the brief with the court. You should be familiar with your local court rules pertaining to the form of the brief, the number of copies needed, and the time for filing.

COORDINATING TRIAL LOGISTICS

Coordinating the logistics of a trial is often the paralegal's responsibility. If the trial is held at the local court where your attorney usually works, coordinating the logistics will be a routine matter. However, when the trial is held in another district or another county, or when your client and many of the witnesses are from out of town, you may be asked to arrange for hotel and office space near the courthouse. Also, for both local and out-of-town trials you will have to examine the courthouse and contact local court personnel.

Arranging for Accommodations

When the trial is to be held in another district or county, or when your client and several of the witnesses are from out of town, you as the paralegal may be responsible for travel, hotel, and food arrangements. Often a suite of offices in a hotel near the courthouse is set up as a war room. The war room is an area containing additional trial documents and supplies. It also doubles as a conference room where the legal team, the client, and the witnesses may gather during trial recesses or at the end of the trial day to regroup and prepare for the next day of the trial.

You should locate hotels near the courthouse and determine whether your firm has a corporate account with any of them. An actual review of the available hotel accommodations is necessary to ensure that the site contains the space and setup required for your particular trial needs. Once the hotel has been selected and the necessary rooms reserved, make any travel arrangements that may be required for the client and out-of-town witnesses, and confirm the travel arrangements in writing. Write to the client and the witnesses informing them of the location of the hotel and the details of the travel plans. Remember to enclose the airline tickets and hotel confirmation, if requested, along with a map of the area around the courthouse and the hotel.

Once the trial is under way, the paralegal may be called upon to arrange for catered meals in the war room to avoid crowded, noisy restaurants near the courthouse. Having catered meals also prevents the awkwardness of being seated in a restaurant next to the opposing counsel or several of the jurors. However, often these arrangements should be delegated to another member of the legal team. This delegation is especially important at the relatively short lunch breaks that occur during the trial because the paralegal may be needed elsewhere. For example, the paralegal may have to use this valuable break time to locate a witness, secure another copy of an exhibit, or locate a case for inclusion in the trial brief.

Visiting the Courthouse

If the trial is to be held in another district or another county, or if you have never been to the courthouse where an upcoming trial is scheduled, you should visit that courthouse several weeks before the trial begins. You may need to locate a work area for meeting with the client or witnesses during the trial.

In many courthouses all of the courtrooms are identical; in others each courtroom is configured differently. If possible, locate and examine the exact courtroom where the trial will be held. Determine the amount of space available for exhibits, briefcases, and supplies. Also check for the potential location of easels, charts, chalkboards, overhead projectors, slide projectors, video equipment, and audio equipment. This check is critical because you will have to bring any equipment that your attorney will need that is not provided by the court. Note whether the courtroom is equipped with enough electrical outlets for the operation of a VCR or laptop computers. If the number or location of these outlets is inadequate for your needs, you will have to arrange for adapters or extension cords.

A *trial box*, consisting of all supplies needed during the trial, should be put together after the visit to the courthouse. Any special items noted during the courthouse tour should be included in the trial box. Exhibit 15-10 lists items you may want to consider placing in your trial box.

Contacting Court Personnel

The paralegal should schedule a meeting with the court clerk and the court reporter before the trial. Determine whether the courtroom will be available on the evening before or early on the morning of the trial for the delivery of exhibits, documents, and equipment. You may need to arrange for security clearance and access to the courthouse elevators and

EXHIBIT 15-10 Contents of a Trial Box

✓ Exhibit stickers	✓ Court rules (federal or state and local rules)
✓ Business cards for attorneys and paralegals	✓ Manila folders
✓ Roll of quarters (for copier, vending machines, etc.)	✓ Pencils
✓ Copy card (for law library or clerk's office copy machine)	✓ Pens
✓ Bus pass	✓ Stapler
✓ Aspirin	✓ Staple puller
✓ Cough drops	✓ Staples
✓ Antacid	✓ Rubber bands
✓ Kleenex	✓ Paper clips
✓ Extension cord	✓ Binder clips
✓ Tape recorder	✓ Post-It notes
✓ Blank tapes	✓ File labels
✓ Batteries for tape recorder	✓ Hole punch
✓ Boxes of CDs	✓ Yellow pads

the loading dock after hours. The paralegal should ask the clerk whether trial exhibits and other trial material can be left in the courtroom throughout the trial or arrangements must be made to remove those items at the end of each trial day.

During the trial, the court clerk will receive many calls and inquiries concerning the case. If the paralegal furnishes the clerk with a list of the law firm personnel who will be present in the courtroom, the possibility of missing an important telephone call is diminished. The court reporter will make a transcript of the trial proceeding. You should meet with the court reporter prior to the trial and give him your business card just in case there are any problems in the transcription of trial testimony. At this point, you will need to inform the reporter of any special transcript requirements. For example, daily transcripts are often available several hours after the completion of each day's proceeding. This expedited service is normally rather expensive. However, the availability of the day's testimony is a valuable asset for your attorney as she prepares for the next day's witnesses.

PRELIMINARY STEPS IN THE TRIAL PROCESS

The *Delgado* case, which served as the Commentary case opening this chapter, has not settled, despite lengthy settlement discussions and mediation efforts. Consequently, the time for the trial has arrived.

Although most cases are settled or dismissed before reaching the trial stage, you must proceed on the assumption that eventually the case will reach trial. Your attorney will make the determination of whether a jury trial or a trial by a judge alone will be in the best interests of your client. If you are going to face a jury, one of the first steps in the trial will be to select the jurors. This selection process must be done with great care because the jurors play a key role in the success or failure of your case.

Decisions Regarding Jury Trials

The Seventh Amendment to the U.S. Constitution guarantees the right to a trial by jury in certain types of civil cases. The amendment states, "In Suits at common law, where the value in controversy shall exceed 20 dollars, the right of trial by jury shall be preserved, and no fact tried by a jury, shall be otherwise re-examined in any Court of the United States, than according to the rules of common law." The amendment clearly preserves the right to a jury trial in cases involving common law for those litigants who wish to take advantage of that right. It does not, however, give the litigants a right to a jury trial in cases tried in equity. Therefore, jury trials are not allowed in divorce proceedings, in disputes involving custody rights, or in other equitable cases.

Factors in Choosing a Judge or a Jury Trial   Several factors should be considered by your attorney as she attempts to decide whether it would be in the best interests of the client to try the case before a judge or before a jury. The first factor to consider is the complexity of the case. If the case involves legal issues and concepts that may be difficult for the layperson to grasp, your attorney may prefer to present the case before a judge. The same might be true if the facts in the case are extremely complicated. Another factor to consider is available time. In general, the attorney can be relatively certain that a trial before a judge

will take less time than a jury trial because in a trial before a judge there is no need to select the members of the jury and no need to explain the law or the legal process to the judge—he will already be well versed in both.

Another factor to consider is the condition of the client. If the case is a personal injury case involving a client who has been disfigured or otherwise permanently disabled, the attorney representing the plaintiff would probably want to ask for a jury trial. In the *Delgado* case, for example, your attorney would most likely decide to demand a trial by jury. Because the plaintiff has been badly burned through absolutely no fault of his own, your attorney would want to rely on eliciting the sympathy of the jury. In contrast, attorneys who represent large, impersonal corporate defendants, like Bio-Med Pharmaceuticals in the Commentary, might prefer to have a judge decide the case. Naturally, any party requesting a jury trial will have that request honored because, as noted earlier, trial by jury is a constitutional right.

Even the location of the trial can be a factor in the decision to demand a jury trial. If your client is a local community member, and the opposition is someone from out of town, your attorney may elect to demand a jury trial. In the *Delgado* case, for example, the plaintiff is a locally prominent CPA who was born and raised in the town of Red Forest, Alabama, and the defendant is a large corporation formed in Delaware. This would seem to indicate that your attorney would prefer a jury trial. However, she might also consider the fact that Bio-Med is one of the largest employers in town and is therefore an integral part of the local economy. Knowledge of its importance to the economic health of Red Forest might cause her to reconsider the advisability of demanding a jury trial.

Requesting a Jury Trial   The fact that the Constitution guarantees the right to a jury trial does not prevent the courts from making the request for such a trial the responsibility of the litigants. For example, Rule 38(b) of the Federal Rules of Civil Procedure requires the litigants to demand a trial by jury. Such a demand must be made in writing at any time after the lawsuit has begun, but not later than 14 days after the last pleading in the case has been served. If such a demand is not made by either party, the right has been voluntarily surrendered by the parties. This means that the trial will be conducted before a judge. In such a trial the judge acts as both the finder of fact and the determiner of law. In a jury trial the jury plays the role of fact finder.

THE JURY PROCESS

In the past, planning for, conducting, and winning a case before a jury were to some degree matters of chance. Today, however, attorneys have a wide variety of tools at their disposal to help them maximize the effectiveness of a jury trial. These techniques include the juror profile, the mock jury trial, and the shadow jury.

Preparing a Juror Profile

Social psychologists and litigation specialists are often utilized to provide law firms with valuable statistics and jury sampling information to create not only the image of the preferred jurors but also a profile of the jurors that your attorney will want to avoid.

mock trial
A practice trial prior to the date of the actual trial, intended to reveal the strengths and weaknesses of a party's case.

mock jury
A group of independent individuals chosen to reflect the probable makeup of the actual jury.

shadow jury
A group of persons (selected to be similar to the real jurors) paid by one side in a lawsuit to observe the trial and give their reactions.

For example, in the *Delgado* case, the litigation specialist may conclude that well-educated, white-collar workers will be more sympathetic to your client. One reason for this may be that your client is a well-educated, white-collar professional. Another reason may be that well-educated jurors tend to be skeptical of the motives of large corporations such as the defendants in this case. The social psychologists and litigation specialists also may indicate that lower-income, less-educated jurors may be swayed by the presence of the corporate defendants. Your attorney would therefore try to steer away from including such people on the jury as often as possible. It is important to remember that the cost of this service may be prohibitive for smaller cases. If the expense results in a favorable decision or reduces the judgment against a client, though, the cost will certainly be justified.

Holding a Mock Jury Trial

Complex cases often require a jury trial of several months. To help facilitate a favorable jury decision, many firms stage a mock trial prior to the actual trial. A **mock trial** is a practice trial. Again, social psychologists and litigation specialists can be retained to arrange the mock trial. Legal directories, litigation journals or newspapers, and Internet sites are excellent sources for locating companies that specialize in conducting mock trials.

The paralegal is often responsible for arranging the mock trial. The first step in the mock trial is to select the mock jury. A **mock jury** is a group of independent individuals chosen to reflect the probable makeup of the actual jury. Again, social psychologists and litigation specialists can interview and hire the persons to make up the mock jury. Once the mock jury panel is selected, your firm presents the mock trial. Key witnesses and principal exhibits are presented to the jury in the same way that they will be presented at the actual trial. Part of your legal team also presents the case that you envision being presented by the opposition. To ensure an impartial evaluation, the jurors should not know which side your law firm represents. The mock jury evaluates the testimony and exhibits and renders the verdict.

Following their decision, the jurors may be questioned about their perceptions of the strengths and weaknesses of the case. For example, in the *Delgado* case, you may discover that the medical model you intended to present at trial is far too complicated for the jury to understand. Or you may discover that your attorney's cross-examination of the opposing witnesses offended certain jurors. In contrast, you may find that some of the evidence presented by the corporate defendants was very convincing. You would then concentrate your forces on countering this evidence. The period between the mock trial and the actual trial should be devoted to correcting these and other weaknesses pointed out by the mock jury.

Using Shadow Juries

The increasing complexity of litigation has resulted in the introduction of a technique known as the shadow jury. A **shadow jury** is a secret jury selected by the law firm or the outside consulting firm to match as closely as possible the individuals who will serve on the actual jury. The shadow jury then attends the trial. To assure fairness, these individuals are not told which party has retained them. During each break and at the end of each day's court session, the shadow jury reports to another paralegal or legal team member on their impressions of the trial witnesses, the exhibits, and the attorneys. The shadow jury's reports are given considerable weight. Adjustments in the order of witnesses, changes in the trial exhibits, or alterations in the attorney's examination technique may result from the observations and the suggestions made by shadow jury members. A substantial amount of expense and time is involved in this exercise. If the shadow jury strengthens a case, however, both the expense and the time are justified.

THE TRIAL

A civil trial consists of six main phases:

1. Jury selection
2. Opening statements
3. Witness testimony and cross-examination
4. Closing arguments
5. Jury instructions
6. Jury deliberation and verdict

Jury Selection

Although a trial does not technically begin until the jury is seated, the process of jury selection or seating the jury is generally referred to as the first stage of the trial process. The jury members are selected from a jury pool that has been gathered from among the local citizenry. Most jury pools are taken from the ranks of registered voters. The introduction of the eJuror program for U.S. District Courts in late 2008 greatly simplified the prospective juror process. Potential jurors now may go online to respond to juror questionnaire forms and summons, update their personal information, request a deferral or excuse from jury duty, select an alternative time for jury service, and check to see when they need to report for jury service. As of March, 2013, 72 of the 94 district courts have adopted eJuror. A national directory of courts participating in the program is available on the U.S. Courts Web site. Each court's Web site has a jury service page link, enabling a potential juror to access the site from any location 24 hours a day. Exhibit 15-11 is an example of the eJuror feature on a U.S. District Court Web site.

Once a jury pool has been assembled at the courthouse, members of the pool are asked to fill out preliminary information forms, copies of which are given to the attorneys in the case. Exhibit 15-12 is an example of a Juror Information Sheet. Once the juror information sheets have been received by the trial team, the paralegal may be asked to assist in researching the potential jurors. Exhibit 15-13 is a chart of sources for information on potential jurors. These forms are used as part of the jury selection process.

Technology has significantly changed the jury selection process. Several software packages and applications are now available to trial attorneys for the construction of a searchable database of prospective jurors. One example of such products is JuryPad, an application for the iPad and iPad mini, which allows attorneys to view jury demographics by race, age, or gender. It also permits searches regarding marital status, employer, and

EXHIBIT 15-11

UNITED STATES DISTRICT COURT
Northern District of Texas

Please enter your 9-digit juror participant number (just above your name and address on your summons) and your 5-digit zip code.

Participant Number: [   ]

Zip Code: [   ]

| Reporting Instructions | Request Postponement or Excuse | Request Certificate of Service |

Instructions by Phone: Your reporting instructions are also available by phone toll free at 1-800-488-0903. You will be asked by the automated attendant for your 9-digit participant number.

508 **Bobby** APPROVED

Source: https://jury.txnd.uscourts.gov/AppearWeb/Default.aspx

EXHIBIT 15-12 Juror Information Sheet

Name: _____

Address: _____

Home phone: _____

Work phone: _____

Birth date: _____

Place of birth: _____

Education (highest level completed): _____

Employer: _____

Employer's address: _____

Employer's telephone number: _____

Dates of employment: _____

Job title: _____

Marital status: _____

Location of childhood home: _____

Parents' names: _____

Father:

      Name: _____   Age: _____

      Level of education: _____   Occupation: _____

EXHIBIT 15-12 Juror Information Sheet (*continued*)

Mother:

        Name: _____ Age: _____

        Level of education: _____ Occupation: _____

Spouse:

        Name: _____ Age: _____

        Education (highest level): _____

        Occupation: _____

        Employer's name: _____

        Employer's address: _____

Political party: _____

Military experience: _____

Hobbies: _____

EXHIBIT 15-13 Sources of Juror Information

1. Jury panel. Many clerks' offices provide a list of all jurors for the upcoming court term.
2. Voter registration records. The county clerk's office maintains information that could be beneficial in evaluating potential jurors, including political party.
3. Internet searches. Using the juror data sheet, Westlaw databases or search engines will reveal information such as the potential juror's assets, type of automobile driven, number and sizes of residences owned, and any lien or bankruptcy filings.
4. Trial psychologist/jury consultant. Specialists often maintain databases of area jurors. In addition, they are equipped to offer special insights into what type of juror should be selected and what type of juror should be avoided for your particular case. This process is expensive, but the results obtained may more than offset that expense.
5. Friends, coworkers, and attorneys. It is worthwhile to review the juror information sheets with friends and other law firm personnel.

home address. Using the home address of a potential juror, you are able to take a virtual tour of the neighborhood.

The ability to track juror challenges, both peremptory and for cause, using a list of jurors, seating chart, or both tools, is a valuable asset. JuryPad notifies your attorney when she is down to her last peremptory strike.

Instead of the yellow notepad or yellow sticky note process previously used during voir dire, JuryPad permits the attorney or paralegal to take notes, sort, and evaluate jurors online, in a speedy and orderly fashion.

In federal court, a civil trial uses 12 jurors. However, the parties are allowed to stipulate that fewer than 12 jurors will hear the case. Many state courts require only eight jurors for a civil trial. Most states also allow parties to stipulate that fewer than eight jurors may hear their case. The federal court and most state courts also allow for the use of alternate jurors.

The Voir Dire Process

Literally, *voir dire* means "to speak the truth." In trial practice, voir dire is the process by which the jurors are questioned to determine any bias that they might have that would affect their ability to be fair and impartial in the case. For example, in the *Delgado* case your attorney would want to determine whether any potential jurors are related to or are friends of the officers and employees of Bio-Med Pharmaceuticals, Diversified Security Solutions, Inc., or the Rawlings Maintenance Corporation. She might also want to know if any of the potential jurors has any financial interest in the outcome of the trial. Such information would indicate bias on the part of the juror and would be grounds for a challenge. Each side in the suit has an unlimited number of these *challenges for cause*.

Peremptory Challenges

Each side also has a limited number of **peremptory challenges**. The federal courts and some states allow only three such challenges; other states allow as many as four. Additional peremptory challenges are allowed when alternate jurors are to be chosen. However, the number of peremptory challenges is always limited because an attorney making a peremptory challenge does not have to give a reason for the challenge. He simply exercises the peremptory challenge, and the juror is dismissed. The objective of the peremptory challenge is to allow attorneys an opportunity to dismiss jurors for certain "intangible" reasons that cannot be logically explained to the court. For instance, your attorney may feel that there is a certain air of hostility about a certain juror, or she might feel that the "chemistry" is not right between them.

Opening Statement

Once the jury is seated, the second phase of the trial process begins—the presentation of **opening statements**. The objectives and scope of these statements are not as precise and definitive as one might expect in a profession that prides itself on both accuracy and clarity. Still, the opening statement is one of the most important steps, if not the most important step, in a jury trial. Consequently, a skillful attorney will know that he should keep the opening statement brief, use ordinary language in the statement, make the statement interesting, and use appropriate body language in delivering that statement.

Definition and Limitations of the Opening Statement

Each side in a jury trial is allowed time to make an opening statement. An opening statement presents facts to the jury and introduces the evidence that the attorney intends to use to prove those facts. A general rule of trial procedure states that attorneys are not permitted to argue their cases during opening statements. The exact meaning of this rule is not clear. Consequently, the judge has an enormous amount of discretion in what the attorneys can and cannot say during opening statements. Some judges are strict in adhering to the general guideline that attorneys cannot argue their cases in the opening statement; others are more lenient, allowing attorneys to introduce points that another judge would almost certainly label as argument. To be successful in an opening statement, an attorney must have an understanding of just how much "argument" a particular judge will allow. Such an understanding comes from experience and from a willingness to ask questions about the processes when the attorney is unfamiliar with a court and its judges.

Importance of the Opening Statement   The imprecise nature of the opening statement is even more critical because of its importance. Some legal scholars argue that the opening statement is the most important part of the trial. First, because the opening statement occurs so early in the trial, the jurors are very attentive. This attentiveness heightens their awareness of what is being said and done during the opening stages. As the trial progresses and they become more comfortable and secure in the courtroom, their attentiveness lessens. Also, although jurors are counseled to remain as objective as possible, they are, nevertheless, human beings who have a natural tendency to pick sides in any adversarial contest. When they watch a television show or a movie, they know whose side they are supposed to be on. When they attend a sports event, people are quick to pick sides.

The jurors carry this tendency to choose sides with them into the courtroom, and as early as the end of the opening statements may have unconsciously decided who is the "good guy" and who is the "bad guy." This places a heavy burden on the attorney who has been labeled the bad guy and gives an edge to the one who has been labeled the good guy. The advantage given to the good guy has been termed by some scholars as the "halo effect" and by others as the "white hat syndrome." Basically, the halo effect or the white hat syndrome means that everything said by the good guy and every piece of testimony and evidence that is introduced in support of the good guy's argument is interpreted favorably, while everything damaging to that side's case is somehow rationalized or explained away. Of course, this does not mean that a juror will never change her mind. It just means that attorneys who have been labeled bad guys have a much more difficult time getting jurors to believe them.

Characteristics of a Good Opening Statement

Because so much of the success of a jury trial seems to depend on the opening statement, an attorney should take great care in fashioning it. A good opening statement should be brief, interesting, understandable, sympathetic, and tactful.

Delivering a Brief Opening Statement   Setting an absolute minimum or maximum length of time for an opening statement beyond which an attorney should never wander is difficult. It is, however, safe to say that an attorney should rarely, if ever, pass up the opportunity to make an opening statement, unless both parties waive that right. Waiving the opening statement, or even postponing it, gives a psychological advantage to the other party. The opening statement should be long enough to capture the attention and imagination of the jurors, but not so long that it puts them to sleep. Most opening statements can be limited to 30 to 45 minutes. Occasionally, when the facts are extremely complex, more time is needed.

Delivering an Interesting Opening Statement   An experienced attorney will take advantage of the jury's high attention level at the beginning of the trial by delivering an interesting, even captivating, opening statement. The opening statement involves facts, and nothing conveys facts in a more interesting or convincing fashion than a story. Cold, antiseptic facts, exhibits, and statistics should be avoided in favor of conveying a sense of the people and the action involved in the case. For instance, in presenting the case of Mr. Delgado to the jury, your attorney might begin by stating that, "On the morning of March 4, 2013, Mr. Delgado awoke and prepared for a routine day conducting an audit at the offices of Bio-Med Pharmaceuticals here in downtown Red Forest. At that time he had no idea that this day would be one of the worst of his entire life." From this point on, your attorney would follow the events of that day much as if she were telling a story. Such an opening statement is much more likely to capture the attention and sympathy of the jurors than one limited to a long procession of facts.

Delivering an Understandable Opening Statement

Your attorney will be more likely to gain the interest and sympathy of the jury members if she avoids legal jargon and speaks the language of the jurors. Opening statements that are full of legal terms and unintelligible Latin phrases are guaranteed to alienate jury members, who may already view all attorneys with a certain degree of distrust, if not downright hostility. If your attorney, for example, buries the *Delgado* opening statement in references to *respondeat superior*, *vicarious liability*, *piercing the corporate veil*, and *alter egos*, she may bury her case along with it. In addition, depending upon the opinion of the judge in the case, the use of such terms may be considered arguing the case. Your attorney will do better to speak in ordinary, everyday language.

Delivering a Sympathetic Opening Statement

To make the opening statement as convincing and sympathetic as possible, the attorney must show the jury that he believes in the client's cause. If the jury members doubt the attorney's dedication to vindicating the client's rights, they will have little faith in anything that he says on behalf of that client. For these reasons an attorney should immediately identify himself with the client's cause. The jury will be much more convinced by the attorney who says, "We will prove that our case against the defendant is as solid as a rock," than one who says, "Don't believe everything the other side has to say about the plaintiff."

Delivering a Tactful Opening Statement

As noted earlier, the attorney should be brief, interesting, understandable, and sympathetic in the opening statement. However, this can go for naught if jurors are intimidated by the presence and actions of the attorney. For this reason, the delivery of the opening statement should be as tactful as possible. Attorneys should not be overly emotional, too loud, or excessively boastful in the opening statement. Rather, they should be soft-spoken, even-tempered, and genuine. It is important for the attorney to keep her distance from the jury. Moving close to the jurors may make a powerfully dramatic scene in a movie or television show, but in real life it invades the space of the jurors, intimidates them, and destroys their concentration on what the attorney is saying.

The Presentation of Evidence

Four types of evidence are presented during a civil trial: (1) witness testimony and cross-examination, (2) exhibits, (3) stipulation, and (4) judicial notice.

Witness Testimony and Cross-Examination

The heart of a civil trial is often referred to as the "case-in-chief," the stage at which both sides present key evidence and arguments to the jury. The plaintiff presents his evidence by calling witnesses to testify, placing those witnesses under oath, and then beginning his direct examination. The defendant then has the right to conduct a cross-examination of each witness. The roles are then reversed. The defendant places her witnesses on the stand for direct examination. The plaintiff then has the opportunity to engage in cross-examination.

Exhibits As a second type of evidence, and to bolster the witness testimony phase of evidence, the plaintiff may also introduce physical evidence, such as documents, photographs, and medical records, discussed earlier in this chapter, throughout the case-in-chief. The admissibility of exhibits is governed by the Federal Rules of Evidence.

Stipulation The third type of trial evidence is the **stipulation**. A stipulation is an agreement between the parties that certain facts are not in dispute. A stipulation may be shown or read to the jury. The parties in the *Delgado* case might stipulate that an expert witness for the opposition is indeed an expert, thus avoiding wasted trial time establishing the witness's credentials.

stipulation
An agreement between the parties in a lawsuit that certain facts are not in dispute.

Judicial Notice This fourth type of trial evidence, *judicial notice*, occurs when the trial judge takes judicial notice of a fact that is commonly known in the jurisdiction where the trial is held, easily determined and verified, and that fact is assumed true and admitted as evidence. For example, the trial court in the *Delgado* Commentary in this chapter might take judicial notice of the location of the facility where Delgado sustained the alleged injuries. The primary purpose of this type of evidence is to move the pace of trial with regard to evidence that is relevant but not in dispute.

The Plaintiff's Case-in-Chief

In its case-in-chief, the plaintiff's attorney methodically sets forth its evidence in an effort to persuade the jury that the defendant is legally responsible for the plaintiff's damages or that judgment for the plaintiff is warranted.

Direct Examination by the Plaintiff The plaintiff's attorney subjects each of the witnesses who will provide facts to verify the validity of the plaintiff's version of the case to direct examination. This is a question-and-answer period conducted under oath and recorded by the court stenographer. In general, the plaintiff's attorney may not ask her own witnesses leading questions. A leading question is one containing the answer. For example, your attorney could not call Mr. Delgado to the witness stand and ask him, "Isn't it true that the storeroom next to the room where you conducted the audit for Bio-Med Pharmaceuticals contained combustible material?" Such a question would be considered leading and would not be permitted.

Leading Questions by the Plaintiff There is an exception to the rule that prohibits asking leading questions. When an attorney is faced with an adverse or hostile witness, he is permitted to ask leading questions. For example, in the *Delgado* case, your attorney has elected to call several adverse witnesses, including Mario Montalvo, CEO of Diversified Security Solutions; Sam Guzman, CEO of Bio-Med Pharmaceuticals; Angie Guzman, treasurer of Bio-Med Pharmaceuticals; Alex Rawlings, CEO of Rawlings Maintenance and vice-president of Bio-Med Pharmaceuticals; and Mercedes Herrera, treasurer of Rawlings Maintenance and vice-president of Bio-Med Pharmaceuticals. Each of these witnesses could, therefore, be the legitimate target of leading questions by Delgado's attorney. For instance, Delgado's attorney would be permitted to ask Sam Guzman the following question: "Isn't it true that the storeroom next to the room where the audit was conducted contained combustible chemicals?"

Rules Regarding the Plaintiff's Direct Examination

The process of asking precisely the right questions during a direct examination session is not as easy as it may appear. Advance preparation is essential. All friendly witnesses should be properly and thoroughly prepared before the day of the trial. They should meet with the attorney and discuss the questions that will be asked, the answers that the witness intends to give, and the probable questions to expect on cross-examination. An attorney should never ask a question to which she does not already know the answer. The time for exploratory questions is during the discovery process, not at trial. An attorney also needs to know when to stop asking questions. Once the attorney has elicited the facts that she wants, questioning should stop. Continuing questions after that point can be very damaging.

Cross-Examination by the Defendant

When the plaintiff's attorney has completed the direct examination of each witness, the defendant's attorney has the opportunity to engage in cross-examination. In federal court and in most states, the scope of cross-examination is limited to facts covered in direct examination. If the defendant's attorney wants to explore new territory with a witness, he will have to call the witness during the defendant's direct examination session. The objective of cross-examination is to discredit the witness, to cast doubt on the accuracy of the witness's testimony, or to show that the witness is somehow biased in favor of the plaintiff. One way the defendant can do this is to show that the testimony delivered at trial by the witness contradicts the testimony presented during the discovery process. Another way is to use leading questions that require simple "yes" or "no" answers from the witness, thus limiting his ability to elaborate on those answers.

Redirect Examination by the Plaintiff

When the defendant has completed the cross-examination of a witness, the plaintiff's attorney has the opportunity to redirect questions to that witness. The objective of this part of the trial process is to allow the plaintiff's attorney the chance to reestablish the credibility of her witnesses and to clear up any factual disputes raised on cross-examination. To make redirect examination as efficient as possible, the plaintiff's attorney is limited to those matters addressed by the defendant's counsel during the cross-examination period.

The Defendant's Case-in-Chief

Once the plaintiff has completed her case-in-chief and rests, the roles are switched. The defendant's efforts are directed to discrediting the case that was presented by the plaintiff. The objective is to demonstrate that the plaintiff's version of the facts is not supported by the evidence. In addition, if the defendant raised any affirmative defenses, now is the time to present evidence that demonstrates the validity of these defenses.

Direct Examination by the Defendant

The defendant's attorney calls his witnesses and subjects them to direct examination. This is the same type of question-and-answer period that was conducted by the plaintiff. As was the case with the plaintiff's attorney, the defendant's counsel may not ask his own witnesses leading questions. For example, the defendant's attorney could not call Lon Anderson, an employee of both Diversified Security Solutions and Rawlings Maintenance, to the witness stand and ask him, "Isn't it true that Diversified Security Solutions and Rawlings Maintenance management decisions were made separately from any and all management decisions made for Bio-Med Pharmaceuticals?" Such a question would be considered leading and would not be permitted.

Leading Questions by the Defendant   As is the case with the plaintiff's counsel, when the defendant's attorney is faced with an adverse or hostile witness, he is permitted to ask leading questions. For example, in the *Delgado* case, if the defense attorney has elected to call Mr. Delgado to testify, he would be the legitimate target of leading questions by Bio-Med's attorney. For instance, Bio-Med's attorney would be permitted to ask Mr. Delgado the following question: "Isn't it true that you knew of the risk imposed by the combustible chemicals located in the storeroom next to your office?"

Rules Regarding the Defendant's Direct Examination   The same rules governing the plaintiff's strategy on direct examination also apply to the defendant's direct examination. Thus, the defendant's attorney should prepare in advance by meeting with friendly witnesses before trial. The defendant's attorney should never ask a question to which he does not already know the answer, and he should develop the discipline to know when to stop asking questions.

Cross-Examination by the Plaintiff   When the defendant's attorney has completed the direct examination of each witness, the plaintiff's attorney has the opportunity to engage in cross-examination. The scope of plaintiff's cross-examination is limited to facts covered in direct examination. Like the defendant, the plaintiff wants to discredit the defendant's witnesses, to cast doubt on the accuracy of their testimony, or to show that the witnesses are somehow biased in favor of the defendant.

Redirect Examination by the Defendant   When the plaintiff has completed the cross-examination of a witness, the defendant's attorney has a chance to redirect questions to that witness. This step allows the defendant the same chance that the plaintiff had to reestablish the credibility of his witnesses and to clear up any factual disputes raised on cross-examination.

The Presentation of Rebuttal Evidence

After each side has had the opportunity to see the entire case-in-chief presented by the other party, both have the chance to present rebuttal evidence. **Rebuttal evidence**, or evidence in rebuttal, is designed to discredit the other side's evidence and to reestablish the credibility of the side presenting the rebuttal. To make the rebuttal as efficient and as fair as possible, the scope of rebuttal is limited to the evidence presented during the case-in-chief. No new evidence is to be presented during the rebuttal. When the plaintiff has completed her rebuttal, the defendant has the same chance to call rebuttal witnesses. Some states use the term *surebuttal* to describe the defendant's rebuttal. Others use the phrase *evidence in rejoinder* or *rejoinder evidence*. Regardless of the terms used to describe it, the defendant's rebuttal is limited to the rebuttal evidence presented by the plaintiff.

rebuttal evidence
Formal contradiction of statements made by an adversary.

Closing Argument

As the trial begins to wind down, one of the final steps is the presentation of the closing argument. The objective and scope of the closing argument are more precise and definitive than for the opening statements. The evidence has already been presented, so it is clear that the closing arguments must refer to that evidence and must attempt to convince the jury that the attorney's interpretation of that evidence is the correct one.

Definition and Limitations   Each side in a jury trial is allowed time at the end of the presentation of evidence to make a closing argument. The closing argument will help jurors review the evidence that the attorneys introduced during the trial. Unlike the procedure followed during the opening statements, which prevents the attorneys from arguing their case, during the closing arguments attorneys are permitted to do their best to persuade jurors of the validity of their case. Moreover, they are also permitted to attack the presentation of the other side's evidence.

The Strategy of the Closing Argument   During closing arguments, each attorney will explain her theory of the case and will demonstrate how the evidence presented at trial supports that theory. Each attorney also will do her best to destroy the jury's belief in the credibility of the other side's witnesses. Destroying the credibility of the opponent's witnesses can be accomplished in a number of ways. The attorney may demonstrate that the witness has contradicted himself on the stand. The attorney may point out discrepancies between the witness's testimony in a deposition or interrogatories and his testimony during the actual trial. It also may be demonstrated that the witness lacks credibility because of bias or because of the inability of the witness to really know the facts that he testified to.

Characteristics of a Good Closing Argument   As noted earlier, the jury has a heightened awareness of the trial process at the beginning of the trial. The same is true, though to a lesser degree, at the end of the trial. This fact, plus the fact that this is the attorney's last chance to reach the jury, makes the closing argument very important. Because so much of the success of a jury trial depends on the closing argument, an attorney should take great care in fashioning the closing. It is critical to know the characteristics of a good closing argument. A closing argument must be well-planned and persuasive.

Delivering a Well-Planned Closing Argument   Planning the closing statement is important because the attorney must organize a mass of evidence and testimony into a coherent pattern that the jury can understand. The attorney begins the closing argument with his theory of the case and then moves to an explanation of the burden of proof and the evidence that strengthens his theory. The attorney also attempts to point out weaknesses in the evidence the other side has presented and to discredit the witnesses upon whom his adversary has relied.

Delivering a Persuasive Closing Argument   The closing argument must be persuasive. Persuasiveness is difficult to manufacture, so it is extremely helpful if the attorney is convinced of the righteousness of her client's cause. If jury members doubt the attorney's dedication to vindicating the rights of the client, they will have little faith in anything she says on behalf of that client. For these reasons, in the closing argument, as in the opening statement, an attorney should identify herself with the client's cause. In the *Delgado* case, for instance, the jury will be much more easily convinced by your attorney if she concludes her argument by saying, "We have proved that the officers and directors of Bio-Med Pharmaceuticals attempted to hide behind the facade of Diversified Security Solutions and Rawlings Maintenance in a feeble attempt to escape their legal obligation to protect all those who used their offices," than if she were to say, "The defendant's attorney did not prove that Diversified Security Solutions and Rawlings Maintenance were not the alter egos of the defendants."

Jury Instructions   In both federal and state courts, the judge has the responsibility of delivering jury instructions. These instructions include an explanation of the law, the burden of proof, the weight that should be given to the evidence, the process to be followed during the deliberations, and the verdicts that can be rendered, all based solely on the evidence presented during the trial. Usually, such instructions are given to the jury after the closing arguments, immediately before the deliberation process begins. However, the judge may instruct the jury on some things, such as the law relating to the procedure at trial, the duties and the functions of the jury, the law that pertains to the case, and the use of evidence, before the trial begins and whenever needed during the actual course of the trial. Also, although the responsibility of final jury instructions belongs to the judge, the attorneys have, at the close of evidence, the opportunity to file a written request with the judge to deliver the instructions in a particular way. Before closing arguments the judge will inform the attorneys how she will instruct the jury. After closing arguments, the judge delivers the jury instructions. Before the jury retires to consider its verdict, the attorneys may, out of the hearing of the jury members, object to the instructions. The objection must specifically explain the grounds for the objection.

Jury Deliberation and Verdicts

Actual Deliberations   Following the judge's instructions, the jury as a group considers the evidence in light of those instructions and attempts to arrive at a verdict. If the jurors are confused about some point or unsure of the law, they can ask for clarification from the judge. The jury can also see any of the evidence presented at trial. In a civil case tried in federal court, a unanimous verdict is required unless the parties have agreed on some number less than a majority. In many state courts, a three-fourths majority is sufficient for a verdict in a civil case.

Rendering a Verdict   Once the jury reaches a decision, the foreperson notifies the judge. In most jurisdictions, parties and lawyers are not required to wait at the courthouse for a verdict. The clerk or bailiff may telephone them when a verdict has been reached. Some lawyers even elect not to be present when a verdict is returned. The verdict is generally read aloud by the judge and then filed with the clerk of court.

Types of Verdicts   In civil cases, the court has the broad discretion to decide which of three types of verdicts a jury will use: general verdict, general verdict with interrogatories, or special verdict. That decision does not depend on the type of litigation but rather on the complexity of the legal issues. Often the court waits until the end of the trial before determining which type of verdict to use and, in some cases, may submit some issues on a general verdict form and others on a special verdict form.

general verdict

A verdict in which the jury must simply decide in favor of the plaintiff, by specifying an amount of money damages, or decide in favor of the defendant.

general verdict with interrogatories

Requires that the jury find for the plaintiff or the defendant, and requires that the jury members answer specific fact questions.

special verdict

The jury answers specific questions about the case, and the court then applies the law to the facts found by the jury to determine which party is entitled to judgment.

motion for judgment as a matter of law

In a jury trial, a request from one party that the judge decide the case in that party's favor on the basis that no facts have been proved that would support a jury's decision for the other party.

The **general verdict** is a verdict in which the jury must simply decide in favor of the plaintiff by specifying an amount of money damages, or decide in favor of the defendant.

Rule 49 of the Federal Rules of Civil Procedure provides for a **general verdict with interrogatories** and not only requires that the jury find for the plaintiff or the defendant, but requires that the jury members answer specific fact questions. Questions are phrased so that they may be answered with a short response, generally a "yes" or "no." In the event of inconsistencies in the answers, the court may ask the jury to deliberate further in an attempt to correct the inconsistencies. The court also has the option of declaring a mistrial and trying the case again with a new jury.

The verdict form used most often currently is the **special verdict**, in which the jury answers specific questions about the case. It is the responsibility of the court then to apply the law to the facts found by the jury to determine which party is entitled to judgment. (See Rule 49(a) of the Federal Rules of Civil Procedure.)

Polling the Jury   *Polling the jurors* involves asking each juror if the verdict announced was the verdict that he or she rendered. As long as the required number of jurors answer that the verdict announced is the verdict that they agreed to, there is no problem and the jury is dismissed. For example, suppose in the *Delgado* case eight jurors were involved in the deliberations. Suppose further that three-fourths of those jurors were required for the rendering of a verdict. If six of the eight answer during the polling process that they agreed with the verdict, the jury members are discharged. If, however, fewer than six concur with the verdict, then the jurors are sent back to continue their deliberations.

Motions during Trial

While a trial is still in progress, the litigants have the opportunity to end the dispute in a number of different ways. As discussed in Chapter 14, settlement may occur even after the trial has commenced. During the trial, a party may attempt to arrive at a speedy conclusion by asking the court to grant a motion for judgment as a matter of law. Also, throughout the trial, both parties have the opportunity to present a variety of motions to the court, including a motion for involuntary dismissal, a motion to strike, or a motion for mistrial.

Motion for Judgment as a Matter of Law   A **motion for judgment as a matter of law** (JMOL), formerly known as a motion for directed verdict, allows the trial judge to remove a case or issues in a case from the jury's consideration when the facts are sufficiently clear that the law mandates a particular result.

The moving party for a JMOL must wait until the opposing party has rested its case. After the JMOL has been urged, the opposing party must be given an opportunity to cure any deficiency in its proof. Two situations generally result in the court's granting a JMOL:

1. There is a total absence of pleading or proof on an issue that is material to the claim or defense.

2. There are no controverted issues of fact on which reasonable persons could differ.

The court is required to view all evidence presented for a JMOL in the light most favorable to the nonmoving party and grant all inference in favor of the nonmoving party.

Motion for Involuntary Dismissal
In a nonjury trial, a defendant might, upon completion of the presentation of plaintiff's evidence, move for dismissal upon facts and law, without waiving the right to offer evidence if the motion is not granted. This motion is similar to a motion for directed verdict in cases tried by a jury. The judge can rule on the motion at the time it is made, or wait until the close of the trial. Requirements for a **motion for involuntary dismissal** are discussed in Rule 41(b) of the Federal Rules of Civil Procedure.

If the court denies the motion or renders judgment on the merits against the plaintiff, the court must make findings of fact required by Rule 2(a) of the Federal Rules of Civil Procedure. In the event that the court denies the defendant's motion or reserves its decision until the conclusion of the presentation of evidence, the defendant may renew its motion after all of the evidence has been presented.

Motion to Strike
A party may move to strike evidence that has been improperly admitted. For example, if a witness blurts out an answer to opposing counsel's question quickly, before her counsel can object, the witness's counsel may move to strike that testimony. The **motion to strike** should include a request that the judge instruct the jurors, in a jury trial, to disregard the improper evidence during its deliberations.

Motion for Mistrial
In a **motion for mistrial**, a party asks the court to terminate the trial before judgment and set the case for trial at another time, on the basis of improprieties. This motion should be reserved for an impropriety so severe that a party cannot receive a fair trial before that particular jury. Usually, improprieties can be corrected by instructing the jury to disregard the impropriety. Possible improprieties might include improper and inflammatory argument, or improper contact between a party and a jury member or members.

Motions at the End of Trial

After the jury has rendered its verdict, and the court has entered its judgment, a dissatisfied party has the opportunity to file a motion to have a judgment set aside.

Renewed Motion for Judgment as a Matter of Law
A **renewed motion for judgment as a matter of law**, formerly known as a *motion for judgment notwithstanding the verdict*, asks the district court to disregard the jury findings and enter judgment for the movant in spite of the jury's verdict for the nonmovant. Rule 50(a)(2) of the Federal Rules of Civil Procedure permits the consideration of a renewed motion only if the moving party made a motion for JMOL before the case was submitted to a jury. Additionally, if the party made a pre-verdict JMOL, but not a renewed motion for JMOL after the judgment, the district court and the appellate court are powerless to direct entry of judgment in favor of the party.

Rule 5(c)(J) of the Federal Rules of Civil Procedure allows the filing of a renewed motion for judgment as a matter of law no later than 28 days after the entry of judgment, "or if the motion addresses a jury issue not decided by a verdict, no later than 28 days after the jury was discharged."

motion for involuntary dismissal
A motion requesting dismissal of a lawsuit by the court, either prior to judgment or by virtue of a judgment against the plaintiff based on the verdict of the jury or the decision of the court after trial.

motion to strike
A request that immaterial statements or other things be removed from an opponent's pleading.

motion for mistrial
A motion asking that the judge terminate a trial prior to its conclusion because the jury is unable to reach a verdict, because of prejudicial error that cannot be corrected or eliminated by any action the court might take, or because of the occurrence of some event that would make it pointless to continue.

renewed motion for judgment as a matter of law
Asks the district court to disregard the jury findings and enter judgment for the movant in spite of the jury's verdict for the nonmovant.

AUTOMATED LITIGATION SUPPORT

Presentation Software

SCENARIO

You are the only paralegal on the trial team for the *Delgado* case. Because you used litigation support software throughout the discovery phase of the trial, you feel confident that you will be able to retrieve documents, prior deposition testimony, answers to interrogatories, requests for disclosures, and admissions easily and readily. However, after a brief meeting with your attorney you find that you still have work to do. Your attorney wants to be sure that she has the full attention of the jurors during her opening statement and closing argument. She anticipates that both will be lengthy and complex, and she wants to be sure the jurors remember some important points. She has asked you to help her put together a visual presentation to emphasize the important aspects of her opening statement and closing argument.

PROBLEM

How do you create a visual presentation to meet the attorney's needs, and what equipment will be needed in court for that presentation?

SOLUTION

Professionals in all areas realize the importance of visual aids in any type of presentation. Trial attorneys also recognize this. Software, known as presentation software, helps a trial attorney or paralegal put together a visually appealing computer slide show. Using templates provided in the software, the user creates "slides" containing both colorful text and graphics to help emphasize points. Software, such as Microsoft PowerPoint or Corel's Presentation, enables you to insert graphs and charts designed with the companion spreadsheet programs. Relevant photographs taken with a digital camera can be inserted into the slide presentation. These slides are displayed to the jury on a screen or monitor with the use of a special projector connected to the computer running the program. In a trial situation, the attorney would use a laptop computer. This same laptop computer can be used to run litigation support software, such as Summation.

If your attorney plans to use a laptop computer (or any specialized hardware) in court, you should check the courtroom ahead of time. You may need extension cords or plug adapters in order to use your equipment. Remember that some courtrooms are old and were not designed for today's technology. Check with the court clerk to make sure that the judge does not have any special limitations on the use of technology in his or her courtroom. With adequate preparation and planning, presentation software can greatly enhance a trial attorney's presentation to the jury.

---

motion for new trial

A motion asking the trial court to order a new trial when prejudicial error has occurred or when, for any other reason, a fair trial was prevented.

Objections by the nonmovant are permitted under Rule 50, with no deadlines for the filing specified. The court may grant the renewed motion for JMOL and render judgment for the movant or grant a new trial.

Motion for New Trial A **motion for new trial** asks the district court to correct a trial error by granting a new trial. (See Rule 50(d) of the Federal Rules of Civil Procedure.) This motion must be filed within 28 days after the entry of judgment. When a motion for new trial is based on affidavits, they must be filed with the motion. The time limit cannot be extended by the district court or by the parties.

The opposition may file a responsive affidavit within 14 days after being served with the motion for new trial.

The court has the authority to grant a new trial for any reason that would justify granting one on a party's motion.

THE PARALEGAL'S ROLE AT TRIAL

The paralegal's role at the trial involves many of the same areas that the paralegal was involved in during the preparation stages. These areas of participation include witnesses, exhibits, note taking, jury selection, and general trial coordination tasks.

Ensuring the Presence of Witnesses

The paralegal may be responsible for locating and having the witnesses present in the courtroom for their testimony. Your witness control log, discussed earlier, will assist you in coordinating the production of witnesses at the appropriate times. You also may be asked to provide for transportation of witnesses. This task may even include picking up out-of-town witnesses arriving at the airport. If possible, delegate this responsibility to another member of the legal team so that you are not away from the courtroom for any extended period of time. The paralegal may be called upon to calm or reassure a nervous witness. It may even be your responsibility to work with hostile witnesses whom your attorney is forced to call to the stand. Your demeanor must be firm but relaxed when dealing with hostile witnesses. If a contact person for witnesses has been designated at the law firm, you should check with that person frequently to ensure that all witnesses will be present in court as scheduled.

Keeping Track of Exhibits

During the trial, you must keep track of exhibits introduced by both sides. The exhibit log reflects which exhibits have been offered and admitted, which exhibits have incurred objections, and whether the exhibit was ultimately admitted into evidence. At each break in the trial, you should compare the court reporter's original exhibits against the exhibit log to be sure that all exhibits are accounted for. During the trial, you should confer with your attorney at the end of each day to determine which exhibits will be introduced the next day. Review your exhibit files to make certain that adequate copies of these exhibits are ready for the next trial session.

Participating in Jury Selection

As the paralegal assigned to the case, you may be asked to prepare a jury seating chart similar to the one depicted in Exhibit 15-14. The purpose of this chart is to track voir dire examination. While your attorney is conducting the jury examination, you should note the verbal and nonverbal communication of potential jurors, particularly with respect to factual issues or prejudices that are germane to the case.

The paralegal must record the information learned through the voir dire process to assist the attorney with her decisions regarding which jurors to strike and which to retain. Unless you are fortunate enough to have a remarkable memory, it is very difficult to process and record all of the requisite information while your attorney is in the process of questioning the potential jurors.

The use of a spreadsheet that lists the potential jurors in either alphabetical or seating order will make this process much less cumbersome. This spreadsheet enables you to enter on your laptop computer all personal and case-specific information that will go into your

EXHIBIT 15-14 Juror Seating Chart

Delgado v. Bio-Med Pharmaceuticals
Civil Action NO. 12-71891
Jury Seating Chart

1. Pete Anderson	2. Nancy Rodriquez	3. Carole Peczniak	4. Joy Speigel	5. Gaspar Ortega	6. Christine Calderone

—Back Row—

7. Hubert Conaughton	8. Hedeki Seki	9. Andrew Glanzburgh	10. Monroe Szarkowski	11. Gustave Schoenborn	12. Chifton Wheeler

—Front Row—

Copyright © 2015 Cengage Learning ®

electronic courtroom
A courtroom equipped with electronic equipment to be utilized in trial presentation.

attorney's decision-making process for each potential juror. Additional information that should be entered includes notes of strikes, including who struck the individual, how many strikes each side has used, and potential jurors who have been excused for cause by the judge. This chart preserves critical and complete information on the jury selection process in the event that becomes an issue on a subsequent appeal of the final decision in the case.

Taking Notes during the Trial

Your attorney's full energy and concentration must be directed toward the witness on the stand, the objections raised by opposing counsel, and the court's rulings on particular motions. You should, therefore, assume responsibility for taking full and accurate notes of the trial proceedings. A lined notebook with a wide left margin will assist you in noting inconsistencies in testimony, incomplete answers to questions, and exhibits that have not yet been admitted into evidence. You may want to use red ink to record "things to do" that arise during the trial. Note the beginning time of each session and all breaks. These notations will enable you to quickly locate a particular piece of information.

THE ELECTRONIC COURTROOM

The **electronic courtroom**, a courtroom equipped with electronic equipment to be utilized in trial presentation, is not a new phenomenon. Rather, it has evolved, becoming more sophisticated and pervasive over the past 30 years. Courtrooms fall into two categories, a courtroom wired for evidence presentation systems, or a traditional courtroom, a courtroom not wired for evidence presentation systems. To determine which category your trial courtroom falls into, you will need to check the court's Web site, or tour the courtroom early in the trial preparation stage. Most federal court Web sites contain information regarding the electronic capabilities of your assigned courtroom. For example, if you check the Northern District of Texas' Web site at www.ndtx.uscourts.gov, you will find information regarding the court personnel to contact regarding evidence presentation systems, training available, and the specific equipment found in each judge's courtroom.

In the event your courtroom is a traditional courtroom, you will need to contact the appropriate court representative to arrange for a portable video cart with evidence presentation equipment, or make arrangements to bring your own equipment to the courtroom.

Evidence presentation systems are technologies that present evidence electronically and simultaneously to everyone in the courtroom. The technology may include all or part of the following:

- Document camera
- **Laptop computer with presentation software**
- Electronic whiteboard
- Annotation equipment
- Digital monitor, projector, and projector screen
- Integrated lectern
- Kill switch and control system

The **document camera**, a compact, high-resolution camera, is the successor to the projector. Evidence utilized with the document camera is not limited to documents, but includes photographs, X-rays, maps, and diagrams. The unit is approximately 12 inches wide and 16 inches tall. A magnification zoom lens permits enlargement of a particular portion of evidence for the fact finder.

Laptop Computer with Presentation Software

The laptop is the most frequently used type of computer in the courtroom because of its built-in monitor and portability. The laptop may utilize external monitors also. Another advantage of the laptop is that it generally offers the same amount of storage capacity as desktop models. Document exhibit retrieval for view on a monitor or monitors in the court room can be accomplished by storing the documents/exhibits in files and retrieving them through software, or by a touch screen sensor through which exhibit numbers are stored on the display, and through use of a bar code system. With the latter system, the attorney runs a handheld bar code scanner over the bar code and the document appears.

Two major types of presentation software are utilized in the courtroom. The first type, standard software that has sufficient capability for litigation purposes, generally consists of Microsoft's PowerPoint and Corel's Presentations. Changes to the slides generated with these programs must be made prior to their use in the courtroom, not at the last moment when a witness is testifying regarding the slide. The second type of presentation software, often referred to as "high-end" includes all the attributes of the standard software, but permits changes to be made to the document as it is presented in the courtroom. There are many commercial software packages, including ANIX from DOAR Communications, Inc., Sanction from Verdict Systems, and Trial Director from InData Corp., in addition to proprietary packages developed by specific companies or law firms for their individual purposes.

evidence presentation systems
Technologies that present evidence electronically and simultaneously to everyone in the courtroom.

laptop computer with presentation software
A laptop containing software to create a slideshow presentation.

document camera
A compact, high-resolution camera.

electronic whiteboard
A surface that can be written on and erased, display computer images, and send commands to the computer.

annotation tools
Hardware devices that coordinate with the document camera and laptop to mark screen images.

monitor
A device that displays signals on a computer screen.

projector
Digital equipment, either portable or a standard unit, that projects rays of light or images onto a screen.

projection screen
A white or silvered surface where a projected image may be viewed by an audience and may be wall-mounted or stand-mounted.

integrated lectern
A lectern that incorporates the equipment, connections, and controls in one location for an attorney to operate the courtroom technology from a single position.

kill switch
The switch at the bench that permits the judge to turn off monitors until a particular piece of evidence is admitted or in an instance where the judge determines that certain images should not be shown to the jury.

real-time reporting
A service provided by court reporters who utilize software that matches the keystrokes on a stenograph machine to corresponding entries in a database and then translates the keystrokes into words.

The **electronic whiteboard**, is a surface that can be written on and erased, display computer images, and send commands to the computer. The whiteboard may contain a pressure sensitive surface for writing, or it may utilize markers that are embedded with a tracking device. Sensors in or around the board capture the position, movement, and color of the marker. A personal computer saves the writing, including any deletions, or changes. Images on the whiteboard can be transmitted instantly to all monitors in the courtroom.

Annotation tools are hardware devices that coordinate with the document camera and laptop to mark screen images. Three such tools are the touch screen monitor, which responds to pressure on the surface, the telestrator tablet and the light pen, which works only with a CRT monitor.

Monitor, Projector, and Projection Screen

In a standard courtroom setup, **monitors**, devices that display signals on a computer screen, are usually placed on the bench, at the witness stand, on counsel table, and in a position visible from the jury box. Monitors may be built into the jury box. The **projector** used with a laptop is digital equipment, either portable or a standard unit that projects rays of light or images onto a screen. A projector with a rating of 1,000 or more lumens of light is needed in the courtroom. The distance between the projector and the screen will determine the lumens requirement. Newer digital projectors contain built-in converters to display the output from both analog and digital devices. The **projection screen** is a white or silvered surface where a projected image may be viewed by an audience and may be wall-mounted or stand-mounted. In some courtrooms, the screens are recessed into the wall so that they are out of the way when not in use.

The **integrated lectern** incorporates the equipment, connections, and controls in one location for an attorney to operate the courtroom technology from a single position.

A **kill switch** is the switch at the bench that permits the judge to turn off monitors until a particular piece of evidence is admitted or in an instance where the judge determines that certain images should not be shown to the jury.

Real-time reporting is a service provided by court reporters who utilize software that matches the keystrokes on a stenograph machine to corresponding entries in a database and then translates the keystrokes into words. The court reporter's computer transmits these words immediately to connected monitors. Voice writer reporters record courtroom proceedings by speaking into a stenomask. Voice writers also have the ability to produce real-time transcripts. Speech recognition software translates the voice to digital format, and the digital is matched with database entries, and the English words then appear on the courtroom monitors in a transcript format.

Real-time service may be available only to the court (the most common procedure currently) or may be made available in other courtroom locations. Attorneys in federal court cases may receive real-time services upon payment of the fees authorized by the Judicial Conference. Because of the extensive costs, this service to attorneys is normally cost-effective only in larger cases. The second level of real-time service delivers the court reporter's output to a laptop loaded with special software to make the output more useable. In most courtrooms, attorneys must provide their own laptops to receive this second level of real-time output. The operator of the receiving computer can copy, add notes or highlights, and search the transcript. Any receiving laptop can copy the file to a disk, print the transcript, or send the file via e-mail to another computer. There are numerous real-time software packages currently utilized by attorneys, including Summation Realtime from Summation Legal Technologies, Inc., LiveNote from LiveNote, Inc., CaseView from Stenograph LLC, and e-Binder from RealLegal, Inc.

Videoconference equipment is equipment that facilitates a two-way real-time transmission of audio and video signals between specialized devices or computers at two more locations. There are two sites in a videoconference call, the "local site," normally the courtroom, and a remote site where the conference participant who is not in the courtroom is located. The videoconference may be between two or more points.

The **telephone interpreting system** permits interpreting services from English to a foreign language or vice versa. The foreign language translation is heard by a witness or defendant in the courtroom through telephone handsets or headsets. The balance of the courtroom hears the English translation of foreign language testimony through either a speaker telephone or the court's audio system. Two telephone lines are required. One line is connected to a digital conference telephone, while the second is connected to a conventional telephone handset or headset. The interpreter listens to the English or foreign language from the courtroom through the conference call and interprets into the foreign language or English. The interpretation is sent by a hand switch to either the conventional receiver or the conference phone.

videoconference equipment

It is equipment that facilitates a two-way real-time transmission of audio and video signals between specialized devices or computers at two more locations.

telephone interpreting system

A system that permits interpreting services from English to a foreign language or vice versa.

FINDING IT on the Internet

The Lectric Law Library maintains a search engine titled "Law Looker-Upper" at <**http://www.lectlaw.com/search.html**>.

a. Access the search engine and use the key word function to find articles relating to jury research. Use the information from that search to prepare a memo relating to the advisability of employing a jury consultant for the *Delgado* case.

b. As an alternative assignment, research your state's pattern jury charge and draft jury instructions for the *Delgado* case.

SUMMARY

- One trial preparation task that can be completed during the preliminary stages of a lawsuit is the organization of litigation files. It is best if files are kept current as the case develops. Each time a pleading is filed by either side, it should immediately be placed in the pleadings binder. One problem that might surface during organization of the file is the need to amend the pleadings in the case before the time to do so expires. The paralegal should check federal or local rules to determine the procedure to be followed if a pleading must be amended after the trial date has been set. The paralegal must also prepare a trial notebook. The form of the trial notebook is dictated by the type of case, the number of pleadings, the complexity of the legal issues, the number of exhibits and witnesses, and the anticipated length of the trial. However, most trial notebooks include the following basic sections: (1) list of the parties and attorneys, (2) the pleadings and motions, (3) information regarding the witnesses, (4) information regarding the expert witnesses, (5) document indices, (6) deposition summaries, (7) chronology, (8) the cast of characters, (9) legal research, (10) trial exhibits, (11) jury profiles and instructions, (12) the trial outline, (13) the attorney's notes, and (14) the "things to do" list.

- The paralegal must consult with the attorney to determine whether any witnesses will require a subpoena. In some instances attorneys prefer to subpoena only witnesses who are not considered "friendly." However, a friendly witness may request a subpoena to present to an employer as evidence that he has been ordered to appear and testify. The paralegal may be asked to communicate with the witnesses early in the trial preparation period about the basic details of the trial, including the date, the location, and the anticipated length of their testimony. The witnesses should be informed that they will need to meet with the attorney and the paralegal closer to the time of the trial. Shortly before trial, the paralegal should arrange a witness preparation meeting, during which your attorney will explain the trial process to each witness.

- Often the paralegal is called upon to gather and organize exhibits in a case. This responsibility may require obtaining enlarged exhibits or unusual graphics. The paralegal also may have to set up a chronology or organize a set of statistics. Whatever the case, it helps to know what to look for in the evaluation of those exhibits. It is possible that the paralegal may be called upon to help conduct research for or assemble a notebook of cases referenced in the trial brief.

- The paralegal is often responsible for coordinating the logistics of a trial. Logistics can be a matter of routine. However, when the trial is held in another district or another county, or when the client and many of the witnesses are from out of town, the paralegal will have to arrange for hotel accommodations and travel arrangements. Also, the paralegal will have to examine the courthouse and contact local court personnel.

- The purpose of the jury profile is to determine a composite profile of the ideal jurors for a particular case. Social psychologists and litigation specialists can provide law firms with valuable statistics and jury sampling information to create not only the image of preferred jurors but also a profile of the jurors that your attorney will want to avoid.

- The paralegal is often responsible for arranging a mock trial, often coordinating the arrangements with a jury consultant. The first step in the mock trial is to select the mock jury. Key witnesses and principal exhibits are presented to the jury in the same way that they will be presented at the actual trial. The mock jury evaluates the testimony and the exhibits and renders a verdict. Following their decision, the jurors may be questioned about their perceptions of the strengths and weaknesses of the case. The period between the mock trial and the actual trial should be devoted to correcting the weaknesses pointed out by the mock jury. The increasing complexity of litigation has resulted in the introduction of a technique known as the shadow jury, a secret jury selected by the law firm or an outside consulting firm. The shadow jury attends the trial and at breaks and the end of each session is questioned about the effectiveness of the witnesses and exhibits.

- The paralegal may be asked to prepare a jury seating chart to track voir dire examination. While the attorney is conducting the jury examination, the paralegal notes the verbal and nonverbal communication of potential jurors.

- During the trial, both parties have the opportunity to present a variety of motions to the court, including a motion for involuntary dismissal, motion to strike, or motion for mistrial. Another option open to a party at the conclusion of the evidence is to file a motion for directed verdict, asking the judge to instruct the jury to render a verdict for the party filing the motion.

- The paralegal may be responsible for locating and having witnesses present in the courtroom. During the trial, the paralegal keeps track of exhibits. The exhibit log must be maintained to reflect which exhibits have been offered and admitted, which have incurred objections from opposing counsel, and which were ultimately admitted into evidence. The paralegal must assume responsibility for taking full and accurate notes of trial proceedings. A lined notebook with a wide left margin will assist the paralegal in noting inconsistencies in testimony, incomplete answers, and exhibits that have not yet been admitted into evidence. Paralegals often use red ink to record "things to do" that arise during the trial.

KEY TERMS

theory of the case
proof chart
pretrial conference
motion in limine
trial notebook
curriculum vitae
on point
jury instructions
voir dire examination
trial brief
cite check
mock trial
mock jury
shadow jury
peremptory challenges
opening statement
stipulation

rebuttal evidence
general verdict
general verdict with
    interrogatories
special verdict
motion for
    judgment as a
    matter of law
motion for involuntary
    dismissal
motion to strike
motion for mistrial
renewed motion for
    judgment as a matter
    of law
motion for new trial
electronic courtroom

evidence presentation
    systems
document camera
laptop computer with
    presentation software
monitor
electronic whiteboard
annotation tools
projector
projection screen
integrated lectern
kill switch
real-time reporting
videoconference
    equipment
telephone interpreting
    system

REVIEW QUESTIONS

1. Describe the paralegal's duties in trial preparation.
2. What is the purpose of the trial notebook?
3. List the contents of the trial notebook.
4. What responsibilities does the paralegal have in preparing witnesses for trial?
5. Describe the standards by which a trial exhibit is evaluated.

6. What duties does the paralegal have in preparing the logistics of the trial?

7. Identify motions that might be appropriate during a trial.

8. What are the paralegal's duties in preparing for the jury process?

9. What duties does the paralegal perform during the trial?

10. List the major components of a trial.

CHAPTER EXERCISES

Where necessary, check with your instructor prior to starting any of these exercises.

1. Review your local court rules relating to jury selection. Check to see if these rules differ in any substantial way from the rules enumerated in the Federal Rules of Civil Procedure.

2. Prepare a memorandum describing what a paralegal should look for during a visit to an out-of-town courthouse.

3. Prepare a trial exhibit list for the *Delgado* case for both parties.

4. Draft a memorandum to your attorney reflecting the trial tasks that you have completed for the *Delgado* case and listing outstanding trial assignments. Use the information related to paralegal trial duties in this chapter.

CHAPTER PROJECT

In this chapter, locate the detailed explanation of the contents of the trial notebook. Next, review the facts presented in the *Delgado* case, which appears in the opening Commentary. Draft a memorandum to a new paralegal in your law firm instructing him on the contents of a trial notebook for the *Delgado* case. Make certain to include instructions for each area of the notebook.

THE *BENNETT* CASE
Assignment for Chapter 15: Preparing a Trial Notebook

The *Bennett* case is going to trial. You have been asked to create a trial notebook. Organize all of the documents you have prepared in connection with the case and create sections in the notebook for information to be inserted prior to or during trial.

THE *DOUGLASS FINANCIAL SERVICES INC.* CASE
Assignment for Chapter 15: Preparing Trial Subpoenas

Your attorney is preparing for trial and asks that you prepare subpoenas for two witnesses listed in the police report. Locate the proper subpoena forms for your state and complete them. Trial is set to begin on the 28th of the following month.

CHAPTER 16 Posttrial Practice

CHAPTER OUTLINE

THE *TRAN-STAR* CASE

A federal court jury recently awarded $10 million to the owners of Paragon Centre, a 10-story office building in downtown Dallas, Texas. The decision stated that the Tran-Star Company, a major national gasoline distributor incorporated in Delaware and headquartered in Pennsylvania, was negligent in permitting a leak from its abandoned gas station, a block from Paragon Centre, to spread through the elevator shaft of the office complex. The building was evacuated for less than two hours. Three employees in the building suffered nausea and dizziness from the fumes. They were treated and released from a local hospital. There was no structural damage to the building. However, the jury found that the future value of the building was diminished because of the stigma associated with the gasoline incident. The firm that represented Tran-Star at trial is unable to prosecute an appeal and has withdrawn from its representation of the client. Tran-Star has hired your local firm to appeal what it feels is an excessive jury award in light of the minimal injury to the building. Tran-Star also suspects that the large jury award was due in part to local prejudice in Dallas against a large, out-of-town corporate entity that the jurors felt damaged a small, local real estate developer. Your attorney has requested that you immediately obtain a copy of the testimony from the six-week trial. This testimony encompasses 20 volumes and more than 100 exhibits. Accordingly, your attorney asks that you summarize the transcript and draft the necessary posttrial documents. You also may be asked to participate in the preparation of an appellate brief. This chapter covers the details of the posttrial process.

The posttrial process is the final stage in the litigation process. After reading this chapter, you should be able to:

- identify posttrial motions.
- define appeal.
- identify the two major parties to an appeal.
- explain the nature of a notice of appeal.
- explain the purpose of a supersedeas bond.
- determine the paralegal's duties in drafting an appellate brief.
- describe the paralegal's role in the oral argument.
- discuss the final procedures in an appeal.

FEDERAL RULES CHANGES REGARDING CALCULATING DUE DATES IN THE APPEAL PROCESS

A variety of technical, but significant, changes to the Federal Rules of Appellate Procedure went into effect on December 1, 2009. These new rules, referred to as "Time-Computation Project," were designed to simplify the method of calculating various deadlines. The Federal Rules of Civil Procedure also received substantial changes regarding the calculation of due dates. Under the new rules, intermediate weekend days and holidays count no matter how many days are provided for any given deadline. The provision of 14 days for a filing now literally means 14 days.

Previously, there was ambiguity in 26(c) of the Federal Rules of Appellate Procedure on how to account for the three extra days that are accorded to parties who have been served with a filing by mail or via electronic service. The revision now specifies that you must first calculate when the time period would expire, and then add three days. For example, if you are the appellee in a case and are served with the appellant's brief via overnight delivery, you would calculate your due date by counting the 30 days under Federal Rules of Appellate Procedure 31(a)(10), adjusting that due date if it falls on a weekend to the following Monday, and then adding three days because of the lack of hand service.

Normally, due dates are determined by counting forward from a triggering event. However, a party may occasionally need to count backwards; for example, 10 days before a trial, seven days before argument. The rule has been amended to eliminate any ambiguity in how to account for weekends and holidays when counting backwards and now specifies that the parties should continue to count backwards to arrive at a due date (Federal Rules of Appellate Procedure 26(a)(5)). Thus, if a party is ordered to file a brief 10 days before a trial, and the 10-day period would fall on a Saturday, the brief would be due the previous Friday. The last time for an e-filing in the appellate court is midnight in the time zone of the court's principal office (Federal Rules of Appellate Procedure 26(a)(4)).

POSTTRIAL MOTIONS

Motion for a New Trial

Rule 59 of the Federal Rules of Civil Procedure allows a dissatisfied party to file a motion asking for a new trial. A motion for a new trial must state the legal grounds on which a new trial should be granted. The court may grant such a new trial on the following grounds: (1) the verdict was contrary to law, (2) the verdict was totally defective, (3) irregularity in the court proceeding, (4) excessive or insufficient damage awards, (5) jury misconduct, or (6) newly discovered evidence. For example, in the *Tran-Star* case, your attorney may feel that some irregularity in the court proceedings may have resulted in the excessive damage award. She may, for instance, feel that the closing remarks of Paragon's attorney inflamed the jury, igniting a prejudicial passion against your client. Such a situation would call for the filing of a motion for a new trial.

Under Rule 59 of the Federal Rules of Civil Procedure, a motion for a new trial or a motion to alter or amend a judgment must be filed with the court within 28 days of the entry of judgment. It is important for the paralegal to realize that the actual entry of a judgment could be several weeks or even months after the decision itself has been rendered. You should therefore monitor the court's docket to determine the actual date of the entry of judgment. This date begins the official posttrial time clock.

Indicative Ruling and Remand to the District Court

Rule 12.1 of the Federal Rules of Appellate Procedure was enacted on December 1, 2009, in conjunction with Rule 62.1 of the Federal Rules of Civil Procedure to allow a party to request an "indicative ruling" in the district court on a motion that the district court lacks authority to grant because of a pending appeal. Rule 12.1 facilitates remand to the district court of a ruling on the motion when the district court has indicated that

appeal
Asking a higher court to review the actions of a lower court in order to correct mistakes or injustice.

appellant
The person who appeals a case to a higher court.

appellee
The person against whom an appeal is taken.

cross-appeal
An appeal by the appellee.

pro se
A person representing himself or herself (as a defendant or plaintiff) without a lawyer in a court proceeding (and whether the matter is civil or criminal).

the motion raises a substantial issue or that the district court would grant the motion if the court of appeals remanded for that purpose. Federal Rule of Civil Procedure 62.1(a) will allow a district court to "(1) defer consideration of the motion; (2) deny the motion; or (3) state that it would grant the motion if the court of appeals remands for that purpose or that the motion raises a substantial issue." It is only when the district court selects the third "indicative" option that Federal Rule of Appellate Procedure 12.1 will come into play.

PRELIMINARY STEPS IN THE APPEAL

As a paralegal, you will be instrumental in preparing the appeal. An **appeal** is filed by a party who has lost a case or who is dissatisfied with a judgment or a court order. The appeal asks that a higher court review the lower court's decision. A person bringing an appeal is referred to as the **appellant**. The person who opposes an appeal is the **appellee**. The appellee may also file a cross-appeal. A **cross-appeal** is an appeal filed by the appellee based on a different legal rationale than the appeal filed by the appellant. Only questions of law are subject to review. The appellate court has no authority to consider questions relating to the facts of a case. For example, in the *Tran-Star* case, no facts may be introduced concerning the safety record of Tran-Star over the 10 years it has operated in the Dallas area. However, your attorney may argue that the judge erred in his instructions to the jury. This argument relates only to the law that should have been applied in the case. Appeals are expensive, time consuming, and often unsuccessful. However, the appeal is an essential element in the legal system. Without appeals there would be no check on the legal decision making of the trial courts.

In recent years, the appellate process has been simplified in the federal courts. The clerk in the district court supervises the preparation of the court record—that is, all pleadings and transcripts in the case—for an appeal. The clerk also provides the attorneys with the appropriate forms and copies of the local rules. In contrast, involvement in the state appellate process generally requires more attention to the state court procedural rules.

Rule 25 of the Federal Rules of Appellate Procedure authorizes courts to require electronic filing by local rule, with reasonable exceptions allowed. One exception might be for a solo practitioner whose offices do not include computer technology. Another exception might be for an individual who files **pro se**. The paralegal should carefully review local appellate rules at the beginning of an appellate process. Electronic filing has been implemented in federal district court rules for several years, so there should be a seamless move to electronic filing on your appellate cases.

You should be familiar with federal, state, and local rules for the appellate process. The preliminary steps in an appellate procedure generally include (1) notice of appeal, (2) bond for costs or a supersedeas bond, (3) transcript order and preparation of pertinent record sections, and (4) filing of briefs by both parties. Following these preliminary steps, oral arguments are presented to the court, and the court renders its decision. Exhibit 16–1 charts the stages of an appeal in the federal court up to and including the time for filing the briefs. The chart also notes the time limits for completing each stage and the underlying federal appellate court rules.

EXHIBIT 16-1 Appellate Timetable and Procedures—Federal Courts

ACTION	TIME DUE	FED. APP. RULE
Notice of Appeal	30 days after entry of judgment or order in a separate document.	4(a)(1)(A)
	60 days in cases involving United States, its offices, agencies, or parties.	4(a)(1)(B)
	If timely motion for new trial, judgment as a matter of law, motion to amend or alter judgment, or motion to amend or make additional findings of fact, time for appeal for all parties runs from entry of order denying.	4(a)(4)(A)(4)
Supersedeas Bond	Supersedeas bond given at or after time of filing notice of appeal or order allowing appeal.	7
Record and Transcript Appellant	Within 14 days after filing notice of appeal or entry of an order disposing of the last timely remaining motion of a type specified in Rule 4(a)(1)(A), whichever is later, appellant places written order for transcript or files a certificate stating that no transcript will be ordered. At or before time for perfecting appeal, appellant makes written request designating portion.	10(b)
Record and Transcript Appellee	Within 14 days after service of appellant's order for transcript, appellee designates additional parts of transcripts.	10(b)(3)(B)
Transcript-Reporter	If transcript cannot be completed within 30 days of receipt of order, reporter shall request extension of time from clerk of court of appeals.	11(b)(1)(B)
Briefs	Appellant must file a brief within 40 days after record is filed. Appellee must file brief within 30 days after service of appellant's brief. Reply brief must be filed within 14 days after service of the appellee's brief, and at least 7 days before argument, unless the court, for good cause, allows a later filing.	31(a)

Note—when a party is either required or permitted to act within a designated time period after service on that party, three days are added to the response period, unless the paper is delivered on the date of service reflected in the proof of service. Rule 26(c) of the Federal Rules of Appellate Procedure states that a paper that is signed electronically is not treated as delivered on the date of service shown on the proof of service.

Notice of Appeal

Only one document is required to file an appeal. That document is the **notice of appeal**, which lists the party or parties taking the appeal, the judgment, the order or the portion of the judgment appealed (including the caption of the case in the trial court), and the court to which the appeal is taken. Exhibit 16–2 is an example of a notice of appeal.

According to Rule 4(a) of the Federal Rules of Appellate Procedure, the original of the notice of appeal must be filed with the clerk of the district court from which the appeal is taken within 30 days after the entry of the judgment or the order. Rule 4(a) also

notice of appeal
A document filed with the appellate court and served on the opposing party, giving notice of an intention to appeal.

EXHIBIT 16-2 Notice of Appeal

**IN THE UNITED STATES DISTRICT COURT
FOR THE NORTHERN DISTRICT OF TEXAS, DALLAS DIVISION**

Paragon Centre,   )
)
    Plaintiff,   )   CIVIL ACTION NO. 12-81891
)
    v.   )
)
Tran-Star Company   )
)
    Defendant.   )
)
)
)

NOTICE OF APPEAL

Notice is hereby given that the Tran-Star Company, Defendant herein, hereby appeals to the United States Court of Appeals for the Fifth Circuit from the final judgment entered in this action on February 7, 2013

Respectfully submitted,

By: _____
Attorney for the Defendant
Kirchendorfer, Lehane, Zuer, and Musil
14710 Merit Drive
Dallas, Texas 75230
[Telephone number]
[Facsimile number]

---

states, however, that if the United States or one of its agencies or officers is a party in the case, the notice of appeal must be filed within 60 days after entry of the judgment or the order. Rules 58(a) and 79(e) of the Federal Rules of Civil Procedure answer the controversy of the meaning of "entered" with regard to a judgment or order. These rules direct that a judgment or order is "entered" in a civil case when it is set forth in a separate document approved by the court, signed by the court or court clerk, and entered in the clerk's docket.

This requirement for a separate document is intended to clarify the beginning of the appeal period. Parties have argued in the past that the appeal time begins with the judge's announcement of the ruling from the bench or the judge's filing of a memorandum decision. Rule 12(b) of the Federal Rules of Appellate Procedure requires that the attorney who filed the notice of appeal must, within 14 days after filing the notice, file a statement with the circuit clerk naming the parties that the attorney represents on appeal. Another party may file a notice of appeal within 14 days after the date the first notice was filed, or within the time period prescribed by Rule 4(a) of the Federal Rules of Appellate Procedure, whichever period ends later.

The appellant must pay two separate docketing fees to the clerk of the district court upon filing the notice of appeal. The district court clerk then forwards these fees to the clerk of the appellate court. These fees consist of the filing fee of $5 (under 28 U.S.C.A. § 1917) and the docketing fee of $450 (under 28 U.S.C.A § 1913). An appeal is valid even if these fees are not paid with the filing of the notice of appeal. The clerk of the district court is required to serve notice of the filing of a notice of appeal by mailing a copy of the notice to counsel of record for each party other than the appellant, or to the last known address of a party not represented by counsel. A note is made in the court docket of the names of the parties to whom the clerk mailed copies of the notice of appeal and the date of the mailing. Docketing an appeal occurs when the notice of appeal and certified copies of docket entries are received by the clerk of the court of appeals.

Appeal Bond

An appeal does not automatically stay, or halt, the judgment or the execution of the judgment in the lower court. A party must apply to the district court for a stay. Therefore, an appellant in a civil case may be required to post a bond to cover the cost of the appeal and a supersedeas bond to stay the enforcement of the judgment. A **supersedeas bond** is a promise, supported by a form of surety, to secure suspension of a judgment and delay execution upon the judgment, pending the outcome of the appeal. The appellant and its surety, usually an insurance company, agree to pay to the appellee the amount of any damages sustained due to the delay caused by the appeal if the appellant loses the appeal. The court has the authority to set the amount of the supersedeas bond, based on a monetary value set to the risk taken in the appeal. For example, in the *Tran-Star* case, the court might establish a supersedeas bond of $2 million because of the amount of the verdict and because of the additional devaluation of the real estate as the appellate process continues.

Under Rule 7 of the Federal Rules of Appellate Procedure, the district court may require an appellant to file a bond or provide other security in such form and amount as the court finds necessary to ensure payment of costs on appeal. Security costs for the appeal include the cost of filing fees for docketing the appeal, the cost of the clerk's preparing and transmitting the record, and the cost attributed to the losing party for transcribing and printing the necessary copies of the briefs, appendixes, and records. Costs are eventually paid by the party losing the appeal. Exhibit 16–3 is an example of a bill of costs.

Ordering the Transcript

According to Rule 10(b) of the Federal Rules of Appellate Procedure, within 14 days of filing the notice of appeal the appellant is responsible for making a written request, on a form supplied by the district court clerk, to the court reporter for the complete transcript, the official daily record of the court proceeding, or desired portions of the transcript. A copy of the request is filed with the clerk of the district court. If the appellant does not order a copy of the transcript, the appellant must file a certificate stating that no transcript will be ordered. The appellant also must notify the clerk of the appellate court that the transcript has been ordered. Exhibit 16–4 is an example of the Transcript Purchase Order form available on the various courts of appeals Web sites.

supersedeas bond

A bond put up by a person who appeals a judgment. Supersedeas is a judge's order that temporarily holds up another court's proceedings or, more often, temporarily stays a lower court's judgment. The bond delays the person's obligation to pay the judgment until the appeal is lost.

EXHIBIT 16-3 Bill of Costs

AO 133   (Rev. 12/09) Bill of Costs

UNITED STATES DISTRICT COURT

for the

_____ District of _____

	)	
	)	
v.	)	Case No.:
	)	
	)	

BILL OF COSTS

Judgment having been entered in the above entitled action on _____ against _____ ,
                                                                                              Date

the Clerk is requested to tax the following as costs:

Fees of the Clerk . . . . $_____

Fees for service of summons and subpoena . . . .   _____

Fees for printed or electronically recorded transcripts necessarily obtained for use in the case . . . . . .   _____

Fees and disbursements for printing . . . .   _____

Fees for witnesses *(itemize on page two)* . . . .   ____0.00____

Fees for exemplification and the costs of making copies of any materials where the copies are
necessarily obtained for use in the case. . . . .   _____

Docket fees under 28 U.S.C. 1923 . . . .   _____

Costs as shown on Mandate of Court of Appeals . . . .   _____

Compensation of court-appointed experts . . . .   _____

Compensation of interpreters and costs of special interpretation services under 28 U.S.C. 1828 . . . . .   _____

Other costs *(please itemize)* . . . .   _____

                                                                                       TOTAL $____0.00____

SPECIAL NOTE: Attach to your bill an itemization and documentation for requested costs in all categories.

Declaration

    I declare under penalty of perjury that the foregoing costs are correct and were necessarily incurred in this action and that the services for which fees have been charged were actually and necessarily performed. A copy of this bill has been served on all parties in the following manner:

☐   Electronic service   ☐   First class mail, postage prepaid

☐   Other: _____

s/ Attorney: _____

       Name of Attorney: _____

For: _____   Date: _____
           Name of Claiming Party

Taxation of Costs

Costs are taxed in the amount of _____ and included in the judgment.

                            By: _____   _____
_____
     Clerk of Court   *Deputy Clerk*   *Date*

Source: http://www.uscourts.gov/uscourts/FormsAndFees/Forms/AO133.pdf

EXHIBIT 16-3 Bill of Costs (*continued*)

AO 133 (Rev. 12/09) Bill of Costs

UNITED STATES DISTRICT COURT

Witness Fees (computation, cf. 28 U.S.C. 1821 for statutory fees)							
NAME , CITY AND STATE OF RESIDENCE	ATTENDANCE		SUBSISTENCE		MILEAGE		Total Cost Each Witness
	Days	Total Cost	Days	Total Cost	Miles	Total Cost	
							$0.00
							$0.00
							$0.00
							$0.00
							$0.00
							$0.00
						TOTAL	$0.00

NOTICE

Section 1924, Title 28, U.S. Code (effective September 1, 1948) provides:
"Sec. 1924. Verification of bill of costs."
    "Before any bill of costs is taxed, the party claiming any item of cost or disbursement shall attach thereto an affidavit, made by himself or by his duly authorized attorney or agent having knowledge of the facts, that such item is correct and has been necessarily incurred in the case and that the services for which fees have been charged were actually and necessarily performed."

See also Section 1920 of Title 28, which reads in part as follows:
    "A bill of costs shall be filed in the case and, upon allowance, included in the judgment or decree."

The Federal Rules of Civil Procedure contain the following provisions:
RULE 54(d)(1)

Costs Other than Attorneys' Fees.
    Unless a federal statute, these rules, or a court order provides otherwise, costs — other than attorney's fees — should be allowed to the prevailing party. But costs against the United States, its officers, and its agencies may be imposed only to the extent allowed by law. The clerk may tax costs on 14 day's notice. On motion served within the next 7 days, the court may review the clerk's action.

RULE 6

(d) Additional Time After Certain Kinds of Service.

    When a party may or must act within a specified time after service and service is made under Rule5(b)(2)(C), (D), (E), or (F), 3 days are added after the period would otherwise expire under Rule 6(a).

RULE 58(e)

Cost or Fee Awards:

    Ordinarily, the entry of judgment may not be delayed, nor the time for appeal extended, in order to tax costs or award fees. But if a timely motion for attorney's fees is made under Rule 54(d)(2), the court may act before a notice of appeal has been filed and become effective to order that the motion have the same effect under Federal Rule of Appellate Procedure 4(a)(4) as a timely motion under Rule 59.

Print	Save As...		Reset

EXHIBIT 16-4 Transcript Purchase Order Form

AO 148
(Rev. 6/88)

UNITED STATES COURT OF APPEALS
FOR THE FEDERAL CIRCUIT

) Appeal from ☐   U.S. District Court for _____
                  ☐   Court of International Trade
                  ☐   Claims Court

–VERSUS--   ) TRIAL COURT NO. _____

) CIRCUIT COURT NO. _____

TRANSCRIPT PURCHASE ORDER
(See Rules 10(b) and 11(b) of the Federal Rules of Appellate Procedure)

PART 1 -   TO BE COMPLETED BY APPELLANT WITHIN 10 DAYS OF FILING OF NOTICE OF APPEAL.
            Copies to be distributed by appellant as follows: Copies 1, 2, and 3 to court reporter; Copy 4 to Trial Court;
            Copy 5 to appellee; Copy 6 retained by appellant.

    A.   Complete one of the following:
         ☐   A transcript is not needed for the appeal
         ☐   A transcript is already on file
         ☐   Request is hereby made to the reporter for a transcript of the following proceedings (give particulars):
             Note: voir dire and closing arguments are not prepared unless specifically requested.

         Note: Unless the entire transcript is ordered, appellant must attach a statement of the issues to Copies 4 and 5.
    B.   I certify that financial arrangements have been made with the reporter. Payment is by:
         ☐   Private funds
         ☐   Government expense (civil case). A motion for transcript has been submitted to the trial judge.

SIGNED _____ Date _____ COUNSEL FOR _____
ADDRESS _____
TELEPHONE _____

PART II - TO BE COMPLETED BY COURT REPORTER.
            Copy 1 and 3 retained by the reporter; Copy 2 to be transmitted to the Court of Appeals on same date transcript
            order is received.
            Date Purchase Order received: _____ .
            Estimated completion date: _____ .
            Estimated number of pages: _____ .

I certify that satisfactory financial arrangements ☐ have ☐ have not been completed with appellant for payment of the cost
of the transcript.

                                    _____   _____
                                              Signature   Date
                             Telephone: _____

PART III-NOTIFICATION THAT TRANSCRIPT HAS BEEN FILED IN THE TRIAL COURT.
            (To be completed by court reporter on date of filing transcript in Trial Court and this notification must be
            to Court of Appeals on same date.)

This is to certify that the transcript has been completed. _____ volumes of transcript have been filed with the Trial Court
today.

_____   _____
            Date   (Signature of Court Reporter)

DISTRIBUTION: COURT REPORTER (3 copies),   TRIAL COURT,   TRIAL,   APPELLANT
(Two of Court Reporter's copies are for completion of Part II and Part III and transmittal to Clerk, U.S. Court of Appeals, Federal Circuit, 717 Madison Place, N.W.
Washington, D.C. 20439.)

Source: http://www.cafc.uscourts.gov/images/stories/rules-of-practice/forms/form22.pdf

Responsibilities of Appellant and Appellee   Under Rule 10(b) of the Federal Rules of Appellate Procedure, if the entire transcript is not included in the appeal, the appellant, within 14 days of filing the notice of appeal, must file a statement of the issues that will be presented on appeal. This statement, along with a copy of the order for the transcript or a copy of the certificate stating that no transcript will be ordered, must then be served on the appellee. Under the provisions of Rule 10(b), the appellee then has 14 days to file and serve on the appellant a designation of any additional parts of the transcript that the appellee wants included. If the appellant does not order the additional parts, the appellee may order those parts or apply to the district court for an order requiring the appellant to do so.

Responsibilities of the Court Reporter   Rule 11(b) of the Federal Rules of Appellate Procedure requires that the court reporter acknowledge receipt of the order for the transcript. According to Rule 11(b), the reporter must also note at the bottom of the order the date on which the reporter expects to complete the transcript. The reporter then transmits the order to the clerk of the court of appeals.

Rule 11(b) also provides that if the transcript cannot be completed within 30 days of receipt of the order, the court reporter must request an extension of time from the clerk of the court of appeals. The clerk then notes the extension of time granted on the docket and notifies the parties. The court reporter files the completed transcript with the clerk of the district court within 30 days after receipt of the transcript order form and notifies the clerk of the court of appeals of the filing. Under Rule 11(b), if the court reporter does not file the transcript within the allotted time, the clerk of the court of appeals notifies the district judge and takes such steps as may be directed by the court of appeals, including sanctions.

Responsibilities of the Paralegal   The paralegal will have a variety of responsibilities in relation to the transcript. You should, first of all, maintain close contact with the court reporter to make sure of the timely filing of the transcript. Contact the reporter periodically to determine the projected release time for the transcript. If the reporter is unable to complete the transcript within the designated time frame, designate the order in which you would like to receive parts of the transcript. For example, in the *Tran-Star* case, if your attorney plans to base the appeal on the judge's erroneous instructions to the jury and on the opposing attorney's inflammatory closing arguments, you would want to request those portions of the transcript first. Once the transcript has been received, review it for accuracy, comparing the transcript with any notes taken by the attorney or the paralegal from the law firm that originally tried the case.

Transmitting the Record

The district court clerk is responsible for arranging in chronological order the original papers filed with the district court and numbering and indexing those documents. Once this has been accomplished, the clerk must transmit the record and a certified copy of the docket entries to the court of appeals. This must be done within 14 days of the filing of the notice of appeal, or 14 days after the filing of the transcript, whichever is later. If the deadline cannot be met, the district court clerk must notify the court of appeals of the reasons for the delay and request an extension.

motion for enlargement of time
A motion requesting additional time for an appeal, including the reasons that the additional time is needed and the number of additional days required.

amicus curiae
A person allowed to give argument or appear in a lawsuit (usually to file a brief, but sometimes to take an active part) who is not a party to the lawsuit.

The district clerk will not send to the court of appeals unusually bulky or heavy documents, physical exhibits other than documents, or other parts of the record designated for omission by the local rules of the court of appeals, unless directed to do so by either a party or the circuit clerk. In the case of unusually bulky or heavy exhibits, a party must make arrangements with the clerks of both courts in advance for their transportation and receipt.

The parties may stipulate, or in response to a motion the district court may order, that the district clerk retain the record temporarily for the parties' use in preparation of the appeal. In such an event, the district clerk must certify to the circuit clerk that the record on appeal is complete. Upon receipt of the appellee's brief (or earlier in the event the parties agree or the court orders), the appellant must request that the district clerk forward the record to the circuit court.

Enlargement of Time

If your attorney determines that the time permitted for the appeal is insufficient, you may be asked to draft a **motion for enlargement of time**. Such a motion is authorized by Rule 26 of the Federal Rules of Appellate Procedure. This motion should set forth the reasons that the additional time is needed and the number of additional days required. The court of appeals generally will grant additional time for a new firm taking over an appeal, especially if the case is lengthy and complex. The motion for enlargement of time must be served on all counsel of record. Exhibit 16–5 is an example of a motion for enlargement of time.

THE APPELLATE BRIEF

Often the paralegal is called upon to assist with the drafting of the appellate brief. Your research, writing, organizational, and analytical skills must be employed in this vital part of the appellate process. Because the court of appeals will not hear witnesses nor see evidence, the brief must be well researched and well written to have the necessary persuasive power.

Drafting the Appellate Brief

The appellate brief is an integral part of the appeal. This formal document consists of the legal issues, the important facts, the legal arguments, and the legal authorities. You may be called on to help draft several types of briefs. These are the appellant's brief, the appellee's brief, and the reply brief. It is also possible for your attorney to, at some time, write and file an amicus curiae. An **amicus curiae** (literally, "friend of the court") or intervenor brief is one that is voluntarily filed by an attorney who is not a part of the case but who has been granted permission to present some legal argument before the court. Before beginning work on a brief, you should locate and review the format of the appellate briefs filed either in that particular case or in that appellate court. You may be asked to assume responsibility for compiling and organizing the various sections of the brief.

EXHIBIT 16-5 Motion for Enlargement of Time

**IN THE UNITED STATES COURT OF APPEALS
FOR THE FIFTH CIRCUIT**

Paragon Centre,	)	
	)	
	)	APPEAL NO. 12331753
Plaintiff-Appellee,	)	
	)	
v.	)	
	)	
Tran-Star Company,	)	
	)	
Defendant-Appellant.	)	
	)	
	)	

Appeal from the United States District Court
For the Northern District of Texas
Dallas Division, Civil Action No. 10-81891

MOTION FOR AN ENLARGEMENT OF TIME

Now comes Appellant, Tran-Star Company, and files this motion to request that the time for filing its brief be enlarged by 30 days, to April 25, 2013, and, in support of this motion, Appellant shows the following:

I.

The judgment from which this appeal is taken was rendered in cause No. 10-81891 in the Federal District Court for the Northern District of Texas, Dallas Division, on January 18, 2013. The appeal was perfected on January 31, 2013. The transcript was filed on February 4, 2013, and the statement of facts was filed on February 4, 2013. Appellant's brief is to be filed on or before March 25, 2013.

II.

The undersigned attorney is solely responsible for the preparation of the Appellant's brief.

III.

The undersigned is lead counsel for a medical malpractice action involving complex issues, Cause No. 10-31791, *Montgomery v. The Stepford-Carmichael Medical Institute*, which is set for trial in the Federal District Court, Southern District of Texas, Houston Division, beginning next week. The court has scheduled three weeks on its docket to hear the case.

EXHIBIT 16-5 Motion for Enlargement of Time (*Continued*)

WHEREFORE, PREMISES CONSIDERED, Appellant requests the court to enlarge the time for filing Appellant's brief to April 25, 2013,

Respectfully submitted,

By: _____

Attorney for the Defendant-Appellant
Kirchendorfer, Lethane, Zuer, and Musil
14710 Merit Drive
Dallas, Texas 75230
[Telephone number]
[Facsimile number]

CERTIFICATE OF SERVICE

I hereby certify that a true and correct copy of the foregoing has been mailed by first class mail, postage prepaid, to Simon Zuercher, 35713 Marion Road, Arlington, Texas, on this 20th day of March, 2013.

By: _____

Attorney for the Defendant-Appellant

Format of the Brief   Exhibit 16–6 contains a summary of the requirements for appellate briefs, including page length, fonts, color of brief covers, and so forth. Check local appellate rules for variances in such requirements as the number of copies required for filing or whether electronic filings are permitted in your appellate court.

A brief submitted under Rule 28.1(e)(2) or 32(a)(7)(B) must include a certificate by an attorney that the brief complies with the type-volume limitation. The person signing the certification may depend on the word or line count features of the word-processing system used to prepare the brief. Exhibit 16–7 is an example of such a certification.

Researching the Law   An experienced paralegal is often asked to assist in researching the law in preparing the appellate brief. Responsibilities in this regard may include researching potential legal theories, locating supporting authority, researching pertinent parts of the record, and verifying the correctness of both the citations and the brief format.

Drafting the Statement of Facts   Good writing skills and an analytical mind are requirements for drafting the statement of facts. Knowing where to find the pertinent facts to incorporate in the appellate brief is critical. It is also important to be able to figure out which facts should be included in the relatively short statement of facts. To accomplish these tasks, you may be required to summarize the transcript and index testimony for inclusion in the appellate brief. Familiarity with the transcript will enable you to effectively assist your attorney with the drafting of the brief. Indexed summaries of the transcript and exhibits should be incorporated into a three-ring binder and provided to each member of the legal team working on the brief. The binder might also include pertinent pleadings, trial exhibits, statutes, and cases that will be relied on in the brief.

EXHIBIT 16-6 Checklist for Preparation of Appellate Brief and Appendix

SUBJECT	REQUIREMENTS
Length of Brief	**Options:** **Page Limit Option** 14 point or larger for text and 12 point or larger for footnotes in proportional typeface. No more than 10 1/2 cpi for text and no more than 12 1/2 cpi for footnotes in mono-spaced type. **Principal briefs 30 pages and reply briefs 15 pages.** **Type-Volume with monospaced (nonproportional) type. Text Line Option** At least 10 1/2 cpi for text and 12 1/2 cpi for footnotes. **Principal briefs 1,300 lines of text and reply briefs 650 lines of text.** **Type-Volume with proportional or monospaced type. Word Count Option** At least 14 point for text and at least 12 point for footnotes in proportional typeface. 10 1/2 (12 1/2 cpi) for monospaced typeface. **Principal briefs 14,000 words and reply briefs 7,000 words.** Generally, the corporate disclosure statement, tables of contents and citations, statement with respect to oral argument, addendums containing statutes, rules or regulations, and certificates of counsel do not count toward the word or text line limitations.
Paper Size	8 1/2 × 11. Only one side of the paper may be used.
Text	Double-spaced; quotations over two lines and footnotes may be single-spaced.
Margins	1" on all sides
Typeface	Plain roman style is required. However, italics or boldface may be used for emphasis. Case names must be either italicized or underlined. Sans serif typeface (example "I" and "1" don't have a horizontal line at the bottom of their letters) is not permitted in proportional typeface, except for headings and captions.
Legibility	A clear black image on light paper with a clarity that is equal to or exceeds that of a laser printer.
Binding	Briefs must be bound securely, not obscuring the text, and permitting the brief to lie reasonably flat when open (i.e., spiral binding).
Cover of Brief and Appendix	1. Name of the court 2. Number of the case, centered at the top 3. Title of the case 4. Nature of the proceedings 5. Name of the lower court 6. Title of the brief 7. Names, addresses, and telephone number of counsel representing the party on whose behalf the brief is filed.
Color of Covers	Appellant—Blue Appellee—Red Reply Brief of Appellant—Gray Intervenor or Amicus Curiae—Green Supplemental Brief—Tan Appendix (if separate from the brief)—White
Number of Copies	Twenty-five copies must be filed with the clerk and two copies must be served on each unrepresented party and on counsel for each separately represented party. Check local rules as individual courts often require a different number of copies.

EXHIBIT 16-7 Form 6. Certification of Compliance with Rule 32(a)

FORM 6. CERTIFICATE OF COMPLIANCE WITH RULE 32(a)

(PLACE THIS AS LAST DOCUMENT IN YOUR BRIEF BEFORE THE BACK COVER)

Certificate of Compliance with Type-Volume Limitation, Typeface Requirements, and Type Style Requirements

1. This brief complies with the type-volume limitation of Fed. R. App. P. 32(a)(7)(B) because:

    ✔ this brief contains [*state the number of*] words, excluding the parts of the brief exempted by Fed. R. App. P. 32(a) (7) (B)(iii), *or*

    ✔ this brief uses a monospaced typeface and contains [*state the number of*] lines of text, excluding the parts of the brief exempted by Fed. R. App. P. 32(a)(7)(B)(iii).

2. This brief complies with the typeface requirements of Fed. R. App. P. 32(a)(5) and the type style requirements of Fed. R. App. P. 32(a)(6) because:

    ✔ this brief has been prepared in a proportionally spaced typeface using [*state name and version of word-processing program*] in [*state font size and name of type style*], *or*

    ✔ this brief has been prepared in a monospaced typeface using [*state name and version of word-processing program*] with [*state number of characters per inch and name of type style*].

(s) _____

Attorney for _____

Dated: _____

(PLACE THIS AS LAST DOCUMENT IN BRIEF BEFORE BACK COVER)

Source: http://www.ca5.uscourts.gov/clerk/docs/32cer.pdf

appellant's brief
Brief of the person bringing an appeal.

Appellant, Appellee, and Reply Briefs

As noted previously, the three most important briefs that you may be required to work on are the appellant's brief, the appellee's brief, and the reply brief.

Appellant's Brief   The requirements for the **appellant's brief** vary slightly among the federal circuit courts of appeal, but they generally include the following in this order:

1. A corporate disclosure statement if required by Rule 26.1
2. Table of contents, with page references
3. Table of cases in alphabetical order, with page references and list of statutes, treatises, and law review articles, including the author's name where appropriate, with page references
4. Statement regarding oral argument required by Rule 34(a)(1)
5. Statement of jurisdiction
6. Statement of issues
7. Statement of the case, the nature of the case, the course of the proceedings, and disposition in the court below
8. The statement of facts relevant to the legal issues, including appropriate references to the record

AUTOMATED LITIGATION SUPPORT

Submitting an Appellate Brief

SCENARIO

Your attorney calls you into her office and tells you that the *Tran-Star* case has been appealed. The appellate brief is due in three days. The attorney advises you that she has researched the case and written a draft of the opening brief. It has been some time since the attorney has handled an appeal and she wants to be certain that the brief conforms to all the local rules of court. Also, before submitting the brief, your attorney would like you to cite check the document, making sure that all citations are current and verified. She also wants you to prepare a table of authorities for the brief.

Your office does not have a copy of the local rules of court for the appellate court in which you must file the brief. You can obtain a copy of the rules from the court, but the court is more than an hour's drive from your office. Also, even though you took courses in legal research, you remember that manually checking citations was a nightmare, not to mention time consuming.

PROBLEM

You are under a time pressure. Not only are you working on this case, but you are working on another case as well that is getting ready to go to trial. How do you get a copy of local appellate rules without making a lengthy trip? How can you cite check the brief quickly but accurately? How can you prepare a table of authorities without spending hours of time?

SOLUTION

Many courts, including federal appellate courts, maintain home pages on the Internet. On these Web sites they generally post the latest local rules of court and may even have downloadable forms. Your local federal appellate court can be located through the following site: **<http://www.uscourts.gov>**. If you know the number of the circuit you can go directly to that home page by typing **<http://www.ca[#].uscourts.gov>** (e.g., Texas would be **<http://www.ca5.uscourts.gov>**). If for some reason you did not have a site address (URL), you could use any of a variety of search engines and look for the "United States Courts of Appeals."

Your second problem is also easily solved. *Shepard's* is now available through the online LexisNexis service. Verifying authorities this way is simple and current. The citation to be checked is entered, and the authority is instantly verified. There is no need to check multiple supplements or to read and interpret numerous abbreviations found in *Shepard's* in print. Westlaw contains a product called KeyCite, which is similar to *Shepard's* and also verifies cites. Additionally, Westlaw provides special software known as WestCheck®, which is an automated citation-checking software product that verifies citations in a legal document or in a manually entered citations list. This software, used in conjunction with your Word or WordPerfect document, automatically reads and verifies the citations included in the document. Thus your appellate brief can be cite checked in only a few minutes, and your results will be up to date.

Generating a table of authorities is easily done. Both Word and WordPerfect have features that will automatically generate a table of authorities. As the document is typed, authorities to be placed in a table of authorities are specially "marked." A table of authorities, in proper format, can be automatically generated when the brief is completed.

9. Summary of the argument

10. The argument, including the reasons for the contentions regarding issues, as well as citations to authorities, statutes, and parts of the record relied upon, and so on

11. A short conclusion listing the exact relief sought

12. Certificate of compliance, if required by Rule 32(a)(7) of the Federal Rules of Appellate Procedure

appellee's brief
Brief of the person who opposes an appeal.

The appellant is also required to file an appendix to its brief, which includes the following parts:

1. Relevant docket entries in the lower court proceeding
2. Relevant portions of the pleadings, charge, findings, or opinion
3. Judgment, order, or decision in question
4. Any other parts of the record to which the parties wish to direct the attention of the court

Ten copies of the appendix must be filed with the clerk. One copy is served on each counsel of record. Rule 30(d) of the Federal Rules of Appellate Procedure specifies the arrangement of the appendix as follows:

1. Table of contents, with page references to the beginning of each part of the appendix
2. Relevant docket entries
3. Other parts of the record in chronological order

Exhibits designated for inclusion in the appendix may be placed in a separate volume. The cover of a separately bound exhibits volume must be white. Four copies of this separate exhibits volume must be filed with the appendix, and a copy served on counsel for each party.

Appellee's Brief   The **appellee's brief** should follow the requirements of the appellant's brief, with the exception that none of the following are required unless the appellee is dissatisfied with the appellant's statement: (a) the jurisdictional statement, (b) the statement of the issues, (c) the statement of the case, (d) the statement of the facts, or (e) the statement of the standard of review.

Reply Brief   Rule 28(c) of the Federal Rules of Appellate Procedure permits the appellant to file a brief in reply to the appellee's brief. The appellee may also file a cross-appeal. As noted earlier in this chapter, cross-appeal is an appeal filed by the appellee based on a different legal rationale than the appeal filed by the appellant. If the appellee files a cross-appeal, the appellant will file a brief in response to the issues presented in the cross-appeal. The appellee can then file a reply to the appellant's response. No further briefs are permitted, except by leave of the court. A reply brief must contain a table of contents, with page references, and a table of authorities that includes cases arranged alphabetically, and statutes and other authorities, complete with references to the pages of the reply brief on which the authorities are cited.

Filing and Service of Appellate Briefs

According to Rule 31 of the Federal Rules of Appellate Procedure, the appellant must file and serve its brief within 40 days after the date on which the record is filed. The appellee has 30 days after service of the appellant's brief to file and serve its brief. Under Rule 31(a), the appellant's reply brief is due seven days after service of the appellee's brief. It must, however, be filed at least seven days before the argument of the case, except for good cause. A brief is deemed timely filed if it is mailed within the time permitted by the pertinent court rule. It does not have to actually reach the clerk's office by that day.

Rule 31 of the Federal Rules of Appellate Procedure allows a court of appeals to require the filing of a greater, as well as a lesser, number of copies of briefs than the 25 copies noted in the rule. This rule also requires that two copies must be served on each unrepresented party and on counsel for each separately represented party. As the paralegal, you should refer to the local rules published by your particular circuit to determine the appropriate number of copies to be filed. If the appellant fails to file its brief within the time allowed, the appellee may move for a dismissal of the appeal. If the appellee fails to file a brief, it will not be heard at the oral argument, except by permission of the court.

oral argument
The presentation of each side of a case before an appeals court. The presentation typically involves oral statements by a lawyer, interrupted by questions from the judge.

COORDINATING THE ORAL ARGUMENT

The **oral argument** is the presentation of the basis for the appeal before the court of appeals. Oral arguments are permitted in all appellate cases unless, pursuant to local rules, a three-judge panel, after examination of the briefs, unanimously decides that oral argument is not needed for any of the following reasons:

1. the appeal is frivolous;
2. the dispositive issues have been authoritatively decided; or
3. the briefs and record adequately present the facts and legal arguments, thereby reducing the possibility that the decision-making process would be significantly advanced by oral argument.

If such a local rule exists, the party desiring the oral argument may file a statement with the court listing the reasons that it should be granted the oral argument. The court notifies the parties of the date, time, and place of the oral argument. The court also notifies the parties of the amount of time allotted for each side's presentation. The appellant opens and closes the oral argument. Even though the parties do not request oral argument, the court may direct that the case be argued.

Preparing for the Oral Argument

The paralegal's duties related to oral argument may vary, depending on the complexity of the case, the economic constraints, or the paralegal's experience. As an experienced paralegal, you may be asked to prepare for and attend the oral argument.

Outline of the Argument You may be requested to assist your attorney in preparing the written outline for the oral argument. This outline is incorporated into the oral argument notebook, which may include copies of pertinent cases and pleadings. Capsule summaries of the trial transcripts also may be included in the oral argument notebook.

Research Notebook for Justices For the convenience of the court, you may be asked to prepare a notebook of research for each justice, consisting of cases that your attorney anticipates the court will need to consider in its decision. The cases may be indexed by the court rendering the decision or alphabetically by the parties. Additionally, the notebook may include summaries of the records that have been organized and indexed.

petition for rehearing
A request for a new hearing to reconsider an action that may have been wrongfully taken or overlooked in a previous hearing.

petition for certiorari
A request to a higher court for review, but which the higher court is not required to take for decision. Certiorari is a writ from the higher court asking the lower court for the record of the case.

judgment debtor
A person who has yet to satisfy a judgment that has been rendered against him or her.

judgment creditor
A person who has proved a debt in court and is entitled to use court processes to collect it.

postjudgment interrogatories
Written questions that the judgment debtor must answer in writing about his or her assets.

Delivery of the Exhibits to Court   You may be given the responsibility of delivering the exhibits to the court of appeals for the oral argument. You also will have to make arrangements for the prompt removal of these exhibits. This is especially important because Rule 34(g) of the Federal Rules of Appellate Procedure provides that any physical evidence not removed within a reasonable time after notice to the counsel by the clerk is to be destroyed or disposed of.

Assisting at Oral Argument

As in the deposition or the trial, you may be asked to attend the oral arguments and make complete notes for your attorney's use during her portion of the oral argument. Thus, your attorney will be free to concentrate on her argument, without the distraction of making notes during the opposition's argument.

FINAL PROCEDURES

We are nearing the end of the litigation process. After the court of appeals has rendered a decision, a dissatisfied party may seek to continue the appellate process. However, should the defendant eventually lose the case, the plaintiff may use certain posttrial judgment procedures to secure payment of the award.

Further Appeal Procedures

Under provisions of Rule 40 of the Federal Rules of Appellate Procedure, if the losing party desires to appeal the decision of the court of appeals, a petition for rehearing should be filed. A **petition for rehearing** asks that a higher court's decision be reviewed. This petition must be filed within 14 days after the judgment is entered, unless the time is either shortened or enlarged by order of the court. If the United States or its officer or agency is a party, the filing must occur within 45 days after entry of judgment, unless the time is shortened or extended by court order. The requirements for a petition for rehearing are the same as those for briefs, and, therefore, subject to Rule 32 of the Federal Rules of Appellate Procedures, unless the court permits or a local rule provides differently. A petition for rehearing must not exceed 15 pages unless the court permits or a local rule provides otherwise. A petition for a rehearing is not a prerequisite to the filing of a petition for certiorari. A **petition for certiorari** is a request for a rehearing before the U.S. Supreme Court.

Posttrial Judgment Procedures

Statutory remedies allow for the execution of a judgment within 30 days after the entry of judgment. The party seeking to execute on the judgment is known as the **judgment creditor**. The party who must pay the judgment is known as the **judgment debtor**. Often it is helpful for the judgment creditor to uncover details about the financial condition of the judgment debtor. To facilitate this process, the law permits postjudgment discovery. Exhibit 16–8 provides a checklist for an assets search of the debtor. Postjudgment discovery procedures offer the judgment creditor a relatively simple and inexpensive method of determining the amount and the location of a party's assets. **Postjudgment interrogatories**, for example, are written

EXHIBIT 16-8 Checklist for Assets Search—Debtor

1. Law firm files, including discovery and interrogatories that might list homes, business ownership, and so forth.
2. Motor vehicle registrations.
3. Litigation filings, both as plaintiff and defendant. (Potential awards due the debtor?)
4. Deed records.
5. Mortgage records.
6. Tax assessor records.
7. Probate records. (Debtor might be due funds from settlement of the estate of a parent, spouse, etc.)
8. UCC and lien searches. (Existence of such a filing might indicate a checking, savings, or investment account at the same financial institution.)
9. Secretary of State filing. Search for ownership in companies, service on a board of directors, and so forth.
10. Westlaw people and asset searches.

Copyright © 2015 Cengage Learning®

postjudgment deposition
A deposition that can be taken after judgment, with only a dictating machine or a tape recorder, with no court reporter present.

notice of intent to take oral deposition by nonstenographic means
A notice sent to opposing counsel of an intent to take a deposition after the judgment by use of only a dictating machine or a tape recorder, with no court reporter present.

writ of execution
A document that orders a court official to take a debtor's property to pay a court decided debt. Execution is the official carrying out or completion of a court's order or judgment.

posttrial garnishment
A separate, but ancillary, lawsuit, filed in the court that rendered the judgment, to permit the judgment creditor to collect on a judgment.

garnishment
A legal process, taken by a creditor who has received a money judgment against a debtor, to get the debtor's money. This is done by attachment of a bank account or by taking a percentage of the debtor's regular income.

garnishee
A person who holds money or property belonging to a debtor and who is subject to a garnishment.

questions that the judgment debtor must answer in writing about his assets. A **postjudgment deposition** can be taken after sending the opposing counsel a **notice of intent to take oral deposition by nonstenographic means**. This type of deposition is taken with only a dictating machine or a tape recorder, with no court reporter present. The judgment creditor also could use a postjudgment request for production of documents to obtain necessary financial information from the judgment debtor.

Without the filing of a supersedeas bond, a writ of execution may be issued 14 days after entry of a final judgment order. A **writ of execution** is a court order compelling the seizure of the judgment debtor's property to satisfy the judgment (see Exhibit 16–9). Proper notice must be given to the public and to anyone who has an interest in that property before it can be sold at a public auction. In addition, the judgment debtor must be given the opportunity to pay the judgment creditor before the auction is held. The law also prescribes the order in which certain types of property can be seized and sold at auction. Usually, personal property is seized and sold before real property is subject to seizure. After the auction has been held and the debt satisfied, any remaining amount goes to the judgment debtor.

Another means by which the judgment creditor could collect is by using a **posttrial garnishment**. A posttrial garnishment is a separate but ancillary lawsuit, filed in the court that rendered the judgment. The **garnishment** is brought against a third-party **garnishee** that is holding assets belonging to the judgment debtor. The judgment creditor must obtain a writ of garnishment (see Exhibit 16–10). The garnishee is then served with the writ and a summons. The garnishee will be compelled to reveal how much of the judgment debtor's money or property is in its possession. Once this is known, the judgment creditor can seize the money or property or prevent the judgment creditor from receiving any of that money or property. Bank accounts and wages can be the targets of a posttrial garnishment. However, state and federal laws protect a certain percentage of the debtor's income so that she can still make a living, despite the garnishment.

EXHIBIT 16-9 Writ of Execution

United States District Court
Northern District of Texas

Writ of Execution

Case No. _____

_____
Plaintiff

v.

_____
Defendant

(Complete the following if judgment was rendered in another district.)

District _____

Docket No. _____

Date Entered _____

TO ANY UNITED STATES MARSHAL IN THE STATE OF TEXAS:

WHEREAS, on the ____ day of _____, A.D., ____ in a cause styled as above, judgment was rendered in this Court, or other United States District Court as indicated above and registered herein, in favor of

_____
_____

against _____,

hereinafter called judgment debtor, for the sum of $ _____ with interest thereon at the rate of _____

percent per annum from the _____ day of _____ , A.D., ____ until paid, together with costs which have

been taxed to date by the Clerk of Court in the sum of $ _____ ;

AND WHEREAS, according to an affidavit on the reverse side hereof, executed by or in behalf of the judgment creditor, there remains due and unpaid the following sums:

$ _____ Unpaid balance of costs specified hereinabove taxed by the Clerk of Court

$ _____ Judgment

$ _____ Interest on Judgment

and further interest will accrue on the unsatisfied judgment in the sum of $ _____ per day from date of the aforesaid affidavit;

THEREFORE YOU ARE COMMANDED, that of the goods and chattels, lands and tenements of the said judgment debtor you cause to be paid the full amount of said judgment, interest, and costs, with the further costs of executing this writ.

HEREIN FAIL NOT, and have you the said monies, together with this writ, before this Court within ninety (90) days from the date of this writ.

WITNESS my hand and the seal of this Court at _____ , Texas, this _____ day of _____ , _____ .

KAREN MITCHELL, CLERK

By _____
Deputy Clerk

EXHIBIT 16-9 Writ of Execution (*Continued*)

AFFIDAVIT AND REQUEST FOR ISSUANCE OF WRIT OF EXECUTION

I,_____ , judgment creditor or duly authorized agent or attorney acting in the capacity specified under my signature, do hereby swear or affirm that all of the recitals on the reverse side of this instrument relating to the entry of judgment and costs are true and correct; and, after application of all credits, first against costs, second against accrued interest, and third against the judgment as entered, there remains unpaid and unsatisfied the sums specified, and that further interest will accrue as shown.

Dated this _____ day of _____ , A.D., _____ .

Signature and capacity in which signed: _____

_____

Address: _____

_____

Telephone Number: _____

STATE OF _____

COUNTY OF _____

On this date there appeared before me, the undersigned authority, the person whose name is subscribed to the foregoing instrument and on his oath did swear or affirm that he has knowledge of the facts stated therein, that such facts are true and correct, and that he has authority to execute the instrument in the capacity stated therein.

Date: _____

_____

_____

Title

MARSHAL'S RETURN

Received this writ at _____ , on _____
and executed as follows:

_____

UNITED STATES MARSHAL

By _____

Deputy Marshal

EXHIBIT 16-10 Writ of Garnishment

**IN THE UNITED STATES DISTRICT COURT
FOR THE NORTHERN DISTRICT OF TEXAS, DALLAS DIVISION**

Paragon Centre,   )
)
     Plaintiff,   )   CIVIL ACTION NO. 12-81891
)
        v.   )
)
Tran-Star Company,   )
)
     Defendant.   )
)

WRIT OF GARNISHMENT

TO: THE TEXAS LONGHORN BANK AND TRUST COMPANY, 444 Houston Plaza, Houston, Texas, 75429, Garnishee;

1. Paragon Centre is the plaintiff in the case of Paragon Centre v. Tran-Star Company, in Civil Action No. 12-81891, in the Federal District Court for the Northern District of Texas, Dallas Division. In this case the plaintiff has a valid, uncollected judgment against the defendant for the sum of $750,000 with interest charged at a rate of 10% per year and costs of the suit.

2. Plaintiff has applied for a writ of garnishment against The Texas Longhorn Bank and Trust Company.

3. You are hereby commanded to appear before this court at 9 a.m. on November 22, 2013. You will at that time be required to answer under oath what property belonging to the defendant you have in your possession or had in your possession when this writ was served upon you, and what money owing to or belonging to the defendant you have in your possession or had in your possession when this writ was served upon you. At that time you will also be required to answer under oath what other persons you know of who have property belonging to the defendant in their possession or had in their possession at the time this writ was served upon you, and what other persons you know of who owe the defendant money or have possession of money belonging to the defendant or had in their possession when this writ was served upon you money belonging to the defendant.

4. The official who served this writ upon you is also charged with serving the defendant, Imperial Gasoline Company, with a true copy of this writ.

Dated and Issued on October 21, 2013.

ATTESTED TO BY:

_____
Clerk of the Federal District Court,
Northern District of Texas,
Dallas Division

_____
Presiding Judge

FINDING IT on the Internet

The Federal Rules of Appellate Procedure, together with appellate rules for the Fifth Circuit, can be accessed at <**http://www.ca5.uscourts.gov/clerk/docs/frap2007.pdf**>. Access this site and determine the following information relating to an appeal of the *Tran-Star* case.

A. Review the appellate rules for the Fifth Circuit and determine the final date to file a Notice of Appeal, assuming an entry of judgment or order date of January 10, 2013.

B. Determine the number of copies of the appellant's brief that must be forwarded to the Fifth Circuit.

C. Research the Fifth Circuit's Web site and report to your attorney the median length of time that an appeal takes in that circuit, based on the most recent statistics available.

Appellate rules for the Supreme Court are located at the following site: <**http://www.law.cornell .edu/rules/supct/**>.

SUMMARY

- If the court has denied a motion for judgment as a matter of law made at the close of evidence, the motion may be renewed by service and filing within 28 days after entry of judgment. A motion for new trial under Rule 59 of the Federal Rules of Civil Procedure may be combined with this renewal of the motion for judgment, or, in the alternative, only a motion for new trial may be filed. The motion for new trial will state the legal grounds for the new trial.

- An appeal is filed by a party who has lost a case or who is dissatisfied with a judgment or a court order. The appeal asks that a higher court review the lower court's decision. A person bringing an appeal is referred to as the appellant. The person who opposes an appeal is the appellee. Only questions of law are subject to review. The appellate court has no authority to consider questions relating to the facts of a case. The preliminary steps in an appellate procedure generally include (1) notice of appeal, (2) bond for costs or a supersedeas bond, (3) transcript order and preparation of pertinent record sections, and (4) filing of briefs by both parties. Following these preliminary steps, oral arguments are presented to the court, and the court renders its decision.

- The appellate brief is an integral part of the appeal. This formal document consists of the legal issues, the important facts, the legal arguments, and the legal authorities. You may be called on to help draft several types of briefs: the appellant's brief, the appellee's brief, and the reply brief. It is also possible for your attorney to write and file an amicus curiae or intervenor brief, which is voluntarily filed by an attorney who has been granted permission to present some legal argument before the court. The appellee may also file a cross-appeal. A cross-appeal is an appeal filed by the appellee based on a different legal rationale than the appeal filed by the appellant. If the appellee files a cross-appeal, the appellant will file a brief in response to the issues presented in the cross-appeal. The appellee can then file a reply to the appellant's response.

- Oral argument is the presentation of the basis for the appeal before the court of appeals. Oral arguments are permitted in all appellate cases unless, pursuant to local rules, a three-judge panel, after examination of the briefs, unanimously decides that oral argument is not needed. The paralegal may be requested to assist the attorney in preparing the written outline for the oral argument. This outline is incorporated into the oral argument notebook. For the convenience of the court, the paralegal may be asked to prepare a notebook of research for each justice, consisting of cases that your attorney anticipates the court will need to consider in its decision. The paralegal may be given the responsibility to deliver the exhibits to the court of appeals for the oral argument. As in a deposition or trial, the paralegal may be asked to attend the oral argument and make complete notes for the attorney's use during her portion of the oral argument.

- If the losing party desires to appeal the decision of the court of appeals to a higher court, a petition for rehearing should be filed. A petition for rehearing asks that a higher court's decision be reviewed. A petition for certiorari is a request for a rehearing before the U.S. Supreme Court. Statutory remedies allow for the execution of a judgment within 30 days after the entry of judgment, or sooner. The party seeking to execute the judgment is known as the judgment creditor. The party who must pay the judgment is known as the judgment debtor. Often it is helpful for the judgment creditor to uncover details about the financial condition of the judgment debtor. To facilitate this process, the law permits postjudgment discovery. Without the filing of a supersedeas bond, a writ of execution may be issued 14 days after entry of a final judgment order. A writ of execution is a court order compelling the sale of the judgment debtor's property to satisfy the judgment. Another means to collect a judgment is by using a postjudgment garnishment.

KEY TERMS

amicus curiae	judgment creditor	petition for certiorari
appeal	judgment debtor	petition for rehearing
appellant	motion for enlargement	postjudgment deposition
appellant's brief	of time	postjudgment
appellee	notice of appeal	interrogatories
appellee's brief	notice of intent to take	posttrial garnishment
cross-appeal	oral deposition by	pro se
garnishee	nonstenographic means	supersedeas bond
garnishment	oral argument	writ of execution

REVIEW QUESTIONS

1. Define "motion for judgment as a matter of law."
2. What is a motion for a new trial?
3. What is an appeal?
4. Who are the parties to an appeal?
5. What is a supersedeas bond? What is its purpose?
6. List and define four types of appellate briefs.
7. Describe the paralegal's duties in relation to oral arguments.
8. What postjudgment discovery devices are available to a judgment creditor?
9. Define "petition for certiorari."
10. List posttrial judgment procedures available to collect a judgment.

CHAPTER EXERCISES

Where necessary, check with your instructor prior to starting any of these exercises.

1. Review the laws of your state and find all state appellate court rules. Compare the state and federal court rules to determine the differences between the two.
2. Prepare a memorandum describing the duties of the paralegal during the appellate process in relation to the transcript.
3. Use the facts contained in the *Tran-Star* case to draft 10 postjudgment interrogatories to Paragon Centre.
4. Prepare a notice of intent to take oral deposition by stenographic means for Jackson R. Towery, chief financial officer of Paragon Centre. Draft 10 questions for your attorney to include in her deposition of Mr. Towery to determine the actual damages sustained by Paragon Centre because of the loss of tenants following the gas leak.

CHAPTER PROJECT

Review the *Tran-Star* case in the opening Commentary. Recall that the case originated in Dallas, Texas: the appeal must therefore be brought in the Fifth Circuit Court of Appeals. Remember also that each circuit has local rules that must be followed, in addition to the Federal Rules of Appellate Procedure. Draft a memo in which you tell a new paralegal in your firm about the requirements for the appellant's brief in the *Tran-Star* case.

THE *BENNETT* CASE
Assignment for Chapter 16: Filing an Appeal

The *Bennett* case went to trial. The plaintiff lost and now wants to appeal. Prepare the notice of appeal and request for reporter's transcript.

THE *DOUGLASS FINANCIAL SERVICES INC.* CASE
Assignment for Chapter 16: Preparing a Motion for a New Trial

The Hewitt trial is over and your attorney is very disappointed in the verdict. The jury rendered a verdict for the plaintiff and against both Evan Portman and your client, Douglass Financial, Inc. Your attorney tells you that it was just learned that one juror, Marie Davis, was previously injured by a drunk driver and failed to disclose this during voir dire. Your attorney learned about this from a different juror, Nathan Dugan. Evidently Ms. Davis revealed this to other jurors during deliberation. Your attorney has asked you to review your state law on motions for new trial and then help prepare the necessary documents. Your attorney also tells you that Mr. Dugan is willing to sign a declaration or affidavit as to what Ms. Davis revealed. You are to prepare the notice of motion, motion and the declaration of Nathan Dugan. Your attorney will draft the memorandum of points and authorities supporting the motion but asks you to try to find and copy the state law or rule dealing with motions for new trial.

APPENDIX A

Sample Deposition

1 SPENCER FLANNIGAN	)
2	) Civil Action No. 1015-7507
3 Plaintiff,	)
4	)
5	)
6 v.	)
7	)
8 LASSITER CENTRAL CLINIC OF VERMONT, et al.	)
9	)
10 Defendants.	)
11	)
12	)

13
14
15
16 **APPEARANCES:**
17
18 Bradford, Miller, and Hutchinson
19 By: Roger Hutchinson
20 For the Plaintiff
21
22 Reeves, Allyn, and Cain
23 By: William Radcliffe
24 For the Defendants
25
26 **STIPULATIONS:**
27

1   It is hereby stipulated and agreed by and between counsel that all objections, except as to the form of the
2 questions, be reserved until the time of the trial.
3
4   Jonathan Harbinger, Certified Radiologic Technologist, sworn
5
6 BY MR. HUTCHINSON:

7   Q.   Would you please state your full name for the record?

8

9   A.   Jonathan Harbinger.

10

11   Q.   Where are you employed, Mr. Harbinger?

12

13   A.   Lassiter Central Clinic of Vermont.

14

15   Q.   At what address is Lassiter Central Clinic of Vermont located?

16

17   A.   17810 Glessner Avenue, in Burlington.

18

19   Q.   Mr. Harbinger, would you briefly list your educational background?

20

21   A.   I attended Concord County Community College, where I earned an associate of applied science

22   degree in radiologic technology.

23

24   Q.   Do you have any board certification?

25

26   A.   Yes. I became a registered radiologic technologist in 2012 and a certified radiologic technologist

27   in 2013.

[Page 3 of 20]

1   Q.   Would you explain the process required to become a certified radiologic technologist?

2

3   A.   At least an associate's degree is required, plus satisfactory performance on a state-administered,

4   nationally recognized examination.

5

6   Q.   How many hours of clinical work were you required to perform as part of your education?

7

8   A.   I was required to perform 320 hours of supervised radiologic work at an approved center.

9

10   Q.   At what approved center did you perform your clinical work?

11

12   A.   At LCCV

13

14   Q.   And LCCV is . . .

15

16   A.   I'm sorry. LCCV is Lassiter Central Clinic of Vermont.

17

18   Q.   So, prior to being hired by LCCV, you had 320 hours of clinical experience in their X-Ray Department.

19

20   A.   Radiology Department.

21

22   Q.   I beg your pardon?

23

[Page 4 of 20]

1   A.   It's called the Radiology Department.

2   Q.   So, at LCCV you had 320 hours of clinical experience in their Radiology Department?

3

4   A.   Actually, I had a lot more experience than that.

5

6   Q.   Why is that?

7

8   A.   Under state rules, once you're in your second year of an accredited radiologic program, you can work
9   in a department as long as you're under the supervision of a CRT.

10

11   Q.   What exactly is a CRT?

12

13   A.   A Certified Radiologic Technologist.

14

15   Q.   So, you were hired by LCCV during your second year in the program at Concord County Community
16   College?

17   A.   That's correct.

18

19   Q.   How many hours per week did you work?

20

21   A.   Well, it varied, but usually around 20.

22

23   Q.   So, before being hired on a full-time basis, you had worked how long for LCCV?

24

                                                                                          [Page 5 of 20]

1   A.   About six months.

2

3   Q.   When were you hired on a full-time basis?

4

5   A.   Right after graduation.

6

7   Q.   Totaling all this time, how long have you worked for the X-Ray, that is, the Radiology Department at
8   LCCV?

9

10   A.   Two years.

11

12   Q.   Are you familiar with the procedure manual at LCCV?

13

14   A.   Yes. Everyone is required to read it and sign a form that indicates that they have done so.

15

16   Q.   And did you read it and sign the appropriate form?

17

18   A.   Yes, I did.

19

20   (Deposition Exhibit 1 marked for identification)

21

22   Q.   Mr. Harbinger, I'd like you to take a look at the document that I have marked Exhibit 1 and tell me if
23   that is the form that you signed.

24   A.   Yes. That's it.
25
                                                                        Page 6 of 20]

1   Q.   And is that your signature?
2
3   A.   Yes, it is.
4
5   (Deposition Exhibit 2 marked for identification)
6
7   Q.   Mr. Harbinger, I'd like you to take a look at the document that I've marked Exhibit 2 and tell me if that
8   is a copy of the policy and procedure manual used at LCCV.
9
10   A.   Yes, it is.
11
12   Q.   Mr. Harbinger, in a typical day at the hospital, how many patients do you see in the Radiology
13   Department?
14
15   A.   Typical day—there's no such thing as a typical day. I probably see on an average of 30 to 40 patients
16   a day.
17
18   Q.   Since you see so many patients, it is unlikely that you'd remember any single patient.
19
20   A.   That's true.
21
22   Q.   Mr. Harbinger, do you remember a patient named Spencer Flannigan?
23
24   A.   I sure do.
25
26   Q.   But you've just testified that you don't remember most of your patients.
27
                                                                        [Page 7 of 20]

1   A.   He's the first one I ever saw come close to dying, so I'll always remember him.
2
3   Q.   Do you remember why Mr. Flannigan was taken to the Radiology Department?
4
5   A.   Yes. He was scheduled for an IVP.
6
7   Q.   And what is an IVP?
8
9   A.   An intravenous pyelogram.
10
11   Q.   Is this procedure dangerous?
12
13   A.   Not usually.
14
15   Q.   But it can be.

16 A.   Oh sure, if the patient is allergic to the contrast material.

17

18 Q.   Mr. Harbinger, let's back up for a moment. Explain the procedure you performed on Mr. Flannigan.

19

20 A.   Well, we inject the patient with a contrast material. The contrast material acts sort of like a dye. That

21   allows the radiologist to see things that he ordinarily wouldn't see absent the contrast material.

22

23 Q.   And you say that this is a dangerous procedure.

24

25 A.   It can be if the patient has an allergic reaction to the contrast medium.

26

[Page 8 of 20]

1   Q.   Mr. Harbinger, did Mr. Flannigan realize the dangers involved in this procedure?

2

3   A.   I don't think so.

4

5   Q.   And why do you say that?

6

7   A.   Well, the radiologist never explained it to him.

8

9   Q.   And who was the radiologist on March 17 of last year when Mr. Flannigan underwent this examination?

10

11

12 A.   Dr. Bethany Randall.

13

14 Q.   How do you know that Dr. Randall did not explain the procedure to Mr. Flannigan?

15

16 A.   Well, she gave me the informed consent form and told me to get his signature on it.

17

18 Q.   And what is an informed consent form?

19

20 A.   It's a form that explains the dangers of the procedure and tells the patient what alternatives

21   are available.

22

23 Q.   And did you get his signature?

24

25 A.   Yes.

26

27 Q.   Did he ask you what the form was for?

28

[Page 9 of 20]

1   A.   Yes.

2

3   Q.   And did you tell him?

4

5   A.   I never got the chance.

6   Q.   Why not?

7

8   A.   Dr. Randall came into the room and told him it was just for insurance purposes.

9

10 Q.   Is that standard procedure?

11

12 A.   That depends.

13

14 Q.   What does it depend on?

15

16 A.   Well, it depends on the radiologist.

17

18 Q.   What does the policy and procedure manual say?

19

20 A.   Oh, the procedure manual is clear as a bell. It says the radiologist is required to explain the dangers of

21   the procedure to the patient and to get his signature.

22

23 Q.   How often did Dr. Randall violate this explicit procedure?

24

25 BY MR. RADCLIFFE:

26

[Page 10 of 20]

1   A.   I object. Mr. Harbinger has not been present every time Dr. Randall has performed her job in the

2   Radiology Department. Therefore, he is not qualified to answer that question.

3

4   BY MR. HUTCHINSON:

5

6   Q.   How many times have you observed Dr. Randall violating this procedure?

7

8   A.   Every time I've worked with her.

9

10 Q.   Mr. Harbinger, are there any procedures that should be followed to help prevent an allergic reaction

11   to a contrast material?

12

13 A.   Well, you really should ask patients if they have any allergies.

14

15 Q.   On the day in question, did Dr. Randall ask Mr. Flannigan about his allergies?

16

17 A.   No.

18

19 Q.   Do you remember why she did not ask him about his allergies?

20

21 A.   I guess she thought we didn't have the time.

22

23 Q.   Would the patient's chart include this information?

24

25 A.   Yes.

[Page 11 of 20]

(Deposition Exhibit 3 marked for identification)

1 Q. Mr. Harbinger, I'd like you to look at the document that I've marked Exhibit 3 and tell me what it is.
2
3 A. It's a copy of Mr. Flannigan's chart.
4
5 Q. And what does it say about his allergies?
6
7 A. It just says that he answered "yes" when he was asked about his allergies.
8
9 Q. Is there any other information on his chart about his allergies?
10
11 A. No.
12
13 Q. Is that unusual?
14
15 A. No, not really.
16
17 Q. Why not?
18
19 A. Sometimes the patient doesn't know exactly what he's allergic to, and sometimes the admitting nurse
20 doesn't ask or gets busy with something else, things like that.
21
22 Q. I see. Now, to your knowledge, did Dr. Randall check Mr. Flannigan's chart?
23
24 A. No, she didn't.

[Page 12 of 20]

1 Q. You're certain?
2
3 A. Yes.
4
5 Q. How can you be so certain?
6
7 A. I asked her if she wanted to see the chart, and she said no.
8
9 Q. Why was that?
10
11 A. Well, like I said before, she thought we didn't have the time for petty details.
12
13 Q. Were those her words?
14
15 A. Which words?
16
17 Q. You said that Dr. Randall didn't think you had time for "petty details." Did she use the words "petty details"?
18
19 A. Yes. That was one of her favorite sayings.

20	Q.	Now, since Mr. Flannigan's chart indicated a long history of allergies, would the IVP have
21		been canceled?
22		
23	A.	Not necessarily.
24		
25	Q.	Why not?
26		

[Page 13 of 20]

1	A.	There are a few relatively new contrast materials that could be substituted for the one that we
2		usually use.
3		
4	Q.	Such as?
5		
6	A.	Well, let's see, there's Iopamidol and Iohexol.
7		
8	Q.	Why would these be preferable?
9		
10	A.	The risk of anaphylactic shock is much lower if you use them.
11		
12	Q.	Just what is anaphylactic shock?
13		
14	A.	That's what happened to Mr. Flannigan.
15		
16	BY MR. RADCLIFFE:	
17		
18	A.	I object. The witness is not in a position to say exactly what happened to
19		Mr. Flannigan
20		
21	BY MR. HUTCHINSON:	
22		
23	Q.	Mr. Harbinger, Could you rephrase your answer without referring to Mr. Flannigan?
24		
25	A.	I've forgotten the question.
26		
27	Q.	What is anaphylactic shock?
28		

[Page 14 of 20]

1	A.	That's the medical term for an allergic reaction.
2		
3	Q.	And is it life-threatening?
4		
5	A.	It can be, yes.
6		
7	Q.	If the risk of shock is much less with these materials, why didn't Dr. Randall use them?
8		
9	A.	She told me that she thought they were much too expensive.

10	Q.	Are there any other precautions that can be taken to lessen the risks that go along with an IVP?
11		
12	A.	Yes. You're supposed to have some intravenous epinephrine nearby and ready to go just in case.
13		
14	Q.	And what is intravenous epinephrine?
15		
16	A.	It's sort of like an antidote.
17		
18	Q.	And was that antidote available?
19		
20	A.	Not exactly.
21		
22	Q.	Would you explain what you mean by that?
23		
24	A.	We had some in the hospital, but we didn't have it in the Radiology Department.
25		

[Page 15 of 20]

1	Q.	Was Dr. Randall aware of this?
2		
3	A.	Yes.
4		
5	Q.	How can you be so certain?
6		
7	A.	Because I told her so.
8		
9	Q.	And how did she react?
10		
11	A.	Well, she got really angry. You see, we were really swamped that day and I think she just didn't
12		want to take the time.
13		
14	Q.	And what did you do?
15		
16	A.	Well, I told her again that we really shouldn't perform the test without the epinephrine.
17		
18	Q.	What did she do then?
19		
20	A.	Well, she told me she was running the department and to mind my own business.
21		
22	Q.	What did you say to that?
23		
24	A.	I told her it was my business.
25		
26	Q.	How did she react?
27		

[Page 16 of 20]

| 1 | A. | She told me to go to the pharmacy and get the epinephrine. |

2   Q.   And did you?

3

4   A.   Yes.

5

6   Q.   What transpired next?

7

8   A.   Dr. Randall went ahead with the test after I left. When I got back, the crash cart
9   was already there. Mr. Flannigan had apparently suffered cardiac arrest.

10

11   Q.   Is it standard procedure to begin such a test without the antidote present?

12

13   A.   Absolutely not.

14

15   Q.   You're certain of this?

16

17   A.   Yes, I am. I was so shook up I double-checked the manual about 500 times. Without the epinephrine
18   you're not supposed to do anything.

19

20   Q.   Yet Dr. Randall went ahead with the test?

21

22   BY MR. RADCLIFFE:

23

24   A.   I object. Mr. Harbinger was not present in the room when the alleged test took place. He cannot
25   possibly know whether Dr. Randall administered the test.

26

[Page 17 of 20]

1   BY MR. HUTCHINSON:

2

3   Q.   Mr. Harbinger, what is hospital policy at LCCV when something like this event occurs?

4

5   A.   You're supposed to fill out an incident report.

6

7   Q.   And was one filled out in this case?

8

9   A.   Not to my knowledge.

10

11   Q.   Do you know why not?

12

13   A.   Dr. Randall said it wasn't necessary.

14

15   Q.   Is that standard procedure?

16

17   A.   No, like I said, the manual says to fill out an incident report.

18

19   BY MR. HUTCHINSON:

20

21   A.   I have no further questions.

22   BY MR. RADCLIFFE:
23
24   Q.   Just for the record, Mr. Harbinger, you were not actually present in the X-Ray Department when
25   Mr. Flannigan suffered his trauma, is that correct?
26

[Page 18 of 20]

1   A.   No, it's not correct.
2
3   Q.   It's not correct? How so?
4
5   A.   It's called the Radiology Department, not the X-Ray Department.
6
7   Q.   Very well, then. You were not present in the Radiology Department when Mr. Flannigan
8   suffered his trauma?
9
10   A.   Yes. Like I said, I'd been sent to pharmacy.
11
12   Q.   So you really don't know what happened in your absence?
13
14   A.   No. I only know that when I came back to the department the crash cart was already there.
15
16   Q.   Mr. Harbinger, do you know in fact that an incident report was never filed?
17
18   A.   No. I only know that Dr. Randall told me that it wasn't necessary to fill out an incident report in this case.
19
20   Q.   How often have you seen that happen?
21
22   A.   See what happen?
23
24   Q.   How often have you witnessed events that you thought needed an incident report when none was filed?
25

[Page 19 of 20]

1   A.   Practically every day.
2
3   Q.   Mr. Harbinger, if Mr. Flannigan's heart attack had not resulted from an allergic reaction to the contrast
4   medium, but had resulted from natural causes, would an incident report be required?
5
6   A.   No. An incident report is required only when someone has made a mistake.
7
8   Q.   Mr. Harbinger, are you still employed at LCCV?
9
10   A.   Yes. But not in the Radiology Department.
11
12   Q.   Why not?
13
14   A.   I left the department about six months ago.

15   Q.   Why was that?

16

17   A.   I decided I couldn't take the pressure.

18

19   Q.   Pressure like the day Mr. Flannigan suffered his alleged allergic reaction?

20

21   A.   I guess so.

22

23   Q.   Isn't it possible that you were the one who made the mistake on the day that Mr. Flannigan suffered
24   his trauma?

25

26   A.   I don't see how.

27

[Page 20 of 20]

1   Q.   Well, you just said that you couldn't take the kind of pressure you said you were under that day in the
2   Radiology Department.

3

4   A.   I didn't say that I couldn't take the pressure on that particular day.

5

6   Q.   Admit it, Mr. Harbinger, you cracked under pressure that day and decided that you, and not Dr. Randall,
7   a well-trained and highly respected radiologist, knew what was best for the patient.

8

9   BY MR. HUTCHINSON:

10

11   A.   I object. You're badgering the witness. Move on with the examination.

12

13   BY MR. RADCLIFFE:

14

15   Q.   Mr. Harbinger, between the radiologist and the radiologic technologist, who is presumed by the medical
16   profession to know what's best for the patient?

17

18   A.   The radiologist, I guess, but . . .

19

20   Q.   That's all. I have no further questions for this witness.

APPENDIX B

Bennett and *Douglass* Research Files

CASE FILE 1: THE *BENNET EMPLOYMENT DISCRIMINATION* CASE

CASE FILE 2: THE *DOUGLASS FINANCIAL, INC.* CASE

CASE FILE 1: THE *BENNETT* CASE

THE PARTIES AND THEIR ATTORNEYS

Plaintiff	Alice Bennett
Defendant	Rikards-Hayley 45 Prospero Place New York, New York
Witnesses	Darren Blackwood General Manager Rikards-Hayley Martina Yardly Manager, Training and Development Rikards-Hayley Rhees Bradley Director, Personnel Rikards-Hayley
Attorney for Plaintiff	Anthony Righetti, Esq. Righetti, Morgan and Blake 34 Court Ave. Greenville, New York 555 222-2222 arighetti@rmb.com
Attorneys for Defendant	Vanessa Graves, Esq. Miller, Graves and Klein 1 Main St. New York, New York 555 222-1111 Vanessa.graves@mgkesq.com Monica Ruiz, Esq. In-House Counsel Rikards-Hayley

SELECTED DOCUMENTS FROM THE PLAINTIFF'S FILE

Client Interview Summary

Personal Data

Name	Alice Bennett
Home Address	2367 Meadow Ln., New York, New York
Address for Billing	Same
Home Telephone	212 555-1212
Work Telephone	None
Cell Phone	212 555-3987
Fax Number	None
E-mail	aben@yahoo.com
Date of Birth	09/15/1974
Social Security No.	215-90-1111
Spouse's Name	Robert Bennett
Employer	None

Information Relating to Claim

Client, Alice Bennett, provided the following information: Client believes that she was a recent victim of employment discrimination based on gender which occurred at Rikards-Hayley, an investment banking firm located at 121 Centre St., New York, New York. She began working for Rikards-Hayley four years ago (she started work on January 5). Her first job was in training and development, where she received nothing but superior evaluations from her supervisors. Approximately two years ago she was promoted to acting manager of the department. As acting manager she received superior evaluations.

Five months ago the company decided to fill the manager position permanently. Bennett applied for the position. She was told by her supervisor, Darren Blackwood, that management liked her work but that she did not quite fit the image they were seeking. She needed to lose weight as well as change her attitude toward male employees. She was perceived as being "too assertive." It would be better, she was told, if she could show more deference. Bennett was not hired as manager. Instead, the company hired Martina Yardly.

After Yardly was hired, Bennett states that her life was made miserable. Yardly criticized her work constantly. She also made comments about her appearance, stating that even though she was not hired as manager, she should still try to lose weight and "fix herself up." Two months ago, Bennett was fired.

When male employees in Bennett's position are terminated from Rikards-Hayley, they commonly receive a severance package consisting of one year's salary. Bennett received a severance package consisting of six months' salary.

As a result of her treatment at work, Bennett claims that she suffered physically and emotionally. She is still seeing a doctor for physical and mental side effects of the stress. To date her medical bills total $2,500. She has also been unable to find other work. In the year before she was terminated, Bennett earned $150,000.

Correspondence
"Demand" letter from Plaintiff's Attorney

Anthony Righetti, Esq.
Righetti, Morgan and Blake
34 Court Ave.
Greenville, New State
555 222-2222
arighetti@rmb.com

Monica Ruiz, Esq.
Counsel, Rikards-Hayley
45 Prospero Place
New York, New York

Re: Bennett v. Rikards-Hayley

Dear Ms. Ruiz,

This office was recently retained by Alice Bennett, a former employee of Rikards-Hayley. Ms. Bennett worked for your company for several years and was terminated approximately six months ago. Based on information provided by Ms. Bennett, I believe that her termination was in violation of the employment discrimination provisions of both federal and state law. In particular, according to Ms. Bennett, she was denied a promotion and eventually terminated because of her sex. Furthermore, she was deprived of compensation equal to that of male employees.

I would like to meet with you to discuss this matter in hopes of resolving it without unnecessary litigation.

Sincerely,

Anthony Righetti, Esq.
Attorney at Law

Response to demand letter from Defendant's Attorney

Vanessa Graves, Esq.
Miller, Graves and Klein
1 Main St.
New York, New York
555 222-1111
Vanessa.graves@mgkesq.com

Anthony Righetti, Esq.
Righetti, Morgan and Blake
34 Court Ave.
Greenville, New York
555 222-2222
arighetti@rmb.com

Re: Bennett v. Rikards-Hayley

Dear Mr. Righetti,

Monica Ruiz, in-house counsel for Rikards-Hayley, forwarded me your recent letter regarding the claim of Alice Bennett. I have spoken with Ms. Bennett's prior supervisors, Darren Blackwood and Martina Yardly, as well as the Manager of Personnel Services, Rhees Bradley, and have determined that your client's claim is without merit. Although Ms. Bennett was a valuable employee of Rikards-Hayley for some time, her termination and compensation were in no way a result of any discriminatory practice.

Several months ago, Ms. Bennett interviewed for a position as Manager of the Department of Training and Development. Another, more experienced candidate, also a woman, was hired for the position. After this, Ms. Bennett, who was still an employee in training and development, developed a hostile attitude toward her new supervisor, creating an extremely uncomfortable work environment. In an effort to resolve matters, and in view of Ms. Bennett's prior contributions to the firm, she was offered a position in another department. She refused this position and eventually was terminated.

My client emphatically denies any wrongdoing on its part and will not consider any settlement.

Sincerely,

Vanessa Graves, Esq.
Attorney at Law

The Law

Relevant U.S. Code Sections—Employment Discrimination Title 42

§ 2000e. Definitions

For the purposes of this subchapter—

(a) The term "person" includes one or more individuals, governments, governmental agencies, political subdivisions, labor unions, partnerships, associations, corporations, legal representatives, mutual companies, joint-stock companies, trusts, unincorporated organizations, trustees, trustees in cases under Title 11, or receivers.

(b) The term "employer" means a person engaged in an industry affecting commerce who has fifteen or more employees for each working day in each of twenty or more calendar weeks in the current or preceding calendar year, and any agent of such a person, but such term does not include (1) the United States, a corporation wholly owned by the Government of the United States, an Indian tribe, or any department or agency of the District of Columbia subject by statute to procedures of the competitive service (as defined in section 2102 of Title 5), or (2) a bona fide private membership club (other than a labor organization) which is exempt from taxation under section 501(c) of Title 26, except that during the first year after March 24, 1972, persons having fewer than twenty-five employees (and their agents) shall not be considered employers.

§ 2000e-2. Unlawful employment practices

(a) Employer practices

It shall be an unlawful employment practice for an employer—

(1) to fail or refuse to hire or to discharge any individual, or otherwise to discriminate against any individual with respect to his compensation, terms, conditions, or privileges of employment, because of such individual's race, color, religion, sex, or national origin; or

(2) to limit, segregate, or classify his employees or applicants for employment in any way which would deprive or tend to deprive any individual of employment opportunities or otherwise adversely affect his status as an employee, because of such individual's race, color, religion, sex, or national origin.

§ 2000e-5. Enforcement provisions

(e) Time for filing charges; time for service of notice of charge on respondent; filing of charge by Commission with State or local agency; seniority system

> **(1)** A charge under this section shall be filed within one hundred and eighty days after the alleged unlawful employment practice occurred and notice of the charge (including the date, place and circumstances of the alleged unlawful employment practice) shall be served upon the person against whom such charge is made within ten days thereafter, except that in a case of an unlawful employment practice with respect to which the person aggrieved has initially instituted proceedings with a State or local agency with authority to grant or seek relief from such practice or to institute criminal proceedings with respect thereto upon receiving notice thereof, such charge shall be filed by or on behalf of the person aggrieved within three hundred days after the alleged unlawful employment practice occurred, or within thirty days after receiving notice that the State or local agency has terminated the proceedings under the State or local law, whichever is earlier, and a copy of such charge shall be filed by the Commission with the State or local agency.

(2) [Omitted]

(3) (A) For purposes of this section, an unlawful employment practice occurs, with respect to discrimination in compensation in violation of this subchapter, when a discriminatory compensation decision or other practice is adopted, when an individual becomes subject to a discriminatory compensation decision or other practice, or when an individual is affected by application of a discriminatory compensation decision or other practice, including each time wages, benefits, or other compensation is paid, resulting in whole or in part from such a decision or other practice.

(f) Civil action by Commission, Attorney General, or person aggrieved; preconditions; procedure; appointment of attorney; payment of fees, costs, or security; intervention; stay of Federal proceedings; action for appropriate temporary or preliminary relief pending final disposition of charge; jurisdiction and venue of United States courts; designation of judge to hear and determine case; assignment of case for hearing; expedition of case; appointment of master.

(3) Each United States district court and each United States court of a place subject to the jurisdiction of the United States shall have jurisdiction of actions brought under this subchapter. Such an action may be brought in any judicial district in the State in which the unlawful employment practice is alleged to have been committed, in the judicial district in which the employment records relevant to such practice are maintained and administered, or in the judicial district in which the aggrieved person would have worked but for the alleged unlawful employment practice, but if the respondent is not found within any such district, such an action may be brought within the judicial district in which the respondent has his principal office. For purposes of sections 1404 and 1406 of Title 28, the judicial district in which the respondent has his principal office shall in all cases be considered a district in which the action might have been brought.

(g) Injunctions; appropriate affirmative action; equitable relief; accrual of back pay; reduction of back pay; limitations on judicial orders

(1) If the court finds that the respondent has intentionally engaged in or is intentionally engaging in an unlawful employment practice charged in the complaint, the court may enjoin the respondent from engaging in such unlawful employment practice, and order such affirmative action as may be appropriate, which may include, but is not limited to, reinstatement or hiring of employees, with or without back pay (payable by the employer, employment agency, or labor organization, as the case may be, responsible for the unlawful employment practice), or any other equitable relief as the court deems appropriate. Back pay liability shall not accrue from a date more than two years prior to the filing of a charge with the Commission. Interim earnings or amounts earnable with reasonable diligence by the person or persons discriminated against shall operate to reduce the back pay otherwise allowable.

(k) Attorney's fee; liability of Commission and United States for costs

In any action or proceeding under this subchapter the court, in its discretion, may allow the prevailing party, other than the Commission or the United States, a reasonable attorney's fee (including expert fees) as part of the costs, and the Commission and the United States shall be liable for costs the same as a private person.

Relevant Code of Federal Regulations—Claim to EEOC

Title 29 Part 1601

PART 1601—PROCEDURAL REGULATIONS—Table of Contents
Subpart B—Procedure for the Prevention of Unlawful Employment Practices
Sec. 1601.12 Contents of charge; amendment of charge.

    (a) Each charge should contain the following:

        (1) The full name, address and telephone number of the person making the charge except as provided in Sec. 1601.7;

        (2) The full name and address of the person against whom the charge is made, if known (hereinafter referred to as the respondent);

        (3) A clear and concise statement of the facts, including pertinent dates, constituting the alleged unlawful employment practices: See Sec. 1601.15(b);

        (4) If known, the approximate number of employees of the respondent employer or the approximate number of members of the respondent labor organization, as the case may be; and

        (5) A statement disclosing whether proceedings involving the alleged unlawful employment practice have been commenced before a State or local agency charged with the enforcement of fair employment practice laws and, if so, the date of such commencement and the name of the agency.

    (b) Notwithstanding the provisions of paragraph (a) of this section, a charge is sufficient when the Commission receives from the person making the charge a written statement sufficiently precise to identify the parties, and to describe generally the action or practices complained of. A charge may be amended to cure technical defects or omissions, including failure to verify the charge, or to clarify and amplify allegations made therein. Such amendments and amendments alleging additional acts which constitute unlawful employment practices related to or growing out of the subject matter of the original charge will relate back to the date the charge was first received. A charge that has been so amended shall not be required to be redeferred.

Federal Rules of Civil Procedure

Rule 7. Pleadings Allowed; Form of Motions

    (a) Pleadings. Only these pleadings are allowed:

        (1) a complaint;

        (2) an answer to a complaint;

        (3) an answer to a counterclaim designated as a counterclaim;

        (4) an answer to a crossclaim;

        (5) a third-party complaint;

(6) an answer to a third-party complaint; and

(7) if the court orders one, a reply to an answer.

(b) Motions and Other Papers.

(1) *In General.* A request for a court order must be made by motion. The motion must:

    (A) be in writing unless made during a hearing or trial;

    (B) state with particularity the grounds for seeking the order; and

    (C) state the relief sought.

(2) *Form.* The rules governing captions and other matters of form in pleadings apply to motions and other papers.

Rule 15. Amended and Supplemental Pleadings

(a) Amendments before Trial.

(1) *Amending as a Matter of Course.* A party may amend its pleading once as a matter of course within:

    (A) 21 days after serving it, or

    (B) if the pleading is one to which a responsive pleading is required, 21 days after service of a responsive pleading or 21 days after service of a motion under Rule 12(b), (e), or (f), whichever is earlier.

(2) *Other Amendments.* In all other cases, a party may amend its pleading only with the opposing party's written consent or the court's leave. The court should freely give leave when justice so requires.

(3) *Time to Respond.* Unless the court orders otherwise, any required response to an amended pleading must be made within the time remaining to respond to the original pleading or within 14 days after service of the amended pleading, whichever is later.

Complaint Form—Employment Discrimination

5B Am. Jur. Pl. & Pr. Forms Civil Rights § 103

American Jurisprudence
Pleading and Practice Forms Annotated
Database updated April 2013

Civil Rights
III. Discrimination In Particular Matters
E. Employment
4. Sexual Discrimination
Topic Summary Correlation Table

§ 103. Complaint, petition, or declaration—Discrimination in employment based on sex—Damages for discrimination, unlawful discharge, and fraud

UNITED STATES DISTRICT COURT
FOR THE DISTRICT OF _____
_____ DIVISION

,
[Party]

                        Civil Action, File Number

v.   *[Designate name of document]*

,
[Party]

                        COMPLAINT

Plaintiff alleges:

FIRST CAUSE OF ACTION
Discrimination

1. Plaintiff, *[name of plaintiff]*, is a resident of *[county]*, residing at *[address 1]*.

2. Defendant, *[name of corporation]*, is a corporation duly organized and existing under the laws of *[state]*, engaged in the business of *[type of business]*, with its principal place of business located at *[address 2]*, *[county]*.

3. *[If applicable, description of allegations regarding other defendants.]*

4. The acts alleged took place primarily within *[county]*, *[state]*, at *[description of location where discriminatory acts took place]*.

5. On *[date 1]*, plaintiff filed a verified complaint with *[name of administrative agency]*, alleging that defendant had committed an unlawful employment practice against plaintiff in violation of *[citation of statute]* within the preceding *[period of time]*.

6. On *[date 2]*, *[name of administrative agency]* issued plaintiff a right-to-sue letter informing plaintiff of the right to file suit against defendant within *[period of time]*. On *[date 3]*, plaintiff informed *[name of administrative agency]* that plaintiff had determined to file suit against defendant privately and requested that the accusation filed with *[name of administrative agency]* be dismissed.

7. Plaintiff is a female, *[number of years]* years of age, born on *[date 4]*. Plaintiff began working for defendant on *[date 5]*. From plaintiff's hiring to *[date 6]*, she worked for defendant in numerous clerical positions. On *[date 7]*, plaintiff was promoted by defendant to *[description of position 1]* at defendant's *[name of facility 1]*. On *[date 8]*, plaintiff was again promoted by defendant to the position of *[description of position 2]* at *[name of facility 2]* and served in that position until *[date 9]*. Plaintiff has worked competently and loyally for defendant throughout her *[number of years]* years of employment.

8. As *[description of position]*, plaintiff was one of a group of *[description of job classification]*, *[number in job of male employees in classification]* men and *[number in job of female employees in classification]* women. On *[date 10]*, defendant decided to attempt a consolidation of *[description of job classifications]* into a smaller number of offices. As the initial step in this process, defendant organized at *[name of facility 2]* a pilot program that would serve as a model for such consolidations.

9. To head the *[description of office]* defendant promoted *[name of male employee]* from *[location of facility]*. *[Name of male employee]*, a man, is *[number of years]* years of age and substantially less qualified for that position than plaintiff. *[Name of male employee]* had *[number of years]* years of experience with defendant. He started as a *[description of position]*, and was promoted to *[description of second position]*. *[Description of facts regarding any further promotions affecting employee.]* By the time of male employee's promotion to head the new office, plaintiff worked for defendant for *[number of years]* years in *[description of job title]* and had held the position of *[description of other position]* for *[number of years]* years. By *[date 11]*, plaintiff was not only substantially more experienced than *[name of male employee]*, but was more competent at *[description of managerial position]*.

10. In spite of this overwhelming difference in suitability for *[description of position]*, defendant entirely overlooked and rejected plaintiff for *[description of position]*. *[Name of male employee]* was placed in *[description of position]*, at a pay level and a benefit level substantially above plaintiff's.

11. *[If applicable, description of any further facts supporting claim of defendant's promotion of other parties less qualified than plaintiff.]*

12. *[If applicable, description of any further facts supporting plaintiff's claim of promotion requests to males and defendant's refusal to promote her.]*

13. Instead of a promotion to *[description of position]*, defendant offered plaintiff a position as a *[description of lesser or equal position]*. At such time, defendant did offer plaintiff a *[percentage 1]%* pay increase to accompany the move, but stated that her salary would be "red-circled," or frozen at the new level subsequently.

14. *[If applicable: description of any further facts supporting claim of defendant's general or systematic discriminatory pattern in favor of equivalently less experienced and qualified males and against equivalently more experienced and qualified females.]*

15. After plaintiff's service and qualifications were persistently ignored in favor of less able and qualified male employees, and after defendant informed plaintiff that she would not be considered for positions she was amply qualified for in favor of less qualified men, plaintiff found her position completely untenable and resigned on *[date 12]*.

16. The conduct of defendant, as set forth above, constitutes unlawful discrimination against plaintiff on the basis of sex, in violation of *[citation of statute]*.

17. As a proximate result of defendant's conduct, plaintiff has suffered and continues to suffer substantial losses in earnings, job experience, retirement benefits, and other employee benefits that she would have received absent defendant's discrimination. Furthermore, plaintiff has incurred additional costs and expenses due to defendant's discrimination. Plaintiff does not know at this time the exact amount of her damages, but is informed and believes, and thereon alleges, that the amount of her loss will be $*[dollar amount 1]* or more. Plaintiff requests leave of the court to amend the complaint when these damages are more fully known.

18. As a further proximate result of the above-mentioned acts, plaintiff has suffered humiliation, mental pain and anguish, all to plaintiff's damage of $*[dollar amount 2]*.

19. The above-mentioned acts of defendant were willful, wanton, malicious, and oppressive, and justify the awarding of exemplary and punitive damages of $*[dollar amount 3]*.

SECOND CAUSE OF ACTION
Breach of Contract

20. Plaintiff refers to the allegations of Paragraphs 1 through 15 of the First Cause of Action, and by such reference repleads and incorporates them as though fully set forth here.

21. At all times relevant to this action, defendant has represented to employees in various writings, including but not limited to, personnel policies and procedure manuals, retirement and profit-sharing plan and employee guidelines, that their employment relationship with defendant would be based on good faith, that employees would be treated fairly and equitably, that employees would be judged on the basis of individual merit and ability, and that employees would receive just compensation for their services rendered to defendant. These provisions and representations form part of plaintiff's express employment contract with defendant.

22. Prior to plaintiff's constructive discharge by defendant on *[date 13]*, plaintiff had performed all conditions, covenants, promises, duties, and responsibilities required of her to be performed in accordance and in conformity with her employment contract.

23. On *[date 14]*, defendant breached plaintiff's contract and wrongfully failed to judge plaintiff on the basis of merit and ability, and wrongfully and without cause forced plaintiff to resign by committing such deliberate actions that rendered plaintiff's working conditions intolerable.

24. As a result of defendant's breach of contract as mentioned above, plaintiff has suffered and will suffer damages in excess of the jurisdictional requirements of this court. Plaintiff requests leave to amend this complaint on learning the extent of the damages.

THIRD CAUSE OF ACTION
Breach of Implied Covenant of Good Faith and Fair Dealing

25. Plaintiff refers to the allegations of Paragraphs 1 through 15 of the First Cause of Action and Paragraphs 21 through 23 of the Second Cause of Action, and by reference repleads and incorporates them as though fully set forth here.

26. The above-described employment agreement has implied in law a covenant of good faith and fair dealing by which defendant promised to give full cooperation to plaintiff in her performance under the employment agreement and to refrain from any act that would prevent or impede plaintiff from performing all of the conditions of the agreement.

27. Beginning on approximately *[date 15]*, and culminating with defendant's constructive discharge of plaintiff on *[date 16]*, defendant breached its implied covenant of good faith and fair dealing with regard to plaintiff by:

(a) discriminatorily refusing to judge plaintiff on the basis of her ability and merit;

(b) refusing and failing to make available to her equal opportunity for promotion and advancement;

(c) failing and refusing to reconsider plaintiff's merit and ability for promotion or transfer;

(d) failing to give any consideration to plaintiff's long-term record of employment service;

(e) violating company procedures regarding job interviews for openings and transfers, including but not limited to, interviews of qualified candidates who have expressed a desire to be considered; and

(f) failing to consider fairly plaintiff for either *[description of position 1]* or *[description of position 2]* despite plaintiff's abundant qualifications and the impending elimination of plaintiff's present position by defendant, all with the object of denying plaintiff the opportunity to continue in *[description of position 1]*, forcing plaintiff to quit her employment, reducing salary costs, and avoiding its obligation to pay plaintiff employment and retirement benefits.

28. As a proximate cause of defendant's breach of the covenant of good faith and fair dealing, plaintiff has suffered and continues to suffer substantial losses in earnings, retirement benefits, and other employee benefits that she would have received had defendant not breached the agreement. Plaintiff requests leave to amend this complaint on learning the extent of the damages.

29. As a further proximate resulting of the above-mentioned acts, plaintiff has suffered humiliation, mental pain and anguish, all to plaintiff's damage of $*[dollar amount 4]*.

30. The above-mentioned acts of defendant were willful, wanton, malicious, and oppressive, and justify the awarding of punitive and exemplary damages of $*[dollar amount 5]*.

FOURTH CAUSE OF ACTION
Wrongful Discharge

31. Plaintiff realleges and incorporates by reference each allegation contained in Paragraphs 1 through 15 of the First Cause of Action, Paragraphs 21 and 23 of the Second Cause of Action, and Paragraphs 26 and 27 of the Third Cause of Action, and by reference repleads and incorporates them as though fully set forth here.

32. The above-described actions of defendant constitute a wrongful discharge entitling plaintiff to general, compensatory, and punitive damages.

FIFTH CAUSE OF ACTION
Intentional Infliction of Emotional Distress

33. Plaintiff realleges and incorporates by reference each allegation contained in Paragraphs 1 through 15 of the First Cause of Action, Paragraphs 21 and 23 of the Second Cause of Action, and Paragraphs 26 and 27 of the Third Cause of Action, and by reference repleads and incorporates them as though fully set forth here.

34. Defendant, in committing the above-described acts, intended to and did inflict severe emotional distress upon plaintiff. Defendant acted with a reckless disregard of the probability of causing emotional distress to plaintiff.

35. As a direct result of the outrageous acts and omissions, conduct, and discrimination, plaintiff became physically distraught and sustained shock to her nervous system and suffered severe emotional distress, all resulting in damages to her in excess of $*[dollar amount 6]*.

SIXTH CAUSE OF ACTION
Fraud, Deceit, and Misrepresentation

36. Plaintiff realleges and incorporates by reference each allegation contained in Paragraphs 1 through 15 of the First Cause of Action, Paragraphs 21 and 23 of the Second Cause of Action, Paragraphs 26 and 27 of the Third Cause of Action, and Paragraph 34 of the Fifth Cause of Action, and by reference repleads and incorporates them as though fully set forth here.

37. Defendant made material misrepresentation of the fact that plaintiff be judged on the basis of merit and ability, and that plaintiff would be given an opportunity to interview and be evaluated for all the positions opening up in the *[description of office]*.

38. Defendant concealed facts from plaintiff which defendant had an affirmative duty to disclose to the effect that defendant would not provide plaintiff with an opportunity to be evaluated on a nondiscriminatory basis for transfer or promotion.

39. Defendant held itself out as being situated so that plaintiff would reasonably rely on defendant. Defendant made the material misrepresentations and concealed facts with the knowledge of the falsity of the representations made, with the intent to induce plaintiff to rely on such representations. As a consequence, plaintiff reasonably relied on the fraudulent and material misrepresentations.

40. As a result of defendant's fraud, deceit, and misrepresentations as set forth above, plaintiff has suffered and will suffer damages in excess of the jurisdictional requirements of this court. Plaintiff requests leave to amend this complaint on learning the extent of the damages.

41. Defendant's fraudulent actions toward plaintiff were willful and intentional, and were made with the intent to vex, annoy, oppress, and injure plaintiff, and therefore plaintiff is entitled to punitive damages of $*[dollar amount 7]*.

WHEREFORE, plaintiff requests judgment as follows:

On Second Cause of Action

1. Actual damages against defendant of $*[dollar amount 8]*, with interest thereon from the date of judgment until paid.

On First, Third, Fourth, Fifth, and Sixth Causes of Action

1. Actual damages of $*[dollar amount 9]*, or to be established at trial;
2. General and compensatory damages of $*[dollar amount 10]*;
3. Punitive damages of $*[dollar amount 11]*.

On All Causes of Action

    1. Costs of suit;

    2. Reasonable attorneys' fees; and

    3. Such other and further relief as the court may deem just and equitable. Dated: *[date 17].*

[Signature and address]

Notes

West's Key Number Digest

West's Key Number Digest, Civil Rights 158.

Legal Encyclopedias

Sexual discrimination in employment in general. Am. Jur. 2d, Job Discrimination §§ 135 et seq.

Reprinted with permission of Thomson Reuters.

SELECTED DOCUMENTS FROM DEFENDANT'S FILE

Interview Transcript

Interview Transcript of Darren Blackwood
by Thomas Perth, Paralegal

Q. Good morning Mr. Blackwood. My name is Thomas Perth and I'm a paralegal
    working for Vanessa Graves. She's the attorney who is representing your employer,
    Rikards-Hayley. I am going to ask you some questions about Alice Bennett, a
    former employee of Rikards. I think you know that she is claiming to be a subject of
    employment discrimination by the company. Do you recall Ms. Bennett?

A. Yes.

Q. When did you first meet her?

A. I was actually on the interview committee that recommended her hiring. That must
    have been about 5 years ago.

Q. And what was the position she was hired for?

A. It was as assistant manager of training and development.

Q. And what was your impression of Ms. Bennett when you hired her?

A. Well, she seemed very competent. She had good academic credentials and she
    had experience in training employees. I can't remember all the details, but the
    information would probably be in her personnel file. She seemed very self-confident
    and I thought she would be good in a managerial position.

Q. Aside from being on the interview committee did you have other contact with
    Ms. Bennett?

A. Yes, I was the General Manager of the division where she worked, so I had quite a bit
    of contact with her.

Q. And what was your impression of her as an employee?

A. She was a very good employee and when the manager of training and development
    left, I had no hesitation about making her acting manager.

Q. And how did she do in that position?

A. Well I thought she was doing a very good job. There may have been one incident
    with an employee she fired, but that was all resolved.

Q. How did she get along with other employees in her department?

A. Aside from the one incident, she seemed to get along just fine. I thought she was a
    good manager.

Q. Can you describe that one incident?

A. It really wasn't anything. One employee, a man who had worked for the company
    for several years, occasionally took a little too long for lunch. Alice really came down
    hard on him and he took offense. I spoke to Alice, though, and told her that some
    of our older male employees had a hard time adjusting to female supervisors and it
    would probably be better if she went easy on them. She seemed to understand.

Q. You mention that Ms. Bennett was made acting manager. Was there a process in
    place to fill the position permanently?

A. Yes. It really just requires that a group of partners approve a candidate. Sometimes
    the interview is limited to internal candidates and sometimes a broader search is
    conducted.

Q. What was the process for the position in which Ms. Bennett was acting manager?

A. I was a strong supporter of Alice. I thought she would be a great manager, so I recommended that she be interviewed and hoped that would settle it. In fact I sent a memo to Rhees Bradley, the Personnel Director, indicating my support. I brought a copy of that memo with me.

Q. Great. I'll include that in our file. What happened after Ms. Bennett's interview?

A. It seems that others were not as impressed with Alice as I was. They seemed to want someone with more experience. They decided to expand the search and interview more candidates. I also have a copy of a memo from personnel explaining this.

Q. Did anyone ever say anything to you about not wanting her in the position because she was a woman?

A. Absolutely not.

Q. Did anyone ever say anything to you about her physical appearance?

A. Well, off the record, Alice was a little over weight. Someone, I don't remember who, did mention that we needed a person with a better image as manager. But that wasn't why she didn't get the job. Martina was just much more qualified.

Q. After Ms. Yardly was hired, did Ms. Bennett continue working for Rikards?

A. Yes. She went back to her former position as an assistant manager.

Q. How did that work out?

A. It didn't. There were all sorts of problems and complaints and it became obvious that the two women could not continue to work together. I felt a little bad for Alice because I think she could have handled the manager's job. I offered to let her transfer to a different department, in a sales position, but she didn't want this.

Q. Eventually, I take it, she was terminated?

A. Yes, there was just no other way. But we did give her a generous severance package—six month's pay.

Q. Does the company have a uniform severance package?

A. No. Each case is different.

Q. Who decides?

A. It's a joint decision of the partners, personnel, and the individual's supervisor.

Q. To your knowledge, have male employees ever received a greater severance package than Ms. Bennett.

A. They may have. You probably should double check with personnel.

Q. One other matter, Mr. Blackwood. Do all employees use computers?

A. Of course. We're all networked.

Q. Including personnel?

A. Sure.

Q. How about the partners?

A. Some of them are resistant to using them, but they all have them.

Q. Do employees use other devices at work, such as tablets, smartphones?

A. I'm sure they do. I think you probably need to speak to our IT people about this.

Q. I'll do that. Thank you for speaking with me today. Attorney Graves may have more questions later. We appreciate your cooperation.

A. Of course.

Documentary Evidence

Document 1

Interoffice Memo

From: Darren Blackwood
To: Rhees Bradley, Director Personnel Services

Date: May 15

In the several months since Ms. Bennett assumed the position of acting manager of Management Training, she has performed in an outstanding manner. She is organized, efficient, and productive. Most importantly, she has been instrumental in rebuilding the morale of her staff. As you know when she assumed the position of acting manager, she encountered a department that was extremely dysfunctional. I do hope that when the company appoints a permanent manager for Management Training, Ms. Bennett will be given strong consideration.

Document 2

Interoffice Memo

From: Rhees Bradley, Director Personnel Services
To: Darren Blackwood
cc: Monica Ruiz, Esq., Counsel for Rikards-Hayley
Date: June 13

The Interview Committee completed its interview of Ms. Bennett for the Management position. We appreciate your comments concerning Ms. Bennett. However, the interview committee has some hesitation about Ms. Bennett and wants to widen our search. We know that Ms. Bennett has done a good job as acting manager, but her overall experience in this area is very limited. There are some additional problems. We have heard that she has difficulty managing some male employees, who seem to be reluctant to take direction from a woman. Some of the members on the interview committee were also concerned about her physical appearance.

CASE FILE 2: THE *DOUGLASS FINANCIAL INC.,* CASE

THE PARTIES AND THEIR ATTORNEYS

Defendant	Douglass Financial Services Inc. 1 State St.
Contact	Braedon Douglass 111-555-3333
Co-Defendant	Evan Portman 3256 Adelaide Way
Co-Defendant	Creative Catering
Plaintiff	Jessica Hewitt
Witnesses	Laura Green 456 Camino Seco Dr. 111-555-7677
	Adam Ortiz 1456 Olive Ave. 111-555-3890

Attorneys

Defendant, Douglass Financial	Manning Law Group 876 Courthouse Circle
Defendant, Evan Portman	Pearce, Solomon, and Ng 111 Juris Drive.
Defendant, Creative Catering	Unknown
Plaintiff, Jessica Hewitt	Crane, Gomez & Holliday 67 Walnut Ave.

INTRODUCTION

Jessica Hewitt v. Douglass Financial Services, Inc., Creative Catering and Evan Portman

This action results from an automobile accident involving Jessica Hewitt and Evan Portman, as a result of which Ms. Hewitt suffered serious injuries. The accident occurred in an intersection controlled by traffic lights. The accident occurred when the front of the vehicle driven by Hewitt (a Ford) hit the passenger side of a vehicle driven by Portman (a Honda). Independent witnesses indicate that Hewitt entered the intersection just as the traffic light turned green and that Portman entered the intersection on a yellow or red light. Witnesses also indicate that both parties were traveling fast.

Police were called to the scene of the accident and when they spoke to Portman noted that he appeared to be intoxicated. A subsequent blood test confirmed that he was over the legal limit. Portman told police that he had just left work, and that there had been a social gathering for employees during which alcohol was provided by his employer. Ms. Hewitt has hired an attorney to pursue a claim for her damages against Mr. Portman, his employer Douglass Financial Services, and Creative Catering. You work for the law firm that represents Douglass Financial Services, Inc.

SELECTED DOCUMENTS FROM THE DEFENDANT'S FILE

Client Interview

Interview of Braedon Douglass,
3/12/XXXX

Present: Gretchen Reilly, Esq.
              Natalie Ortiz
              Braedan Douglass

Questioning by Gretchen Reilly, Esq.

Q. Good morning, Mr. Douglass. I'm Gretchen Reilly, one of the attorneys with the Manning Law Group. I'd like to introduce, Natalie Ortiz, a senior paralegal with our firm. We will both be working on your case. I believe you spoke with Mr. Manning and you have retained this firm to represent your company.

    As you know, Jessica Hewitt is making a claim against Douglass Financial Inc. and its employee Evan Portman arising out of an accident at the end of last year. Mr. Portman is represented by attorneys in the firm of Peace, Solomon and Ng. It's my understanding that you received a letter from Ms. Hewitt's attorneys advising that she is making a claim. Is that right?

A. Yes. I gave a copy of the letter to Mr. Manning. I really don't understand why they are making a claim against us. We had nothing to do with the accident.

Q. We have quite a bit of investigation to do, Mr. Douglass, but in the meantime, she is making a claim and we cannot ignore it. It's really much too early to say what's going to happen. Could you clarify your relationship to Douglass Financial Inc.?

A. Sure. Douglass Financial is a corporation, but I am the sole owner. I am also the president of the company.

Q. How long has the corporation been in existence?

A. We incorporated about 6 years ago, on the advice of my accountant.

Q. Did you have an attorney take care of the incorporation?

A. Yes, but I don't remember who, right now.

Q. How large is your company?

A. We have about 20 employees.

Q. Okay. What can you tell me about Evan Portman?

A. Well, he's been working for us for a couple of years. Nice young man with a lot of potential.

Q. Have you ever had any problems with him?

A. No.

Q. How well do you know him?

A. As well as I know any of my employees.

Q. Do you work with him on a daily basis?

A. No. I don't work with many of the employees on a daily basis. I have two managers and they handle day-to-day operations. But we are a small company, and if there are any problems I usually hear about them.

Q. Okay. Let's talk a little about the office party that preceded Mr. Portman's accident. According to the letter from Ms. Hewitt's attorneys this accident happened on December 19 of last year. I am assuming that the office party was a Christmas party?

A. Yes, although we call it a Holiday Celebration.

Q. Tell me about the party.

A. Because our business tends to slow down between Christmas and New Years, we generally close the office during that time. A few days before we close we typically have an office party. This is held at our offices. I hire a caterer and provide food and drinks. This year we closed the office around 3 p.m. and everyone socialized with food and drinks.

Q. Did you provide alcohol?

A. We did have beer and wine, but no hard alcohol.

Q. What was the name of the caterer?

A. Creative Catering.

Q. Did they provide the beer and wine?

A. Yes.

Q. And did they serve the alcohol?

A. Yes.

Q. Were you at the party?

A. Of course.

Q. How long did the party last?

A. Everyone left by about 7 p.m.

Q. How about Evan Portman?

A. He left a little earlier than that.

Q. Do you know what time?

A. I'm not sure.

Q. Did you observe Mr. Portman during the party?

A. Well, some. I try to mingle with all the employees.

Q. Did you notice if Mr. Portman was drinking beer or wine?

A. No. I really wasn't paying attention.

Q. Did you have the opportunity to observe Mr. Portman when he left?

A. Yes. He wished me a Merry Christmas when he left.

Q. How would you describe his state of sobriety?

A. He looked fine to me.

Q. Does Evan Portman have any close friends at work?

A. I'm not sure.

Q. Well, at the party, did he seem to be socializing with anyone in particular.

A. I couldn't say.

Q. Does he work closely with any specific individuals?

A. Yes. He does work in a small group.

Q. I will want to get their names and probably talk with them.

A. That shouldn't be a problem.

Q. Just a few more questions. Are employees required to come to the office party?

A. Required?

Q. Yes. You mentioned that the party starts around 3 p.m. I assume that's before the regular work day ends. Could an employee skip the party and just go home?

A. That issue has never come up. They all come, although some do leave before 5.

Q. I think that's all I have for now. I would like to get a copy of Evan Portman's employee personnel file from you. We will get a copy of the police report of the accident and after that we may need to meet again.

A. Just let me know.

Police Report

POLICE DEPARTMENT
INCIDENT/OFFENSE REPORT

Type of Offense: Reckless Driving/Driving Under the Influence of Alcohol

Name of Suspect:	Address:	Phone: 111-555-1234		
Evan Portman	3256 Adelaide Way[1]	Gender:	Race:	DOB:
		Male	C	2-26-81

Driver's License Number:	Business Address:
B123215	Douglass Financial Services, 1 State St.,
	Business Phone:
	111-555-3333

Location, Date and Time of Offense:	Date and Time of Report:
Intersection of Park Avenue and Third Street; December 19, 7:00 P.M.	December 19, 7:00 P.M.

Vehicles Involved:
(1) Suspect Portman's: 2012 Honda CRV, white, VIN# 398293028378887
(2) Victim Hewitt's: 2013 Ford Focus, red, Vin# 3871738902766084

Witness(es) Name, Address, & Phone
Adam Ortiz, 1456 Olive Ave., 111-555-3890
Laura Green, 456 Camino Seco Dr. 111-555-7677

Victim:
Jessica Hewitt

Narrative Report, Interviews, Evidence
I was dispatched to the corner of Park Avenue and Third Street at approximately 7:00 P.M. on December 19, 20XX, in response to a 911 call indicating a motor vehicle collision. I was advised that medical assistance was also dispatched to the scene. When I arrived at the scene, medical personnel were rendering aid to the victim, who was being placed in an ambulance. I was advised by medical personnel that the victim sustained serious injuries and needed to be transported to the nearest hospital. Because of her physical condition, I could not interview her at the scene. At the scene, I interviewed the suspect, Evan Portman and 2 witnesses, Laura Green and Abel Ortiz.

Statement of Suspect, Portman
Suspect was interviewed at the scene. Portman was obviously shaken and upset and before I could question him, rambled about a "stupid office party." When I asked him what the office party had to do with the accident, he related the following. His employer, Douglass Financial Services, held an after-work office party to celebrate the holiday season. As a result he was forced to stay at work much later than he normally does. He and his wife had plans for the evening and he was running late. He seemed overly concerned about the reaction of his wife to his being late. I also observed that

---

[1]Assume that all addresses are within the city and state in which your school is located.

his speech was somewhat slurred and his eyes were bloodshot. I asked the suspect how much he had to drink at the party. He indicated that he just had a few beers. I then asked him to perform some field sobriety tests. He had trouble performing these and I then requested that he submit to a breathalyzer test. The test was positive for alcohol (.14%). Suspect was then placed under arrest for driving under the influence.

Statement of Laura Green

Mrs. Green related the following at the scene. She first noted the suspect's Honda SUV vehicle as it was driving north on Park Avenue toward the intersection of Third Street. Mrs. Green stated that the Honda SUV passed her on the right (at that point Park Avenue is one lane in each direction with a right shoulder used for street parking). The witness estimated the speed of the Honda at 45 m.p.h. The speed limit for that part of the road is 30 m.p.h. The witness further stated that the traffic signal turned yellow for traffic in her direction a few seconds before the Honda entered the intersection. The Honda vehicle was struck by a Ford Focus that had entered the intersection travelling west on Third Street. The Ford came from the suspect's right. The witness did not see the color of the light for the Ford as it entered the intersection. The witness thinks the Honda entered the intersection on a yellow light, but was not certain.

Statement of Adam Ortiz

Mr. Ortiz related the following. Prior to the collision of the Ford and Honda SUV, Ortiz was stopped for a red light at the intersection of Park Ave. and Third St. At that point, Third Street has two lanes in each direction. Ortiz was traveling west on Third St. Just as the light turned green for traffic traveling on Third Street, a Ford Focus came along side his vehicle. The Ford Focus entered the intersection without stopping, although the witness indicated that the light was green when the vehicle entered the intersection. Ortiz indicated that the Ford seemed to have been travelling "pretty fast" as if anticipating that the light was going to change. Shortly after the Ford entered the intersection, the vehicles collided, the front of the Ford hitting the passenger side of the Honda.

Recommendations

I recommend that when investigation is complete, this case be referred to the District Attorney's office for prosecution for driving under the influence.

Report Made By: Officer Donald Ramirez **Date**: 12/19/20XX

Complaint Form—Civil Liability For Selling or Furnishing Liquor
14C Am. Jur. Pl. & Pr. Forms Intoxicating Liquors § 140

American Jurisprudence Pleading and Practice Forms Annotated
Database updated April 2013
Intoxicating Liquors

VII. Civil Incidents and Liabilities
B. Civil Liability For Selling or Furnishing Liquor
2. Forms

Topic Summary References Correlation Table

§ 140. Complaint, petition, or declaration—Against sponsor of function where alcohol was served—Collision between car driven by intoxicated attendee and another car—For personal injuries

[Caption, see § 14]

COMPLAINT

Plaintiff, _____, alleges:

    1. Plaintiff now is, and at all times relevant to this action was, a resident of _____ County, _____*[state]*, residing at _____*[address]*, _____*[city]*, _____ County, _____*[state]*.

    2. Defendant, _____*[name of intoxicated driver]*, now is, and at all times relevant to this action was, a resident of _____ County, _____*[state]*, residing at _____ *[address]*, _____*[city]*, _____ County, _____*[state]*.

    3. Defendant, _____*[name of liquor provider]*, now is, and at all times relevant to this action was, a corporation duly organized and existing under the laws of _____ *[state]*, engaged in business as a restaurant, with its principal place of business located at _____*[address]*, _____*[city]*, _____ County, _____*[state]*.

    4. Defendant, _____*[name of sponsor of event]*, now is, and at all times relevant to this action was, a corporation duly organized and existing under the laws of _____ *[state]*, engaged in the business of _____, with its principal place of business located at _____*[address]*, _____*[city]*, _____ County, _____*[state]*.

    5. Sometime prior to _____*[date]*, defendant _____*[liquor provider]* was hired to provide facilities and a bar for a party which took place on _____*[date]*, which party individual defendant attended. Defendant _____*[liquor provider]* provided liquor which was offered for sale to those attending the party, a bartender who mixed and sold drinks to those attending the party, and parking facilities to enable those attending the party to park their cars. At all times relevant to this action, defendant _____*[liquor provider]* was in control of the premises where the party took place and where liquor was sold.

6. Sometime prior to _____*[date]*, defendant _____*[liquor provider]* was hired by defendant _____*[sponsor of event]*, through its agents, servants or employees, for the purpose of holding _____*[a Christmas]* party for the employees and staff of defendant _____*[sponsor of event]*. Defendant _____*[sponsor of event]* knew or should have known that liquor would be served at the party and that people attending and leaving the party would do so by automobile.

7. As a result of the negligence of defendant _____*[sponsor of event]*, its agents, servants, and employees, individual defendant was permitted to become intoxicated and to leave the party by car, a fact which defendant _____*[sponsor of event]*, through its agents, servants, and employees knew or should have known. Due to the intoxicated state of individual defendant, _____*[his or her]* automobile collided with the vehicle in which the plaintiff was riding while the automobile was in the immediate vicinity of the parking lot of defendant _____*[liquor provider]*.

8. As a result of the collision, plaintiff was severely and permanently injured, suffered and continues to suffer great pain of body and mind, has incurred great expense for hospitalization, medicine, medical attention, and nursing, and was prevented from transacting _____*[his or her]* usual business and carrying on _____*[his or her]* usual activities.

WHEREFORE, plaintiff requests judgment against defendants, jointly and severally, for:

1. Damages according to proof;
2. Costs of suit; and
3. Such other and further relief as to the court seems just and proper.

Dated: _____.

_____ *[Signature]*

Reprinted with permission of Thomson Reuters.

Glossary

accidental spoliation   The destruction of ESI that occurs when ESI is ruined despite a reasonable attempt to prevent that destruction.

active data   Computer-generated records within a computer system that are in current use.

adverse inference   *An adverse inference* is a ruling by a judge that declares that the jury may interpret any missing evidence against the interests of the party that failed to produce the evidence.

affidavit   A written statement sworn to under penalty of perjury before a notary or other person permitted by law to administer an oath.

affirm   An appellate court's upholding of the lower court's decision.

affirmative defense   Facts alleged by a defendant in an answer, which if proven, defeat plaintiff's claim, even if plaintiff can prove all the elements of his cause of action.

agent for service of process   Party designated by a corporation who is authorized to be served with a lawsuit against the corporation.

allegation   A contention or claim made within a pleading, regarding a fact that the party intends to prove at trial.

alternative dispute resolution (ADR)   Ways to resolve a civil dispute without resort to a legal action.

amicus curiae   A person allowed to give argument or appear in a lawsuit (usually to file a brief, but sometimes to take an active part) who is not a party to the lawsuit.

annotation tools   Hardware devices that coordinate with the document camera and laptop to mark screen images.

answer   The initial pleading filed by the defendant in a lawsuit, contesting the factual and/or legal basis for the lawsuit.

appeal   Asking a higher court to review the actions of a lower court in order to correct mistakes or injustice.

appellant   The person who appeals a case to a higher court.

appellant's brief   Brief of the person bringing an appeal.

appellate jurisdiction   The power of a court to review the decision of a lower court or administrative agency.

appellee   The person against whom an appeal is taken.

appellee's brief   Brief of the person who opposes an appeal.

app platform providers   An app platform provider is an organization, institution, or business, that creates and operates a mobile application.

arbitration   An out-of-court process in which disputing parties present their case to a neutral third person who listens to evidence from each disputing party and makes a decision; the decision is sometimes binding and sometimes not binding.

arbitrator   The neutral third party who presides over the arbitration process and makes a decision.

arb-med   An arbitrator is allowed to act as a mediator after hearing the arbitration.

attachment   Seizing property pursuant to a court order and giving the court the right to make orders regarding disposition of the property.

attorney–client privilege   A privilege that belongs to the client in an attorney–client relationship that requires the attorney to treat all information revealed to him or her, or to anyone employed by the attorney, as confidential. Because the privilege belongs to the client rather than to the attorney, only the client can give permission for the revelation of such confidential matters.

authorization   A signed statement empowering someone (such as a doctor or employer) to give out information that might otherwise be treated as confidential.

backup data   Computer-generated records within a computer system that are stored as a precautionary measure.

baseball arbitration   Each side presents its evidence to the arbitrator, each party informs the arbitrator what one number it believes the award should be, and the arbitrator must choose one of those proposed awards, based on the evidence heard.

bates numbering   The numbering of documents in a lawsuit using a machine.

brief   A written analysis of the facts and law related to a case, written by the attorneys handling the case, and filed in a trial or appellate court. Briefs are also filed in the Supreme Court.

bring-your-own-device (BYOD) policy   The practice of permitting, and sometimes even expecting, employees to use their own smartphones or tablets on the job.

capacity   Having the legal ability to do something such as initiating a lawsuit.

caption   The heading found in all pleadings, usually identifying the court, the parties, the nature of the pleading, and the docket number.

cause of action   A legal basis for a lawsuit based on the facts of the case and applicable law.

certiorari   A term used in connection with appellate proceedings indicating that the reviewing court wants the lower court to send the higher court its record, so that the proceedings can be reviewed. When parties ask the U.S. Supreme Court to hear a case, they often file a petition for writ of certiorari, which, if granted, means that the Supreme Court will review the record in the case.

chain of custody   A precise record of who received, handled, evaluated, and safeguarded the evidence in a legal proceeding.

character evidence   Evidence of a person's character or character trait shown by testimony regarding that person's reputation. This is admissible only in limited situations.

chronological deposition summary   A written abridgement of a deposition that records the information produced by the deposition based on a specified temporal sequence.

circumstantial evidence   Indirect evidence that helps to prove a fact, often requiring the trier of fact to draw reasonable and logical inferences.

cite check   Verifying the accuracy and proper form of all the citations in a document.

civil laws   Laws dealing with private disputes between parties.

civil litigation   The process of resolving private disputes through the court system.

civil procedure   The rules that apply in a civil case and determine how a civil case proceeds through the legal system; in federal courts many of the rules are found in the Federal Rules of Civil Procedure and the Federal Rules of Appellate Procedure.

claim statute   A type of law that requires a written notice describing a claim to be presented to the defendant before a lawsuit can be filed.

class action   A lawsuit brought by a limited number of parties on behalf of themselves and other persons with the same or similar issues.

clawback agreement   An agreement, sometimes called a nonwaiver agreement that allows the parties to agree that privileges can be asserted after evidence has been sent to the other party if the data retriever discovers that it has accidentally included privileged information in the evidence sent to the data requester.

cloud computing   Electronic file storage where files are stored on the Internet rather than on the office computer.

cloud storage   A way for an institution to preserve ESI by eliminating the need to store the ESI on hard drives and flash drives and passing that responsibility to a third party, the ESI or data center.

common interest privilege   The rule that protects any communication that takes place between attorneys for different clients when those clients share a common interest.

company-owned, personally enabled (COPE) device policy   The practice of providing employees with business-owned handheld e-devices, such as smartphones and tablets, that include separate apps for the employee's personal use.

compensatory damages   An award of money damages that compensates the plaintiff for actual loss, including pain and suffering.

complaint   Usually the first document filed in court in connection with a lawsuit; this sets forth the allegations or contentions of the plaintiff and states the basis for the action and the type of relief requested from the court.

compound request   A request made by a party in a lawsuit to another party in that lawsuit to admit in a single statement the truthfulness of two or more facts.

compulsory counterclaim   A defendant's claim against a plaintiff that must be brought in the lawsuit or is forever barred; one that is based on the same subject or transaction as the original claim.

compulsory examination   An examination that a party to a lawsuit has been ordered by the court to undergo concerning a physical or mental condition.

compulsory joinder   A party who should be included or named in a lawsuit; in federal court, Federal Rule of Procedure 19 sets out the criteria for compulsory joinder of parties.

computer   During the planning stage, it is important to remember that the term *computer* includes desktop PCs, laptops, notebooks, mobile phones, personal digital assistants (PDAs), digital recorders, GPS units, smartphones, scanners, fax machines, tablets, wireless reading devices (WRDs), and home computers that are part of a network. This is true whether the device is owned by the employer or the employee, if the employer is involved in the lawsuit and if work-related ESI has been programmed into the device.

concurrent jurisdiction (concurrent)   Power or authority of more than one court system to hear a case.

confessor–penitent privilege (clerical privilege)   A privilege designed to protect the confidentiality of any communication between an individual and his or her confessor when the relationship involves the spiritual support of the penitent. The privilege belongs to the penitent rather than the confessor. However, the law also protects the confessor who has taken a religious oath not to reveal the content of such counseling sessions.

confidentiality agreement   An agreement that is designed to protect confidential information, trade secrets, and other secret data from being revealed during the discovery process in a lawsuit.

conflict of interest   A situation in which, due to competing factors, one party (i.e. an attorney or paralegal) might be unable to act entirely for the benefit of party to whom a fiduciary duty is owed.

consent decree   A settlement of a lawsuit or prosecution in which a person or company agrees to take certain actions without admitting fault or guilt for the situation causing the lawsuit.

consideration   The reason or main cause for a person to make a contract; something of value received or promised to induce (convince) a person to make a deal. Without consideration a contract is not valid.

contingent fee   A legal fee based on a percentage of the final settlement or recovery from a lawsuit.

contribution   The right of a person who has paid an entire debt (or judgment) to be reimbursed a proportionate share of the judgment from another person who is also responsible for the debt.

costs   Out-of-pocket expenses incurred in pursuing a legal action (e.g. filing fees)

count   Separate claims stated in one complaint.

counterclaim   In a civil lawsuit, a claim for some relief made by a defendant against the plaintiff.

court of appeals   A court of review; this court reviews decisions from a trial court.

court reporter   An individual who records word for word the testimony of sworn witnesses in court or at depositions and who may be required to compose a written transcript of that testimony.

covenant not to sue   A type of settlement agreement in which the plaintiff agrees not to commence or maintain an action against the defendant, but does not release the defendant from liability arising from the incident.

criminal law   Laws that prohibit conduct that society deems harmful and provide for punishment in the form of jail, fines, or probation.

criminal procedure   The rules that apply in a criminal case and determine how a criminal case proceeds through the legal system; these are based on federal and state constitutions, codes, rules of court, and cases.

cross-appeal   An appeal by the appellee.

cross-claim   In a civil lawsuit, a claim made by one defendant against another related to the plaintiff's claims.

curriculum vitae   A list of an expert's credentials, including each educational and professional credential, and a summary of publications and research projects.

damages   Money that a court orders paid to a person who has suffered damage (a loss or harm) by the person who caused the injury (the violation of the person's rights).

declaration   A statement under penalty of perjury that certain facts are true or believed to be true.

declaratory relief   A court order defining or explaining the rights and obligations of parties under some contract or other document.

deemed admitted   A principle that holds that an undenied request for admission is treated as if it were admitted.

default   Failure to file an answer or other responsive pleading within the proper time; can eventually lead to a default judgment.

defendant   The party who is sued in either a civil or criminal case.

deliberate spoliation   The destruction of ESI that results from conduct that is "willful or in bad *faith*."

demand for inspection   A discovery technique that involves a request to enter property to inspect that property to gain facts in relation to the lawsuit.

demeanor   The appearance of a person and the way in which a person acts as opposed to what he or she says.

demurrer   A legal pleading in some state jurisdictions that attacks the validity of another pleading (usually a complaint) in that on its face, the pleading does not state facts that satisfy the requirements of the pleading.

deponent   An individual who responds to questions during a deposition.

deposition   An out-of-court question and answer session under oath, conducted in advance of a lawsuit as a part of the discovery process.

deposition summary   A written abridgement of a deposition that condenses the question-and-answer period to a concisely written, understandable account.

deposition upon written questions   A deposition before a court reporter that consists of oral responses by the deponent to written questions.

direct evidence   Proof that establishes a fact without the necessity of other evidence or the drawing of inferences.

disclosure   The process of revealing some information that was previously unknown or difficult to comprehend.

discovery   The procedure that the parties to a lawsuit follow in order to uncover the facts that are involved in the suit. The system involves an exchange of information among the parties using certain established discovery techniques including depositions, interrogatories, requests for real evidence, requests for physical and mental examinations, and requests for admissions.

dismissal with prejudice   A court order or judgment that ends a lawsuit. No further lawsuit may be brought by the same persons on the same subject.

dismissal without prejudice   A court order or judgment that ends a lawsuit. A further lawsuit may be brought by the same persons on the same subject.

diversity of citizenship   A basis for federal court subject matter jurisdiction under 28 U.S.C. § 1332 existing when no plaintiff and no defendant are citizens of the same state and the amount in controversy exceeds $75,000, or when one party is a citizen of a state and the other is a citizen of a foreign state.

docket number   A number assigned to a lawsuit by the court; each pleading or document filed in the action must bear this number.

document   An artifact that contains written matter, such as words or figures, in the form of a message or record.

document camera   A compact, high-resolution camera.

document production log   A method of keeping track of documents in a lawsuit by categorizing those documents based on source and file location. The document production log should indicate whether the documents have been excluded as privileged.

duplicative   A request made during discovery that replicates a request that was made at some previous time during the lawsuit.

early neutral evaluation   An ADR technique in which litigants meet with an outside neutral person who is an expert in the subject matter of the case. The evaluator provides a nonbinding evaluation of the merits and value of the case in an effort to facilitate settlement.

e-discovery (also electronic discovery and digital discovery)
A series of techniques and tools that involve the use of a wide variety of electronic resources to conduct discovery of electronically stored information in an efficient and economical way.

e-forensics (cyber-forensics or computer forensics)   A strategy that employs certain processes to retrieve, examine, analyze, and authenticate ESI.

electronically stored information (ESI)   Electronically stored information encompasses all computer-generated records such as those found in app records, backup tapes, blogs, "cookies," databases, data-processing cards, digital recorders, documented image technology, embedded chips, e-mail messages, metadata, fax machines, financial data, GPS tracking records, home computers, input data, Internet use records, instant messages, music files, PDAs, photos, scanners, smartphones, statistical data, system and network data, tablets, text messages, Web-based bulletin-board postings, Web-based discussions, widget records, wireless reading devices (WRDs), word-processed documents, videos, and voice mail, among others.

electronic courtroom   A courtroom equipped with electronic equipment to be utilized in trial presentation.

electronic deposition (e-deposition)   A deposition that is recorded by the use of a laptop, a smartphone, a tablet, or some other electronic device, thus allowing the participants involved in the deposition to be located at separate sites, often hundreds or even thousands of miles apart.

electronic transcript (e-transcript)   An electronic transcript or an e-transcript is a word-for-word account of a proceeding that is handled electronically

electronic whiteboard   A surface that can be written on and erased, display computer images, and send commands to the computer.

engrossed (or engrossment or engrossing)   The process of creating the final form of a document just before that document is used in a formal setting.

entry of default   Action by a court clerk noting that the defendant has failed to file a proper response to the complaint.

ephemeral data   Data that was created to self-destruct after a short period of time.

equitable relief   A judicial remedy other than money damages, such as specific performance of a contract or an injunction.

ESI center   A third party in a cloud storage agreement that is paid to receive, organize, and store data and to make it available to the ESI or data owner.

ESI or data center   An ESI or data center is a remote, secure facility designed to store and save electronic data for data owners who have quick and easy access to that data.

ESI owner (ESI depositor)   The owner of ESI in a cloud storage agreement.

ESI requester   The party in a lawsuit who requests data, including ESI, from the other party.

ESI retriever   The party to a lawsuit from whom data, including ESI, is requested during the discovery stage.

evidence in a legal proceeding   Relevant and admissible testimony, ESI documents, photographs, records, reports, objects, and other tangible items used by a party in a legal procedure to demonstrate the veracity of the party's claims to the finder of fact in the case.

evidence log   A document attached to an item of physical evidence recording the chain of possession (chain of custody) of that piece of evidence.

evidence presentation systems   Technologies that present evidence electronically and simultaneously to everyone in the courtroom.

exclusive jurisdiction (exclusive)   Power or authority to hear a case that belongs to one court system only (i.e. federal or one state court system).

ex parte   A legal proceeding in which only one party needs to be present.

expert witness   A person who possesses special knowledge on a topic because of education and/or experience. An expert witness is allowed to give opinion testimony concerning facts within his or her expertise.

extant data   Computer-generated records within a computer system that are hidden in the system, generally because they have been deleted.

fictitiously named defendants   Defendants in a lawsuit who are not identified by their correct names; usually refers to the practice in some state courts of including several "Does" as defendants to provide for discovery of additional defendants after the statute of limitations has run.

filing   Presenting a paper to the court clerk to be included in the court file for the case.

flat fee   A legal fee based on a fixed sum rather than on an hourly rate or a percentage of a recovery.

form books   Books containing sample forms for legal professionals to follow in preparing pleadings and other documents.

garnishee   A person who holds money or property belonging to a debtor and who is subject to a garnishment.

garnishment   A legal process, taken by a creditor who has received a money judgment against a debtor, to get the debtor's money. This is done by attachment of a bank account or by taking a percentage of the debtor's regular income.

general appearance   Either a physical appearance or filing of documents in a court, without specifically limiting the purpose of the appearance; a general appearance confers personal jurisdiction on the court on the party appearing.

general denial   A type of answer in which all of the allegations of the complaint are denied.

general jurisdiction   The power or authority of a court to hear cases that are not within the exclusive jurisdiction of a different court.

general release   A document by which a claim or right is relinquished.

general verdict   A verdict in which the jury must simply decide in favor of the plaintiff, by specifying an amount of money damages, or decide in favor of the defendant.

general verdict with interrogatories   Requires that the jury find for the plaintiff or the defendant, and requires that the jury members answer specific fact questions.

good cause   A legally acceptable reason for doing something or for refusing to do something.

guardian ad litem   A person who is appointed by the court to represent a party in a lawsuit, where the party lacks the capacity to file the action; guardians ad litem are usually appointed for minors or those who are mentally incapacitated.

habit   Evidence of a party's routine practice, used to show that on a particular occasion the party acted in accordance with that practice.

hearsay   A statement made out of court used to prove the truth of what was said.

higher court   Another term for a court with appellate jurisdiction.

high-low agreement   The parties agree that the outcome of the case will be no less than "X" dollars (the low) and no more than "Y" dollars (the high).

hourly billing   A legal fee based on a fixed amount for each hour the law firm spends on the case.

inactive data   Computer-generated records within a computer system that are relatively up to date but are not used on a routine basis.

in camera   A hearing or other proceeding that is held in the judge's private chambers out of the sight and hearing of any spectators; in private; in chambers.

in controversy   In the case of any physical or mental examination, the prerequisite that states that the condition to be examined must be at issue in the lawsuit.

indemnification   A concept allowing a defendant who has paid a judgment to seek reimbursement from another more culpable party, usually where the defendant seeking indemnification has done nothing wrong, but is nevertheless liable or where the parties have an agreement that one party will indemnify the other.

indispensable party   A person who must be joined in the lawsuit and whose absence makes it impossible for a court to render a judgment.

injunction   A court order requiring a party to take some action or to stop some conduct.

in rem jurisdiction   The authority of a court to hear a case based on the fact that property, which is the subject of a lawsuit, is located within the state in which the court is situated.

integrated lectern   A lectern that incorporates the equipment, connections, and controls in one location for an attorney to operate the courtroom technology from a single position.

interpleader   A type of action in which a party deposits money or property in the court because, although the party clearly owes money or the return of property, the parties to whom it is owed is unclear; after the property is deposited, the court determines its proper distribution.

interrogatories   Written questions requiring written answers under oath and directed to a party, in which another party seeks information related to the litigation.

judgment   In a civil court action, the final decision from the trial court.

judgment creditor   A person who has proved a debt in court and is entitled to use court processes to collect it.

judgment debtor   A person who has yet to satisfy a judgment that has been rendered against him or her.

judicial admission   A statement or other piece of evidence that has been admitted and that can, therefore, be introduced during the trial.

judicial notice   A court's acceptance of the truth of a fact without the necessity of evidence, often because the facts are official acts or are so universally known that they cannot reasonably be disputed.

jurisdiction   The power that a court has to hear a particular case; requires that a court have the power to hear the type of case (subject matter) and that a court have power to render a decision against a particular defendant (personal) or over property (in rem).

jury instructions   Directions given to the jury explaining the law that applies in the case and spelling out what must be proved and by whom. These instructions are given just before the jury is sent out to deliberate and return a verdict.

kill switch   The switch at the bench that permits the judge to turn off monitors until a particular piece of evidence is admitted or in an instance where the judge determines that certain images should not be shown to the jury.

laches   An equitable doctrine preventing a party from pursuing certain types of lawsuits (equitable) because that party has delayed to the extent that it would be unfair to the opposing party.

laptop with presentation software   A laptop containing software to conduct a slideshow presentation.

leading question   A question that generally calls for a yes or no answer and suggests the answer by the way it is phrased (e.g., beginning the question with "Isn't it true . . .").

legacy data   Data that was initially recorded on what is now an outmoded media format such as a floppy disk.

legal error   A mistake in the way the court interprets or applies the law.

limited jurisdiction   Authority to hear only certain kinds of cases.

linear document review   Linear document review is a technique used during the discovery phase of a lawsuit that involves compiling, accessing, examining, and assessing documents, using a traditional hands-on, manual approach.

litigation hold   An order issued by an attorney to a client telling that client's employees and associates to stop the routine handling of all ESI, especially as that routine involves the deletion of ESI.

litigation response team   A group of highly trained individuals who are charged with the job of learning all there is to know about the client's ESI system, including all backup, retrieval, formatting, deletion procedures, and so on.

loan receipt agreement   A contract between a claimant and settling tortfeasor by which they agree that one of them will prosecute the claim against another tortfeasor.

local rules of court   Rules that are adopted by individual courts and apply only in those courts.

long-arm statutes   A state law that defines the right of state courts to exercise jurisdiction over non-resident defendants.

lower court   Another term for a trial court.

Mary Carter agreement   A secret or semisecret agreement between the claimant and one or more, but not all, the tortfeasors.

med-arb   The dispute is mediated first, and if the dispute is not settled, the parties then move into the arbitration phase, which would generally be binding.

mediation   A non-binding process in which a neutral third party helps disputing parties reach a settlement.

mediation statement   A statement of facts and legal argument for your case.

mediator   The neutral third person who facilitates the mediation process.

medical diary   A document in which the client keeps track of medical treatment, daily health complaints, type and amount of medication, mileage to physicians' offices, and other related medical expenses.

medical privilege (physician–patient privilege)   The medical privilege exists between a patient and a medical practitioner and is designed to protect the patient's confidential communication with the practitioner. The privilege covers communications made between the patient and physicians, psychiatrists, podiatrists, psychologists, and dentists.

memorandum of points and authorities   A legal argument in the form of an explanation and analysis of the law that applies to the case.

metadata   Computer data about data, including such things as a tracking record that shows how the data was compiled, who compiled it, what it was used for, where it is stored, and so on.

metadata mining   The process of searching metadata for evidence.

minitrial   A proceeding in which high level executives of all the parties are brought together to hear a summary version of each other's case as presented by its lawyers and presided over by a neutral party (often a retired judge).

mobile applications (apps)   Mobile applications or apps are miniature dedicated programs downloaded to an e-device to provide a variety of services, such as game playing, calorie counting, music playing, photo editing, and so on. .

mock deposition   A practice session that attempts to duplicate the question-and-answer period that will occur during a real deposition. The objective of a mock deposition is to help the party or witness rehearse for an upcoming deposition.

mock jury   A group of independent individuals chosen to reflect the probable makeup of the actual jury.

mock trial   A practice trial prior to the date of the actual trial, intended to reveal the strengths and weaknesses of a party's case.

Model Rules of Professional Conduct   American Bar Association rules setting standards for the ethical conduct of lawyers; while not binding in themselves, these rules form the basis for most state ethical rules.

monitor   A device that displays signals on a computer screen.

motion   A request that a judge make a ruling or take some other action, most often in connection with a pending lawsuit.

motion for a more definite statement   A motion made in response to a complaint in which the defendant challenges the clarity or specificity of the complaint.

motion for a new trial   A motion made after a trial requesting that the judge set aside the verdict or judgment and grant a new trial to the parties.

motion for a protective order   A motion made during discovery asking the court to limit a discovery request.

motion for change of venue   A request from a party that the court transfer the case to a another geographical location.

motion for enlargement of time   A motion requesting additional time for an appeal, including the reasons that the additional time is needed and the number of additional days required.

motion for involuntary dismissal   A motion requesting dismissal of a lawsuit by the court, either prior to judgment or by virtue of a judgment against the plaintiff based on the verdict of the jury or the decision of the court after trial.

motion for judgment as a matter of law   In a jury trial, a request from one party that the judge decide the case in that party's favor on the basis that no facts have been proved that would support a jury's decision for the other party.

motion for judgment notwithstanding the verdict   A motion made in some state courts after a jury verdict; a request from one party that the judge reverse the jury's verdict against that party and enter a different judgment in that party's favor.

motion for judgment on the pleadings   A motion claiming that the allegations in the pleadings are such that no controversial issues remain and that judgment can be entered for only one party.

motion for mistrial   A motion asking that the judge terminate a trial prior to its conclusion because the jury is unable to reach a verdict, because of prejudicial error that cannot be corrected or eliminated by any action the court might take, or because of the occurrence of some event that would make it pointless to continue.

motion for new trial   A motion asking the trial court to order a new trial when prejudicial error has occurred or when, for, any other reason a fair trial was prevented.

motion for relief from a judgment or order   A request to the court by one party that the court relieve a party from any judgment, order, or proceeding.

motion for sanctions   A request to the court from one party that penalties be imposed on the other party for violating the provisions of Rule 11 of the Federal Rules of Civil Procedure.

motion for summary judgment   A motion requesting that judgment be entered immediately because there is no genuine dispute as to any material fact in the case and the movant is entitled to judgment as a matter of law.

motion in limine   One of the first motions filed before or at the beginning of trial, frequently used to prevent opposing counsel from introducing certain evidence at trial.

motion to amend   A request by one party to the court to allow a change in a pleading.

motion to compel   A request by one party to the court for an order requiring the other side to comply with a discovery request.

motion to dismiss   A party's request that the court strike or terminate the case before any judgment.

motion to quash service of summons   A request that the court declare that service of the complaint and summons is invalid, either because the court lacks jurisdiction over the defendant or because of some procedural problem with the service itself.

motion to quash the return of the service   Motion made by a defendant who claims that he was improperly served with the summons and complaint.

motion to strike   A request that immaterial statements or other things be removed from an opponent's pleading.

motion to tax costs   A motion made after a trial challenging the costs of suit that are claimed by the prevailing party.

movant   Party in a lawsuit who makes a motion.

mutual release   An agreement by which each party relinquishes its claims against the other.

negotiation   A situation in which the parties discuss their problems with one another.

negotiation (negotiate)   Discussion between opposing parties in an attempt to settle a case; usually involving compromise by both sides.

night baseball arbitration   The parties submit their proposals in confidence to the arbitrator after evidence is presented, the arbitrator then assigns a value to the case, and the parties agree to accept the high or low figure closest to the arbitrator's value.

nonbinding arbitration   An adversarial hearing before a neutral party or arbitrator who listens to each side and then makes a decision (an award) regarding the dispute.

nonresponsive documents   Documents that need not be presented to a party in answer to a request from that party for the production of those documents.

notice   A formal notification of intent; the knowledge of a particular set of facts; the formal acquisition of the knowledge of a fact or set of facts.

notice of appeal   A document filed with the appellate court and served on the opposing party, giving notice of an intention to appeal.

notice of hearing on the motion   The part of a written motion that describes the nature of the motion being made and tells when and where a hearing on the motion will occur.

notice of intent to take deposition upon written questions   A notice spelling out the date, time, and place of a planned deposition upon written questions. The notice will also indicate the name and address of the intended deponent as well as the identity of the officer who will attend the deposition. A subpoena must accompany any such notice served upon a nonparty to the lawsuit.

notice of intent to take oral deposition by nonstenographic means   A notice sent to opposing counsel of an intent to take a deposition after the judgment by use of only a dictating machine or a tape recorder, with no court reporter present.

notice of intent to take oral deposition   A notice spelling out the date, time, and place of a planned deposition. The notice will also indicate the name and address of the intended deponent as well as the identity of the attorney who will ask the questions during the deposition.

not reasonably accessible ESI   ESI that cannot be retrieved without unwarranted difficulty or without unfair cost.

on point   A law or prior case that directly applies to the facts of the present case.

opening statement   The introductory statements made at the start of a trial by lawyers for each side. The lawyers typically explain the version of the facts best supporting their side of the case, how these facts will be proved, and how they think the law applies to the case.

open stipulation   An agreement between parties or their attorneys that a defendant need not answer a complaint within the time directed by law and need not answer until specifically notified by the plaintiff to do so.

oral argument   The presentation of each side of a case before an appeals court. The presentation typically involves oral statements by a lawyer, interrupted by questions from the judge.

order   A judge's ruling in response to a motion.

order shortening time   A ruling from the court, often in connection with motions, allowing a moving party to give less notice of a hearing on a motion than is required by statute.

original jurisdiction   The power of a court to conduct a trial in a case; confers a court the right to be the first court to hear the matter.

overbroad   A request made during discovery that is so wide-ranging and inclusive that it asks for more evidence than could ever be useful to the other party in the lawsuit.

page-line deposition summary   A written abridgment of a deposition that records the information produced by the deposition in the order in which it was actually presented during the deposition process.

paper data   ESI that has been reduced to a hard copy for filing purposes as a safeguard against the loss of that data caused by the breakdown of the computer system.

partial release   The relinquishment of some claims and the retention of others by a party.

peremptory challenges   The automatic elimination of a potential juror by one side before trial without needing to state the reason for the elimination. Each side has the right to a certain number of peremptory challenges.

permissive counterclaim   A defendant's claim against a plaintiff that a defendant is allowed, but not required to make; one that is not necessarily related to the plaintiff's claim.

permissive joinder   A concept allowing multiple parties to be joined in one lawsuit as plaintiffs or defendants as long as there is some common question of fact or law.

personal jurisdiction The power or authority of the court to make a ruling affecting the parties before the court.

personal service of process Notice of a lawsuit or other proceeding that is given to a party by personally delivering a copy of the papers to that party.

petition An initial document filed with the court asking the court for some order. Sometimes petitions are filed in conjunction with a complaint (for example, asking the court to appoint a guardian for a party who cannot file a lawsuit); sometimes petitions are filed in lieu of a complaint (for example, in certain jurisdictions petitions and not complaints are used in divorce cases.)

petition for certiorari A request to a higher court for review, but which the higher court is not required to take for decision. Certiorari is a writ from the higher court asking the lower court for the record of the case.

petition for rehearing A request for a new hearing to reconsider an action that may have been wrongfully taken or overlooked in a previous hearing.

physical or mental examination An examination that a party to a lawsuit must undergo concerning a physical and/or mental condition that is at issue in a pending legal action.

plaintiff The party who initiates a civil or criminal lawsuit in court.

pleadings Documents that describe the claims and defenses of a lawsuit, including the complaint and the answer to the complaint.

postjudgment deposition A deposition that can be taken after judgment, with only a dictating machine or a tape recorder, with no court reporter present.

postjudgment interrogatories Written questions that the judgment debtor must answer in writing about his or her assets.

posttrial garnishment A separate, but ancillary, lawsuit, filed in the court that rendered the judgment, to permit the judgment creditor to collect on a judgment.

prayer The part of the pleading (usually at the end) where the party asks the court to either grant or deny some relief.

predictive coding A document retrieval strategy that employs a digital cataloging process that involves several well-orchestrated steps.

preliminary injunction A court order made prior to final judgment in the case, but after all parties have had the opportunity to present evidence, directing that a party take or refrain from some action until the trial in the case takes place.

presumption A conclusion or assumption of fact that the law requires to be made from the proof of another fact. Presumptions can be rebuttable or conclusive.

pretrial conference Meeting between the presiding judge and attorneys to facilitate both the preparation for and management of a trial.

primary sources Print or electronic publications that contain the actual law (i.e., case reporters, codes, constitutions).

privilege A protection afforded by the law to prevent or limit the discovery of evidence created within a setting such as that provided by the attorney–client or the physician–patient relationship.

privilege against self-incrimination A privilege granted by the Fifth Amendment to the Constitution that prevents a criminal defendant from being forced to testify against himself or herself, but which can, under certain circumstances, be used in a civil case.

privileged documents Documents that are shielded by the attorney–client privilege, the work product privilege, or the common interest privilege.

privilege log A method of keeping track of documents that are shielded by the attorney–client privilege, the work product privilege, or the common interest privilege.

procedural law Laws that set forth legal procedures or methods used by parties to enforce their rights or to oppose claims made against them.

projection screen A white or silvered surface where a projected image may be viewed by an audience and may be wall-mounted or stand-mounted.

projector Digital equipment, either portable or a standard unit, that projects rays of light or images onto a screen.

proof chart A list of the elements of the case that must be proved, witnesses to prove the various elements, exhibit/s that should be introduced to prove up the element, and any anticipated objection/s to the exhibit.

proof of service (certificate of service) Verification that a copy of a pleading, motion, or other document has been served to another party or attorney.

prose A person representing himself or herself (as a defendant or plaintiff) without a lawyer in a court proceeding (and whether the matter is civil or criminal).

protective order An order that is issued by the court in a lawsuit that protects a party in the suit from revealing information, documents, data, or other types of evidence to another party who has previously requested the production of that evidence.

punitive or exemplary damages Damages that punish a defendant for intentional or malicious conduct that causes injury.

qualified denial A type of answer denying all of the allegations of the complaint except those that are specifically admitted.

quasi in rem jurisdiction Authority of a court to hear a case based on the fact that the defendant owns property that is located within the state, even though that property is not the subject of the lawsuit.

quick peek agreement An agreement that allows the data retriever to give evidence to the data requester for a preliminary assessment while still preserving all privileges associated with that evidence.

quiet title action A legal proceeding to determine ownership of real property.

real party in interest The person who is entitled to the relief requested in a complaint, even though not named as a plaintiff.

real-time reporting A service provided by court reporters who utilize software that matches the keystrokes on a stenograph machine to corresponding entries in a database and then translates the keystrokes into words.

reasonably accessible ESI   ESI that can be retrieved without unwarranted difficulty and without unfair cost.

rebuttal evidence   Formal contradiction of statements made by an adversary.

redaction   A procedure that involves removing information from a document before duplicating the document and turning the duplicate over to another party in a lawsuit in response to a request for production.

release   Giving up a claim or right to sue.

relevant evidence   Evidence that tends to prove or disprove any fact that is of consequence to the determination of the action.

remand   The act of an appellate court sending a case back to the lower court after reversing a decision, often with specific instructions as to how the lower court must deal with the case.

removal   Generally, the transfer of a case from a state court to a federal court where concurrent jurisdiction exists and the case was initially filed in a state court.

renewed motion for judgment as a matter of law   Asks the district court to disregard the jury findings and enter judgment for the movant in spite of the jury's verdict for the nonmovant.

reply   In federal practice, a pleading in response to an answer sometimes required of a plaintiff.

representation letter   A letter from an attorney to a new client establishing the ground rules of the litigation, including fees, billing rates, retainer, and work to be performed by the law firm.

request for admission   A request made by a party to another party in that lawsuit to admit to the truthfulness of a fact or the genuineness of a piece of evidence.

request for a physical or mental examination   A request made by one party to another party in that lawsuit to undergo a physical or mental examination provided that the examination involves a condition that is at issue in the pending action.

request for documents   A request that a party or other individual involved in a lawsuit provide specific documents or other physical evidence to the party making the request for such documents or physical evidence.

request for the production of documents, electronically stored information (ESI), and tangible things, or entry upon land for inspection and other purposes   A request that a party or other individual involved in a lawsuit provide specific documents or other physical evidence to the party making the request.

rescission   To "undo" or abrogate a contract.

residual data   Fragments of data that may be left over on a computer's hard drive.

responsive documents   Documents that must be presented to a party in answer to a request from that party for the production of those documents.

restitution   Returning property to the original owner where fairness requires that it be done.

retainer   A legal fee imposed at the beginning of a legal action, usually intended to be applied to future attorney fees actually incurred.

retainer agreement   An agreement between an attorney and a client setting forth the fee arrangement and details of the attorney's obligations.

reverse   The act of an appellate court setting aside the decision of a lower court.

scope of discovery   The amount and type of evidence that can be sought during the discovery process.

secondary sources   Print or electronic publications about the law, such as articles, treatises, and encyclopedias; these are not binding on a court.

self-induced trigger event   A self-induced trigger event is an incident or a discussion about litigation that occurs completely within the confines of an institution but that, nevertheless, still produces the need to issue a litigation hold.

settlement   To come to an agreement about; disposition of a lawsuit.

settlement agreement   A contract between two or more parties to settle a case; it involves the voluntary, mutual assent of the parties and the give-and-take element of consideration. The agreement must be legal and must be made by parties with the capacity to contract.

settlement brochure   A summary of facts designed to get the other side to settle a case.

settlement conference   A meeting of the parties to discuss settlement of the case.

settlement letter   A detailed account of the information needed to determine the benefit of settling a case.

settlement summary   A summary of all essential information outlining the benefits of settling the case at an early stage in the litigation.

shadow jury   A group of persons (selected to be similar to the real jurors) paid by one side in a lawsuit to observe the trial and give their reactions.

social media   Sites that include a wide variety of communication and networking spots, such as Facebook, LinkedIn, StumbleUpon, Twitter, YouTube, Pinterest, WordPress, Snapchat, and MySpace, on which individuals record their thoughts, beliefs, events, photos, videos, and texts with great regularity.

special appearance   An appearance in court (either in person or by filing documents) for a limited purpose, often contesting jurisdiction.

special verdict   The jury answers specific questions about the case, and the court then applies the law to the facts found by the jury to determine which party is entitled to judgment.

specific denial   A type of answer in which the defendant specifically replies to each of the contentions alleged in the complaint.

specific performance   A court order requiring a person to fulfill his or her promises in a contract.

spoliation letter   A letter sent by an attorney to all opposing parties in a lawsuit placing those parties on notice that they should make an affirmative effort to preserve all ESI related to the case.

statute of limitations   The maximum time period in which any lawsuit must be filed in court.

stipulation   An agreement between the parties in a lawsuit that certain facts are not in dispute.

subject matter jurisdiction   The authority that a court has to hear a particular type of case.

subpoena   A written order issued by a court or an administrative agency commanding the presence of a person in order for that person to give testimony in an official proceeding. The word *subpoena* is an abbreviated form of the Latin term *subpoena ad testificandum*.

subpoena duces tecum   A written order issued by a court or an administrative agency commanding the presence of a person in order for that person to give testimony and to surrender the evidence that is enumerated in the subpoena. Generally, such evidence takes the form of documents, records, letters, memos, and so on.

subscription   A signature at the end of a document.

substantive law   Laws that determine parties' rights and obligations as opposed to the procedures used to enforce those rights.

summary bench trial   A trial before a judge rather than a jury in which evidence is introduced in a condensed manner.

summary jury trial   A trial in which the parties present their evidence before a six-person or eight-person jury which renders a nonbinding decision.

summons   A form served with a complaint informing a person of a lawsuit against him or her, the time limit for responding to the lawsuit, and the consequences of failing to respond.

supersedeas bond   A bond put up by a person who appeals a judgment. Supersedeas is a judge's order that temporarily holds up another court's proceedings or, more often, temporarily stays a lower court's judgment. The bond delays the person's obligation to pay the judgment until the appeal is lost.

supplemental jurisdiction   A federal court's right to decide a claim based on a nonfederal issue if this claim depends on the same set of facts as does a federal claim in the case before the court.

supreme court   A name given to the highest court in the federal court system and to many, but not all, of the highest court in state court systems.

technology assisted review (TAR)   Technology assisted review is a technique used during the discovery phase of a lawsuit that involves compiling, accessing, examining, and assessing documents by employing a computer-run protocol such as predictive coding.

telephone interpreting system   A system that permits interpreting services from English to a foreign language or vice versa.

temporary restraining order (TRO)   An order from the court requiring a person to act or refrain from acting in a certain way, issued for limited time until a full hearing on the matter can be scheduled.

theory of the case   The plan for where you are going with the case and how you will shape the law and the facts to achieve your ultimate destination.

third-party complaint   A complaint brought by a defendant in a lawsuit, based on the claims in that lawsuit, against someone not named in the original lawsuit.

tickler system   A calendaring system.

topical deposition summary   A written abridgment of a deposition that records the information produced by the deposition according to certain designated topics.

tortfeasor   A person who commits a tort (civil wrong) either intentionally or through negligence.

traditional oral deposition   A deposition that involves the actual presence of the deponent who responds aloud to the questions asked by an attorney.

transcript   A typed, electronic, or word-processed copy of the testimony of a witness produced by a court reporter following the oral testimony of the witness at trial or at a deposition; an official record of the proceedings of a court.

trial   A court proceeding in which parties to a lawsuit present their evidence to a judge or jury and the judge or jury make a decision in favor of one party.

trial brief   A document prepared by a lawyer to use at trial. It usually contains lists of witnesses, evidence, and citations as well as arguments to be presented.

trial court   A court where the parties to a lawsuit file their pleadings and present evidence to a judge or jury.

trial notebook   A binder that contains, in complete or summary form, everything necessary to prosecute or defend a case.

trigger event   A trigger event is any set of circumstances that sparks the duty to issue a litigation hold.

trust account (trust deposit)   A special bank account used exclusively for handling money belonging to another, usually a client.

unduly burdensome   A set of interrogatories made during discovery that is so complex and detailed that it will require the party answering the interrogatories to spend excessive time, effort, and expense, and which will result in a burden on that party that far exceeds any benefit gained by the opposing party.

venue   Among all the courts that have jurisdiction, venue defines the specific geographical location of the court or courts where an action should be brought. In the federal system this determines which is the proper district. In state court systems this often determines the proper county or counties.

verification (verify)   Statement at the end of a document and under penalty of perjury that the contents of the document are true.

videoconference   An electronic conference setup that permits several individuals at separate locations to discuss the planning of the case.

videoconference equipment   It is equipment that facilitates a two-way real-time transmission of audio and video signals between specialized devices or computers at two more locations.

voir dire examination   The preliminary in-court questioning of a prospective witness (or juror) to determine competency (or suitability) to decide a case.

webcam A video camera that is connected to a computer by a USB port or other cable connector that facilitates the transmission of real-time images to a personal computer.

webchat (webinar, online chat, online workshop) An online process that permits individuals at separate locations to meet via the Internet using personal computers, smartphones, or tablets.

web conference An electronic conference setup that permits individuals at separate locations to meet online via the Internet.

work product privilege (the litigation privilege) A privilege that protects any information prepared by an attorney in a lawsuit if that information is prepared by the attorney or anyone employed by the attorney in anticipation of litigation or to present at trial.

writ of execution A document that orders a court official to take a debtor's property to pay a court decided debt. Execution is the official carrying out or completion of a court's order or judgment.

***Zubulake* proportionality test** An analytical process that provides the court with seven factors for determining who should pay how much in a search for ESI.

Index